Buying Time

NEW AFRICAN HISTORIES

SERIES EDITORS: JEAN ALLMAN, ALLEN ISAACMAN, AND DEREK R. PETERSON

David William Cohen and E. S. Atieno Odhiambo, *The Risks of Knowledge*

Belinda Bozzoli, *Theatres of Struggle and the End of Apartheid*

Gary Kynoch, *We Are Fighting the World*

Stephanie Newell, *The Forger's Tale*

Jacob A. Tropp, *Natures of Colonial Change*

Jan Bender Shetler, *Imagining Serengeti*

Cheikh Anta Babou, *Fighting the Greater Jihad*

Marc Epprecht, *Heterosexual Africa?*

Marissa J. Moorman, *Intonations*

Karen E. Flint, *Healing Traditions*

Derek R. Peterson and Giacomo Macola, editors, *Recasting the Past*

Moses E. Ochonu, *Colonial Meltdown*

Emily S. Burrill, Richard L. Roberts, and Elizabeth Thornberry, editors, *Domestic Violence and the Law in Colonial and Postcolonial Africa*

Daniel R. Magaziner, *The Law and the Prophets*

Emily Lynn Osborn, *Our New Husbands Are Here*

Robert Trent Vinson, *The Americans Are Coming!*

James R. Brennan, *Taifa*

Benjamin N. Lawrance and Richard L. Roberts, editors, *Trafficking in Slavery's Wake*

David M. Gordon, *Invisible Agents*

Allen F. Isaacman and Barbara S. Isaacman, *Dams, Displacement, and the Delusion of Development*

Stephanie Newell, *The Power to Name*

Gibril R. Cole, *The Krio of West Africa*

Matthew M. Heaton, *Black Skin, White Coats*

Meredith Terretta, *Nation of Outlaws, State of Violence*

Paolo Israel, *In Step with the Times*

Michelle R. Moyd, *Violent Intermediaries*

Abosede A. George, *Making Modern Girls*

Alicia C. Decker, *In Idi Amin's Shadow*

Rachel Jean-Baptiste, *Conjugal Rights*

Shobana Shankar, *Who Shall Enter Paradise?*

Emily S. Burrill, *States of Marriage*

Todd Cleveland, *Diamonds in the Rough*

Carina E. Ray, *Crossing the Color Line*

Sarah Van Beurden, *Authentically African*

Giacomo Macola, *The Gun in Central Africa*

Lynn Schler, *Nation on Board*

Julie MacArthur, *Cartography and the Political Imagination*

Abou B. Bamba, *African Miracle, African Mirage*

Daniel Magaziner, *The Art of Life in South Africa*

Paul Ocobock, *An Uncertain Age*

Keren Weitzberg, *We Do Not Have Borders*

Nuno Domingos, *Football and Colonialism*

Jeffrey S. Ahlman, *Living with Nkrumahism*

Bianca Murillo, *Market Encounters*

Laura Fair, *Reel Pleasures*

Thomas F. McDow, *Buying Time*

Jon Soske, *Internal Frontiers*

Buying Time

Debt and Mobility in the Western Indian Ocean

Thomas F. McDow

OHIO UNIVERSITY PRESS ∽ ATHENS

Ohio University Press, Athens, Ohio 45701
ohioswallow.com
© 2018 by Ohio University Press
All rights reserved

To obtain permission to quote, reprint, or otherwise reproduce or
distribute material from Ohio University Press publications,
please contact our rights and permissions department at
(740) 593-1154 or (740) 593-4536 (fax).

Printed in the United States of America
Ohio University Press books are printed on acid-free paper ∞ ™

28 27 26 25 24 23 22 21 20 19 18   5 4 3 2 1

Library of Congress Cataloging-in-Publication Data

Names: McDow, Thomas F., 1970– author.
Title: Buying time : debt and mobility in the western Indian Ocean /
  Thomas F. McDow.
Other titles: New African histories series.
Description: Athens, Ohio : Ohio University Press, 2018. | Series: New African
  Histories | Includes bibliographical references and index.
Identifiers: LCCN 2017061019| ISBN 9780821422816 (hc : alk. paper) |
  ISBN 9780821422823 (pb : alk. paper) | ISBN 9780821446096 (pdf)
Subjects: LCSH: Indian Ocean Region—Commerce—History—19th century. |
  Africa, Eastern—Commerce—History—19th century. | Africa, Eastern—
  Civilization—Oriental influences. | Credit—Indian Ocean Region—
  History—19th century. | Credit—Africa, Eastern—History—19th century.
Classification: LCC DT365.65 .M33 2018 | DDC 967.601—dc23
LC record available at https://lccn.loc.gov/2017061019

Contents

List of Illustrations		vii
Acknowledgments		ix
Note on Terms, Translation, and Transliteration		xiii
Introduction	Temporizing across the Indian Ocean	1
Chapter 1	Drought and New Mobilities in the Omani Interior	24
Chapter 2	The Customs Master and Customs of Credit in Zanzibar	44
Chapter 3	Sultans at Sea: Mobility and the Omani States	61
Chapter 4	Halwa and Identity in the Western Indian Ocean World	86
Chapter 5	Tippu Tip's Kin, from Oman to the Eastern Congo	117
Chapter 6	Freed Slaves: Manumission and Mobility before 1873	145
Chapter 7	Acts for Consuls and Consular Acts: Documents, Manumission, and Ocean Travel after 1873	165
Chapter 8	A Dhow on Lake Victoria	190
Chapter 9	"Everything Is Pledged to Its Time": Salih bin Ali, Debt, and Rebellion in the Omani Interior	215

Epilogue	260
Notes	277
Bibliography	337
Index	359

Illustrations

FIGURES

0.1	Juma bin Salim's acknowledgment of ivory debt, 1869	2
0.2	Juma Merikani's house in the Congo, 1870s	11
1.1	Nizwa fort, 1901	25
2.1	Zanzibar waterfront, 1847	47
4.1	Thani bin Amir's house in Kazeh, late 1850s	90
4.2	Swahili man in Omani Arabic dress, 19th ce	98
4.3	Mwinyi Kidogo, 1850s	101
5.1	Muhammad bin Said al-Murjebi and Hamed bin Muhammad al-Murjebi at Stanley Falls, 1888	134
5.2	Women of Rumaliza's houshold in Ujiji, 1890	142
7.1	Sultan Barghash bin Said al-Busaidi, 1875	167
7.2	Stopping a slave ship and examing her papers, 1880s	176
8.1	Building the first dhow on Lake Victoria, 1877	209
9.1	Approaching Muscat from the interior, 1890s	238
9.2	Transaction in Zanzibar that temporarily sold the rights to a property in Sharqiya, Oman, 1877	245
9.3	Inside the gates of Muscat, 1890s	256
10.1	The Barwani family tree, 2000	271

Maps

0.1	The western Indian Ocean in the nineteenth century	3
1.1	Oman and its surrounding regions	27
5.1	Eastern and Central Africa in the age of Tippu Tip	126
6.1	Itineraries of manumission	153
8.1	Lake Victoria region	199
9.1	Salih bin Ali al-Harthi's Arabia and Africa	218

Acknowledgments

THIS BOOK IS MY own portfolio of debts, and I would like to acknowledge the range of creditors and patrons who have made my own mobility and modest success possible. The financial support of a Fulbright-Hays Fellowship, the Mathy Junior Faculty Fellowship from George Mason University (GMU), and small grants from the Department of History and Art History at GMU and the Department of History at Ohio State University made the research and writing of this book possible. A subvention grant from the Arts and Humanities division of OSU's College of Arts and Sciences supported the publication. I am grateful to the librarians and archivists who maintain important collections in Tanzania, Oman, India, the United Kingdom, and the United States. The Zanzibar National Archives are at the center of this book, and I am grateful to the staff and leadership there who maintain this wonderful collection. The magic of libraries—Thompson Library at Ohio State, Fenwick Library at GMU, and Sterling Library at Yale—and their assorted book-sharing consortia have made it possible to complete the research. Several people have provided me with research assistance at various stages of this project, and I am grateful for their aid: Mohamed Abdou, Sylvia Alexander, Pearl Harris-Scott, Steve Harris-Scott, Melvin C. S. Jenkins, Hamisi Ally Jumalhey, and Matthew Smith Miller. Likewise, Rob Squires was a patient cartographer.

An early version of chapter 6 was published as "Deeds of Freed Slaves: Manumission and Economic and Social Mobility in Pre-Abolition Zanzibar," in *Indian Ocean Slavery in the Age of Abolition*, eds. Robert W. Harms, Bernard K. Freamon and David W. Blight, (New Haven, CT: Yale University Press, 2013): 162–179. An earlier version of one section of chapter 4 originally appeared as "Being Baysar: (In)flexible Identities in East Africa" in *The MIT Electronic Journal of Middle East Studies* 5 (Fall 2005): 34–42.

For the opportunity to present and refine my work I am grateful to Gwyn Campbell and his crew at the Indian Ocean World Centre in Montreal; to

Kai Kresse and Edward Simpson at the Zentrum Moderner Orient in Berlin; to Pier Larson and the African Studies colloquium at Johns Hopkins; to Hans Gaube, Michaela Hoffmann-Ruf, and Abdulrahman Al-Salimi for inviting me to their Ibadi Studies conference at Tuebingen; to Engseng Ho and his Indian Ocean workshop at Duke; and to Ann Biersteker at Michigan State University. Anne Bang, Jonathan Glassman, Mandana Limbert, Brian Peterson, and Scott Reese provided important feedback on the book proposal.

Robert Harms has helped this book grow from a seminar paper to a dissertation, a series of articles, and now, a book. I hope that this book reflects his astute criticism, keen editorial eye, and commitment to good stories. I have also benefited from Abdul Sheriff's generous mentorship and his willingness to share the research he collected for his own first book decades ago. The year I spent as a fellow at the Zanzibar Indian Ocean Research Institute was formative for this project.

The editorial team at Ohio University Press has made this book better. I am grateful to the series editors Jean Allmen, Allen Isaacman, and Derek Peterson for their careful reading and feedback. Derek was an early champion of the manuscript, and his earnest encouragement is greatly appreciated. Two anonymous reviewers helped me sharpen my focus. Gillian Berchowitz's kind leadership, patience, and professionalism set a high standard, and I am happy to join the ranks of authors who she has published.

In Oman, in Zanzibar, and mainland Tanzania, many people have been extraordinarily welcoming. I am particularly grateful for the hospitality and friendship of the following people and their families: Mariam Aboud, Taharia Said Aboud, Hamisi Ally Jumalhey, Fatma Khamis, Hilda Kiel, Leyla Said, Ibrahim Noor Shariff, Salum Saidi Suliman, and Ali al-Zefeiti. I regret that several people who influenced this project did not live to see its completion. I acknowledge my debt and sense of loss for Zein Hafidh al-Busaidi, Jan-Georg Deutsch, Suleiman Ali Suleiman al-Murjebi, and Randolph Whitfield.

This book has been written in many places, and several wonderful families have hosted me for writing retreats of various lengths including Croom and Sandy Coward, Christopher and Heather Gergen, Jonathan Holloway and Aisling Colon, and Jennifer Siegel. I owe an extra special thanks to Mike Thomas and Nancy Balfour, Chris and Dennis Harrington, Tim and Maggie Hobbs, and Randy and Suzanne Whitfield who, due to their weeks-long hospitality, got to see just how boring I am while working. Their generosity created this book.

I have benefitted from smart, engaged departmental colleagues at George Mason and at Ohio State. I am grateful to Benedict Carton, Michael Chang,

Rob DeCaroli, Matt Karush, Brian Platt, and Joan Scully for their encouragement in Fairfax. In Columbus Sarah van Beurden, Nick Breyfogle, Theodora Dragistinova, Jane Hathaway, Robin Judd, Ousman Kobo, Scott Levi, Jennifer Siegel, Ahmad Sikainga, Mytheli Sreenivas, Christina Sessa, and Ying Zhang read, commented on, and discussed parts of this project with me and made it better. I am also grateful to the smart folks in the Space and Sovereignty Working Group, including Lisa Bhungalia, Melissa Curley, Becky Mansfield, Katherine Marino, Nada Moumtaz, Juno Parrenas, and Noah Tamarkin, for workshopping two chapters and generally being great intellectual company. Roxanne Willis's editorial pen, friendship, and guidance helped me solidify chapters into a draft manuscript, and her encouragement made it fun.

I am also indebted to other academic friends who have helped me think through my work and sustained me: Eric Allina, Fahad Bishara, Bill Bissel, Justin Beckham, Sarah Beckham, David Bernstein, Lori Flores, Matt Hopper, Erik Gilbert, Sarah Igo, Pranav Jani, Arash Khazeni, Steve Lassonde, Jesse Kwiek, Lisa Moses Leff, Roger Levine, Nate Mathews, Christian McMillen, Ole Molvig, Ben Siegel, Wendy Warren, Eric Worby, and Ali al-Zefeiti. The friendships and insights of Todd Keithley and Ron Birnbaum have enriched me for nearly three decades.

Since I first started following people moving across the Indian Ocean, I have had three amazing children. While they have been incredible sources of inspiration, I could not have completed this project without the work of those who helped us take care of them, especially Kathleen Bergin, Abbie Carver, Bryna Harrington, Matt Miller, Kim Moore, Paige Phillips, Leyla Said, and Marielle Schweickart. A cadre of like-minded parents and neighbors has also sustained us: Seth Abel and Steffanie Wilk, Dana and Brent Adler, Tom and Andrea Easley, Maggie and Jeff Gumbinner, Gretchen Eiselt and Matt Harding, Elena Irwin and Brian Roe, Kelly Lynch and John Wix, Gillian Thomson and Kent Johnson, Cindy and Scott Tyson, and Kit Yoon and Jim MacDonald.

This is also a book about kinship. Thank you to my extended family, especially my own parents Croom and Sandy Coward, Thomas and Lucy McDow, and Bob and Peg Norris. Randy and Suzanne Whitfield read and patiently commented on a draft, and Clarkson McDow gave key feedback on the proposal. Maggie and Jeff Gumbinner, Randolph and Lauren McDow, Will and Leslie McDow, Mary Rincon, Eston Whitfield, and Louisa Whitfield unwittingly helped write chapter 5 by blurring the lines between siblings and cousins. Abby and Piers Norris Turner have been invaluable collaborators in all aspects of life. Maggie, Franklin, and Solomon McDow make every day better. The last person is always the most important: Without Alison Norris, this book, and my life, would not be complete.

While these pages may be poor recompense for everything that I have gained in writing them, I appreciate that the debts I have accrued bind together a wonderful network of colleagues, friends, and family that make this all worthwhile.

Note on Terms, Translation, and Transliteration

IN AMITAV GHOSH'S IBIS trilogy of historical novels that move across the worlds of the Indian Ocean in the nineteenth century, the characters speak in a variety of argots and cants specific to their particular social milieu. These include phrases from dialects of English, Hindi, Chinese, and Malayan languages, among others. Ghosh renders these wonderfully, yet I suspected that one of his goals in immersing the reader in this linguistic confusion is to underscore the multiethnic, polylingual world his characters inhabited. In this book, I would like to avoid this.

Certainly linguistic puzzles are one of the charms of the Indian Ocean. In an early round of research, I realized that the hard-to-decipher letter in front of me was not in Arabic, despite the script, but Portuguese. In this book, I have tried to solve all those puzzles for the reader by using common English spellings, where they exist, for words from other languages. In the text, I have dropped diacriticals from common names (Said for Sa'īd, Muhammad for Muḥammad), though included them in the index. I have also used the historical place names for the period (Kutch for Kachchh, Bombay for Mumbai, Lake Nyasa for Lake Malawi). For Arabic terms and phrases that I transliterated, I have followed the standards of the *International Journal of Middle East Studies* for the first usage, and dropped the diacritical marks subsequently. Unless otherwise noted, all currencies are listed in Maria Theresa dollars (MT$).

Although I hope to evoke a world like Ghosh does, I am not a novelist. As a historian, one of my goals has been to translate this Indian Ocean world and ease your journey through it.

Introduction
Temporizing across the Indian Ocean

HE PROMISED TO DO it in two years. In 1869, Juma bin Salim wrote a contract, in his own hand in Arabic, to deliver 10,500 pounds of ivory to Zanzibar in two years. In exchange for a substantial advance, he agreed to bring the ivory to Ladha Damji, a Hindu financier and the leading creditor on that Indian Ocean island. In authoring the contract, Juma used the most formal version of his name—Juma bin Salim bin Mbarak bin Abdullah al-Bakri—and identified his hometown, Nizwa, in distant Oman. More than a decade before, Juma had left Oman and joined the caravan trails in central Africa, where he became known as Juma Merikani. He was famous for importing *merikani*, American-made cotton sheeting, which he exchanged for elephant tusks. Juma identified Ladha with an honorific title, the Arabicized version of his name, and by his position as the agent of "our lord," the sultan of Zanzibar. The contract spelled out the exact weight of ivory and established that Ladha would pay the taxes on it. This was convenient, since Ladha and his firm collected all the taxes for the sultan.[1]

While Juma's Arabic contract was very detailed, its formality left many things—not just Juma's colorful nickname—unwritten. It did not mention money or acknowledge that Ladha had ever lent money to Juma. Those arrangements were kept separate to avoid the Islamic prohibition on interest. The elements of the contract reveal a historical process rooted in Islamic finance and adapted to a burgeoning global commodity trade. Fulfilling the contract's promise required the cooperation (and coercion) of people from

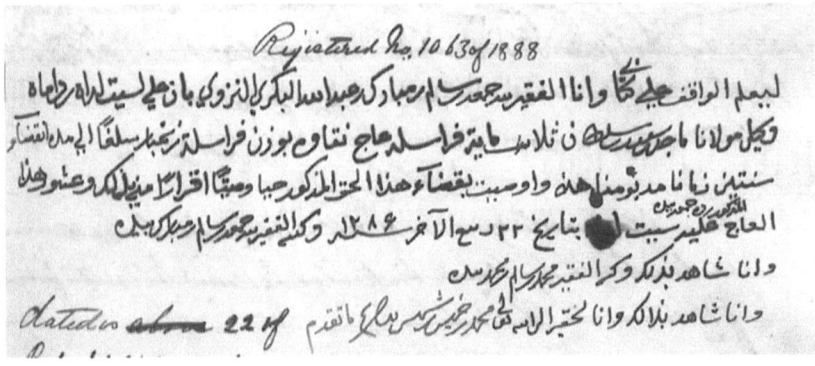

FIGURE 0.1. Juma bin Salim al-Bakri al-Nizwi's 1869 acknowledgment of ivory debt. Registered deed 1063 of 1888, AM 12/20, Zanzibar National Archives.

the Indian Ocean littoral and the residents of its interior hinterlands: Africans, Arabs, and Indians. Juma's contract also spanned a vast geography: his hometown was in the interior of eastern Arabia, and his debt would require him to travel to new ivory outposts near the Congo's tributaries. This contract for African ivory included a set of global exchanges: the capital financing his journey came from Bombay, and the cotton sheeting he exchanged for ivory came from American mills in Massachusetts. When the contract was written, the ivory was still attached to elephants in upland Africa, and at least fifty of them would need to be killed to meet the contract's terms. All this would take time, and time mediated the relationships between the people, geography, and commodities in this contract. As for the intermediaries, complex negotiations, and travel required to repay the debt to Ladha, Juma bin Salim had two years to figure it out.

Juma bin Salim was one of a multitude of migrants in the western Indian Ocean in the nineteenth century, and his life course represents one path among a wide range of trajectories that transformed the region. Juma bin Salim was originally from Nizwa, an ancient city in the interior of Oman, but he made his name as an ivory trader in central Africa, where he would eventually be buried in 1887. At the time of his death, he had been an active trader on Lake Tanganyika and the Congo tributaries for thirty-some years. Juma bin Salim controlled large stores of ivory, managed plantations of rice and maize, had several African wives, and was a vital source of geographic knowledge for the few Europeans who had reached the center of the continent.[2]

What set this world into motion? Why would date farmers and city dwellers from Arabian oases leave their homes for uncertain ventures in East Africa?

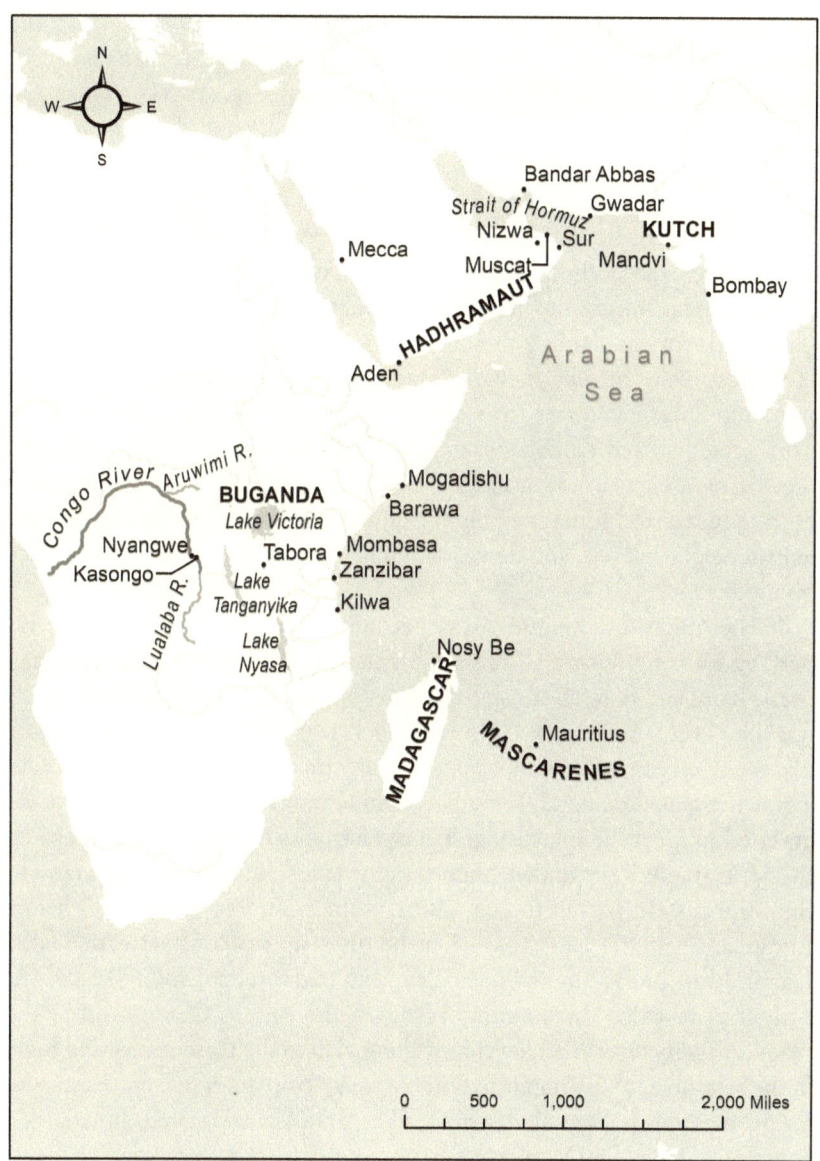

MAP 0.1. The western Indian Ocean in the nineteenth century

Part of the explanation is environmental. In the late 1830s, three decades before Juma bin Salim wrote his promissory note, an extreme drought in the interior of Oman led many residents to leave for the Arabian coast and the Indian Ocean world. But economics and politics also contributed. Around

Temporizing across the Indian Ocean ⤳ 3

the same time as the drought, the Omani sultan—motivated by trade and strategy—relocated his court and his capital from Muscat to Zanzibar, over two thousand miles away. The sultan's move was just one part of a larger pattern of migration from Arabia and India to Zanzibar and the African coast in the nineteenth century. Zanzibar was where Juma bin Salim promised to deliver ivory to Ladha Damji, who had himself been born into poverty in Kutch in western India. Ladha Damji became notoriously wealthy in Zanzibar as the head of the island's most important commercial house, as well as the sultan's master of the customs revenue. Ladha invested heavily in slaves and ivory by lending money to caravan leaders like Juma bin Salim. His investment portfolio included loans for ivory, plantations, and houses. Juma bin Salim's contract gave him two years to fulfill its terms. He set to work, crossing from Zanzibar to the mainland, hiring a band of porters, and organizing a caravan to travel hundreds of miles into the African interior. During his travels, Juma bin Salim acquired great stores of ivory, gave loans to European explorers, and eventually chose not to return to Zanzibar to face his creditor.

In the nineteenth century, ivory became East Africa's most valuable export, and it complemented a rise in plantation culture on the East African coast. Ivory and plantations spurred an economic boom in Zanzibar. Ivory was the plastic of its day, used in manufacturing a wide array of items, and, like copal, cloves, and coconuts, one of many East African commodities with a growing global demand. Juma bin Salim and other caravan leaders of his era tried to meet the increasing demand for tusks by venturing deeper into the African interior to find elephants. In the 1840s, Juma's colleagues crossed from the eastern part of the continent to the west, two generations before Europeans.[3] By the late 1860s when he drew up his contract with Ladha Damji, Juma bin Salim had been a caravan trader for at least a decade. His early trips revealed the amount of ivory in the eastern Congo, and by the 1860s an "ivory fever" had developed there akin to the California Gold Rush or the scramble for diamonds in South Africa.[4] Ivory fever had consequences for peoples and polities across east and central Africa. Indeed, Juma's 1869 contract with Ladha Damji was part of a cresting wave that thrust residents of the Indian Ocean basin into deeper and more frequent contact with peoples of Central Africa. These waves of contact created pools of Indian Ocean culture far into the interior. Juma settled in the eastern Congo, and many travelers observed "second Zanzibars" in Africa. The undertow of this movement swept away ivory and the Africans who harvested it—first to the littoral and then out to sea. An ocean away, these same tides pulled Arabs from interior towns, while the wealth from East Africa reconfigured Arab settlements and local politics.

❦

Buying Time is a history of how nineteenth-century credit and mobility knit together a vast region, extending from the deserts of Arabia to the equatorial forests of Africa's Congo watershed. Juma bin Salim and others who created this western Indian Ocean world—Africans, Arabs, and Indians—used monsoon winds and ancient trade routes to link port cities to distant hinterlands. They relied on Islamic financial instruments with deep roots in Indian Ocean exchanges to record obligations of creditors and debtors. From the 1820s onward these men and women endeavored to take advantage of the new opportunities—as traders, as patrons, and as clients—available in an increasingly globalized economy. When their initial strategies failed, or when they met resistance from entrenched hierarchies, they bought time. Time allowed them to escape drought, seek new markets, acquire ivory, reconfigure life paths, and often—but not always—pay off debts. In the half century before European colonization, Africans, Arabs, and Indians used credit and new circuits of mobility to seek out new opportunities, establish themselves as men of means in distant places, and maintain families in a rapidly changing economy. To tell this story, this book traces people's movements and the financial flows that underwrote their activities. It is a story told in previously unexplored Arabic contracts. The documents that lie at the heart of this book illustrate the startling reach of the Indian Ocean world even as they convey the individual aspirations of the people who inhabited it.

As a social history of interconnected Indian Ocean worlds, this book is foremost about people: families who left date farms in Arabia; freed slaves who bet on the ivory trade; sultans and their rivals; displaced Swahili elites; religious ideologues; mixed race Indo-Africans; dissident traders; sophisticated scribes; African porters; Arab confectioners; and an eloping Arab princess who became a German housewife and author. The members of this diverse group inhabited overlapping regions in Arabia and Africa. They also shared a set of scribal practices and used fixed formulas to carry out transactions. Their documents cut across a world now rife with national boundaries. At the same time, they created obligations between creditors and debtors. These obligations fit into broader Indian Ocean patterns of patronage and clientship, which crossed ethnic, geographic, and cultural groupings. By focusing on the strategies that individuals developed in the face of broader changes, this book examines the complex, interwoven, and mobile societies that existed in the western Indian Ocean in the years before formal colonialism would undermine these ties.

~

This book joins a growing body of scholarly literature in oceanic history, a field pioneered by Fernand Braudel, whose 1949 history of the sixteenth-century Mediterranean "world" recognized that the sea was not a true boundary during that period. In many ways, Braudel anticipated the work of more recent scholars examining the latest wave of globalization. He noted that the civilization of the Mediterranean "spreads far beyond its shores in great waves that are balanced by continual returns," and suggests, "We should imagine a hundred frontiers, not one, some political, some economic, some cultural." Without looking at this zone of influence, it would be difficult to grasp the sea's history.[5] In his formulation, the Mediterranean pulsed, creating a dynamic "world" over time. Braudel's work became the foundation for a new scholarship of oceanic spaces, and comprehensive histories of the Indian Ocean have explicitly attempted to adopt Braudel's model.[6] The proliferation of Braudel-inspired studies around the world gave rise to a "new thalassology" (the study of the sea), and the Indian Ocean has emerged as an important space in this new field.[7]

Despite the Indian Ocean's much longer standing as an arena of human interaction and cross-cultural exchange, the Atlantic Ocean has attracted more scholarly attention. One result of this has been a lopsided sibling rivalry between oceanic adherents—lopsided in the sense that scholars of the Indian Ocean have been the ones to call attention to the slights of inclusion and perceived inequalities. For example, the Indian Ocean was left out of a forum on "Oceans of History" in the *American Historical Review* that focused only on the Mediterranean, the Atlantic, and the Pacific.[8] Scholars of slavery in the Indian Ocean have been particularly diligent in trying to provincialize Atlantic plantation chattel slavery as but one of many forms of bondage and dependence.[9] In both oceanic worlds, however, Africa has historically been given short shrift, generally characterized by slavery and its human contributions to the slave trade. Recent scholarship by Atlantic Africanists, however, although focused on slavery generally, offer models and insights that can enrich Indian Ocean histories through biography and microhistory, paying attention to the dynamic changes in port cities, and mapping oceanic actors in broader hinterlands.[10] A focus on Africa's relationship to its western ocean has profitably expanded the scope of Atlantic world studies, and in this book the Indian Ocean world is inconceivable without Africa.

The boundaries of the Indian Ocean world varied over time, and this book demonstrates how the nineteenth century was the time of their greatest extent and their greatest incorporation of Africa. Many anthropologists and social scientists have grappled with late twentieth-century (and early twenty-first-century) globalization. From their perspective, nation-states and continents break down, failing to be useful containers of human activity. Arjun Appadurai calls them "problematic heuristic devices," and scholars have approached subjects across national boundaries that have revealed new insights about the global order.[11] One of these approaches replaces standard geographic considerations with "process geographies" that can shift (like Braudel's pulsing Mediterranean) and focuses on "congeries of language, history, and material life."[12] Newer historical studies of the Indian Ocean have used innovative and unconventional sources (like genealogies of diasporic communities) and have read colonial archives against the grain to find new connections between nodes.[13] This study attempts to do both. The Arabic transaction records in the Zanzibar Archives describe a type of process geography, a world of credit and debt. This information is embedded in Arabic contracts about assets and people, from Arabia to central Africa. Commodity chains (like those of ivory) and foodways (such as the production, consumption, and social practice around the Omani sweetmeat *halwa*) have spatial dimensions and dispersed geographies in this Indian Ocean world. By focusing on debt—both as an economic relationship and as part of a network of social relationships—this book describes human mobilities and a unified geography by pursuing connections across boundaries of race, ethnicity, status, class, and religion. This book considers time, debt, mobility, kinship, and environment to show how individuals took advantage of credit and mobility to temporize and to reshape their lives.

This book concentrates on the hinterlands of the western Indian Ocean, during the long nineteenth century. In European terms, we can define this period as spanning the French Revolution to World War I. This era encapsulates the Anglo-French rivalry in the Indian Ocean; British attempts to gain more control over India and its dependencies, both before and after 1857; and the explosion of colonization in the last decades of the century. While such global processes affected many people in this story, local events governed their lives in more profound ways. In eastern Arabia, local rulers chose either to accommodate or to challenge Wahhabi expansion, and rulers in Muscat, Oman, struggled to shore up their power in the face of challenges from their families and coreligionists. Omani sultans sought to balance this opposition with cooperation—both commercial and political allegiances—with British officials and their Indian subjects.

On the African coast and in the interior, Zanzibar's economic boom made the island an important node. Local trade in cloth, gunpowder, ivory, and slaves reconfigured polities and practices near and far. Formal Omani rule in Zanzibar was a novelty during this period. Said bin Sultan al-Busaidi brought the East African coast under his control, moved his court to Zanzibar in the 1830s, and ruled dominions in Arabia and Africa until his death in 1856. His sons became sultans in Oman and Zanzibar, and their rivalries and their reluctant British clientship paved the way for international treaties that limited the slave trade and later ceded territory and created colonial sovereignty.

The western Indian Ocean is the stage for the action in this book, and it includes not just the cosmopolitan port cities long connected to maritime trading networks but also the distant hinterlands of Arabia and Africa. This area includes the rugged mountain-to-desert landscapes of eastern Arabia, the Indian Ocean seascape, the fertile islands of Zanzibar and Pemba, the mangrove-guarded coasts of East Africa, the central plateau of the eastern African mainland, the Rift Valley lakes, and the tributaries that pushed the Congo River to the Atlantic Ocean. Remarkably, by the end of the nineteenth century, this diverse geography had some things in common. Arabs from Oman and Swahili speakers from the coast inhabited trading outposts across the east central African plateau, built dhows on the shores of the Great Lakes, and navigated the Congo River. Africans from the interior lived on the east coast and traveled—some as slaves, others free—to coastal and interior Arabia. Human mobility connected interior regions to global trade networks, expanded the Islamic ecumene, and broadened the boundaries of the Swahiliphone world.

Throughout this period and across these spaces, this book focuses on five factors—time, debt, mobility, kinship, and environment—to elucidate the patterns and disjunctures around which people in the western Indian Ocean structured their lives.

TIME

The notion of "buying time" is an organizing metaphor for this book. It frames both historical contingency and the many time-mediated exchanges that were vital to the region. Buying time is shorthand for a particular type of historical agency: temporizing. To temporize is to adopt a course of action to conform to circumstances; to wait for a more favorable moment; or to negotiate to gain time.[14] By seeing the actions of Indian Ocean actors in this framework, we recognize the limited choices and difficult decisions they had to make, often with incomplete knowledge.[15] This also allows us to focus on people of middling and low status, such as impoverished migrants, freed slaves, and nonsheikhly Arabs, and recognize that even sultans and tribal leaders had to make decisions between an uncomfortable status quo and a possible threatening future. In the western Indian Ocean, slaves often had more power than an outside observer would expect, and sultans often had less. Western Indian Ocean actors used temporizing strategies to improve their circumstances, enhance their autonomy, and increase their security. The strategies for buying time provide a lens to view the actions and choices of individual actors to go along, to parley, and to see what would happen in a world of uncertain outcomes.

This approach preserves a sense of historical contingency that has often been overlooked in teleological approaches to the history of East Africa and Oman. Some Marxian and world-systems analyses have tended to treat economic processes, class formation, and European colonialism as foregone conclusions. Likewise, racial and ethnic categories that hardened in the violent politics of Zanzibar in the 1950s and 1960s have tended to cloud fluid identities from the previous century.[16] The combination of these sets of arguments that map class and race ends up ignoring poor and low-status Arabs, outcast Indians, and African elite traders. If, as Isabel Hofmeyr has suggested, the Indian Ocean has become "the subaltern sea," we need to employ a temporal approach that leaves room for agency and contingency as a wide range of actors created the interlinked Indian Ocean world.[17]

But what was "time" in the context of the western Indian Ocean? Jürgen Osterhammel reminds us that there were a multitude of methods for reckoning time in the nineteenth century, and prior to the nineteenth century time was far from "universal."[18] Then, in 1884, the same year that the Congress of Berlin met to divide up Africa, the Prime Meridian Conference met in Washington, DC, to divide the world into time zones and to create a universal day that began at midnight.[19] This movement was tied to technological innovations like railways, telegraphs, and steamships, which required something more than nonstandardized local times.[20] Excellent recent histories of the movement to adopt a universal time narrate their stories beginning in the 1870s and emphasize the way various actors contested the imposition of new time schemes.[21] The long history of movement and exchange in the Indian Ocean, however, had created many overlapping units for rendering time before the late nineteenth century. The monsoonal calendar governed ocean travel for millennia, and it created the seasonal rainfall patterns that dictated growing seasons. In the African mainland, dry season trading ventures set the stage for long-distance trade. The date harvesting cycle shaped the patterns of life in eastern Arabia, which stands outside the monsoon rainfall system. Consequently, the need for irrigation and shared water resources led to systems for measuring time with stars and to elaborate units of time—the smallest was one-sixteenth of a second—to measure the water flow in irrigation canals.[22]

In East Africa, the time of day was measured in hours from the sunrise, so that noon was "*saa sita* (six hours)." Islamic time had a lunar calendar that included months for fasting and pilgrimage, but the start of these months was locally determined by moon sightings. Likewise, the Islamic calendar did not synchronize with other natural, seasonal calendars, so for instance, Ramadan could occur during Oman's date harvest one year, slip back through the "agricultural" year, and not coincide with the date harvest again for thirty-three years.

While nineteenth-century technologies helped define parameters of time and space, multiple time scales persisted in the western Indian Ocean. Jeremy Prestholdt has shown that, when the sultan of Zanzibar installed a clock tower in the 1880s, he "domesticated" the clock by setting it to Swahili time, the local standard, in which one o'clock is the first hour after sunrise. Thus he "did not Europeanize time in Zanzibar; rather he adapted the European timepiece to Zanzibari perceptions of time."[23] Erik Gilbert has further demonstrated that dhow travel on monsoon winds was prominent until late in the twentieth century. The flexible logic of dhow sailing—as opposed to the rigid schedule of steamships—allowed dhows to compete on favorable terms with freighters for coastal cargoes.[24] Given the ways that those in the western Indian Ocean incorporated or challenged "universal" or "bureaucratic" time, what does it mean to say that people in the western Indian Ocean and its hinterlands bought time?

In Oman, people bought time when they needed to buy water. The country's interior needed elaborate irrigation schemes to make agriculture possible. The water was distributed by shares. Yet, while some people owned permanent shares, others bought shares in regular auctions. They were not, however, buying certain volumes of water. They were buying units of time, during which the water would flow into their channels.[25]

The Arabic contracts that people like Juma bin Salim used to acknowledge debt explicitly involved time. One subset of these documents suggests that individuals were literally buying time. Although Juma bin Salim did not put up collateral for his 1869 ivory deal, many others received credit by pledging houses or land, with an agreement to redeem them after a fixed period by paying in ivory. Others took part in *bayʿ al-khiyār* (optional, reversible sales) that gave the creditor rights to rent or usufruct for a fixed period of time, after which the original owner could withdraw the original sale. When clerks in Zanzibar copied these deeds—sometimes decades later—for the British consul, they often called the deeds "time sales."

The Arabic documents also demonstrate the imposition of bureaucratic time, which was out of sync with time in the Islamic legal system. The deeds followed Islamic formularies, and the scribes recorded dates in the Arabic calendar. Time for redeemable sales was also measured in Arabic years. Yet the Islamic dates were much less important to the clerks who recorded them for British consular courts. Clerks duly noted, stamped, and indexed the documents by the date they were registered. Sometimes these documents were registered decades after the transactions took place. Juma bin Salim's 1869 promissory note was registered at the consular court in 1888. This suggests that Juma bin Salim never satisfied this debt despite his promise to return in two years. Operating in and among these overlapping and unstable boundaries of time in the nineteenth century, the concept of "buying time" reflects the literal sense of some transactions, and it also metaphorically explains agency and historical contingency.

This book focuses on debt and mobility as temporizing strategies. Omani Arabs from nonsheikhly lines went overseas when they could no longer

FIGURE 0.2. Juma Merikani's house in the Congo. From Verney Lovett Cameron, *Across Africa* (New York: Harper & Brothers, 1877).

access irrigation water. Freed slaves sold property to join the caravan trade, and during their journeys they maneuvered among categories and statuses. Arabs, Africans, and other Indian Ocean actors who took to the caravan trails founded and populated settlements in mainland East Africa. Their opportunistic traveling took them to places where they could find personal autonomy and could attract clients of their own, while the distance from the coast loosened their ties to creditors. In Oman, tribal leaders played cat-and-mouse games with the sultan and his allies—parleying at times and attacking at others. These opportunities to strike, however, were organized through a financial interface—namely credit from Zanzibar—that shaped political tensions with the sultan. These temporizing strategies across the long axis of the western Indian Ocean demonstrate how the constrained agency of multiple actors worked to maintain an interconnected region.

DEBT

Notions of time are inextricably linked to the concepts of debt and indebtedness, a second core concept of this book. The anthropologist David Graeber has called debt "just an exchange that has not been brought to completion," and it follows that what remains in that equation is time. And, as Graeber notes, the time between contracting a debt and repaying is when "just about everything interesting happens."[26] As Juma bin Salim's two-year promise makes clear, debt was an essential part of acquiring ivory, and thus it was a vital link in a commodity chain that stretched from East African forests to Victorian parlors.[27] In this way, ivory was similar to other natural products from the Indian Ocean world—cloves, copal, pearls, and dates—that the growth of global capitalism helped deliver to distant centers.[28] The procurement and delivery of these goods around the Indian Ocean depended largely on Indian merchants, like Ladha Damji, who served as key creditors and intermediaries within commodity chains. It was credit and debt from these lenders that drove the commercial expansion of the Indian Ocean world in the nineteenth century.[29]

Assuming debt and accessing credit allowed people to take advantage of new opportunities in the Indian Ocean in the nineteenth century, and they did so through contracts rooted in Islamic law. Juma bin Salim's promissory note acknowledging his ivory debt to Ladha Damji represented one of many types of *waraqa* (literally paper) that were flexible instruments used to extend credit and confirm debts. Although non-Muslims like Ladha Damji used these documents widely, the writings followed well-known Islamic formulas so that they would be legitimate in the eyes of *qadis* (jurists). Thus, one of the goals of such contracts was to avoid the appearance of usury (*ribā*) because charging interest would invalidate the legality of the contract. Does this mean that merchants and moneylenders did not charge interest in the Indian Ocean?

While European observers in the nineteenth century claimed that merchants charged exorbitant interest rates—up to 100 percent—this was not true. The nature of the transactions, however, and the surviving documents make it difficult to determine the actual rates with precision. Certainly European traders paid interest at a rate that was eventually standardized to 9 percent in the 1860s.[30] When financiers like Ladha Damji lent money to Muslims like Juma bin Salim, however, the interest was obscured through two separate transactions, both of which were legal. To begin, the financier advanced a certain value of trade goods—*merikani* cloth, trade beads, and other goods. In a separate transaction, like the one Juma bin Salim completed, the debtor acknowledged that he would deliver a certain value of goods at a future date. The "interest" was thus the discount between the value of goods advanced and the value of the payment promised. In the late 1850s Burton noted that secured loans included interest of 15 to 20 percent, and Livingstone reported in the 1870s that the rates were between 20 and 25 percent.[31] Stanley, also writing in the 1870s, claimed that the effective interest was between 50 and 70 percent.[32] The initial agreement may have been negotiated orally, and only the second contract was written down. In these cases, the "interest" was charged initially on the transaction so there was no compounding over time, and the debt could be ongoing.

Another common way to avoid the sin of interest was through a set of incomplete sales that created debt. These included optional sales (*bay' al-khiyār*) in which the seller could undo the sale by returning the sale price, and sales with pledged property (*rahnan maqbuḍ*). In both cases, the creditor would retain the right to the property sold, such as a house or a farm, and would profit from the rent on the house or the produce of the farm. One common version of this arrangement included the debtor renting his own house back from the creditor. In this case, the sale of the house from A to B would be written in one contract, and a separate contract would be issued for B to rent the house from A at a fixed rate each month. In this case, the "interest" was the rent and could, in theory, continue indefinitely. These optional sales, *bay' khiyār*, became a way for many different actors with even a small amount of property to leverage themselves into positions to participate in and profit from the lucrative trade booms of the Indian Ocean world.

In all of these cases, indebtedness created a set of obligations that mirrored patron-client relationships elsewhere in the Islamic world. In the western

Indian Ocean, as on the caravan trails of the Sahara, commercial dealings did not depend entirely on faith or ethnicity.[33] The portfolios of merchants represented the diversity of peoples present in port cities. In Zanzibar, debtors included Arabs of many social strata, Hindu and Muslim Indians, indigenous Zanzibaris, Swahili, mainland Africans, and enslaved people. In this sense, debts created overlapping networks of obligation that implicated both sultans and slaves. The sultans in Oman and Zanzibar were, after all, chronically in debt to their customs masters. Within these networks of patronage and obligation, creditors cultivated clients to build their own reputations and firms while clients and debtors sought to balance powerful patrons with their own autonomy.[34]

When the autonomy of clients as debtors threatened to undercut the loan, Indian Ocean creditors did not rely solely on reputation mechanisms.[35] One reason Hindu creditors like Ladha Damji followed Islamic contractual prescriptions was so that they could appeal to jurists (*qadis*) to help enforce their claims. *Qadis* themselves sometime turned to the local rulers for enforcement. Punishments included fines, confiscations, and imprisonment.[36] In the second half of the nineteenth century, however, British consular courts in Indian Ocean port cities came to assume an outsized role in settling disputes that involved Indian merchants, which eventually reshaped commercial law and practice in the Indian Ocean by the early twentieth century.[37] These enforcement mechanisms, however, depended on the debtors being close at hand. Debtors could escape enforcement in a region marked by mobility.

MOBILITY

Time, debt, and mobility expanded the boundaries of the Indian Ocean world in the nineteenth century, and mobility features as the third major theme of this book. The Indian Ocean was a world in motion from earliest times because monsoon winds made long-distance travel possible. Jewish merchants in old Cairo traded and settled in western India in the eleventh century, Ibn Batuta sailed the breadth of the ocean in the fourteenth century, and Vasco da Gama found mariners on the East African coast who could guide him to western India at the end of the fifteenth. From the Hadhramaut in southern Arabia, generations of sayids traveled and settled as teachers, scholars, and advisors at court in distant Malaysia and Indonesia.[38] From Malacca to Kilwa, cosmopolitan port cities have long been a hallmark of the region.

The nineteenth century, however, introduced new forms of mobility and new circuits of movement that disrupted people at every rank in Indian Ocean societies, from sultans to slaves. The introduction of steamships and opening of the Suez Canal increased the speed and routes of sea travel in the Indian Ocean, but older forms of transport persisted and allowed poorer people to cover great distances. Juma bin Salim was born in the Omani interior and died on the banks of the Congo River. Although it is difficult to reconstruct his early movements with precision, travel from Nizwa to Muscat required a hundred-mile trek walking or on camelback, sailing more than 2,500 nautical miles from Muscat to Zanzibar, and, once he reached the African continent, another eight-hundred-mile trek on foot to his settlement in the Congo. For his part, Ladha Damji had been born impoverished in Kutch on the west coast of India before making his way to Zanzibar and clawing his way to the top of the region's financial elite. One Omani sultan moved his capital to Zanzibar, and his heirs went as far as Bombay and London as exiles and supplicants, biding their time in pursuit of succeeding him. The slave trade forced Africans from the interior to the Indian Ocean islands, Arabia, India, and even the Americas, and indenture transported Indians to the Mascarene islands and southern Africa. In turn, many freed slaves managed their own mobility, and their skillful manipulations of debt and time made them part of a larger group of Indian Ocean actors who populated the East African interior.

Juma bin Salim was part of a much larger movement that made upland East Africa a far shore of the Indian Ocean. Classic histories of the Indian Ocean have marginalized Africa in the early modern period, but it is impossible to overlook the movement of people into and out of Africa in the nineteenth century. The pursuit of ivory and slaves attracted traders from Arabia and the coast most prominently, but Comorians, Baluchis, and even Khojas traveled and lived in the new commercial centers that sprang up in this period on the eastern African plateau, near the Great Lakes, and on the Congo River.

The mobility of Indian Ocean actors in the African interior has had profound long-term consequences across the region, yet scholars have given inadequate attention to this process. While debt enabled their mobility to far-flung destinations, they did not always return to repay their creditors. Scholars have frequently fallen prey to a kind of coastal chauvinism that privileges the coast in the Indian Ocean world. Accounts frequently assume that all those who traveled to the interior did so to enrich themselves and return to their own distant homes or at least the shores of the Indian Ocean. These circumstances were true for a small subset of successful migrants, and it is clear that others repatriated wealth or invested in their home areas. But these cases overshadow the degree to which Indian Ocean actors were able to establish themselves in the trading depots of East Africa or in small settlements along the caravan routes and achieve a degree of wealth and autonomy that would not have been possible at home. By building local allegiances and marrying African women, Indian Ocean men became heads of polygynous households with many clients and agricultural holdings. Some enjoyed privileged access to trade, and many of those of lower status in Indian Ocean hierarchies—recently freed slaves, nonsheikhly Arabs, former Baluchi mercenaries—found greater degrees of freedom. While they might move beyond the reach of their creditors, they remained part of an expanding Indian Ocean milieu, and some status distinctions—like the Arab disdain of nontribal *bayāsirah*—traveled too. Nineteenth-century mobility and the commodity-focused credit that underwrote it brought Indians, Arabs, and Africans to new places on the Indian Ocean rim and its hinterland in much greater numbers than at any point in history. Assessing this mobility helps us balance both individual agency and the results of unintended consequences. If Juma bin Salim intended, at some point, to leave his plantations and trading hub and return with his dependents and his store of ivory to Zanzibar, settle his debts, and perhaps even go back to Oman, he died before he could do so. He ran out of time.

KINSHIP

Kinship was a vital factor in the organization of trade and mobility in the Indian Ocean. Likewise, trade and mobility led to the reconfiguration of family and broadened the purview of kin. Genealogy was a key strategy of self-representation in documents and, as a result of exogamous marriages, descent also became a discourse of belonging for Indian Ocean actors. Across the Indian Ocean, scholars have documented the family trees of rulers, descendants of the Prophet, and Sufi scholars, but new sources make it possible to reconstruct kin networks and clan memberships for other Indian Ocean actors.[39]

Although little evidence exists for us to see Juma bin Salim amid his own kin networks, he proudly listed three generations of paternal ancestors in a promissory note, and he established a household in the Congo with a Ugandan wife who helped oversee his ivory stores. Even from this limited information we can see how kinship functioned on two levels. The first level was an official genealogical one—the patrilineal line and clan—that created differences between people and ordered and legitimated a social order.[40] On the second level, the idiom of kinship described connections to other people, and these connections or relationships could be used in certain circumstances. For Juma bin Salim, this was his African wife, and for others in East Africa these included maternal uncles and uterine brothers. Indeed, in the Indian Ocean world, the calculus of kinship was important. Said bin Salim al-Lamki was born on the Swahili coast to an Omani Arab father and a Malagasy mother. Said bin Salim served as the *wali* (governor) of Saadani on the Swahili coast before the sultan appointed him in 1857 to lead Richard Burton and John Hanning Speke on their expedition in search of the Nile. Burton was scaldingly dismissive of Said bin Salim al-Lamki's obsession with kinship, complaining of Said's "ignorance and apathy concerning all things but A. bin B., and B. bin C., who married his son D. to the daughter of E."[41] But Said's focus makes clear that genealogy, kinship, and marriage were vital. Birth and genealogy were tools that mobile Indian Ocean actors could use to establish new statuses and roles by calling on new categories of kin.[42]

Familial networks served as an infrastructure linking to production and reproduction in the western Indian Ocean. In her work on Indian networks between western India and East Africa, Hollian Wint challenges narrow conceptions of trading diasporas and static views of kinship to show the centrality of families and households. They were "neither peripheral to trading networks nor unchanging units within them, rather, they were at the core of trans-local connections and transformations."[43] These transformations are clear when we see kinship as socially constructed and use it as a way to analyze social inequalities through gender, power, and difference. Within Arab families in East Africa, for example, family structures changed with mobility and new marriages, and in some cases these resulted in pronounced inequalities among kin.

ENVIRONMENT

Itinerant people in the western Indian Ocean reacted to environmental challenges and reshaped local ecologies.[44] This book prioritizes environmental histories alongside human histories, heeding anthropologist Anna Tsing's call to take seriously nonhuman actors, disturbance-based ecologies, and their shared roles in histories of capitalism.[45] The Indian Ocean monsoon system has structured mobility around the ocean; likewise, periodic droughts outside the ocean's intertropical convergence zone created difficulties for date farmers in Arabia's marginal lands. Arabs left Arabia in greater numbers in times of drought. When cyclones and floods came—wiping out palm groves and settlements—Omanis also took to the sea. Repatriated monies from migrants helped finance new irrigation channels and expand Arab settlements into marginal lands, but the threat of silting water channels and drought made for precarious livelihoods. The plentiful rain in coastal East Africa must have been a welcome relief to Arabian migrants. In Zanzibar, clove mania led to the confiscating and repurposing of farmland in the 1830s. A disastrous hurricane in 1872 destroyed substantial portions of the clove crop and undermined the sultan's independence. On the mainland, people pursuing the lucrative ivory trade changed elephant ecologies: herd populations, habitats, and dispersal. In 1875, Livingstone's biographer suggested that 44,000 elephants a year were killed to supply England with ivory.[46] While not all of these elephants were from East Africa, the demand for cheaper tusks created a moving East African ivory frontier, which encouraged hunters to travel deeper into the continent. Some Indian Ocean migrants and their dependents settled alongside Africans in the interior, and some carved out their own small communities. They planted the trees and field crops they wanted to feed themselves. They spread rice cultivation into the central African lake regions and the Congo River's tributaries. People living in western Tanzania still associate mango trees with early Arab settlers.

THE WESTERN INDIAN OCEAN, NEW SOURCES, AND ORGANIZATION OF THE BOOK

Buying Time uses a unique set of sources to complement and build on histories of East Africa and Arabia. By connecting the regions of the western Indian Ocean, this book argues for a more synthetic view of the processes that set people and goods in motion in the nineteenth century. An oceanic perspective has always helped explain the history of East Africa, but an oceanic turn in the approach to history—what some have called a "new thalassology"—in the first decade of the twenty-first century has made it easier to assess connections between distant regions through the sea.[47] The earliest twentieth-century histories of East Africa posited that the Indian Ocean was a source of "invaders" who "exploited" the region.[48] Important classic works noted the role of Indian Ocean trade networks for coastal entrepôts linked to trade and production in the African interior.[49] Some scholarship specified the role of "Arabs" (loosely defined) from the Indian Ocean as oppositional to Europeans in Africa, missing the opportunity to describe both groups as part of a broader regional historical trajectory.[50] Close study of coastal societies revealed waves of immigration from both the sea and the interior that shaped political discourse and rebellion on the eve of European colonization, and Africans from the interior shaped forms of labor on long-distance trade to and from the coast.[51] While many of the historical actors had ties to distant shores, and these regional histories acknowledge the role of the ocean as a source of trade goods or migrants, they do not cross it.

A willingness to cross the sea and engage the Indian Ocean as an organizing framework also deepens our understanding of the history of Arabia. The initial histories of Oman deemphasized oceanic connections, while more recent work on the nineteenth century has focused on the Muscat-Zanzibar nexus in terms of trade and British imperial politics.[52] The historian Nile Green disaggregated "the Middle East" into three arenas, one of which is the Indian Ocean. (The others are the Mediterranean Sea and Inner Asia.) A benefit of this formulation, he argues, is "bringing Africa into view as a crucial component in the development of Middle Eastern societies."[53] Certainly recent excellent work on Africans in Arabia shows the merit of this approach.[54] *Buying Time* works from both the Arabian and African shores of the western Indian Ocean to show how the movement of people between them was a crucial component of the development of both regions in the nineteenth century. Within histories of the Indian Ocean in the imperial age, India, as a subimperial power, and Indians moving within "greater India" have been prominent.[55] Hadrami Arabs have received the most attention as an Arabian diaspora.[56] While these groups certainly figure into our story, the focus of this work will be primarily on the broad social array of Omani Arabs and Africans in western Indian Ocean networks that stretched into continental hinterlands.

~

While this new thalassology adds an oceanic perspective, new sources make it easier to trace the movements of people across this broad, complicated region. These new sources include thousands of Arabic business contracts—sales, mortgages, and promissory notes—that have been sitting—uncatalogued and untranslated—in the Zanzibar archives for over 130 years.[57] These documents record the activities of Africans, Arabs, and Indians within social and financial networks—networks that included the caravan stations of East Africa and the oasis villages of interior Arabia. The unique information in this archive reveals new and important details about the Indian Ocean's past. First, these documents show complex variations on the financial transactions that underwrote ivory trading and mortgaged property—in Arabia, on the eastern coast of Africa, and in the African interior. Second, they list names, genealogies, statuses, and clan names of a wide variety of people—Africans,

Indians, and Arabs; men and women; free and slave—who bought, sold, and mortgaged property in the nineteenth century. These genealogies illustrate the vast diversity of actors involved in these transactions. Third, the documents were created outside colonial and European influence and adhere to long-standing Islamic legal forms, but they also exhibit local inflections. Each deed provides a snapshot of an interconnected world before European colonialism.

The challenge of these documents has been to provide sufficient context to bring them to life. On the one hand, these transaction records have provided nuanced backstories for known individuals like Juma bin Salim. Starting from an interesting deed, on the other hand, I have been fortunate to fill in details of overlooked actors in Indian Ocean history by turning to nineteenth-century colonial archives, travelers' accounts, missionary journals, Swahili biographies, and Omani scholars. I also gathered family histories by following the routes that the deeds set into motion: up and down the Swahili coast, across the old caravan route to Lake Tanganyika, and to the capital and interior towns of Oman. These sources and methods cannot account, however, for more informal credit networks or arrangements that were never registered. Indeed, the source base is slanted toward those who relied on Indian creditors. During the 1860s and 1870s changes to consular courts and to the definition of who was a British subject meant that Hindu and Muslim Indian businesspeople brought their documents to be registered at the consulate. Fortunately, some of these were decades old so that it becomes possible to reconstruct a range of social worlds from the 1840s and, occasionally, earlier. The breadth of the archive makes clear that throughout the nineteenth century a wide variety of people engaged in these transactions. These exciting new sources provide a way to understand the uses of credit and debt, to see previously overlooked groups, and to map individuals into Indian Ocean circuits.

This book is organized around nine chapters. It begins in Arabia, examining the conditions in Oman during the first decades of the nineteenth century. Chapter 1 argues that a novel combination of environmental, social, and political factors influenced Arab immigration to East Africa. Drought and political disturbances that aligned with periods of intense migration demonstrate that emigrants from the interior of Oman left their villages as a temporizing strategy. These migrants dealt with challenges such as drought, water courses running dry, and palm groves dying, with the seemingly temporary solution of transoceanic migration. This movement was made easier by the Omani sultan's relocation to East Africa in the 1830s. Omani Arab rule in Zanzibar helped formalize a commercial culture, and chapter 2 analyzes the Arabic business documents that comprise the heart of this book by looking at the 1840s. These documents record agreements between buyers and sellers, creditors and debtors, and each one reflects the enmeshed social and economic relations in the port city of Zanzibar, even as they implicate a broader Indian Ocean seascape.

The third chapter details the enmeshed politics of Zanzibar and Muscat, especially during the rule of Said bin Sultan al-Busaidi (r. 1804–56) and the period after his death. His heirs' intrigues and rivalries led to civil war in 1859, a division of dominion in 1861, and a revival of the Ibadi Imamate in Muscat in 1868–71. The political and economic relationships between these two capitals remained influential for the rest of the century. Chapter 3 focuses on the Omani rulers' mobility around the western Indian Ocean and on their exertion of authority through property seizures in Zanzibar and Oman. The 1859 rebellion led to more Arab settlement in the East African interior during the burgeoning ivory trade.

Chapter 4 examines the movements of people. Mobility shifted notions of identity as Indian Ocean peoples established themselves in the East African interior. The nineteenth century marked the delinking of ethnonyms from specific geographies: Arabs were not just in Arabia; Swahili people left the coast; and Nyamwezi and other interior people took to the sea. This movement produced new configurations of people and geographies, which had implications for identity, kinship, and belonging for Arabs and Africans. Chapter 5 focuses on the kinship networks of the most famous trader of this period, Hamed bin Muhammad al-Murjebi, better known as Tippu Tip. Reading his autobiography through the lens of kinship reveals that, rather than being a self-made man, Tippu Tip benefited from elaborate webs of kinship, stretching from Oman to the eastern Congo. His trade organization—like many during this period—relied on siblings, and his marriage into an elite Omani family provided him with property in Zanzibar and Oman. Kinship emerges as a vital way to understand business and family networks.

While both the slave trade and slavery itself have been associated with this period of African history, freed slaves have often been overlooked. Chapter 6 first examines manumission and the mobility of freed slaves in the western Indian Ocean up to the 1850s. Islamic manumission was an important social practice long before European colonization disrupted slavery in East Africa. The chapter then addresses the moral economy of manumission and insincere manumission after the 1850s to meet the demand for labor in the Indian Ocean islands. Chapter 7 looks at the period following the 1873 antislavery treaty to examine Indian Ocean mobility amid the rise of a British documentary regime. New consular courts, a redefinition of British Indian subjecthood, and naval antislavery enforcement all contributed to a focus on new kinds of writing and a return to insincere manumission. By this time, however, African slaves and former slaves were tightly connected to Arab and Indian households, and when households left Africa for Arabia or India they revealed a racial gradient of mobility. By examining the lives of freed slaves—including their economic activity, their relationships with their former masters, and the routes they traveled—the broader history of the western Indian Ocean comes more sharply into focus.

Each of the final two chapters focuses on an individual who represents a microcosm of the Indian Ocean world: a freed slave and an Omani tribal leader. They both built lives and transformed environments far from the sea, but they depended on Indian Ocean credit, mobility, and kinship to advance their own agendas when the deck was stacked against them.

The eighth chapter focuses on the extraordinary career of the man who built the first dhow on Lake Victoria. He was a freed slave who entered the ivory business on the mainland with his partner, another freed slave. They became entangled with Zanzibari creditors and the complex local politics of their African patron. The freed slave and ivory trader created tight kin networks with his patron on the island of Ukerewe in Lake Victoria, and he built "a second Zanzibar" on the lake's shore. This trading post attracted missionary attention in the 1870s, and it created a collision among the local ruler, the missionaries, and the ivory dealer, which led to many deaths. It sent reverberations across the lake and down the caravan trails to Zanzibar. At the center of the dispute were attempts at the manipulation of credit, misunderstood documents, and a contest in the interior over Indian Ocean trade.

During this period in Arabia, the political history of interior Oman proved to be intricately tied to Indian Ocean networks, specifically credit markets in Zanzibar. Chapter 9 traces the history of Salih bin Ali al-Harthi (1834–1896), a major religiopolitical leader in the Omani interior, to show how his challenges to the Omani sultans were connected to Zanzibar. The second half of the century also saw ongoing migration (and circulation) from Arabia to East Africa, despite the political division of the territories in 1861. Salih bin Ali was preceded in death by his former ally Barghash, the sultan of Zanzibar (r. 1870–88), and by his bête noir Turki, the sultan of Muscat (r. 1871–88). The death of these two sultans marked a turning point in the western Indian Ocean: European hegemony resulted in the partition of East Africa and an unofficial protectorate in Oman. An epilogue connects these nineteenth-century events to the present, including twentieth-century Omani migration; the violent revolution in Zanzibar in 1964, which killed and expelled thousands of Arabs; the 1970 palace coup in Oman, which paved the way for East African Arabs to "return" to the homeland of the predecessors; and the place of these so-called Zanzibaris in modern Oman.

⌇

When Juma bin Salim wrote his two-year ivory contract with Ladha Damji in Zanzibar in 1869, he identified himself by genealogy and origin. He included his tribal name, al-Bakri, and appended a signifier of his place of origin, Nizwa, one of the most important cities in the eastern Arabian interior. The circumstances in Oman and Nizwa that thrust Juma bin Salim out into the Indian Ocean, into debt, and into the heart of Africa begin our story.

1 ❦ Drought and New Mobilities in the Omani Interior

بُو يَاكِل حَلْوَاهَا يَصْبُرُ عَلَى بَلْوَهَا
"He who eats her halwa must [also] patiently endure her misfortune"

إِذَا مَا طَاعَك الدَّهَر طِيعُه حَتَّى تَكُون رَبِيعُه
"If fortune does not obey you, follow it so that you may become its companion."

—Nineteenth-Century Omani Proverbs

IN THE 1840S, Nizwa, one of the largest and most important towns in the Omani interior, and its environs were struck by a severe drought. This drought lasted for more than five years, disrupted the normal patterns of life, and resulted in mass emigration. The festival (*'eid al-adha*) marking the culmination of the Hajj in 1845 reflected the impact of this environmental crisis. Because of the drought, Nizwans were unable to celebrate in their normal manner. The eighty-foot-tall fort at the center of Nizwa commanded a view of what had been, in more prosperous times, extensive date groves. As a meeting place of four streams, Nizwa was generally well watered, and, consequently, its citizens were well off. Writing forty years after the drought, S. B. Miles noted that Nizwa surpassed "all the towns of Oman in its supply of water, natural wealth, and the industry of its inhabitants."[1] Before the drought in the 1840s, the area's agriculture supported a population whose size was second only to Muscat, and its industry included "famous and extensive" textile and embroidery works. Nizwa grew cotton and indigo, and women spun and men worked looms to produce blue cotton goods.[2] Nizwa was also a religious capital, known as *bayḍat al-Islam*, the core—literally, "egg"—of Islam, for its historical role in maintaining the Ibadi Imamate.[3] The people of Nizwa prayed and studied in three hundred mosques.

During the December 1845 festival (*'eid*), however, something was amiss. A procession of drummers and horn players led cheering men to the central square for mock fighting with swords, spears, and matchlocks. Women watched the festivities from the rooftops. But the normal celebrations lacked something important. The *'eid al-Adha* celebrations of the *Hejira* year 1261 went on for a typical three days, but the circumstances—namely, the five years of drought—meant that anxiety plagued people from every social class. With the central market closed and commerce suspended, adults worried about rain. Would this be the year? More immediately, those who anticipated the delectable sweetmeats for which Nizwa was famous felt the sting of the drought. There was no *halwa*. None of the sweet delicacies were procurable. And it was not simply a question of obtaining the ingredients. Many families had left Nizwa because of the drought and mysteriously, the departed in-

FIGURE 1.1. Nizwa fort, silent witness to the 1840s drought. Percy Cox took this photograph in 1901. "Some Excursions in Oman," *Geographical Journal* 66, no. 3 (September 1925).

cluded all of the confectioners.⁴ The out-migration of confectioners, who were people of humble status, offers new clues on the mobility and circulation of people within Arabia and beyond.

The long drought and the loss of viable agricultural lands around Nizwa caused people to flee. While some moved to places in the interior or to the coastal towns of Oman, others went farther afield. One Nizwan became an important property broker in Zanzibar. Juma bin Salim al-Bakri, whose story was introduced earlier, amassed huge ivory holdings at his headquarters in the eastern Congo. And, fifteen years after the *halwa*-free Hajj festivities, a confectioner who had traveled through Muscat to East Africa became a trade agent and "big man" in the most important trading depot in central Africa. Thus, in that drought-stricken festival in 1845, while the men of Nizwa sipped coffee in the evening and listened to a poet sing his verses, they were likely worrying about the ruin of the whole province. They probably could not have imagined how far the drought would compel their neighbors and countrymen to travel.

This chapter examines eastern Arabia in the early nineteenth century to explain the environmental, social, and political conditions that prompted Arab migration to East Africa. The Omani ruler Seyyid Said bin Sultan al-Busaidi's reasons for shifting his capital to Zanzibar in 1832 were financial and geostrategic, but what motivated others?⁵ Despite the important connections, many histories focused on East Africa have taken Arab migration for granted and overlooked push factors.⁶ Surprisingly, many of the Arab migrants who traveled to Africa in the nineteenth century were people of modest means from interior towns, not wealthy traders from port cities. Rather than neglect the Omani interior, this chapter focuses on the patterns of circulation that connected Arabian oasis towns like Nizwa to far-off Zanzibar and new settlements in eastern and central Africa.

This story necessarily begins with the underlying geographical and environmental factors that shaped human settlements in interior Oman and ends with threats that periodically upset these settlements. The management of water shaped Omani settlement patterns, and this chapter takes up the technological adaptations and religious traditions that addressed environmental limitations. Scholarly approaches that have presupposed a false dichotomy between static interior societies and enterprising coastal peoples have misread Omani history and misunderstood the processes that linked the interior regions of Arabia and Africa. Seyyid Said bin Sultan's activity in the Indian Ocean, and his outposts in Africa in particular, renewed circuits of

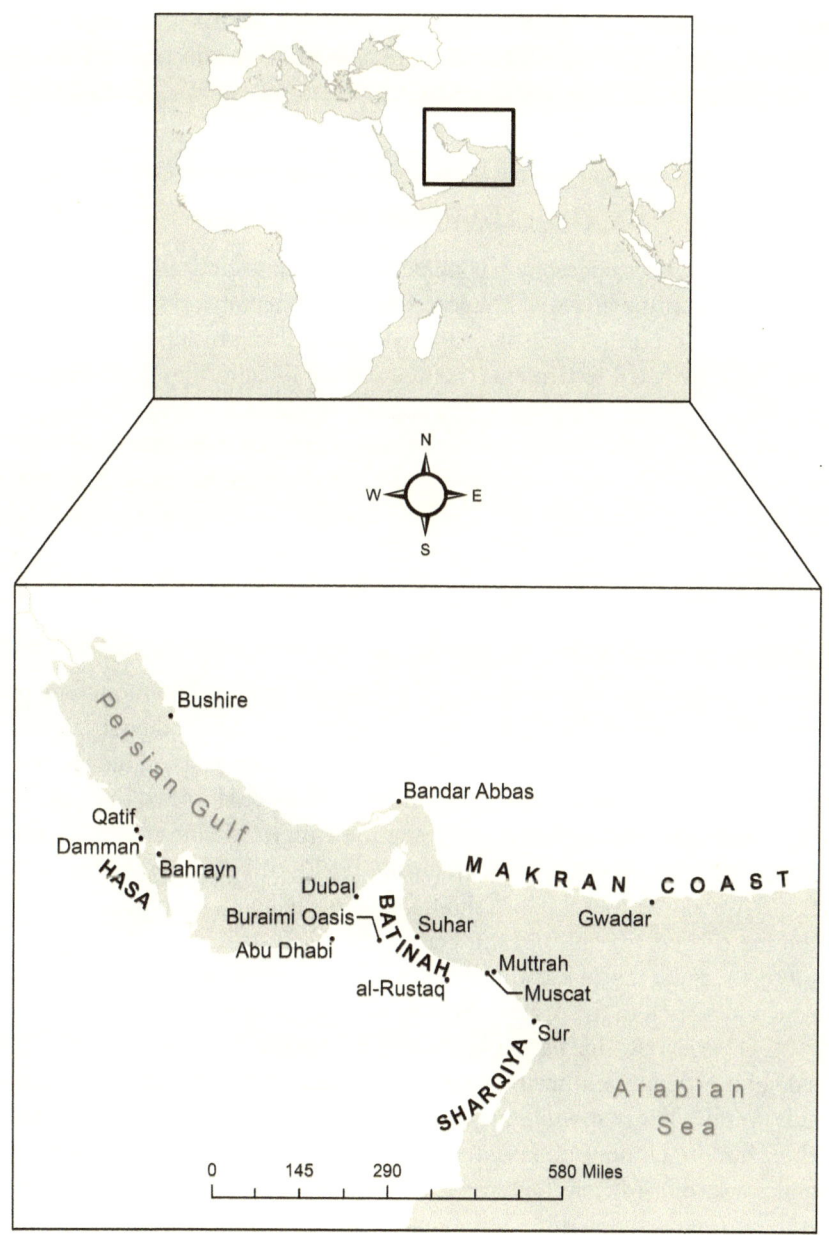

MAP 1.1. Oman and its surrounding regions

travel and created new opportunities. Thus, when Arabs in Oman were faced with progressively more difficult choices about how to handle constricting droughts or devastating floods, a new temporizing strategy—decamping to Africa—was open to them.

GEOGRAPHY

Oman's peculiar geography has made it both relatively isolated from the Arabian Peninsula and well connected to maritime networks. The region's geography has created unusual patterns of rainfall and runoff, and humans have built irrigated settlements that are well adapted to these arid, rugged conditions. Oman's seemingly contradictory forces of isolation and integration have also sustained Ibadism, a sect of Islam that is neither Sunni nor Shi'a, though regional dynamics have also undermined Ibadism's ideal form of governance, the imamate.[7] These forces have also tempted scholars to mistake the country for a static interior cutoff from the littoral, a view derived from the country's twentieth-century history, when it was known as the Sultanate of Muscat and Oman, than from the preceding century, which is our focus.

Geography is inherently visual and most easily understood through maps or metaphors. It is useful to imagine the Arabian Peninsula as a boot. Viewed from the side, the boot has a heel, Yemen, which nearly rests on the Horn of Africa. The boot's spiked toe pokes into the Straits of Hormuz, the passage into the Persian Gulf. The countries of the eastern Mediterranean (Syria, Lebanon, Israel, and Jordan) serve as the boot's pull straps at the top, and Saudi Arabia is the boot's thick shaft. Oman is the boot's toe box. The top of the toe box curves out into the Persian Gulf's entrance, and the toe box meets the outer sole at Ras al-Hadd, the eastern-most point of the peninsula, which juts out into the Arabian Sea of the Indian Ocean.

As it turns out, this particular boot is steel-toed: mountains line the inside of the toe box and seem to cut off (or protect) the interior from the outside world.[8] These mountains, called the Hajar range, run for more than three hundred miles (500 km), are seventy-five miles (110 km) at their widest, and reach to nearly ten thousand feet (3,000 m) at their highest point, Jebel Akhdar (green mountain). The range only breaks at a few points, where drainage has created passes through the mountains. On the sea side of the mountains, a coastal plain known as the Batinah (*al-Bāṭinah*) fills the gentle arc at a width of twenty miles. The mountains draw close to the shore again, and the Batinah ends at an important pass—the Sumayl Gap—through the mountains, right before the twin ports of Muttrah and Muscat.

The steep mountains plunging to the sea create the natural harbors of Muttrah and Muscat, and the Sumayl Gap is the broadest break in the mountains. Historically, Sumayl was a vital link between the coast and the interior for the movement of people and goods; control of the pass had military implications for the ruler and those who wished to challenge him.

The Omani interior lies between the landward side of the Hajar range and the desert forelands of central Arabia. This region was historically known as Oman, so the modern nation-state derives its name from its interior rather than its more famous coasts. Thus, referring to the "Omani interior" is something of neologism. In the interior, the mountains give way to a bajada zone of alluvial fans that reach out to a vast waterless plain before running into the desert sands.[9] Primary settlements exist in the mountains, on the piedmont, and out in the plain. Movement along the outwash fans is much easier than crossing the mountains or the desert, facilitating exchange between interior settlements. In this sense, if we imagine the desert as the sea, the Omani interior shares characteristics with littoral societies: greater similarities in location, occupation, and culture to those on the littoral than to those in the hinterland.[10] The interior settlements fall into two general regions, al-Dakhiliya and al-Sharqiya. Al-Dakhiliya (literally, "the interior") is the central region, snugged south and west of the Jebel Akdhar massif. To the east, al-Sharqiya (literally, "the east") is hemmed in by the Hajar Mountains to the north and east. The region gives way in the south to the Wahiba Sands. The Sumayl Gap connects Dakhilya and Sharqiya to the ports of Muscat and Muttrah, and Sharqiya also has a connection to the port of Sur to the southeast.

IBADISM

Another defining aspect of the Omani interior has been its religious character. Oman has been the home of Ibadi Islam for 1,200 years. Ibadism (*Ibaḍiyya*) is a sect that separated from mainstream Islam in 37 AH/657 CE, before the better-known divisions of Sunni and Shia took place. Ibadis refer to themselves as "the people of straightness" (*ahl al-istiqāma*), and they believe they are the practitioners of "the oldest and most authentic form of Islam."[11] Ibadi theology centers on a longing for a righteous imam who scholars and pious leaders select to facilitate the believers' ability to live in an ideal society defined by piety and justice.[12] Striving to achieve this righteous imamate has been a touchstone of Omani history, and Wilkinson has proposed an "Imamate Cycle" as a means to explain the Omani past. In this view, new imamates have strong ideological power, but when the ideological basis of the Ibadi imamate weakens, the struggle for power and wealth increases, and this struggle leads to a revival of tribal factionalism.[13] Elected imams ruled Oman from the interior towns, generally Nizwa or al-Rustaq.

While the first Busaidi ruler of Oman, Ahmad bin Said, was proclaimed an Imam in 1749, his descendants who have ruled the country have not been elected as imams since the late eighteenth century. In 1785, Imam Ahmad's grandson, Hamed bin Said bin Ahmad (r. 1784–1792), shifted his seat of power from al-Rustaq, where his father had ruled, to Muscat in order to take advantage of the Indian Ocean trade.[14] While trade connections and migration to Africa led some Ibadis to adopt Sunnism, Ibadism thrived in the Omani interior and remained a potent political discourse for challenging the Busaidi sultanate over the last two hundred years. Ibadism has only recently attracted broader scholarly attention, and the Omani interior's distinctive relationship with this religion contributed to broader misunderstandings of the region.

MISREADING THE INTERIOR

While the coastal Indian Ocean port cities of eastern Arabia have long been cosmopolitan centers, scholars have considered the interior of Oman to be isolated, static, and conservative. Yet it was interior Arabs, from Oman proper, who took to the Indian Ocean in great numbers in the nineteenth century. The imagined dichotomy between an outward-looking coastal people and an inhospitable interior inhabited by backward, fearsome people echoes the view that both contemporaries and scholars held about East Africa's coast and interior. In this false geographical determinism, the mountains and deserts of Arabia played the same role as the supposedly impenetrable "jungles" in Africa. Some scholars mapped this geography onto Omanis themselves. One historian of nineteenth- and twentieth-century Oman declared, "The coastal Omani often considered the entire western Indian Ocean his world; his vision was not restricted by the rim rocks of a narrow mountain valley as was so often the case with an inhabitant of Oman's interior."[15] In this view, the interior was "a highly static society" organized to "preserve a fundamentalist, conservative Ibadi environment."[16] Following this argument, geographical barriers limited residents' mobility, and their particular practice of Islam further narrowed their horizons. A picture of an isolated, simple people dominated by Ibadi Islam emerges from this view.

These characterizations, however, break down under scrutiny. A typical historical account from the twentieth century imagined an Arab of the interior within an isolated, static society and noted that his "idea of wealth was limited to such things as the number of date palms trees, camels, goats, wives, or slaves" he might possess. Spiritual possessions supposedly trumped material ones: "Even these material belongings would have to rank behind the spiritual virtues of knowledge of the Koran and Ibadi law in the hierarchy of desired possessions; ostentatious display was, of course, forbidden."[17] During the nineteenth century, however, the primary market for dates was overseas; slaves arrived from distant shores; and the seat of Ibaḍi learning and scholarship moved to Zanzibar. While dichotomous thinking about Oman is suspect in any period, the nineteenth-century connections between Oman and East Africa thoroughly undercut imagined distinctions between coast and interior. These new patterns of migration to East Africa that began in the nineteenth century did not subside until the last third of the twentieth century. Only the 1964 anti-Arab revolutionary bloodshed in Zanzibar and a new 1970 regime in Oman—led by a man who committed newly found oil wealth to transforming his Arabian sultanate—would reverse the flow of interior Omanis to Africa. In the nineteenth century, however, new links to Indian Ocean networks and the wealth generated in East Africa expanded settlements in the Omani interior, attracted migrants, fueled political rivalries, and discounted the myth of an isolated interior.

WATER AND PRECARITY

Oman's geography—or more accurately, its topography—has allowed for irrigated agriculture in all but the most arid parts of the country. The mountain massif that separates the coast from the interior traps moist air from the Indian Ocean and Arabian Sea, and during the cool months rain falls in the mountains. The average yearly rainfall over the whole country from 1900 to 2012 was 98.1 mm (3.86 inches).[18] This volume provides sufficient moisture for pluvial farms in the mountain valleys, and some people even made their own wine. More important, rain drains from the mountains into wadis that fan into the plains. The wadis filter the water into underground aquifers, and using ancient engineering techniques, inhabitants have tapped these aquifers to extend agriculture far from the central mountains and to water-thirsty date palms, their most important crop.

The *falaj* (plural: *aflāj*) irrigation system in the interior connected water sources to distant points underground. These engineered channels, some of which ran for miles underground and others that had shafts more than forty feet deep, awed the British naval officer James R. Wellsted when he visited the interior of Oman in 1835. Wellsted noted that most of the interior towns "owe their fertility to the happy manner in which the inhabitants have availed themselves of a mode of conducting water to them, a mode, as far as I know, peculiar to this country, and at an expense of labour and skill more Chinese than Arabian."[19] This irrigation scheme actually originated in ancient Persia, and an underground channel built sometime before 681 BCE still delivers water to Arbil, in Kurdish Iraq. The techniques of building these *qanāt*, as they are known in Persian, spread from Persia to Oman and Egypt, among other places, during the Achaemenian Empire (650–330 BCE), and later with the spread of Islam.[20] Wellsted was correct, however, in appreciating the expense of labor and skill required to create and maintain *aflaj*.

The *aflaj* system was necessary to sustain life in the interior, and organization and management of water resources drove settlement patterns for the villages and towns. The result was self-contained, nucleated settlements spaced wide apart.[21] Within villages, the flow of the *falaj* created the principles for spatial organization. The place where the *falaj* emerged was a site from which everyone could take drinking water, and the *falaj* was sometimes divided into channels from there, depending on the size of the settlement and the flow of the water. Residential clusters and mosques were often at the top of the flow, and palm gardens received irrigation first, followed by other permanent cultivation, and then by seasonal crops.[22] Unlike the relatively well-watered Batinah, the Omani interior depended on the careful use of water through the *aflaj* to grow dates, fruits, and fodder. Of these, dates were the most important agricultural product for both individual people (in terms of caloric intake) and the economy (as the most valuable export). Omani farmers thus depended on careful allocations of water to ensure their survival.

Management of the *falaj* system required an elaborate set of practices for allocating water shares, for measuring both time and water, and for maintaining the upkeep of the water courses.[23] These irrigation channels required constant care, which demanded, in turn, a well-organized group to tend to them.[24] The Ibadi rules of war made clear the centrality of the *falaj* systems and the tree crops they supported. People laying siege against other Muslims could remove crops and cut off the water supplies, but cutting down a palm tree was extreme and the destruction of a *falaj* was verboten.[25] Rules also governed access to abandoned or silted up *aflaj* and the rights of those who undertook the immense effort and expense to build new *falaj* systems. Those who originated a *falaj* or renewed a dead (*mawāt*) falaj could claim permanent shares in the system for a fixed period. The other permanent shares in the *falaj* were sold, and all shares were subject to Ibadi inheritance law.[26] Because the seasonal flows of water varied, these shares were not for units of volume, but for units of time for water flow. Regular auctions of shares that belonged in trust (*waqf*) to the *falaj* provided income for the upkeep of this intricate system. Such auctions also allowed people who did not own permanent shares in the *falaj* to purchase access to irrigation water. This practice was a literal example of people buying time, purchasing units of water flow to ensure that their crops could survive.

The *falaj* system, a solution to inhabiting marginal lands, created a distinctive form of settlement in Oman that required a delicate balance of human ingenuity and labor with the right amount of rain. Too little—or too much—precipitation had disastrous consequences. During the nineteenth century, drought and its extreme opposite—violent rainstorms—periodically wreaked havoc on the interior of Oman. While some drought was expected, irregular, extreme patterns of drought like the one that left Nizwa without any *halwa* in the 1840s ended the water supply to some *aflaj* when the water table fell. These were the kinds of ecological disruptions that temporarily reset Omani society. One can see a halting pattern throughout Omani history: villages were abandoned and reopened at different times when, either through good fortune or hard work, the *falaj* flowed again. Large-scale expansions of the *falaj* system tended to occur only when strong imams ruled with links to maritime trade. These were the conditions best suited to major extensive development and falaj building.[27]

Along these lines, it is worth noting that the nineteenth century emerges as anomalous because new mobility resulted in both the abandonment of settlements (albeit sometimes temporarily) for the coast and for Africa, and in new sources of wealth linked to Indian Ocean commodity trades, which made it possible in a limited number of cases to renovate or extend *aflaj*. The advent of Omani rule in Africa broadened mobility and could relieve temporary pressure on precarious settlements.[28] Even in times of typical rainfall, however, *falaj* communities faced pressure to divide the irrigation supply fairly among many shareholders, to use the water efficiently, and to ensure the maintenance of the system. The way that each community made these compromises around the *falaj* system, Wilkinson has argued, reveals "some of the fundamental aspects of social organization in an Omani village."[29]

Extreme drought threatened the social organization of villages and the livelihoods of families. Individuals and families had to choose from among a range of limited options open to Omanis in the interior. As water courses slowed to a trickle—or dried up completely—families could no longer water fields, fruits, or fodder. Famine followed drought. Paradoxically, water was not always a blessing. Cyclones or hurricanes sometimes delivered massive deluges, and the compromised hydrology of the country made it vulnerable to flash floods that uprooted palm trees, damaged *aflaj*, and devastated settlements. Indeed, periodic environmental setbacks undercut livelihoods in interior Oman, and they also provided reasons to abandon settlements. In the nineteenth century, however, a new option presented itself: emigration from Oman to the burgeoning Arab settlement on the Indian Ocean coast of Africa, a route made possible by the Indian Ocean activities of their ruler, Said bin Sultan.

SAID BIN SULTAN AND THE INDIAN OCEAN CONTEXT

For interior Omanis, a new connection to the Indian Ocean world emerged in the nineteenth century because of changes in trade and alliances. Said bin Sultan bin Ahmed al-Busaidi was at the center of these changes. Known by the honorific *seyyid* (lord), Said had been the ruler of Muscat and its dependencies since 1804, and he had played an important role in an Omani commercial expansion.[30] While Europeans insisted on calling him the Imam of Muscat, he was never elected to that Ibadi rank. Instead he focused on external relations, continuing a tradition of Busaidi rulers. In the first half of the eighteenth century, Said's grandfather, Ahmad, led the resistance to a Persian invasion and cast off the Omani Ya'arubi dynasty that had allowed the Persians in. These heroics—and Ahmad's exemplary character—led to his election as Imam in the 1740s. Seyyid Said, his grandson, came to the throne through adroit personal maneuvering in the early years of the nineteenth century, and became Oman's greatest sultan. Domestic politics in Arabia demanded smart tactics, and Said bin Sultan used the same political flair (and willingness to use force) to expand al-Busaidi control beyond Arabia. He deftly balanced the competing interests and animosities of four regions—Oman, the Persian Gulf, the Indian Ocean, and East Africa—to rule an empire that connected three sides of the western Indian Ocean.[31] His family and close allies controlled Oman's principal towns and both sides of the Straits of Hormuz. Across the Arabian Sea, Oman's Busaidi rulers claimed the Makran coast, in what is now part of Pakistan, and in the 1820s and 1830s, Said subdued the towns of the Swahili coast.

Seyyid Said was a ruler of international standing. He corresponded with Muhammad Ali, the pasha of Egypt, and Andrew Jackson, the president of the United States. He finalized commercial treaties with the United States, Britain, and France. In 1846, he sent his most trusted ambassador to New York City with a cargo of merchandise. In the Indian Ocean region, he sought strategic marriages with regional powers, taking a Persian royal for a bride, and he sent proposals to the widowed Sakalava Queen of western

Madagascar.[32] In Oman, he leveraged his power to check challenges on religious grounds, both from Omani Ibadis and from reformist Wahhabis outside his realm. In the Persian Gulf he battled other regional maritime powers and allied with Great Britain to suppress piracy.[33] After 1819, when Great Britain effectively limited the Omani role in the Persian Gulf trade and threatened the robust exchange between Muscat and the ports of western India, Said looked to Africa.[34]

The relationship between eastern Arabia and East Africa was an enduring one. People from Arabia had settled on the east coast for more than a millennium, and slaves from the Swahili coast revolted in southern Iraq in the tenth century.[35] Monsoon winds propelled seasonal traders to Africa and back, and other Arab migrants established themselves on the Swahili coast in medieval city-states like Kilwa.[36] Direct Omani involvement in East Africa began after the Omani Arabs wrested the coast from the Portuguese in 1698. This involvement in East African affairs waxed and waned over the next two hundred years, dictated as much by politics in Arabia as by matters on the coast. Under the eighteenth-century Omani Ya'arubi dynasty, more Arabs had settled along the East African coast—especially from Lamu to Mombasa, and further south at Kilwa—as they were attracted by profits from trade. These settlers retained their loyalty to the Ya'arubi rulers even after the 1740s, when Imam Ahmad displaced them in Oman. During that period, Imam Ahmad tried to capture Mombasa, and he sent assassins from Oman to eliminate certain rulers, but he was unsuccessful.[37] It was tenacious Arab clans like these, foremost among them the Mazrui of Mombasa, that Said bin Sultan faced in the early nineteenth century when he attempted to assert al-Busaidi control over the coast.

Said had begun his conquest of East Africa in 1817, and he tried to balance Arab and European rivalries in the Persian Gulf and on the African coast, along with a tenuous domestic situation in the Omani interior. Once he secured Zanzibar, an island situated twenty miles from shore in the middle of the long Swahili coast, Seyyid Said used it as a base of operations. Some East African outposts, especially Mombasa, did not readily submit to al-Busaidi rule. Elsewhere on the Swahili coast by the late 1820s, Said had established effective control over important coastal towns, appointing a governor, a customs master, and in some cases, a garrison chief. Zanzibar was the most important for Said bin Sultan, and he moved his court from Muscat to Zanzibar in 1832. With this direct attention (and substantial intrigue), he was able to subdue the Swahili coast and exile the Mazrui governor of Mombasa and his followers to the Persian Gulf in 1837.[38]

Despite his nominal control of both Arabia and East Africa, Said bin Sultan faced challenges to his rule from his subjects and from European political interests in the western Indian Ocean. In Arabia, he favored the coastal towns like Muscat, Muttrah, and Suhar, over the interior centers of Ibadi power, such as Nizwa and al-Rustaq. During his reign, Said bin Sultan failed to earn the confidence of Ibadi leaders, and he sought to balance their needs with the demands and attractions of Indian Ocean (and global) trade.[39] The Busaidis had aggressively pursued international trade since 1783, focusing more on Muscat and port cities than the interior. By moving their capital from al-Rustaq to Muscat in the eighteenth century, al-Busaidi rulers distanced themselves from the tribal politics of the interior.[40] Consequently, Muscat and its sister city Muttrah became vibrant, multicultural ports, attracting merchants, traders, and slaves from the Persian Gulf and the western Indian Ocean. A visitor in 1824 noted Muscat had become "a sort of emporium for the Coasts of Africa, Madagascar, the Red Sea, the Persian Gulf, and India in general; and in being so, it has rather added to than diminished the trade of Cutch, Surat, Bombay, &c."[41] The strong connection to India was clear: this observer noted that the lingua franca of Muscat was Hindustani, and the only Arabic speakers were native Arabs, whom he called "by far the smallest portion of the inhabitants."[42]

Within Arabia, Said had to contend with the threat of Wahhabi pressure. The violent, reformist ideology that Muhammad ibn 'Abd al-Wahhab expounded in the eighteenth century became the theological basis for the expansion of Muhammad bin Sa'ud's state from highland central Arabia. The Wahhabi antagonized the Ottomans to their north and the Omanis to their east.

Said bin Sultan's challenges in Arabia from the Wahhabi forces demonstrated the complex calculus of local and regional rivals. Between 1800 and 1820, the area around Wadi Ma'awil was home to a series of violent destructive conflicts. The Wahhabi attacks on the well-watered date-farming region at the southern end of the Batinah coast and the areas northwest of Muscat and near Wadi Sumayl were retribution for Said bin Sultan's activity in the gulf. Said bin Sultan had allied with the East India Company in 1809 to thwart his rivals the Qawasim of Ras al-Khayma and their Wahhabi allies.[43] When the East India Company's ships withdrew, however, the Wahhabi staged multiple punitive expeditions against Oman, and the Wadi Ma'awil was hit hard. In response to the Wahhabi alliance with Said's local rivals, the Omani ruler requested military support from the Persian shah and received 1,500 cavalrymen.[44] Some of the pitched battles lasted nearly two weeks. Foreign troops occupied local settlements, and fighting spilled into the marketplace.[45] Both sides destroyed their enemies' date plantations, cutting down trees in contravention of Ibadi laws of war, and crushing the local agricultural economy.⁴⁶ Seyyid Said failed to bring peace when he captured the fort at Nakhl, because the governor he appointed abused the local populace. They insisted that the governor be removed or they would emigrate, but the replacement was also cruel.⁴⁷ Even as Said bin Sultan launched attacks on Bahrain in the gulf, the war in Wadi al-Ma'awīl continued until the late 1810s when, after sending a large contingent from Sharqiya, Said bin Sultan negotiated a temporary settlement in the region.⁴⁸ The fight with the Wahhabi and their allies threatened Said bin Sultan's rule and destabilized the local population. These rivalries also pushed Said bin Sultan to ally frequently with British forces, and he spent much of his career negotiating with Europeans in the Indian Ocean.

As with domestic forces, Said engaged in a subtle balancing act with European nations, and his move to Africa brought him into closer contact with them. He sought trading advantages through commercial treaties, but he tried to limit the role of European traders, especially in his African dependencies. For much of his reign, Europeans were forbidden from trading on the African mainland. He funneled all business through Zanzibar. There, Indian merchants and financiers, some of whom had followed him from Muscat (where their families had lived for generations), oversaw trade on behalf of Said, and they imposed customs duties on all goods. In Oman, foreign merchants were limited to the port cities. In the 1840s, British traders desired direct access to the products of the African mainland, and their government wanted to curtail the slave trade. Said bin Sultan signed treaties in 1822 and 1845 to limit the trade of slaves within his dominion. Although these treaties only applied to European subjects and did not prohibit Said's subjects from keeping, selling, or transporting slaves within East Africa, the measures were not popular in Said's African territories. European observers noted the limited strength of the Zanzibari state and its inability to control Africa beyond its primary trading ports.

Said had been forced to balance these interests and strategize among their connections to maintain his precarious command of these far-flung realms. To maintain his interests, he often needed to be present in Arabia or Africa, and even after he had moved his court to Zanzibar in 1832, events in Oman or the Persian Gulf frequently beckoned him north. Such absences, dependent on the twice-yearly monsoon winds to facilitate his voyage, could easily stretch over a year. Seyyid Said's rule thus relied upon loyal governors, mercenaries, and tax collectors. When Said traveled, he did so warily, sometimes insisting that rivals from tribal factions, prominent families, or learned Ibadi ulama travel with him.⁴⁹ In this increasingly connected Indian Ocean world of Seyyid Said's dominions, the ruler compelled some elites to move with him. Others, facing desperate circumstances, chose to move in his wake.

Temporizing in the Face of Drought

The drought that struck across the Nizwa region in the 1840s created dwindling resources and mounting desperation. People had to make choices about their very survival, and their reactions to the drought demonstrate how and why mobility became a solution. In Manaḥ, seven miles from Nizwa, the prolonged drought dried up seven of the eight springs that watered the town. Formerly cultivated land lay in ruin, and the lack of water destroyed date groves. Dead trees marked the approach to the walled town, where two-storied stone and mud houses lined the narrow streets. In wetter, more prosperous times, the settlement had produced sugar cane in abundance. In the small date groves that persisted, the people had no spare fodder for the animals. Only one plantation northeast of town continued to flourish, presumably because it had access to the only remaining water source. Want of water reduced the population in Manaḥ. In the decade of drought (1835–45), the town lost half of its population: only 500 residents remained.[50]

As the drought's realities set in, people had to make difficult choices about how to use the water that came from the *falaj* and how to guarantee their own survival. We have no intimate portrait of drought in the interior during the first half of the nineteenth century. Given the continuities of agriculture and life ways, however, a more recent example provides a basis for comparison. The experience of the village of Ghayzayn, in Wadi Hawasina on the eastern side of the Hajar Mountains, where "drought began to erode the wealth of the community" in the 1970s, is illustrative.[51]

The people of Ghayzayn, having faced three years without rainfall, initially tried to use water more efficiently. They opened only one of the two irrigation streams from the *falaj*, halving the normal irrigation cycle. Next, they filled a cistern above the *falaj* to increase the flow when they did let the water run. As the months wore on, however, decreased irrigation took its toll. Young palms, which were future assets, died, as did the lime trees growing with them. Villagers took more drastic steps, allowing crops to wither. They first cut water to their field crops (wheat, tomatoes, and onion) and then to their fodder crop (alfalfa). All the remaining water was used for date palms, but the year's yield was nevertheless diminished. The drought's effects were both immediate and ongoing. Dates and alfalfa served as feed for domestic animals; the poor date harvest and lack of fodder led to the sale of livestock.[52]

In addition to the short- and medium-term hits to household economies, the drought created difficult living conditions and exacerbated infrastructural problems. As the volume of water fell in the *falaj*, the water contained more dirt, and women had to walk further upstream to get drinking water that was only marginally cleaner. The only other source of drinking water, a shallow well in the wadi, had dried up in the early days of the drought.[53]

The *falaj* also suffered. Unsealed channels lost more water to infiltration when underground water in the *wadi* disappeared. Less flow and more dirt resulted in faster silting. The channel needed to be relined and cleaned, and *falaj* repair was expensive. The village had already delayed maintenance before the rains stopped. Raising money for repair was even more difficult in the depths of the drought. The longer the people waited, the more difficult the *falaj* was to repair.[54]

While some members of the community were optimistic that the rain would eventually return, clouds of pessimism hung over the village. The drought "had broken the spirit of the community, and many had begun to accept an inevitable end to the settlement." Three families left the community as the drought set in, and many others prepared to do so. In a village of five hundred people, this was a tremendous demographic shift. The people who departed were "some of the most dynamic and astute economically," so the loss to the community was in disproportion to the number who left.[55]

Although this example comes from the early 1970s, the fact that the village relied so heavily on the *falaj* and on irrigation provides important insights into the process a century before. Where the people of Ghayzayn used cash remittances to pay for the water, dates, and alfalfa brought in by land rover, individuals in Nizwa and Manaḥ in the nineteenth century did not have these options. The author of the modern study suggests that people in the past, with fewer options, would have most certainly have taken earlier action to repair the *falaj* and to protect their crops.[56] Judging by the extreme drought in Nizwa in the 1840s, however, the people's ability to palliate was limited; every aspect of their lives was affected; and departure—if only until the end of the drought—was a ready solution. For example, a half century earlier, during an intense drought in the late eighteenth century, date palms died, and some Arabs, like Nasir bin Ahmad al-Riyami, abandoned small villages for larger interior settlements.[57] Others, including "the greater portion of the inhabitants," fled from the interior to coastal towns in the Batinah and near Muscat. In the port city trading town of Muttrah the recent arrivals drove up the price of well water. When the drought broke, they returned home.[58] Likewise for the Nizwans, some took temporary refuge at the coast and, given the new circumstances in Africa, others may have made their way there.

Be Careful What You Wish For

The solution to the eighteenth-century drought that had displaced interior Omanis and driven up well water prices in Muttrah was intercession from the sultan. Hamed bin Said al-Busaidi (r. 1784–1792) took decisive action to end the drought: he gathered people and led them in prayer for rain in three different wadis around Muscat on three subsequent days. As a result, "clouds covered the sky, and the rain descended, as if poured from buckets." Hamed bin Said mounted his horse and rode quickly back to his house in Muscat before waters coursed down the wadis and washed into the sea. The outcome in this case was favorable—great fertility followed, crops were abundant, and prices were low.[59] Some storms, however, brought too much rain, and the consequences of downpours were also dire.

Evidence from the nineteenth century shows that, in the face of devastating flash floods in Oman, out-migration to East Africa increased. One exception to this was the Sumayl valley, where a newly robust market for their particular dates created economic resiliency. In most other regions of the interior, however, environmental damage prompted some to move across the Indian Ocean. In general, most Omanis welcomed rain. In 1835, a cold drenching rain from a December downpour delighted the Jenebeh of eastern Oman by ensuring pasturage for the coming months.[60] People knew that violent rains sometimes fell, and the community expected them with some regularity, as often as every three years. These rains turned the valleys into dangerous streams, so swollen and swift that camels could not pass through them.[61]

Voluminous, unseasonable rains could also turn sinister and flash floods in wadis could carry date palms and houses as far as the sea. Writing in the early twentieth century, Ibadi scholar and historian Abdullah bin Humayd al-Salimi recounted Oman's worst flood, a heavy June downpour in 251 (Hegira) / 865 that swept down the wadis, washed away whole villages, pulled date palms from their roots, and carried bodies out to the sea. The same floods inundated the *aflaj*.[62] In addition to the immediate loss of life and livelihood, floods compromised the irrigation system by damaging watercourses, filling them with detritus, and hastening the silting of the *falaj*.[63] Damage to *aflaj* increased the cost of maintaining the water source. Beyond their economic consequences, floods and storms contributed to out migration from Oman across the Indian Ocean in an era of new mobility.

Data from the 1870s suggest a variable pattern of heavy rains and storms that destroyed large numbers of date palms, dismantled houses, and led to transoceanic emigration. In 1874 and 1875, unseasonably heavy rains destroyed the date crop in central Oman. The next year, however, rains fell plentifully at the appropriate time (at the beginning of the year), and this precipitation pattern promised an abundant date harvest.[64] The following year, severe storms in December flattened five thousand date palms in the Ma'awīl and Sumayl valleys.[65] At that time the Sumayl valley was rapidly expanding its production of *fard* dates for the United States market. In 1875, an American visitor to Muscat estimated that six million pounds of dates traveled from Muscat to New York that year.[66] Farmers in Sumayl discovered that they could sell all the dates that they could harvest, and the value of this export peaked in the 1880s.[67] Thus, while we have insufficient data to quantify the effects of a storm that toppled five thousand palms, it is likely that the loss of thousands of trees producing the region's most valuable export devastated some residents.

In the following season—from 1877 to 1878—heavy floods overran "the whole of Oman," and the country's date crop was almost entirely lost. The environmentally marginal Sharqiya region was hardest hit, with an estimated crop loss of 90 percent. Surrounding districts suffered almost as much. By harvest time, the specter of famine was clear, and the British resident in Muscat expected distress and possible political disturbances.[68] While political grievances simmered, some people whose lives depended on date farming in the 1870s made the same decision as those who faced the catastrophic drought in Nizwa the 1840s: they left their homes. In Muscat, observers reported a steady emigration to Zanzibar. Between 1877 and 1878, an estimated one thousand Arabs decamped in response to the poor date harvest.[69]

In March 1885, a cyclone hit central Oman, inundating villages and settlements. A flash flood ripped down the Sumayl valley, destroyed thousands of date trees, and rendered homeless the poorest inhabitants who lived in makeshift shelters of matted palm leaves. The recovery from such destruction was slow. Nine months later, a visitor still found wrecked houses, ruined date gardens, and many headless palm trees broken or bent to the ground.[70] The strong international market in *fard* dates from Sumayl may have been a saving grace. In response to demand in the 1870s, farmers in Sumayl had greatly increased the number of date trees they planted. The loss of thousands of trees was proportionately smaller than the preceding decade's loss. Still, Sumayl producers exhibited some resilience, probably because of the thriving production and high prices of dates. Throughout the 1880s, the date trade to the United States was at its peak, averaging more than $100,000 per year. The producers earned about 80 percent of the export value.[71] Unfortunately for most Omanis, the lucrative, particularistic market for fard dates from Sumayl had no cognates in other sectors of the economy. As the nineteenth century closed, Sumayl fell more in line with the rest of the country, as both local political disturbances and a North American recession significantly diminished export earnings.[72] This set the groundwork for waves of emigration to East Africa that would continue until the 1960s.

﹌

What conclusions should we draw from the people of Oman's relationship to their environment in the nineteenth century? The sometimes tenuous balance that Omanis sought in maintaining their date groves and their livelihoods faced the same challenges in the nineteenth century as they had in previous periods. Droughts and floods were endemic. What was strikingly different about this era, however, was that Indian Ocean emigration was an option for many more people than it had ever been before. A close connection between the interior of Oman and Zanzibar and other East African locales became firmly established during this period. For example, Nasir bin Ahmad al-Riyami escaped drought in the eighteenth century by moving his family from the village of Al Jede'iya to the larger settlement of upper Ibra (Ibrā' 'Alaya). After Said bin Sultan had paved the way to East Africa in the early nineteenth century, however, Nasir bin Ahmad led his family there in the 1820s, and his family prospered.[73] Africa became a refuge and a source of wealth. The degree to which environmental difficulties prompted people to move is hard to isolate, yet the extreme droughts of the 1840s and the destructive, variable rain patterns of the 1870s both preceded periods of Arab migration. Desiccated water sources and ruined date groves put individuals and families in precarious conditions. When their homes and farms were unsustainable, and an absent sultan was unable to lead prayers for rain, Omani Arabs could temporize. Moves to the Arabian coast and to East Africa bought time for droughts to end, rain to come, and land to revive.

Following historian Claude Markowitz's terminology, this movement should be seen as a pattern of circulation.[74] Some Arabs did settle in East Africa, but emigration began as a response to particular factors in Oman, and nothing suggests that individuals left Arabia with no intent of returning. As we shall see, some of these migrants used wealth gained abroad to invest in their homelands. Some renovated *aflaj* or built new ones, while others underwrote the construction of impressive houses. Far from being isolated, the interior of Arabia continued to be connected to the Indian Ocean world, not just through the circulation of goods, but also through the circulation of people, their wealth, and the religious and political ideologies that motivated them. By understanding the temporizing strategies that individuals pursued in the face of difficult conditions, we can appreciate the contingent nature of mobility in the western Indian Ocean in the nineteenth century. The evidence of this mobility can be found among the former halwa-makers of the caravan routes of central Africa, and in the business contracts that these men and women from drought-stricken Nizwa and other places wrote in Zanzibar. The sweetness of halwa must wait, and it is to these deeds and the world they describe that we now turn.

2 ～ The Customs Master and Customs of Credit in Zanzibar

WHEN PASSENGERS DISEMBARKED in Zanzibar from the booms and buggalas that sailed the western Indian Ocean in the early nineteenth century, they found a city in transition. Those who had recently left the interior of Arabia and had never sailed with the monsoon may have been overwhelmed by the hubbub of the port, or just happy to be on dry land, and they may have been too disorientated even to notice what was going on around them. On the other hand, the seasoned sailors who made this journey every year or two would certainly have noticed differences in the city. Zanzibar had begun to transform from the relatively simple fishing settlement of a few decades earlier to the biggest and most prosperous town on the east coast of Africa. Zanzibar was becoming a commercial center from which networks of indebtedness reached across the Indian Ocean and far into the East African interior. This chapter examines the formalization of Zanzibar's commercial culture by unpacking the Arabic business documents that underwrote the city's far-flung credit networks. It focuses on the 1840s, the earliest decade for which Arabic business contracts are available, to help reveal the enmeshed social and economic networks of Zanzibar.

Among the thousands of Arabic language contracts that have been preserved in Zanzibar, only a small number deal with the period before the late 1860s. This is a result of the process of registering documents (as detailed in chapter 7), though the difference between official, bureaucratic senses of time and the sense of time embedded in these contracts meant that some creditors submitted documents that were decades old. The documents considered in this chapter are thus a subset of a vast collection that informs the whole book. As such, these examples from the 1840s stand in for what were inevitably a great number of transactions that were completed (and thus not disputed), lost, or never registered. Contracts and agreements that were not resolved were more likely to be registered. In any case, the sample that remains makes clear that a dynamic Indian Ocean economy included a wide variety of mobile economic actors who used Arabic language transactions to forward their own goals in Zanzibar, the place that welcomed the most travelers from the Omani interior.

The journey to Zanzibar from Oman took a couple of weeks with favorable monsoon winds. As the dhows made their way from Muscat or Sur, they sailed close to the coast. The passengers may have stopped at Mogadishu, a place Ibn Batuta had visited in 1331, and even if they had not stopped, they certainly would have seen the minarets of four of the largest mosques that were visible ten miles from the shore.[1] The views of Mogadishu and Barawa on the northern Swahili coast would have been somewhat familiar, as these cities resembled the coastal cities of Arabia and Persia, with low, square, flat-roofed houses built of stone and mud.[2] When the travelers crossed the equator south of Barawa, they would have approached the Lamu archipelago, and the landscape would have changed.

We do not know how Arabian migrants saw this, but the verdant shores may have struck them as the view struck a British captain sailing this route in 1811: "The numerous richly-clothed islands which line the shore separated by beautiful and frequently spacious inlets and bounded behind by a delightful continent, rich in all the charms of luxuriant vegetation, present to the eye a prospect extremely enchanting, and would seem to indicate a degree of natural wealth equal of the most favored regions of the known globe."[3] Sailing past Mombasa, travelers could not have helped but see the massive Fort Jesus, built by the Portuguese in the late sixteenth century to anchor their burgeoning Indian Ocean empire. The Portuguese had constructed similar forts in Muscat. In the seventeenth century, when the Omanis expelled the Portuguese from Muscat and then from Mombasa, the Omanis took over the Portuguese thick-walled forts. In the 1830s, Fort Jesus was once again the site of dispossession, but this time rival Omani factions, emissaries of Said bin Sultan, seized the fort from the Mazrui ruler, killing some and exiling others to the gulf. Thus, Said bin Sultan, the Busaidi ruler in Zanzibar, could claim control of this entire coast, from southern Somalia to Lamu and Mombasa; including the island of Pemba (Mombasa's bread basket) and, south of that, Zanzibar.

Ras Nungwi at the northern tip of Zanzibar provided the first sight of the island, but sailing vessels had to continue down the island's western edge, skirting the small island of Tumbatu, before spotting the large white buildings of Zanzibar town. These multistory buildings were the visible markers of Zanzibar's boom. While they shared an architecture with Omani buildings, they shared space with the waddle and daub houses—thatched with palm fronds—that were interspersed in the narrow lanes and neighborhoods of the town's tidal peninsula. During the nineteenth century, the mix of buildings shifted. The big houses built of coral rag predominated, and the humbler dwellings disappeared. The process of becoming "Stone Town"—as the city became known in the twentieth century—had its roots in the economic prosperity of the nineteenth century and in the market for land (and mortgages) that developed during this period.

For first-time visitors, figuring out the underlying order of Zanzibar would have been difficult. While travelers who were familiar with other Indian Ocean ports would have found some similarities, the first British agent (representative) assigned to Zanzibar in the 1840s did not believe that the city's port or its commercial aspects were ordered or rational. He reported in 1844 that the port had no quarantine regulations, no charges for wharfage or buoys, and no regular supply of local pilots. It was assumed that the captains either knew the reefs on the approaches to the port or could send someone up the mast to point them out. The merchants employed several currencies at no fixed rate of exchange, but the Spanish dollar and the German crown were considered equal in the 1840s. It seemed as though the only rule was that all goods, whether they were coming or going, had to pass through the customs house, a small thatched shed near the shore.[4]

The unpresuming thatched shed belied the vital role of the customs master, who was the linchpin of the economic, social, and political orders. His constant access to cash and elaborate networks of patronage made him the island's apex creditor. Indebtedness—both fiscal and social—became the common language of this multiethnic society, connected through webs of patron-client relations that stretched far from Zanzibar, to the African interior, the islands of the Indian Ocean, and the shores of Arabia. Within this network in 1840, the customs master Jairam Shivji was a vital node. He lent money to the sultan and bought houses from freed slaves. He underwrote American merchants and oversaw a network of Indian financiers. Not surprisingly, his name was among the most common written on the contracts, sales, and mortgages that are left from this period. These documents—an

FIGURE 2.1. Zanzibar waterfront, 1847. Image courtesy of the Melville J. Herskovits Library of African Studies, Winterton Collection, Northwestern University.

archive within an archive—reveal intriguing details about the social and financial interconnections of Zanzibar and its hinterlands. Let us first look at Jairam Shivji's role in financing both the Zanzibar state and foreign trade before turning to his dealings with the more common African and Arab people living in or passing through Zanzibar.

JAIRAM SHIVJI FROM KUTCH TO ZANZIBAR

Jairam Shivji, a Banyan Hindu, was born in 1792 in Kutch, on the west coast of India. The Indian Ocean entrepôt trade shaped his family's life. His father, Shivji Topan, was part of the Banyan merchant community in Muscat, and from there, Shivji Topan traveled to East Africa in 1785 in the company of the Muscati ruler Said bin Ahmad al-Busaidi. In the following years, Shivji Topan moved his business to East Africa. His decision was influenced by Muscat's new ruler, Seyyid Said bin Sultan, who had his sights on Zanzibar. Early Omani governors in Zanzibar had either been slaves of the royal family or appointed from loyal Omani clans. These governors were also responsible for collecting customs duties. One of Seyyid Said's innovations in East Africa was to remove the customs duty from the portfolio of the governor and to transfer it to a merchant house. In 1835, Shivji Topan won the contract to "farm the customs" at Zanzibar for 84,000 Maria Theresa dollars.[5] This meant that his firm paid an advance to the ruler and then kept all customs revenue for themselves. His son Jairam took over this duty from Shivji, and although they paid increasingly higher prices for the privilege, Jairam and his family firm held this vital (and remunerative) position for fifty years. The family firm also maintained branches in Muscat, Bombay, and Kutch.[6]

From the 1830s until his retirement in 1853, Jairam remained focused on his firm's revenue and the customs house in Zanzibar. As a Kutchi merchant, this was not unusual. An observer noted in 1836 that the port of Mandvi, in Kutch, was connected to the entire western Indian Ocean: "From Mandavee a maritime communication is kept up from Zanguebar and the whole east coast of Africa, with the Red Sea and Arabia, with the Persian Gulf, Mekrom, and Sinde, and with India as far as Ceylon."[7] Jairam's commitment was legendary. In 1837, a visitor who called on him when he was ill noted that Jairam had ivory stored under his sickbed. This was evidence of his "ruling passion," which remained "strong in sickness."[8]

Jairam did indeed indulge his ruling passion for finance. An American merchant in Zanzibar estimated that Jairam Shivji earned $100,000 profit in 1839.[9] One historian guessed that Jairam had thirty million dollars in a Bombay bank.[10] While this may be exaggerated, he was the wealthiest man in East Africa, in part because of his extensive commercial network. From his post in Zanzibar, Jairam controlled customs collectors in many of the major ports on the Swahili coast. Thus, he was well informed about prices and news from every part of the sultan's realm. His financial heft and his intelligence networks made him a formidable ally and daunting foe. Foreign merchants were keenly aware of the importance of staying on Jairam's good side. One foreign merchant noted Jairam's ominous power over traders in 1842: "Refuse to comply with his terms and they would be driven from the market with doing little or nothing."[11] The ruler and the foreign merchants in Zanzibar were indebted to him, and they needed his capital to run their ventures.

CREDIT AND STATECRAFT IN EARLY BUSAIDI RULE IN EAST AFRICA

The availability of credit was essential to the commercial expansion of Zanzibar. This credit, largely supplied by Indian Ocean commercial firms originating in India, financed the expansion of American and European firms in East Africa and of the Arab state in Zanzibar.[12] The wealthiest Indian merchants at Zanzibar provided staggering amounts of credit.[13] In 1849, Jairam Shivji, the customs master and head of his eponymous firm, was "the best and only certain way of obtaining a supply of cash for immediate service."[14] Shivji stood out among merchants of that time. The other merchants and traders required fifteen to twenty days to collect MT$300,[15] whereas Jairam could secure MT$5,000 in a matter of hours.[16] His firm used its substantial wealth to dominate Zanzibar for the first three quarters of the nineteenth century. Jairam Shivji's firm advanced huge sums to foreign trading interests to finance their operations in Zanzibar. Jairam had three main groups of debtors: the Arab rulers of Zanzibar, American and European trading firms, and a large group of everyday people, including Indians, Arabs, and Swahilis in Zanzibar and on the mainland.

Jairam Shivji's firm advanced large sums of money to the al-Busaidi rulers in Zanzibar. The al-Busaidi state in Oman and Zanzibar had a long history of relying on credit from Hindu Banyan commercial houses. In the eighteenth century, firms from Kutch, in western India, lent the Omani ruler Sultan bin Ahmad al-Busaidi warships in exchange for protection and favorable commercial treatment.[17] As Zanzibar grew in commercial importance, however, the customs duties collected on imports and exports had high income potential. Because the al-Busaidi rulers had relatively little wealth, they sought cash up front by farming the customs to powerful, cash-rich firms like Jairam Shivji's. This practice—functionally the same as tax farming—was a very common way to raise cash for Muslim rulers or state treasuries.[18] Tax farming entailed selling the right to collect taxes over a specific time period to an individual or private firm. The person or firm who collected the taxes kept them as profit. Jairam Shivji farmed the customs both in Zanzibar (after 1819) and on the mainland (after 1837).[19] The sultan had the guaranteed income, and Jairam and his firm enforced the customs collection and kept the profits.

During al-Busaidi rule, the finances of the ruler and the state were intimately connected, and the customs master was central to providing credit to the sultan and his government. When Said bin Sultan needed to raise additional funds to pacify resistance to his rule in Oman, he turned to the customs master. In 1851, Jairam Shivji gave Said a year's advance against the customs receipts, and Said went to Muscat with MT$500,000. He later wrote to Jairam for an additional MT$50,000.[20] Said used these funds to raise forces to quell the rebellion and to buy the loyalty of various leaders. These debts passed on to Seyyid Said's heirs, and they would be one source of ongoing tension between Zanzibar and Muscat after his death.

American and European merchants also depended on credit in Zanzibar to finance their trading ventures. American whalers' early efforts at trading in Zanzibar floundered because of the poor circulation of credit. They could not secure cargoes because they had no way to advance capital to themselves. By the 1840s, however, Indian firms like that of Jairam Shivji provided capital to American and European merchants on a regular basis. These loans were unsecured, but they had generous interest rates to provide Jairam Shivji and other lenders with good returns on their investments.[21] In 1851, an experienced American agent explained to his superior back in Massachusetts why he had decided to keep MT$25,000 of Jairam Shivji's money on a permanent loan. First, he considered the capital an "absolute necessity" to have funds on hand, and second, he noted that borrowing it from the powerful customs master would bring certain commercial advantages in Zanzibar, including collecting on debts and finding suitable business partners.[22] They believed that the customs master would have a strong interest in the firm's success. By the 1860s and early 1870s, Jairam Shivji's firm had advanced loans of MT$665,000 to American, British, and French companies.[23] These infusions of credit went along with commercial treaties and informal alliances between commercial houses to help build international trade in Zanzibar. The cloth and beads coming from North America, Europe, and South Asia were necessary to meet the demands of the East African market. The peddlers, traders, and commodity producers in these markets were not foreign merchants or state officials, but a diverse group of Africans, Arabs, and Indians who were part of an expanding Indian Ocean world in the 1840s.

The 1840s was a dynamic period in the economic history of Zanzibar. Seyyid Said bin Sultan signed commercial treaties with the United States (1833), Great Britain (1839), and France (1844) that resulted in each sending consuls to represent their national and trading interests at Seyyid Said's court in Zanzibar. In this period after the Napoleonic Wars, the British and the French were engaged in strategic maneuvering in the western Indian Ocean, and they also heralded more forceful global approaches to so-called free trade, as best exemplified in the first Opium Wars (1839–1842). The letters and records that these consuls created are invaluable historical sources for Zanzibar and the western Indian Ocean, but they emphasize diplomatic and commercial relations of the powerful, and obscure the actions of the Africans, Arabs, and Indians that made up most of the population of Zanzibar.

A trove of Arabic-language documents in the Zanzibar National Archive provides important sources for the history of East Africa. These materials demonstrate how credit markets in Zanzibar connected much of the western Indian Ocean, from the interior of Oman to the interior of East Africa. These documents—preserved for more than one hundred years—reveal important new details about the Indian Ocean past. They record thousands of sales, loans, and transactions between Africans, Arabs, and Indians. These documents present multiple variations on the complex financial transactions that allowed people to buy time: they underwrote the ivory trade; and they mortgaged property in Arabia, on the east African coast, and in the interior of Africa. These sources are unparalleled in their listing of individual names, genealogies, statuses, and clan names of a wide variety of people (Africans, Indians, and Arabs; men and women; free and slave) who bought, sold, and mortgaged property in the nineteenth century. They also provide insight into the world of the judges, scribes, and clerks who created them. Finally, the individuals who created these documents did so outside of any colonial or European-influenced sphere. As noted earlier and explained in Chapter 7, their registration occurred during a time of increasing British activity, but the documents were produced in a different milieu. The writers adhered to long-standing Islamic legal forms, and they inflected them with local usage. Each of these transactions provides a snapshot of an interconnected world before European colonialism.[24] As a whole, these exciting new sources allow us to understand the inner workings of credit and debt, to see previously overlooked groups, and to map individuals into Indian Ocean circuits.

The dozen documents that have survived from the 1840s give a sense of the regional economy in transition, especially regarding the value of land. The material also points to a wide variety of actors. A very small number of wealthy people sold large farms—some with slaves attached—or houses. In most of the transactions, small holders sold their property to the customs master, who may or may not have been speculating on the land.

Jairam Shivji was the biggest buyer and creditor, participating in twelve of the fourteen transactions from the 1840s. While he was an important creditor to foreign merchants and to the sultan, he also transacted business with a wide variety of other people in Zanzibar. The range of people involved in transactions in the 1840s included an indigenous man from Tumbatu, freed slaves of early Omani migrants, a wife of a Swahili notable, and Omani families established in Zanzibar, including members of the sultan's clan. Most people sold agricultural land (*shamba* in Swahili). Judging by the prices, indigenous Zanzibaris, Swahili elites, freed slaves, and some Omanis held small parcels of land. Those on the island of Zanzibar sold for between MT$15 and $70, while the only farm on the sister island of Pemba sold for a paltry MT$1.50!ized 25: Because this was a time of growing commercial agriculture—especially cloves—land was increasingly valuable to those who could afford the labor to work it.

For some larger holdings, the labor was included in the sale. In 1845 Jairam Shivji bought a *shamba* in Mwera (outside of town) from Ali bin Muhammad al-Busaidi for MT$650. This sale included the clove and coconut trees on the property and eight slaves.[26] Indians commonly owned African slaves, although this became contentious after the 1850s, because the British were attempting to limit the trade in slaves and to claim all Indians as British subjects. Ebji, Jairam's younger brother, was frequently implicated in the sale of slaves. British intervention led to the forced manumission of Indian-owned slaves during and after the 1860s. Judging by Jairam's business documents from the 1840s, other slave owners were manumitting slaves for different reasons. The twelve sales records that exist from the 1840s indicate four properties that Jairam Shivji bought from manumitted slaves. Three of the sellers had been slaves of Omani Arabs, and one was the slave of a Swahili man. As Chapter 6 elaborates, formerly enslaved people often gained property as part of the manumission process, and they either used it for cash or to finance trading ventures into the interior.

From the 1820s, Omani rule replaced or co-opted Swahili elites in Zanzibar on the East African coast, and two documents from this period help understand this process. Consider the two sales of *shambas* in the 1840s. One of the sellers was a member of the Swahili elite identified as Diwan Makambi (or Mwekambi) Juma bin Ahmad. Both Diwan and Makambi are honorifics here. In 1847, he sold a *shamba* that belonged to his wife Binti Bana (Bwana) Waziri al-Mufazii.[27] Her *nisba*, al-Mufazii, marks her as a member of a patrician Swahili family, and it suggests origins in Faza, in the Lamu archipelago. Her father might have been Bwana Waziri, a ruler of Pate, also near Lamu, in the 1820s. During local disputes, Bwana Waziri made an alliance with Seyyid Said bin Sultan, the great Omani ruler, while his enemies called on the Mazruis in Mombasa. Bwana Waziri's alliance with Seyyid Said was part of an elaborate contest with the Mazruis that gave Seyyid Said a foothold on the coast.[28]

Mwekambi Juma, Binti Bwana Waziri's husband, represented her in the sale. He was born in Zanzibar, but he became the Diwan (ruler) of the coastal town of Saadani on the African mainland. He also led caravans to the interior.[29] When Mwekambi Juma first reached Ugogo, several hundred miles from the coast, the local residents had never seen anyone as fat as he was, and they assumed he had extraordinary rainmaking powers. He denied this and refused to make rain for them. As the story goes, if it had not been for some opportune showers that fell, he would have faced certain death. Such conflicts were not uncommon for him. Around the time he sold his wife's farm, Juma led an expedition against the Wadoe, a group of troublesome neighbors to the residents of Saadani.[30] Whether the sale of his wife's property to the Zanzibar customs master for $50 paid off a debt or helped to support a trading expedition, a military conquest, or his rule in Saadani, Mwekambi Juma's activities were indicative of the changes in mobility and of the scale of trade that were taking place in East Africa.

A second aspect of this story also points to changes under Omani rule when newly arrived Omanis threatened the place of Swahili patricians. Bwana Heri bin Juma al-Mafazii, Mwekambi Juma's son, was a trader and the Diwan of Saadani for at least twenty years. He maintained strong connections in the interior, and he was the only non-Omani governor on the Swahili coast during a late 1880s uprising that challenged the ruling Arabs and their German allies. This later event marked the onset of formal European colonialism in East Africa. Historian Jonathon Glassman has argued that Bwana Heri's longevity and political savvy were the result of his "ability to straddle two worlds, the world of the hinterland, still dominated by values associated with village agriculture, and the world of the coastal towns, where new values were rapidly being forged in the context of expanding international commerce."[31] The interactions between these two worlds accelerated in the second half of the nineteenth century, but these processes had started more than a generation before. Bwana Heri's parents had used connections to the Indian Ocean world through Zanzibar to convert property into cash.

The new presence of Omani rulers displaced indigenous people in Zanzibar. The second notable sale from the 1840s includes someone from among the WaTumbatu, one of Zanzibar's indigenous groups. The identification on the sale of his *shamba* to Jairam Shivji in 1845 demonstrates both his rootedness and his mobility. His name was written Maqame bin Māsibu bin A'ami of Tumbatu and his title was Serang.[32] Tumbatu, a prominent island on Zanzibar's northwest side, was one of the two most important trading towns and ports on Zanzibar before 1500.[33] When Seyyid Said and his followers moved to Zanzibar, their demand for land put pressure on the indigenous inhabitants.

The WaTumbatu and the WaHadimu were the two groups who lived in Zanzibar and its outlying islets before the arrival of the Arabs. Through the middle of the nineteenth century, they had their own ruler, known as the Mwinyi Mkuu. When Burton visited Tumbatu in 1858, he said the people of Tumbatu were of a new race, and he was "now beyond Semítico-Abyssinian centres." He noted that the Omani Arabs called the people of Tumbatu "Makhádim—helots or serviles," and the name Hadimu shares a root with the Arabic word for servant.[34] In 1841, Zanzibar's British agent explained to his superiors in Bombay about the Omani Arab view of the indigenous inhabitants: "The whole of the Native inhabitants of the Islands of Zanzibar and Pemba are considered by the subjects of His Highness as slaves." When new arrivals were given land by the sultan or bought land from other Arabs, the land's inhabitants became slaves who were expected to work for the landowner and to provide their own subsistence. These slaves were expected to expand the clove production of the island.[35] Although Hamerton's account is likely exaggerated, the inhabitants of Zanzibar definitely faced difficulties as the island's property regime changed. As historian C. S. Nicholls notes,

The Customs Master ⇜ 53

the effects of the Arab arrival on the Hadimu and Tumbatu are difficult to measure. Some people may have altered their ways of life; some may have changed where they lived. One outcome was clear: by the second half of the nineteenth century, many Hadimu no longer lived in the parts of Zanzibar that had the best soil. Some had moved east and south.[36]

The example of Serang Maqame, however, suggests a different kind of mobility. *Serangs* have been alternately described as crew leaders, indigenous boatswains, petty officers, and "native bosses" in the Indian Ocean. The root of the word is from Malay. *Serangs* oversaw the maritime workers known as *lascars*, and *serangs* were vital to the functioning of the ship and the organization of the multiethnic crews of the Indian Ocean.[37] The men of Tumbatu had reputations as skillful pilots and good seamen.[38] With the advent of steamships, the work crews from the age of sail were incorporated into a highly regulated labor regime, controlled by a set of British laws called the Asiatic Articles. By 1855, as historian Janet Ewald notes, British merchant ships employed as many as twelve thousand *lascars* under the Asiatic Articles, 60 percent of whom were from India.[39] *Serangs* oversaw all these men and kept a certain kind of rough order onboard. As a *serang*, Maqame would have been a skilled negotiator, an experienced traveler, and a comfortable visitor in many ports. Because of this, Maqame represents an unusual category—the indigenous cosmopolitan—and his land sale in 1845 implies a strategy of mobility in the face of increasing land pressure on the WaTumbatu and WaHadimu. His strategy may have been possible because of his relatively high status in the maritime world of the western Indian Ocean.

Sales of property and credit derived from mortgage-like arrangements were crucial to accessing mobility across the western Indian Ocean. Two more of Jairam Shivji's financial deals in the 1840s illustrate this point. Both arrangements involve Ali Muhammad al-Busaidi, the man who sold the *shamba* with the slaves attached. In July 1845, a month after selling his *shamba*, Ali bin Muhammad al-Busaidi sold his house in Zanzibar and the adjoining property to Jairam Shivji for $400. On the day he sold his house, he agreed to rent it from Jairam Shivji for $40 per year. Ali bin Muhammad's actions, written in two documents, demonstrate a business logic that challenged Islam ideals. They also provide an important window into Zanzibar society at that time.

The deed of transaction makes clear that this mud and mortar house and the adjacent land were surrounded by property owned by prominent individuals. Jairam Shivji already owned the house to the west. To the north was the house of Humud bin Sayf bin Msellem, a young clove grower who would later become a close advisor to two sultans. The Banyan Hari, presumably a merchant, owned the property to the east. In the south was empty land that belonged to Sulayman bin Hamed al-Busaidi, the long-standing governor of Zanzibar, a large landowner, and one of the most powerful men in East Africa.[40] Other bordering properties belonged to the Indian Hima, whose son would become a prominent landlord.

Why would someone sell a house and rent it back? Such a maneuver allowed the property owner to receive cash (in this case, $400) and then pay a portion of this over time. In Ali bin Muhammad's arrangement, he would have paid the value of the house in rent after ten years. Arrangements like this allowed those with fixed property to capitalize their assets. By completing two separate transactions with two different contracts, one also avoided the Islamic prohibitions on interest. From Jairam Shivji's perspective, the rent served as interest on the $400 he had granted. This kind of double contract would become an increasingly common method of generating credit in East Africa, especially when paired with a redeemable sale, in which the original owner could buy back the property after a fixed period of time. These deals financed the ivory and clove trades for people of varying social classes. An understanding of these debt arrangements and the mobility they engendered can be achieved through close study of Arabic business documents in Zanzibar.

AN ARCHIVE OF TRANSACTIONS

Business deeds fill several volumes within the Zanzibar archives, and they detail more than two thousand transactions that span the nineteenth century. The languages of these documents reflect underlying commercial forms and Indian processes: the vast majority of them were written in Arabic; a substantial number are in Gujarati; and a much smaller number are in English. Although some deeds describe partnerships or the settling of estates, most directly relate to the flow of cash and credit. These documents clarify the terms of sales and the conditions under which creditors supplied money. They describe the security or collateral involved (if any) and specify the terms and time frame of repayment. The length of these documents varies from a few lines of text to several pages of subclauses. The collection, as a whole, offers a portrait of the interconnected world of the Indian Ocean. While most of the documents were written in Zanzibar, they implicate property and people who traveled far across the ocean and into the interiors of Africa and Arabia.

"Said bin 'Umar bin Muhammad bin Salim al-Kharūsi acknowledged that he owes Wala bin Banji al-Hindi one hundred frasila and twenty frasila pure ivory in the measurement [weight] of Zanzibar frasila."⁴¹ So begins a typical contract written in Arabic, following the precepts of Islamic legal practice. Said bin 'Umar, the borrower, stated his obligation to deliver ivory to Wala Banji, the creditor (and one of the agents of the customs master), within a period of one year, from the date of the contract, 10 Dhu al-Qa'da 1293 (November 26, 1876). This type of document is among the most common written Islamic agreements, an acknowledgment or *iqrār*, and this type is well-represented in the Zanzibar collection. These documents acknowledge a debt or obligation, and they take their name from the Arabic verb root q-r-r in its fourth form (أقر).⁴² The verb denotes acknowledgment, admission, or concession, and the documents take the form of declarations. These declarations are generally quite flexible and applicable in many areas of Islamic law. S. D. Goitein, a scholar whose masterful work includes translations of Arabic documents discovered in the Cairo Geniza that date from the tenth century, called *iqrār* "a legal instrument of a rather technical and abstract character."⁴³ Indeed, because of the documents' wide usage, scholars have suggested that the translation of *iqrār* as "an acknowledgment" is too narrow, and these declarations should be considered as the recognition of rights, such as the right of patrimony or the right to collect a debt. Historically, many *iqrār* dealt with family rights, acknowledging relationships and dealing with inheritance,⁴⁴ but most samples in the Zanzibar archive are related to financial relationships.⁴⁵ In his large sample from Cairo, Goitein noted that *iqrār* were also the most frequently represented mechanisms for credit and debt.⁴⁶

One of the most striking aspects of Islamic contract law, however, is that written agreements are not required for any transaction. Theoretically, a written contract is only valid after the oral testimonies of qualified witnesses verify its content.⁴⁷ Thus, written agreements in Islamic commercial life have had an uneasy history. The Quran explicitly instructs people to write down their agreements and to make contracts: "Believers, when you contract a debt for a fixed period, put it in writing. Let a scribe write it down for you with fairness; no scribe should refuse to write as God has taught him. . . . So do not fail to put your debts in writing, be they small or big, together with the date of payment. This is more than just in the sight of God; it ensures accuracy in testifying and is the best way to remove all doubt."⁴⁸ This injunction reflects the transactional relations and the commercial world of seventh-century Arabia, and it lays the groundwork for prohibiting two Islamic commercial practices: usury (*riba* in Arabic, which means an increase with an implication of illegal means, such as bribery, profiteering, and fraud) and speculation (*gharar* in Arabic, which means risk, hazard, or jeopardy).[49]

The Quranic injunction to write contracts notwithstanding, early Islamic legal theory emphasized the primacy of witnesses' oral testimony and downplayed the role of documentary evidence.[50] Oral testimony and the qualification of witnesses have been central to Islamic legal epistemology. Despite the tension between oral testimony and written documents, however, paper contracts have been fundamental to Islamic commercial practice from the earliest days.[51] These contracts rested—much like oral agreements—on the testimony of witnesses. Thus, while written documents shadowed testimonial evidence, scholars and practitioners linked these by writing formularies and templates that only had to be witnessed to be valid.[52]

Signing formulae arose so that witnesses could state their acknowledgment of the agreement. And written documents increasingly followed boilerplate texts to avoid standard objections and pitfalls, while still remaining legally sound. Getting the details correct in such documents would guarantee that transactions were legal and rights were respected. In the case of property sales, for instance, deeds were required to list the owners of all adjoining properties, because these people had a right to preempt the sale under Islamic law. These forms and contracts were easily replicated with the formularies that allowed people to create contracts that met Islamic legal standards.[53] Parties to these agreements wanted them to be legally impeccable, and formularies were especially important to non-Muslims who wanted to ensure the documents' validity in Muslim courts.

Iqrār documents acknowledge rights (as in the right to collect a debt). Legal scholars consider the people making these declarations to be doing so unilaterally. Hence, these acknowledgments, if properly witnessed, are irrevocable. Any person making an *iqrār* must have reached the age of puberty and be of sound mind. Slaves could theoretically make *iqrār*, although there were some exceptions to this. If the declaration had been properly witnessed, the person who made it could not repudiate it, and only in a few cases did grounds exist to invalidate them. An *iqrār* written under duress was considered invalid, for instance, and each school of Islamic law has its own strict rules to determine the acceptability of *iqrār* created when the declarer is near death. Recognition of rights granted in an *iqrār* can be extinguished if the beneficiary of the acknowledgment refuses to accept the recognition.

The generic formula for *iqrār* includes the name of the person acknowledging the obligation, the beneficiary, the object of acknowledgment, the terms of payment, the date, and the signature of witnesses.[54] The formula demands a degree of specificity to ensure the validity of the document and to avoid ambiguity. After the initial verb expressing intention, a clause identifies the declarant (*al-muqirr*, the acknowledger) and the person to whom the rights are given (*al-muqarr lahu*; the "acknowledged," or the one to whom something is acknowledged).

In the example above, Said bin 'Umar bin Muhammad bin Salim al-Kharūsi acknowledged his debt to Wala bin Banji al-Hindi. Manuals of instruction make clear that the names of both the declarant and the person "acknowledged" should include their personal names (Said and Wala, respectively); the names of their fathers ('Umar and Banji); the names of their grandfathers (Muhammad, for the former); and the *nisba* (clan name or descriptive adjective: al-Kharūsi—of the Kharūsi clan—and al-Banyani—the Banyan) or *laqab* (nickname), which are further means of identifying individuals. This degree of specificity makes the documents in Zanzibar especially useful, because connections among members of the same families and clans can be made.

To return to the exchange in the Introduction, Juma Merikani was identified by his whole name, Juma bin Salim bin Mubarak bin Abdullah, which traces not only his patrilineal genealogy to the name of his great-grandfather, but also includes his clan name, al-Bakri, and a *nisba* of origin, al-Nizwi. This information linked him to the interior Omani town of Nizwa, the site of the drought in the 1840s that had compelled many families to emigrate. Ladha Damji, the person to whom he owed the ivory, was identified in the document as Ladha bin Damha al-Baniani.[55] After the naming clauses, the object of the acknowledgment (*al-muqarr bihi*) must be detailed in full. Because of the flexible nature of the *iqrār*, the object might be the price of something for sale, the sum of a debt, or the weight of ivory. For example, the document of Said bin 'Umar al-Kharusi states the good (ivory); its quality (pure); its unit of measure (frasila, a unit of thirty-five pounds); the number of that unit (one hundred twenty); and the basis for the unit of measure (the Zanzibar frasila).

The document should include description of how payment is to be made. In the case of debt, the debtor should clarify his ability to pay in the future. Liabilities for someone pledging or guaranteeing on the behalf of the acknowledger should also be stated. The formula for marking calendar dates follows, and the witnessing statements come at the end. The witnesses are the key to making the document legitimate, and the witnessing formula should be free of ambiguity. The date of the testimony is included, and the witnesses must specify whether or not they wrote it in their own hand. Witnesses attest to the declarations and their names are included in the document.

In our example, the attestation was given by the author of the document (Humūd bin Said bin Salim al-Fera'i) and it was endorsed by the sultan (Barghash bin Said al-Busaidi).

The Zanzibar archives contain hundreds of writings (*waraqa*), and these illustrate microeconomic transactions based on relationships, kinship, and small-scale commerce. These small interactions collectively permit us to assess the macroeconomic trade system that linked Oman and the Indian Ocean to Zanzibar and the East African interior. In East Africa, these deeds provided people in the 1840s with new ways to conduct financial relations over long distances.

MORTGAGES AND PLEDGES OF PROPERTY

More sophisticated *iqrār* functioned as mortgages, providing credit against fixed assets. Two types of credit-generating transactions are found in the Zanzibar archives. The first was a *rahnan maqbudan* (رهنا مقبوضا), or a mortgage in which the person providing the credit takes full possession of the house or property.[56] More frequent, however, was a conditional or redeemable sale called *bay' al-khiyar* (بيع الخيار) or sometimes *bay' al-iqāla* (بيع الإقالة). British officials referred to these as "time sales," because this transaction permitted the seller to buy back the property at the same price within a fixed period of time. In some cases, the seller also rented the property from the person to whom he had mortgaged it.[57] If one *iqrār* contained the sale, the purchaser might create a second *iqrār* to lease the mortgaged property to the original owner.

For example, Muhammad bin Rashid bin Ahmed al-Riyami sold his farm in Pemba through a time sale for one year to Gopal Takarsi for MT$700. During that same year, he agreed to rent the farm from Gopal for MT$175 per annum.[58] Muhammad bin Rashid was permitted to buy back the farm for the original price of MT$700. At the end of the year, he would also have to pay the rent, meaning he would have paid a total of MT$875 to redeem his property. Through arrangements like this, many Arabs in Zanzibar and elsewhere forfeited property.

Scholars have viewed this rent as a form of interest. Consequently, these sales have been condemned by legal purists for their "very questionable orthodoxy," given the Islamic prohibitions of interest and speculation.[59] Others accepted the practices out of necessity. Islamic judges (*qadis*) in Zanzibar ruled that these kinds of sales were legal "to enable persons needing money to obtain credit without incurring the possible guilt of dealing in transactions by way of interest."[60] Thus, these methods of conducting business allowed observant Muslims to stay (narrowly) within Islamic prohibition on interest and speculation.

Time sales gave anyone who had property the ability to raise cash. Although the creditors resided in Zanzibar and operated their businesses from there, they extended credit to property owners in many directions. In Oman, where many Arabs relied on date farming and attenuated irrigation channels for their income, this form of mortgage was already established. Arabs in Oman sold houses and date trees to secure loans to cover the lean period between harvests.[61] This practice moved to Zanzibar with the Arab migrants who followed Said bin Sultan when he shifted the capital in 1832. Arabs who retained property in Oman were able to use it to capitalize their ventures in Zanzibar.

While Jairam Shivji was the apex creditor, the relationships of debtors and creditors crossed social and ethnic boundaries, forming the basis of Zanzibar's cosmopolitan culture. Arabic business contracts provide new insights into the temporal and spatial aspects of debt and credit and the tension between obligation and opportunity. Webs of indebtedness linked Zanzibar, the African interior, and Oman, creating the common commercial culture of the western Indian Ocean. Historian Philip Curtin has argued that the development of common commercial culture reduced the need for brokers to serve as intermediaries between groups.[62] The mechanisms of credit and debt (especially Arabic-language contracts) allowed individuals to conduct business across racial, ethnic, and confessional lines and across the long distances of the Indian Ocean and its continental interiors. By the 1840s, Zanzibar was emerging as an important financial center, a place where deals were struck, credit advanced, and repayment, eventually, was due. These contracts derive from a long history of Islamic legal practice and provide an intimate view of the business and societal connections emanating from Zanzibar. They also provide unusual insight into the position of freed slaves and the microeconomics of the ivory trade.

3 ∽ Sultans at Sea
Mobility and the Omani States

ON THE NIGHT OF OCTOBER 25, 1856, a small band of Arab men rowed toward the flickering oil lights of Zanzibar town. They had waited at anchor behind a small island in the channel since late afternoon. During the day, Zanzibar's shore buzzed with activity. Gangs of laborers unloaded cargo from the African mainland, animal hides, gum copal, and mangrove poles. Merchants supervised ivory shipments while their workers scraped and washed the tusks.[1] The Indian customs master and his assistants hovered around the port, eager to collect levies on the shipments arriving from Bombay, Manchester, and Salem. At night, however, the waterfront was quiet. Against a rising storm, the oarsmen pulled the travelers on the final leg of their journey from Arabia. Most likely, the passengers kept silent, due both to their cargo and their errand. Among them were three important men—including one who was anxious to prove his manhood and another who was six days dead.

The corpse was Seyyid Said bin Sultan al-Busaidi, the Omani merchant prince who had brought East Africa under his sway. Said bin Sultan was a contemporary of Napoleon Bonaparte and Mohammed Ali Pasha of Egypt, and, as a British official observed, he was "hardly inferior" to either man, "except in as far as the stage on which he acted was more restricted."[2] This "restricted" stage touched all sides of the western Indian Ocean, and, as hard as it would be to calculate, Seyyid Said probably covered more lifetime miles than either of these other men. After nearly three decades of shuttling between Arabia and the East African coast, to establish himself in East Africa and then to maintain his rule in both places, Seyyid Said bin Sultan died at sea on a return trip to Zanzibar. A unified Omani realm did not survive him. The other men on the ship, including his young son Barghash and the leader of the Harthi confederation in Zanzibar, hoped to bury Seyyid Said quietly and then seize power.[3] This proved impossible, and Seyyid Said's death set off contests for control in Zanzibar and Muscat that lasted fifteen years and reverberated into the twentieth century.

Seyyid Said's death has become a periodizing marker in the histories of both Oman and East Africa.[4] This framing, however, ignores the continuities across the nineteenth century, including the mobility of Arab rulers in Muscat and Zanzibar. This mobility allowed them to buy time when faced with a reconfiguration of power in the Indian Ocean. This chapter examines the remarkable nineteenth-century itineraries of the Busaidi rulers and traces the correlation of mobility and debt to state power. In doing so, it also provides an overview of Oman's and Zanzibar's nineteenth-century political history. State power tended to be weak, and travel and mobility reinforced the tentative nature of central authority, especially in an era of encroaching British suzerainty. Mobility as a temporizing strategy allowed sultans and aspirants to make claims on new territories, escape confrontations, and wait out challenges. Mobility and indebtedness also posed challenges to state formation when distance weakened loyalties or credit dried up. Although the first half of the nineteenth century witnessed Omani territorial control at its zenith, this changed dramatically during the second half when circuits of mobility shifted, deracinated rulers became protégés of empire, and state political cultures became increasingly rooted. A formerly unified Indian Ocean realm became two territorial sultanates in 1861, one in Muscat and one in Zanzibar. Greater imperial hegemony and global economic integration produced a hardening of territorial boundaries in the Indian Ocean that challenged older practices of mobility in the region and ultimately undercut Busaidi authority.

This chapter begins with Seyyid Said bin Sultan's travels on the Indian Ocean, when, in response to constrained opportunities in Arabia, he worked to expand and solidify his domain in Africa. He practiced a form of mobile governance to rule a vast dominion across the western Indian Ocean. As he moved between Arabia and Africa, he bought temporary loyalties with pensions and subsidies. These gave Said bin Sultan flexibility in the short term but did not provide lasting solutions to the unique challenges of a dispersed territory. To maintain mobile governance, Said used thinly veiled hostage-taking and depended increasingly on his own sons as governors. Fraternal rivalries among the younger generation led to exaltations for some and exile for others, ultimately undermining the unity of Said's dominions. The movements and maneuvers of five of his sons—Hilal, Thuwayni, Turki, Majid, and Barghash—deserve special attention because they illuminate a new geography of power in the western Indian Ocean that included travels to London, and, more importantly, Bombay. Said's firstborn, Hilal bin Said, traveled to London in the 1840s to appeal to British authorities and to improve his standing in his father's realm, but he was unsuccessful and died in exile in Arabia. After Seyyid Said's death in 1856, an unfolding succession dispute among Thuwayni, Turki, Majid and Barghash created an opportunity for British intervention that circumscribed the mobility of the winners and their territorial mobility. The losers—Barghash in Zanzibar, Turki in Muscat—faced temporary exile in Bombay, while Barghash's allies in his failed 1859 rebellion escaped to the caravan trails of mainland Africa. British arbitration in 1861 led to the Canning Award that formalized the political separation of Muscat and Zanzibar. While the British officially framed the brothers' rivalry as involving succession and sovereignty, the sons of Said bin Sultan used the language of debt. Between them, the seizure of property became the idiom of power, and their access to credit governed their standing with allies and in the region.

In the second half of the century, Barghash's exile in Bombay and his partisans' sojourns in the East Africa interior stretched the boundaries of the western Indian Ocean circuits, which had its poles in Muscat and Zanzibar. Yet the rulers in Zanzibar and Muscat had less space in which to operate. From Zanzibar, Majid (r. 1856–70) moderated his ambitions and reached for the coast of East Africa to found his own modern city at Dar es Salaam, was inspired by a trip to Bombay. Instabilities in Oman in the 1860s illuminated the degree to which three successive regimes were hemmed in territorially and by debt (Thuwayni, r. 1856–66; Salim, r. 1866–68; and a new imamate, 1868–71). Bombay provided refuge for Turki bin Said to wait out the political turmoil in Muscat, and credit from Zanzibar allowed him to choose when to reassert himself in Oman. His story also highlights an underappreciated aspect of mobility: some members of households, especially women and children, were not as mobile in Indian Ocean circuits and suffered for it. In the early 1870s, the more mobile younger brothers, losers of the early succession disputes who each endured exile in Bombay, succeeded at last. Barghash's reign in Zanzibar (1870–88) and Turki's in Muscat (1871–88) marked turning points in Arab sovereignty in the western Indian Ocean. While British intervention compromised their authority, their successors would claim even less independence, mobility, and territory.

SAID BIN SULTAN AND MOBILE GOVERNANCE, 1820S TO 1856

Said bin Sultan, whose shrouded corpse had been carried ashore in Zanzibar in 1856, was not an elected imam, but his territorial expansion and his legacy reflected principles of the Ibadi imamate ideal. For Ibadis in Oman, the imamate was the historical and religious ideal of government. Historically, male leaders and religious scholars sought to elect an imam who was righteous and fair. The imam would then make a contract with the electors, who pledged their support.[5] Thus in its ideal form, imamate rule depended on personal qualities and on the imam as being first among equals. The Ibadi imamate did not have a fixed capital in Oman, and transferring the capital—between Nizwa, al-Rustaq, Bahla, and other places—became a key aspect of Omani political culture.[6] In this way, the imamate's approach to territoriality also influenced the later Busaidi state.

Said bin Sultan's rule was also a legacy of contradictory forces within Ibadi politics. While the proscribed pattern of imamate election and rule worked in theory, in practice the imamate tended to revert from elected rule to a pattern of inherited, dynastic rule, at which point electors and religious leaders withdrew their backing. Dynastic rule depended on tribal confederations rather than religious legitimacy, so this imamate cycle, as Wilkinson details, also fed Omani tribal politics and rivalries. The first imam of the Busaidi line was Ahmad bin Said, who had helped rescue Oman from civil war and Persian invasion in the 1740s and was formally elected imam in 1753–54. From Ahmad bin Said's election up to the present, his heirs have been the rulers of Oman, though two distinct familial lines emerged in the 1780s. At that time, one line eschewed the support of the interior ulema, moved its capital to Muscat, and staked their future on trade in the gulf and the Indian Ocean. These were Said bin Sultan's direct ancestors, and he benefited from their dynastic rule. The other line maintained itself at al-Rustaq in the interior and enjoyed more support from Ibadi scholars.[7]

As in the imamate ideal, the Busaidi sultans were not all powerful rulers, but their personal qualities helped forge allegiances and loyalties. One way sultans demonstrated the power of their personalistic rule was in settling disputes—and enforcing settlements—between factions. For the rulers' own rivals, however, coopting them by providing access to income from trade or to credit became a way to ensure fealty, although these allegiance were usually temporary. Indeed, one aspect of statecraft that was vital to the mobile governance of the nineteenth century was offering subsidies or pensions to rivals.

Said bin Sultan employed techniques of mobile governance throughout his reign to consolidate state power and unify dispersed territorial holdings in the gulf, Arabia, and East Africa. In order to take over the Swahili coast and subdue his rivals in Mombasa, he made three separate journeys to East Africa between 1828 and 1837. He relied on local allies, superior naval power, and some old-fashioned chicanery to defeat the Mazrui in Mombasa and to take the fort there in 1837. This victory allowed him to encourage trade on the East African coast and to move his court to Zanzibar. His absences from Oman, however, brought challenges to his rule from rivals and tribal coalitions.

He countered these challenges by offering trade perks and stipends. When these failed, he resorted to hostage taking, essentially making his rivals mobile, too. To the first case, the Yal Sa'd tribe in Oman were frequent dissenters, and to win their favor Said bin Sultan granted them tax-free exportation privileges for their dates and other goods. Other tribal leaders received healthy annual payments to ensure their loyalty. In East Africa, Said bin Sultan faced recalcitrant governors and established Arab families. One solution to this problem was to insist that certain tribal leaders, such as Salim bin Abdullah, the senior al-Harthi man from Zanzibar, always traveled with him. He handled prominent Ibadi leaders in a similar way. Nasir b. Abi Nabhan al-Kharusi, a well-known Ibadi scholar feared and admired for his ability to make talismans, accompanied Said to Zanzibar.[8] Said thus kept powerful rivals close at hand even while on the move.

At the center of the essentially weak state structures was a ruler who depended on personal politics. Maintaining a semblance of control over such a large realm required frequent movement back and forth, and this evolved into a form of mobile governance that held together a dominion that touched three coasts of the western Indian Ocean: eastern Arabia; the port of Bandar Abbas in the gulf; the port and area surrounding Gwadar on the Arabian Sea (in what is now western Pakistan); and Zanzibar and some important towns along the Swahili coast.

While Said bin Sultan's move to Zanzibar in 1832 shared continuities with Omani patterns of rule, it became an essential shift in the history of the western Indian Ocean in the nineteenth century. This relocation precipitated the process of incorporating the East African interior into the Indian Ocean world. Fundamentally, the move to Zanzibar allowed Said to buy time when faced with a rapidly shifting set of regional relations and uncertain outcomes in the context of a renewed European presence. Arabs had for millennia gone to East Africa for trade, and Indian Ocean monsoon winds facilitated their travel. The Omanis had successfully expelled Portuguese interlopers during the seventeenth century and enjoyed hegemony in the western Indian Ocean. The situation changed in the nineteenth century when, in the wake of the Napoleonic Wars, the British began to assert themselves into trade dealings in the Persian Gulf and in the Indian Ocean. These maneuvers were tied broadly to Britain's growing interest in India, and led to an allegiance with Said bin Sultan to quash "piracy" in the gulf in the 1810s. Britain made truces with the sheikdoms of Abu Dhabi, Ras al-Khayma, and others on the southern coast of the gulf in 1820 and in so doing severely limited Said bin Sultan's and his subjects' activity in the region. At the same time, Omani traders faced stricter scrutiny in Bombay.[9] In response to setbacks in the gulf and in Bombay, Said bin Sultan took an active approach to East Africa, using his naval power and allegiances with Omani Arab families in the region when he could. This set of moves established outposts of the Omani state astride the Swahili coast and regional maritime networks. The historian M. Reda Bhacker makes clear that the pull factors in Zanzibar—a secure island that promised economic growth and had close relations with Indian traders—were partial solutions to Said bin Sultan's "need to survive" British moves in the Indian Ocean, and served to delay any confrontation.[10] Said bin Sultan's temporizing moves paid off with the early commercial success of Zanzibar, but maintaining his rule relied on his mobility.

Said bin Sultan traveled between East Africa and Arabia to settle disputes, to protect his interests, and to ensure his rule would continue. He initially relied on slave governors or appointed governors from prominent local families but eventually began to appoint his sons as governors in key port cities. His oldest son, Hilal bin Said, was the *wali* (governor) of Barka, on the Batinah coast, in the late 1830s, and another son, Thuwayni bin Said was the governor of Muscat from this period.[11] When Thuwayni bin Said captured the port city of Suhar in 1851 from the rival branch of the Busaidi, Said appointed another son, Turki bin Said, as its governor. The expelled governor, Qays bin Azzan bin Qays, and his followers moved to al-Rustaq, the interior stronghold of their line. Said bin Sultan needed loyal sons as governors while he moved back and forth to maintain control. Indeed, after Said had settled affairs at Suhar, he returned to Zanzibar in 1852 and then left once again for Muscat in 1854 to address Wahhabi encroachment and a dispute with the Persians at Bandar Abbas.

The characteristics of Said's mobile governance are evident during the period when he concluded trade agreements with foreign powers. He signed a commercial treaty with the Americans in 1833, and they enjoyed great influence in Zanzibar. Said bin Sultan hoped that his relationship with them would led to a steam-powered ship for him. This cutting edge technology would allow him to defy the monsoon winds and move back and forth more easily. In December 1839, rumors flew that the US Government was going to give Said bin Sultan a steamship in exchange for access to one of the mainland trading towns.[12] This trade never came to pass, and Said would not acquire his first steamship for more than a decade.[13] In 1840, shortly after Said bin Sultan concluded a similar commercial treaty with Britain, the British appointed a consul to oversee their interests. Fittingly, the new agent, Atkins Hamerton, was not assigned to a specific place, but to the ruler, so he, too, moved between Zanzibar and Oman in the 1840s and 1850s.

All told, Said bin Sultan ruled for nearly fifty years (1806–56) and was present in East Africa for nearly one-third of this. The proportion was much higher in the second half of his tenure. Between January 1828 and his death in October 1856, Said spent more than 80 percent of his time in East Africa (211 of 345 months).[14] He had also spent many months at sea, and perhaps it is fitting that he died at sea in October 1856 en route from Muscat to Zanzibar. It was then that Barghash tried to bury his father surreptitiously and seize power from his brother Majid. Said bin Sultan's reliance on his sons was an aspect of mobile governance that held his dominions together during his lifetime, but it also fostered a rivalry between his sons. These rivalries fractured their father's carefully nurtured realm and delineated new circuits of mobility in the Indian Ocean.

MOBILITY TO SEEK NEW SUPPORT FOR POWER, 1844 TO 1851

While Said bin Sultan was still alive, his sons had already begun to jockey for position, and their actions demonstrated both the shortcomings of Said's system of mobile governance and the importance of credit for Arab rulers. Said bin Sultan's governors had been allies, near relatives, and trusted slaves earlier in his rule. As his own sons became old enough, however, he began appointing them as governors. His first son's rise and dramatic fall from grace revealed the shifting contours of power emerging in the Indian Ocean during this period. Hilal bin Said had received foreign visitors in the palace in Muscat and served as the governor of Barka (c. 1838–41) in Oman before his father lost faith in him and recalled him to Zanzibar in 1841.[15] In 1844, Atkins Hamerton called Hilal "the most shrewd and energetic of all the Imam's sons," and he noted that Hilal had "the sympathy and good view of all His Highness's Arab subjects . . . and [was] loved by the tribes of Oman."[16] Said did not feel the same affection. Some attributed Hilal's downfall to the fact that his mother, an Abyssinian, had died when he was a child so he had no advocate for him in household politics. In contrast, Khalid, Hilal's main rival, had the active support and behind-the-scenes lobbying of his mother, a concubine from the Malabar coast of India.[17] The real reason for Hilal's fall may have been something darker. Said later referred to Hilal's "wickedness and evil deeds—such as cannot in any way be tolerated or overlooked amongst Arabs." Said felt "overwhelmed" that Hilal "might do things not approved of by either God or the Prophet."[18] As a result, Said bin Sultan exiled Hilal from Zanzibar in 1844.

Hilal's subsequent movements suggest the new contours of power in the western Indian Ocean. Although he moved through the typical circuits of the region (Zanzibar, Muscat, Mecca), he also went to London to seek allies. From Zanzibar in 1844, he went first to Jeddah, perhaps on the way to Mecca where his wife and children remained, and the next year he sailed to London from Alexandria. He undertook this trip to win favor from the British by asking them to intercede, thus clearly acknowledging their growing role in the Indian Ocean. In London, Hilal procured a letter for his father that he believed would set things right. Following his return to Zanzibar, he sought a powerful governorship—Muscat, Zanzibar, or Lamu—with an annual allowance of MT$30,000. Instead, Said offered to appoint him governor of a lesser port like Pemba or Bandar Abbas. When their negotiations failed in 1849, Said stripped Hilal of his horses and slaves and exiled him again.

Hilal died destitute in exile, and his family's ongoing hardships make clear the gendered nature of mobile governance and the limited possibilities for advancements without allowances or access to credit. Hilal went first to Lamu in a "state of destitution" because his father had not given him any financial support.[19] Hilal's wives and children were still in Mecca, also in distressed circumstances.[20] Elite men had much more mobility than women during this period, and stranded relatives became a common theme of the Busaidi sovereigns and mobile rule in general. From Lamu, Hilal made his way to Aden and then to Mecca to rejoin his family. Hilal died there in June 1851, after which his family moved to Muscat.[21] By happenstance, Said bin Sultan and Hamerton were both in Muscat when Hilal's family arrived. The British official lectured Su'ud, one of Hilal's older sons, on the importance of complying with his grandfather's wishes.[22] Perhaps the better lesson for Su'ud was that mobility alone was not a path to power. When Hilal's younger brothers had become governors—Thuwayni in Muscat and Majid in Zanzibar—they enjoyed their father's financial support. Without an allowance or access to credit, certain positions were untenable. Hilal predeceased his father, but their failed negotiations presaged the in-fighting among Hilal's brothers that marked the period that followed his death.

TURMOIL AND TRANSITION, 1856 TO 1861

When Barghash attempted to sneak Said bin Sultan's body to shore on that dark October night in 1856 he was part of a plot. Barghash, in cooperation with the Harthi sheikh who had traveled as Said bin Sultan's hostage, attempted to usurp control of Zanzibar from Majid. Their plans failed but set into motion a series of disputes that would lead to armed rebellion three years later, create an opening for British intervention, and inadvertently broaden the circuits of mobility to include the East African interior and Bombay.

After Said bin Sultan's death, Thuwayni bin Said, who had ruled in Muscat during his father's absences, believed that he should control the entire dominion, while his younger brother Majid bin Said, who had become the Zanzibar governor in 1854, thought that he should be the one to take over his father's rule. They had to contend with each other and with their local rivals. Thus, each of them faced similar circumstances: they had a sibling rival at the other end of the former empire who was angling to control the whole realm, and they each had a nearby brother hoping to usurp local power. In Oman, there was Turki bin Said, a brother younger than Thuwayni, who served as the governor of the port city of Suhar. In Zanzibar, Barghash bin Said was only twenty years old but his allegiance with the Harthi gave him additional heft.

The three years following Said bin Sultan's death saw an unsettled state of affairs as Thuwayni and Majid squabbled over dominion and over an estate marked by debt. During the same period, two prominent people, the customs master and the British agent, exited. In Zanzibar, Majid had laid claim to Said bin Sultan's ships, and in Muscat, Thuwayni claimed landed property. Yet they were also faced with debt because during Said's rule the line between state assets and personal assets did not exist. Said had depended heavily on Jairam Shivji, his customs master, for loans and liquidity to underwrite mobile governance. Both before and during Said's last trip to Arabia, he had taken loans from the house of Jairam Shivji to engage in diplomacy with the Persians and to offer stipends to win the loyalty of the rebels. Thus one of Said's legacies was a great debt to the firm of Jairam Shivji. Shivji had retired in 1853 from Zanzibar and returned to Kutch, his birthplace.[23] Likewise, Hamerton died in Zanzibar shortly after Said bin Sultan, and was not replaced immediately, in part due to the northern Indian uprising in 1857.

Thus when Colonel C. P. Rigby arrived in Zanzibar in 1858, he wanted to reassert British influence and tamp down the slave trade. This fit into the new increased control in India, with the Crown—in the form of the Raj—taking over the British East India Company's rule in the subcontinent.[24] The dispute between Thuwayni and Majid lasted for nearly three years, with accusations back and forth and property seizures in Zanzibar and Muscat.

By early 1859, Thuwayni, the senior brother, was frustrated by his penury and sought to break the impasse by coordinating with allies in Zanzibar and launching an invasion. Instead, he ran into British attempts to assert control in the western Indian Ocean. Thuwayni complained about the hierarchy and wealth of the status quo between Muscat and Zanzibar: "The man who is given a bone . . . can only suck it, but he who gets the flesh eats it. I am the elder brother and I have the bone in Muscat. Majid, my junior, has the flesh in Zanzibar."[25] Thuwayni outfitted an expedition to sail to Zanzibar in February, seize the island, and overthrow Majid.[26] The previous year, he might have executed this plan without difficulty, but in 1859, post-uprising in India, British consular and naval officers intervened. In late February 1859, the Political Resident for the Persian Gulf sent a commodore from the British Navy to Muscat to use "friendly counsel and remonstrance" to persuade Thuwayni to cease hostilities against Majid. The commodore delivered a letter to Thuwayni and explained that he should discuss his claims against Majid with the British. The naval officer was to follow Thuwayni in his ship to assure that he returned to Muscat.[27] This left Thuwayni's allies in Zanzibar, led by Barghash, on their own. In short, the death of Seyyid Said had allowed the British to increase their role as arbiters in the region, and the unified Arab rule of this western Indian Ocean dominion was being dismantled.

Although the officer successfully intercepted Thuwayni bin Said and called back his ships, arbitration did not resolve the situation. The result was a breaking point with historiographical implications. Thuwayni sent a representative to Zanzibar to meet with Majid but after several months of negotiations, they remained at a stalemate. Historians have seen the moment in two ways: beset by internal dissent or a gallant move for unity. British officials, writing twenty-five years after the fact—at a time with Harthi activism in Oman was challenging the sitting sultan—claimed that Thuwayni's 1859 representative had not come in good faith, but rather had come "to distribute money among the Harthi tribe & induce them to rise." In this version, Thuwayni withdrew because he had been double-crossed by the Harthi, who held great sway over a young Barghash.[28] The Omani historian al-Hashimy, following al-Salimi, has framed this as an Omani national issue: the 1859 negotiations were the last chance to preserve the supposed unity of the trans-Indian Ocean Omani empire.[29]

Either way, the breakdown of negotiations allowed the British to intervene in the succession dispute. As historian Rheda Bhacker explains, "From now on it was to be the paramount power, Britain, who assumed the role of kingmaker in Zanzibar as well as in Muscat."[30] In April of 1859, before the matter was formally settled, however, the government in Bombay had already split the African and Arabian realms bureaucratically, assigning Muscat to Persian Gulf officials. "I am desired in conclusion to observe that the Resident in the Persian Gulf should [. . .], now that Zanzibar and Muscat are disunited [. . .], be regarded as the officer in charge of Political relations as with the Imam of Muscat."[31] The bureaucratic wheels had begun to constrain the mobility of Arab rulers in the western Indian Ocean. Said's sons would never move so freely or so frequently as he had. Events in Zanzibar would only compound this.

BARGHASH'S REBELLION AND EXILE, 1859 TO 1862

In early 1859, while Thuwayni schemed his invasion of Zanzibar, Barghash and the Harthi chiefs conspired to overthrown Majid. The cloak and dagger maneuvers, related in breathless detail by a surprising narrator, were not successful and resulted in a scattering of the conspirators into exile, from the ivory depots of central Africa to cosmopolitan, industrial Bombay. Barghash's machination aligned with the plot in Muscat, attracted allies of questionable character, and split the royal family. In 1859, Barghash was only in his early twenties and aside from some loyal young relatives, did not have a natural base of support in Zanzibar. He was more client than patron. The British consul called him "a morose discontented man."[32] The consul noted in 1858 that, while Barghash had few followers in Zanzibar, his alliance with Thuwayni put him among the leaders of a group in Muscat that planned to dispossess Majid.[33] In these circumstances, with few funds of his own to attract allies, Barghash encouraged others to bet on the future, promising influential positions when his plot succeeded. He invited them to meetings, held in the darkest part of the night, based on when the moon was rising or setting.[34]

These meetings, according to the memoirs of Salme bint Said, Barghash's younger sister, were steeped in secrecy, and the conspiracy played out with delicious intrigues. Salme, who had a falling out with Barghash decades later, lends a suspenseful narration to the events of the rebellion. At fifteen years of age she was the youngest female member of the conspiracy and served as the "secretary-general" of the alliance, due, in part, to her literacy, unusual for this era.[35] She supervised correspondence with the chiefs and ordered the bullets, powder, and muskets that were to be used in the rebellion.[36]

Given Barghash's approach, it is not surprising that the brewing rebellion attracted diverse opportunists. People that Salme considered more reputable—including the majority of her half-siblings—distanced themselves from Barghash's faction. The followers were "ambitious and important people who feel grieved and overlooked," seeking revenge for perceived injustices. "Dozens of discontented saw themselves already as Barghash's ministers or in other high places; hundreds reckoned undoubtedly with property and titles, of which they would not even have dreamed before." These strivers came from far and wide to join the conspiracy, "apparently to serve Barghash, but in reality to serve themselves." In hindsight, Salme noted that, when building the coalition of rebels, "the most miserable were also received with open arms."[37]

Yet, as the conspiracy grew, secrecy was more difficult to maintain. Hotheaded Barghash no longer feigned loyalty to his brother the sultan. He stopped attending Majid's regular *baraza* (court and public reception), and his imprudent behavior raised suspicions across society. Majid took action to block the conspiracy in Oman and in Zanzibar. He sent MT$30,000, two large iron guns, and two hundred barrels of gunpowder to Turki in Suhar so that Turki could challenge Thuwayni in Oman.[38] In Zanzibar, before the conspirators could finalize their rebellion, Majid put Barghash under house arrest, essentially laying a siege against his house. Most houses in Zanzibar did not have wells, and a lack of fresh water would have forced concessions from Barghash. But the tempestuous young lord communicated with his sisters from the high balconies on the narrow lanes of Zanzibar, and one sister sewed a canvas hose to deliver freshwater surreptitiously.

Meanwhile, Salme corresponded with the Harthi leaders, key confederates of the plotters who had escaped house arrest. Salme does not name "the influential, energetic chief" of the al-Harthi with whom she cooperated, but she notes that he remained free to recruit soldiers to the rebellion.[39] While this possibly could have been Salih bin Ali, a young man of the sheikhly line of the Harthi, who was in Zanzibar at the time, it is more likely, that her correspondent was Abdullah bin Salim al-Harthi. Abdullah bin Salim was one of Zanzibar's wealthiest men, with immense holdings of both land and ships and command of a retinue of 1,500 armed slaves. Majid had tried to win Abdullah bin Salim's loyalty by paying him an annual allowance of

$1,200 and permitting him to import his goods duty-free.[40] Abdullah bin Salim, however, chose Barghash over Majid, and brought most of the Harthi with him.

With Barghash and his close allies under house arrest, the conspirators altered and accelerated their plan. They hatched a scheme to spring Barghash from house arrest to rendezvous with the conspirators on a plantation in the countryside. The guards at Barghash's house turned back the women when they arrived, but Salme and her sister Khole stepped forward and addressed the soldiers and their commanding officer directly. These elite women conversing with nonkin "conflicted with customs and usages," and the men were, in their bewilderment, unable to formulate a reply. "When they regained their composure a little," she reported, "they launched forth in so many excuses that I, conscious of our evil intentions, felt deeply ashamed." The two women insisted, indignantly, that they should be able to visit their brothers. The guards—armed with muskets and fixed bayonets—relented.[41]

Inside the house, the women had to convince their proud brother of their plan: to dress him like a woman and to smuggle him out of the house. He initially resisted on grounds of masculinity.[42] He agreed, however, armed himself, and was wrapped in a large, black silken shawl with a gold border. Only his eyes were uncovered. His twelve-year-old brother Abdulaziz bin Said did the same. The tallest women walked beside the men and they exited nonchalantly, engaging in idle chatter. To their surprise and relief, the guards moved aside respectfully.[43] The party of women moved carefully to the outskirts of the city, and then they ran as fast as they could through the countryside, "totally unconcerned" about their fine urban dress and gold embroidered slippers. At the meeting point, Barghash and Abdulaziz proceeded to the plantation headquarters, and Salme and the other women slipped back to town.

Despite the Harthi strength and supporters who flocked to Barghash's side, Majid's forces—reportedly numbering in the thousands—advanced on the semifortified plantation. They pummeled the rebels. Hundreds of people were killed, although Barghash and the other leaders escaped back to town. Barghash barricaded himself and his closest supporters in his house and refused to negotiate. In response, Majid and Rigby, the British Consul, summoned a troop of Royal Marines from the harbor. The British force launched an assault on Barghash's house, briefly turning the neighborhood into an urban war zone. As bullets whizzed by, Salme's household members ran for cover, some falling into prayer amid the confusion.[44] When Barghash surrendered, his sister Khole ran to Rigby's house to report the news. He was not at home, but the people in Barghash's house were calling out for peace, so the marines stopped firing. The rebellion had been defeated before Thuwayni's forces could arrive from Muscat.

Although Majid agreed to Barghash's exile, he did not treat him as harshly as their father had treated their brother Hilal. Barghash received a monthly allowance of 700 crowns after the rebellion, and Majid asked the customs master, Ladha Damji, to pay Barghash a total of 14,000 crowns, one part (4,000 crowns) as his inheritance and the balance (10,000) to support him in exile.[45] On his way into exile in Bombay aboard the steamer H.M.S. Assaye, Barghash stopped briefly in Muscat.[46] Whether he saw Thuwayni, whose naval support may have turned the battle against Majid, is unclear. Their father's era of mobile governance had ended, but the ambit of the western Indian Ocean expanded. As a result of the uprising and British intervention, one son of Said who was not allowed to move (Thuwayni) and another who was forced across the Indian Ocean to Bombay (Barghash). Meanwhile, Barghash's array of followers and Harthi allies fled to the African mainland and settled in the new towns of the caravan trails. The Harthi ringleaders were imprisoned in Lamu where they died under suspicious circumstances.[47] The defeat of Barghash's rebellion further enhanced the separation of Muscat and Zanzibar and marked growing British influence. Majid retained control of Zanzibar, Thuwayni held Muscat, and Barghash, like his brother Hilal before him, was exiled.

Barghash lived in Bombay for two years. This modernizing, industrial city of the mid-nineteenth century was what historian Nile Green has called "the cosmopolis of the Indian Ocean."[48] With a population of more than five hundred thousand (about a fifth of whom were Muslim), the city was experiencing a second wave of urbanization. A professional class of city planners emerged who oversaw elaborate public works. In early 1860, Barghash wrote a beseeching letter to Lord Elphinstone, asking to return to Zanzibar: "I beg your lordship to send me to Zanzibar in one of your vessels." Barghash asked for transport and a mediator who could help him with Majid. He vowed "that no objectionable act will ever be committed by me," and he appealed to a notion of homeland and property, writing that he could not abandon Zanzibar because it was his birthplace and he had estates there.[49] Barghash returned to Zanzibar in 1861 and took up a life in seclusion; "resid[ing] in his old house, and attend[ing] durbar; 'but is it is well understood throughout town that Syud Barghash is a marked man and that no person is to call on him or address him.'" Receiving no salary, in part because Majid was unable to afford it, Barghash was more of a state prisoner than a principal courtier.[50]

In this situation, Barghash opted to bide his time in Zanzibar and wait out Majid. The new British agent, Pelly, had made arrangements to send Barghash abroad, but Barghash did not want to depart and arouse Majid's suspicions.[51] Having returned from exile, Barghash's most direct path to power was not mobility but patience. In 1870, his stoicism was rewarded when Majid died, and almost a decade and half after he had tried to bury his father in secret, Barghash bin Said was the ruler of Zanzibar. In time, he became Zanzibar's modernizing sultan, famous for his improvements in the technology and infrastructure on the island. For instance, he brought printing presses from Bombay, and as historian Anne Bang has argued, the Ibadi *nahda* (renaissance) took place in Zanzibar rather than Oman in part because of Barghash's leadership. Barghash seems to have imbibed the lessons of Bombay's modernization from his time in exile. Majid, constrained by his success in Zanzibar, had been less mobile and had no such exposure, so his British allies had contrived a trip to inspire him.

MAJID AND THE MODERN CITY, 1861 TO 1865

In aftermath of the 1859 rebellion and the 1861 Canning Award, Majid bin Said was the undisputed sultan of Zanzibar and his father's African dominions. British forces had helped him protect his rule, and now they sought to influence it by refocusing his ambitions from Arabia to within the East African sphere. The key to this, however, was a trip to Bombay. The city had become a key point in the new geography of power in the Indian Ocean: a waypoint for mobile sultans.

The new British agent, Pelly, who arrived in 1862, contemplated the results of the Canning Award, which untethered Omani rule in East Africa from Muscat. Despite this political division, East Africa was not territorially distinct from long-standing Indian Ocean processes, including the movement of Indian merchants, slaves, and credit. How could the British coach their new client to adapt to changes and continuities? Pelly believed the biggest question the British had to answer was, "Is it the permanent intention of Government to accept an Arab State of Zanzibar?" And, if so, how should the British exert pressure upon it? Pelly understood credit as Zanzibar's lifeblood and recognized three flaws with the sultanate. First, Indians—who he called British Indian subjects—were the center of the economy, and the wealth of Zanzibar depended on them.[52] Second, Majid lacked modernizing impulses, while Pelly wanted him to build roads, clear jungles, clean up the towns, and drain swamps. Third, the place of slaves in both the economic and social order was distasteful and difficult to address. Pelly understood the role of credit in the economy as well as the emerging role of fixed property. He warned the British government to avoid any action "to shake credit in the Zanzibar market or to unsettle the value of landed property or to disturb society by any sudden or sweeping radicalism, such as the dictatorial abolition of slavery."[53]

Pelly made plans to turn Majid into a modern ruler by focusing on the African mainland and drawing inspiration from India. This transformation would require mobility, both within his realm and beyond it. Majid's power on the mainland was "very slight and undefined" because, like the Portuguese of an earlier era, he held islands and forts along the coast. Majid held more authority among people along the coast—Pelly referred to them as "the softer & agricultural tribes & mixed breeds of the low shore"—than he did in the interior. Beyond the coast, the frontier of his realm was ill-defined and relationships were based only on commercial exchanges. The remedy to this situation necessitated both travel and force. Pelly suggested to the Indian government that for Majid to consolidate his hold on the mainland, he "should himself travel through it from time to time, at the head of a sufficient Force, requiring, en route, the salaams of the Chiefs in token of submission & if necessary taking Hostages there!"[54] Thus, Majid's new territorially subscribed rule would require crossing the Zanzibar channel to the African mainland and crossing the Indian Ocean to Bombay.

To build a modern city, Majid had to see a modern city, and for the western Indian Ocean, this meant Bombay. Majid's trip to Bombay in 1865 was the culmination of three years of planning. The two goals for the trip were to reconcile Majid with his younger brother Abdulaziz and to expose Majid to Bombay and its Public Works Department. Abdulaziz bin Said had initially departed Zanzibar with Barghash in 1859, but after their return in 1861 Abdulaziz offended Majid and was sent away again. A meeting in Bombay would set the stage for Abdulaziz's return.

R. L. Playfair, Pelly's successor, was even more enthusiastic about impressing Majid with the infrastructure of Bombay, but he realized some delicacy would be required in introducing a conservative Ibadi ruler to the region's cosmopolis. The plan was to waive docking fees, borrow a private rail car from a wealthy Parsi businessman, and "show him everything of interest in Bombay & Poona." Playfair was conscious that opulence and development of Bombay, not to mention habits of everyday living, might be out of step with the sultan's practices. Playfair warned the officials that no one should smoke in Majid's presence because it was "abhorrent" to Majid and "all belonging to his sect." Playfair claimed that Majid had "never seen a road or a carriage" and believed that, in Bombay, the sultan of Zanzibar might hire a surveyor and builder from the Public Works Department to oversee road building efforts in Zanzibar.[55] Majid left Zanzibar on September 13, 1865, among a convoy of four ships.[56]

In Bombay, Majid presented the governor with gifts, including diamond ornaments, and the governor gave Majid a screw steam yacht with a dubious history.[57] In the official account of this exchange, the yacht was valued at 45,000 rupees, while Majid's gifts were only estimated to be worth 26,000. The disparity attracted official scrutiny, but the Indian government allowed the difference in light of "the extreme liberality of the Sultan in all his dealings with the British Government."[58] Majid returned to Zanzibar after an absence of nearly three months. .[59]

Although the idea for a city on the mainland had been talked about since the 1862, building a trading port that would allow Majid to tap into the caravan trade did not begin until the year Majid returned from Bombay (1865) or the next year. He built this city near a fishing village on the mainland southwest of Zanzibar and called it Bandar al-Salaam, the haven of peace, generally shortened to Dar es Salaam. Historians James Brennan and Andrew Burton's argument that Majid modeled the city on his experience in Zanzibar fails to account for the peregrinations of a mobile sultan and his Indian Ocean itinerary.[60] In the years that Majid was building a new city, however, his less mobile brother, Thuwayni in Muscat, was struggling with many forces that were nearly out of his control. He lacked a haven of peace.

THUWAYNI'S TROUBLES IN MUSCAT, 1856 TO 1866

The decade from 1856 to 1866 was a trying one for Thuwayni bin Said. He had aspired to be ruler of all his father's dominions: in the Persian Gulf, along the Makran coast, in Oman, and also in Zanzibar and its opposite coasts where customs agents collected massive revenues. His aborted mission to invade Zanzibar, however, and his capitulation to the Canning Award hemmed him in Muscat, where he faced multiple threats and had few allies. As territorial boundaries became more rigid in the western Indian Ocean, Thuwayni in Arabia was highly circumscribed. His inability to maneuver makes clear the reasons that his father had moved his capital from Muscat in the 1830s. Thuwayni had begun as the *wali* (governor) of Muscat and learned the exigencies of the Arabian capital during his father's frequent trips to Zanzibar. As governor, Thuwayni maintained his rule by negotiating with Arabs from both interior Oman and the coast. He tried to stave off incursions from the Sunni orthodox Wahhabi of central Arabia, sought conciliation with the Persian Shah over Muscat's control of the gulf port of Bandar Abbas, and engaged with the British. After his father's death these challenges were amplified.

The arbitration that led to the Canning Award severed Thuwayni's claims of Zanzibar and entangled him more closely with the British, who proved to be fickle allies. In 1860, Thuwayni had agreed to arbitration over the succession dispute and felt certain that his position as the rightful ruler of his father's entire domain would be vindicated.[61] He was disappointed by the 1861 Canning Award. Thuwayni, who had once likened his position in Muscat to being thrown a bone while Majid in Zanzibar feasted on the flesh, was not content with the bone or with the hand that offered it. Thuwayni found the British were hard to please and slow to help. They made demands of him in the gulf, in his actions against Persia, and over the slave trade. Yet when his rule was in jeopardy they were reluctant to join a fight. This became clear in 1864 when their empty promises and his empty coffers exposed Thuwayni's vulnerability.

Thuwayni's highly circumscribed rule left him isolated when the rival Busaidi line allied with the Ibadi ulema in the interior in 1864. When he sought external support, sheikhs in the gulf declined, and the Wahhabi ruler in Nejd promised swift retribution if Thuwayni attacked the rebels. Thuwayni's precarious balancing act between internal and external rivals was failing, and his lack of funds made it difficult to attract support. Four years earlier, Thuwayni had extinguished a rebellion on the Batinah coast and, in the process, killed Qays bin Azzan al-Busaidi, the scion of the rival line. Later, Qays's son Azzan, however, allied himself with the Ibadi leaders of the interior, including Said bin Khalfan al-Khalili, and they headquartered themselves at al-Rustaq. Thuwayni moved against them in December 1864, but he lacked the funds to attract allies. The sheikhs of Abu Dhabi and Ras al-Khayma were reluctant to support Thwuayni. The British agent at Muscat noted cattily that the shaykhs "probably having learnt the embarrassed state of the latter's finances (which unfortunately has become a common topic of conversation) they are loath to incur expense without some good prospect of repayment."[62] The Wahhabi contingent that controlled the strategic Buraimi oasis on Oman's border supported the rebels. The Wahhabi *naib* promised to attack Muscat if Thuwayni assailed al-Rustaq, the latest indignity for the Omani ruler from his Saudi rivals. Wahhabi forces were both a fiscal and physical threat to Thuwayni's rule, and their command of Buraimi oasis halfway between the Persian Gulf and the Gulf of Oman allowed them to assert themselves into local allegiances and force the sultan to pay *zakat* as protection money.[63] Thus, Thuwayni was checked against al-Rustaq at the end of 1864, hemmed in by Omani rivals, a woeful treasury, and Wahhabi power.

Thuwayni's fickle allies, the British, initially refused his request to attack the Wahhabis in the gulf. Escalating Wahhabi violence against Oman and British Indian subjects in 1865, however, spurred the British to half measures. They had rejected Thuwayni's blockade of the Hasa coast to cut off the Wahhabis there. Unrestrained, a Wahhabi agent arrived in Muscat in August 1865 and demanded a threefold increase of Thuwayni's *zakat* payment. The sultan refused, and the Wahhabis swept into Oman from Buraimi, teamed with Thuwayni's rivals, and captured Sur, one of Oman's principal ports of exchange with East Africa. In the fighting, the invaders killed one British Indian and captured others. This alerted the British to the Wahhabi ruler Faisal's rising power, and they promised to send Thuwayni arms to attack Buraimi and to blockade the Hasa coast. All three plans were for naught. The naval action fizzled because the Wahhabis preemptively struck Oman's Batinah coast, disrupting trade and driving Indian merchants into the sea, at least one of whom drowned. Meanwhile, the two eighteen-pound guns the British granted to Thuwayni were impossible to transport to Buraimi. Even if Thuwayni's forces had moved the guns, no one knew how to fire them.[64] The arms, like the allies who supplied them, were more a burden than a help.

Thuwayni had no room to maneuver and no way to buy time. A serendipitous death in Nejd and unexpected British vigor created a short-lived windfall for Thuwayni in 1865 and early 1866. In the midst of the British demands for restitution from Faisal, the Wahhabi emir, for the attacks on British subjects, the Wahhabi leader died unexpectedly. The British agent Pelly, recently reassigned from Zanzibar, insisted on shelling the Wahhabi ports without waiting for a response from the new emir. Pelly then trained his sights on Wahhabi sympathizers in Thuwayni's territory and demanded payment from the Janabah sheikhs near Sur who had assisted in the previous year's attack. The sheikhs plead for more time to raise the money—their dhows were trading in the gulf—but Pelly opened fire upon arrival. His forces destroyed the Janabah forts and continued to Sur the next day and demolished all the boats in the creek.[65]

The fortuitous news of his rival's death and the meaningful assistance of a capricious ally likely had not yet reached Thuwayni in Suhar on February 13, 1866. He probably felt that his circumstances left much to be desired. His brother was still conniving against him in Zanzibar, Azzan bin Qays in al-Rustaq had allied with his Ibadi detractors, the Wahhabi supported his close enemies, and the British interventions had been bungled. And yet, there was another unsuspected threat. In the night, Thuwayni was killed by his son Salim. Salim bin Thuwayni murdered his father as part of a plot backed by the Wahhabi and endorsed by Thuwayni's Omani rivals, the Ibadi leaders and Azzan bin Qays.[66] The post-Canning circumstances had pinned Thuwayni into an untenable position, and his murder inaugurated a period of greater political and economic fragility in Oman.

SALIM BIN THUWAYNI, 1866 TO 1868

In February 1866, Salim declared himself sultan. Thuwayni's struggles had shown the challenges of ruling post-Canning Oman, and although Salim enjoyed short-lived support from Azzan bin Qays and his allies, the British regarded the young sultan with deep suspicion, and he faced a potent rival, his uncle Turki bin Said. Salim immediately imprisoned Turki in Suhar, but it was his own unsavory route to power and shaky legitimacy that most undermined his authority. He lacked too many things: access to wealth and the support of the commercial classes; wide acceptance from both the interior tribes and the Ibadi scholarly elite; and the acquiescence of British officials in the gulf. Turki also remained an active threat and was freed from prison six months later.

Salim's ascension was another blow to the battered economy of Oman. Political machinations influenced trade and economy in Muscat and the Arabian interior. When news of the palace coup reached the Indian merchants in Muscat and in Muttrah, they boarded boats in the harbor to escape any threat of violence. Pelly ordered their property to be embarked for good measure.[67] Disturbances like this one in Muscat and the previous Wahhabi attacks in Sur and Saham undermined the local and regional economies in which Kutchi and Khoja merchants increasingly played an important role. Muscat's economy unraveled in the five years following Salim's ascent to power. This was a result of the dynamic political (and religious) order and dissent within the merchant communities. Indeed, while the sultan's mobility was constrained by the Canning Award, the confluence of events after 1866 created favorable conditions for everyday Omanis to emigrate. The decline in commerce and the merchant population in Muscat contributed to the rise of Zanzibar as a commercial center.

Turki bin Said was also on the move. Having slipped his captors, he fled to the gulf in September 1866 to shore up support. His mobility was a strength. The threat of attack on Muscat made rumors fly, and the Bombay government authorized Pelly to take action in "an extraordinary crisis."[68] In April 1867, Turki left Dubai, where he enjoyed the support of the sheikh but had failed to woo the new Wahhabi emir, and attacked Suhar. Pelly warned both Turki and the sheikh of Dubai that they were playing a dangerous game, and he sent warships to Dubai to back up his complaint. Turki lost his position there but, with Wahhabi assistance, he retreated to the Buraimi oasis.[69] Turki reorganized and successfully captured Muttrah, the commercial port that controlled access to Muscat.

When Salim bin Thuwayni was unable to dislodge Turki, he sought British intervention. Pelly steamed to Muttrah and took a page from Said bin Sultan's mobile governance. He convinced Turki to retire to Bombay, where he would receive a monthly stipend of six hundred dollars, as long as he remained in British India. Bombay was once again a site of exile for one of Said bin Sultan's sons. Turki's exile bought Salim some time, though his days as a sultan were numbered.

THE IMAMATE, 1868 TO 1871

Salim's reckoning with his erstwhile Ibadi allies occurred in 1868. They rallied tribal levies, expelled Salim from Muscat, and held the first imamate election of the nineteenth century. They elected Azzan bin Qays al-Busaidi, Thuwayni's rival, as imam. This signaled a victory for the Ibadi activists of the interior over the branch of the Busaidi clan that had moved to Muscat in the 1780s and staked its future on the gulf and Indian Ocean trade. For Salim's enemies, achieving the Ibadi ideal had been a rallying point, but their unity did not last. The disturbed economy was a major factor. With the already declining revenues that had begun with the diminution of trade in Salim's reign, the imamate faced stark budget shortfalls. They chose to augment the state treasury by confiscating the property of those who were enemies of the state, especially the deposed Busaidis and their allies[70] They defended this with a slim legal justification under Ibadi ideals, but some supporters regarded it as immoral, and tribal leaders gradually withdrew their support from the regime.[71]

Salim bin Thuwayni also demonstrated, in defeat, the importance of mobility and access to capital in controlling Oman. After his overthrow, Salim fled to Bandar Abbas and tried to rally supporters in Suhar and the northern region of the country to challenge Muscat.[72] He had very little money and very little success. Enlisting supporters required direct payments or at least the promise of financial reward. Salim had overborrowed from his creditors, and his few supporters incurred "extravagant expenses." This limited his mobility within the gulf, and in early 1869 it seemed he would be stuck in Dubai.[73] He forged an allegiance with the Wahhabi state and backed their incursion into Suhar in the middle of 1869.[74] Lacking sufficient capital to assure the loyalty of supporters, however, Salim was ultimately unsuccessful. He spent the rest of his life in the Persian Gulf and the western Indian Ocean in fruitless attempts to reclaim power in Muscat.

With the defeat of Salim and the rise of the imamate, Turki's retirement in India did not go as planned. When news reached Turki that the imamate had failed to consolidate its hold on the country, he saw his opening. In Bombay, however, he lacked the funds to mount an effective challenge. His only source of income was his subsidy of $600 per month, which he believed was meant to support his family and was predicated "on the condition that, and so long as, he [Turki] shall reside in British India, or such other place as the British Govent. may allot to him, without molestation of the Muscat territory."[75] Such conditions echoed the Canning Award's constraints on the sultans of Muscat and Zanzibar, and Turki faced a choice between his family and his future.

Turki and Exile in Bombay, 1867 to 1870

In August 1870, Venayek Wassoodew, the Oriental Translator to the Government of Bombay, reported on an unusual case. He had been asked to investigate a foreign family living in Bombay, and found two Abyssinian women living with four young children. One of the women was the children's mother, and one was their paternal grandmother. The household also contained a retinue of fifteen servants. Although this number of dependents suggested a wealthy family, Mr. Wassoodew was asked to inquire because the government had heard for some months that this family was "in great pecuniary distress."[76] This turned out to be true, and Wassoodew reported that the family members were in "an actual state of starvation."[77]

While there were many starving individuals in booming, industrial Bombay in 1870, one would not expect these to include the grandchildren of the illustrious Seyyid Said bin Sultan bin Imam Ahmad al-Busaidi. Yet, indeed, these were the family and followers of Turki bin Said. They were starving in Bombay while Turki was trying to reclaim Muscat and reestablish his father's line as the rulers of the country. To take advantage of unfolding circumstances since 1866, Turki had moved between the coast and the interior of Oman, between Oman and the gulf, back to Oman, and into exile in Bombay. He later negotiated an exit from Bombay, and, with financing from Zanzibar, a return to Oman.

When Turki arrived in Bombay in 1867, he was an outsider. He noticed this most pointedly when he tried to raise funds or secure credit, the lifeblood of Indian Ocean mobility. He complained to the governor of Bombay that he was "a poor stranger," untrusted and unable to secure a loan.[78] An

Arabic promissory note in the Zanzibar archive shows that Turki secured a loan from the firm of Jairam Shivji for four thousand rupees in 1868, but other sources of credit were fleeting.[79] Indeed, based on his experience in his father's administration as a governor in Suhar, he understood where he might find a creditor. In his few years in Bombay, Turki became quite knowledgeable about the customs department. On the one hand, he sought to import personal goods from the Persian Gulf duty-free.[80] On the other hand, he recognized the power of that office to control the flow of goods, and he asked that the customs office impound the Arabian horses that his main rival, Imam Azzan bin Qays, had exported from Oman.[81]

Lacking access to credit elsewhere, Turki beseeched the Bombay government to grant him $80,000 of the Zanzibar subsidy that was supposed to be given to the sultan of Oman. Thus, Turki asserted himself as the legitimate head of state in Muscat.[82] While his letters proclaimed his legitimacy as a ruler, they also emphasized his fealty to and reliance on the government of Bombay. By early February 1870, Turki was eager to reenter the contest for Muscat. He explained that he would leave Bombay soon for Oman, but that he did so with the governor's permission. He invoked the allegiance the British had with his father and stated explicitly that he was "a guest and someone who yields obedience to Government."[83] As with his brothers, Turki's mobility was compromised by entanglements with British officialdom.

As Turki made plans to invade Muscat, he had to balance his relationship with Bombay officials, his access to other forms of credit, and his ability to move across the Arabian Sea and in the gulf. In March 1870, Turki departed to challenge Azzan bin Qays in Oman, and mistakenly assumed that his allowance would continue to support his household in Bombay.[84] Turki made no other provisions to maintain his household.[85]

Before he realized what had happened to his relatives, Turki's two greatest challenges in his campaign were credit and mobility. Bombay officials undermined his efforts to return to the gulf. When he telegraphed to Gwadar, an Omani outpost between Persia and India, in March 1870 to try to raise his allies there, the Assistant Political Agent in Gwadar forbade Turki from embarking armed men from that port.[86] In the following months, Turki bounced around the gulf, trying to amass the human and financial resources to attack the imamate. On May 10, 1870, he wrote from Dubai to secure a loan from the Bombay government. He knew he would not persuade the sheikh of Abu Dhabi to support him, and he assumed incorrectly that the Wahhabi emir might back him.[87]

By late June, Turki's efforts flagged in Bandar Abbas, not because of military or political news from Oman, but because of personal news from Bombay.

Sultans at Sea ⇆ 83

He learned that his stipend had been discontinued and that his household was destitute. He was deeply disappointed with the Bombay government because his family was under its protection. They lived in a government-owned residence. Turki's distress made it impossible for him to conduct the business at hand. "I now labor under two anxieties.... One about myself personally and the other about my children." Just as his brother Hilal's wives and children had been stranded in Mecca some thirty years before, Turki's family's plight underscores the gendered nature of mobility in this period, especially within elite households. Turki had miscalculated. If he had known that the stipend would be discontinued, he said that he would have sent his family to Zanzibar before he left Bombay.[88] In these regrets, Turki sees clearly the new geography of power that had emerged in the western Indian Ocean in the nineteenth century for contesting authority in the Omani states. Muscat and Zanzibar were still the poles, but Bombay had become an essential meridian.

In the last months of 1870, Turki's twin anxieties dissipated. Wassoodew's desperate reports led to an emergency grant of one thousand rupees from the Bombay government for Turki's dependents. Meanwhile, in the gulf, Turki gathered followers from Oman and financial resources from Zanzibar. He retook Muscat in 1871, overthrew the imamate, and gained British recognition. In defeating the imamate, however, Turki's actions echoed Majid's after the 1859 rebellion. Majid let his al-Harthi enemies be murdered in a Lamu prison, and Turki was party to the execution of a key figure in the imamate, Said bin Khalfan al-Khalili, and Khalili's son. This earned him deep enmity from Ibadi leaders, a problem that would plague his seventeen-year rule.

⸻

Although Turki bin Said may be among the least heralded of the Busaidi rulers of Oman and Zanzibar, his accession and reign were key to the continuation of the Busaidi dynasty. When Turki bin Said reclaimed his father's Arabian dominions in 1871, he reestablished the Said bin Sultan's line in the wake of a patricide and the subsequent Ibadi-backed coup. He did not come to power as his father did, deftly negotiating the politics of Oman and its interior. Turki's rise depended on his ability to move in the gulf and the western Indian Ocean and his use of the overlapping networks of wealth, clientship, and imperial power in this broader world. Specifically, Turki strategized his return and augmented his alliances with interior tribes through money raised in Zanzibar's credit markets and through delicate negotiations for British support, both in Bombay and in the gulf.

SULTANS AT SEA

When Seyyid Said bin Sultan died at sea in 1856 he governed a dispersed realm in Africa and Arabia, with outposts in the Persian Gulf and the Makran Coast. His son Barghash's ill-fated attempt to smuggle the body ashore in Zanzibar foretold a decade and a half of struggle among Said's heirs. The politics of Oman were no longer disputes and alliances between port cities and oasis towns. Seyyid Said's mobile form of governance had redrawn the map of state power. He did this at the same time that growing British influence and the industrialization of western India's biggest port made London and Bombay new nodes in circuits of Omani power. From the 1840s, Seyyid Said's sons visited these new junctions as they attempted to claim portions of their father's realm for themselves. After Said's death, British intervention made Oman and Zanzibar separate sultanates. Internal dissent and external threats challenged Thuwayni in Oman more than they did Majid in Zanzibar. In the 1860s, while Majid's visit to Bombay helped launch a vision for his own new settlement, Dar es Salaam, on the Swahili coast, Thuwayni in Muscat was hemmed in by regional and intimate enemies. In the wake of his death, two short-lived regimes followed. By the early 1870s, however, Turki and Barghash, younger brothers initially shut out in succession disputes, had each returned from an exile in Bombay to rule in Muscat and Zanzibar, respectively. While nominal British power in the Indian Ocean mediated their exiles and their eventual accessions, subsequent Busaidi rulers were much less mobile, or perhaps, more aptly, they were much less able to chart their own course in establishing or disputing sovereignty.

4 ∽ Halwa and Identity in the Western Indian Ocean World

IN THE EARLY 1840S, at the time of the Nizwa drought, Thani bin Amir al-Harthi was a humble confectioner making halwa in Oman.[1] Less than twenty years later, he was one of the wealthiest traders in Kazeh, an ivory depot on the East African plateau, over four hundred miles from the Indian Ocean.[2] In Africa, Thani participated in trading caravans as early as 1845, and he was thus part of the expanding commercial world of the 1840s. Thani traveled and traded extensively—from the coast to the kingdoms on the lakes—and his knowledge underlays Richard Burton's seminal book that explained interior Africa to the English-speaking world. Thani was both participant and witness to the incorporation of upland East Africa into the Indian Ocean world.

Marginal and displaced Indian Ocean actors like Thani inadvertently connected the East African interior to a distant shore of the Indian Ocean. When people like Thani left Oman to escape instability, they often went to the East African coast. The Omani sultanate at Zanzibar tried to dominate Swahili towns, and networks of debt created new obligations to Indians, among others. Thani's rapid reversal of fortune—from low-status confectioner to wealthy ivory trader—might suggest an effortless movement through Indian Ocean circuits. Yet the caravan trails were full of hustlers from many backgrounds, including Arabs, Swahili, Nyamwezi, and those of servile (or recently liberated) status. The mobility of these groups created new encoun-

ters among them and demonstrated the need to work out ethnic and status hierarchies. These individuals built new settlements that looked like Indian Ocean towns and spread Swahili language and culture. To understand how the newcomers did this, we first must tackle coastal chauvinism, the myth of return, and how buying time led to the growth of settlements.

Examination of towns in the interior, such as Kazeh, where Thani lived, indicates that identity distinctions among Indian Ocean migrants shaped settlement patterns and suggests the need to disaggregate groups who arrived from the Indian Ocean's shores. Throughout the region in the nineteenth century, new mobilities created a contest between Arab newcomers and Swahili elites, even those who had been reduced to slavery. Even among people considered Arabs, extreme mobility could not outrun the taint of being *baysari* (a low status identity in Arabia). The process of transforming upland East Africa into an Indian Ocean world was not a grand strategy implemented from Zanzibar, Muscat, Bombay, or London. It was the result of thousands of individuals trying to make the best from limited options.

ON THE BRINK OF THE INDIAN OCEAN WORLD: UPLAND EAST AFRICA

In July 1845 Thani bin Amir's caravan reached the village of Dege la Mhora and stumbled upon a murder. They had walked three days from the coast and had seen where a man had been tied to a post, his throat slit, and his limbs cut. The deceased was named Maizan, a twenty-six-year-old Frenchman, who was hoping to open up African trade for his countrymen. He carried a letter of introduction from Said bin Sultan, the ruler of Zanzibar and Oman, who had fought for the previous two decades to establish sovereignty on the coast.[3] The Zaramo chief Mazungera had ordered the murder, but no one was ever convicted of the crime. This was not, as some hinted at the time, because the sultan was complicit in the murder, but because the sultan lacked control over chiefs in the hinterland, a point Said bin Sultan admitted in 1846.[4] Maizan's presence threatened the balance of power in coastal trade between the sultan and the Zaramo chiefs. The chiefs controlled a monopoly in copal, a forest product used to make varnishes. Copal and ivory were the two most important exports from the mainland, and Thani's caravan sought ivory.[5]

Although Thani was not among the first Arabs to travel to the interior, his trading activities (and eventual settlement) helped institutionalize the caravan route between the Swahili coast and Lake Tanganyika. Travel beyond the coast required perseverance, good negotiation skills, and toughness.

Thani bin Amir possessed these qualities, and he covered great distances in the 1840s and 1850s. In the wake of the murder, Mazungera demanded a *hongo* (payment) from Thani's caravan, threatening them with the very knife that had killed Maizan. In Thani's recollections, these negotiations did not trouble him, and he boasted that he left the impression that he was "not a man to be trifled with."[6] His subsequent achievements bear this out. In the early 1850s, the Bugandan *kabaka* (king) Suna was unable to persuade Thani to deliver ivory on his behalf to Said bin Sultan, the ruler of Zanzibar. Kabaka Suna had hoped to create closer relations between the African kingdom and the Arab sultanate.[7] Suna was well-informed about Said bin Sultan and Zanzibar because of another Indian Ocean migrant, Isa bin Husayn, a Baluchi man and one of the sultan's former mercenaries. Isa bin Husayn had fled his debtors on the coast, establishing himself in Buganda as an advisor and bodyguard to the *kabaka*. In return, Suna provided Isa with ivory and wives.[8] Thani turned down a similar offer to be Suna's broker because he did not want to settle in Buganda. On the return from this three-year sojourn, Thani formed other temporary allegiances with African rulers. In Usukuma, for instance, Thani and a group of Arabs assisted a chief in a local dispute. Such ventures were risky, however, and in a six-day skirmish with their enemy, Thani and his group almost died.[9]

Thus, in 1852, after nearly a decade of caravan trading, Thani built a house and sunk a well in Kazeh, an area in Unyanyembe, a central district of Unyamwezi. His partner in establishing this village was another trader, Musa Mzuri, an Indian Muslim.[10] Musa, born into poverty in Surat, western India, had come to Zanzibar as a young man. In the 1820s, an Arab governor of Zanzibar sponsored Musa's older brother in the ivory trade. In the 1830s, Musa joined him, helping him pioneer the route to Unyamwezi. Musa took over the business after his brother died.[11] Musa and Thani's new settlement attracted other Omani Arabs, and Thani established himself as a general agent for traders and caravan leaders.[12] By 1858, Thani was well settled, and a contemporary account noted that he and his compatriots "live comfortably, and even splendidly, at Unyanyembe. The houses—though single-storied—are large and capable of defense. Their gardens are extensive and well planted; they receive regular supplies of merchandise, comforts, and luxuries from the coast; they are surrounded by troops of concubines and slaves, whom they train to diverse crafts and callings; rich men have riding-asses from Zanzibar, and even the poorest keep flocks and herds."[13] This life stood in marked contrast to the existence of the halwa-maker in Oman.

Like other Indian Ocean migrants in the East African interior, Thani established a household, maintained diverse clients, and engaged in agriculture, including introducing new crops. Thani's quarter of the town was like its own village, marked by storehouses and depots for the cloth and beads he exchanged for ivory and slaves. Thani's many dependents, clients, and slaves populated the area. The details of Thani's personal household are not clear. Opportunities to marry Arab women in Kazeh were extremely rare. Despite comments about "troops of concubines" in Kazeh, Thani had eschewed relationships with slave women in Uganda.[14] The closest woman to him in Kazeh was his "buxom housekeeper," Mama Khamisi. It is unclear whether she was Arab, Swahili, Nyamwezi, or another African ethnicity. Mama Khamisi had a son named Khamis, and she knew how to cook Omani delicacies, including *kawurmeh* (a meat dish), and the proper way to boil rice, a crop that the Indian Ocean migrants had planted in Unyanyembe. Not surprisingly, Mama Khamisi also knew how to prepare various confections—*firni* (rice pudding), rice-jelly, and, of course, halwa—presented in a variety of shapes.[15]

Thani keenly observed the world he inhabited. His knowledge—documented principally by the explorer Richard Burton—has profoundly shaped understandings of this period. Burton wrote that Thani "was as familiar with the languages, the religion, the manners, and the ethnology of the African, as with those of his natal Oman." Thani was, in fact, Burton's principal informant. Burton credited much of the information in his popular 1860 volume, *The Lake Regions of Central Africa*, to the "instructive and varied conversation" he had with Thani during his more than four months in Kazeh in 1857 and 1858.[16] Burton's ten-page obituary in the *Proceedings of the Royal Geographical Society* in 1890 called his report of the trip "a perfect mine of information on every aspect of the country traveled," and credited Thani bin Amir for his information.[17] Burton's writings on this subject were the first English language reports on the East African interior and they remain rich ethnographic and historical sources for scholars. While none of Thani's writings have survived, Burton's account provides a useful window into Thani's life in East Africa, the social worlds of the caravan trails, and how the African interior became part of an Indian Ocean world.

Thani abandoned an uncertain life in Oman, crossed the Indian Ocean, acquired fifteen years of hard-won, valuable knowledge about the East African interior, and established himself as the respected leader of a thriving settlement. Given this passage of time and the profound changes in his circumstances, it may seem obvious that Thani did not return to the precariousness of life in Oman. Yet his example does not accord with how scholars and contemporary observers have written about Indian Ocean migrants in the East African interior.

FIGURE 4.1. The house of Thani bin Amir in Kazeh. He was a halwa maker in Muscat in the 1840s and a principal trade agent in east central Africa by the late 1850s. From Richard Burton, *The Lake Regions of Central Africa* (New York: Dover, 1995).

COASTAL CHAUVINISM AND THE MYTH OF RETURN

A persistent story has Indian Ocean migrants in Africa eventually returning to the coast or to Arabia. This archetypal myth of return, when combined with many scholars' prejudice against the interior, has made it difficult to understand the history of Indian Ocean migrants who established themselves in the interior, making continental Africa part of their extended oceanic world. European observers frequently characterized the goal of Arab traders in the interior of East Africa as simply earning enough money to retire to Zanzibar or Oman. The missionary Alexander MacKay told a particularly vivid version of this story after living for more than a decade in Uganda, and though they never met, MacKay's tale paralleled the life of Thani bin Amir. In MacKay's telling, the typical scenario unfolded with a "pure Arab" of Oman finding "a passage for a few dollars in a native dhow bound for Zanzibar."

> He has no capital to begin with but accompanies a richer friend, whom he finds fitting up a caravan for the interior; by-and-by he makes small ventures of his own on the strength of a tusk or two he may have come by on his first journey inland. If successful, he will get credit to almost any extent from the Indians at the coast, and profits are such that he can, after twenty years' labour, return to Muscat a rich man, his ambition being to purchase an estate there,

dig wells make a canal for navigation [he must mean irrigation], and let patches for the cultivation of dates.[18]

While this may have represented an ideal outcome to Europeans—and perhaps even to Arab and Indian Ocean migrants who went to the interior—it overlooks the contingencies of life in the interior. In this version of the story, small success in trade could lead to almost unlimited capital, but even this would require twenty years of labor. The eventual outcome would be a landed estate, investments in infrastructure, and control of agriculture in either Oman or Zanzibar. This trope left out the possibility for individuals to achieve greater autonomy in the interior, and even meeting their goals in their new milieu. While this narrative was primarily applied to Arabs, versions of it also featured Swahili and Indian Ocean actors. They were all, it seems, biding time, plotting for a return to coastal society.

European observers at the time, and some historians since, have fallen prey to a kind of coastal chauvinism that privileges the Indian Ocean coast over continental interiors. Similarly, they claimed that those who went to the interior to trade did so only temporarily and wanted to return to the coast (or in the case of some Arabs, to Oman).[19] While a small subset of successful migrants may have returned home, the historical record suggests that many more Indian Ocean actors—including low-status Arabs, former Baluchi mercenaries, and Swahili pawns—established themselves in East African trading depots or small settlements near caravan routes. They achieved degrees of wealth and autonomy that would have been impossible at the coast or in Oman. They built allegiances, married African women, and became polygynous household heads, with many clients and plentiful arable land. If we assume all migrants wanted to return home, we overlook agency and contingency in their movements. We also miss the ways that their households and activities were transforming the interior of East Africa into part of an Indian Ocean world.

By imaging incentives for mobile Indian Ocean actors to remain in the interior, we raise questions about their activities and relationships there. We also create a more nuanced understanding of agency, which showcases temporizing and unintended consequences. Some individuals may have intended to return, even if it seemed unlikely to outside observers. The swashbuckling Henry Morton Stanley ruminated on Arab migration to the interior: "While many of the descendants of the old settlers who came with Seyyid [Said bin] Sultan still cling to their homesteads, farms, and plantations [at the coast] . . . a great number have emigrated into the interior to form new colonies. . . . A number of other prominent Arabs may be cited to prove that, though they themselves firmly believe that they will return to the coast some day, there are too many reasons for believing that they never will."[20] For many Arabs and coastal peoples, even if they hoped to return to the coast, they never did. Temporizing strategies turned into long-term settlement in the interior.

IDENTITIES ON THE MOVE: NYAMWEZI, ARAB, SWAHILI

As the Indian Ocean spilled into the East African interior, new identity categories arrived in places where they had never been before. Arabs and Swahili people ventured upcountry, and people from the interior—like those from Unyamwezi—more frequently traveled to the coast. Thani bin Amir's move from Arabia to Africa—and his knowledge of Omani Arabic and culture—marked him as an Arab to Richard Burton, but the labels for these groups were unclear to writers at this time, and even those who came later. The question of who was an Arab and who was Swahili has long been debated among scholars.[21] Most have resorted to collective terms for all Indian Ocean actors, glossing them under one rubric: either "Arabs," "Swahili," or "Muslim."[22] The lack of precision creates confusion. As one author states about the Lake Malawi region, "The influence of the Swahili before 1800 was indirect, and evidently did not involve large numbers of Swahili from the coast, although it did involve peoples who were in close contact with the Swahili."[23] What does Swahili mean in this context? Similar labeling has occurred at the coast. The 1888 "Arab Uprising" on the East African coast was, in fact, a movement of upcountry Africans and Swahili patricians, challenging both Omani Arab hegemony and early German colonial rule.[24] "Nyamwezi" became a catchall phrase that outsiders applied to people from the area around Kazeh, those associated with the chiefdom at Unyanyembe, and even those from the vast territory east of Lake Tanganyika and south of Lake Victoria.[25] Scrutinizing and disaggregating "Swahili," "Arab," and "Nyamwezi" groupings illuminates the social contours of the western Indian Ocean world as it expanded to the Great Lakes of central Africa. Furthermore, the historical actors themselves perceived and acted on distinctions of race, ethnicity, and faith, which shaped the settlements and activities in the interior.

The rising global demand for East African products reoriented the regional economy toward Zanzibar, where credit was available. New mobilities challenged received notions of social order and clientship. On the coast, as historian Jonathon Glassman has shown, the relationships between Swahili and Arab elites, between townsmen and rural folk, and between masters and slaves were all being renegotiated in the nineteenth century.[26] In the interior, such contests of status played out in novel ways. Before turning to Swahili and African notions of identification, we should first consider the flexibility of Nyamwezi identities. The social hierarchies on the coast were not shared by all Africans. Arab and Swahili people sought to establish their status relative to each other and the African groups among whom they lived.

Whether Swahili or Arab traders remained in the interior for one safari, several years, or the remainder of their lifetime, they negotiated their social statuses and identities in the interior. These negotiations took place among Africans, like the Nyamwezi people who were famous as traders and porters. For those who moved back and forth, the fluidity of some identities and cultural practices made this easier. Migration and mobile populations invited self-fashioning and encouraged individuals to present themselves in ways that would provide greater social advantage—especially when identities were distinct in time and space. Consider Nyamwezi traders and porters arriving at the coast with caravans from the interior. While some town dwellers may have considered them *washenzi* (barbarous unbelievers), some of these up-country men claimed the mantles of urban gentility to improve their position in Swahili social and economic hierarchies. They took on coastal styles of dress, converted to Islam (or presented themselves as Muslims), and used idioms of belonging to identify themselves as *waungwana*, *waswahili*, or *wamrima* (people of the Mrima coast). By doing this, Nyamwezi and other interior people avoided enslavement and gained access to juridical and moral frameworks that they could use to defend their rights.[27]

The Nyamwezi's reasons for taking on these new identities at the coast relate to what it meant to be Nyamwezi. Thus, claiming to be *mwungwana* was not just a strategy to ensure safety at the coast. It served a larger goal of fulfilling one's role as a Nyamwezi man. Many observers noted that successful trading ventures to the coast became a rite of passage for Nyamwezi men, and their mobility gave them status at home. "A young man is looked down upon as a milksop until he has made a least one journey down to the coast," noted Bishop Edward Steere, an amateur linguist and ethnographer in 1872 Zanzibar.[28] Travel and trading were linked to masculinity and reproduction for the Nyamwezi as they were to the Yao on the southern caravan route. As the London Missionary Society representative Swann recalled after years on Lake Tanganyika, "Not one of [the Nyamwezi men] was allowed to marry before he had carried a load of ivory to the coast, and brought back one of calico or brass-wire. It was the tribal stamp of true manhood, at once making him a citizen and warrior."[29] Yet at the coast, presenting oneself as an aspiring Nyamwezi head of household, citizen, and warrior carried danger.

The need to protect oneself and avoid slavery meant taking on aspects of identity incompatible with standard notions of Nyamwezi-ness.

Nyamwezi men who wanted the status of man or citizen at home might take on another identity abroad. This suggests that identities in labor systems in East Africa were more fluid than many have argued. In a related example from elsewhere on the continent, Dunbar Moodie's work on twentieth-century migrant workers in South Africa shows that some men took part in same-sex "mine marriages" while they were migrant workers, even though they had become migrants to earn money to pay for marriage in their home communities. As Moodie states, "Being a 'wife' on the mine, for all its apparent gender reversals, eventually reinforced the potential for male hegemony at home."[30] Thus, being *mwungwana* at the coast allowed a porter man to be Mnyamwezi at home.

Glassman suggests that upcountry people would refute other identities by converting to Islam and abandoning "one's noncoastal, nonurban identity."[31] This assumption of a hegemonic coastal society is the same one that drove incorrect notions of retirement to the coast. This view does not account for people moving beyond the coast or living independently in the interior. Indeed, people who originated in the interior and lived for some time at the coast could and did return to their home areas. These included Nyamwezi porters, who left the coast where they were entangled in debt or in danger of being enslaved, and they escaped their coastal identities in Tabora or other interior towns. Caravan leaders had trouble tracing them, and those who were found were often protected by local allies.[32] Likewise, residents of Urua, in the eastern Congo, who were taken to the coast as slaves, were said to have returned to Urua "single-handedly," even though they inevitably traveled with caravans as porters or craftsmen.[33]

Furthermore, coastal discourses of identity and power did not have the same traction in the interior. Some Arabs attempted to enforce racial and religious hierarchies in the interior, but they did so with limited success. In the 1870s, for instance, an Arab who "failed to make his fortune in the interior" tried to dispossess a Nyamwezi caravan by calling them heathens and disputing their right to trade goods, invoking coastal idioms of *ushenzi*.[34] On his trip down to the coast, the disgruntled Arab picked out Nyamwezi traders traveling in a larger group and harassed them, disputing their right to possess trade goods. He tried, unsuccessfully, to assert his own status as a Muslim. Tellingly, this Arab man failed to rally his companions to press his claims on the Nyamwezi traders.[35] The caravan routes and the new towns of the interior became places where individuals could wriggle out of claims of coastal creditors, employers, and other social ties.

WHO WERE THE SWAHILI IN THE INTERIOR?

Scholars attempting to discern identities in the interior of East Africa face two challenges: the way that European travelers wrote about them and the inconstancy of "Swahili" as an identity. Taking the first idea, knowing who was "Swahili" was difficult even for long-standing residents in the region. For instance, after nearly a decade in East Africa, the missionary Charles New wrote in the 1870s, "the modern Msuahili is a medley of almost everything oriental, and is perhaps not without a spice of something occidental in his blood." When New tried to describe the appearance of a Swahili person, he felt lost: "Every physical type is to be found among them, from the high Asiatic of the noble Arab to the lowest negro type of the people who come from the regions of the Lake Nyassa. There is also a great variety of colour among them, every shade between jet black and light brown."[36] In addition, Charles New and other writers failed to appreciate that people who *others* might consider Swahili might identify *themselves* in other ways. One early twentieth-century writer declared: "A true Swahili will generally mention the name of his tribe," calling himself an Mkilindini, that is, a person from Kilindi, or Mpate, someone from Pate, as the case might be, "and will not mention the word Swahili at all."[37] In his Swahili-language autobiography, Hamed bin Muhammad al-Murjebi, better known as Tippu Tip, consistently refers to *"watu wa Mrima"* (people of the coast) rather than call any group Swahili.[38]

One reason someone from the coast might identify as Swahili is tied to the second point. During the nineteenth century, people of upcountry origins—like the Nyamwezi caravaners—and those of servile status began to call themselves Swahili. An observer at the time noticed, "Generally speaking when a man, on being questioned as to his nationality, replies that he is an Mswahili, the probability is that he is an Mzalia [slave born at the coast]."[39] The strategy of presenting oneself as part of the coastal urban gentility (*mwungwana / waungwana*) was motivated by not wanting to be perceived as a slave (*mzalia / wazalia* or *mtumwa / watumwa*). Indeed, this practice of claiming Swahili identity began during the mobile nineteenth century, and it accelerated in the 1890s with colonial rule and the abolition of slavery.

In the 1870s, New opted for a simple bifurcation of the "Swahili" population into *waungwana* and *watumwa*, even though he acknowledged the shades of identity—"many distinctions of rank and station . . . among them"—with the label "Swahili." For him, the labels *mwungwana* and *mtumwa* portray the contrasts between "the free and the bond, masters and slaves," defined in opposition to one another.[40] This dichotomy reflects New's familiarity

Halwa and Identity ⌇ 95

with Atlantic slavery. While this division may explain one social tension in this Indian Ocean world, it is clumsy.

During the nineteenth century, labels such as Swahili and *mwungwana* shifted in both geographic and social scope. *Mwungwana* was, among Swahili speakers of the East African littoral, a term for people from nonservile origins that suggested one had the values of coastal urban gentility.[41] This meaning changed as one moved further from the coast. As an early dictionary suggests, "In the hinterland, [*mwungwana* was] often used of any person who professes to be a Muhammadan and wears a *kanzu* [a flowing robe]."[42] Indeed, *mwungwana* became a widely used term in the Congo, where it was associated with everyone from the east coast. The variety of Swahili still spoken in eastern Congo is called Kingwana, the language of the *waungwana*. The meaning of *mwungwana* changed depending on location, underscoring the relative nature of this identity, the ways in which mobility contributed to mutability, and the ways people in distant parts of Africa began identifying with Indian Ocean idioms.

The broader category of *waungwana*—that is, Swahili-speakers on the move—influenced African linguistic and cultural practices in the interior more than Arabic practices did. Like the Nyamwezi porters who took on coastal characteristics to live and work near the sea, Swahili and coastal people who ventured into the interior adapted themselves to the people there. When coastal men became husbands in Nyamwezi households, they conformed to Nyamwezi norms of gifting and reciprocity.[43] And while Nyamwezi porters set the tone for a "caravan culture," as historian Stephen Rockel has argued, Swahili and *waungwana* porters participated in and influenced these practices.[44] Like Burton's informant Thani bin Amir, Swahili voyagers knew a great deal about the lifeways, languages, and customs of the Africans among whom they traveled.

As a group, Swahili and *waungwana* were also influential in the interior—partly because they were more numerous than Arab traders. They were more likely to live among interior Africans and marry them. In 1884, a British missionary remarked on the effect of Swahili and coastal people on his mission on the western side of Lake Tanganyika: "It is a remarkable fact that these Zanzibar men have had far more influence on the natives than we have ever had—in many little things they imitate them, they follow their customs, adopt their ideas, imitate their dress, sing their songs, and it was with great difficulty I could get those of the Baguha on the station to speak their own language [instead of Swahili]. I can only account for this by the fact that the Wangwana live amongst them, and to some extent partake of their notions."[45] This willingness to "partake of their notions" demonstrates the flexibility of identities and social practices. The Nyamwezi porters' strategy at the coast suggests a path for mobile individuals making their way in a changing world.

SWAHILI VERSUS ARAB

In the 1840s, Thani bin Amir had witnessed the limits of the Zanzibar state in the coastal hinterlands. Still, the imposition of Arab rule at the coast—and the economic transformation that it brought about—had profound effects on the social standing of Swahili patricians compared to newly arrived Arabs. As the Swahili coast became increasingly under the sway of the Omani state at Zanzibar, it was also increasingly linked to the East African interior because of the growing ivory trade. The once-independent patrician leaders of the Swahili coastal towns and city-states found themselves protecting their coastal interests by reaching further into the interior. Swahili men became well-seasoned travelers. Omani Arabs—both from old coastal families and from the newly arrived Omanis like Thani—posed threats to these Swahili adventurers because of their ties to Zanzibar and their competing caravan aspirations. When Burton and Speke set off from Zanzibar in early 1857, they traveled the central caravan route from the Indian Ocean to the new coastal settlements in the interior. During this trip, they bore witness to the expansion of Swahili notions of social status, as well as to social tensions between Swahili and Arab men.

The Swahili social hierarchies placed *diwans* (patricians) at the top, above the *waungwana* (town gentlemen). In the 1850s, the *diwans* on the coast opposite Zanzibar set themselves apart in their dress, bearing, and other marks of distinction. They alone wore turbans and special sandals. They also enjoyed the prestige of sitting on fancy woven mats and of taking the lead in sword dances on feast days. Burton noted that a *diwan* expected to live with dignity and "to support his family with the fat of the land, and without sweat of the brow."[46] In earlier times, the lives of *diwans* may have been more comfortable, but by mid-century, they struggled for commercial dominance at the coast by acting as intermediaries to interior trade.

The Sultan of Zanzibar and his customs master sent Indian tax collectors and Baluchi-run military garrisons to coastal towns to collect duties and impose order. The *diwans* worked within this system, trying to exploit advantage from both the Indian tax collectors and the African caravan traders. They employed "every petty art of mercantile diplomacy" to bring caravans returning from the interior to their towns. If they succeeded, they would be able to negotiate the price of ivory and extract a tax or tip. These

FIGURE 4.2. Swahili man in Omani Arabic dress. Image courtesy of the Melville J. Herskovits Library of African Studies, Winterton Collection, Northwestern University.

activities, which included sending "armed parties of his kinsman and friends, his clients and serfs" to the interior to entice caravans to their towns, were far from living off the fat of the land.[47] Indeed, the *diwan*'s brow must have been often drenched in sweat as he exhorted his kinsmen to forward his interests and wheedled over taxes under the equatorial sun.

As these groups of kinsmen, friends, clients, and serfs, traveled further inland—perhaps only to persuade caravans to come to their sponsor's station—notions of Swahili social structure spread to the interior. These people founded some of the earliest settlements in the interior, sometimes by making local alliances or starting their own settlements. By mid-century, Burton and Speke encountered scattered pockets of people from the Mrima coast (*Wamrima*) in the interior. However, identifying and mapping these people in the interior was not an easy task. They appear in the sources indirectly, attached to retinues of important Arab men.

Some scholars have suggested that the social distinctions that were contested at the coast blended in the interior. This was not true, however, at least in the short run. In her pioneering study of Ujiji, Beverly Brown suggested that the common elements that Arab and Swahili traders shared—religion, social habits, and possibly language (Swahili)—and the common experience of being "alien settlers" in the interior erased differences (Ibadi vs. Sunni Islam, relationship to Arabia) between these two groups.[48] This erasure of difference, however, took decades. At mid-century, the process was far from complete, and Swahili and Arab migrants found themselves in contests over identity.

A long, simmering dispute in the caravan of Burton's and Speke's East African Expedition of 1856–1859 is, in this case, more important than the epic dispute between its European leaders. Burton's and Speke's disagreements and their lingering enmity about the source of the Nile persisted, even after Speke's death from a self-inflicted gunshot wound in 1864.[49] The running squabble between Arab and African caravan leadership, however, demonstrates the social dynamics of identity and mobility, a story that would have been forgotten had Burton not inadvertently recorded it in his diary. The principals here were Said bin Salim al-Lamki, the caravan leader appointed by Seyyid Majid, sultan of Zanzibar, and Mwinyi Kidogo, the chief of the expedition's armed escort. On the surface, Said bin Salim's and Mwinyi Kidogo's ongoing disputes appear to be about the leadership of the expedition, but the undercurrent was a contest over the status and authority of Swahili gentlemen in comparison to Omani Arabs (and others) in the East African milieu.

Said bin Salim al-Lamki represented the new kind of Arab authority on the nineteenth-century Swahili coast. He was a member of an Omani clan that served the sultan of Zanzibar, enforcing the sultan's will in Swahili port cities. His father had been the governor of the important port of Kilwa, and his mother, most likely a concubine, was from Madagascar. Prior to joining Burton and Speke, Said had been the governor of Saadani, one of the terminal ports for the northern (or Maasai) caravan routes.[50] An Ibadi, Said bin Salim met his religious obligations by praying and fasting "uncompromisingly." Said bin Salim was short and thin, with a faint beard and scant mustaches. He enjoyed chewing betel nut, and his teeth were often flecked with the characteristic crimson. Burton described Said's skin as "yellow." Although he was an Arab, Said bin Salim's mother tongue was Swahili. He also spoke Muscati Arabic and knew some classical, Quranic Arabic. While Burton, a proven Arabophile, appreciated Said bin Salim's knowledge of grammar, his fine handwriting, and his ability to sprinkle proverbs into conversation, Said's erudition paled next to that of Thani bin Amir.[51] Burton also thought Said was overly concerned with genealogy.

In 1856, Said bin Salim was about forty years old when Sulayman bin Hamid al-Busaidi—the trusted advisor and relative of the sultan—tapped him to lead Burton's and Speke's expedition. Unlike Thani bin Amir, Said bin Salim had no experience in the interior. Burton later wondered why they had taken "a guide apparently so little fit for rough-and-ready work." Burton listed Said bin Salim's qualifications as respectability, knowledge, courteousness, temperament, generosity, and honesty.[52] He was also more knowledgeable about East Africa than Burton, who described his guide somewhat uncharitably as "a well-filled knowledge box, and was no churl in imparting its contents."[53] These characteristics matched well with contemporary ideals of Arab gentility. Indeed, it seems that Said bin Salim was better equipped to navigate polite society in Zanzibar and within the Omani elite than he was for the rowdy caravan camps of the East African interior.

In contrast, his rival Mwinyi Kidogo was a man of the coast and had completed many journeys to the interior when he joined the expedition's ranks. Kidogo was the leader of nine Swahili men who joined the expedition as "interpreters, guides, and war-men."[54] Their service illustrated the shifting power of Swahili elites on the coast and the connection between indebtedness and travel. Kidogo considered himself an elite Swahili. He was a freeborn son of a *diwan* and as such received (and when he did not, demanded) respect from the coastal men, porters, and slaves around him. Burton noted that Kidogo "was by no means a common man."[55] He, like Said bin Salim, was short and thin, but his beard was pointed (and presumably fuller), and his skin was "coal black." Kidogo joined the expedition at the behest of Ramji, a Hindu of the Bhatia caste.[56] Kidogo was, despite his high birth, one of Ramji's slaves. His parents or uncles had pawned him to Ramji because of debt and had been unable to redeem the pledge.[57] Despite this status, however, Kidogo still considered himself a Swahili patrician, and many respected his social position.

Kidogo also had legitimate claims to expertise in the interior. He had undertaken several ivory trading ventures that took him far from the coast for two or three years at a time.[58] During one trip, he married in Unyamwezi.

FIGURE 4.3. Mwinyi Kidogo was born on the Swahili coast, became a skilled caravan leader, and had a family in Tabora. From Burton, *The Lake Regions of Central Africa* (New York: Dover, 1995).

His wife and children remained there. Burton praised Kidogo's knowledge of the languages, manners, and customs in the interior. Kidogo also commanded respect from the porters and servants who made up the caravan. He gave rousing exhortations in Swahili—the idiom of the people—before they commenced an important march.[59] Indeed, it was Kidogo and his colleagues' experience that made them valuable to the caravan. According to Speke, their role was not to shoulder loads, but to guard the caravan and to deal "with the native chiefs on the line of the march, as they were familiar with the road to Ujiji and were friends with the chiefs we should find there."[60] Thus, Mwinyi Kidogo was a proven expert in travel whose role as go-between and cultural broker was to smooth the way of expedition.

While part of Burton's and Speke's expedition, Mwinyi Kidogo and his Swahili brethren still needed to defend their position, authority, and expertise, as Said bin Salim and the caravan's leaders asserted their superior rank within the caravan. This discrimination galled Kidogo and the others, but their authority was obvious yet not absolute. Kidogo and his Swahili companions had superior knowledge of local languages, customs, and negotiating techniques, and they were also well armed. Throughout the journey, they negotiated their status through a variety of strategies, including palavers, walkouts, strikes, and shows of force.[61]

Mwinyi Kidogo and Ramji's Swahili men refused to take part in the menial (but necessary) caravan tasks, like carrying loads or stringing beads for local trade.[62] This work of production—altering imported trade goods to fit local tastes—was usually done by porters. Porters also shouldered the bundles of trade goods and were responsible for arranging the correct varieties and denominations of beads for commerce in each area. After some porters deserted, however, Burton insisted that Kidogo and his men carry loads, which they did half-heartedly. They resented this imposition, especially because of their understanding of their own status. Ultimately, they wore down Burton through their resistance. Burton noted in his account that "their dignity was hurt by shouldering a pack, and day after day, till I felt weary of life, they left their burdens upon the ground."[63]

Kidogo and his companions' struggles with Burton paled in comparison to their contest with Said bin Salim. Throughout his writings, Burton never understood the depth of the feud between Kidogo and Said bin Salim. The explorer thought the dispute was over the dependents with whom each man traveled. Said bin Salim used his position to enter his dependents as porters—and thus salaried—while the slaves that accompanied Kidogo were not compensated. The dispute was more deep-seated than this, however, and a quiet war persisted for much of the journey. In Burton's eyes, their dispute played out through backbiting and never through direct confrontation. The remedies each man sought, however, suggest the source of the problem. Mwinyi Kidogo hoped that Said bin Salim would be dismissed for inexperience. Said, for his part, thought that Kidogo's sword should be broken (that is, he should be disarmed) and that he should be disciplined in Zanzibar, the seat of Arab power.[64]

The ongoing dispute hampered the movement of the caravan. Mwinyi Kidogo used his expertise and status to control the group of travelers. He built consensus among the Swahili men and Nyamwezi porters; vetoed the movement of the caravan for days at a time; and rushed the trip to see his wife in Unyamwezi.[65] Kidogo was the only leader who understood the risks and obligations they faced. While the European and Arab members of the party were making decisions to ensure their day-to-day survival, Kidogo's decisions were shaped by his engagement with the caravan trade. At one point, for instance, he forbade Burton and Speke from paying high prices, fearing that they would set unreasonable precedents for other caravans.[66] The Swahili man's expertise and judgment were proven correct several times, and Burton (and even Said bin Salim, albeit grudgingly) seems to have respected his ability. The views of the European and the Arab were clearly tainted by racialized notions of status and hierarchy. Burton was never sure what to make of Kidogo, who on the one hand was a slave, but on the other was knowledgeable and commanded great respect at both the coast and in the interior.

Kidogo's actions forced Burton to reorganize the caravan to accommodate the feud. On their return journey, Burton removed Said bin Salim as the caravan leader and replaced the guide. In Said's place, he installed Sidi Mubarak Bombay, a Yao man and freed slave who had lived in India, before returning to East Africa. Said bin Salim's demotion meant he only oversaw the porter's rations, but this job still returned him safely to the coast. Kidogo maintained his position as the leader of Ramji's servants, so he could refuse some demands made of him until the end of the journey.[67] With the structural conflict in the caravan resolved, the relationship between Said and Kidogo became more congenial.[68]

Later, Said bin Salim joined Speke's and Grant's caravan in 1860, which sought to travel from Zanzibar to the source of the Nile and down the river to its delta. Said bin Salim left the expedition in Unyanyembe, however, to become the representative of the Zanzibar sultan and customs master's there. In the 1870s, when other Arabs forced him out of that role, he retired not to the coast, where his debts and compromised reputation limited him, but to another interior town where he died in 1879. Kidogo's career after leaving

Burton's employ in 1859 is unknown. His caravan expertise, commercial acumen, and family interest in the interior suggest that he was the type of Swahili man who would continue to move among the coast, Tabora, and beyond. His status at the coast relative to Arab encroachment may have encouraged this. At one point in his journey with Burton, Kidogo "felt aggrieved by the sudden yet tardy demand [from the Arab], which deprived him of the dignity and the profits of his stewardship." In general, Swahili people at the coast who had been deprived of their dignity sought roles in the interior.

BIFURCATED SETTLEMENTS

Given the dispute between Mwinyi Kidogo and Said bin Salim, it is not surprising that many interior African settlements of traders were split between Swahili and Arab migrants. The early camps, like Thani bin Amir's at Kazeh, seem to have followed ethnic lines, with Omani Arabs and Swahili traders living in different places. Kazeh was the "capital village" of the Omani merchants in the interior, while Msene attracted Swahili travelers.[69] By examining the founding and growth of these two settlements, we see the way identities shaped the growth of the Indian Ocean world in the East African interior.

Kazeh's growth demonstrates the patterns of trade and settlement among Omani Arabs and their dependents. While Speke noted that Kazeh was "fast expanding into a colony," the number of Arabs there at that time (and in Unyanyembe, its broader region), is difficult to know.[70] Arab traders like Thani bin Amir formed a key population of Kazeh, and their presence was necessary for the growth of the town. Only twelve Arabs lived there in 1857, and the Arab population varied seasonally, fluctuating between as few as three in the traveling season to as many as twenty-five at other times.[71] The population grew quickly after the failure of Barghash's 1859 uprising in Zanzibar. The Harthi confederation and other supporters of Barghash fled to mainland Africa, taking to caravan routes and then settling in new towns like Kazeh.[72] During his second journey in May 1861, Speke noted that the caravan routes were "thronged" with people fleeing Zanzibar. He called Kazeh, "a regular Botany Bay; all the blackguards of Zanzibar are flocking to it."[73]

Many of these people, such as Amran bin Masoud, were out of favor, and others had had property confiscated after the conflict.[74] Although accounts reference many Arabs going to interior locations, it is difficult to account for them individually. They might have dispersed to far-flung settlements, and some might not have stayed in the interior for long. Nearly fifteen years after Burton enumerated the Arabs, Cameron reported that "many Arabs" were in Unyanyembe, but he could make the expected social calls "to all the principal Arabs, and eat with all" in a single day between 10 a.m. and 4 p.m.[75] This suggests a relatively small population, or at least a hierarchal group with a small top strata—depending on who Cameron considered "principal." As the Arab presence in Unyanyembe grew, more clusters of *tembe* (houses) appeared. Land in that area was free, and the Arabs used low-lying damp hollows to begin rice cultivation.[76] They also amassed large herds of cattle. The Arabs in Unyanyembe continued to live in dispersed settlements through the 1870s, when the whole area was called Tabora.[77]

Tabora, with its population of sometimes resident, sometimes transient Arabs, was a hub of trade and communication, linking the East African coast with the far interior. Tabora served as both a crossroads and a port city. Burton called it the place where an Arab merchant from Zanzibar would meet his compatriot coming from the interior.[78] Such merchants did not travel alone, so Tabora also became a meeting place for the Arabs' traveling companions, such as Swahili and other coastal migrants. These migrants accounted for the largest percentage of Indian Ocean actors in towns like Tabora.[79] In 1872, Livingstone estimated that Tabora was home to eighty Arab men, and he assumed that each of these individuals had a retinue of twenty people. So, the whole population "in connection with the Arabs" was sixteen hundred. Livingstone noted that some Arabs returned to the coast after one or two seasons of collecting ivory.[80] He did not explain what happened to their dependents.

The settlement of Msene, about seventy miles northwest of Kazeh, became a coastal enclave.[81] Information about Msene is scarce because it never became a prominent town. By examining Msene, however, population patterns and a nascent urbanism emerges. By the late 1850s, Msene was a multiethnic settlement, the principal trading post of the region, and a favorite stop of up-bound caravans. Msene supported a modest market in an open space between houses, and one could find local produce supplied by nearby agricultural villages; long distance trade goods (cloth, beads, wire); and some luxuries (spices, coffee, tea).[82] The area also had sophisticated mechanisms of exchange, so travelers could acquire the most appropriate trade goods for the region. Burton, for instance, had failed to buy *sofi* (a type of bead) in Zanzibar, but in the interior these beads were a highly desirable medium of exchange. Thus Burton was forced to trade cloth for *sofi*, and Msene was one of the places he could carry out this transaction and stock up.[83]

Msene's rich agricultural hinterland supported a heterogeneous population of interior Africans and coastal migrants. The primary residents of the area were WaSumbwa, migrants from western Uhha who had taken refuge there, and pastoral Watutsi.⁸⁴ Msene also attracted itinerant *fundi* (slave artisans) who came from the coast and could command high wages for their skills.⁸⁵ Msene's growth was reflected in its lack of formal streets, so when caravans entered they passed between the neighborhoods and the houses. The presence of coastal people was also reflected in the surrounding farms where rice cultivation accompanied traditional crops.⁸⁶

Msene was not, however, a generic melting pot and Indian Ocean migrants self-segregated both in moving to and living within the settlement. In the late 1850s, Burton noted Msene was a place that coastal Arabs and Swahili people chose over Kazeh, due to "a natural antipathy to their brethren in Oman."⁸⁷ These Swahili and coastal Arabs also tended to segregate themselves within the areas that they cohabitated. While all lived in the local sultan's two stockaded villages of Kwihanga and Yovu, the Swahili people lived in a part called Mji Mpia ("New Town") and the coastal Arabs inhabited an area called Chyambo.⁸⁸ One of these Arabs was Salim bin Masoud, who lived in Msene and was killed while traveling there from Kazeh.⁸⁹ Thus, the differences among Muslim groups in the interior were great enough initially to prohibit all Omani merchants from visiting Msene. The danger in the countryside—such as the death of Salim bin Masoud—eventually drove Omani Arabs from nearby districts into Msene but their numbers were small.⁹⁰

What caused "the natural antipathy" that created separate settlements for Omani Arabs and African coastal people in Unyanyembe? Burton does not elaborate, but a careful reading of his account demonstrates that Arab and coastal travelers carried with them the social tensions that had arisen in the Indian Ocean littoral. These social tensions, coupled with the attractions of the towns themselves, led to the slow accretion of Indian Ocean populations in the interior.

Msene stood out from similar settlements because its market and lively atmosphere attracted road-weary caravaners. In 1858, perhaps because of this, Msene appeared more prosperous than the more simply built African villages to the west.⁹¹ Trading parties passing Msene experienced a greater number of desertions. "The temptations of the town rendered it almost impossible to keep a servant or a slave within doors," noted Burton. Some of his party traded "vigorously," while others made festive: "Even household slaves, born and bred upon the coast, cannot tear themselves from its Circean charms."⁹² The coastal men who accompanied Burton's and Speke's expedition as "interpreters, guides, and war-men" were, according to Speke "quite in their element" in Msene.⁹³ Indeed, their status and feeling about being in Msene points to a familiarity and comfort in this new settlement.

By the late nineteenth century, interior towns were clearly Indian Ocean outposts. From the early settlements—like Thani bin Amir's initial encampment in Kazeh—new hamlets and trading camps grew into permanent settlements. Even in African market towns like Ujiji, urban spaces came to resemble towns of the Indian Ocean littoral. A missionary observer in Ujiji noted: "The frequent appearance of Arabs in their flowing garments, (sometimes walking, sometimes riding on Muscat donkeys), bands of Waswahili, strings of slaves laden with grain or ivory, flocks of sheep and goats, and small herds of cattle, together with the canoes on the water, all gave the place an appearance not unlike a coast village on the Mlima."[94] Indian Ocean actors used their mobility to reproduce coastal society in the interior. Still, some status distinctions between Indian Ocean migrants traveled with them, and these shaped patterns of settlements and, as we shall see, patterns of marriage.

BEING BAYSARI

Said bin Salim, the caravan official whose squabbles with Mwinyi Kidogo reenacted coastal grievances, also took a dim view of Thani bin Amir, the prominent trader who had been a sweetmeat seller. Thani reciprocated. Their mutual disparagements help disaggregate Arabs in the interior, and also make clear that social categories forged in the specific circumstances of Oman could travel, be redefined, and become markers of identity in the diaspora. Indeed, while Said bin Salim may have simply regarded Thani's prominence with jealousy, Thani may also have been tainted as *baysari* (plural, *bayāsirah*), a member of a low-status group rooted in Oman. While the case against Thani as *baysari* in the 1850s is not clear, these Omani social categories certainly operated in Tabora and became grounds several decades later to halt a marriage.

During Said bin Salim's first visit to Unyanyembe, he regarded Thani bin Amir—the Omani halwa-maker-turned-commercial agent—quite warily, and their open conflict points to status rifts among Omani migrants. Said bin Salim, born at the Swahili coast to an Omani father and Malagasy mother, could not join the learned Arabic conversations on history and religion that Thani bin Amir and Burton held each evening. The barrier was not really language, Burton noted, but Said bin Salim's "ignorance and apathy" about everything except people and relationships. He wanted to talk about kinship, genealogy, and marriage ties.[95] Further, Said bin Salim, even after the long up march from the coast, lacked the expertise of the interior that Thani's fifteen years' experience gave him. Thani was used to auditing

Halwa and Identity ⌒ 107

the flow of cloth and beads in his own establishment, so he scrutinized Said bin Salim's fiscal and managerial practices. Apparently, Said bin Salim used his control over the expedition's resources to grant extra cloth and beads to his own slaves—part of his dispute with Mwinyi Kidogo—and he was willing to look the other way when they siphoned off the expedition's gunpowder. From inexperience and against Thani's advice, Said bin Salim also tried to secure porters too far before the downward march. When these issues came to a head in Kazeh, Said bin Salim was caught in several lies, justified his decisions, and asserted his position as an official of the Zanzibari sultan. Burton, in exasperation, walked out of the room, and Thani bin Amir was left to deliver "rough language" to Said bin Salim.[96]

The tension between these two Arab men points to disunity among Omani Arabs in the interior. While some Arabs found common cause and worked together, on many occasions they pursued separate agendas and even worked at cross-purposes. Omani Arab identity was not an all-powerful unifier. This was true in the 1850s when Thani was the leader of the Arab community at Kazeh. It still held true in the early 1870s when Said bin Salim had returned to Tabora as the governor of the growing settlement. While it is tempting to write off Said bin Salim's and Thani bin Amir's conflict in the late 1850s as differing conversational interests or a professional rivalry about managing caravans, the distinctions were more deeply rooted in social categories. One man was from an "old Arab" family from the coast, with limited experience in the interior, and the other was a recent migrant from Oman with a wealth of knowledge and—at least according to Burton—a gracious manner. Diving more deeply into Omani social prejudices, however, Said bin Salim's personal disregard for Thani may have emerged from the latter's taint of *baysari*.

People known as *bayāsirah* within Omani society faced social sanction in everyday settings and strict limitations on who they could marry. Tribal Arabs considered *bayāsirah* as either outsiders of dubious origins or no tribal background. The concept of *bayāsirah* is well known in Oman and has been mentioned incidentally in connection to Zanzibar. People with this unusual status—and the status itself—also moved through the expanding Indian Ocean world, up the caravan trails, and into central Africa.[97]

As a status category, *bayāsirah* has deep roots and contemporary resonance. The earliest account of *bayāsirah* links them to an old Indian Ocean trading diaspora. The Muslim geographer al-Masudi described them as Muslims living in Gujarat in the tenth century. These people originated in Oman, Basra, and Baghdad, among other places, and they wore "the same dresses and having their beards grow in the same manner as the infidels."

Some of them were wealthy merchants.⁹⁸ In this connection, the etymology of the word is linked to Gujarati (*adh-besra,* meaning mixed blood), but all other explanations tie the concept to Arabia.⁹⁹ The historian Wilkinson identified *bayāsirah* as the earliest inhabitants of eastern and southern Arabia, a group without origin (اصل) who—even though some became Muslim—never assimilated into the dominant Arabic social order after the rise of Islam.¹⁰⁰ Through his informants in the 1960s and 1970s, Wilkinson was interested in "the underlying layers in the palimpsest of present traditional social organization in South East Arabia." He argued that explanations of *bayāsirah* that rested on a deep history of Arabia and Islamic conversion might have had more social truth than historical truth. These explanations of *bayāsirah* origins still circulate in Oman.¹⁰¹ Despite efforts to create a national culture that minimizes social distinctions of race, tribe, and status, *bayāsirah* remains, for some, a concept with strong negative connotations.

Whatever the deep historical truth, *bayāsirah* was part of nineteenth- and early twentieth-century Oman. In 1876, when the British officer S. B. Miles was traveling near the town of Nakhl, in the Batinah region of Oman, he was surprised by the "mixed character of the population," and noted that the "Bayâsir" made up a large part of the community. He described them as "industrial and peaceable folk," many of whom were wealthy, although not given positions of command or authority.¹⁰² Tribal Arabs considered them aliens, claiming they originated in the Hadramawt.¹⁰³ Five years later, when Miles estimated the population of Oman, he listed "the foreign element, viz., African, Belooch, Indians, Persians, Byasir, and Gipsies."¹⁰⁴ Despite the long history of Indian Ocean migrations, Miles imagined a monoethnic Oman, and all non-Arabs as foreign. At the same time, this list puts *bayāsirah* among the littoral peoples who came from the Indian Ocean (and gulf) regions. This knowledge was enshrined in J. G. Lorimer's encyclopedic *Gazetteer of the Persian Gulf, Oman and Central Arabia* (1908), in which *bayāsirah* received its own entry, probably based on Miles's earlier notes. *Bayāsirah* were "a community or tribe of inferior social status," members of which were living throughout Oman, but especially in the interior towns of Nakhl (where Miles had visited), Nizwa (whence the halwa-makers fled drought), and Bahla. They also lived in greater numbers in the primary coastal cities, from Muscat north and west.¹⁰⁵

At the beginning of the twentieth century, *bayāsirah* lived in and around Muscat and Muttrah. They most commonly resided in heterogeneous groups outside the walls of Muscat with Baluchis, freed slaves, and mixed Arab tribes. Those outside the city walls often lived in simple *barsati* huts, and others lived within the confines of Muttrah.¹⁰⁶ The questions that circled around *bayāsirah* concerned their uncertain origins. Lorimer assumed South Arabian (Hadhramaut) origins, but he noted that others said, "most of them are merely the children of 'Omāni Arabs by slave mothers."[107] Yet slaves and *bayāsirah* were not frequently in the same locations. Wilkinson's fieldwork revealed that some locations in the Omani interior had substantial numbers of *bayāsirah* inhabitants, with little or no evidence of an imported slave population.[108]

The presence of *bayāsirah* in interior and coastal Oman in the nineteenth century makes their existence in coastal and even far interior East Africa less surprising, because of the increasing mobility between these regions. What is surprising, however, was that Richard Burton, the most astute observer of Arab society in East Africa among the nineteenth-century European travelers, did not mention *bayāsirah*. The trader and autobiographer Hamed bin Muhammad al-Murjebi makes an oblique reference to *bayāsirah* in the interior, and the archival record in Zanzibar also attests to their presence. Hamed bin Muhammad—better known as Tippu Tip—recalled an incident from the late 1860s, in which porters warned him against moving into Chief Isamu's territory, southwest of Lake Tanganyika. Isamu had large stores of ivory, but he was cruel: he had already killed various Arabs, bayāsirah, and people from the Mrima (i.e., Swahili).[109] In Whitley's English translation, he leaves Tippu Tip's Swahili phrase "Wabisar" untouched, offering no explanation or comment. In the context, however, Tippu Tip added a Swahili personal plural prefix (wa-) to the Arabic root *baysir*. Tippu Tip's order might hint at his understanding of the social standing of *bayāsirah*—below true Arabs, but above coastal people.

In both Oman and East Africa, *bayāsirah* faced social restrictions, and Arabs expected them to conform to the behavior of servants. In Oman, a *bayāsirah* man meeting a member of the sheikhly class could not approach him as a social equal, by going to him, kissing his hands, and greeting him. *Bayāsirah*—like slaves and other inferiors—were expected to drop their sandals at the path before greeting.[110] In both Oman and East Africa, *bayāsirah* were expected to defer to Arabs in social situations and greet Arabs of higher status—meaning those with a tribal name—as "Hababi" (master).[111] One of the *bayāsirahs*' strategies was to attach themselves as clients to the most important lineages in their home areas.[112] This way, some could claim the *nisba* (clan name) of prominent clans, like the Harthi. Despite this ability to affiliate, *bayāsirah* faced restrictions on whom they could marry. Thus social proscriptions reified the *bayāsirah* as a category in everyday practice.

Beyond these social restrictions, *bayāsirah* enjoyed economic leeway, pursued a variety of occupations, and, in some cases, amassed great wealth. In the 1920s, a British traveler in southern Arabia noted that the social position of *bayāsirah* was subordinate, but this status did not limit occupation.[113] In the 1870s, a *baysari* man served as a qadi in Zanzibar. Because of his rank he refused to use the deferential language expected of *bayāsirah*, and became known for the social criticism in his poetry.[114] The status also did not limit their accumulation of wealth. One of the three wealthiest men in Zanzibar in the 1850s was Sulayman bin Habib, who some have identified as *baysari*. He built a house in the Malindi section of town, which spurred competition with two rich al-Harthi men. His wealth was obvious, but his status leaves historians guessing. He was described as belonging to "a very degraded tribe of Omani Arabs; but they were rich."[115] The freedom to amass wealth and raise their status became important to *bayāsirah* in East Africa. In a region where people from Oman were the minority, the differentiations of status among Omanis became less important. The majority population considered both non-*bayāsirah* and *bayāsirah* people from Oman as Arab.

The social standing of *bayāsirah* and clues about their relations emerge from the records of the British consulate in Zanzibar in the 1870s. An English-language record from the end of that decade indicates that people identifying as "Beasur" and "Beaser" had manumitted slaves. Their former slaves sought documentation to travel by sea. In this case, the *bayāsirah* included both men and women, each of whom was connected to a prominent Omani tribe. A woman named Asma bint Said bin Khamis, who was a *baysari* to the Harthi, freed two female slaves, Zohara and Ziyada, girls in their late teens.[116] These young women arrived at the consulate to make their deeds of freedom official, a process that usually preceded traveling abroad with their former masters.[117] In other consular records, the office's translations between Arabic and English confound servitude and *bayāsirah* status. An English clerk, for instance, identified one man as the "beaser" of the Harthi, while the Arabic text identifies him as a *khadim* (servant) of the Harthi.[118] This may be in keeping with shifting senses of identity for *bayāsirah*, slaves, manumitted slaves, and other clients during a time of great social (and physical) mobility.

But what of Thani bin Amir? His contemporaries Burton and Tippu Tip did not label him *baysari*, but Tippu Tip's German biographer Heinrich Brode states unequivocally that Thani was *baysari*. Brode called Thani the most prominent Arab in Kazeh, but he also noted that as a "besar," he was "an Arab from Oman, only not of pureblood, the issue of the slave caste."[119] Writing nearly fifty years after Thani died, Brode's allegations would be easy to dismiss were it not for his close relationship with Tippu Tip, one of the rare Indian Ocean actors who made good money and retired to the coast

Halwa and Identity ~ 111

(though the encroachment of the Congo Free State on his trade might have produced further incentive). Brode lived in Zanzibar for several years during Tippu Tip's retirement, during which Brode convinced him to write an autobiography. Brode transcribed this text into Roman script, then into German, and published it.

Brode then wrote a biography to make Tippu Tip's life "generally intelligible," an obvious contrast to the sometimes rambling and disjointed autobiography, which, as Brode noted, served "primarily a linguistic purpose."[120] Brode's biography uses both Tippu Tip's written account and additional materials that he gained working with Tippu Tip in the early twentieth century. The book, however, leaves Thani's status difficult to determine. Marriage prohibitions against *bayāsirah* might help reveal Thani's status, but the only woman mentioned in his household was Mama Khamisi.[121] Thani's relationship with halwa production offers a clue to his earlier low status and his relationship with the Khoja Indian trader Musa in Kazeh rather than other Arabs could also suggest an outsider status.[122] On the other hand, Tippu Tip was critical of other Arabs in the interior but does not disparage Thani, someone more of his father's generation.

Burton's interest in Arab life and his insistence on referring to Thani with the honorific *sheikh* suggests that Thani's upward mobility had removed the taint of his previous status. Despite their inferior social status with respect to the tribal Arabs, Brode noted *bayāsirah* were "far superior to them in intelligence" and could amass great personal wealth. Such wealth mattered in a multiracial and multiethnic society with burgeoning global connections, since "money everywhere is in good repute." As Brode reflected, Thani was "one of these honorable exceptions to his class" and therefore enjoyed a good reputation among the Arabs. In fact, Thani was the person who rallied Arab communities to take action against a Nyamwezi leader.[123] Brode's identification of Thani as *baysari* cannot be substantiated, but the general consideration of the *bayāsirah* in the African context sheds new light on the social mobility and fluid construction of identity in the interior. It also helps us understand an aborted wedding.

While Thani may have been "an honorable exception," other *bayāsirah* from Oman who traveled to the East African interior were unable to shake the status. More than thirty years after Thani's death, a marriage between two Arabs came to a skidding halt when the bride's representative recognized the groom's status. The wedding was to take place in Tabora, which, by the 1890s, had grown into the principal way station for interior caravans. An estimated eighty to one hundred thousand people passed through each year.[124]

The circumstances of the failed wedding point to the mobility of Arabs from Oman, even in the 1890s, when, in the wake of the Berlin Conference, European colonial forces dispossessed Arabs and tried to limit their movements. It was during this time that Sulayman bin Sleyum al-Hamzi brought a proposal to marry Zuwayna bint Muhammad. Sulayman bin Sleyum was a recent arrival from Oman, and Zuwayna had not been in Tabora for long either. Her father, Muhammad bin Khamis al-Kiyumi, an Arab born in Oman, had emigrated to East Africa in search of new opportunities.[125] Whether he secured credit on his own or joined a kinsman's caravan is unknown. Muhammad bin Khamis, like Tippu Tip and Juma Merikani, established himself near the plentiful ivory supplies of the eastern Congo. By the 1890s, however, representatives of Belgium's King Leopold and their mercenaries were competing with the Indian Ocean traders. They fought openly for the first half of that decade, and some Arab and Swahili people were killed, while others fled.[126] In the mid-1890s, Muhammad bin Khamis died while fighting the Belgians in the Congo.[127] Zuwayna and her two sisters went east, crossed Lake Tanganyika to Kigoma near Ujiji—in what had recently become German East Africa—and then went to Tabora, where their father's business partner, Sulayman bin Zahir al-Jabri, resided.

Sulayman bin Zahir al-Jabri (d. 1910) was born in Oman and was a trader in the East African interior from the 1860s, when he led (or sent) caravans west of Lake Tanganyika.[128] His close relationship with Barghash's court in Zanzibar is recounted in letters and family history.[129] Sulayman bin Zahir received a grant of land near Tabora from the Nyamwezi ruler Isike (r. 1876–93) as a reward for Sulayman's role in fighting the rival Nyamwezi chieftain Mirambo.[130] By the early 1880s, Sulayman bin Zahir was trading in Buganda, with massive credit tabs secured from important financiers in Zanzibar.[131] Sulayman bin Zahir was, for some time in the 1880s, a fixture at the *kabaka's* court in Uganda. He offered stiff (and sometimes fierce) opposition to the newly arrived Christian missionaries. In 1888, he had a hand in the plot against Kabaka Mwanga, which led to the death of Christian converts and drew the ire of British officials. When he returned to Zanzibar, the British representative urged the sultan to punish Sulayman by seizing his ivory and exiling him from Zanzibar. Sulayman paid a fine and retained his freedom of movement.[132]

Whereas Tippu Tip returned to Zanzibar when colonial encroachment curtailed his trading career, Sulayman bin Zahir remained in Tabora.[133] Sulayman's large household and many dependents included the orphaned daughters of one of his Arab trading partners. The bride-to-be, Zuwayna, lived with Sulayman bin Zahir and his family. The trader served as her guardian for the wedding. As his descendants narrate, old Sulayman bin Zahir was ill on the wedding day and asked his trusted slave Marjani bin Othman to finish the wedding arrangements.[134] Everyone wore their finery, and when Sulayman bin Sleyum arrived, he was dressed in Omani style, with a long white *kanzu* (dishdasha) and a *joho*, the woolen cloak favored by well-to-do Arabs for occasions such as these. Sulayman bin Sleyum greeted Marjani and the assembled group, "Al-salaam 'alaykum," and the servant Marjani answered, "Wa'alaykum al-salam, ya shaykh Sulayman"(And peace be upon you, Sheikh Sulayman). Here, Sulayman bin Sleyum corrected the slave. He was not a sheikh, he said, but a servant of sheikhs. This humble admission tipped off the Omani Arabs and their trusted slaves that the groom was *baysari* and thus unfit for marriage to an Omani of noble birth. And with that, the wedding was called off.[135]

This failed marriage attempt between two people of Omani descent in Tabora—several hundred miles from Zanzibar and several thousand miles from Oman—hinged on ideas of status imported from Oman. The tensions here were between the constructed and fluid identities in frontier places and the kind of identifications and fixed social statuses in established communities.

The prohibition of marriage between *bayāsirah* men and Arab women was strong, and it followed the Islamic legal principle of *kafā'a* (equality and sufficiency for marriage). In classical Islamic legal doctrine, *kafā'a* relates to the social status, fortune, and profession of the groom (vis-à-vis his father-in-law to be) and the parity of birth of the couple. *Kafā'a* protects Muslim women from "inadequate" matches, although Muslim men were permitted to marry women "below" them in the social—or economic—hierarchy.[136] Differences of descent as part of parity of the couple could be mitigated over time. For example, a freed slave or Islamic convert was to be considered an equal to all Muslims after three generations.[137] It seems, however, that even though *bayāsirah* were Muslim, they were subjected to more stringent social codes.

Zuwayna was the daughter of an Arab man and probably an African wife or concubine.[138] Standards of *kafā'a* may have been important in a few cases in the interior, but as was likely the case with Zuwayna's father, marriages involving Arab or *bayāsirah* migrants tended to follow the pattern of Omani men marrying African women. Both Arab and *bayāsirah* men were free to marry African women or take them as concubines. The immediacy of the debate over sufficiency was removed, but was still applicable to Arab women in later generations, as in Zuwayna's case. Zuwayna's guardian later found her a suitable match. She married Sayf bin Hamed al-Busaidi, a man who shared a name with the ruling family of Zanzibar and Oman. They had one child, Hamedi bin Sayf, born near Tabora.[139]

Sulayman bin Sleyum, the bachelor, arrived in Tabora sometime in the last decade of the nineteenth century. Born in Oman, he possibly migrated first to Zanzibar where—either through clientship with a wealthy Arab, access to credit, or his own wits—he joined a caravan to the interior. Acquiring patronage was common among migrants and freed slaves, because established Arabs had greater access to capital in Zanzibar in the late nineteenth century. Thus, they could more easily finance trading ventures for ivory into the interior.[140]

Zuwayna's guardian did not know Sulayman bin Sleyum or his status, which suggests that the bridegroom had not been in Tabora long. He remained in the town afterwards and he appears in German land records not far from his once-betrothed's guardian, Sulayman bin Zahir. Both were identified as Arab.[141] In his neighborhood he was called "Sulayman Chai," because whenever a guest would appear he would call into his house for someone to prepare tea (*chai* in Swahili). His descendants still own property in Tabora, not far from the soccer stadium.

Tabora today has few people who identify with early Arab settlers or know their stories.[142] The fact that the memory and idea of *bayāsirah* is fading in East Africa indicates a longer-term assimilation of nineteenth-century migrants. It also suggests that important oral sources for understanding Omani migrant identities and the process of assimilation are limited.

The presence of the category *bayāsirah* in the interior of East Africa adds another layer to the circulation of people, goods, and concepts between Oman and the East African coast and interior in the nineteenth century. Though relevant only for a seemingly tiny group within a small migrant community, the category of *bayāsirah* persisted into the early twentieth century. This demonstrates the incomplete process of racial assimilation in Oman and the ways in which such attitudes traveled and operated in a new multiethnic context. In the same way, coastal categories of Swahili and Arab also traveled to the East African interior, and discourses about these identities shaped settlement patterns.

﹌

The remarkable arc of Thani bin Amir al-Harthi's life—from humble halwa maker in Oman to an important trader in east central Africa—illuminates the expansion of the Indian Ocean world in the nineteenth century. His travels and settlement placed him in the middle of contests over identity between Arabs and Swahili people and between Omani migrants themselves.

Thus, even as Swahili people at the coast negotiated their position vis-à-vis Omani Arabs and the Zanzibar state, a broader Swahili and Indian Ocean world took root in the interior. Such a shift can only be understood by recognizing that some Indian Ocean people went to the interior and chose to stay there. They founded settlements, married, and established themselves, often in coastal enclaves. Just as interior people took on aspects of coastal identity, Swahili and coastal people "partook of notions" by invoking aspects of local cultural practices to make local claims. Allowing for situational identities and recognizing that some people who left the coast stayed in the interior makes it easier to understand the movements of people like Thani bin Amir and the ways the African interior became part of an Indian Ocean world. Mobility allowed travelers greater autonomy in self-presentation, but fluid identities had limits. Such limits underscore the connection that the East African interior had with the Indian Ocean world. Attitudes about relative identities followed travelers great distances, only to be activated in new encounters of familiar tropes. We see this in Thani's relationship with Arabs from old coastal families, in the tensions between Swahili elite and coastal Arabs on the caravan trail, and finally, in retrospective accusations about Thani's social standing.

5 ～ Tippu Tip's Kin, from Oman to the Eastern Congo

HAMED BIN MUHAMMAD AL-MURJEBI was the most famous coastal trader in the interior of East Africa in the nineteenth century. He led caravans of thousands of people, acquired hundreds of tons of ivory, earned the trust of Zanzibar's major creditors, had the ear of the sultan, befriended European explorers, and controlled such a large area of the Congo that, following the incorporation of the Congo Free State in the 1880s, the Belgians appointed him a provincial governor. To Europeans, Hamed was better known by his nickname, Tippu Tip, and his name and visage appeared in many places during the last decades of his life. An 1886 feature in the *New York Sun* featured him as "Central Africa's Richest Man," and informed their readers that "The World's Greatest Slave and Ivory Dealer on his Way to Zanzibar." Visitors to the 1894 World's Fair in Antwerp who walked past Mr. Thomas Edison's new-fangled phonograph in the American exhibit could also see a wax figure of Tippu Tip in a panorama of the Congo exhibition.[1] For contemporary observers, Tippu Tip was both the archetype and the pinnacle of traders. "Tippoo was the greatest ivory-raider of them all. He was a character that only Oriental Zanzibar, Darkest Africa, and the wealth of savage treasure ever could have produced; and never can there be another like him." So wrote Ernest D. Moore, a Connecticut ivory merchant, in his 1931 book *Ivory: Scourge of Africa*.[2]

Certainly Tippu Tip was exceptional. He achieved a degree of celebrity that wealth alone could not generate, and he was unique among his peers in writing an autobiography.³ Contrary to what Moore suggests, however, there were many more traders who, on the surface, seemed like Tippu Tip. They were Arab and Swahili men of modest means nonelite families. They took on debt to access small amounts of credit, and used the time between loan and repayment for the uncertain prospects of cheap ivory deep in the interior. What set Tippu Tip apart was his network of kin. He was a third-generation caravan trader with claims of kinship to Oman, the Swahili coast, and several points in the East African interior. Tippu Tip used a vast infrastructure of kinship networks that cut across racial, ethnic, and geographical boundaries to be successful. Tippu Tip was born Hamed bin Muhammad in Zanzibar in the late 1830s and died there in 1905. In between, he relied on his mother's lineage, his father's lineage, his half-siblings, his strategic marriages, and his offspring to organize, staff, and conduct his trading ventures. While his own initiative and fortuitous timing fueled his career and contributed to his ability to retire to Zanzibar as a wealthy man, his kin provided a network unmatched by any contemporary.

ARAB KINSHIP AND THE ORGANIZATION OF TRADE

Whereas the previous chapters have established the way that debt worked in Zanzibar, how sultans and others used mobility, and how Indian Ocean actors built the new settlements of the East African interior, this chapter focuses on Arab kinship at a time of population movement and expansion in the western Indian Ocean, from Oman and from Zanzibar to the East African mainland and interior. It unfolds in four sections, using Tippu Tip as a focal point to examine patrilineal and matrilineal kin, the predominance of siblings in long-distance trade, and kinship through marriage. Tippu Tip's extended family's involvement in trading and settlement in the East African interior is the touchstone for this analysis. His autobiography, his debt contracts in Zanzibar, and from the accounts of Europeans who encountered him make it clear that kinship was vital to many Arabs' activities in the interior.

Kinship has been overlooked as a means to examine the activities of Arabs in East Africa, as most analysis has focused on economic and racial characteristics. Yet it is central to understanding both Arab production and reproduction at the coast and in the interior. The change in the economy of East Africa is well attested; the results of this process have been shown to include a much greater incorporation into global capitalist systems and the creation of alternate modernities in places like Zanzibar.⁴ Indeed the changes in the connections between Arabia, the Swahili coast, and mainland East

Africa can be traced much more intimately through the changes in family structure and makeup.[5] As Arab and coastal people moved from the Indian Ocean shores to the interior, the family as an organizational framework served as an agent of this expansion, and at the same time, the constitution of the family was rearranged to incorporate the expanded scope and distribution of family members.

Though other scholars have noted the connections of kinship that existed among Arabs in the nineteenth century, they have not used kinship as a way of understanding the organization and expansion of a population into the interior. Norman R. Bennett's *Arab versus Europeans* acknowledges, for instance, that Tippu Tip gained from his father's strategic marriage and that some of Tippu Tip's relatives were in the interior with him. But kinship is not an analytical factor in his analysis. Instead, Bennett portrays Tippu Tip as a "wandering trader" who "followed the example of many of his generation" by taking to the caravan trails as a young man, gaining experience, and making allies with Africans wisely. Bennett noted that "The transition undergone by the young Arab, from a wandering trader to a locally based ruler . . . marked the inauguration of the most important commercial and political component of East Central Africa."[6] Perhaps this discursive approach to Tippu Tip draws from the trope of the European traveler who, making his way through Africa, was perceived (and portrayed himself) as self-propelling and independent. Anthropologist Johannes Fabian gives lie to this myth created by European travelers in central Africa. Fabian demonstrates that such men were not independent, but depended on Arab, Swahili, and other African people who had expertise and knowledge.[7] Likewise, Tippu Tip's familial relations greatly shaped the form of his engagement with the East African interior and influenced the way that Tippu Tip transformed himself from a mobile trader to a ruler of a territory.

Historian Walter Brown suggests that family structure provided an advantage in trade, but his focus was on immigrants from India who settled on the coast. Echoing nineteenth-century physician and long-time Zanzibar resident James Christie, Brown explains that Khoja Ismailis shopkeepers gained an advantage over Hindus because the Khojas were willing to bring their wives across the Indian Ocean or to marry locally, and the Hindus, generally, were not. Thus, Khojas gained "a trusted devoted non-salaried employee," and were able to divide economic tasks: the husband could concentrate on the wholesale business while his wife minded the store.[8]

These forms of kinship that Bennett and Brown touch on—patrilineal descent and marriage—are the most obvious and easily traceable. A close reading of Tippu Tip's autobiography, however, reveals an account suffused with relatives of many types. This chapter contextualizes this information and uses kinship as an analytical category and a vital way to understand the organization of business and family networks. Indeed, understanding the links of marriage, the bonds that tied half-brothers to each other, and the attachments between uncles and nephews reveals a new layer in the history of Arabs in East Africa and helps explain movements of people and settlements.

KINSHIP

The academic study of kinship was born during Tippu Tip's lifetime and has been closely related with cultural anthropology, another field that came into being in the nineteenth century. As one practitioner noted, "Kinship is to anthropology what the nude is to art."[9] But scholars should not leave it to anthropologists. As this chapter demonstrates, the scaffolding of kinship provided stability to an extended network of Arab traders from the Indian Ocean to the far interior of East Africa. Any inquiry into kinship must begin with the assumption that all understandings of kinship and relatedness are culturally bounded.[10] This short section charts the changing scope of kinship studies as a way of anticipating the format of the chapter, from formal horizontal kinship (patrilineal and matrilineal relations) to associative kin through partnering (siblings, marriages). The distinctions here parallel what Bourdieu has called "official kin" and "practical kin."[11]

The formal study of kinship as a science began in North America and Europe in the nineteenth century, and its early development aligns historically with Tippu Tip's professional life as a trader. Around the time that Tippu Tip undertook his first trip into the East African interior, an American, Lewis Henry Morgan (1818–1881), was scrutinizing consanguinity among the Iroquois of his native upstate New York. Early pioneers like Morgan focused on the study of "unchangeable" kinship among Native Americans. These "unchanging" structures invited comparisons with other ethnic groups, and Morgan undertook ethnological field trips and sent surveys to missionaries who worked among various groups.[12] He published the results of this research in *Systems of Consanguinity and Affinity of the Human Family* (1871). Morgan met and corresponded with leading lights of social science, Charles Darwin, E. B. Tylor, and Henry Sumner Maine, and became known as the "Father of American Anthropology."[13]

The heavy focus on kinship structures influenced the next generation of scholars. A. R. Radcliffe-Brown and Bronislaw Malinowski formalized the study and applied it to many other world peoples. The emphasis remained on structure, and studies of kinship became so bogged down in specialized terminology and hypotheses that Malinowksi wrote in 1930: "the average anthropologist... has his doubts whether the effort needed to master the bastard algebra of kinship is really worthwhile."[14] Arabic studies of kinship as an Islamic science also have a long history and difficult calculus.[15]

More recent scholarship asserts that kinship, rather than being immutable, is in fact socially constructed in all forms.[16] Scholars have tried to utilize kinship as a tool for broader understanding. In this way, kinship has also been a study of gender, power, and difference that offers analysis of social inequalities. This chapter borrows from these innovations to see gender as a core component of kinship, even though limited sources prevent a full inquiry in this direction. As family structures changed with the mobile population of Arabs in East Africa, inequalities, even among kin, became pronounced.

Kinship functioned on two levels. First, an official genealogical one that came into play in formal situations and served as a way to create differences that ordered the social world and legitimated this order.[17] For Arab kinship especially, these were ties to the paternal line that determined not only people's names (X bin Y bin Z), but also their formal membership in society through their inherited tribal or clan adjective (*nisba*, like al-Murjebi). On the second, less formal, level, kinship provided connections to others that could be utilized in certain circumstances. These connections include maternal uncles, uterine brothers, and strategic marriages. All three of these were vital to the organization of Arab society in East Africa and served as an infrastructure that undergirded mobility and access to credit. Indeed, birth and genealogy were tools that Arabs used in Africa (and Arabia) to establish new statuses and roles by calling on new categories of kin.[18]

PATRILINEAGE

The relatives of Tippu Tip on his father's side linked him to East Africa and to Oman, served as trusted deputies, and, through marriage, provided important allies. Arabs take their names from their fathers, and Arabic naming practices tightly bind children to the patriline, so Tippu Tip's patrilineage is a natural place to begin. Patrilineal descent linked given names (Arabic: *ism*) to genealogies (*nasab*) and clan names (*nisba*). In the case of the man who came to be known as Tippu Tip, his parents named him Hamed, and his full name indicates that he was the son of Muhammad, the son of Juma.[19] Using a more robust *nasab* (pedigree), the patrilineage can be traced back five generations: Hamed bin Muhammad bin Juma bin Rajab bin Muhammad bin Said.[20] Generally only two names are given, and Tippu Tip refers to himself throughout his autobiography as Hamed bin Muhammad. Daughters followed the same naming pattern, but the word *bint* (daughter of) followed the given name and preceded the father's name, for example, Moza bint Khalfan bin Khamis al-Barwani.

In addition to the names of the members of the patrilineal line, naming practices also attach a clan name, known as a *nisba*, the Arabic grammatical term for a noun of relation. Although the *nisba* adjective of medieval Islamic usage could demonstrate a relationship between a person and a variety of things (a group, another person, a concept, or an object), in contemporary usage a *nisba* serves as a family name.[21] As such, a *nisba* "implicitly contains the genealogy of the tribe," and signifies not just belonging to the group, but also sharing its (often) eponymous ancestor and the achievements, history, and territory. Children inherited the *nisba* of their fathers.[22] Hamed bin Muhammad's *nisba* was al-Murjebi, a clan that traces its ancestry to the Adam region of Oman.[23] In his earliest promissory notes for ivory, however, Tippu Tip identified himself with no *nisba*, but as Humayd bin Muhammad Abu Rajab, only linking him to his grandfather's generation, not an Arab tribal name.[24] The *nisba* al-Murjebi shares the same semantic roots (r-j-b) with Rajab, and may simply be derived from his great grandfather's name. In this case, the eponymous ancestor, achievements, history, and territory of the clan may be much more recent.

The fact that Arab and Swahili practices of naming children linked them inextricably to their patrilineage has led some observers of Arabic society to overstate the importance of these connections in the past. As one prominent anthropologist of the Middle East wrote in 1965: "a man's patrilineal descent counts for everything; his matriline counts for nothing."[25] Such views have come to be challenged more broadly.[26] Certainly both patrilineal and matrilineal relations were vital components of Tippu Tip's success.

Tippu Tip's patrilineage linked him both to Oman and to East Africa, and he regarded it as important. Tippu Tip's father's line is well established in his autobiography and is remembered today by members of his family.[27] Family history of Tippu Tip's branch of the Murjebi clan in East Africa begins with Rajab bin Muhammad al-Murjebi. Rajab bin Muhammad, Tippu Tip's paternal great-grandfather, was born in the Adam region of Oman and arrived in East Africa as a young man in what must have been the last decades of the eighteenth century.[28] He traveled with a peer, a son of Juma bin Muhammad al-Nabhani. The Nabhani have a history in Oman entwined with imamate politics, and they were also among the longest-standing Arab clans on the African coast. Indeed, the Nabhani man with whom Tippu

Tip's great-grandfather traveled was following in his own father's footsteps. The father, Juma bin Muhammad al-Nabhani, had previously journeyed to the East African coast and settled at least temporarily in Mbwamaji, an important trading town in the nineteenth century.[29] He married there and sired children. A generation later, when Juma bin Muhammad's son returned to Mbwamaji with Rajab bin Muhammad al-Murjebi, the Murjebi man married an al-Nabhani sister, a woman identified in the account only as Bint Juma Muhammad al-Nabhani, the half sister of his traveling companion. Bint Juma had been born in Mbwamaji to an African mother. Her father had returned to Oman, but may have continued to travel to East Africa seasonally for trade as other Arabs did.[30] The connection with the Nabhani family persisted in later generations. Tippu Tip referred to a well-known al-Nabhani trader and adventurer, Muhammad bin Saleh al-Nabhani, as *baba yetu* (our father).[31] This Muhammad bin Saleh had traveled with two other members of the Murjebi clan into the central African kingdoms of Kazembe, in what is now Zambia and the southeastern Congo.[32] Tippu Tip commended David Livingstone to Muhammad bin Saleh when they met in the late 1860s and Livingstone was bound for the Lunda territory further west. When Livingstone met him in 1867, Muhammad bin Saleh had already spent ten years in Lunda territory.[33] But the connection with the Nabhani started generations before, with Tippu Tip's great-grandfather.

Rajab bin Muhammad al-Murjebi and Bint Juma al-Nabhani together had a son, Juma, and Rajab bin Muhammad had five other sons. Whether Bint Juma was the mother of these sons, and whether he sired any daughters, is impossible to determine because Arab family trees only record men.[34] Juma bin Rajab al-Murjebi, one generation removed from Oman on his father's side, traveled and traded in East Africa with several of his brothers and their sons. Trading connections made early in the nineteenth century benefited their grandsons. Juma bin Rajab traded in the interior, and in one of his transactions dealt with a Nyamwezi man named Moura. Moura became a chief, and one of his descendants, himself a powerful chief, credited Juma bin Rajab's support as one of the forces that propelled Moura to the chieftaincy.[35] Thus the mobility of Indian Ocean actors created new kin networks and linkages that paid dividends over time.

Juma bin Rajab bore three sons—Sayf, Muhammad, and Abdullah.[36] The younger two continued their father's trade activities in the interior, and the first was also likely involved in these undertakings. Building on his father's knowledge and contacts, Muhammad bin Juma bin Rajab, two generations removed from Oman on his father's side, established trading partnerships in Unyamwezi by the late 1840s. In this he was a contemporary of Thani bin

Amir al-Harthi and the Khoja Musa Mzuri, the founders of Kazeh (see chapter 4). Unlike these two, however, Muhammad bin Juma built on his father's relationships with Nyamwezi traders. Muhammad bin Juma established a bond of kinship with the important Nyamwezi ruler Fundikira, who governed the large area surrounding Kazeh, by marrying his daughter Karunde. Muhammad bin Juma married Karunde, or at least contracted to marry her, when she was still a child.[37] This was not his first marriage—he had previously married Bint Habib bin Bashir al-Wardi in Zanzibar—and it was she who bore his son Hamed.

Muhammad bin Juma's trading activities built on his father's previous journeys and his own ties to Fundikira, but they also depended on his kin. Groups of kinsmen offered protection and advantages in long-distance trade. "An Arab can walk through Africa armed only with a cane," was proverbial wisdom of the period, according to the same nostalgic, American ivory trader who waxed on about Tippu Tip.[38] While Moore was given to exaggeration, he was pointedly contrasting the early period with a later, more violent time.

Kinship, via blood brotherhood, was a cornerstone to the trade deals that Arabs made with Africans. Linking this fictive kinship with negotiations and agreements was their mode of exchange because they were greatly outnumbered in the early years. The American clarified that "this was the only way in which the Arabs could enter and emerge from the country, for, armed with only daggers in their belts, and the swords and spears carried by their bodyguards, their safety, once in the interior, depended on their good relations with native chiefs."[39] While traders like Muhammad bin Juma took care to secure good relations with local rulers, they also maintained their position by traveling with a force of kinsmen. On one journey in 1859, Muhammad bin Juma traveled with a group of more than thirty relatives, many of whom were the sons of his paternal uncles and each of whom had his own body of servants.[40] These relations shored up Muhammad bin Juma's positions vis-à-vis both Africans of the interior and other Arabs and coastal people they met there. To the Africans, the group of Arab kinsmen appeared to protect each other and to be well-armed. To Arabs and other coastal people, a group of kinsmen appeared to be a cohesive faction even among potentially like-minded people. In 1859 Muhammad bin Juma's kin represented roughly 10 percent of the Arabs and coastal people in Unyamwezi. Muhammad bin Juma and his group of al-Murjebi men held sway there, as the aftermath of the great chief Fundikira's death makes clear. The Murjebi party counseled that the Omani traders be patient and forestall any rash action toward Fundikira's successor. This flew in the face of those who wanted to depose the new sultan. When the Murjebi had taken the measure of the new leader, they changed course and rallied support for a rival.[41] Muhammad bin Juma's group of kinsmen and marriage link to a Nyamwezi clan made these machinations possible.

One of the kinsmen in the group with Muhammad bin Juma was his son Hamed (later nicknamed Tippu Tip). Tippu Tip had started trading expeditions with maternal kin at the coast as a very young man. He began his long-distance trading journeys far into the interior when he was eighteen years old by his own reckonings, so this must have been in the mid-1850s. They traveled north of Lake Nyasa to Ugangi, an area between the Uranga and Luwego rivers, and shortly thereafter visited the Arab depot at Tabora in Unyanyembe. The continued on to Ujiji on the shores of Lake Tanganyika in pursuit of ivory.[42]

As our focus turns to Tippu Tip in the interior as a trader, it is worth recalling that far from a wandering young man, he was deeply embedded in the legacy of his father's family. He was a member of the third generation of his family to trade in Unyamwezi, he had the support of a large number of paternal relatives on the caravan trails, and he had the advantage of relatives by marriage who were autochthonous rulers in the interior.

How did he use such advantages? The central Unyamwezi settlement of Unyanyembe, with its cluster of Arab villages (including Kazeh), became both a stronghold and safe haven for Tippu Tip, allowing him to shore up his supply lines to the coast as he pushed west into the Congo. Unyanyembe was a vital resupply point and the place that caravans formed (or reformed) before heading to the coast. Contemporary observers noted Tippu Tip's advantage in moving from the coast to interior: "he had permanent stations under responsible sheiks, for the reception and forwarding of his ivory and goods, and also for keeping the road open."[43] Other Arabs maintained connections in Unyanyembe and other settlements, but it was Tippu Tip who could lay claim to slaves, property, and a large network of indigenous kin.

Few other Indian Ocean lineages could claim multigenerational experience trading in the interior of Africa. One was the Wardi clan, to whom Tippu Tip was tied through his mother's side. Muhammad bin Masoud al-Wardi was an intimate associate of Tippu Tip's, and he was the third generation of Wardi clan members to travel in the interior: his maternal grandfather had traveled to the Congo. François Bontinck suggests in his scholarly translation of Tippu Tip's autobiography that Muhammad bin Masoud's father was a trader in the interior who met Richard Burton at the end of 1857.[44] These al-Wardi relatives of Tippu Tip's were important, as were the kinsmen within his paternal line who took to the caravan trails and served as his loyal deputies.

Several members of the Murjebi clan of Tippu Tip's generation were vital to his trading efforts, and he in turn helped them secures loans. Men like Muhammad bin Said bin Hamed and Juma bin Sayf bin Juma were cousins and Tippu Tip's age mates. This special bond made them like siblings. The Arabic business documents in Zanzibar make clear that Tippu Tip served as a patron within his paternal kin networks. When his father's brother, Abdullah bin Juma bin Rajab al-Murjebi, borrowed 175 Maria Theresa dollars (MT$175) from Tharia Topan for one year in 1887, Tippu Tip served as a guarantor as he had done for his cousin twenty years earlier.[45] By his own account, Tippu Tip bought goods worth more than MT$50,000 in order to stake others in business in the late 1880s.[46] Thus the relative pittance that Tippu Tip guaranteed for his uncle hints at limits of kinship. Tippu Tip did not lend the money himself (he borrowed MT$17,218 from Tharia Topan the next month), and the fact that Tharia Topan required a written guarantee from one of his best customers suggests Tharia's rigorous business practices and the importance of recording such debts.[47]

Arab and Swahili kinship relations also contained ambiguity. As the sons of Omani and Zanzibar ruler Seyyid Said bin Sultan demonstrated, rivalries among elite kin shaped state policies and actions. Other, more typical

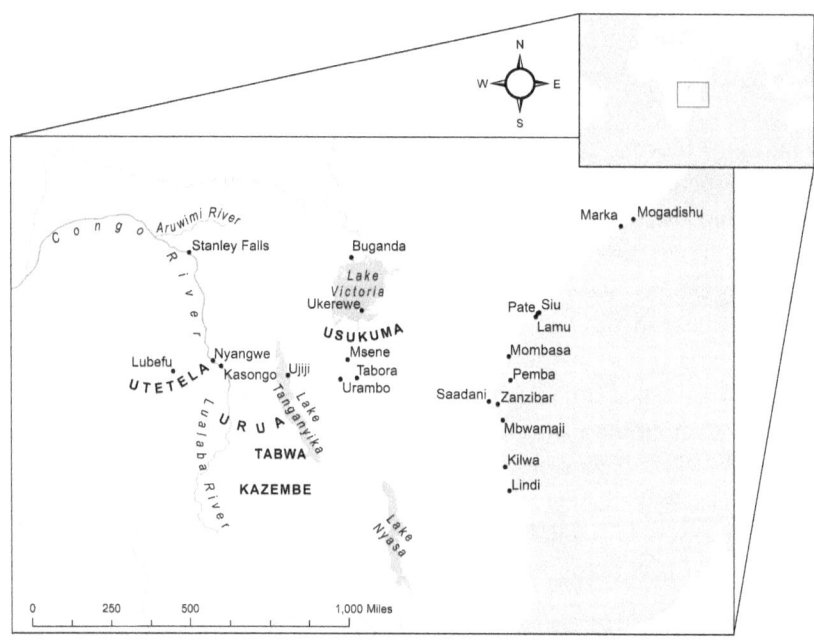

MAP 5.1. Eastern and Central Africa in the age of Tippu Tip

men did not automatically side with their paternal kin, and aspects of generational conflict among Arabs in the interior are clear, even within a patrilineage. In one case Tippu Tip found himself on the other side of a dispute from his powerful father, Muhammad bin Juma. Tippu Tip and his retinue, by his telling, had stumbled into a fight after a misunderstanding in one of the interior settlements where his men were trying to pound their grain. The fight soon involved dozens of local people. In the midst of the scuffle, Tippu Tip ordered the chief shot. Although this ended the fight for the time being, the result was a greater degree of dislocation for local people. The Arabs in Unyanyembe, five days of travel away from the site of the fighting, were concerned about the disarray in the countryside and sent a party of Baluchi soldiers to encourage Tippu Tip to desist. Muhammad bin Juma sent a letter with this group and subsequently arrived with the Arab leaders from Unyanyembe. The other Arabs refused to enter Tippu Tip's camp or receive his hospitality, a grave stand against custom. They sent Muhammad bin Juma to negotiate, and his son acceded to all of the demands the Tabora Arabs made.[48] Other stories that circulated among Arabs and Europeans in the interior suggested that Tippu Tip and his father stopped trading and traveling together because of disagreements.[49] This echoes Said bin Sultan's falling out with his son Hilal in the 1840s (see chapter 3).

Sayf bin Hamed, Tippu Tip's son, was deeply enmeshed in his father's enterprises, and his death in the Congo in the 1890s represented a new era of European encroachment. Sayf took part in trade in the interior and carried out sensitive negotiations on his father's behalf. In 1882, Sayf met with Mirambo, a powerful Nyamwezi chief who, over the span of twenty years, fought with the Arabs based in Tabora to benefit from trade. Sayf eventually became his father's representative in the Congo territory.[50] Sayf, like his father, spent his early years in Zanzibar, but some of Tippu Tip's collaborators arranged for Sayf to travel with them to Unyanyembe where he could join his father and paternal grandfather.[51] In 1881 the Belgian traveler Jerome Becker met Sayf, then about twenty years old, with his father at the Murjebi headquarters near Tabora.[52] Sayf then traveled with his father to Nyangwe in eastern Congo, where Tippu Tip left him with another Murjebi relation, Muhammad bin Said.[53] Sayf bin Hamed remained there for some time and was put in charge of the Arab settlement at Kasongo on the Lualaba River. When he traveled to the coast in the late 1880s, he did so with his father's permission, representing his father before the new Zanzibar sultan, Khalifa, who had come to power upon Barghash's death in 1888.[54] Sayf returned to the Congo by the early 1890s, and became embroiled in machinations between the Free State authorities and his father's supposed surrogates. Tippu Tip later remembered his son's efforts and noted that although he had been a young man, he was smart and feared his father.[55] Sayf died in the Congo in the violent conflicts with Europeans in the 1890s.

Arab kinship was central to the organizational logic of the caravan trade, and patrilineal descent was central to the logic of Arab kinship. Tippu Tip ventured into the interior with his fathers, his uncles, and his uncles' sons, covering ground upon which his grandfather had also trod. But for Tippu Tip, these agnatic kin represented a small portion of his network. His most intimate colleagues were maternal kin.

MATRILINEAGES

While matrilineages are frequently difficult to surmise among patrilineal people in the past, matrilineal kin proved vital to Tippu Tip's trading efforts, and his closest confidants were members of his mother's clan. As noted previously, paternal genealogy among Arabs has received great emphasis from scholars, but in practice in East Africa maternal relations remained tight-knit kin.[56] Tippu Tip's first trading trips, all close to the coast, were with his uterine half-brother Muhammad bin Masoud al-Wardi and two of his maternal uncles, Bushir bin Habib al-Wardi and Abdullah bin Habib al-Wardi.[57] Loyal support from several members of the Wardi clan helped launch and sustain Tippu Tip's career.

Little is known, comparatively, about Tippu Tip's mother, the daughter of Habib bin Bushir al-Wardi. Like many Arab women her name was not recorded, only her relationship to her paternal line. The fact that we do not know her name should not diminish her standing. Anthropologists of a previous generation made this mistake, and one argued for the irrelevance of matrilineal kin: "this lack of importance [of the maternal line] is best illustrated by the inability of even the best tribal genealogists to recall the names of their grandmothers or great-grandmothers, although they are able to rattle off the names of their male ancestors up to ten or more generations."[58]

Tippu Tip invoked the names of his maternal line to his great advantage, and his maternal grandmother provided a vital connection for him. As a young man, Tippu Tip's maternal grandfather, Habib bin Bushir al-Wardi, traded between the Swahili coast and Urua in the eastern Congo. In the course of his commerce, he saw a beautiful woman named Daramumba, and he bought her. She returned with him to the coast and joined his household as a concubine. Daramumba bore him a daughter, Bint Habib bin Bushir (the daughter of Habib). This was Tippu Tip's mother. When Tippu Tip was young, Daramumba told him tales of her country, Utetera, and of her family who had been rulers there when she was captured in war and enslaved.[59] When, as an adult, Tippu Tip traveled to Utetera, he arrived as part of a large caravan and invoked his grandmother's name and lineage, appealing to the ruler there on the basis of shared kinship. Tippu Tip claimed a connection to Utetera ("Utetera is our place") and its ruler Kasongo ("Kasongo is my grandfather").[60]

Contemporaries of Tippu Tip claimed that this story is embellished, and that Tippu Tip manipulated intelligence he had gathered in order to impress the local ruler.[61] Even if this is the case, it is clear from Tippu Tip's narrative that his kinship connection was seen as important. The fact that Tippu Tip, as author, invoked the medium of kinship, indicates the legitimizing power of this discourse.

The relationship between Tippu Tip's parents' lineages suggests the relative lack of prestige that his father may have endured. Bint Habib al-Wardi, Tippu Tip's mother, was married before she wed Mohammed bin Juma al-Murjebi. Bint Habib had previously married a man from her own clan named Masoud bin Muhammad al-Wardi. Such endogamous marriage would have fulfilled certain ideals of marriage and kinship for Habib bin Bushir, the father of Bint Habib (and the husband of Daramumba), dovetailing with Burton's observation that, "Men of pure family will not give their daughters to any but fellow-clansmen."[62] This marriage produced at least one offspring, a son named Muhammad bin Masoud al-Wardi, who became one of Tippu Tip's frequent collaborators and closest partners. The marriage of Bint Habib and Masoud bin Muhammad, like many in the nineteenth century, ended in divorce.[63]

First marriages for women like Bint Habib were governed by their families and accorded prestige. As the failed marriage in Tabora made clear, Arabic notions of sufficiency (*kafā'a*) in marriage put forth rules to protect women from marrying men beneath their station, but these were most commonly invoked only in first marriages. Divorced or widowed women had much greater social and commercial leeway, so women like Bint Habib had greater latitude in deciding who they would agree to marry. Because unattached women also faced certain constraints and lacked social protections that marriage provided, they might seek remarriage. Jonathon Glassman has shown that men of marginal social status on the Swahili coast used marriages to widowed or divorced women of higher status to improve their own standing.[64] Although she had been married before, Bint Habib appears to be Muhammad bin Juma's first wife. Their son's autobiography mentions no other senior (paternal) brothers and does not mention any other wives of Muhammad bin Juma at the coast. This marriage therefore raises questions about the relative status of Muhammad bin Juma and his family, but explanations as to why his first wife was from a different clan and was previously married are unavailable.

Through his mother's first marriage, Tippu Tip gained a close confidant, and through her clan he developed relationships with uncles who became trusted business partners and associates. Indeed, Tippu Tip first traded on local trips in the 1860s along or near the coast, not with his father or any paternal relatives, but with his mother's other son Muhammad bin Masoud and two of his maternal uncles, Bushir bin Habib and Abdullah bin Habib. The earliest registered documents related to Tippu Tip's ivory trading show that he and Muhammad Masoud embarked on ivory trading together in July 1867. They secured their advances within days of each other from Tharia Topan, but Tippu Tip's debt was 320 frasilas and MT$3,000 while Muhammad bin Masoud's was only twenty frasilas of ivory.[65] While Muhammad bin Masoud's direct stake in the business may have been smaller in financial terms, he became one of Tippu Tip's constant collaborators and oversaw relationships with creditors and suppliers.

Tippu Tip's maternal uncles advised him, protected him, and attacked those who challenged him.[66] In the late 1860s, when Tippu Tip's trading venture into Nsama's territory became a war, Tippu Tip looked to Bushir bin Habib al-Wardi for advice and leadership of the coastal forces. In the battle, Tippu Tip was incapacitated by arrow wounds and was unable to fight. Bushir defended their position with a small force that was ultimately victorious.[67] In the interior, Bushir bin Habib protected his nephew, and took risks to help his young relative.[68] At several points on their joint trip to Urua in 1870, Bushir led a portion of the caravan. Bushir died on one of these side trips, a journey to Refu (Lubefu) to the west of Utetera in the early 1870s, when he and his large force were attacked by Kusu people. Perhaps motivated by notions of honor and kinship, Tippu Tip sought revenge against the Kusu, justifying his attack both on his loss and on the supposed Kusu practice of cannibalism.[69]

Tippu Tip's other maternal uncle, Abdullah bin Habib al-Wardi took part in early trips but was not as prominent as his brother Bushir in later journeys. Rather than trading on his own, Abdullah may have settled in a trading town as a representative of other traders, such as his nephew. In February 1874, explorer V. L. Cameron, met a man named Abdullah bin Habib in Kawele (near Ujiji) and identified him as Mrima, a man from the coast, opposite Zanzibar, and included him in a group of secondary traders who "acted as agents for large merchants."[70] Abdullah bin Habib knew something about trade and geography of the territory west of Lake Tanganyika, but was unable to translate this information to a map that was useful to Cameron.[71]

Other members of the Wardi clan were also linked to Tippu Tip, maintaining connections between the interior of East Africa, Zanzibar, and Oman. Salum bin Omar al-Wardi traveled with Tippu Tip's son to join the famous trader in the interior, and Hamed bin Said al-Wardi accompanied Tippu Tip on at least one journey from the interior to the coast in the early 1880s.[72] Hamed bin Said's brother, Sayf bin Said bin Salim al-Wardi (d. 1887 or 1888) was a caravan leader who traveled to the interior as early as the 1850s. In 1882 Sayf dedicated his house in Zanzibar town as *waqf*, a form of Islamic trust, to benefit his heirs and the poor of the Wardi clan. Income from this endowment was sent to Wardi people in Oman at least through the 1920s.[73] In this example we see how profits from trade in the interior supported a household in Zanzibar that later benefited impoverished kin in Oman.

Few sources offer sufficient information to allow such a detailed reconstruction of relationships through matrilineal links. Maternal kin are difficult to trace and require a broad source base. The extensive evidence in Tippu Tip's autobiography when measured against his numerous transactions suggests that Arabs who were able to take advantage of networks of maternal kin gained great advantages in organizing and conducting their economic enterprises.

SIBLINGS

For mobile individuals like the Arabian traders and migrants of eastern Africa in the nineteenth century, horizontal, intragenerational ties of kinship were arguably more important than vertical links to paternal or maternal lines. A close analysis of these sibling relationships offers several insights that other types of kinship study do not.[74] First, for groups of mobile individuals in periods of great change, like the Arabs of East Africa in the nineteenth century, evidence for sibling relationships is more readily available than intergenerational data. Patrilineal descent is easily noted in Islamic naming systems, but the meaning of these relationships is less easily understood. Matrilineal data is only available in rare cases. In both realms, the analysis of descent in kinship lends more readily to structural interpretations. The content of relationships among those in the same generation highlights relational practice across society, specifically the way Arabs built business networks and ensured their security in the interior. The study of siblings also reveals overlapping descent structures, and more easily incorporates idioms of affiliation that were common in East Africa among Arab and Swahili people.

Arabs and coastal people depended on siblings when they went to the interior of East Africa. The trope of siblingship was prevalent and seems to have been the most common form of partnership among Arabs and coastal traders in the nineteenth century. More important, those who were most successful in the interior almost always worked with their siblings. Tippu Tip had several sibling partners that will be the focus here, and broader evidence suggests the pervasiveness of this organizational model.[75] Siblingship made for ready bonds of partnership because familial ties reinforced those bonds. In some instances, siblings were not related within one nuclear family, but established relationships along the lines of siblings with those who were more distant kin. Such arrangements were especially useful among a highly mobile population. Tippu Tip had relationships with two people he described as his brothers, Muhammad bin Masoud al-Wardi and Muhammad bin Said al-Murjebi.

The first person mentioned in Tippu Tip's autobiography is Muhammad bin Masoud al-Wardi. Muhammad bin Masoud, sometimes known by the caravan name Kumbakumba ("he who has seized everyone"), was Tippu Tip's uterine half-brother, several years his senior.[76] In the late 1840s or early 1850s, when Tippu Tip was only twelve years old he accompanied his older brother on local trading ventures. Soon afterwards they went in separate directions. Tippu Tip traveled far into the interior with his father and traded in ivory. In recalling this period of separation, Tippu Tip explains that Muhammad bin Masoud traveled to Ngao, near Lindi on the southern Swahili coast; to the Lake Nyasa region; and from there to Benadir (Somalia), on the northern end of the Busaidi sultan's realm.[77] The route to Lake Nyasa supplied most of the slaves to the East African market, and both Brode and Bontinck interpret Tippu Tip's reference to these areas to mean that Muhammad bin Masoud had been involved in the slave trade.[78] Muhammad had partnered with Muhammad bin Said al-Harthi (known as Utelezi, "slipperiness") who, Brode suggests, mismanaged the partnerships' funds and brought on losses or greater debt. This financial mismanagement made Muhammad bin Masoud eager to join his younger sibling whose trading to the interior had been successful in the intervening twelve years.[79] Muhammad bin Masoud could only muster MT$5,000 in credit for this trip, and Tippu Tip had more than MT$30,000.[80] Perhaps it was this financial difference that subtly altered the dynamics of the brothers' relationship, allowing the younger brother to assume the more dominant role in their trading ventures. In any case, they joined forces around 1860 and developed an extremely close working relationship that continued until their retirement in the 1890s.

Muhammad bin Masoud served as Tippu Tip's lieutenant and agent, representing him in trade, war, and politics. When they traveled, Tippu Tip and Muhammad bin Masoud were rarely together—they divided their forces to cover a greater area. Tippu Tip recorded that his brother either preceded the main body of the caravan by several days or followed behind it.[81] In their journey to Tabwa country in 1870, Muhammad bin Masoud remained for five years, consolidating coastal power and coordinating trade, while Tippu Tip traveled elsewhere.[82] The brothers seem to have remained in communication throughout this time, with goods moving between them through intermediaries.[83] When they did meet in person after long separations, they rejoiced.[84] When both men were in Zanzibar in the early 1880s, Tippu Tip took the lead in trading the ivory that they had collected, but when Tippu Tip was absent, his brother registered an Arabic deed of *wakala*, or power of attorney, and thus acted as his agent and secured credit on his behalf.[85]

Tippu Tip also sought Muhammad bin Masoud to undertake diplomacy for him. When, in late 1888, Tippu Tip learned of European intentions to portion eastern and central Africa between the Belgians, Germans, and British, he wrote to his brother in Zanzibar. He explained what he had learned, noted several stations he controlled over this broad area, and instructed his brother and son Sayf to assess the news of Zanzibar and take action: "If you see that it would be of an advantage to us to join with the Germans . . . [and] if you find the strongest of all, please go and tell them that Ahmed bin Mohammed, I, Tippu Tib, has sent you a letter asking you to seek their friendship." At the same time, Tippu Tip instructed, "before you do anything, you should go quietly to the British consul and approach him by stratagem" to complain that Tippu Tip had not heard from them. He also hinted to Muhammad bin Masoud that, should the Germans try to use force, his strength could match them.[86] Thus Tippu Tip entrusted his brother Muhammad bin Masoud with extremely sensitive negotiations and diplomatic posturing. In the same packet of letters Tippu Tip sent a missive to his son, Sayf bin Hamed, that focused on contractual disputes with European traders. Tippu Tip also asked his son to convey information to the British consul, but it was not nearly as sensitive, and Tippu Tip suspected that the consul might already know the details.

Muhammad bin Said al-Murjebi (known in the interior as Bwana Nzige, "Sir Locust"), was another of Tippu Tip's siblings, though not of the same mother or father. Tippu Tip referred to Muhammad bin Said as his *ndugu*, a Swahili word that indicates a brother or cousin; they were in fact cousins.

FIGURE 5.1. Like brothers: Muhammad bin Said al-Murjebi (Bwana Nzige) and Hamed bin Muhammad al-Murjebi (Tippu Tip) at Stanley Falls, 1888. From Alexandre Delcommune, *Vingt années de vie africaine: Récits de voyages d'aventures et d'exploration au Congo Belge, 1874–1893* (Brussels: Ferdinand Larcier, 1922), 300.

As members of the same clan, of roughly the same age, and both in the interior of East Africa, they formed a close bond. Tippu Tip referred to him as his brother, as did European observers.[87] Muhammad bin Said was "a tall, light-coloured Arab with a long beard, the most benevolent and piouslooking old gentleman," according to James S. Jameson who met him in early 1888.[88] Muhammad also apparently had a well-known taste for chocolate and a marked generosity toward less fortunate Arabs.[89]

It is unclear whether Muhammad bin Said's early career in the interior was linked to Tippu Tip's, but his later activities certainly were. Muhammad bin Said had established himself at Kasongo on the Lualaba River of the greater Congo basin by the 1870s, but conditions for trade and daily life were not always good there, and the Arab position was not secure. When Tippu Tip arrived in Kasongo in the 1870s, seeking out his *ndugu*, the state of affairs in the settlement was poor: famine had affected the region and, perhaps because of this disruption, local people challenged the Arab presence.[90] The Arab and coastal traders in Kasongo were a small group at that time, and they had limited arms. They suffered losses from pilfering and raiding, even after Tippu Tip arrived. The traders apparently welcomed Tippu Tip, and according to his account ceded leadership of the settlement to him. Tippu Tip acknowledged his brother's strong position and opted to fight the Africans for local control. After three months of fighting, the coastal traders gained an upper hand. The conditions for the settlement of hostilities suggest the coastal traders' priorities. The Arabs insisted on exclusive rights to sell ivory and demanded a supply of labor. Under the control of Tippu Tip and his sibling (and loyal deputy) Muhammad bin Said, the settlement of Kasongo thrived, just as the other Indian Ocean settlements like Kazeh had grown in the previous decades. Muhammad bin Said's leadership attracted many people to live there, made travel so safe that even women traveled regionally, and produced agricultural surpluses. The coastal travelers had introduced rice to the region, and Tippu Tip noted that the quantity of rice grown in Kasongo was so great that contemporaries compared it with Bengal.[91] The efforts led by Tippu Tip and his *ndugu* transformed the town. Tippu Tip's decision to move his capital to Kasongo in the mid-1870s set the town "on a path to development to the largest of all Arab centers in the East Central African interior."[92]

Throughout their association, Muhammad bin Said often deferred to Tippu Tip, and in so doing gained his trust. He did not travel from his appointed station without securing his brother's permission, and in this way he ventured with Tippu Tip's imprimatur.[93] When Tippu Tip returned to the coast with his huge caravan in 1881, Muhammad bin Said accompanied him. Tippu Tip counted on his judgment and experience to travel ahead of the ponderous caravan—it was so huge that one part of the trip to Lake Tanganyika that normally took one month required six—and when Tippu Tip went ahead he entrusted Muhammad bin Said with the heavily laden caravan.[94] Muhammad bin Said also oversaw Tippu Tip's operations in the Congo during the period of European encroachment and served until the downfall of the Arabs in the region.[95]

The downfall of the Arabs occurred between 1892 and 1894. The Congo Free State, the colony established by King Leopold II, in 1885, had initially needed Tippu Tip's support and installed him as the governor at Stanley Falls in 1887. He took up his post by traveling from Zanzibar, via South Africa, and up the Congo river from the Atlantic. The appointment made him the governor of a vast region centered on Stanley Falls. This was a fragile arrangement, and skirmishes broke out in 1892 that led to a series of military campaigns. Tippu Tip and his siblings retreated east, but many Arabs and coastal people were killed. When the Indian Ocean center of Nyangwe was besieged, a thriving city of thirty thousand was reduced in six weeks by fighting and fire to an abandoned city; only one principal building remained standing.[96]

In March 1893, Kasongo fell much more quickly, and without such destruction, to Free State forces. The invaders were astounded at the transformation the Arabs and their allies had made in their time there. Great swaths of cleared land supplied abundant produce, the buildings were large and spacious, and the soldiers slept on carved beds outfitted with silk and satin mattress and mosquito nets. The leader of the group, Sydney Hinde, forgot he was in Central Africa.[97] He did not acknowledge that the siblings who had built up the town had created an outpost of the Indian Ocean world from whence they came.

In considering the organization of Tippu Tip's network, the important role of siblings as partners is clear. Among the loose association of Arab and coastal traders who connected central Africa to the Indian Ocean world, intergenerational kin provided an organizational advantage.

MARRIAGE

Like siblingship, marriage was a way for Arab migrants to choose allies, and in doing so they expanded the idiom of kinship. Arabs living at the coast attempted to conform to Arabian endogamous cultural practices when they could. Arabs who took part in caravans and traveled to the interior, however, followed more diverse practices and received other benefits. Marriages in the interior created bonds between Arab men and local women, and by extension their families. Some women, married at the coast, worked to assert their rights vis-à-vis marriage and mobility, and refused to travel. While discourses of sufficiency in marriage applied most often in first marriages, subsequent marriages could reveal the relative status of the participants.

Tippu Tip married a woman of the Barwani clan, one of the Harthi subgroups who were long resident in East Africa and mobile between Oman and Zanzibar. By starting with Tippu Tip's marriage, and the ways that marriage might grant access to credit, we can consider other marriage outcomes within the Barwani family in the nineteenth century. The relationship between husbands and wives helped to link the coast and the interior, and marriage interacted with business dealings. Of particular interest is the manner in which women negotiated the terms of their marriages.

Tippu Tip's kin network, while valuable in coastal East Africa and the interior, was not a prestigious family. Tippu Tip had a dispersed group of kin he could claim, but he did not have wealth in the form of property to leverage himself into trade. This makes the way he described his marriage to the wealthier Barwani family all the more intriguing. In his autobiography, Tippu Tip wrote that he married the daughter of Salim bin Abdullah al-Barwani, and implies that this marriage helped him secure credit for a journey. When Tippu Tip mentioned that he borrowed MT$50,000 to finance a caravan, he also noted pointedly that he did not own any property but that his wife did. "As for me at this time, I had no plantation or houses either in Zanzibar or any other place, but I had a wife here in Zanzibar, the daughter of Salum bin Abdullah al-Barwani. She had a great deal of wealth [property] here in Zanzibar and in Muscat."[98] He used "Muscat" in the generic sense for Oman, and it is most likely that the property that he refers to was in Sharqiya, perhaps near Ibra, the main center of the Barwani clan. The implication in his account is clearly that her wealth and position helped him. Brode, however, was dismissive of this idea, suggesting that Tippu Tip's marriage played no role in the loan because "the Banyan," meaning the Indian creditor, knew that Bint Salim would not cover Tippu Tip's losses, should they occur.[99] Although Brode may have had additional information about this matter because of his interviews with Tippu Tip, his written account seems to misinterpret Tippu Tip's suggestion.[100] Certainly other people used property in Oman as the basis for entering the ivory trade.[101] Unfortunately no documents from the Zanzibar deeds collection shed more light on this moment. It seems clear from Tippu Tip's account, however, that the wealth and prestige deriving from a link by marriage to this leading clan would have been to his advantage, just as his relationships with families in the interior helped in other ways.

The challenge in Tippu Tip's marriage, however, is determining exactly who it was he married and how she fit into the Barwani and Harthi clans in Zanzibar. The Salim bin Abdullah al-Barwani mentioned previously was born in 1835. Of Salim bin Abdullah's eight children, four of them were girls, but, if family records are to be trusted, none of them would have been born before 1878.[102] Other members of the family, including Salim bin Abdullah's grandson, do not mention a marriage between Tippu Tip and a daughter of Salim bin Abdullah al-Barwani.[103] The Barwani clan with property in Zanzibar and Ibra was Salim bin Abdullah's line; thus it is difficult to reconcile this description of a Barwani woman with property with the known facts. Possible explanations for this discrepancy include that his wife may have been a daughter of Salim bin Abdullah and a secondary wife or concubine, or the fact that Tippu Tip's later notoriety as a slave trader made him a distasteful relative to acknowledge. Alternatively, he may have married into another branch of the Barwani family, perhaps some of those who fled to the interior following the upheaval in Zanzibar in 1859 with the failed attempt to overthrow Sultan Majid.[104]

Barwani family marriages also illuminate how marriages strengthened kinship and business relationships, even as kin made status distinctions about children of concubines. Arabic ideals favored endogamous marriage, and the highest form of this was *bint amm*, in which a man married his paternal uncle's daughter. Such a marriage cemented relationships between siblings. As Arabs migrated to East Africa, however, it was difficult to follow such practices because of the uneven patterns of migration. An example from the Barwani family demonstrates that recent migrants tried to marry within their clan, but also married *masuria*, or concubines. These same families, once successive generations were established in East Africa, returned to the expected marriage patterns.[105]

The prominent merchant Abdullah bin Salim al-Barwani (d. 1860) was the second generation of his direct Barwani line to live in East Africa. He became a very wealthy merchant and leader of the Harthi in Zanzibar, a counterweight to Busaidi power. To neutralize this threat, Said bin Sultan had insisted that Abdullah bin Salim travel with him to Muscat from Zanzibar. Abdullah bin Salim was onboard when Said bin Sultan died at sea in 1856, and he cooperated with Barghash to seize the throne and also rose against Majid bin Said in 1859 (see chapter 3). Abdullah bin Salim's first marriage was to Salma bint Muhammad al-Barwani. His exact kinship relationship to her is unclear because the family tree maintained by the Barwani family does not include daughters, and the other detailed family history concentrates on a different line of the family.[106] She may have been Salma bint Muhammad bin Isa al-Barwani, and thus Abdullah bin Salim's first cousin, but the record is not clear. Abdullah bin Salim and Salma bint Muhammad had two sons, Salim and Said.

Abdullah bin Salim al-Barwani's other wife Bint Nangomwa, was likely from the Lindi area of the southern Swahili coast where members of the Barwani clan had engaged in both trade and agriculture since the late eighteenth century.[107] As a *suria*, her status within coastal households was better than that of other slaves, but likely not as high as Arab or free-born wives. All of the children of the Omani ruler Said bin Sultan were born of his concubines, and within the palace compounds these wives were subordinated to Said bin Sultan's Arab wife.[108] In more common coastal households, like other wives, *masuria* had their own bedrooms.[109] Abdullah and Bint Nangomwa had one son, Juma who was born in 1854.[110]

Within one family, the children of endogamous marriages and of marriages to concubines operated under different constraints. Abdullah bin

Salim and his brother Isa bin Salim arranged a marriage between their children. Salim bin Abdullah bin Salim (1835–1925), who was raised both in Ibra, Oman, and in Zanzibar, married Sharifa bint Isa bin Salim al-Barwani. This *bint amm* marriage fulfilled the ideal of marriage among Arabs and consolidated this Barwani line. Such marriages were easier to contract as immigration to Zanzibar continued and more members of the clan were living in East Africa.

Because Abdulla bin Salim did not have daughters, his brother Isa bin Salim had to look elsewhere to arrange his son's marriage. His son Ali bin Isa married Moza bint Khalfan al-Barwani from the Lindi branch of the Barwani family. Moza's brothers traveled to the interior to trade, and one of them, Muhammad bin Khalfan, better known as Rumaliza, became one of the most notorious Arab traders in the interior.[111] Moza bint Khalfan's first marriage linked branches of the Barwani family. Her subsequent marriage demonstrated the degree to which the family practiced endogamy. After Moza's husband Ali bin Isa died in 1889 or 1890, she married Abdulla bin Salim, her late husband's uncle.[112]

From a religious point of view, the children of *masuria* were equal to the other children of one father. This was not always the case, however, in social practice among Arabs in East Africa. This may explain why Juma bin Abdullah was the only one of Abdullah bin Salim's sons who needed to buy time or increase his standing by undertaking the hazards of long-distance trade to the interior.[113] While his brothers from another mother likely continued business at the coast, sometimes traveling to Oman, he entered into the rough-and-tumble ivory trade.

In the interior, Juma bin Abdullah demonstrated both the breadth and limits of kin. He provided his kinsman Muhammad bin Khalfan (Rumaliza) of the Lindi Barwanis an entrée into trade in the interior.[114] Tippu Tip, who also had a claim on Barwani kinship links through marriage, explained that after Juma and Muhammad bin Khalfan had gone to Ujiji together, Juma preceded him back to the coast. Rumaliza was to sell the remaining goods and transport the ivory to the coast. Rumaliza, however, fared poorly in trading, and lacked the trade goods necessary to secure porters to deliver the ivory to the coast. His delay in returning raised anxieties at the coast among his kinsmen and allies. Juma's accounts at the coast were overseen by Ali bin Isa al-Barwani, Juma's first cousin and the husband of Rumaliza's sister Moza.[115] Ali bin Isa wrote insisting that Rumaliza forward the tusks to the coast, but Rumaliza lacked the credit to do so. Tippu Tip, who was in Ujiji at the time and knew Ali bin Isa "like a brother," perhaps due to his Barwani marriage, underwrote Rumaliza's journey. Rumaliza repaid this, in part, by becoming one of Tippu Tip's junior partners.[116] According to Tippu Tip, whose view of Rumaliza was negatively colored by their subsequent falling out, both of the Barwani men, Ali bin Isa and Juma bin Abdullah, refused to extend further credit to their kinsmen. Relations of kinship and credit had definite limits.[117]

MARRIAGES IN THE INTERIOR

Newcomers in the interior used marriages as new relations of kinship to cement business and social ties for newcomers. In 1887, a British missionary in Buganda mocked an Arab man who lived and traded there, chiding that as soon as the Arab collected his ivory he would leave. The target of this critique, Ali bin Sultan, retorted, "I am more of a Muganda [person of Buganda] than you. My wives are all Baganda."[118] The plurality of wives and the assertion of belonging demonstrate clearly a strategy in the East African interior. By marrying daughters of chiefs or other local women, Arab, Swahili, and coastal migrants gained commercial and political footholds among autochthonous groups. Muhammad bin Juma al-Murjebi, Tippu Tip's father, provides the most prominent example of such marriages, though other traders pursued the same strategy.

Muhammad bin Juma married Karunde, the daughter of the Nyamwezi chief Fundikira. This provided the Arab traders a valuable foothold in the interior and gave Fundikira's Nyamwezi clan a set of important allies. As noted earlier, part of Muhammad bin Juma's strength in the interior was the number of Arab and coastal kinsmen with whom he traveled. The complement to this power was his local kin.

Karunde was the daughter of Fundikira's first wife. Tippu Tip points out that in those days the first wives of Nyamwezi rulers had power comparable to that of their husbands. Thus, Muhammad bin Juma was able to trade on favorable terms—as Fundikira's kin—because of his connection with the local rulers.[119] This relationship also insulated Muhammad bin Juma from other Nyamwezi rulers. The other Arabs in Tabora, for instance, deferred to Muhammad bin Juma before interfering in Nyamwezi affairs.[120] When there was cause for action—Fundikira's successor tormented Karunde's mother and brother—Muhammad bin Juma framed his appeal to the Arabs, whose intervention against Fundikira's successor he sought, in the language of kinship, especially that of maternal kin.[121] The implication was that kinship created a set of obligations. Muhammad bin Juma sought revenge, and when enough Arabs, including his son, were present he made war.[122]

Muhammad bin Juma underscored the importance of his relationship with the Nyamwezi line when, after his wife Karunde died, he married Nyaso, Fundikira's other daughter. In doing so, Muhammad bin Juma spurned the proposal floated by Mkasiwa, the then-ruler, to compel him to wed one of his daughters instead.[123] By marrying again within the same family, however, Muhammad bin Juma centralized his wealth. Tippu Tip noted that in Ituru, his father's settlement near Tabora, all the people and property belonged to Muhammad bin Juma's and his Nyamwezi wives.

Relationships between Arab men and African women were not simply strategic. Tippu Tip's account suggests real intimacy with his Nyamwezi kin.[124] Descendants living in Tabora from both sides of the family recount ongoing close relationships. The ruling family of Unyanyembe and the Arabs came to rely heavily on each other in commercial, political, and social realms.[125]

Muhammed bin Juma married twice into the Nyamwezi ruling line, but for most traders, marrying one daughter of an influential African family was enough. For example, Mwinyi Kheri, a Swahili merchant and prominent resident in Ujiji, married a daughter of a local ruler in the 1870s.[126] However, strategic marriages had to be sustained to be valuable. Kinship required a living relationship that was either ongoing or renewed. Thus, marrying two daughters within the same family was not unique among Arab traders in the interior. Said bin Habib al-Afifi was one of the most intrepid traders from Zanzibar. He left the island in 1845 and traveled to the Katanga region to trade. He proceeded to the Atlantic coast, reached Benguela in 1852, and returned to Zanzibar in 1860.[127] His subsequent career also took him to these trading areas, and he married the daughter of Major Coimbra, a Portuguese trader in the region. When she died, he married another daughter in about 1875, cementing his relationship with the well-established commercial family.[128] In a sense, these marriages united the Indian Ocean and Atlantic worlds through cross-cultural family ties in central Africa.

For most migrants in the interior, however, the main benefit of marriage was social production (and reproduction). Arab men relied on African women as free and slave wives to maintain their households. African wives were the most common, and the rare presence of Arab women may have disrupted the household. Rumaliza's home in Ujiji had many women attached to it. When the women of the household posed for a picture in 1890, two of them were not photographed with the others. They were said to be Arabian women from Muscat, a clear indication of the way Indian Ocean travel became more routinized in the last decades of the nineteenth century.[129] Although some Arab men traveled with their wives, others moved

FIGURE 5.2. Women from the household of Muhammad bin Khalfan al-Barwani (also known as Rumaliza) in Ujiji, 1890. From Edward C. Hore, "An Arab Friend in Central Africa," *The Chronicle of the London Missionary Society*, 1891.

between two households: one at the coast and another in the interior. Observers liked to make much of the grand style in which the wives of elite traders traveled, but these were rare occurrences.[130]

MARRIAGE BETWEEN THE COAST AND THE INTERIOR

While Tippu Tip's accounts show the importance of maternal kin, the claims on one's maternal line, and the potential credit benefits of marriage to wealthy women, his autobiography reveals little about the relative autonomy of women. In general, women had limited autonomy throughout the region, but the little evidence there is suggests that Indian Ocean women were more able to control their circumstances at the coast than in the interior. Some families protected the rights of their daughters by creating favorable marriage contracts with clear terms that protected the bride from upcountry travel and from a bridegroom's misrepresentations. The brother of one Swahili woman negotiated a marriage contract with her upcountry fiancé that stated that the woman would remain at the coast. If the groom attempted to take her upcountry, it would constitute grounds for divorce. The contract also protected the bride in case the upcountry suitor, presumably not well known at the coast, turned out to be a slave. This would also be grounds for divorce.[131] These conditions show that families agreed to marriages with only partial knowledge of grooms' origins and plans.

Without similar contracts, women might assert their autonomy to remain at the coast when their husbands traveled to the interior. Such negotiations did not always end well, and some women risked violence. In 1871 an English missionary, Bishop Tozer, witnessed an Arab man beating a woman. The bishop himself intervened and delivered the man to the sultan for punishment. The sultan, Barghash, determined that the woman had been a slave and confiscated her but did not charge the man. The sultan reported that the man had broken no law.[132] Tozer was certain that the man was known about town, but he was unable to establish his name. Furthermore, the Arab was preparing to depart for the interior, where he would certainly avoid punishment.[133] Was his departure, however, linked to his violence? Perhaps the assault was motivated by the woman's unwillingness to accompany him to the interior where she would give up town life and erode even more of her ability to negotiate.

As previous scholars have suggested about Mombasa in the 1890s, the behavior of women on the Swahili coast did not always follow the norms established for them.[134] Salme bint Said (b. 1844), the daughter of Said bin Sultan, certainly exceeded expected norms by learning to write in secret, managing her own plantations, carrying on an affair with a German merchant, and eloping to Aden in 1866. She converted to Christianity, moved to Germany, and became a bit player in the German scramble for Africa. More commonly, however, as early as the 1850s, a visitor to Zanzibar noted that widows refused to marry again and used their independence to engage in trade, including running plantations and dealing in slaves.[135] From available evidence, although Tippu Tip was born into a family with strong links to the caravan trade and the East African interior, his own mother and his wives remained at the coast.

As families stretched across the Indian Ocean, new kin allowed Arabs to establish themselves in new places, which in turn permitted them to practice older forms of kinship. Tippu Tip's well-known account of trade in the interior, when lined up with new archival and genealogical research, provides a framework for understanding how kinship served as an infrastructure for Arab mobility. To wit, Tippu Tip's successes in trade and diplomacy were linked tightly to his complex web of patrilineal and matrilineal kin relationships. Siblings were important as "practical kin" through which trusting and mutually beneficial relationships created influential men. Finally, marriage, like other kin relationships, was vital to the social and economic well-being of Arab migrants. Strategic marriages were sought differently at the coast, where traditional endogamous relationships were possible as a means to centralize family holdings. In the interior, links with new families were essential for survival. Freed slaves occupied a space between dependents and kin, and it is to processes of manumission that we now turn.

6 ~ Freed Slaves
Manumission and Mobility before 1873

SAID BIN MUHAMMAD AL-AGHBARI, an Omani governor in Zanzibar in the 1820s, "possessed the entire monopoly of the traffic" in slaves.[1] Even though he had a public role as a slave trafficker, he also freed many of his slaves, founded a mosque, and owned houses and farms to support the mosque and his freed slaves. The slave trade on the western shores of the Indian Ocean was obvious to the nineteenth-century European visitor who noted al-Aghbari's slave monopoly. The processes of manumission and the roles of freed slaves, however, were nearly invisible. The group of freed slaves, identified in Arabic documents as *sarīḥ*, typify the strategies of temporizing in the face of economic and social challenges. Before European pressure ended the slave trade in the late nineteenth century, manumitted slaves—like those freed by this Omani governor—owned urban and rural property, participated in trade on land and sea, and were major players in the social and economic worlds of East Africa. The practice of manumission also utilized the different juridical frameworks through which Arabs, Africans, and Indians moved in the western Indian Ocean world.

This chapter first outlines manumission from social and religious perspectives in early to mid-nineteenth-century Zanzibar to demonstrate the hidden—yet integral—roles of freed slaves in the region's economy. In response to British antislavery treaties at midcentury, a contradictory process of insincere manumission emerged. Europeans participated in a system to "free" slaves to supply labor to island plantations in the 1850s, but Muslims in Zanzibar regarded this as outside the moral economy of manumission. In contrast, slaves who were legitimately manumitted often received property and retained bonds of clientship with their former masters. Freed slaves identified themselves in formal documents using their patrons' names and lineages. These formal documents were the instruments that allowed them to buy time by selling or mortgaging property to improve their situation. As a result, *sarīḥ* developed Zanzibari neighborhoods, entered Indian Ocean commerce, and migrated to the African mainland for trade and settlement.

The dynamic regional economies of the western Indian Ocean drew European interest and slowly transformed the status of slaves. The growth of plantation economies on oceanic islands and the African mainland undercut older Indian Ocean notions of slaves as dependents and clients and created new demands for slaves as laborers. Slaves bound to their masters under the old system were more likely to gain independence or legal freedom. Like the plantation slaves in the Atlantic, western Indian Ocean plantation slaves were unlikely to be freed by their masters. At the same time, the integration of eastern Africa into the global economy brought with it an antislavery ideology that justified European interventions to end the slave trade in the western Indian Ocean.

Independent of these external pressures to end slavery, however, slaves continued to secure their freedom through local processes of manumission in accordance with Islamic practices. These manumitted slaves (*sarīḥ*) used their property holdings and Arab family ties to participate in East Africa's expanding economy by producing cloves, procuring ivory, or dealing in property. These freed slaves and their descendants took on important roles in the social and political spheres of early twentieth-century Zanzibar. Still, the nineteenth-century origins of manumitted slaves and their pivotal roles in the western Indian Ocean and its hinterlands require greater attention.[2]

For researchers, freed slaves from the mid-nineteenth century have existed only as disembodied names on lists that documented the African slaves who were captured at sea and then released to missions or members of the consular staff, as was the European practice in Zanzibar. Many of these individuals—like the freed woman Swema in the 1860s or the children of the Kiungani mission in the 1880s—were enslaved but never worked as slaves before they were freed. Their memories before and during their capture were fragmented, and their stories were passed through the filter of European missionaries.[3] These people, enslaved on the African mainland and intended for coastal plantations, would have been on the lowest rungs of the coastal social hierarchy. Coastal elites identified these slaves as uncultured and pagan, below slaves of more refined categories, such as those born into slavery at the coast, those who worked for wages outside their master's ambit, or those who were accomplished traders or tradesmen who might compete for status with freeborn individuals.

In the Indian Ocean, slaves were not simply property, and the distinction between the enslaved and the free is not the best way to understand a slave's position. Like free individuals, slaves existed in hierarchies of dependency. Individuals sought to improve their social standing by securing powerful patrons under whom they had the greatest degree of autonomy. Across such continua, freedom was not necessarily preferable to slave status, and some people were content to remain slave clients to powerful patrons.[4] Given that slave status encompassed varying degrees of autonomy within hierarchies of patronage and clientship, manumitted slaves gained greater autonomy even as they made claims as clients. As such, from at least the 1840s, manumitted slaves were active in vital sectors of the economy, and freed slaves occupied unappreciated roles in the growth of the city of Zanzibar and its suburbs.

Atkins Hamerton, the representative of the East India Company to the court of Zanzibar, estimated that one-third of the population of the archipelago in 1844 were slaves, totaling as many as 150,000 people. The proportion of slaves in the population had grown quickly in the previous decade, as Arab planters profited handsomely from clove cultivation. At least 20,000 captives per year came from the African mainland. The number of imported slaves had remained roughly steady for the first four decades of the century, enabling the economy to be scaled up, most notably in plantation agriculture. At the same time, the expanding plantation sector bifurcated the slave population, creating a new category of agricultural slaves that was distinct from the older forms of client servitude.[5] Hamerton claimed that among the latter, "The slave is well fed generally and ill-treatment of the slave on the part of the master is of very rare occurrence." These slaves were also more likely to be freed. The lives of agricultural slaves, however, were more difficult, and their annual mortality rate ranged from 22 to 30 percent. In Hamerton's opinion, though, the outlook for all slaves was not good, and their chances for collective freedom were dim. In 1844, he found that Zanzibar had "no party favourable to the abolition of slavery."[6] While no one may have advocated the broad scale abolition of slavery, private acts of manumission occurred during this period in accordance with Islamic precepts.

Freed Slaves ⤚ 147

VOLUNTARY MANUMISSION

During the nineteenth century, freedom for slaves in the western Indian Ocean came in three forms: European intervention, African resistance, and Muslim manumission. The first two represent their own historiographical categories, and they are well covered in scholarly work. The first modern historians writing about East Africa viewed slavery as the central theme of the region's history—Coupland called it a "scarlet thread" that ran through the history of East Africa—and historical accounts detailed European intervention motivated by a desire to end the slave trade. Such views have come under great scrutiny, partly because British and German colonial governments in East Africa were slow to end slavery in the late nineteenth and early twentieth centuries. These governments also worked hard to maintain local economies and comfortable relations with elites, even as they disrupted the social relations of labor. Subsequent generations of scholars—drawing on nationalist histories, neo-Marxist ideals, and the insights of subaltern studies—focused on the roles of slaves in creating more independence (and sometimes even outright freedom) for themselves.[7] The "Europeans freed the slaves" and the "slaves freed themselves" models do not account for the role of slave owners in local practices of manumission.

Slavery in Islam has not been as straightforward as most scholars have assumed, but manumission has been promoted from the earliest days of the faith. Historian Ghislaine Lydon points out that, since the time of the Prophet Muhammad, scholars and commentators have reinterpreted sources of Islamic law to justify enslavement. More recently, some scholars have argued that the sources of Islamic law do not justify enslavement.[8] Manumission, on the other hand, has always been endorsed. The Quran directs Muslims to write contracts of emancipation when sought by slaves and encourages Muslims to bestow part of their God-given wealth on freed slaves. Freeing slaves was also considered a pious act, so Islam provided both a justification and a reward for manumission. In classical jurisprudence, manumission did not sever the relationship between master and former slave, but created a new legal tie (*walā' al-'itiq*) between the parties as patron and client.[9] Thus, freed slaves had a prescribed legal relationship of rights and obligations, not with the state or with a lineage, but with an individual.

Although early Islamic legal sources laid out normative rules for manumission, they did not create a "single, coherent ideology" that structured interactions in East Africa.[10] In fact, Omani Arabs in the western Indian Ocean faced a great deal of uncertainty around manumission and patronage. They wrote numerous letters to learned Ibadi *qadis* for guidance and fatwas on these topics.[11] While Islamic legal norms were one source of motivation, Muslims who freed slaves in East Africa also followed local practices and were shaped by historical contingency. For instance, the rise of plantation slavery in the mid-nineteenth century created new categories of slaves who were much less likely to be freed. At the same time, European treaties attempted to disrupt the trade and transportation of slaves, and by the end of the century they insisted on manumission by the state. Individual manumission before and during this period was a way out of slavery that has been neglected by scholars studying the routes to freedom in the western Indian Ocean.

Local practices of manumission were invisible to outside observers. These manumissions required no state mediation and took place in the private sphere between masters and their dependents. Occasionally, when Islamic manumission did fall under the purview of European observers in Zanzibar after 1845, it was employed insincerely to subvert the escalating British treaty regime.

After considering local practices of manumission to understand who was freed and under what circumstances, this chapter considers the midcentury treaty regimes and the (mis)use of Islamic manumission to thwart them. After establishing an understanding of the process of manumission, the focus shifts to the roles that freed slaves played in the economy and society of East Africa and the western Indian Ocean. Throughout the nineteenth century, the nature of slavery changed, and European pressure on the trade increased. Men and women in bondage found freedom through Islamic processes of manumission, and freed slaves played significant roles in East African society.

Who freed their slaves? Despite the fact that well-to-do individuals were more likely to own large numbers of slaves in the nineteenth century, people in every stratum of Zanzibari society owned slaves. Fragmentary evidence suggests that voluntary manumissions also took place within every social class. For instance, a man named Baraka—who was himself a freed slave of an Indian Muslim—granted his slave Songoro freedom in October 1877 through a deed of manumission.[12] In tracing the lives of freed slaves, however, individuals linked to prominent families and powerful patrons are the most easily located through business transactions. Said bin Muhammad al-Aghbari, the monopolistic slave dealer, and Sulayman bin Hamed al-Busaidi, a kinsman and plenipotent advisor to the sultan, both freed numerous slaves. These powerful Arabs had served as governors of Zanzibar in the first half of the nineteenth century. Although it is difficult to pin down the motivations of these individuals, patterns of manumission can be seen.

The three primary influences on manumission were Islamic piety, a slave owner's circumstances, and the actions of slaves themselves. As noted above, early Islamic law encouraged manumission and provided both the incentive and justification for freeing slaves. In the nineteenth century, these early teachings found continuity Shafi'i and Ibadi ideals in the western Indian Ocean.[13] While broad notions of Islamic piety and atonement influenced masters, personal circumstances and specific social standings affected manumission. Enslaved people also shaped practices of manumission through their own accomplishments.

Islamic piety offered a justification for freeing slaves, and testamentary manumission occurred with other acts of religious charity. Wills were the last chance individual Muslims had to demonstrate piety, and freeing slaves was one way to do this. The explorer John Hanning Speke visited Zanzibar around 1860, and while he considered testamentary manumission an obligation under "the Mohammedan creed," he found that these acts were more common in Arabia than in Zanzibar. Another British visitor observed, however, that manumission at an owner's death was a common occurrence, "to give themselves a lift into the next world." The fact that slave owners saw their slaves who were autonomous clients as different from agricultural slaves may explain the discrepancy in these two opinions. Said bin Sultan, who ruled Oman and Zanzibar, composed his will in 1850 (six years before his death) and stipulated that all of his slaves should be freed after his death, except for those who worked on his plantations.[14]

In 1875, Said bin Sultan's son Barghash wrote his will before traveling to Europe. Barghash's testament demonstrates both the broad ethnic makeup of his servants and the demarcation between most of his slaves and his plantation slaves. The document specified which slaves should be freed after his death: "Georgians, Abyssinians, Baluchi, Nubians, people of the Grand Comoro, and of East Africa, who speak Arabic, all who dwell in town, and who are sailors, engineers, stokers, and all others, whoever they may be, male or female." The catalog of his slaves, their origins, their acculturations, and their occupations bear witness to the circulation of people within the western Indian Ocean. Barghash's will continued, however, with the statement that "the slaves on the plantation and in the environs excepted." The document explicitly stated that he did this to "obtain the acceptance of God" and to "escape from punishment." He commanded his heirs not to interfere with the slaves, except in service as a *wala* (i.e., a trustee or patron).[15] Several generations earlier, some of the slaves of the governor Said bin Muhammad bin Said al-Aghbari also appear to have been freed at his death, and they were bequeathed property both in and out of town.

In addition to freeing slaves, testators performed other pious acts, such as offering money for individuals to complete a pilgrimage to Mecca on their behalf or sponsoring people to fast in atonement for the deceased's failings during their lifetime. Like his father, the later sultan Barghash bin Said (d. 1888) freed slaves and provided funds to support people to fast for fifty months on his behalf.[16] Manumission was not only linked to death but occurred in accordance with the yearly religious calendar or the rhythms of a slave owner's life. The end of Ramadan, the holy month of fasting, was the most popular time for Muslims to free slaves. When Baraka manumitted his servant Songoro, the deed of freedom was dated the sixth day of the month Shawwal, less than a week after the end of fasting. The same impulse that compelled masters to write wills granting slaves their freedom might have affected aging residents of East Africa. As individuals grew older, they were more likely to free slaves, either to do something good or to acknowledge their long service.[17]

Individuals also freed slaves as penance for their marital problems. An Ibadi man who was considering divorce could take an oath of abstinence with his wife for a four-month period. At the end of this time, the couple could divorce, renew their vow of abstinence, or return to conjugal life. The only two ways to break this vow, according to the renowned Omani jurist Abdullah bin Humayd al-Salimi, was to free a slave or to foster an orphan.[18] In these cases, manumission sanctioned other actions and permitted Muslim men to return to their marriage beds.

Slaves also influenced manumission decisions. Accomplished slaves were sometimes granted freedom. Khamis wad Mtaa had been a slave as a young man, but after he demonstrated prowess as a trader on the African mainland, he was freed sometime before 1867. His name meant Khamis, the child of the neighborhood or street, and he met success along the northern Maasai caravan routes into what is now Kenya and in the slave-rich area of Lake Nyasa, near what are now the borders of Tanzania, Mozambique, and Malawi. He then became "the principal Arab" of a settlement in the eastern Congo and connected to "one of the most influential native mercantile houses in Zanzibar."[19] He thrived in the far interior, trading in both ivory and slaves.

His strategic alliances added to his trading moxy. In September 1867 he married the daughter of the Tambwe chief Nsama. Another time, when Khamis was down on his luck, he brokered a deal for Tippu Tip to buy four Yao elephant hunters.[20] Khamis had been highly mobile even when he was a slave, which led observers like David Livingstone to conflate his status (successful trader; good source of credit) with a certain race (Arab). But Khamis was almost surely of African descent.

One way female slaves could influence their manumission was by bearing the children of their masters. Such children were born free, and they were not sold or called slaves. If they were not already free, their mothers were liberated at the time of their master's death. Among highly mobile people, however, it was not always possible to know when a husband had died. Omani jurists made provisions for this scenario when a slave woman's master was presumed dead. The jurists instructed that a woman who bore her master's child and whose husband was lost at sea was freed after a waiting period of three years.[21]

Not all female slaves bore children, however, and not all slaves in the western Indian Ocean were African. While most plantation slaves in Zanzibar and the East African mainland were born in or traced their origins to Africa, urban centers were also home to captured people from the Middle East and South Asia. Some of these slaves also gained freedom. For example, an Indian woman named Mariam came to the attention of British officials in Bombay in 1846. She had been born to Hindu Rajput parents in Baroda (modern Vadodara), Gujarat, in western India in the 1820s or 1830s. After they died, she was sold to an Arab man in Bombay's Bhendi Bazaar. He first took her to Mukulla, in the Hadramawt region of Arabia, and eventually they moved to Zanzibar.

Mariam was bought and sold by a succession of Arab Muslim and Indian Khoja men. She moved among Zanzibar, Kilwa, and Bombay with her various masters, one of whom emancipated her, perhaps making it easier for her to travel at sea. In Bombay, the British officials did not know what to do with her. Mariam had become a Muslim, and she did not want to return to Baroda, her place of origin. She was willing to remain in Bombay or to return to Zanzibar, as long as someone would provide for her.[22] Mariam had been manumitted, but state intervention disrupted her position as a client. She did not seek abstract freedom, but rather a guarantee of support.

To the surprise of many nineteenth-century observers, some slaves in Zanzibar did not want to be free. In the 1860s, a man identified as Buckett (perhaps properly spelled Bhukhīt) worked as an interpreter for the Royal Navy and dressed in crimson and fine linen. Although he was the slave of an aged Arab woman, he did not seek freedom from slavery. Buckett had achieved a degree of autonomy that transcended the dichotomous relationship between free and slave. As Glassman has pointed out, slaves on the Swahili coast "did not struggle for 'freedom' and a complete break with slavery," but for "powerful patrons who would give them the opportunity to participate vigorously and autonomously in coastal society."[23] Buckett worked

MAP 6.1. Itineraries of manumission

independently of his mistress and dressed as he pleased. And though he worked for the British navy assisting in their enforcement of antislavery treaties and their attempts to end the slave trade, his autonomy did not require manumission.

ANTISLAVERY TREATIES AND INSINCERE MANUMISSION

British treaties with the Arab rulers of Zanzibar increasingly tightened restrictions on the transport and trade of slaves in 1822, 1839, 1845, 1873, and 1890. These treaties, which also promoted British trade, were a cause and consequence of the growing leverage that British merchants and diplomats imposed on the rulers of Zanzibar. The more restrictive treaties after 1845 also had an unintended consequence: increasing Islamic manumissions. Muslims complicit in the sale and transport of slaves granted manumissions to move their slaves more easily across the Indian Ocean. These insincere manumissions ran afoul of both local understandings of Islam and imperial policy, but they illustrate how plantation slavery transformed slave practices in the Indian Ocean. These insincere acts also demonstrate how Islamic mechanisms of manumission complemented British predilections for written documents.

Despite the treaties, the East African slave trade continued because neither the British nor the sultan could enforce laws against it. The 1845 treaty, for instance, made it illegal to export slaves from the sultan's domains, but neither Britain nor the sultan committed naval resources to suppress the slave trade. Early assumptions that the all-powerful sultan could bring an end to the slave trade were incorrect. As Hamerton observed in 1850, Said bin Sultan's "orders to his people on any occasion are or are not obeyed by them just as it suits their own interests to do so."[24] The relative independence of the sultan's Arab subjects typified the Ibadi political ideology of Oman, which regarded a just ruler as the first among equals. The sultan's forces also felt deep ambivalence about the treaty regime. Hamerton informed the Foreign Office "that the Imam of Maskat has not an officer in his service who pays the slightest attention to His Highness's orders relative to the suppression of the slave trade."[25]

While British officials doubted the effectiveness of the 1845 treaty, slave traders and labor agents did in fact change their practices to conform to the letter of the treaty. Since the 1770s, the slave trade from the Swahili coast had been oriented toward Ile de France and Ile de Bourbon in the Indian Ocean.[26] In subsequent years, French traders and their agents negotiated contracts with the Sultan of Kilwa and other coastal residents, and they sent representatives to Oman to palaver there. In 1814, following the Napoleonic Wars, the British took control of Ile de France and renamed it Mauritius, and the demand for labor on both islands remained high. The Moresby Treaty of 1822 had attempted to limit the import of slaves to the islands, and the 1845 treaty aimed to replace slave labor with free labor by outlawing the export of slaves from Zanzibar. Neither treaty, however, managed to end slavery in the sultan's domain. In fact, the conditions of the treaty created a loophole that was easy to exploit. In Zanzibar, Said bin Sultan had agreed that free laborers in his dominions could become contract laborers on Mauritius or Bourbon. What he did not anticipate, however, was that slaves would be bought and freed specifically to fit this designation.[27]

In September 1851, the sultan's forces stopped a French brig sailing from Zanzibar and found twelve men aboard who had recently been purchased at the Zanzibar market. Surprisingly, in the brief time since their purchase, these slaves had been manumitted and had agreed to a five-year labor contract in Mauritius. A subsequent investigation found that French traders and their agents had co-opted local practices of manumission to create "free" labor.[28] Muslim agents in Zanzibar—some Arab, some Swahili, some free, and some slave—bought and freed slaves. French recruiters paid them for each manumission, so pecuniary motivations likely overshadowed pious ones. It was not long before Omani and British authorities challenged these insincere manumissions.[29]

The British representative Atkins Hamerton feared that the Gulf Arabs who traded seasonally in Zanzibar would exploit this same loophole, rendering the 1845 treaty moot. These so-called Northern Arabs sailed with the monsoon winds in October or November from Persian Gulf ports and the coastal Omani town of Sur to the Swahili coast. Said bin Sultan, the Omani ruler in Zanzibar, was intimidated by their seasonal presence, and British consuls viewed Northern Arabs as the prime culprits in the slave trade. Earlier in 1851, Hamerton wrote to the British naval commander in the Indian Ocean, expressing his pleasant surprise that slave brokers had heeded the sultan's admonition against selling slaves to the Northern Arabs: "this is the first time I have ever known the Imam's orders strictly obeyed by any of his people."[30]

Six months later, the implications of the manumission loophole that created opportunities to secure "free" labor worried Hamerton immensely. He predicted the Northern Arabs "will furnish these Free labourers in thousands because it will be the best and indeed almost the only market open to them in the dominions of the Imam of Maskat—for the sale of slaves."[31] Official British documents ascribe a wiliness to the Arabian dhow captains that recalls historian Lauren Benton's notion of "pirates as lawyers." Benton argues that pirates—or in this case slave traffickers—were not lawless, but rather steeped in normative legal practices and the documents that supported them.[32] Their efforts to conform to the letter of the law reveal their savvy. The manipulation of documents and laws became increasingly common practices in the face of more stringent British enforcement. Initially, however, the primary challenge to the treaty's loophole came from Arabs in Zanzibar.

Among the Arab elite in Zanzibar, the opposition to insincere manumission was moral and religious in nature. Said bin Sultan and "all of the respectable Arabs," in Hamerton's view, opposed the French maneuvers on Islamic grounds: "man may call it what he likes but . . . God knows what it really is." Three years later, insincere manumission had not abated, and the sultan wrote to the British Secretary of State for Foreign Affairs to condemn the recruiters from Ile de Bourbon who were paying Arabs to buy and free slaves. He explained, "such business is at variance with the Mahammedan [sic] religion."[33]

The sultan did not detail the reasons he opposed the practice, but they may have stemmed from the moral economy of manumission as much as any Islamic tenet. Freeing low status, unacculturated slaves who could not function as clients did not fit local practices of manumission. In fact, slave owners might have seen such slaves as unfit for *walā' al-'itiq* and thus undeserving of their good intentions. As Said bin Sultan's will demonstrated, he did not believe that such slaves should be freed. They were a different class of slaves, bound for plantation labor. For some local traders and their French partners, however, this moral economy of manumission mattered less than the simple certification of freedom. With the imposition of the treaty regime, older forms of writing took on new authority. But this would change.

WORDS IN DEEDS

For both the owner and the slave, a deed of manumission was at the center of the act of freeing a slave. From these deeds and Arabic business contracts, it is possible to see clearly how freed slaves shaped the evolution of Zanzibar town and how they participated in all sectors of the economy.

Deeds of manumission were written in Arabic, and they followed a prescribed formula to establish the slave's freedom. Although a late nineteenth-century Swahili speaker recalled that some slave owners wrote these documents themselves, the technical nature of these deeds led most owners to enlist a *qadi* (Islamic judge) or scribe to write for them. For instance, the *qadi* Abdullah bin Ali bin Muhammad al-Mundhri wrote the 1877 deed when Baraka—himself a freed slave—manumitted his servant Songoro. Documents like these from earlier periods are rarely found in the archives of Zanzibar, but the formulae used in these manumissions served as the basis for the deeds of freedom issued by the British protectorate government after

1897.³⁴ These documents held the most value for the freed slaves, since they established their autonomy and offered protection from reenslavement. Some freed slaves even stored these "writings," as they called them, in small silver boxes and wore them around their necks.³⁵

Arabic deeds that recorded business transactions have been vital in the identification of the slaves and freed slaves in mid-nineteenth century Zanzibar. In these documents, freed slaves positioned themselves in relation to their former owners and identified themselves following Arabic naming practices, including names, lineages, indications of status, and clan membership. Such discursive practices should not be seen only as signs of subordination. When slaves became free, they assumed *walā' al-'itiq*, the legal category of client to their former master. This contractual relationship formalized the reciprocal demands that both individuals could make.³⁶

The practice of slaves and freed slaves identifying with their masters' lineage and clan began in the mid-nineteenth century, if not before. In 1846, for example, Mgingira—the freed slave (*sarīḥ*) of Gharib walid Musa, the slave of Sultan Arshad al-Ghaythi—sold his farm at Bonde la Mzungu, Zanzibar, to the customs master, Jairam Shivji.³⁷ In the document that recorded the transaction, Mgingira included all his names and associations—indicating his status as the freed slave of another slave—and his seemingly distant tie to an Omani clan active in Zanzibar. These ties remained important: More than a decade later Mgingira arranged a loan with a Zanzibar creditor that would be paid back, in part, with ivory. The loan was guaranteed by the son of his former master, Muhammad bin Gharib, a successful ivory trader working in the eastern Congo.³⁸

While scholars should not believe that the identities recorded in legal documents were a slave's only identities, these documents still offer more details with which to identify slaves than had previously been available. Scholars have convincingly argued that slaves' names and identities were unstable over time. Both enslaved and free residents of the coast changed their names to disguise their identities or to create new ones. Both owners and abolitionists gave slaves and freed slaves new names, and freed slaves refashioned names and identities to suit their own purposes.³⁹ Against the fluidity of identity, fixed documents remain an important way to identify individual freed slaves and their activities.

Arabic-language business documents provide a wealth of information about slaves, including their individual names, stories, and histories, which were all deeply embedded in the social and economic processes of the western Indian Ocean. These documents include an individual's first name followed by his or her lineage. The terms *bin* (son of) or *bint* (daughter of)

Freed Slaves ⇌ 157

introduce the lineage and show the gender of slaves in cases of unusual names. Sometimes the father's name is included as the lineage, but because of the slaves' place as outsiders, not all records include lineage information. Following first names and lineages, individuals are identified by their status and relationship to others. Statuses included *sarīh* (manumitted slaves), *khādim* (slaves or servants), *wakīl* (representatives), and *dalāl* (brokers), and these statuses preceded the person's name to whom they were linked. That individual was also identified by name, lineage, and an adjective that often revealed the clan's place of origin.

For example, in 1847, a freed slave named Twakali sold a plot of land to Jairam Shivji's firm for MT$23.50. The name and identifying details of the seller as translated from Arabic are *Twakali sarīh Haramil bin Said al-Ghaythi*. Twakali listed no father or lineage information. Instead, Twakali was the freed slave of Haramil, the son of Said. Haramil bin Said was a member of the al-Ghaythi clan, a group that originated in the Sharqiya region of Oman. Many members of this clan relocated to Zanzibar during the reign of Said bin Sultan. Although there is little specific information about Twakali, this brief contract makes larger patterns more apparent. For instance, from the few details about Twakali's property, its location, and associated clan name, it appears that several freed slaves and members of the al-Ghaythi family sold land in the 1840s.[40] Because the naming practices encoded the relationship of freed slaves and masters, it is possible to trace the actions of an extended group of freed slaves, all of whom were connected to one family.

THE FREED SLAVES OF AL-AGHBARI

Said bin Muhammad al-Aghbari, a governor of Zanzibar in the 1820s, was said to have a monopoly on the slave trade. What did not survive in any European accounts, however, is the frequency with which he liberated his slaves. While his pious endowments became some of the most important (and fought over) lands in Zanzibar at the start of the twentieth century, the activities of his manumitted slaves in the first half of the nineteenth century shaped the development of Zanzibar and its suburbs.

Said bin Muhammad al-Aghbari's governorship preceded Said bin Sultan's relocation of his capital to Africa. Little is known of al-Aghbari's life, but documents attest to his pious endowments, his property holdings, and his manumissions, which formed his legacy. He built a mosque that bears his name in the Forodhani neighborhood of Zanzibar town and dedicated seven houses and a plot of land to support the mosque's upkeep. The al-Aghbari clan has its roots in Wadi al-Tayyin in Oman, and it is considered part of the al-Ruwahi grouping. Historian Calvin Allen has suggested that in the early decades of the nineteenth century, substantial property holdings in Oman were a prerequisite for a governorship on the Swahili coast. Seyyid Said bin Sultan wanted to be able to ensure his governors' loyalty, and as a precaution he changed governors frequently.[41]

Despite his service and legacy in East Africa, Said bin Muhammad al-Aghbari maintained his connections with Oman. Shortly after he served as governor of Zanzibar, at a time when others suggested that he enrich himself through the slave trade, al-Aghbari's family gave their name to a mosque in Oman's Sumayl valley. One inscription on that mosque quotes the Quran, urging men not to let merchandise or sales beguile them away from their faith.[42] This hints at the tensions in Oman between the draw of trade and mobility on the one hand, and the settled life of the Ibadis in the interior on the other. We can also read it as self-justifying: profits from East Africa's trade made it possible to underwrite new mosques and sites of Islamic learning.

Perhaps financial success and religious piety both motivated Said bin Muhammad al-Aghbari to manumit his slaves. One cannot reconstruct his entire household and its dependents, but records indicate that Said bin Muhammad liberated at least five of his slaves, giving them allotments of land in and beyond Zanzibar. The freed slaves of al-Aghbari owned property outside of town, where other slaves and freed people lived, but they also had houses in town, close to well-respected religious and trading families.[43]

In the 1850s, Fundi Warya bin Makabangi, a *sarīh* (freed slave) of Said bin Muhammad al-Aghbari, owned a house in the Baghani section of Zanzibar town. "Fundi" as a name or title suggests that Fundi Warya had skills and already possessed a degree of autonomy before manumission. Like other skilled men in his position, he bought this property as a way of attracting clients. Since he was the son of Makabangi, he was probably born at the coast and was thus more acculturated than slaves of lower status. Baghani was one of the town's most prosperous quarters and was home to the Zanzibar branch of the Barwani clan, an illustrious group in the histories of Zanzibar and Oman.

While most of Zanzibar in 1850 was "covered by small square mud huts" with thatched roofs and low doorways, new buildings were sprouting up. As profits from plantations and trade grew, Arabs built imposing stone houses in Zanzibar and took great pride in them. These giant stones houses, fronted with elaborately carved doors, served as warehouses, reception halls, and dwellings. In 1856, a visitor to Zanzibar commented on the competition between merchants: "The higher the tenement, the bigger the gateway, the heavier the padlock, and the huger the iron studs which nail the door to heavy timber, the greater is the owner's dignity." One of the grandest stone houses was a seafront building not far from Baghani called, tauntingly, "Mambo Msiige," Swahili for "Something Not to be Imitated."[44]

Fundi Warya was in no position to imitate this. In 1857, his house was wattle and daub, topped with a thatched palm roof. Fundi Warya's dwelling was typical in Swahili settlements, and it demonstrates the heterogeneity of Zanzibar's "Stone Town" in this early period. Historian Felicitas Becker has recently called for work that "brings the mud huts back into [town] history, alongside the patrician palaces," to integrate the analyses of town and country in East Africa.[45] In the early 1870s, a Zanzibar resident observed that "negro huts" were all over the city, though in greater concentrations in Malindi and Ng'ambo. Houses such as Fundi Warya's in Baghani were valuable for their locations, although still a fraction of the value of their thick-walled neighbors. When Fundi Warya sold his house in 1857, he received MT$730 from Jairam Shivji, the customs master. For comparison's sake, in 1877, a stone house adjacent to Fundi Warya's plot sold for MT$8,000.[46]

Other freed slaves of al-Aghbari owned property in Sokomuhogo, the commercial quarter of Zanzibar. The house of Amur bin Swedan, another *sarīḥ* of al-Aghbari, was adjacent to two ends of Zanzibar's social ladder. On one side he neighbored Salim bin Būrūt, also a freed slave of al-Aghbari, and on another, Ahmad bin Sayyid Ahmed Jamal al-Layl. The Jamal al-Layl clan was from the Hadramaut region of Yemen, and had spread throughout the Indian Ocean from Borneo to the Swahili coast and further south to Madagascar. Noted for their religious learning, this family included scholars and poets renowned in East Africa from as early as the sixteenth century. Migration of the Jamal al-Layl clan within East Africa and from the Hadramaut increased in the nineteenth century because al-Busaidi rule fostered both trade and religious learning.

This particular Ahmad Jamal al-Layl might have been more closely involved in commerce than religious teaching but his presence alongside these freed slaves shows that, based on the limited evidence available, freed slaves controlled property in the heart of the city. As the nineteenth century progressed, however, they sold these houses. The heterogeneous composition of the town in this earlier period reflects the vital economy and the fluid lines within it. Not only could slaves gain their freedom through their own efforts or their master's inclinations, freed slaves also associated with elite members of society. This illustrates older Indian Ocean forms of layered sovereignty that later colonial governments sought to stifle and realign.[47]

Freed slaves also controlled property outside the town, and the settlement of these lands shaped the city's growth. The peninsula of Zanzibar's old town was separated from the main part of the island by a tidal creek. The area across the creek and east of town came to be called Ng'ambo (literally "the other side"). Due to changes in land tenure and Zanzibar's expansion during the late nineteenth-century economic boom, Ng'ambo became the African quarter. Slaves freed by Islamic means helped to facilitate this transition, and by the early twentieth century, as historian Laura Fair has shown, freed slaves and their descendants were leading political organizations and demanding rights for people living in Ng'ambo.[48]

In the early nineteenth century, however, Omani Arabs acquired large tracts of land in Ng'ambo through claims, grants, and seizures. The plantations they established were known as *viunga* (singular *kiunga*), denoting land close to town. They were used to cultivate fruit trees. Over time, as property passed from Arab landowner to manumitted slaves and their descendants or to Indian creditors, *kiunga* came to mean "suburb" or "outskirt." Some of the largest holders of *kiunga* lands were Omani Arabs. Sultan bin Muhammad bin Habis al-Muharmi, for instance, had extensive fields in the Welezo area of Ng'ambo. Arab governors in Zanzibar, with links to the royal family and political power did even better. Sulayman bin Hamed al-Busaidi (c. 1782–1873) was a member of the royal family who also served as governor of Zanzibar and used his position to confiscate land. His predecessor as governor was Said bin Muhammad al-Aghbari. While others observed that al-Aghbari used his position to profit from the slave trade, he may also have leveraged the governorship to acquire large *viunga* landholdings. Part of al-Aghbari's *viunga* holdings were in Welezo, and he divided his property among his manumitted slaves.[49]

These manumitted individuals and their property holdings in Welezo were indicative of the change in ownership and occupancy in Ng'ambo in the late nineteenth and early twentieth centuries. In 1895, an English visitor described Welezo's hill as "one of the most beautiful sites on the island." She went on to note that, "in the morning light, with the sunshine full on it, the town looked like a city full of palaces set in the bluest of blue settings. The native quarter is hardly visible, but we could see the Cathedral spire and the Sultan's Clock Tower."[50] By 1895, Zanzibar had been a British Protectorate for five years, and the abolition of slavery was still two years away. The city and its suburbs, however, had been undergoing a transformation for some time. In the early 1870s—when at least three of al-Aghbari's slaves sold their plots in Welezo—the Sultan's clock tower and cathedral spire were not yet built, and the "native quarter" was just coming into being.

Although the ruling elite created the links between the town and Ng'ambo in the 1840s, Ng'ambo's centrality as a site of commerce and residence resulted from the efforts of petty traders and small-scale property owners like the people manumitted by al-Aghbari. In the 1840s, the sultan built a bridge over the tidal creek that separated Stone Town from the rest of Zanzibar so that he could more easily reach his palace in Mtoni. This made movement easier between town and its periphery. The area on the other side of the bridge became an important commercial center, where merchants rented small shops and lived above or near them. During this time, the *viunga* areas near town became the residential neighborhoods of current and former slaves who worked as contract or domestic laborers. Some lived rent free on the properties of their masters; others owned their own small plots.

The Zanzibar economy grew quickly in the 1870s, and Indian merchants began to invest in land to generate income for other ventures. These ventures included redeemable sales and mortgages to underwrite ivory caravans. Historian Laura Fair has shown that property ownership in Zanzibar was not usually based on deeds of title, yet freed slaves held paper titles to their properties in Ng'ambo for more than a quarter century before the abolition of slavery. While some freed slaves sold their land during the 1870s and after, many others retained their rights to it. Fair demonstrates how freed slaves and their descendants were vital to twentieth-century development in Ng'ambo, and they were the first to challenge the depersonalization of tenancy and they led the groundrent strike in the 1920s.[51] The roots of these associations, however, were in the nineteenth century, when freed slaves—such as those of al-Aghbari—gained control of property in Ng'ambo. The impact of freed slaves, however, was not limited to Zanzibar town and its suburbs.

FREED SLAVES IN THE INDIAN OCEAN AND AFRICA

Using their relationships with their former masters or their ability to mortgage properties that they owned, manumitted slaves from Zanzibar traded across the Indian Ocean and along the African caravan trails. Freed slaves played a vital and unrecognized role in the economy of the western Indian Ocean before abolition.

Patronage networks enabled freed slaves to engage in a wide range of activities. Since manumission most often accrued to elite slaves whose efforts had won favor with their masters, it is not surprising that these people continued to be treated as valued clients by their patrons. The powerful governor and chief minister Sulayman bin Hamed al-Busaidi was a cousin and advisor to Said bin Sultan, and he was one of the most powerful men in East Africa. He parlayed his governorship to become one of Zanzibar's most extensive property holders. When Said bin Sultan moved between Oman and Zanzibar in the 1840s he was wary of Sulayman's power. Sulayman outlived the sultan and went on to be a principal adviser to sultans Majid (r. 1856–1870) and Barghash (r. 1870–1888) before he died in his nineties. Sulayman had good relations with foreign dignitaries—Queen Tsiomeko of Nosy Be in western Madagascar singled him out for greetings—and with local indigenous rulers—the Mwinyi Mkuu, Zanzibar's traditional ruler, and his family had multiple ties to him.[52] In Zanzibar, Sulayman possessed town houses, plantations, and slaves. The number of slaves he manumitted is unknown, but two of them used their relationship to their powerful patron to access unusual wealth and power—one in the Indian Ocean trade, and one as an autonomous ruler on the mainland.

Shorkah bin Omah, a trusted former slave of Sulayman bin Hamed al-Busaidi, became wealthy through his Indian Ocean trading activities, and his kinsmen outmaneuvered his former master to claim his estate. Shorkah undertook trading expeditions to Madagascar from the late 1830s, perhaps serving as an agent for his former master. When Shorkah died in Tamatave, Madagascar in 1840, he left property there. Sulayman bin Hamed believed that he was entitled to a share of Shorkah's wealth and agreed to divide the estate with one of the sultan's sons. The sultan dispatched Membec, the late Shorkah's brother, on a British trading ship to recover what he could, and Membec recovered MT$75,000. Membec was not as loyal to his brother's former master as his brother might have been. When the sultan sent another ship from Zanzibar to retrieve Membec, Membec fled to the African mainland.[53] Thus while Shorkah worked within his former master's patronage network to enrich himself, Membec's actions showed that autonomy and mobility allowed those like him to chart their own course.

Another one of Sulayman bin Hamed al-Busaidi's clients ruled a large settlement on the African mainland, near a crossroads for coastal and interior traders. In 1873, Farhan, the autonomous ruler of a large village near Rehenneko, identified himself as a slave of the Zanzibari chief minister, signaling his current status as the minister's client. Although the sources do not indicate whether Farhan had been manumitted, his independence suggests that he had. Farhan's location near Rehenneko, at the base of the Usagara Mountains, was a common place to find freed slaves from Zanzibar, and it was certainly within Sulayman bin Hamed's ambit.

Before this time, an independent leader named Kisabengo had made a strategic alliance with Sulayman bin Hamed to establish a chiefdom near

Freed Slaves ⇝ 163

the Uluguru Mountains on the mainland. Sulayman's powerful reputation and his ready supply of arms and troops helped Kisabengo to victory. The area Kisabengo ruled became an important stop on the east–west caravan route, connecting Zanzibar and the new Indian Ocean settlements of the far interior, and Kisabengo acknowledged his ongoing debt to Sulayman. By the early 1870s, Rehenneko was home to settled Omani Arab traders, disgruntled mixed-race caravaners trying to collect debts, and an African population "all well-dressed after the fashion of the slaves at Zanzibar."[54] While Farhan may not have been the model for such fashion, his dual roles as a patron connected to the caravan sector and a client to a powerful patron demonstrate the embeddedness of freed slaves within the economy and networks of eastern Africa.

Even without powerful patrons, freed slaves could participate in procuring ivory, which was one of Zanzibar's biggest exports. Having received small plots of land in town or in Zanzibar's suburbs, freed slaves entered the lucrative ivory trade by leveraging fixed property in exchange for time to collect the tusks. Some sold their plots outright, and others transacted redeemable sales over fixed periods of time, a long-standing practice in Islamic commerce. Caravan trips to the ivory-rich regions of the far interior frequently lasted more than a year, and redeemable sales provided freed slaves with the capital and time to acquire tusks. Indeed, freed slaves used patronage and property to establish themselves in the western Indian Ocean world.

Islamic manumission was common under Busaidi rule even before Said bin Sultan moved to Zanzibar. In the early years, freeing slaves took place in the family sphere, but antislavery treaties distorted the practice and led to insincere manumissions. These manipulations of Islamic practices followed treaty regimes but offended the moral economy of manumission in Zanzibar. More typical manumissions created a bond of patronage between the master and the freed slave and often granted the freed slave property. Freed slaves identified themselves in relation to their patrons, and they parlayed property to their own advantages, developing new neighborhoods in Zanzibar, trading across the Indian Ocean, or participating in the caravan trade of the African mainland.

7 ∾ Acts for Consuls and Consular Acts
Documents, Manumission, and Ocean Travel after 1873

ON JUNE 2, 1873, the sultan of Zanzibar, Barghash bin Said, had run out of time. British consul John Kirk once again presented a treaty for him to sign that would abolish the trade in slaves from Zanzibar, close all slave markets, protect liberated slaves, and prohibit Indians from owning slaves. Since the 1822 Moresby treaty, created during the reign of Barghash's father, Said bin Sultan, the Zanzibar sultans had walked a tightrope on this issue, trying to appease their British allies while also overseeing a productive and symbolic economy that was dependent on slaves. Barghash had spent the first half of 1873 negotiating the terms, delaying an agreement, and refusing to sign.

Barghash had good reasons to demure. A devastating hurricane had flattened over two-thirds of Zanzibar's clove and coconut trees during the previous year, hobbling the island's economy.[1] The sultan believed that additional slave labor was the only thing that could restore the tree plantations. While the new treaty did not end the status of slavery, it prohibited the trade in and movement of slaves. Faced with the new treaty, Barghash said no so many times in so many ways for over five months that Sir Bartle Frere—the special envoy sent to negotiate the treaty—left the island in a fit of pique.[2] On June 2, Kirk delivered an ultimatum: sign the treaty, or the Royal Navy would blockade the island. This was not a negotiation. "I have not come to discuss but to dictate," Kirk said. Barghash was able to delay briefly once more, but three days later he signed the treaty.[3]

The hurricane of 1872 and the antislavery treaty of 1873 create an inflection point in the history of Zanzibar and the western Indian Ocean. Historian Abdul Sheriff argues that 1873 marks the rise of British paramountcy in Zanzibar.[4] What did this rise mean for the mobility of Africans, Arabs, and Indians in the western Indian Ocean and how did this more aggressive stance against slavery affect the process of manumission? In short, it created more paperwork. The new treaty and its enforcement introduced new layers of bureaucracy that became central to British entanglements with the overlapping political economies of the Indian Ocean rim. Indeed, the treaty was part of what we might call a documentary regime in the Indian Ocean that both created a new juridical framework and gave new prominence to consular courts and to notarized documents that conformed to the new framework.[5] This chapter shows the widespread effects of this documentary regime from the 1850s to the 1870s. During this period new bureaucratic practices reconfigured the manumission of slaves, the subjecthood of Indians, the arbitration of commercial disputes, and the mobility of Africans in the Indian Ocean. The office of the British consul and its consular court became increasingly important in day-to-day interactions, yet consular officials were ill-equipped to deal with the multilayered social relations that defined the Indian Ocean. In the 1870s and beyond, mobile Africans, Arabs, and Indians were linked as kin, as patrons, and as clients, and in some cases as masters and slaves. The 1873 antislavery treaty created new incentives for manumission and the documentary requirements invited insincerity for households on the move. When multiethnic households left Africa to travel to India or Arabia they encountered a racialized gradient of mobility in the western Indian Ocean. Indians and Arabs could move with few impediments, but the Royal Navy assumed that all Africans at sea were slaves unless proven otherwise. The period from 1873 to 1884 marked the Royal Navy's most sustained commitment to antislavery in the Indian Ocean, and throughout this period the *HMS London* was moored at Zanzibar.[6] The crews of the *London* and other ships, however, depended on passes and notarized statements to determine the status of Africans at sea. Thus this racialized gradient of mobility was created and enforced through documents.

This chapter sets the rise of this documentary regime against the background of British efforts from the 1850s to subsume all Indians under consular control, motivated by commercial and antislavery impulses. At the same time that consular courts gained traction for resolving commercial disputes, Afro-Indian families who defied bureaucratic categorization used

FIGURE 7.1. Sultan Barghash bin Said al-Busaidi in 1875. Image courtesy of the Melville J. Herskovits Library of African Studies, Winterton Collection, Northwestern University.

legal fictions abetted by the consulate to leave East Africa. Africans linked to Arab families as wives and dependents also occupied ambiguous statuses, and their movements from the African interior to the coast and onto Arabia threw these into stark relief. While the 1873 treaty and the documentary regime sought to close loopholes and regulate Indian Ocean mobility, African, Arabs, and Indians found ways to forestall its effects while maintaining the fluidity that had long been a hallmark of the western Indian Ocean.

INSINCERE MANUMISSION IN THE AGE OF ABOLITION

In 1877, a man named Mabrook [Mubarak] walked alone into the British consulate in Zanzibar, carrying his deed of manumission and one rupee. The rupee covered the fee to register the manumission document. In exchange, Mabrook walked out with a new paper permitting him to travel by sea to Arabia. No longer enslaved, he was free to move across the ocean. He traveled with Peer Muhammad bin Shahdad, a Baluchi trader and shopkeeper. Peer Muhammad had purchased Mabrook in Kilwa in 1876, three years after the new antislavery treaty went into effect. The pair traveled to Zanzibar but only remained there for one month. During that time, Peer Muhammad wrote a deed of manumission and the sultan signed it. Mabrook registered this document at the British consulate, while Peer Muhammad waited outside.[7]

Whether these travelers had to show their documents at the port in Zanzibar or after they left the sultan's waters on the way to Arabia is not known. When other ships were stopped during this period, however, the presence or absence of consular documents largely determined the outcomes. Africans who lacked proper papers were "liberated," and the Vice Admiralty Court would condemn the ship. "Liberated" Africans were not returned to their home regions, but put ashore and entrusted to particular patrons, such as European missionaries or the consular interpreter.[8] Others were sent to colonies and outposts where labor was needed. One group of liberated Africans was sent from Zanzibar to Natal in South Africa.[9] As historian Jeremy Prestholdt has noted, these practices that followed the freeing of slaves carried many of the symbolic markings and practices of enslavement.[10]

In the late 1870s, Muscat had a diverse population, so Mabrook and Peer Muhammad, as an African and a Baluchi, would have blended in easily. Of the estimated forty thousand people who lived in the area, Africans comprised a quarter of the population, and Baluchis an eighth.[11] It is difficult to ascertain how many Africans in Muscat were slaves. In the early 1860s, a

British officer claimed that the number of slaves in the capital was relatively small, and the wealthiest households only had two or three slaves.[12] In any case, Mabrook and Peer Muhammad lived together near Muscat, and like many residents of the capital they traveled to the Batinah region in the summer for the annual date harvest.[13] Four years later, though, this pattern came to an end. Peer Muhammad wanted to sell Mabrook.

While selling a manumitted slave might seem impossible, the practice was increasingly common after the 1873 treaty. The documents became central to the issue. Officials at Aden sometimes failed to give "free papers" to slaves released by the Vice Admiralty Court, and officials in Zanzibar declared that such people were "unsafe in these dominions without them."[14] In simple economic terms, the abolition of the slave trade had driven up the demand and price for slaves.[15] Thus kidnapping and reenslavement became increasingly common.[16] One notorious kidnapping technique in East Africa involved enticing people with sweetmeats before seizing them for shipment to Arabia. The perpetrators were known as *tende halwa* (sweet dates), and the name came to be slang for northern Arabs visiting Zanzibar.[17] A manumission paper, however, offered a line of defense against slave traffickers. By definition, someone who was manumitted could not be a slave. In Mabrook's case, however, he had no recourse to the manumission document because Peer Muhammad confiscated it sometime after their trip to the Zanzibar consulate in 1877. Four years later, when Peer Muhammad threatened to sell him, Mabrook sought the British consul in Muscat and told his story. Mabrook's conundrum was not a new phenomenon. The British consul noted that it was "becoming a very common practice to import Negroes into Arabia by means of Free papers which are shown to Her M[ajesty]'s Cruizers and afterwards destroyed."[18] The newly required documents enabled the very mobility they sought to suppress.

Mabrook's journey from Zanzibar to Muscat skated the line between licit and illicit movement because the documents were manipulated to satisfy the British naval patrols. His tale highlights how treaties imposed limitations on African mobility; how Islamic processes of manumission—both sincere and insincere—worked long before colonial abolition; how writing and documents were becoming more important in everyday lives; and how overlapping (and sometimes contradictory) regimes of law and sovereignty worked in East Africa, on the Indian Ocean, and in Oman. These factors all influenced the movement of Africans from East Africa. But whereas antislavery policies treated all Africans as slaves, Africans also belonged to mixed-race families, labored as traders, and did contract work. After the 1873 treaty, the documentary regime for Africans to travel in the Indian Ocean created a new round of insincere manumissions, and it also demonstrated that Africans moved in similar ways to Arabs and Indians.

British consular officials oversaw a documentary regime in Zanzibar that both facilitated and controlled the movement of Africans across the Indian Ocean.[19] British naval patrols regularly stopped ships to inspect their cargoes and papers.[20] Whereas Indians and Arabs could move with relative ease through ports, British officials treated Africans with more scrutiny. This scrutiny was the legacy of antislavery campaigns and an ever-tightening noose of restrictions on transporting slaves from the dominions of Zanzibar that began in the 1850s and became most stringent after the 1873 treaty.

EXPANDING CONSULAR COURTS AND GAINING INDIAN SUBJECTS

The late 1850s documentary regime in the British consulate was part of an expansive view of imperial sovereignty in the India Ocean. The new British Consul, C. P. Rigby, arrived in Zanzibar in 1858 two years after the death of Said bin Sultan. Rigby believed that British influence was waning on the island due to the ongoing succession dispute between Said's sons and to the 1857 revolt in India. The flourishing slave trade was evidence to Rigby of lost British prestige, and he used the consular courts to reign in the trade and extend control over Indians in East Africa. He cracked down on slave-trading Indians and freed their slaves. While Rigby's other interventions had helped Majid bin Said fend off his brothers and consolidate power in 1859, by 1861, Majid was arguing against further restrictions on the slave trade and pointing out the deleterious effects of Rigby's actions. Emancipating the slaves owned by Indian Muslims and Hindu traders compromised local businesses, hurt trade, decreased import revenue, and led to individual bankruptcies. Majid protested, "if I put a stop to the traffic in slaves it will ruin these countries, and it will ruin my subjects, and I am certain that the British G[overnment] would agree to this. For the British G[overnment] is far off, and is ignorant of the circumstances of these countries."[21]

Rigby had to confront the fact that many Indians in Zanzibar were not, in fact, British subjects. Given their long residences in the dominion of the sultan of Muscat and Zanzibar, some Indians considered themselves Arab subjects.[22] As British officials in India scrambled to regain control of the subcontinent after the 1857 revolt, their administration made changes that inadvertently affected Indians overseas. Before the uprising, some areas were under control of the East India Company and others had been "dependent" or "independent" states. After 1857, the Crown attempted to erase the distinction. In 1860, Lord Canning wrote that, following the consolidation of British rule, "the Crown of England [as opposed to the Company] stands forth the unquestioned ruler and paramount in all India, and is brought face to face with its feudatories."[23] The bureaucratic result of this standoff with previously independent areas was that all Indians were designated as "British subjects." Consequentially, British consular officers in the western Indian Ocean could claim power over a large number of residents, including subjects of "Indian" territories who had previously been outside of British India.

Kutch, in western Gujarat, which included the port of Mandvi, is a prime example of this. Kutchis had been subjects of an independent ruler, the Rao of Kutch. In 1819, a treaty between the Rao and the East India Company established that the Kutchis were not ruled by the British Crown. Increasing competition in the western Indian Ocean, however, led the British to inveigle the Rao. In 1869 he proclaimed that all of his subjects living or trading in Africa, Arabia, or the Persian Gulf should have their claims settled as if they were British subjects.[24]

On January 12, 1873, when Sir Bartle Frere, the former governor of Bombay, arrived in Zanzibar to push the new antislavery treaty, he traveled with the prime minister of the (now subordinate) Rao of Kutch because of the large number of Kutchis in East Africa.[25] Delicate diplomacy with these new Indian subjects in East Africa was vital because slaves and other African dependents were intimately intertwined with Indian households and businesses. Slave holding and slave trading among Indians was common in early to mid-nineteenth-century East Africa. Some Indians had slave wives or domestic servants, and many received slaves with mortgage contracts or as repayment of debt. In 1860, the British Consul noted that coastal Banians, Khojas, and Bohoras accepted young children as payment for trade goods.[26] Thus Indians were involved in all aspects of the slave trade, and slaves were central to commercial transactions.

When consular courts began enforcing provisions against Indians holding slaves, they undercut networks of obligation and changed the way people wrote promissory notes. British consular officials ruled against Indians who received slaves as part of mortgages, even though slaves had previously been considered part of farms in these transactions.[27] When Ali bin Muhammad al-Busaidi sold his plantation to Jairam Shivji in 1845, the Arabic deed included eight slaves.[28] In the new juridical landscape of the 1860s, however, slaves could no longer be used to repay debts in the consular court. Slaves thus all but disappeared from property descriptions in formal real estate transactions, at least those transactions that involved Indians and that were registered at the consul. Making this formerly legitimate commodity illicit upset the practices of creditors and their clients, but uneven enforcement of these rules left many room to maneuver.

Indian slave holding fluctuated with the consular officials' variable interpretations of who counted as British Indian subjects. By the time Rigby departed in 1861, he had established the British Consul's jurisdiction over "natives of India," whether or not they were born in British territory. Seyyid Majid had acquiesced to this, and Indians protested that they "were never allowed to have any validity whatever."[29] Rigby's successors, Lewis Pelly (1861–63) and R.L. Playfair (1863–65), reopened this question, allowing Hindus and Indian Muslims in Zanzibar to decide whether to register themselves as British Indian subjects. While Rigby had sought to control the most people, Pelly and Playfair saw British protection as a privilege that should not be given indiscriminately to all Indians. Following Playfair's request for a statement on the subject, Seyyid Majid issued a proclamation that declared: "All Indians or Banians from the Dominions of the British Gov[ernment] are British subjects, and those who are from other provinces of Hindustan and have registered themselves as under British protection, they are to be considered as British subjects, and all their slaves who were formerly freed, are not be interfered with. And every Hindee or Banian from other places, except from British territory, who may not have registered himself, they are to be considered as Arabs. Be this known." As a result, some Indians became, or returned to being, subjects of the sultan of Zanzibar.

The proclamation's attempts to clarify citizenship and sovereignty also revealed that concepts of ethnicity during this period were more fungible than fixed. Indians made use of bureaucratic uncertainty and registered "just as it suited their purpose or not," in Consul Prideaux's words. Individuals who trafficked in slaves or held pawns for debts had no reason to register. They became—or remained—subjects of the sultan. Not surprisingly, with the loosening of Rigby's draconian methods, Indian participation in slavery increased in the mid-1860s.[30] The new consul at the end of the decade, H.A. Churchill (1867–70) took another approach—sanctioned by the Government in India—to put down the slave trade "authoritatively and strictly," while permitting possession of existing domestic slaves. This measure essentially divided the domestic sphere from the commercial one and paved the way for Indians to acknowledge the slaves they held. In 1869, 350 Indians (including "half-castes") claimed Sultan Majid's protection, and 76 of these held 171 slaves. Most (274 in number) did not admit to holding slaves.[31]

In this context many Indians avoided consular courts initially because consular authority, Indian subjecthood, and slave ownership were unsettled questions in the 1860s and early 1870s. They preferred to remain within the sultan's jurisdiction and take their cases to a *qadi*'s court. British officials worked against this to eliminate venue shopping and institutionalize consular courts. To do this, consular officials imposed fines on British Indian subjects who failed to bring their suits to the consular courts. When a man from Kutch presented his case to a *qadi*'s court in 1867, the British Consul Edward Seward (1865–67) fined him MT$5, "for having taken his case before the Arab Authorities in contravention of Treaty and prohibiting notification."[32] Several weeks later, Jetha Gopal, an Indian man, attempted to bring a suit against another Indian through the Zanzibari courts, and Seward fined him MT$25.[33] As late as August 1874, an Indian disputed the jurisdiction of the consular court over his affairs because he had been born in Zanzibar and was the sultan's subject. The court did not admit his objection.[34] These litigants were either unaware of the consular court or believed they would receive more favorable judgments from a *qadi*.

Consular courts became more established in the 1870s but were marked by ill-defined jurisdictions and disjointed legal epistemologies. Their tendency to favor British Indian subjects, however, fueled their institutionalization at a time of economic crisis. The dispute between Sumar Widani, an Indian, and Abdullah bin Rashid al-Ghaythi, an Omani Arab, in 1877 illustrates the tangled thicket of debt disputes in Zanzibar and the disjunctures between a *qadi*'s court and a consular court. Sumar Widani and Abdullah bin Rashid initially brought their property dispute to a *qadi*'s court where they reached an outcome that was more favorable to Abdullah bin Rashid. When Sumar Widani pursued the case in the consular court, however, the result went his way.[35] At stake was the question of how much of the debt (MT$3,200) Abdullah bin Rashid had paid. A receipt showed that he had paid MT$1,511. After making that payment, Abdullah said he delivered 65 bags of rice and 40 frasila of *mzugu* (possibly cassava) worth MT$1,000 to Sumar. Sumar alleged that he never received this payment and was thus still owed MT$1,689. The *qadi*—identified only as Hamad—who initially heard the case was an Ibadi scholar. He ruled in Abdullah bin Rashid's favor, deciding that Abdullah only owed Sumar Widani MT$689. Oral evidence from a Muslim would have been sufficient to corroborate Abdullah's in-kind payment.

The next year, Sumar Widani brought the case to the consular court. After considering the evidence and the documents, the consular court affirmed the initial payment, overturned the *qadi*'s ruling on the in-kind payment, and concluded that Abdullah owed the entire balance (MT$1,689). The consular officer based his decision on documentary and religious evidence that would not have been pertinent in the *qadi*'s court. First, the consular court favored written documents over oral testimony. The court found that it was unlikely for an Arab to make a mortgage payment, in this case with rice and *mzugu*, without demanding a receipt. Without such a receipt the claim of payment was suspect. Second, the consular court pointed to one aspect of Ibadi religious practice—*taqiyya* (dissimulation)—to suggest that Abdullah bin Rashid or the *qadi*, both Ibadis, may have willingly made false statements.[36] This court's judgment against Abdullah misunderstood Ibadi practice of *taqiyya*—which was intended for instances of religious persecution—and underscored the growing centrality of documents as the most compelling evidence. The case also illustrates how Indians began to see advantages in consular courts. The mass registration of Arabic business documents by Indian creditors in the 1870s and onward was a testament to their newfound faith in the consular courts and court's strong preference for written documents as evidence.

During the period of the economic uncertainty following the 1872 hurricane and the 1873 antislavery treaty, Zanzibar's consular courts became important places for creditors to settle commercial disputes. The volume of trade and the sophistication of commercial relations were both increasing, and the number and value of cases before the consular courts grew hugely from 1872 to 1874. In 1872, the court heard forty-five cases, valuing MT$32,171.25. In 1873, the number of cases jumped to sixty-eight (a 150 percent increase), with a collective worth of MT$38,909.375. The following year, the consular court heard 221 cases, valued at MT$73,591.90. The number of cases jumped by nearly 500 percent, while the combined worth of these cases more than doubled over a two-year period.[37] This suggests that an increasing number of cases—not just the most valuable—were being heard in consular courts.

The Acting British Consul General W. F. Prideaux (1873–75), a temporary replacement while long-serving John Kirk (1870–86) was on leave, could not account for the tremendous increase in cases in 1874. The only change

TABLE
Consular Court Cases, 1872–1874[38]

Year	Number of cases	Value of cases (MT$)	Change in number of cases from 1872	Change in value of cases from 1872
1872	45	32,171.25	—	—
1873	68	38,909.375	151%	121%
1874	221	73,591.90	491%	229%

he noted was the court had been moved to "an easily accessible building" and that "every facility is given to suitors," but he found this explanation insufficient.[39] Indeed, consular courts encouraged suits by making them easier to file but this increase built on nearly fifteen years of consular efforts to bring British Indian subjects under the court's jurisdiction. The proliferation of cases occurred during a period of great economic insecurity. The hurricane and treaty were both local factors that amplified a larger global economic downturns during this period. At such moments, creditors called in their debts.

Prideaux could not understand the fungibility of time and the flexibility of ongoing debts. The relationships between creditors and debtors mapped onto patron-client relations and as such represented ongoing social relations. In this context, many debts slid past their due dates. The fact that Zanzibar had no statute of limitations presented no barrier to eventual enforcement, so older cases could easily be brought to trial. In the early 1870s, however, the confluence of a financial crisis and a more favorable juridical venue encouraged creditors to reel in outstanding debts. Prideaux noted that he had seen "several claims of many years standing," perhaps due to "the present transitional state of affairs." The 1873 treaty had "induced many people to seek a final settlement with their creditors which in many cases can only be done through the intervention of the Consular authorities."[40] Many Indian creditors took advantage of more robust consular interventions and acknowledged the court's preference for documentary evidence by registering past debts and pursuing repayment. Thus, like Barghash in his treaty negotiations, debtors were running out of time. Against the backdrop of the new antislavery treaty and the growing power of the consular courts, Indian creditors found that the Arabic language contracts that had been prepared within the sultan's jurisdiction for use in a *qadi*'s court were newly valuable in their efforts to enforce debts. While this rising documentary regime privileged Indians as British subjects and the documents they brought to court, African former slaves found that their documents were not valid without consular attestations.

RECONFIGURING MANUMISSION AND MOBILITY

After 1873, Africans traveling to Arabia or India could only do so legally with the imprimatur of the British consulate. The 1877–1879 register of consular acts shows that, in addition to registering contracts and debts, the British representative also approved deeds of freedom. As in Mabrook's case, masters freed slaves following Islamic procedures and local practices, but consular officials had to notarize manumission documents. The consular officials legitimated these Arabic documents with their documentary regime so that naval patrols and imperial officials would accept them. This was a major shift from earlier periods, during which freed slaves could easily move about the western Indian Ocean. By the late 1870s, however, the status of Africans leaving East Africa for Arabia or India was not clear. Because of the aggressive attempts to end the slave trade, Africans who wanted to travel legally across the Indian Ocean needed documents that clarified their status within the bureaucratic regime and imperial legal system.

Limits placed on the movement of free Africans—as compared to Arabs and Indians, who traveled more freely—mirror the distinction between "two worlds of movement," as detailed by historians of the passport. In one of these "worlds," domestic and international governments legitimated people's movements, while the residents of the other "world" were "restricted in their movements both domestically and internationally."[41] Treaty regulations between the British government and the sultan in Zanzibar demarcated a domestic space, within which slavery was legal, and an international space, in which it was not.

Attempts to control the slave trade placed unusual scrutiny on all Africans at sea. Naval squadrons assumed that all Africans traversing the sea could

FIGURE 7.2. The documentary regime in practice: Stopping a slave ship and examining her papers. From *Illustrated London News*, September 9, 1889.

be slaves. Any unmarked case was treated as slavery, and the burden to show otherwise lay with Africans themselves. Since all Africans at sea were presumed to be slaves, the corollary assumption was that their companions were slave owners. Such assumptions underlay an epistemological conundrum: How could one know free from slave? How could one determine whether an individual owned a slave? And how could one differentiate a slave from a client or a slave woman from a wife? For Arabs and Swahili people, these relationships were socially determined. For naval officers and British imperial functionaries, however, boundaries were rooted in (British) legal categories, and only official documents could uphold these distinctions.[42] Naval patrols facing ships with polyglot, multiracial, and multiethnic passengers depended on official documents to ascertain status because they were ill-prepared to read the social landscape accurately.

As the vignette about Mabrook and the manipulation of notarial certification shows, consular documents could only reflect the circumstances presented at the consulate. They sought to attest to whether a person was a freed slave or not. By taking these categories of slave and free as unstable and open to interrogation, however, we find a more complex set of social relations and a British willingness to indulge convenient fictions. In this context, a new variety of insincere manumission emerged in the wake of the 1873 treaty as a result of multiracial and multiethnic households rooted in patron-client relations.

As noted earlier, insincere manumission occurred in the 1850s in the western Indian Ocean, when European desires to move Africans across the Indian Ocean collided with attempts to control the slave trade. This collision affected the attempts to supply cheap or free labor to Indian Ocean plantation islands. Muslims decried the practice and it offended Arabs' moral economy of manumission. In the 1870s, however, Africans who sought to leave East Africa represented a much broader social spectrum. They were not only plantations laborers, but members of families and households headed by Arabs and Indians. In the face of new, stricter enforcement, consular officials attested to deeds of freedom and notarized labor contracts for various Africans. Such acts made these people and their status legible to the consulate, but the same documents obscured the relationships between Africans and their sponsors. The consular need to make categorical distinctions between a free person and a dependent frequently trumped everyday social practice and created legal fictions. From the shades of distinction and mutual obligations that were part of patron-client relationships in the western Indian Ocean, consular acts made contracted workers and freed slaves. To see this process clearly, let us first consider Africans leaving for India and the complex history of Afro-Indian families before examining the African members of an Omani household relocating from Zanzibar to the Arabian interior. These all show how Indian Ocean actors maneuvered within new legal categories to maintain family structures and how consular officials indulged legal fictions.

AFRO-INDIAN FAMILIES AND CONTRACTED PASSAGES TO INDIA

In early 1877, two people, Rehani and Tofiki [Tawfiq] finalized their plans to travel to India. They would accompany Ebji Shivji, and they duly appeared before the British Consul to register their employment contracts. The consul approved these, even though they should have raised obvious red flags in the years after the 1873 antislavery treaty. Ebji Shivji, the man contracting with Rehani and Tofiki, was the brother of Jairam Shivji, who had served as the sultan's customs master until 1866 and become Zanzibar's wealthiest man. Ebji himself was a well-known financier of lucrative trading ventures on the African mainland, and as a partner to his more established brother, Ebji had overseen revenue collection when Jairam was away from Zanzibar. Before going to India in 1877, Ebji contracted to pay Rehani and Tofiki each a quarter of a dollar per month to accompany him, and the consular officer sealed the agreement.[43] Although Ebji was reputed to be a slave dealer and was well known for his dishonesty, the consular office endorsed his contract to take two Africans abroad. The entry in the consular book provided no details about the travelers, besides their names, both of which were common ones given to slaves. (*Rehani* literally meant "a pawn"). Ebji's earlier extensive trading on the mainland had led British officers to suspect him of trafficking slaves, and his willing participation in legal matters at the consulate would have surprised the previous generation of British representatives. In 1851, the consul called Ebji "a most insidious intriguing dishonest man," adding that "he detests our Government and fails not to spread all sorts of false reports regarding us."[44] Twenty-five years later, before his trip to India, Ebji may have brought another "false report" to the consulate, but in the context of the new documentary regime he was simply providing them with the "correct" information about a labor contract to legitimize his travel.

Nearly two decades after Rigby had tried to end Indian slave holding in Zanzibar, many Indians registered labor contracts with Africans before taking trips to Kutch, Bombay, or other ports. With echoes of the earlier practice of insincere manumission, Africans were paid little for their service and these cases from the 1870s suggest a pattern of establishing official labor arrangements to provide documentation needed to travel at sea.⁴⁵ Some contracts followed long-established labor practices for hiring crews for various Indian Ocean sailing ships (such as the *bidan*, *sambuk*, and *batela*) that departed from ports like Lamu, Shihir, or Sur.⁴⁶ For crews these contracts resemble the "Asiatic Articles" of employment that Janet Ewald has identified as common maritime hiring practice in the Indian Ocean. Other entries stipulate the contractual hiring of pilots to guide ships.⁴⁷ The more curious contracts, however, were between Indian men and African women and firmly grounded in the domestic sphere. The requirements of the documentary regime therefore led to the recording and rationalization of relationships between African women and Indian men that had been both common and legally ambiguous in East Africa.

Liaisons between Indian men and African women were not unusual in the nineteenth century and they established families through marriage and concubinage. Most of the thousands of Indian migrants to East Africa were men, and these men—including both Muslims and Hindus—lived with, and sometimes married, African women. These marriages were more common on the African mainland than they were in the growing cosmopolitan city of Zanzibar. On the Swahili coast, communal life for communities like the Muslim Bohora were extremely limited and few (if any) Indian women lived there.⁴⁸ In the 1860s, a Kutchi man, who was a longtime resident of the coast, noted that none of the Hindus who lived there had Indian wives. Instead, he explained, "A few of these buy or engage female negroes who, with their children, if any[,] are invariably left behind when their masters return to India."⁴⁹ Travel records from the 1870s make clear that some men did not abandon these women; they took their partners with them in India. Doing so required them to document these women's relationships to them as contracted laborers or freed slaves. This was a further elaboration of the uncertain legitimacy in the eyes of their communities and imperial officialdom that had existed for Afro-Indian families in East Africa throughout the nineteenth century.

The children of Indian fathers and African mothers were called *chotara* in East Africa. *Chotara* derives from the Gujarati word *jotawa*, which describes Afro-Asians.⁵⁰ Given the multiracial aspect of the ivory trade, it is not surprising that *chotara* also came to describe "mixed" ivory—tusks that combined hard and soft ivory.⁵¹ The value of *chotara* ivory in the marketplace remains unclear, but *chotara* children of Afro-Indian families found themselves between social groups and at odds with communal practices.

Within the coastal communities, Afro-Indian families thrived across generations in the nineteenth century. Hasan Musa Balu (d. 1880) lived in

Kilwa, where the Indian population in 1870 was estimated to be eighty-five people—including sixty Bhatias, twenty Khojas, and five "others."[52] Hasan was at least third generation Afro-Indian. His father was Indian—presumably Khoja—and his mother was Afro-Indian, presumably born in East Africa. Hasan also married an Afro-Indian woman, and after he died in debt, his wife sold her jewelry to settle with his creditors.[53] This family belies assumptions about mobile Indian merchants and short-term liaisons with African women while also revealing Afro-Indian women as embedded in networks of indebtedness.

Indian husbands evaded antislavery rules with the cooperation of their African wives. Consul Lewis Pelly observed that in the period after Rigby tried to divest Indians of their slaves, mixed marriages provided a major loophole in the patchwork juridical framework of East Africa at the time.[54] Pelly noted that an Indian Banyan living on the coast could take a Swahili woman as his concubine. Legal provisions in the 1860s sought to rid British protected subjects of their slaves, but there was no legal means to block their wives who were subjects of the sultan, from owning slaves.[55] This provided Indian men in Afro-Indian households the means to evade antislavery laws.

Legal frameworks also offered some protection to the offspring of Afro-Indian families. For some Indian men, African women were short term domestic companions, a temporary relationship while the men endeavored to become wealthy enough to marry within their own community. A successful trading venture on the coast would permit a man to seek a bride from his own community in Zanzibar or even in India. Such moves created blended, overlapping Afro-Indian households. Jesa Damani, an Indian trader who lived in Kilwa, headed two families. He initially married an African woman named Zanabu, and together they had two sons. He later divorced her and married an Indian woman who bore him a son and daughter. When Jesa died (in late 1877 or early 1878), the probate case clearly distinguished his *chotara* sons from his other children even though all three living sons received equal portions of the estate. His Indian wife and daughter received half a portion, and Zanabu, Jesa's African ex-wife, would have received nothing from the estate. The fact that one of her sons predeceased his father, however, entitled her to some of her late son's share.[56] While we can never know the emotional content of relationships like Jesa and Zanabu's, they underscore both the temporizing strategies of some Indian migrants and the vulnerability of African women.

Some Indian men married Swahili women to escape debt and gain financial advantages. Dhala Sumar—a Khoja, or Indian Muslim—was twenty years old in 1880. He hoped to become a shopkeeper but he was in debt. His father, the wealthy merchant Sumar Widani, had died in the late 1870s with an estate worth nearly MT$6,000. As noted previously, Sumar had collected on outstanding debts by pursuing his Arab client in the consular courts after losing in front of a *qadi*. Sumar's probate was also a consular matter. In his will he provided his son Dhala with a monthly allowance of MT$6 and set aside MT$500 for his wedding.

Dhala recognized that he could rescue himself from debt not by marrying into a wealthy family, but by marrying a Swahili woman. He argued that he was due the full amount of his inheritance regardless of who he married. He clearly understood that consequences of marrying within his community. He explained, "marrying a Khoja wife should not only entail great expense on the occasion of the marriage & require a comparatively more expensive living afterwards but is altogether a very different thing to bring about for a man in my position . . ." He instead sought out a Swahili bride and noted that such a marriage "would save me $400 or 500 and after paying my debts of about $100 more would leave me a capital of $300 to start with." He married Makaa bint Khamis al-Lamiyya (from Lamu), in front of a *qadi* in Zanzibar, and he paid her a dowry of MT$50. Makaa had been married three times before—first to a Comorian man, then to an Indian in Pemba, and then to another Indian in Zanzibar.[57] The marriage between Dhala and Makaa—presided over by a prestigious *qadi* and sealed in a marriage contract in Arabic—appears legitimate from an Islamic point of view. The marriage also met the legal standards of probate for the consular court, yet Dhala's petition demonstrates that he understood the legal performance required to meet his goal.

Men like Jesa Damani and Dhala Sumar pursued relations with African women that seemed to be instrumental, temporizing moves to establish themselves. Another group of Indian men did not leave behind their African concubines and offspring. They sought to legitimate their relationships with African women before consular courts so that they could travel together to India. While some of these African women may have been slaves or other dependents to these men, the narrow legal restrictions reduced these relationships to contract labor or marriage.

Some Indian men took African women to India by making formal labor contracts and registering these at the consulate. These contracts could be quite explicit—a monthly wage; an advance; provisions for cost of the voyage, food, and clothing; and some even set a specific amount of time.[58] These contracts seem to mask a host of relationships. While some arrangements resembled the formal labor contracts that Africans in Zanzibar undertook for overseas employment, others hint at more exploitative relationships. Some laborers were called servants.⁵⁹ But most of these contracts provide very few details. In an agreement between Jamal Rashid and a woman named Faida, Rashid agreed to pay her $2 per month to travel with him to India, saying nothing about an advance or an end date.⁶⁰

Others were more explicit about their domestic arrangements and requested consular endorsement of their marriages to African women who had been slaves. This required a two step process. When Visram Damji and his wife Zenab visited the consular office on October 14, 1878, Visram had two tasks. First, he asked the consular official to attest to his signature on a deed that granted his slave Zenab freedom. He then registered a declaration that Zenab was his wife.⁶¹ These two acts were separate entries carried out sequentially, but taken together they suggest that Visram had taken all the precautions to travel with Zenab to India and withstand the scrutiny of the documentary regime. She had been a concubine, but with a deed of freedom and a certified marriage, they could travel together.

In taking the measure of all of these movements from East Africa to India in the 1870s, we see that the rise of a documentary regime required consular endorsements and notarizations to document the relationships between Indians and Africans. While some of these were straightforward labor contracts that were standard in the Indian Ocean, others obscured the nature of the relationships to fit neatly into legal categories. Consular officials gave their blessing to the contracts of men like Ebji Shivji, who had a reputation for dishonesty and for slave trading, that echoed the insincere manumissions of the 1850s. At the same time, however, the consular acts bring to light the diversity of Afro-Indian households. Some of these were cynical, short-term, or exploitative relationships, but others created multigenerational, mixed-race families; transformed concubines into legitimate, free wives; and provided the means for Afro-Indian families to remain together. Thus even as Indians manipulated documentary practices to pass through naval blockades they revealed how intertwined their lives were with Africans and the ongoing importance of mobility in the western Indian Ocean.

SAILING TO MUSCAT: A HOUSEHOLD ON THE MOVE

The mobility of Arabs in the western Indian Ocean in the nineteenth century created close bonds between Oman and East Africa, and family networks that included Arabs and Africans stretched across this broad region. While Arabs traveled seemingly at will during this period, from the 1870s the African men and women attached to their households were subject to a documentary regime that regulated their movement. In a historical irony, the enslaved or recently manumitted African men and women who were linked to Arab households provide a way of tracing the movements of their elite patrons. Let us consider the household of Rashid bin Amur al-Ghaythi in the late 1870s at the time the family sold a house in Zanzibar and relocated to the Omani interior. While the family patrilineage had roots in Oman and an established history in Zanzibar, the African members of the household originated on the African mainland. Two men and two women, Mubarak, Joohan, Halima, and Sinatendalo, had been manumitted by Rashid bin Amur and were following him to Arabia. By linking their biographies at the moment of departure, we see the overlapping realms of the western Indian Ocean in one household. They passed through the British consulate to certify their freedom on paper, but this process obscured layers of dependency and limits on autonomy.

In 1878 Rashid bin Amur al-Ghaythi sold property in Zanzibar and moved to Ibra, an oasis town in the Sharqiya region of Oman. The Ghuyūth (plural of al-Ghaythi) belonged to a branch of the broader al-Harthi tribal grouping from Oman that was well represented in East Africa. In Oman, the Ghuyuth occupied three neighborhoods in lower Ibra with the Awlad Salim, a related group. At the beginning of the twentieth century, British officials estimated the strength of the Ghuyuth to be 150 men.[62] Long before that time, the Ghuyuth and the Awlad Salim had both benefited from their connections to East Africa. Ghuyuth men had been in Zanzibar from at least the 1840s where they owned property and slaves. They also had a long history of freeing their slaves: one of the earliest surviving contracts executed by a freed slave in Zanzibar shows that the Ghuyuth's former client sold property in 1847.[63]

The Ghuyuth acquired numerous houses and plantations in East Africa, but as Rashid bin Amur's case shows, they also maintained connections to Oman. Rashid bin Amur owned a large stone house in the Shangani quarter of Zanzibar town. His kinsmen, men identified either as al-Ghaythi or Awlad Salim, owned fine houses in Zanzibar and owned plantations outside of town in the 1860s. Edward Seward, the British consul, bought one of these houses.[64] These properties became easy sources of cash and credit in times of crisis.

Although Salme bint Said noted in her autobiography that some Omanis sought to acquire wealth in Zanzibar before returning "to their country and live and die in peace," Rashid bin Amur al-Ghaythi left for Oman during a time of turmoil.[65] In the late 1870s, the acute crisis in Sharqiya caused al-Ghaythi men to sell or to leverage their property in Zanzibar and leave for Oman with their freed slaves. In 1877 the Harthi tribes in Sharqiya, led by

Salih bin Ali, attempted to overthrow the sultan, Turki bin Said al-Busaidi, in Muscat. When the sultan and his British allies quashed the rebellion, they conspired to punish the Harthi by levying fines and interrupting trade.[66] By 1878, Oman was in a bad state. Two weeks before Rashid bin Amur sold his house in Zanzibar, the Omani sultan's brother (and rival) said, "the whole of Oman is full of rebellion, sedition, oppression and disturbances."[67] These disturbances hit Sharqiya the hardest. Along with the political anxieties, heavy rains damaged the date crop that year. Almost 90 percent of Sharqiya's fruit was destroyed. The British Resident in Muscat dispassionately reported, "There will certainly be much distress and this may possibly give rise to disturbances, but I do not apprehend there will be an absolute famine."[68] A famine would have imposed great difficulty on the Ghuyuth in Oman.

The actions of Rashid bin Amur al-Ghaythi, his fellow clansmen, and their relatives of the Awlad Salim suggest that they were mobilizing their resources, and that some were going to Oman. Rashid bin Amur sold his town house in late July 1878 for MT$4,600 to Janbhai, the wife of the Hindu merchant Tharia Topan.[69] Selling his house at the end of July, however, meant that Rashid bin Amur had missed the southwest monsoon that would have powered his sail to Oman in April or May. While he may have traveled against the monsoon via steamship, he more likely departed as soon as possible with the next year's monsoon. In either case, when his former slaves arrived at the British consulate in Zanzibar in late April 1879, Rashid bin Amur had already departed.

Mubarak, Joohan, Halima, and Sinatendalo presented themselves at consulate in April 1879. In seeking endorsement for their manumission papers, they signaled their mainland African origins and their intentions to follow Rashid bin Amur to Oman. All four Africans—two men and two women—had been the slaves of Rashid bin Amur al-Ghaythi.[70] They arrived at the consulate in pairs, man and woman, nearly a week apart. These may have been married couples or their patron might have sent them in pairs to protect the women's propriety. These four people originated from neighboring regions along the southern caravan route that linked Kilwa on the coast to Lake Nyasa in the interior. By connecting the scant details of these four prospective Indian Ocean travelers with the broader history of their home regions, we see mobility embedded in enslavement and manumission and the documentary regime that tried to control this.

Halima and Mubarak registered first. While we know little about Halima besides her name, ascribed ethnic origin, and a particular piercing, these help place her home in the Lake Nyasa region, suggest her route to enslavement, and the place of Yao people in Zanzibar. The consular clerk identified Halima as Yao and noted the hole in her lip. This piercing suggests that she was not born into slavery in Zanzibar but had been captured in her own country. Various groups on the southern caravan route to Lake Nyasa practiced lip piercing, and Yao speakers were both slaves and slave traders in this region. By the end of the nineteenth century, lip rings were "seen rarely" on Yao women, but at midcentury such ornamentation was still common, both among the Yao and among the groups that they raided for slaves. Across this broad region, girls' upper lips were typically pierced when they were young, so it is difficult to pinpoint Halima's origin. In the 1860s, Bishop Steere noted that a group called the Aroro (or Alolo/Walolo) had girls wear small rings of beads through their lip piercings. At the time of Steere's observations, the Aroro were starving due to drought.[71] Such dire circumstances may have led Halima's parents to pawn her to a better-off family or to a merchant with links to the coast. Either way she would have been incorporated as a dependent into a new household. Environmental disasters impoverished people and created pathways to enslavement that Yao traders were well positioned to take advantage of. Whether Halima was born Yao or incorporated into a Yao household, by 1879 she was identified as one of a multitude of Yao people living in Zanzibar.

Zanzibar was full of Yao people like Halima. The slave trade had brought them to Zanzibar, and processes of acculturation in this Indian Ocean port city reconfigured their identities. Slaves and free people of Yao origin presented themselves in Zanzibar as Swahili-speaking coastal people. Indeed, despite the extensive presence of Yao people in the city in the 1860s, the British missionary Steere struggled to find anyone who could teach him the Yao language, ChiYao. He wanted to learn it for missionizing purposes, and he attributed the relative invisibility of Yao speakers to the shame that Africans from the interior felt in the Arabo-Swahili milieu of Zanzibar. Some Yao feigned ignorance of their homelands to avoid talking about their histories. Steere noted that as Yao migrants learned Swahili they often forgot ChiYao, "and for the most part speak neither language at all correctly."[72] While they sought to present themselves as Swahili speakers, they forgot ChiYao and the result was, in Steere's view, an imperfect belonging. Yet Halima clearly belonged to Rashid bin Amur's multiethnic, multiracial household, and sought to have her deed of freedom certified so she could cross the Indian Ocean. When Halima arrived in the Omani interior, the distinctions made in Zanzibar between Swahili and Yao—and even between free and enslaved—would most likely be overlooked. As a dark-skinned African woman with a lip piercing, she would have limited autonomy, especially outside the household of Rashid bin Amur al-Ghaythi.

Halima's companion on the day she went to the British consulate was Mubarak, another slave freed by Rashid bin Amur. Mubarak—whose face showed the scars of smallpox—was from Ngindo, the interior hinterland of Kilwa, which had long supplied slaves to the Indian Ocean world. Mubarak's name and origins may have marked him as a slave or former slave, but his smallpox scars were common to every stratum of East African society. Sultan Seyyid Majid bin Said (r. 1856–70) bore the marks of a smallpox survivor and two of his siblings had succumbed to the disease in 1858.[73] In Mubarak's home area, Yao merchants and their Arab and coastal allies had long captured and sold Wangindo into the Indian Ocean slave trade. By the 1840s, enough Wangindo were slaves in the Mascarenes that their minidiaspora drew notice.[74] In this way, Mubarak's impending trip to Arabia was part of a much larger history of Ngindo mobility. Unlike his countrymen, however, Mubarak traveled not bound for plantation labor.

In the 1860s, Wangindo faced great turmoil in their home region as Nguni-speaking migrants from southern Africa arrived to challenge local rulers and contest Yao slave raiding. These disturbances affected the Wangindo unevenly, depending on where they lived. Some Wangindo moved from Kilwa's hinterland to the port town, speaking Swahili and dressing in the coastal style. Others sought refuge in the countryside from local disturbances. In a relative sense, Mubarak's position as a household member and freed slave of a wealthy Arab was likely better than that of his fellow Wangindo who were trying to avoid capture at home or who had been sold into the Indian Ocean slave trade. In 1874, fewer than five years before Mubarak began preparing for his trip to Oman, British naval patrols stopped a slave ship carrying Wangindo who had been captured and enslaved during a dispute between the Yao and a group of Nguni speakers.[75] They, unlike Mubarak, were not traveling with the appropriate passes, and in this case the documentary regime achieved its goal of stopping the trade in slaves.

It is difficult to compare Mubarak's manumission to the experience of slaves liberated at sea, but the men of the Royal Navy treated the freed slaves in a less than dignified manner. British officers called one large woman "Elephant," and they nicknamed another "Toad." On land, British consular officers also engaged in this chauvinistic racialism. Consul Churchill sneeringly described Ngindo women—who were noted for their facial scars—as "a new species altogether until then undiscovered." He claimed that "for the benefit of natural historians," this species would be called "'Lumpy Keboko' (Lumpy Hippo)."[76] British efforts to curtail the slave trade did not lead to a respect for enslaved Africans, and many Africans liberated at sea were assigned to patrons on shore in relations the resembled slavery in all but name.

Those Wangindo who remained in their home region and evaded capture and enslavement nevertheless lived in fear. Ongoing disputes left the southern hinterland in turmoil. In 1876, a visitor there noticed that the "remains of the Ngindo flee backward and forward as they hear of the approach of their dreaded enemies."[77] While some of Mubarak's countrymen were on the run and others were captured as slaves and smuggled at sea, Mubarak had become—on paper at least—a free man who could travel openly.

Several days after Halima and Mubarak had their deeds of freedom endorsed at the consulate, Joohan and Sinatendalo arrived there. Both were from Nyasa country, an area around Lake Malawi at the terminus of the southern caravan route. If they had been brought from their country, they would have crossed Ngindo territory and Yaoland on their way to Zanzibar. They both had markings near their ears, which were typical of "country marks."[78] Sinatendalo had a Swahili name that was often given to female slaves, which suggested a low status. *Sinatendalo* means: "I have nothing to do with it." In the context of her manumission and her appearance to collect documents to follow her former owner to Muscat, her name raises broader questions about the agency of freed slaves.

With their deeds of freedom certified, Mubarak, Joohan, Halima, and Sinatendalo were free to travel, yet they were not free. The bureaucratic language noted in the consular records shows that these individuals maintained a close relationship with the man who had freed them. While the consular office clerks endorsed the documents and made a clear determination about the Africans' non-slave status in a narrow bureaucratic sense, the clerk's notation belied the ongoing relationship between freed slaves and their former masters. In Sinatendalo's entry, the clerk noted, "she is following her master to Oman."[79]

Thus even as the consulate authorized her movement as a free person, it acknowledged her status as a dependent and her embeddedness in a set of multiracial relations within a mobile household.

FINAL ACTS

Sultan Barghash had temporized as long as possible before submitting to the threats and strongarm tactics Kirk had used to force him to sign the antislavery document in June of 1873. In the devastating wake of the hurricane and the faltering economy, Barghash's grudging attestation legitimized the antislavery treaty and brought it into enforcement. While this marked a turning point in Zanzibari history, it was also part of a growing bureaucratic framework that the British used to encircle the Indian Ocean. This documentary regime softened local sovereignty, sought to control Indians in East Africa, changed the nature of commercial arbitration and strictly scrutinized African mobility. Yet despite this, older practices of manumission, creating documents, and maintaining multiracial households persisted.

Over the course of the nineteenth century, the manumission and mobility of freed slaves highlighted the intersection of Islamic law and imperial interest on the one hand, and the congruence of social and economic ties between former slaves and former masters on the other. As slavery came under greater imperial scrutiny, manumission documents were subsumed to consular attestations. This was a sign of encroaching imperial bureaucracy that focused on both slavery and the presence of Indians in East Africa. These twin pressures created a consular court and a documentary regime that favored British Indian subjects over others, undercuting the *qadi* courts for commercial transactions specifically, and the sultan's rule more generally.

The 1873 antislavery treaty foisted on Zanzibar and Oman was restrictive and tightly enforced. The treaty resulted in a racialized gradient of mobility in the western Indian Ocean. Freed slaves had traveled widely in an earlier period, but in the years after 1873 all Africans at sea were suspect. While the Royal Navy provided the muscle behind antislavery measures from 1873 to 1884, they took their cues from papers, stamps, and seals—and from the absence of these. All Africans at sea were considered slaves unless proven otherwise and thus were subject to British seizure. Furthermore, anyone traveling with Africans was considered a potential slave trader. Thus, Africans needed the correct documents, even if they were obtained insincerely. Well intentioned attempts to stop the slave trade were grounded in racialist assumptions, and the practice of policing the sea reified racial difference. In contrast to a longer Indian Ocean tradition of cosmopolitan mobility, new imperial policies imagined separate interests, rules, and subjecthoods for Indians, Arabs, and Africans.

The process of enforcing these bureaucratic practices, however, created records that reveal the intimate link between Africans (enslaved and formerly enslaved), Arabs, and Indians. African women were wives to Arab and Indian men and mothers to mixed-race children. African men were employees and clients of Arabs and Indians. These layered relations point to the many gradations of servitude, clientship, and patronage that existed in the Indian Ocean. In a seeming nod both to the mobility of Indian Ocean peoples and to the complexities of clientship relations among Arabs, Indians, and Africans, the British established a system that allowed Africans to cross the ocean licitly. Mixed-race households—who linked the multiple shores of the Indian Ocean—could travel legally only with British imprimatur. As a result, we see the mobility of Africans, Arabs, and Indians—bound together as families, patrons, and clients, as well as masters and slaves. These multilayered relations between masters and slaves were characteristic of earlier practices in the western Indian Ocean. Manumission had a long history, and new opportunities and mobilities only reinforced it. Although Islamic manumission was all but invisible to European observers during early visits to Zanzibar, the rise of the British documentary regime after 1873 depended heavily on Islamic manumission. It became the *sine qua non* of African mobility on the Indian Ocean. Likewise, the documentary regime valorized Islamic legal contracts that predated the establishment of consular courts. This was part of a process of making all Indians British subjects and redrawing jurisdictional boundaries for commercial disputes. New rules and boundaries hampered but did extinguish multiracial mobility and social networks that bound together the shores of the western Indian Ocean.

8 ～ A Dhow on Lake Victoria

IN NOVEMBER 1877, the first dhow sailed on Lake Victoria, Africa's largest lake. Dhows, with their characteristic lateen sails angled to the mast, had sailed the Indian Ocean for millennia and remain emblems of that ocean's trade. The arrival of a dhow on Lake Victoria—some five hundred miles from the sea—was another signal that the Indian Ocean world had reached central Africa. The man who built that dhow, a shadowy figure known as both Songoro and Msabbah, is the focus of this chapter. His movements, from slave to free, and from Zanzibar to Lake Victoria, reveals an Indian Ocean story framed by the roles of clients, credit, and kinship. At the coast Songoro appeased or eluded his creditors to become a successful ivory trader. In the interior, however, he ensnared himself in a dispute with a close ally over debt and kinship. He parlayed property holdings in Zanzibar into partnerships with African rulers that aimed to balance debt and establish ivory trading on the lake. For a time, Songoro enjoyed excellent relationships with Indian creditors, African chiefs, and recently arrived European missionaries. Yet, as the result of a simmering dispute about unpaid debt, the meanings of documents, and the values of kinship, Songoro met an untimely demise. He was murdered in December 1877, less than a month after the dhow's maiden voyage.

The story of the dhow's builder—a freed slave from Zanzibar—demonstrates that networks of credit facilitated the integration of the East African interior and the western Indian Ocean. Indeed, Songoro established "a second Zanzibar" on the shores of Lake Victoria and maneuvered around the big men of his era. Songoro is an unlikely protagonist in a story that connects Barghash, the sultan of Zanzibar; Mutesa, the *kabaka* (king) of Buganda; and Mirambo, East Africa's most feared warlord, and that features adventurer Henry Morton Stanley and the arrival of European missionaries on the lake. By focusing on Songoro, however, we see the micropolitics of debt, kinship, and mobility.[1] Songoro temporized by making bets on the future. He did this at the coast, using his connections to an Omani clan for redeemable sales of fixed property that financed ivory trading, and in the interior, through marriages and short term deals. He lived at the interstices of written documents and face-to-face negotiations, between the Indian Ocean and the African interior. He died when he was no longer able to broker between these. The creditor and ally he had duped to forestall a debt repayment exacted the ultimate price. Thus Songoro, imbued with practices and processes from the coast, built a dhow in the 1870s and brought the Indian Ocean to Lake Victoria.

NAMES AND ORIGINS

Who was this mysterious dhow builder? When he died in 1877, the news of his death spread across Lake Victoria, down the caravan trails to the new towns of the East African interior, to the Indian Ocean island of Zanzibar, and on to London. People used two different names for him. The Arabs and coastal traders in Tabora called him Msabbah when they informed the Zanzibar sultan.[2] The European missionaries who had arrived at his settlement on Lake Victoria earlier that year referred to him as Songoro. While both groups had the same person in mind, they used names that had originally belonged to two separate men, slaves who had been freed by the same master and who were business partners and allies. Over time, their close association elided their names and their property, but their commercial transactions from the 1850s and 1860s help clarify the muddled names and relationships that European visitors bestowed upon them. In 1861, British traveler James Grant stayed with "Sungoro-bin-Tabib" en route to Lake Victoria to follow the Nile from its source to Egypt. In 1875, Henry Morton Stanley met "Sungoro Tarib" at Kagei, on the southern shores of Lake Victoria, and identified him as an agent for "Mse Saba." Arabic-language contracts reveal that two people, with the given names Songoro and Msabbah, had a shared past. These two men were manumitted slaves of Talib bin Abdullah al-Mauli, and they both identified themselves in relation to their former master when they sold property in Zanzibar.[3] Thus, the names Tabib and Tarib that the Europeans associated with Songoro were forms of the first name of his former master. Similarly, Songoro's relationship with "Mse Saba" refers to his connection to Msabbah. Msabbah emerged as the more successful partner: he owned more property and signed more lucrative ivory contracts. By 1877, however, Msabbah had died, and Songoro had taken over his name and his trading. A missionary identified Songoro at this time as "the *ci-devant* slave, now successor and inheritor of the name and property of his Arab master."[4] The use of "Arab" here conflates Talib bin Abdullah al-Mauli's Arab ancestry with Msabbah's identity as a successful trader from Zanzibar, but shows how these freed slaves came to share a name.

Songoro and Msabbah's legal identities as former slaves of the Mauli clan link them to that clan's history of mobility that was shaped by the exigencies of warfare and everyday life in Oman and the gulf. Talib bin Abdullah al-Mauli was likely part of an exodus from Oman in the 1810s spurred by the topsy-turvy politics of the region. Seyyid Said bin Sultan al-Busaidi's struggles for dominance in the gulf in the early years of the century led to widespread disturbances, and members of the Mauli tribe preceded him to East Africa by more than a decade.

The Mauli migrants in Zanzibar originated in Wadi Ma'awil, a well-watered date-farming region in Oman, northwest of Muscat, and at the southern end of the Batinah coast. Between 1800 and 1820, Wadi Ma'awil saw intense fighting between the forces of Seyyid Said bin Sultan and the Saudi Wahhabis and their local allies. These violent, destructive conflicts were retribution for Seyyid Said's maritime activities in the Persian Gulf. In 1809, Seyyid Said joined forces with the East India Company to attack the Qawasim of Ras al-Khayma and their Wahhabi confederates in order to stop their harrying shipping in the gulf. The combined force destroyed most of the Qawasim's large ships and compromised their maritime power.[5] These maritime conflicts in the gulf quickly spilled into the Omani interior.

When Said's British allies sailed from the gulf in early 1810, the now unchecked Wahhabi forces mounted punitive raids against Omani territory. Wadi Ma'awil was among the hardest hit areas, and this fighting had local and regional repercussions. Seyyid Said sent a delegation to the Persian court to request military support, and the Persian shah sent 1,500 cavalrymen to his aid.[6] The fighting in Wadi Ma'awil and in nearby towns like Nakhl between Said's forces and his Persian allies, on the one hand, and the Wahhabi their supporters, on the other, put the Mauli clan on both sides of the violence. During a two-week long battle in the wadi, hand-to-hand fighting occurred in the marketplace, and encampments of foreign troops overran settlements.[7] Both Seyyid Said and his local rival punished their enemies by destroying date trees, a vicious practice that crippled local economies.[8]

When Seyyid Said gained control of the fort at Nakhl, he appointed Khalfan bin Sayf bin Said al-Mauli as governor. Residents accused the governor of gross injustice for razing the houses of his enemies, and the region's residents threatened to leave the country if he were not deposed.

While Seyyid Said tried to press his advantage in the gulf, his appointees in Wadi Maʻawil were unable to quell local disturbances. Seyyid Said duly replaced the controversial governor, but the next appointee also mistreated the Mauli.[9] Seyyid Said mustered a large force and negotiated a temporary settlement in the region by the late 1810s.[10] Intense internecine fighting and the destruction of palm trees made migration an attractive option. Family histories claim that Mauli clansmen came to East Africa by the 1820s, and Seyyid Said appointed one of them, Muhammad bin Nasir al-Mauli, to be his first governor of Lamu around this time.[11]

Whether Talib bin Abdullah al-Mauli was in this earliest group of migrants or part of a later movement, by midcentury he and his clansmen had amassed property in Zanzibar, dedicated some as pious endowments, and deeded others to freed slaves. The earliest extant property records show that one Mauli man sold a farm in Zanzibar in 1849.[12] Talib bin Abdullah manumitted his slaves Msabbah and Songoro before the late 1850s.[13] He may have given them property at the same time, or, they may have claimed land from a pious endowment (*waqf*) that one of Talib bin Abdullah's clansmen established. The al-Mauli *waqf* encompassed a huge piece of property in Ng'ambo, Zanzibar's growing peri-urban area. When this property became the subject of a legal dispute in 1907, the original deed of dedication had been lost. The endowment had taken place "considerably more than 50 years ago," and all sources agreed that the property had been left either for the Mauli and their freed slaves or for the Mauli and all poor Muslims.[14] Msabbah and Songoro would have qualified in either case. There was a great deal of land available, and people built huts and houses on the *waqf* property. They did not have to pay rent, so such areas attracted freed slaves and people of minimal means. In the second half of the nineteenth century, however, a market for this land emerged. People like Msabbah and Songoro who had claims to property through manumission or as beneficiaries of *waqfs* used these properties as security for mortgages or sold them outright.[15] This process began the parceling and privatization of nonagricultural land in Zanzibar. Mortgage defaults led to consolidated holdings for a number of landlords by the early twentieth century. For Msabbah and Songoro, access to this property facilitated their entry into the ivory trade and helped finance their caravans. Their ability to move into the East African interior, however, was intertwined with the arc of al-Mauli immigration. The disturbed state of Wadi Maʻawil and the poor treatment the Mauli received in Oman provided incentives to move to East Africa where some of the clan accumulated slaves and property. Their freed slaves took the clan name and identified themselves as *sarīh* (freed slaves) of Talib bin Abdullah al-Mauli. Their link to this family also provided claims to land where they could build houses and sell or pledge them to creditors.

PROPERTY IN ZANZIBAR AND THE INTERIOR

In the 1850s and 1860s, Msabbah and Songoro used their property in Zanzibar to establish themselves as ivory traders. Of the two freed slaves of Talib bin Abdullah, Msabbah was the more prosperous, though Songoro's career as a caravan leader was better known. By tracking their transactions and their movements, their increased engagement and investment in the interior becomes clear. In 1858, Msabbah purchased property from an Omani Arab in Mzambaruni—an urban quarter of Zanzibar town—for MT$325.[16] In the years that followed, both Msabbah and Songoro traveled, traded, and acquired wealth on the mainland. The money that allowed them to purchase property in Zanzibar indicated their own rising standard of living, both in Zanzibar and on the African mainland. In the early 1860s, British traveler James Grant heard about the lavish caravans led by "Sungoro-bin-Tabeeb." Songoro supposedly traveled with a double-poled tent and a harem of sixty women. When Grant stayed at Songoro's camp in 1861, however, he only encountered five women. One of these women was Abyssinian (from Ethiopia) and another was Mtusi (from a region west of Lake Victoria). The presence of both of these women may say less about the extent of Songoro's travels than they do about the regional and extraregional practice of pawning or outright selling women.[17] The number of dependents, while not as extensive as the rumors had suggested, still indicates a man of means. Songoro was a good negotiator. He thrived on the mainland by bending patronage networks to his own advantage through the judicious use of credit and trade goods. In the early 1860s, Songoro traded near Lake Victoria and acquired large stores of ivory. Growing demand for tusks in Zanzibar was fueling the growth of long-distance trade and credit networks into the interior. Traders like Songoro were at the forefront, negotiating with African rulers and taking advantage of promissory notes. His ivory-laden caravan made him a target for local rulers, and when he attempted to return to Zanzibar, a local chief tried to extort half of the haul as an excise tax. Songoro escaped with his goods only through the intervention of Rumanika, the ruler of Karagwe, a kingdom on the western shore of Lake Victoria.[18] During the same caravan journey,

Songoro sold cloth and beads on credit to John Hanning Speke, Burton's former companion and Grant's partner, in Buganda. Speke wrote a chit for $50, payable in Zanzibar. When Songoro presented the chit in Zanzibar, it was cashed immediately.[19] This was not his first encounter with the credit markets and financiers of Zanzibar, and it was certainly not his last.

Msabbah's activities on the mainland are not as well documented. As part of a transaction in Zanzibar in 1866, however, he pledged property he owned in Unyamwezi, the trading hub of the central plateau.[20]

These freed slaves' ability to move easily and successfully between the coast and interior led to rumors about their pasts. Grant heard that Songoro had served time in prison for a robbery committed on his Arab master's orders. Grant concluded that Songoro had inherited his Arab master's "ill-gotten wealth" as compensation for taking the fall.[21] Such justice, were it meted out in Zanzibar, was uneven. The qadis were known for imprisoning people for unpaid debts and even seizing property for punishment. Criminals were also sentenced to jail time, though in the 1860s, the British agent Pelly complained that every year Sultan Majid freed prisoners during the Eid al-Adha—the celebration of the completion of the Hajj—and offered general amnesty to those imprisoned.[22] Thus Songoro may have benefitted from the sultan's largesse, as well as his former master's. Regardless, it was the property that he and Msabbah held in Zanzibar that would underwrite their future ivory ventures.

During the ivory boom of the late 1860s, Songoro and Msabbah used redeemable sales of property to raise capital for another ivory caravan. In 1866, both Songoro and Msabbah had returned to Zanzibar to underwrite their next venture. Redeemable sales had become a key element of financing the ivory trade from Zanzibar for nonelite traders. Both men sold properties to creditors with the option of repaying the price within a fixed time to regain them. The partners made two deals with different creditors under similar terms, and later Msabbah sought out the firm of Jairam Shivji—Zanzibar's most important trading house—to conclude a very large ivory deal. In February, Msabbah sold the property he had bought eight years before to Kurji Ramdas and promised to return within two years with seven hundred pounds (20 frasilas) of ivory.[23] In April, Songoro made a similar arrangement with slightly different terms. He pledged his house in Vuga, Zanzibar—another large *waqf* area—to the brothers Hashim and Qasim Baloo. Songoro promised to return in twenty-six months with 910 pounds of ivory (26 frasilas).[24]

Toward the end of August, Msabbah entered into a major agreement with Jairam Shivji. He contracted to bring 6,650 pounds of ivory (190 frasilas) within two years. In this case, however, Msabbah pledged property in

Unyamwezi, hundreds of miles away on the African mainland. Like Burton's companion Mwinyi Kidogo, Msabbah seemed to lead a double life, with establishments at the coast as well as in the interior. Msabbah offered "all his property" in Unyamwezi, including his slaves. He also guaranteed that Jairam Shivji would be first among his creditors and that no one could be paid until Jairam's debt was satisfied.[25] The terms of this deal, especially when compared to the others, show that Jairam Shivji's firm could make greater demands and presumably offer more in return. In each case, however, the surviving documents do not specify what Songoro and Msabbah received in return for their pledges of property and ivory. To avoid the appearance of usury, such details were usually recorded in a second, separate document. Given the vast weight of ivory promised, Songoro and Msabbah probably received a high value of trade goods. These three deals obligated the two caravan leaders and former slaves to procure more than eight thousand pounds of ivory with a value of nearly MT$13,000.[26] Their caravan experience and wealthy creditors positioned them for success, but triumph in the long-distance ivory trade was never guaranteed, especially during the transformation of the interior in the 1860s and 1870s.

IVORY AND THE EAST AFRICAN INTERIOR IN THE 1860S

The growing demand for ivory and the new Indian Ocean migration to the African interior had profound implications for African polities in the interior. The price of ivory in Bombay had averaged around $MT33 per frasila (a unit of 35 pounds) in the 1830s and 1840s, and the price in Zanzibar was similar in the 1840s. The 1850s saw a much greater demand, and prices over the decade averaged MT$45 per frasila in Zanzibar, but peaked in 1858 and 1859 above MT$52.[27] Political crisis in Zanzibar pushed more people to the caravan trails at the same time that ivory prices were at an all-time high. Msabbah and Songoro's early trading ventures coincided with a flow of political refugees from Zanzibar. The failure of Barghash's rebellion in 1859 brought a wave of Arabs and coastal people into the interior. On the same journey during which Grant had stayed with Songoro, Speke, his traveling companion, noted that the caravan routes in May 1861 were "thronged" with those fleeing Zanzibar. Speke encountered many of these people in Unyanyembe, the trading outpost town of the central caravan route. He called the settlement "a regular Botany Bay; all the blackguards of Zanzibar are flocking to it."[28] This infusion coincided with an ivory rush west of Lake Tanganyika. The high prices in Zanzibar encouraged traders to follow or leap the westward-moving elephant frontier to the unexploited ivory resources of the eastern Congo. Caravan leaders sought to exploit the extensive ivory stores there by using credit mechanisms in Zanzibar to underwrite the ventures. Juma bin Salim al-Bakri of Nizwa (known as Juma Merikani), with whom this book began, and the famed coastal trader Hamed bin Muhammad al-Murjebi (Tippu Tip) were among this group who went to the Congo. Settlements of Indian Ocean migrants grew beyond Kazeh (Tabora), at Ujiji (on the east coast of Lake Tanganyika) and in Nyangwe and Kasongo, which were nascent settlements on the Aruwimi River, a major tributary to the Congo.

While the eastern Congo was the boom region of the late 1860s, Songoro used his previous experience trading around Lake Victoria to establish himself on its southern shore. He built an outpost on the mainland near Kagei, with easy access to the main caravan routes to Unyamwezi, and also had a settlement nearby on the large island of Ukerewe. With these twinned trading stations, he was on the periphery of the expanding Buganda kingdom to the north, the newly established Nyamwezi trading chief Mirambo to the southwest, and the main coastal trading depot of Unyanyembe to the south.

In the East African interior, the ivory trade transformed long-standing kingdoms like Buganda and made it possible for new states and their leaders like Mirambo to become important figures. Songoro, on the southern shore of Lake Victoria, occupied what would become a contested buffer zone between two expansionist states: Buganda, under Kabaka Mutesa (1856–1884), and Urambo, led by the eponymous Mirambo (b., circa 1840).[29] The ancient kingdom of Buganda on the northern shore of the lake sought to adapt to the new Indian Ocean trade. Muslim traders had reached Buganda as early as 1844, and Mutesa enticed Arab and coastal traders to establish a permanent presence at his court. Mutesa sent delegations with presents to the sultan of Zanzibar, hoping to establish a direct outlet for Bugandan ivory, and Buganda also sought to control trade on the lake. Mutesa was especially eager to do this from the 1860s when traders from Egypt and Khartoum began to filter into southern Sudan and Buganda's northern periphery.[30] Historian Robert Reid notes that although Buganda was becoming less influential, the kingdom still wielded military and commercial power under Mutesa. The Bugandans' tremendous war canoes held more than forty people, allowed them to gain control of the lake, and complemented (or compensated for) their army.[31] With their massive canoes, Bugandans had been successful in controlling trade on the north and west sides of the lake and in limiting the roles of Arab and coastal traders. The same economic forces and incentives that Buganda accommodated created a new commercial-guerilla state in Urambo.

Mirambo's rise offers the most compelling example of the how the ivory trade transformed local politics in eastern Africa. The ivory trade created a new resource for rulers to control, and the contests over control also created an array of upstarts usurping power across the region.[32] Mirambo consolidated hereditary rule of a small Nyamwezi kingdom, asserted himself in another local succession dispute, and used his trade ties to build a new kind of state in eastern Africa. Mirambo's fighting forces—called *ruga-ruga*—also reacted to broader changes in warfare in eastern Africa during this time. They drew inspiration, organization, and techniques from the roving Ngoni bands that had reached eastern central Africa in the 1850s after their migrations out of southern Africa. Mirambo's initial territorial claims were north and west of the relatively new Arab settlement in Unyanyembe, but he soon sat astride vital trade routes from Unyanyembe, west to Lake Tanganyika, and north to Lake Victoria. These were the primary corridors of the ivory trade. Reid calls Mirambo's efforts "the most forceful African response" to the growing economic and political influence of coastal traders.[33] As such he became a force to be reckoned with for the coastal traders and their burgeoning ivory trade.

BUILDING A SECOND ZANZIBAR:
DHOWS AND DOWERIES

While Mutesa in Buganda and Mirambo in Urambo provide clear examples of the larger political and economic forces at work with the rise of the ivory trade in the region, Songoro's moves at the lake provide a more granular view of negotiating local allegiances to forge new connections through commerce and kinship. Songoro's two bases on the south-eastern end of Lake Victoria offered strategic advantages and required close allegiances with the rulers in each place. He set himself up on Ukerewe, a large island on the south side of the lake, and had a second headquarters at Kagei on the mainland. Ukerewe and Kagei were two days apart by lake canoe, separated by Speke Gulf, a huge inlet that Speke had visited in 1858 (and there concluded that he stood at the source of the Nile).[34] Ukerewe Island, with an area of more than 200 square miles, is the sixth largest lake island in the world. For Songoro, it offered protection from mainland raids, access to various points of the lake, plentiful timber for boat building, and agricultural bounty. Indeed, the island was a longtime food exporter on the lake. Songoro's station on the mainland, Kagei, in northern Usukuma, had fewer natural resources but was an important lakeside terminus of the caravan routes emanating from Unyanyembe. Songoro's efforts to control the ivory trade on the southern end of the lake had transformed Kagei by the late

MAP 8.1. Lake Victoria region

1870s into "a second Zanzibar" where coastal people felt at their ease.[35] The process of bringing the Indian Ocean to Lake Victoria, however, required Songoro to attend to the relationships with the rulers in both places—Kaduma in Kagei and Lukonge in Ukerewe—although he was more intimately tied to Lukonge.

A Dhow on Lake Victoria ⇆ 199

Songoro developed a close allegiance with Kaduma, the ruler of Kagei on the mainland, and Kaduma used the presence of the trader to raise his own profile. Kagei was a vibrant trade center for the surrounding region, a market where people exchanged foodstuffs, fish, cattle, hoes, iron wire, and salt. Kaduma was a vassal to a larger Sukuma state and was supposed to pay tribute to other regionally powerful men. At the same time, Kaduma ruled over an area of fifteen villages and was the patron of their headmen. He derived his authority from his paternal line and from his ability to make the medicines that brought rain.[36] He maintained his power through networks of half-brothers and other kin—he had four wives who lived in at least two different places within his realm—and through hosting elite men for elaborate beer drinking sessions. Kaduma's wealth had been measured in cattle, sheep, and goats.[37] Songoro, however, brought new idioms of power, and by February of 1875, Kaduma had become Songoro's "faithful ally," and the two were "inseparable friends."[38] Songoro helped connect Kaduma to the ivory trade, and the chief saw great advantage in establishing his own close connection to the Bugandan court. Kaduma wanted to cement this relationship through marriage and thus gain an advantage in the regional ivory trade. In 1877 he was eager to send his sons to Buganda because, he noted, "They will be able to ask Mtesa to send me ivory and a wife."[39] Even without this connection, however, Kaduma had grown more powerful due to the presence of Songoro and the growth of Kagei as a trading port and caravan terminus. As a result, he asserted a new autonomy by refusing to pay an annual tribute to the leader of Mwanza that his father, the former ruler, had traditionally paid.[40]

Songoro became even more deeply intertwined with Lukonge, the *omukana* (king) of Ukerewe Island, a relationship that allowed him to build the dhow and to maintain his standing on Lake Victoria. While Songoro and Lukonge likely slaughtered a goat between them to create a blood brotherhood, their relationship was embedded in credit and kinship, and both men sought advantages from their alliance. Lukonge (also written Rukonge) became the *omukana* of Ukerewe in about 1869 when his father, the previous *omukana*, died. Oral tradition suggests that Lukonge employed magic and deception to succeed his father, and once in power, Lukonge worked assiduously to eliminate his rivals. This included gouging out the eyes of his brother, the presumptive heir. Lukonge also systematically killed members of the three clans most closely associated with sorcery.[41] In addition to these machinations, Lukonge had to prove that he was a rainmaker, one of the sources of legitimacy for the *omukana* of Ukerewe. Lukonge was keen to use every possible resource to maintain his rule. Songoro arrived on the island during the early years of Lukonge's rule. This was likely in the late 1860s, after Songoro and Msabbah had financed their ivory ventures in Zanzibar. If Songoro had come north from Unyanyembe at that time, he would have encountered a famine across the Usukuma region, right up to the lakeshore. One chiefdom's residents called this period "the famine of the profiteers," and they remembered it as a time when the people of Ukerewe, a granary for the lake, sold them food at high prices.[42] Whether Songoro and his well-outfitted caravan took advantage of this imbalance or simply followed the trade to Ukerewe, his connection to the island and its leader soon deepened through marriage, providing benefits to both men.

Songoro's presence in Ukerewe buoyed Lukonge's position at a time when long-distance trade and Indian Ocean goods were increasingly important. Songoro had well-established ties in Zanzibar, and presumably in Unyanyembe, which made him a powerful trade partner. Songoro had established a strong rapport with Kaduma, the ruler of Kagei on the mainland, but he married and put his workshop on the island of Ukewere. As Tippu Tip's case revealed, kinship was a vital infrastructure for traders. Kinship ties influenced Songoro and Lukonge's relationship and became an aspect of the web of credit and indebtedness that arose between them. Songoro married one of Lukonge's sisters, cementing ties of kinship and acquiring great wealth. We do not know the name of the *omukana*'s sister who became the wife of the Zanzibari trader, but Songoro's presents to the family included 350 pounds of beads and 300 yards of cloth.[43] Although prices were volatile, this quantity of beads would have purchased 175 pounds of ivory in Buganda in the next decade.[44] This amount was nearly 20 percent of the ivory that Songoro owed for his house in Zanzibar and provides some measure of the value of this relationship. For Lukonge, this wealth would help him outmaneuver his rivals, and for Songoro, this marriage alliance made it possible to build a dhow. Songoro's relationship with the ruler offered security in Ukerewe, and Lukonge advanced him the timber needed for the boat. Perhaps because of their kin relationship, the two men did not specify the terms of this debt. The differing assumptions about the obligations that this debt created would eventually prove fatal.

IVORY RIVALRIES

Songoro's decision to build the first dhow on Lake Victoria in the mid-1870s highlights the growing stakes in the ivory trade and the differences in trade and regional power between Lake Victoria and Lake Tanganyika. Richard Burton sighted the Indian Ocean vessels on Lake Tanganyika in 1858, nearly twenty years before a dhow sailed on Lake Victoria. At that time, the thriving trade town of Ujiji, on the shores of Lake Tanganyika, had become a point of embarkation for crossing to eastern Congo. Arabs and other coastal traders had built dhows to convey their own trade goods and circumvent protracted negotiations with local boat owners. On Tanganyika there was no dominant lacustrine power equivalent to Lake Victoria's Bugandans and their canoes. Historian Gerald Hartwig has argued that Bugandan hegemony on Lake Victoria limited the movement of people and goods there.[45] Songoro, who had traded in Karagwe and Uganda in the early 1860s, was aware of the Bugandan position. While it is unclear whether Songoro's dhow on Lake Victoria was meant to augment or undercut Bugandan trade, building it permitted him autonomous movement on the lake. His status in Kagei and in Ukerewe depended on good relations with Buganda, and by the 1870s Songoro was orienting the ivory trade on the lake toward the settlement at Unyanyembe and onward to the Indian Ocean coast.[46] He did so at a time when ivory was in great demand and its trade hotly contested.

Rivalries over access to the ivory trade shaped conflicts in the interior, but these were inflected with the language of indebtedness and coastal disdain for African practices. During the early 1870s, Mirambo interrupted the ivory trade to Unyanyembe (and on to the coast) by almost shutting down the caravan routes to the central depot. Mirambo's main blockade occurred between 1871 and 1874, but he harried caravans until his death in 1884. A dispute about credit and ivory sparked this long-running feud with the Arabs at Unyanyembe. At first, Mirambo was friendly with the traders who arrived from the coast. Some benefited from proximity to Mirambo while others received gifts of cattle or opportunities to buy his ivory. Around 1870, at the height of the ivory rush in the eastern Congo, however, one unnamed Arab took ivory on credit from Mirambo but then refused to repay his debt. Mirambo appealed to the other Arabs at Unyanyembe to help enforce his claims, but they demurred. Mirambo then held up a caravan led by the Arab's partner, refusing to let it pass until the debt was paid. The caravan's leader tried to negotiate a partial payment, but Mirambo rejected the offer and attacked the caravan to extract his due.[47] This was neither the first nor the last time that coastal traders reneged on implicit credit arrangements with Africans, but this instance may have had the greatest implications: war and complete disruption of the ivory trade.

This dispute also laid bare racial and cultural assumptions of Omanis in the interior. Said bin Salim al-Lamki, the de facto governor of the Arab settlement in Unyanyembe, wrote to Barghash, the Zanzibar sultan, in February 1872 to report the war and to request help. Said bin Salim feared that "all the Mshenzi" (i.e., heathens, non-Muslims) were against them and the Arabs and Swahili were embroiled in conflict. "We and the people of Mrima are now in great distress," he claimed.[48] This call to the coast for reinforcements communicated that Said bin Salim, descended from an important Omani family (with a mother from Madagascar), had a certain vision of the social order.[49] In these comments, Said bin Salim positioned himself and the other Omani Arabs as one group, and the Swahili and the people from the Mrima (the main coast opposite Zanzibar) as another, two groups allied against the *washenzi*. He refers to Mirambo and his followers as *washenzi*, the Swahili word for wild, uncivilized people, because of their status as nonbelievers.[50] Arab disdain for Mirambo and his followers exacerbated the trade war.

Despite their governor's assertions about cultural superiority, the Indian Ocean migrants in Tabora were unable to gain the upper hand over Mirambo and suffered financial losses. Other Omani Arabs who wrote about the war emphasized the potential loss of property as well as the danger to themselves.[51] In June 1873, when British explorer Verney Lovett Cameron was traveling toward Tabora in central Unyanyembe, he heard that Mirambo had been fighting the Arabs there for three or four years but "was still unconquered; for, although all the Arabs at Taborah, aided by numerous native allies, had taken the field against him, they had been unable to drive him from the vicinity of their settlements."[52] In Zanzibar, Barghash had temporarily aided those in Unyanyembe by dispatching one thousand Baluchi soldiers. In August 1873, Cameron reported that another two thousand people had arrived from the coast. Ironically, these forces sent to quell the disturbances and increase the flow of ivory to Zanzibar were so expensive to maintain that Barghash increased the tax on ivory coming from the Mrima ports by more than 135 percent, from MT$9 to MT$12.25.[53] These Zanzibari forces were ineffective against Mirambo and his *ruga-ruga*, a mobile enemy. The fact that the Zanzibari forces's erstwhile allies, the coastal settlers in Tabora, were plagued by factions and cliques, did not help. Barghash withdrew the forces at the end of 1874 and was determined, according to Vice Consul Elton, "to leave the Arab Colonists to fight their own battles."[54]

The disruption of the ivory trade at this time challenged those in debt to Zanzibar merchants and sparked creative solutions to end the stalemate. This was true for elite Arabs and more humble freed slaves. Historian Abdul Sheriff has argued that coastal traders responded to Mirambo's intrusions by dusting off old ideas and trying new ones.[55] Amran bin Masoud al-Barwani, a political refugee to the interior who had supported Barghash in the 1859 uprising, was a wealthy and successful trader in Unyanyembe who tried to reopen an abandoned caravan route to the coast. Amran bin Masoud came from an elite family, sold a farm in Zanzibar for $7,000 in a redeemable sale, and concluded multiple ivory deals. In Unyanyembe, his huge house, called Baharein ("Two Seas") was "the finest house" in the settlement. It was one hundred feet long, twenty feet high, and surmounted by a door that was "a marvel of carving-work." Inside its thick walls, the rafters were intricately hewn. Amran bin Masoud had spared no expense when he purchased the house for sixty frasilas of ivory at a time when traders from the coast could acquire houses for less than thirty frasilas. He maintained an irrigation system for the gardens that relied on a shadoof (a counterpoised sweep, like those used in Egypt) to draw water.[56] The deadlock in the ivory trade in the 1870s, however, threatened his wealth and his standing. He hoped to go south of Unyanyembe through Usangu to connect to the Ruaha river valley and thus escape Mirambo's depredations. Amran bin Masoud was killed in his attempt to pioneer a new trail to the coast. Songoro's background and wealth paled by comparison with Amran bin Masoud, but his dhow was also an innovation to skirt Mirambo's partial blockage of trade, especially between Buganda and Unyanyembe.[57] He had begun building the boat sometime before 1875.

By 1875, Songoro's establishments on the lake had become important nodes in the networks linking Buganda and the coastal traders at Unyanyembe. As such, they attracted Henry Morton Stanley on his way to Buganda that year. Stanley and his men misunderstood Songoro, characterized a rampant slave trade, and made an urgent plea for Christian missionaries. Stanley and his men imagined a much closer relationship between traders in the interior and Zanzibar. They arrived in Kagei only a few months after Barghash had vowed to let his putative subjects in the interior fend for themselves in the face of Mirambo's challenges, but Stanley and his lieutenants came to some unusual, incorrect conclusions about Songoro's ties. Stanley characterized "Sungoro Tarib" as the agent of "Mse Saba," evidence that Songoro's fellow freed slave was still alive but not with him in Kagei.[58] Then, while Stanley explored the lake and visited Buganda, his lieutenant Frank Pocock spent fifty-eight days in Kagei. Songoro sent Pocock frequent presents (including scarce commodities like rice) and invited Pocock to dine with him. Pocock was a fisherman and a boatsman of modest background who wrote to his parents from Kagei that "I can't get on with the language much." So, despite his long stay and seemingly close relationship with Songoro, Pocock believed that Kagei belonged to the sultan of Zanzibar and that Songoro was the sultan's slave.[59] Thus, at a basic level of language and comprehension, these European visitors misunderstood the man who welcomed them in Kagei.

When Stanley arrived, Songoro and Kaduma, Kagei's ruler, both yearned for the latest news from Zanzibar.[60] We do not know what Stanley told them about the world, but what Stanley told the world about Songoro and the lake was grossly exaggerated and created a missionary scramble for central Africa. This was his second journey to central Africa and his first trip since his much-heralded expedition to find David Livingstone. By lionizing Livingstone, Stanley had drawn attention to both the antislavery and missionary movements.[61] When Stanley met Songoro in Kagei in 1875, both of these topics were very much on his mind. Thus even though Stanley depended on Songoro's hospitality, his supply of rice, and his various clients, Stanley painted his host as an inveterate slave trader. Stanley's purple prose stereotyped Songoro and invoked worn tropes of Arab slave traders around the Indian Ocean. Songoro's unfinished dhow, Stanley concluded, was being constructed so that Songoro could "prosecute more actively his nefarious trade." Stanley knew that the slave trade would attract his Victorian readers' attention. Stanley's earlier dispatches detailed slave abuse and proved influential in the House of Commons in 1872 when Parliament took up the report of the Select Committee on the East African Slave Trade. These parliamentary deliberations called for a stricter antislavery treaty with Zanzibar. After long negotiations, Sultan Barghash had been forced to sign the treaty in 1873 (see chapter 7).

Stanley reached Zanzibar in 1873 after the treaty had been signed and saw obvious changes in the island metropolis. On the mainland, however, he played up the threat of the slave trade on his journey to Buganda. On the site where Zanzibar's old slave market had stood, for instance, an Anglican cathedral was being built. On the mainland, Stanley wished that he had been deputized to execute slavers because he thought the slave trade plagued the region. When Stanley wrote about the lake, Songoro was clearly in his sights. "If ever a pirate deserved death for inhuman crimes, Songoro, the slave-trader, deserves death." Stanley fixated on the dhow and invited his readers to imagine its effect on the regional slave trade. "When Songoro has floated his dhow and hoisted his blood-stained ensign, the great sin will increase tenfold, and the caravan-road to Unyanyembe will become hell's highway."[62]

Songoro—who had personally known bondage—was also no stranger to the complexity of slavery from the Indian Ocean littoral to the far interior. He had been a slave and client, but also became a patron and slave owner. His establishments between Kagei and Ukerewe included approximately eighty people, both freemen and slaves. Some were trusted caravan chiefs who had spent significant time in the interior. One of his men, for instance, had traveled the Maasai route to the lake in the late 1860s.[63] Some of his dependents tended his large herd of cattle. Some women likely worked in agriculture, and others were concubines or pawns, such as the two women—one Ethiopian, one Tutsi—who had accompanied him in the early 1860s. His retinue of slaves included individuals who delighted in terrifying the naive coast men accompanying Stanley by telling them tales of cannibalistic rites.[64] Thus, slavery—with its varying degrees of domination and dependence—was part of everyday life in Songoro's settlements, and he inevitably trafficked in slaves. Yet, Stanley's account of a brutal trade seems overblown. Less than three years later, another British visitor who spent four months around Kagei and Ukererwe reported, "I see and hear nothing of slave gangs. Slavery exists as a domestic institution, and those captured in war are kept as such, but I do not think they are sold to traders."[65]

Following his visit to Buganda, Stanley also exaggerated the kabaka's desire for Christian missionaries. Mutesa professed Islam, but his indication of an interest in Christianity spurred Stanley to issue a fateful call. Stanley's claim that missionaries were needed on the lake may have been as hyperbolic as his characterization of the slave trade and Songoro's role, but it yielded speedier results. In April 1875, Stanley reached Buganda from Kagei and Kabaka Mutesa appeared to be a practicing Muslim. The first Muslim traders had reached the kabaka's court in the 1840s, during Mutesa's father's reign, but Mutesa's submission to Islam came in the late 1860s or early 1870s under the influence of Khamis bin Abdullah, an Arab from Muscat who had lived for more than a year in Buganda.[66] Mutesa proclaimed Islam, dressed in the coastal fashion, and fasted for Ramadan. Indeed, Khamis bin Abdullah's good looks, noble bearing, and firm leadership inspired Arabs, Africans, and Europeans. In Unyanyembe during the early fight against Mirambo in 1871, Khamis rallied the Arabs at Unyanyembe by calling them "Children of Oman" and mustered a force of 250 Africans, the largest contingent of any Arab or coastal trader in the settlement at that time.[67] Khamis bin Abdullah's charms translated well to the kabaka's court. Mutesa "fell in love with him," and Khamis bin Abdullah led Mutesa to Islam. Stanley also gushed about his earlier encounter with the charismatic man, claiming that he "never saw an Arab or Mussulman who attracted me as so much as Khamis bin Abdullah."[68]

When Stanley arrived in Buganda in 1875, Mutesa expressed some interest in Christianity and played to the explorer's ego. As a result of Mutesa's query, Stanley wrote a letter home, published in the *Daily Telegraph* later that year, that contained an exhortatory call for missionaries:

> But, oh that some pious, practical missionary would come here! What a field and a harvest ripe for the sickle of civilisation! Mutesa would give him everything he desired—houses, lands, cattle, ivory, &c., he might call a province his own in one day. It is not the mere preacher, however, that is wanted here. The Bishops of Great Britain collected, and all the classic youth of Oxford and Cambridge, would effect nothing by mere talk with the intelligent people of Uganda. It is the practical Christian tutor who can teach people how to become Christians, cure their diseases, construct dwellings, understand and exemplify agriculture, and turn his hand to anything like a sailor—this is the man who is wanted. Such a one, if he can be found, would become the saviour of Africa.[69]

Stanley's letter arrived in England at an acute moment of interest in heroic Christian missionaries to Africa. David Livingstone, the Victorian ideal of an African missionary, died in May 1873 near the south end of Lake Tanganyika, and his faithful servants embalmed his body and carried it more than a thousand miles to Zanzibar. From there, his body went to England, where it was laid to rest at Westminster Abbey on April 18, 1875, four days after Stanley penned his call for missionaries. When Stanley's letter was published in October, the call to save the souls of Africans touched a popular nerve. Stanley's optimistic take on Mutesa's court prompted the Christian Missionary Society (CMS) to prepare a mission to the lake almost immediately.[70] The missionary scramble for Uganda had begun.

A SALE, A SAIL, AND ASSAIL

When the first CMS missionaries reached Kagei on the southern end of the lake in January 1877, they became immersed in overlapping networks of commerce, credit, and kinship that they did not fully understand. Kaduma and Songoro were among the first people C. T. Wilson and Thomas O'Neill met. Wilson described Kaduma as clad in "filthy clothes," and he called Songoro "a negro trader," who was dressed in "a clean white robe, looking cool and comfortable."[71] The coastal men who had traveled with the missionaries during the six-month journey from the coast found Kagei's environment very familiar, which led the missionary Lieutenant Shergold Smith to describe Songoro's settlement as a "second Zanzibar."[72] Lukonge, Songoro's brother-in-law and ruler of Ukerewe, also invited the missionaries to visit the island, and the Europeans admired Songoro's accomplishments in both places, where he had introduced new crops and new technology. Not only did he grow rice, onions, tomatoes, "and other vegetables foreign to the country," but he was also building a dhow. The missionaries had brought a dinghy and a small boat with them but realized these were insufficient vessels for long distance lake travel. They were unwilling to use the lake canoes and complained about their craftsmanship and about the oarsmen's poor control of the boat. So it is not surprising that by May they had negotiated to buy Songoro's still unfinished dhow for £100.[73]

As the purchase of the dhow revealed, the economy on the lake functioned by connecting the scarcity of materials and labor to the circulation of beads and currency. The CMS delegation members—led by Smith—paid £100 for the dhow and an additional £9 for the sail. In the same transaction they also paid Songoro £25 for beads and gave him £20 as a gift for Lukonge. Smith rationalized these expenses based on his growing knowledge of the regional economy and his isolation from credit networks. If they had built the boat themselves, it would have cost "much time and more money."[74] The scarcity of lumber in Kagei would have made it impossible to build there, and if they had tried to build their own boat on Ukerewe, Smith reasoned, they would have been stuck bargaining with Lukonge on unfavorable terms. As for the beads, Smith guessed that they were four times what they would have cost in Zanzibar, but the price was acceptable when considering the potential losses on a journey from the coast.[75] Besides, Smith desperately needed the beads to finance CMS activities at the lake.

Smith had to rely on Songoro for trade goods to keep his mission solvent and judged Songoro to be fair in his transactions because the delegation had verified some of his deals. The weights that Songoro used, for instance, matched the scale that the CMS had brought with them.[76] In addition, Smith had to rely on Songoro for credit and supplies because he had mismanaged his funds on the journey. In January, Smith had acquired cloth and beads while passing through Unyanyembe. He bought more beads from Songoro in late May or early June, and traveled to Unyanyembe again in August for more goods. He had lost goods on the road and was spending more money than he had. Smith admitted in a letter that "my boast of self-supporting is only in abeyance."[77] Very much like the traders and merchants he had met on his trip from the coast, Smith ended up relying on credit, promissory notes, and the prices of scarce goods. He too was hoping to wait out his difficult situation and receive supplies from the coast or an invitation to Buganda.

While Songoro helped buoy the mission's finances, his own dubious deals endangered them all. Songoro had built his dhow on Ukerewe, the better-wooded island that his brother-in-law Lukonge ruled. Songoro was enmeshed in networks of obligation, and his ability to build the vessel required the cooperation of his host and affine. The missionaries assumed there was a seamless relationship between Lukonge and Songoro; however, multiple layers of obligation and Songoro's attempts to profit unduly from the sale created discord. Lukonge had advanced Songoro the timber to build the dhow, and when Songoro sold it in May 1877 he avoided settling up with Lukonge. Songoro also pocketed the £20 that the CMS has given him for the chief. Thus, in 1877, while the missionaries were trying to finish the dhow and to decide where to build their station, a dispute over unpaid debts simmered on Ukerewe. While the CMS representatives waited for an invitation from Mutesa—who seemed less enthusiastic about the presence of the missionaries than Stanley had suggested two years earlier—the missionaries debated whether to put a permanent station at Ukerewe or Kagei. In June, however, a letter arrived from Mutesa, who invited them to come and expressed special greetings to Lukonge, Songoro, and Kaduma. With this invitation, the missionaries focused on travels to Buganda, even as they completed the

FIGURE 8.1. Building the first dhow on Lake Victoria at Ukerewe. From Thomas O'Neill, *Sketches of African Scenery from Zanzibar to Victoria Nyanza: Being a Series of Coloured Lithographic Pictures, from Original Sketches* (London: Church Missionary House, 1878).

construction of the dhow. When the boat was completed in November, they christened it Chimosi, a pun that played on its being the first dhow of the lake (from the Swahili root, *mosi*, "first") and on the initials of the Church Mission Society.[78] From the missionary point of view, the invitation to Buganda and the finished dhow had resolved some of their problems. However, the completion of the dhow unleashed a dispute between Songoro and Lukonge about debt and ownership.

When the CMS missionaries attempted to launch the boat, Lukonge challenged them and "demanded why his property was being removed."[79] Speaking through an interpreter, Lukonge explained that Songoro told him nothing about a sale, only that the missionaries were helping to finish the dhow. Lukonge knew Songoro still owed him for the material and thought the missionaries were stealing the boat. Claims to ownership of the dhow highlighted overlapping, contradictory practices of commerce, documents, and witnesses that were at play in eastern and central Africa. Attempts to reconcile the debts revealed the layers of obligation and influence that Songoro, the coastal trader, and Lukonge, the local ruler, could exercise over each other. In response to the unpaid debt, Lukonge's men seized the mast from the boat to keep it from sailing.

Songoro had built a career on the interstices of written documents (such as redeemable sales and the acknowledgment of debts) and face-to-face negotiations. These two practices illuminate the contingent space Songoro occupied between the Indian Ocean and the African interior. His attempts to build the boat on credit from Lukonge and profit from its sale to the missionaries brought these practices into conflict. Lukonge believed that the dhow was at least partially his, and he was not persuaded by the written documents and their attestations. When Lieutenant Smith sent his servant to Lukonge with a deed of sale, the illiterate chief scrutinized it and asked, "What is the use of a piece of paper?" He then sent for Songoro, who read the document to the king and explained its contents (and metaphysics), noting that his mark attesting to the sale, "was as good as himself." Lukonge was dismissive. According to Smith, "To him it was merely a bit of paper such as he had seen Mzungu throw away."[80]

The initial confrontation over the dhow, the debt, and the ownership led to three days of intense negotiation grounded in the relationship between promissory notes and property. During this time, the facts that Smith had paid Songoro for the dhow and had given a present meant for Lukonge that was never delivered came to light. Lukonge worried that if the dhow left, he would not be able to recover his debt from Songoro, and he insisted that Songoro fulfill his debt obligation. Lukonge's secondary concern was the credit mechanism and the paper. How, he wanted to know, could a piece of paper be turned into cloth or beads? Lieutenant Smith created a demonstration: he wrote to his colleague O'Neill and requested that he send a cloth by return messenger. He gave the paper to Lukonge, who, after examining the script, asked one of his messengers to deliver it to O'Neill. A cloth came back, and Lukonge was so delighted (or clever!) that he asked to do it again. Secure in his newfound knowledge of written transactions, Lukonge determined that the missionaries did own the boat. Still, Songoro owed him for the wood.

How could Songoro repay his debt? Lukonge insisted on the most valuable commodity available: ivory. He demanded three frasilas (equivalent to 105 pounds) to settle the debt. Songoro counter-offered with traditional commodities: brass wire, cattle, and women. Lukonge would not budge. Songoro needed time. His debts from the coast remained unpaid, and he did not have that much ivory in Ukerewe. Instead, he left twenty coils of wire, sixteen head of cattle, and six children as a pledge to Lukonge. Songoro called them his children, but Smith considered them slaves.[81] Songoro bought time to fetch ivory from the mainland, and Lukonge released his lien on the dhow.

The dispute and ill will with his coastal trading partner occurred at the same time that Lukonge was trying to manage both internal and external threats to his rule. To the Bakwerere subjects, Lukonge's legitimacy as *omukana* and rain maker was in doubt. In February 1877, during a long dry spell that saw millet dying on the stalks, people had threatened to kill Lukonge.[82] Such threats were likely expressed in the idiom of witchcraft and poisons; consequently, Lukonge became obsessed with supplementing his rainmaking techniques and his store of poisons. He beseeched the newly arrived CMS missionaries for both and asked repeatedly for poisons.[83] These threats to his legitimacy were intertwined with external confrontations. Lukonge's challenges on Ukerewe included a chief of the former royal line who wished to depose him, a set of ongoing boundary disputes, and Bugandan aggression. His rivals on the island had recently killed six hundred men and carried away three hundred head of cattle.

While seeking new means of rain and poison, Lukonge also responded with diplomacy and force. First, he took advantage of his enemies' encounter with the Buganda. When Bugandan war canoes approached the island in July 1877, Lukonge's rivals struck preemptively, killing two Bugandans, and the threat of their return led people to abandon their settlement. Building on this, Lukonge sent a request to Mutesa for two hundred canoes to help him press his advantage on the island. Rather than wait for an answer, however, he also deployed troops against his rivals. Some of Lukonge's tactics included ritual demonstrations of power and stand offs in which no one was killed. In another confrontation, however, Lukonge's soldiers returned with twelve severed hands to prove they had killed their enemies.[84] In this broader context of Lukonge's rule, Songoro's dhow and the missionary presence were part of a much larger puzzle.

While Songoro gathered his ivory, the missionaries launched their dhow to great disappointment. To prepare for its maiden voyage from Ukerewe to Kagei, the Chimosi was celebrated in the "Zanzibar fashion" by tying up the overseer and conducting "flea" dances. If the missionaries made merry, however, they did not do so for long. The dhow struggled to reach Kagei. On its initial journey the boat smashed on the rocks and sank with the missionaries' instruments, books, and clothes on board. They managed to recover everything except Smith's bible.[85] Amidst profound disappointment in Kagei, Smith and O'Neill received the message that Songoro had the ivory to pay Lukonge and redeem his property.

Songoro wanted the missionaries to go back to the island to witness the transaction. This socialized pattern of transactions aligned with coastal expectations of a witness. Yet Songoro's seemingly unusual request of the missionaries when they arrived on Ukerewe signaled that this was not a typical transaction. He asked them to take his wives and children aboard their small boat, the *Daisy*, and bring them to Kagei. One of these wives was Lukonge's sister. Smith and O'Neill agreed and sent their boat with Songoro's dependents back to Kagei. The two missionaries remained on the island with six of their men and no boat. Songoro had twenty-three followers with him. He was vastly outnumbered by his hosts' subordinates.

While Songoro had weighed his goods fairly when trading with Smith and the CMS group, he sought to shortchange Lukonge by only giving him two of the three frasilas of ivory. According to Smith, Songoro claimed that the chief would not know the difference.[86] Like the Arab trader who stiffed Mirambo, and his partner who tried to negotiate away part of the debt, Songoro miscalculated. He misunderstood the degree to which a local ruler—spurred by the new ivory economies and beholden to a plethora of local forces—was attuned to the intricacies of trade.

At the root of the dispute between Songoro and Lukonge was an unpaid debt, but this was not an impersonal accounting transaction. The debt was one part of a vast web of connections that included kinship, differential access to the growing trade in ivory, and the credit networks in Zanzibar and beyond. Ambition, jealousy, and greed also played their parts. The dispute between brothers-in-law escalated quickly to violence.

On the night of December 13, 1877, Lukonge launched a deadly attack on Songoro's settlement. When Songoro sustained a spear wound to his head, he fled to the missionaries for refuge. Lukonge demanded that the missionaries surrender Songoro, but they refused. In the ensuing battle, Songoro, Smith, and O'Neill were killed. Missionary O'Neill was said to have shot thirty people before he was hit in the head by an arrow. Meanwhile, Smith supposedly spent most of the battle writing in his book. No one recorded Songoro's actions in the fight, but it was rumored that the trader and the two missionaries were decapitated.[87] Two of Songoro's followers escaped, and one of the missionaries' men—a Zanzibar carpenter—was captured alive. More than fifty people died that day.

In the aftermath of the attack, the far-flung networks that had brought these parties together carried the news of their demise. Messengers were dispatched to Buganda and to Unyanyembe where the reactions showed the importance of Songoro and his position on the lake. When the *Daisy*'s captain returned to the island, two of Songoro's surviving men swam out to meet him. The pilot dropped them in Kagei and went straight to Buganda to inform the CMS representatives and Mutesa. The kabaka offered to send one thousand canoes to punish Lukonge. In the other direction, Songoro's two men landed in Kagei and followed the caravan route to Unyanyembe. On the same day the messengers arrived in Unyanyembe, January 4, 1878, the governor of the Arab colony, Said bin Salim al-Lamki, sent a message to Zanzibar. He informed Sultan Barghash that "the Christians, together with your subject Msabha [Msabbah], have been murdered." The governor conflated the two former slaves and business partners, reported the many deaths at Ukerewe, and explained "there was no immediate cause for this attack, but it was in the hearts of the people of the island to do it."[88]

Said bin Salim's assessment was incorrect. The immediate cause of the attack was an Indian Ocean vessel setting sail on an African lake. But this occurred within networks of mobility and indebtedness that stretched from the tribal wars of the Omani interior to the merchant houses of Zanzibar and the deep interior of central Africa. Relationships of indebtedness and kinship allowed freed slaves to pledge property they owned at the coast and in the interior, to pioneer new trade routes, to accumulate stores of ivory, and to occupy an ill-defined frontier between a traditional power, the kabaka of Buganda, and a new ivory lord, Mirambo in Urambo. Through negotiations, deceptions, and grit, Songoro built "a second Zanzibar" on a massive inland lake and its first dhow became one sign of many that Lake Victoria had become part of the Indian Ocean.

CODA

The story of Songoro offers a challenge and a microcosm of the expanding Indian Ocean world. New evidence of Songoro's slave origins, his partnership with Msabbah, his property holdings in Zanzibar, and his relationships with creditors help us see a little-known historical actor in a new light, firmly grounded in Zanzibar. The older evidence from missionaries and explorers supports a view focused on the interior. Indeed, the death of Songoro and the missionaries was a significant turning point in the history of East Africa and its relationship with the world. Nearly fifty years ago, Hartwig argued that these deaths connected the burgeoning missionary effort, the fortunes of two African rulers (Mirambo and Mutesa) who had benefited from trade, the stability of the coastal settlements at Tabora, and the relationship between Zanzibar and the mainland.[89] But that is only one part of a bigger picture.

Songoro and Msabbah are also important players in the history of the coast and Indian Ocean. They are linked to this history by the way in which they got started in trade: a redeemable sale of property in Zanzibar. One of the properties that Msabbah included in a redeemable sale to Jairam Shivji became the focal point of a legal battle between the customs master and the sultan of Zanzibar in 1887.[90] The fact that this battle took place in a consular court where a *qadi* squared off against an India-trained lawyer makes clear the competing legal norms that beset Zanzibar. Historian Fahad Bishara situates this case within the emerging legal pluralism of an increasing colonized Indian Ocean. At issue was the legality of the original redeemable sale. Clearly the debtor had defaulted (when he died on the mainland), but the customs master and sultan each relied on different documents and witnesses, which raised important epistemological questions.[91] This same legal pluralism in Zanzibar ensnared the large piece of property that had been set aside as a pious endowment (*waqf*) for the Mauli and their freed slaves in the mid-nineteenth century. The Protectorate government had tried to impose a ground rent on this *waqf* land. A man who had bought a plot there from a freed slave refused to pay. The Waqf Commission, led by esteemed Islamic scholars, sued him and lost decisively. This established a precedent in Zanzibar for land tenure and Islamic law.[92]

Thus, while compelling history can focus narrowly on the events in Zanzibar or the series of actions in the interior of East Africa, the sometimes-curious case of the freed slaves Songoro and Msabbah, seen in the broadest context, reveals overlapping and interlinked worlds. The individuals who occupied these worlds and moved between them help us to understand the dynamism of the Indian Ocean and its distant shores in the nineteenth century.

9 ⁓ "Everything Is Pledged to Its Time"
Salih bin Ali, Debt, and Rebellion in the Omani Interior

DURING THE SECOND HALF of the nineteenth century, debt and mobility were critically important to structuring political conflict and shifting power dynamics throughout the western Indian Ocean. The story of Salih bin Ali al-Harthi illuminates how credit from Zanzibar leveraged power and shaped influence in Oman thousands of miles away. Salih bin Ali (1834–1895), the paramount sheikh (*shaykh tamima*) of the large al-Harthi clan, lived in a marginal region of Sharqiya, traveled and studied in the western Indian Ocean as a young man, drew on kinship networks that stretched across the ocean, and manipulated property sales and debt to challenge the sultan in Muscat. His career as a powerful tribal and religious leader was predicated on a sense of timing: when to rise in rebellion and when to abide. Hampered intermittently by debt, he was keenly aware of time as he tried to remake the political order in Oman.

Salih bin Ali was a prominent leader in Sharqiya who led Oman's powerful Hinawi tribal confederation. His credentials as an Ibadi *'alim* attracted students to study under him, and his cooperation with the Ibadi elite made him a prominent force in conservative politics. He could easily be seen as the epitome of a tribal leader embroiled in domestic politics of an isolated Arabian interior, but his reach was much broader, and his Indian Ocean connections were a vital source of power that gave him access to credit to underwrite his efforts to unify Oman under Ibadi rule. In 1868, his personal imprimatur and his military leadership helped to overthrow the sultan and brought to power an imamate, the ideal form of the state for Ibadi Muslims. In the decades that followed the fall of the short-lived imamate, Salih bin Ali's feints and attacks against the sultan Turki bin Said in Muscat destabilized the country, and these challenges continued after Turki's son Faysal assumed the throne in 1888.

From the 1860s to his death in 1895, Salih was second to the Omani sultan in power, and by using his "fine talent for intrigue," he vied for first place by leading multiple assaults on Muscat.[1] No nineteenth-century history of Oman makes sense without considering his role. Historians have portrayed him as a scholar, a scoundrel, a resistance hero, and a caretaker imam in the Omani milieu.[2] Scholars have overlooked, however, Salih bin Ali's Indian Ocean connections that underwrote his actions in Oman. His father had been a widely traveled representative for the sultan, and Salih bin Ali also spent several years in East Africa as a young man. Later, he actively cultivated allies among the Harthi and managed his debts by selling and mortgaging property in the Zanzibar capital markets, which allowed him to underwrite rebellions in Oman. Salih bin Ali's political, military, and religious legacies are apparent in the independent imamate that his sons and students founded in 1913. This imamate undercut the Muscat sultan, and a 1920 treaty formalized a division of power between an interior imamate and a coastal sultanate that would remain in place through the late 1950s. This chapter details Salih bin Ali's activities to show how debt and mobility across the Indian Ocean affected the political landscape of interior Oman.

Salih bin Ali was born in 1834 to a family rooted in the Omani interior but with growing connections to the western Indian Ocean and beyond. Ṣāliḥ bin ʿAlī bin Nāṣir bin ʿIsa bin Ṣāliḥ al-Sumrī al-Ḥārthī spent his early years in oases settlements that dotted Wadi Batha in the Sharqiya region of the Omani interior.[3] Sharqiya's low rainfall and environmental precarity meant that access to *falaj* irrigation was important for survival. Salih bin Ali's father descended from the sheikhly line of the Sumri tribal grouping within the Harthi clan and traveled widely as a representative of the sultan. His mother came from another subclan of the Harthi. She gave birth to him in Mudayrib, and Salih was raised a few miles south of there in al-Qabil, a settlement his forbearers founded. Inscriptions on the intricate prayer niche of the old mosque in al-Qabil testify that Salih bin Isa bin Rashid al-Harthi—the great-great-grandfather of Salih bin Ali—constructed the *falaj* (water channel) in 1758 and built the mosque. Claiming unused land, he dug (or renewed) the *falaj*. At its outflow, he built al-Qabil's first house, known as al-Ḥiṣn (the citadel/fortress).⁴ These activities would have required substantial resources and this construction suggests early Harthi engagement with oceanic trade. Opening a *falaj* also gave the family a permanent share of water, so they would not have to buy irrigation time through the monthly auction. Thus when the *falaj* was running, they enjoyed plentiful access to irrigation.

During Salih bin Ali's childhood in the 1830s, the hamlet of al-Qabil had fifty houses, but according to one British visitor, only three or four were well built.⁵ From this modest settlement, Salih's father Ali bin Nasir traveled widely. Whereas the British visitor in Oman had been disparaging of al-Qabil in the 1830s, less than a decade later, a British ship captain worked to ensure that Ali bin Nasir was properly fêted on their journey from Aden to Zanzibar. In 1843, Ali bin Nasir returned from his second trip to London, where he concluded a treaty as an envoy of Said bin Sultan, the Omani sultan. In 1838, during his first journey to that distant isle, Ali bin Nasir carried congratulations and "presents of great value" to mark the accession of Queen Victoria. Ali bin Nasir had also completed eight trading voyages to Bengal. During the turbulent decades when the Omani state was subduing the Swahili coast, Ali bin Nasir served as the governor of Mombasa. Finally, he also participated in Said bin Sultan's losing naval battle for Siu in 1844, one of the less successful chapters of the Omani conquest of the East African coast. During that engagement, Ali bin Nasir and three hundred Omani troops met their demise.⁶ While his father traveled widely and died abroad, Salih grew up in al-Qabil and pursued a proper Ibadi education that included studying under the renowned Said bin Khalfan al-Khalili (c. 1820–1871), a scholar, mystic, and literary figure who would exert great influence on Salih bin Ali's life.⁷ Thus Salih's childhood was grounded in the rhythms of Sharqiya and the routines of Ibadi education available to sheikhly boys. In the 1850s he set sail for East Africa, a voyage that had become increasingly common for interior Omanis.

ZANZIBAR AND SOMALIA

Salih bin Ali al-Harthi's early movements on the Indian Ocean rim linked him to wealth and kin networks in Zanzibar and Islamic learning in Somalia that would shape the rest of his life. His only known journey to East Africa lasted several years, acquainted him with wealthy clansmen abroad, and gave him the opportunity to acquire property. More important, in Zanzibar Salih bin Ali became embroiled in the 1859 rebellion against the ruler

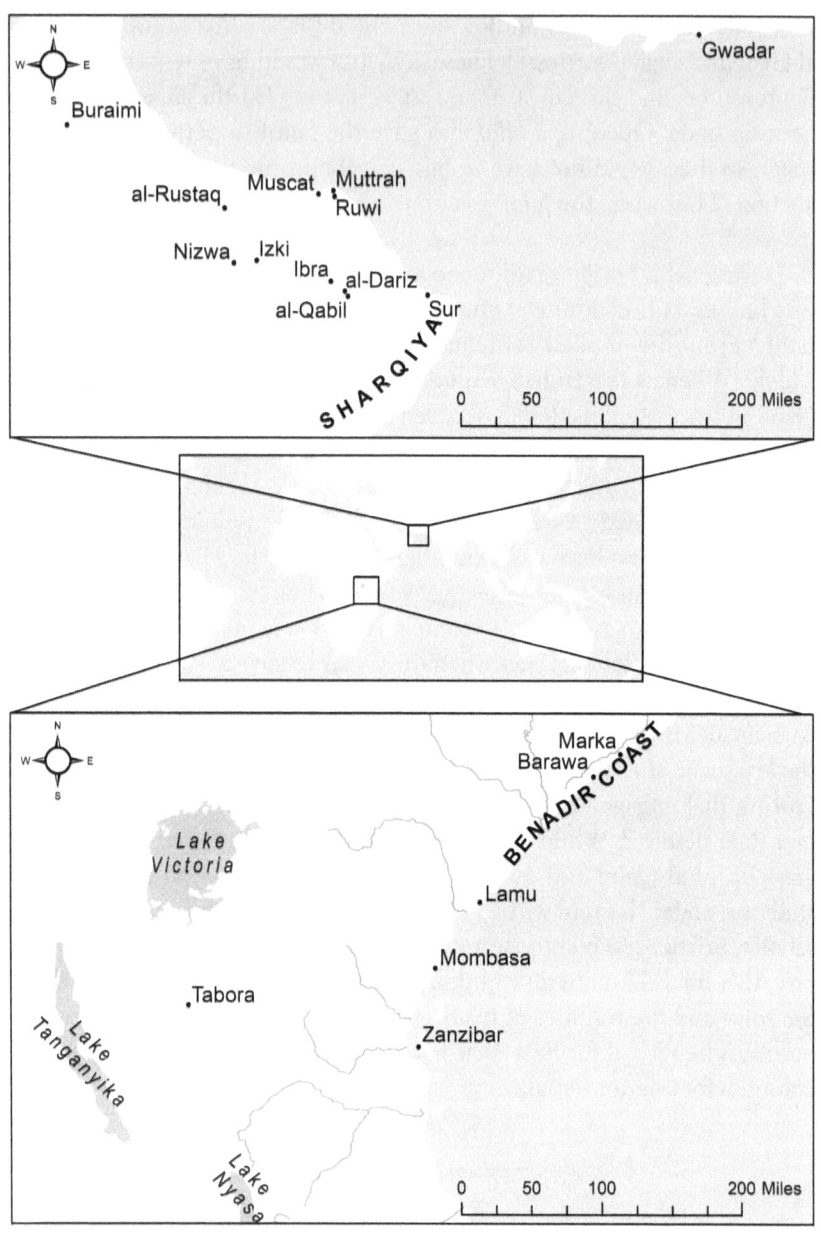

MAP 9.1. Salih bin Ali al-Harthi's Arabia and Africa

Majid bin Said al-Busaidi. The rebellion in Zanzibar was part of a larger contest over the Omani dominions that began when the long-ruling Seyyid Said bin Sultan died in 1856, and his sons Thuwayni and Majid, governors of Muscat and Zanzibar, scrambled to consolidate their positions. The outcome of the 1859 rebellion against Majid framed the political and economic relationship between Zanzibar and Oman for the rest of the century. The aftermath of the rebellion also transformed the Arab presence in the African interior, sending many Omanis to the new towns along the caravan routes and creating an ongoing linkage between Salih bin Ali and the Swahili coast.

In the late 1850s, Salih was caught between the ambitions of two sultans. Thuwayni and Majid had emerged as the rulers of the divided realm, but each held power tenuously, threatened by each other and their scheming siblings. The two sultans each regarded the other with suspicion and cupidity and went to great lengths to disadvantage the other. While the rivalries between some of the sons of Said bin Sultan were linked to palace antagonisms along the ethnicities of their mothers, Thuwayni and Majid were each born of Circassian women, though Thuwayni was raised in Muscat and Majid was reared in Zanzibar. In 1859, Thuwayni supported an attempt to overthrow Majid in Zanzibar by committing funds to sway partisans. From Muscat, Thuwayni dispatched a trusted ally to dispense funds among the Harthi and other Arabs in Zanzibar. He encouraged them to rebel while he prepared a fleet to sail from Oman.[8] In Zanzibar, the Harthi included some of the island's wealthiest merchants. They supported Barghash, another of Said bin Sultan's sons born of an Abyssinian woman, in his attempt to seize power from Majid, his half-brother. Majid, meanwhile, sent cash and arms to his brother Turki, son of an Abyssinian and governor of the Omani port of Suhar, so Turki could challenge Thuwayni's hold on Muscat.[9]

Salih bin Ali was in Zanzibar while dissent fomented in 1859 and he joined his wealthy clansmen in their support of the young Barghash who, like Salih bin Ali, was in his early twenties. Barghash's emerging coalition ran the spectrum from "ambitious and important people who feel grieved and overlooked"—like the Harthi—to some of "the most miserable," self-interested strivers.[10] Abdullah bin Salim, the leader of the Harthi faction, owned plantations and ships and commanded a force of fifteen hundred armed slaves. His power must have impressed the visiting Salih. Despite the Harthi's might and Barghash's serendipitous escape from house arrest dressed as a woman, the coalition failed to overthrow Majid. Hundreds of people died in the battles that took place on the plantations of Zanzibar's interior and in the narrow streets of town. Majid was backed by the British consul

Rigby, who summoned a troop of British marines stationed in the harbor at the time. The fighting was over before Thuwayni's forces arrived from Oman.[11] Barghash, Abdullah bin Salim, and Salih bin Ali, among other leaders, managed to escape with their lives.

In the aftermath of the rebellion, Salih bin Ali, a junior member of the conspiracy, and many others slipped off to the African mainland, but the prominent leaders of the rebellion were punished. Barghash was exiled to Bombay, and Majid arrested Abdullah bin Salim al-Harthi and two of his clansmen, imprisoning them in Lamu. In 1861, Abdullah bin Salim died under mysterious circumstances in that prison. Both Majid and Thuwayni seized the assets of the wealthy merchant. Majid claimed that Abdullah's supposed treachery justified his taking property, and Thuwayni impounded one of Abdullah's valuable ships, asserting that the Harthi men had misused the funds that were meant to support the rebellion.[12] Many of the rank and file survivors fled to the African mainland and caravan trails leading far into the interior. In 1861, Speke reported that the routes were full of exiles, and the number of people from Zanzibar residing at the Kazeh trading depot made it "a regular Botany Bay."[13] Although Arab and coastal traders had been working in the interior for generations, this exodus marked one of the first measurable migrations of Arabs to the far interior.

Salih bin Ali, on the other hand, went from Zanzibar to Somalia to study for two years, a seemingly unusual move for an Ibadi from a sheikhly line. The Somali port cities arrayed along the Benadir coast represent the northernmost reach of the classical Swahili world. Mogadishu was the largest city, but Merka and Barawa also had close trade connections with Zanzibar and southern Arabia. Like other regions of the western Indian Ocean in the nineteenth century, the combination of credit supplied from Indian firms and the demand for commodities from the region fueled an economic boom on the Benadir coast.[14] In 1843, the same captain who had given Salih bin Ali's father passage to Zanzibar wrote from Merka on the Somali coast that he saw boats carrying slaves to Oman. He also noted that the grain trade from Somalia to South Arabia produced profits of 300 percent or more.[15] From Zanzibar, the wealthy trader Abdullah bin Salim al-Harthi agreed to procure hides worth MT$1,000 from Barawa and the Benadir coast.[16] By the time Salih bin Ali arrived in Somalia in the late 1850s, the trade between the Somali coast and the Indian Ocean islands had increased, and Somalia was very much in the orbit of Zanzibar. In the late 1860s, Mogadishu was an important trading town that was "dependent entirely on Zanzibar for sale of produce and purchase of supplies." In addition, the port's chief traders visited Zanzibar every year.[17] Despite the vibrant trade relations with Zanzibar, however, the Benadir coast's most important export to the booming entrepôt may have been Islamic scholars.

The Somali coast was an important seat of Sunni Islamic learning long before Salih bin Ali arrived. Many of Zanzibar's most learned jurists hailed from Bendair or were educated there. In the 1840s, the renowned scholar 'Abd al-'Azīz al-Amawī (1838–1896) studied with three *ulama* in Barawa and then with another Bravanese *qadi* in Zanzibar. They prepared their gifted student well and at the tender age of sixteen he was appointed as a *qadi* at Kilwa.[18] Salih bin Ali did not study with him, but he would have known about Barawa's scholarly prodigy. 'Abd al-'Azīz al-Amawī later became an important advisor to Majid bin Said. In the late 1860s, a prominent, powerful Arab man in Zanzibar noted that Sheikh Abdulaziz was "the cleverest person of the age and that no one was greater."[19] When Salih bin Ali arrived in Somalia in 1859, he could have rubbed elbows with a young student named Uways bin Muhammad. Uways would have only been thirteen or fourteen at the time, but would later leave Barawa for Baghdad and Mecca, among other places, before returning to the western Indian Ocean to lead a flourishing Sufi Qadiriya tariqa (brotherhood).[20] The Somali coast was producing learned young men who became influential throughout the western Indian Ocean. In this scholarly context, Salih bin Ali dedicated two years to studying grammar (*naḥw*) and morphology (*ṣarf*) as well as rhetoric relative to eloquence (*bayān*) and meanings (*maʿani*).[21]

At first blush it would seem unusual for an Ibadi from the Omani interior to study with Sunni scholars in Somalia but within the context of increased mobility in the western Indian Ocean, greater degrees of interaction challenged long-held Ibadi values. Strictly speaking, Ibadis were expected to practice dissociation (*baraʾa*) from non-Ibadis. They were not supposed to be hostile toward them, but encouraged to withhold friendship (*walaya*) from non-Ibadis. Yet mobility around the rim of the Indian Ocean and the growing centrality of Zanzibar as a seat of economic power and Islamic learning catalyzed the mixing of Ibadis and Sunnis. As a result of this contact, some Ibadis became Sunni. Barghash bin Said, who Salih bin Ali supported in the 1859 rebellion, would later play a seemingly double role between these two sects when he became sultan. Barghash was an advocate of Ibadism, founded a printing press that published important Ibadi works, and ushered in an Ibadi renaissance (*nahda*). Barghash bin Said also famously punished a prominent Ibadi scholar (and member of the Barwani tribe of the Harthi clan) for his conversion to Sunnism. Yet, Barghash himself was listed as one of the many *khalīfas* of Sheikh Uways's Qadiriyya tariqa.[22] Historian B. G. Martin argues that this was for political, essentially anticolonial, reasons in the 1880s and also outlines the great extent of the resistance to European colonialism and its close association with Barwani members of the Harthi.[23] In this sense, Salih bin Ali's stay in Somalia may have been a touchstone for the Barawa-Ibadi-al-Harthi nexus that unfolded in the last decades of the nineteenth century.

At the very least, Salih bin Ali's extended stay in Somalia made him more aware of Indian Ocean trade networks and deepened his Islamic knowledge and scholarly credentials, both of which would influence his position in Oman. Indeed, his familiarity with both would pay dividends when he returned to Oman. Before Salih bin Ali left the Swahili coast, however, he traveled to Zanzibar to ask for and receive forgiveness from Majid bin Said for the rebellion.

Salih bin Ali's experiences in East Africa in the late 1850s and early 1860s offer three important insights into the milieu in which he operated—and which he would help to shape—for the next thirty years. First, while Salih would have known something about East Africa before his trip, his time there allowed him to fully understand the size of the Arab presence and the relative wealth of this group. In particular, the Harthi were well-situated in Zanzibar, and their leaders possessed significant economic resources. Second, Salih witnessed in the 1859 rebellion that, although the sultan could summon a large number of followers, the decisive factor in Majid's victory was the intervention of British troops. The sultan's increasing reliance on British support meant that he needed fewer allies among his people. Third, the sultan's levers of power were money and property. Offering allowances and freedom from customs excises were ways that rulers could ensure loyalty. Likewise, the sultans seized property and jailed rivals they could not contain. All three of these factors drove a dynamic in the western Indian Ocean that led Zanzibar to surpass Oman in wealth and prestige. For Salih bin Ali, however, his cognizance of these dynamics better equipped him to face his people's challenges in the Omani interior.

REVIVING THE IMAMATE

Salih bin Ali returned to Oman in the early 1860s. His political star was on the rise during this turbulent decade. The complex political machinations in Oman in the decade after his return included rule by three different sultans from the line of Seyyid Said bin Sultan al-Busaidi that were interrupted by a theocratic rebellion, which controlled the state for three years. One sultan was assassinated (1866) and another overthrown (1868). Salih bin Ali was one of the three leaders who established an Ibadi imamate in 1868, and he defended it until it fell to another sultan in 1871. The unstable nature of rule during this period was related to the weakness of the state and its degree of susceptibility to outside forces. With a relatively balanced array of tribal and religious forces contending to control the state, the influence of money from Zanzibar or intervention from the British could sway a delicate balance. Access to credit was vital to military action and governing, and the imamate foundered on its finances.

Salih bin Ali's emerging prominence was predicated on his position among the Harthi in Sharqiya and his growing tribal and religious network reinforced by kinship. Upon his return from Zanzibar and Somalia, Salih bin Ali immersed himself in the once familiar milieu of interior Oman. He established his headquarters at al-Qabil—with water flowing in its *falaj* only a short distance from the honey-red deserts of the Wahiba Sands. He continued to study with Ibadi teachers and attracted students of his own. The expansion of his home through building and through marriage suggests that he was economically prosperous. During this period, Salih and his brother Nasir further fortified al-Ḥiṣn, the family home, by building a large rectangular wall.[24] In nondrought periods, Salih's *falaj* shares gave him sufficient irrigation for his date palms and enough wealth to support a family.

If Salih bin Ali had not married before his trip to East Africa, he married upon his return. His marriages demonstrate the overlapping intellectual, social, and kin networks of the period. During his life, he was married to five women and divorced three of them. While it is difficult to gauge the content of these marriages besides the children that they produced, they hint at fundamental alliances. Sometime before the early 1870s he married Salima, the daughter of Said bin Ali al-Suqri, a scholar known also as al-'Ālim al-Kabīr (the great theologian). Salih bin Ali had been one of al-Suqri's devoted students. Their relationship took place in the Ibra region of Sharqiya where settlements depended on irrigation, and opening new hamlets required money and labor to bring irrigation. As a young man, Salih may have assisted his teacher in digging a *falaj* to found a new settlement. Said bin Ali al-Suqri had used the new *falaj* to found a settlement at 'Izz in 1856, before Salih went to East Africa.[25] Salih bin Ali's marriage to Salima bint Said added another dimension to his relationship with her father, and these bonds of scholarship, kinship, and mutual assistance all strengthened Salih's standing. Al-Suqri's relatives in Zanzibar would, in time, also provide financial assistance to Salih.

While Salima bint Said was from Sharqiya and the daughter of a household closely aligned with Salih, he also married women from other regions of the country and rival tribal factions. His wife Moza bint Jabr bin Said al-Jabria was from the Sumayil valley, the vital passage between Muscat and the interior. They were married before 1875.[26] Her clan, the Jabri, belonged to the Ghafiri faction in Omani politics, the opposing faction to the Hinawi forces that Salih bin Ali came to lead. Again, we can know little about their relationship, but demographically, a marriage to Moza bin Jabr would suggest an alliance to a member of a rival faction who hailed from a strategically important region. Salih bin Ali had to contend with Ghafiri-Hinawi political rivalries throughout his career, and control of the Sumayl valley was vital to anyone who wanted to control interior Oman.

Shortly after his return from overseas, Salih bin Ali became the *shaykh tamima* (the paramount chief) of the Harthi clan, a role his brother held before him. The historian al-Hashimy suggests that Salih's Indian Ocean journey was vital to his rise to leadership because it was encouragement (تشجيع) from the wealthy and powerful Abdullah bin Salim al-Barwani al-Harthi in Zanzibar that pushed Salih into this prominent position.[27] From his leadership of the Harthi, he came to lead the Hinawi tribal confederation, giving him a broader constituency in the country. Throughout, his connections to Zanzibar would prove to be an important aspect of Salih's tenure.

Salih bin Ali assumed the leadership of the Harthi clan during the rocky rule of Thuwayni bin Said when the sultan faced mounting internal and external challenges. Thuwayni bin Said had struggled to retain power in the years after his father's death in 1856, but the British Canning Award of 1861 recognized Thuwayni as the master of Oman. This intervention also formalized the political separation of Oman and Zanzibar and required Majid in Zanzibar to pay Thuwayni an annual subsidy of MT$40,000. The subsidy, intended to offset the loss of Zanzibar revenue for Muscat, was a welcome source of cash for the sultan. This critical financing from Zanzibar allowed Thuwayni to offer stipends and buy off rivals at a time when he needed all the help he could get. The Canning Award had endorsed Thuwayni's rule, but the British proved to be unpredictable allies when Thuwayni faced rising threats. Rival members of the Busaidi clan vied with Thuwayni for power, and the Wahhabi emirs of the Nejd made increasingly bold incursions into Omani territory. Unbeknownst to Thuwayni, the opposition extended into his own immediate family. In February 1866 his twenty-seven-year-old son Salim murdered him.

Thuwayni's murder demonstrated the forces arrayed against him and ushered in a period of even greater political and economic fragility in Oman. Salim bin Thuwayni had attacked his father with the support of a Wahhabi agent whose orders may have come from the Wahhabi emir himself. In Oman, however, Thuwayni had earned the enmity of a range of Ibadi leaders including his Busaidi rival Azzan bin Qays. They encouraged the plot and were well-positioned in relation to the new sultan's agenda.

Salim declared himself sultan immediately and imprisoned his most likely challenger, his uncle Turki bin Said, in Suhar. When Salim arrived in Muscat his allies Azzan bin Qays al-Busaidi, the Ibadi leader Said bin Khalfan al-Khalili, and throngs of their supporters met him. Said bin Khalfan al-Khalili, who had been Salih bin Ali's teacher, was "the greatest scholar of his generation" and the sheikh tamima of the Bani Rawaha tribe.[28] The new sultan Salim bin Thuwayni began his rule with powerful allies but could not maintain their loyalty.

In the period after Salim's patricide, the commercial classes of Muscat and Muttrah were not as enthusiastic about the new state of affairs. The Indian merchants had boarded boats in the harbor to escape whatever might happen. When the British agent Pelly reached Muscat shortly afterward, he ordered that the Indians' property also be embarked for safety.[29] Just as Rigby had focused on claiming Indians as British subjects to enforce policies in Zanzibar, the economic well-being of British Indian subjects in Muscat became a touchstone for British intervention in Omani affairs.

As the new ruler, Salim was ill-prepared. He faced immediate challenges from aspirants and lacked the financial resources to attract allies. From Sharqiya, Salih bin Ali tried to mediate between the sultan and his rivals, but it was the British who stepped in to buy off the challengers and preserve Salim's shaky rule. When Turki bin Said escaped from prison and launched a military challenge against his obstreperous nephew Salim, Salih bin Ali pointedly kept the Harthi from participating. Later, when Turki came to Sharqiya seeking support, Salih bin Ali attempted to play the mediator and reconcile Turki and Salim.[30] British intervention undercut Salih's role as broker and saved Salim bin Thuwayni. In this instance, they defused Turki's attack and offered him a stipend to retire to India. In doing so, the British followed regional precedents. Payoffs and annual stipends were tools of statecraft that used webs of finance and credit to balance power in the gulf region. Sultans in Muscat and Zanzibar frequently employed them but they were necessarily a temporary fix.[31] For Salim, this British intervention only bought him time. Soon he was overwhelmed and out of money. Zanzibar's riches were denied to him, and he turned to the British again to shore up his administration.

In Zanzibar, Majid bin Said al-Busaidi had used Salim's patricide as an excuse to stop paying the Zanzibar subsidy. Deprived of this guaranteed income to bolster his rule, Salim held an uneasy grip on power as the British agents quailed at further intervention. More than a year into Salim's reign,

Pelly, the British political agent in the gulf, noted that Salim was "in urgent and real need of his subsidy."[32] Although Pelly flirted with the idea of garnishing the customs revenues in Zanzibar to ensure that the subsidy was paid, he rebuffed Salim's requests for other loans. Pelly believed that British support had already exceeded all expectations. He noted the vital role British intervention had played in legitimizing Salim's rule: we "have in short placed him on the throne and maintained him there against what would otherwise have been an overwhelming attack from Sayed Torkee and the Tribes." Further assistance, Pelly believed, was not warranted. To reaffirm the stated policy of nonintervention, Pelly thought the governor of Bombay should remind Salim that earlier military and financial assistance had been "exceptional" and that Salim "must now govern his country for and by himself without aid whether in arms or money."[33] With the economy of Muscat weakening and Salim's religious and tribal allies beginning to doubt his ability to rule, the challenge to Salim of governing for and by himself was daunting.

Salim's missteps converted allies to enemies who formed a coalition to overthrow him and establish an imamate. In late 1867 Salim attempted to capture Salih bin Ali in Barka because he believed Salih's support for him had not been strong enough. This move failed and alienated Salih bin Ali and his Hinawi followers. In 1868 Salih bin Ali allied himself with his teacher Said bin Khalfan al-Khalili to depose Salim and place an imam at the head of the state.[34] They launched a successful rebellion in September 1868, ousted Salim bin Thuwayni, and elected Azzan bin Qays al-Busaidi as the imam.[35]

An imamate led by an elected imam was the ideal type of Ibadi governance. This model stretched back to the rule of Julanda bin Mas'ud, who was elected imam after the province of Oman liberated itself form Abbasid rule around 750.[36] While an imamate has remained an idée fixe for the greater part of Omani history, Wilkinson has demonstrated the pattern of an "imamate cycle." In this cycle, elected imams are pulled toward hereditary rule, which eventually results in the dissolution of the imamate.[37] Indeed, the original Busaidi ruler of Oman had been elected in 1744, but over the next century power had become vested in one hereditary line. While many Europeans visitors called Said bin Sultan al-Busaidi the Imam of Muscat, his Ibadi subjects certainly did not. Thus in 1868 Ibadi partisans in the Omani interior and elsewhere cheered the election of Azzan bin Qays as imam. Salih bin Ali al-Harthi has been called one of its three pillars for his instrumental role in establishing the imamate with his teacher al-Khalili and the imam Azzan bin Qays.[38]

Officials in Zanzibar feared that the imamate revolution in Oman would spill over to East Africa. They worried particularly about Salih bin Ali's influence overseas and his access to property and credit in Zanzibar. British officials had monitored the relationship between Zanzibar and Muscat closely since the 1861 Canning Award and continued to try to influence its direction. In November 1868, in the wake of the imamate's victory, the acting political agent in Muscat worried "that the religious sentiment which has lately been so conspicuous here will be carried across the ocean & play a part equally remarkable amongst the Arabs on the continent of Africa."[39] Salih bin Ali was the linchpin, identified in the dispatch as "an influential chief" and as the person responsible for plotting and carrying out the imamate revolution in Oman. The British officials were wary of underestimating the Harthi chief who, they remembered, had played "an important part in . . . events" in Barghash's 1859 rebellion that compelled him to leave Zanzibar. Although Salih bin Ali fled after Barghash's rebellion failed, the worry a decade later was about the property that he and other Arabs in Oman controlled in Zanzibar and what Majid might do. Events in Arabia, the British agent in Muscat reported to his superiors in Bombay, "may cause Majid to confiscate the property of Shiks [sic] Saleh bin Ali, & Saeed bin Ali & others of the Al Harth & different tribes who own large sugar & clove plantations in this territory."[40] While it has been impossible to confirm the extent of Salih bin Ali's property in Zanzibar during this period, the fact that he and other al-Harthi clansman in Oman had property in Zanzibar demonstrates the ongoing linkages and investments that remained in spite of the political separation. The British agents were concerned that if Majid used the overthrow of Salim bin Thuwayni and the establishment of the imamate as an excuse to seize property in Zanzibar, it might provoke Salih bin Ali and other imamate officials to invade Zanzibar.

For his part, Salih bin Ali used his reputation to fan the flames in Zanzibar and to consolidate imamate rule in Oman. The ongoing circulation of people between Oman and Zanzibar meant that Salih bin Ali posed a constant and destabilizing threat to Zanzibar officials. Salih bin Ali did not shy from the rumors that kept these threats alive. In 1869, for example, he claimed that an uprising against Majid would be extremely popular and that he could easily raise a force of fifty thousand men to lead the attack on Zanzibar.[41] These threats were felt even as Salih bin Ali focused on consolidating the imamate in Oman.

In Oman, Salih bin Ali lent his authority and military leadership to the imamate's struggle to centralize authority and maintain its legitimacy. The imamate state's use of violence to rein in dissident tribes and to establish wide acceptance continued to feed the flow of migrants to East Africa. The imamate depended on Salih to play the role of the enforcer, dispensing justice among the tribes in various parts of Oman. They sent him to 'Aqq to punish those who had raided a caravan and killed four people.[42] Meanwhile, in Salih's home district of Sharqiya, all was not calm, and he was deputized to deal with renegade tribesmen and to recruit men to serve in the imamate's campaigns. While Salih had claimed that he could raise a force of fifty thousand to challenge Zanzibar, the forces he amassed in Sharqiya were much smaller. The Hinawi sheikh led a force of fifteen hundred of his tribesmen and three thousand additional men from al-Batinah in a brutal "pacification" campaign against the Siyabiyin clan in Wadi Sumayl. Salih bin Ali's force destroyed the houses of the Siyabiyin, killed more than one hundred people, and captured others. The Siyabiyin completely capitulated after this devastating loss, and other groups in the area quickly came to terms with the imamate's forces.[43] Given the near annihilation of the Siyabiyin in early 1869, it is not surprising that members fled to other parts of Oman, to Zanzibar, and to the caravan trails of central Africa.[44] A lagging economy exacerbated the effects of such reprisals. Majid had withheld payment of the Zanzibar subsidy during the rule of the imam Azzan bin Qays, a position supported by the government of India's failure to recognize him as the ruler of Muscat.[45] The imamate government, for its part, hampered trade in Muscat and Muttrah and created difficult conditions for many of the Indian merchants. While freed slaves and other less mobile people had fewer alternatives, many Arabs, both from the interior and from the coastal elite, sought refuge in Zanzibar.[46] Indeed, contrary to British concerns, the imamate did not export rebellion to Zanzibar but created new reasons for Arabs to escape, at least temporarily, the strife at home.

ZANZIBAR IS THE FOUNTAIN OF MONEY

Salih bin Ali's harsh reprisals and the imamate's foundering economy were both indications of the state's weakness. The imamate was in no position to export rebellion to Zanzibar. Instead, Zanzibar exported the credit and financing that brought down the imamate and reinstalled the descendants of Said bin Sultan al-Busaidi in Muscat. The contest for Muscat in the early 1870s played out in beseeching letters and promissory notes, which made it possible for armies to take the field. As the imamate stumbled, Turki bin Said worked from Bombay to line up creditors in Zanzibar. Those in Oman, including Salih bin Ali, tried to do the same. In the midst of these pleas for support in 1870, Majid bin Said, the sultan of Zanzibar died, and his brother

Barghash acceded to power. In the waning days of the imamate, a letter from Oman to Zanzibar laid bare the situation: "as you know Zanzibar is the fountain of money and we cannot get on without Zanzibar."[47] In the struggle to gain political legitimacy in Arabia, credit proved to be the key to Turki's success, though before he could seize Muscat he also had to face off against Salih bin Ali, on whom the lesson of overseas finances would not be lost.

Although Turki bin Said had accepted a stipend during the reign of Salim bin Thuwayni to retire to Bombay, the news of widening dissatisfaction with the imamate drew him back into Omani politics. Turki's followers wrote to him that people were changing their minds about the imamate. Shifting views of the new government were making it harder for Salih bin Ali to attract supporters for his military campaigns.[48]

To challenge the imamate, Turki needed political support from allies in the country, the tacit approval of the British Indian Government, and financial backing. His allies were active in Oman in trying to attract supporters, and they also understood the new role that the British played in Muscati politics. British agents had recognized Salim bin Thuwayni after his patricide and grudgingly acknowledged the imamate, though as Wilkinson notes, they did not understand Ibadism at all.[49] Thus, representatives of the Bani Jabir sent a missive to Turki imploring him to return and offered advice: "We pray to God to send you to us in a good state at an early date. When you come, do so, with the support of the British Government, and remove the troubles which your country and your subjects are suffering from."[50] As the British government in India had overseen the terms of his exile, Turki sought their permission to leave. He also asked in vain for their financial support.

Turki was in exile in the wealthiest city in the western Indian Ocean, but funds secured in Zanzibar were vital to financing his time in Bombay and his return to Oman. Turki had great difficulty raising funds in Bombay. He wrote to the governor explaining his plight: "I am a poor stranger in this city [Bombay]. The people here are not acquainted with me and will not trust me. They will not lend me money."[51] On the other side of the Indian Ocean, however, Turki and his family were well known, and he was able to secure credit from Zanzibar. During his first year in exile Turki used connections to the prominent Zanzibar trading house of Jairam Shivji for a personal loan of four thousand rupees.[52] He then turned to the Indian government for assistance, seeking to borrow MT$80,000, suggesting that, if need be, he could borrow against the Zanzibar subsidy.[53] Turki also appealed directly to the sultan of Zanzibar, Majid bin Said. Majid had sent money to Turki in the late 1850s to challenge Thuwayni, and Majid's own position in Zanzibar had been protected by the British in the face of rebellion from Barghash and his al-Harthi backers. Majid demurred on the loan and encouraged Turki to depend on the British. He added, perhaps out of politesse, that Turki should inform him if there was anything that Majid could do for him in Zanzibar.[54] Advancing credit to Turki would have been the most helpful, but Majid was reticent.

Turki's supporters in Oman wondered why Majid, "who is rich and powerful" was silent in supporting his allies in Oman or his brother in exile.[55] Majid's passivity in 1868 and 1869 belied his straitened circumstances and limited diplomatic latitude. Despite the perception in Oman of Zanzibari wealth, Majid's financial outlook was not good. His refusal to pay the Zanzibar subsidy—first to Salim bin Thuwayni and then to the imamate—appeared to be a principled stance, but made virtue out of necessity. Majid had poor cash flow and had devoted a great deal of money to curry favor with the Northern Arabs who sailed to Zanzibar from the gulf each year.[56] Given limited income and the disturbed state of Oman, Majid worried first about the spread of the imamate fervor to Zanzibar and then about whether he should invade Oman.[57] In this scenario, Turki would have been a potential rival for his own designs on Oman. The British dissuaded Majid strongly on his pretension to Oman, and in 1870 the Zanzibar sultan belatedly supported Turki's return from exile with a grant of Rs20,000 drawn on Jairam Shivji. Majid also offered a set of escalating bonuses should Turki succeed in capturing major ports of Sur (Rs30,000) or Suhar (Rs100,000)[58] Thus from Zanzibar, Majid opened the flow of credit and underwrote Turki's political comeback.

With tribal support at home and financial backing from Zanzibar, Turki sought British assent to depart Bombay and received a tepid endorsement. Turki received authorization to depart India but was prohibited from traveling on any of Her Majesty's vessels or even having one of the ships accompanying him. Furthermore, the Government of India refused to pledge to assist or protect Turki if he tried to take Muscat.[59] This official ambivalence did not dissuade Turki, especially as he had Majid's financial backing and supporters in Oman.

After Turki left Bombay, in March of 1870, his brother Majid applied diplomatic and financial pressure from Zanzibar to sway loyalties in Oman. Turki could not enter Muscat, so he went to the gulf to gain support, first to Bandar Abbas and then to the Trucial coast. Majid used his commercial leverage with "Northern Arabs" who visited Zanzibar each year to encourage them to support Turki. While he had sought their favor a few years earlier, he threatened to block them from docking in Zanzibar as long as the imam Azzan bin Qays was in power. Historian J. B. Kelly sees Majid's move as a threat to cut off the slave trade, but Majid was clearly aware of the strategic and commercial value of controlling Sur, as evidenced by the bonuses he promised Turki for doing so. In any case, in June when Turki returned to Bandar Abbas, he met with potential allies from the Omani port of Sur. These were sheikhs from some of the very groups Majid had threatened: the Banu Bu Ali, the Janabah and others from Ja'alan, and the immediate neighborhood of Sur. Indeed, Turki was eager to enlist them to support his efforts in Sur, and he used Majid's first twenty thousand rupees to send four boatloads of Persian and Baluchi fighters to Sur in August 1870. Meanwhile, Turki met with tribal leaders from the Buraimi oasis and the emirates of the Trucial coast in an attempt to win additional support in other parts of the country.[60]

Access to credit and finance were critical to politics and gave Turki the upper hand in his challenge to imamate rule. Majid's funds provided momentum and proved vital in attracting tribal allegiances. As Turki moved through the country he was able to offer subsidies to allies and play on their resentment of Azzan's government.[61] While Turki was flush with credit from Zanzibar, Azzan struggled to meet the subsidies he had promised to the tribes of central Oman and Sharqiya for their loyalty. His government first failed to meet financial obligations to the Ghafiri confederation members who had joined him. During the last months of 1870 and into early 1871, Turki's followers battled the imamate for control of Oman. In this contest, Turki ambushed Azzan in early October and killed several tribal leaders, but the imam and his brother escaped to the coast. As Turki marched through central Oman, his forces swelled as he went. On his way to Sur he left five thousand men behind to control the Sumayl valley and lay siege to Nizwa. Turki and a troop of six thousand men seized Sur at the end of October due to the support of the tribes Majid had coerced. Turki never collected his Sur bonus, however, because Majid died in Zanzibar on October 7 before Turki seized the vital port.

Majid's death and the accession of Barghash offered new hope to the increasingly desperate imamate leaders. Initially, the imamate government had intended to undermine Barghash's rule, but the news that he had been returning property that Majid had confiscated brought pleasure to the imam's government, and they sought his friendship instead.[62] In letters to the new sultan, their congratulations reveal the depth of their disdain for Majid, and their requests of Barghash remind him of their past loyalty and his duty as an Ibadi. They also make clear that Omani politics depended strongly on Zanzibar financing. In his letter to Barghash from early December 1870, Salih bin Ali referred to Majid as God's enemy and reminded Barghash of

Salih's service in 1859: "I and my people were your helpers[,] selling our soul for you and making enemies for your sake." And he had not wavered. He told Barghash, "nor do we go back from this our old faith." Salih bin Ali was solicitous of Barghash's plans ("what you have in your heart for us") and offered his services as a mediator with the imam so that the sultan could make peace and establish friendship. Salih made sure that Barghash knew that Turki had sought loans to raise a force to challenge Barghash's new rule.[63] The other pillar of the imamate, Said bin Khalfan al-Khalili, wrote at the same time to express his happiness for Barghash and to tell him, in stark religious terms, that he should follow God's law and act justly. While he does not directly seek support for his forces in Oman, al-Khalili warns Barghash that if he denies God or departs from his law, God will rise up against him and take his kingdom from him. Al-Khalili offers to be his adviser and make "the right way plain" to him because the sultan's funds and followers cannot protect him from God's wrath: "Your wealth cannot protect you from him nor your people save you."[64]

Yet, the finances of Zanzibar and the relative wealth of the sultan were very much known in imamate circles. Writing from Oman around the same time as Salih and al-Khalili, Abdulaziz bin Said, Bargash's younger brother, wrote to the new sultan requesting money and arms. He had allied himself with the imamate. He requested a large cannon or two other large guns and made clear that Barghash must lend them money because, in the next month, Turki could do anything and that Abdulaziz could be killed. He was without money and asked for a line of credit of MT$5000, stating "this is to you nothing" because, he claimed, the Zanzibar Customs house brings in MT$800,000. In his plea, Abdulaziz cursed Majid and the English, but made clear, "Zanzibar is the fountain of money and we cannot get on without Zanzibar."[65] By the time these requests reached Barghash in early 1871, the tide was beginning to turn against Salih bin Ali, al-Khalili and the imamate. Turki, who had drunk from Majid's fountain of money, was on his way to Muscat. Yet Salih bin Ali stood in his way.

Salih bin Ali proved to be a stout defender of the imamate: He detained Turki from the final assault on Muscat and was the only one of the three pillars still standing when the imamate fell. To capture Muscat, Turki divided his forces in early 1871 to approach the capital from two routes. One group took the coastal route and besieged Muttrah.[66] Turki's path through the interior, however, was blocked by Salih bin Ali. As the forces loyal to Turki tightened their grip on Muttrah in the last weeks of January 1871, Salih bin Ali kept Turki pinned down in Samad, where the imamate forces held the fort. From Muscat, Azzan was unable to relieve Muttrah because the only way to do so was by sea. The British agent in Muscat, A. Cotton Way, followed—in the narrowest sense—the British policy to prevent all hostilities at sea. On January 23, the British gunboat Kwangtung twice turned back a dhow carrying a large field gun and ammunition that was trying to relieve the imamate forces in Muttrah. When the dhow captain tried a third time that day, the gunboat rammed the dhow midship and sank it.[67] Azzan crossed the steep hills from Muscat to Muttrah to take over the defense, but a week later, on the morning of January 30, forces loyal to Turki pressed their attack and took Muttrah. Imam Azzan, one of the pillars of the imamate, was killed in the fighting. Although Turki's side appeared triumphant, their leader was still detained at Samad by Salih bin Ali, another pillar, and did not arrive until several days later. By that time, al-Khalili, the third pillar, had barricaded himself into one of Muscat's forts.

Before the siege was resolved, the British agent for the Persian Gulf, Lewis Pelly, arrived in Muscat and inserted himself into the negotiations between al-Khalili, the senior imamate official, and Turki bin Said, whose followers had secured the town. With Pelly's assurances, al-Khalili agreed to surrender, but Pelly turned him over to Turki, and within a few days, al-Khalili and his son had been buried alive.[68] British interference in the denouement of the imamate resulted in an act of treachery that tainted British-Ibadi relations for the next half century. With the imamate eclipsed, Turki, launched with credit from Zanzibar, was the sultan of Oman.

Salih bin Ali, who had stood with the imamate until the end, returned to Sharqiya having witnessed a sharp shift in Omani-British relations. Like the intervention of royal marines that had halted Barghash's Zanzibar rebellion in 1859, Pelly's partisan intervention—and cold-hearted accessory to murder—in support of Turki sent a message about British support for the heirs of Said bin Sultan. Yet another conclusion from Turki's success was clear: financial support from Zanzibar could help turn the tide in domestic disputes. The face-off between Salih bin Ali and Turki in Samad in early 1871 would be the first of many disputes between the new ruler of Muscat and the sheikh tamima of the Harthi. With the overthrow of the imamate, Salih bin Ali was the de facto leader of the fractured movement. Later historians came to see him as a kind of temporary imam for the period. In his own time, however, he was the sultan's primary challenger, and each run-in they had throughout the 1870s and 1880s underscored the role that debt and finance played in determining the outcome of political contests in Oman.

TUSSLING WITH TURKI

British support helped defeat the imamate, but it did not initially aid Turki in establishing the legitimacy of his rule or offer the fiscal assistance for which he was so desperate. Turki clung to power in the early years and ruled Oman for eighteen years. Throughout this entire period, Salih bin Ali remained extraordinarily attuned to moments of weakness within the regime when he might press his advantages. This occurred several times in the 1870s and more concentratedly in 1883–84. Though Salih bin Ali and his allies were not successful in seizing power, the Harthi chief's attempts to shape Omani politics point to the interplay of coalitions and credit. Within Oman, the overlapping political economies of power between tribal leaders, the sultan, and the British forces in the region shaped coalitions and allegiances. Connections overseas were vital, and throughout the 1870s and 1880s credit from Zanzibar underwrote political activity in Oman.

In the first decade of Turki's rule, the sultan and his rivals all scrambled to secure financing to attract followers and buy off enemies. Turki lacked the funds to cement his position by granting allowances to rivals and by shoring up the allegiance of tribal levies through gifts. For his enemies, posing a credible threat to the sultan was both a means to greater political power and, in the interim, an end in itself. A weakened sultan paid stipends to negate the biggest threats. In the early days, the factions arrayed against Turki were diverse: his nephew—the patricide—Salim bin Thuwayni and his younger brother Abdulaziz bin Said, both from his own line of the Busaidi clan; Ibrahim bin Qays, brother of the deceased imam, who led a rival line of Busaidi men; and of course, Salih bin Ali and his Hinawi allies. As early as April 1871, only three months after Turki's forces overthrew the imamate, Salih bin Ali was rumored to be "restless and intriguing."[69] Fortunately for Turki, his rivals were also insolvent: "the want of money debarred all parties from operations of any magnitude."[70]

In search of funding, Turki and his political rivals sought the wealth of Zanzibar: Salim via family, Turki via subsidy, and Salih bin Ali, eventually, through the sale of property. Salim bin Thuwayni tried to use his kinship connections in Zanzibar in the early 1870s to secure sponsors from the wealthy Arabs of East Africa. Salim's mother and siblings had moved to Zanzibar during the imamate, and their presence in East Africa gave him new access to creditors though he enjoyed limited success.[71] In contrast to Salim, Abdulaziz, who had called Zanzibar "the fountain of money" a few years earlier, struck out with Barghash and seemingly had no other connections in Zanzibar. He sought new overseas sponsors and accepted MT$20,000 from the Aga Khan in Bombay in 1873. The Aga Khan had hoped that Abdulaziz would be able to take Muscat from Turki and help reconcile the dissident Khoja community there.[72] Abdulaziz was not able to do this, in part because Turki was also trying to raise funds overseas.

As sultan, Turki eyed an even larger prize from Zanzibar, hopeful that a new sultan there or the British intermediaries would restore the subsidy. Turki doggedly lobbied the British agent in Muscat, the agent's superior in the Persian Gulf, and the Government of India for the restoration of the Zanzibar subsidy. The 1861 Canning Award required the sultan of Zanzibar to pay MT$40,000 per year to the sultan of Muscat. In practice, however, Majid had curtailed the payment in 1866 on the death of Thuwayni. Majid argued that Salim's palace coup made him an illegitimate ruler and thus not entitled to the subsidy. When the imamate ousted Salim, Majid also withheld payment of the subsidy, a move that paralleled British reticence in recognizing the legitimacy of Azzan bin Qays's rule,[73]

With the death of Majid in October of 1870 and the overthrow of the imamate in early 1871, the presence of two new sultans in Muscat and Zanzibar suggested the possibility of new relations between the two, formerly unified, realms. Turki tried to take advantage of this moment even as British representatives, eager to secure a new anti-slave trade treaty, intervened on Turki's behalf against a truculent Barghash. In June 1871 members of the royal family, including sons of Thuwayni who had moved to Zanzibar, returned to Oman. They brought modest financial support for Turki bin Said from his brother, the new sultan of Zanzibar, Barghash bin Said. In return, the next year Turki sent Barghash an Arabian horse.[74] These tokens did little to advance Turki's position, and when the Government of India facilitated hard bargaining over the restoration of the subsidy in 1873, Barghash laughed off the implication and vowed, "we will never give Muscat a cent."[75] The Government of India, however, was keen to restore the subsidy, in part because the subsidy became a leverage point in negotiating an antislavery treaty in 1873.

Sir Bartle Frere, the former governor of Bombay, carried out diplomatic missions to Muscat and Zanzibar to assess the slave trade and take treaty action against it. Frere openly advocated for Turki to receive the Zanzibar subsidy and authorized an advanced payment to Turki without seeking explicit permission. Frere reasoned that as long as Barghash refused to uphold his obligation to pay the subsidy, Turki would be justified in enforcing his claim and exacting the payment. This would mean a naval attack on Zanzibar, and Frere's memorandum to his superiors was breezily confident that Turki could prevail in this. For his part, Barghash welcomed the challenge. He told the British agent at Zanzibar, John Kirk, that he would never pay the subsidy, and if Turki himself came to Zanzibar, he would find Barghash "the first to meet him outright." Barghash's stridency was, in Kirk's estimation, not due to Barghash's own military might, but to the sultan's certainty that Turki's enemies in Oman would curb his ambitions and restrict his reach overseas.[76] But Frere was looking at a bigger picture. He reminded his superiors of recent Turkish and Persian activity in the gulf, and pointed to Muscat's proximity to India. By permitting Turki to attack Zanzibar, which, according to Frere was a predictable result of turning a blind eye, the British would reverse a long-standing policy of preventing hostilities between the two states. Furthermore, an attack from Muscat would also upset the maritime peace the British committed to in the Persian Gulf and injure the "growing commerce and incipient civilization in Eastern Africa." Frere recognized Turki's acquiescence to the terms of the slave trade and his penury. The results of ensuring a regular payment of the Zanzibar subsidy, he argued, would include political stability in Muscat, peace in Oman, and the protection of British Indian subjects in Zanzibar who controlled "the whole trade" of that port.[77]

At the time Frere conveyed these arguments in a memorandum to his superiors, however, he had already authorized payments to Turki. The ruler of Muscat would be entitled to $120,000 in total: $100,000 in arrears and the payment for that year. Turki could draw $40,000 immediately in April from the political agent in Muscat, and, after three months, could draw an additional $20,000 as half of that year's payment. When Frere wrote his report in May, he suggested that the funds be recovered from Zanzibar. If Barghash should continue to refuse, the British should embargo his customs houses. The consul at Zanzibar should also remind Barghash that while the British government would keep Turki from disturbing the peace in Zanzibar, it would not tolerate Barghash's attempts to "stir up strife" in Muscat.[78] Thus Frere delivered a fiscal lifeline for Turki and set the stage to block financing for Turki's rivals.

Turki quickly collected all that was due to him. The tremendous cash infusion from the Zanzibar subsidy—no longer paid from Zanzibar—bought Turki time to rein in his rivals within his own family and in Sharqiya. By November 1873 he had collected MT$100,000 in arrears and blew through it so quickly that by February 1874 he sought an advance. Only a small portion ($6,000) of his new wealth went to improving the infrastructure of the port of Muscat by enlarging the wharf and landing pier. Turki used the vast majority of the remaining $94,000 to bestow gifts and allowances to rivals within his family and politically powerful leaders and their tribes.[79] Turki's closest familial rivals were his nephew Salim bin Thuwayni, the usurped sultan deposed by the imamate, and Turki's younger brother Abdulaziz bin Said, who a British consul in Zanzibar regarded as the most energetic of Said bin Sultan's sons.[80] Abdulaziz cultivated allies among the Ibadi elite in Oman, and Turki viewed him as more of a threat than Salim bin Thuwayni. To reduce risks to his rule, Turki offered his clansmen a stipend in exile. He paid them each $300 per month as long as they left Oman and stayed in British territory.[81]

Turki also used his newly acquired wealth to ally with the Hinawi tribal confederation that had so frequently opposed him. Salih bin Ali presented himself as a credible threat at a vulnerable moment and secured a handsome stipend. In the midst of his spending spree, in late 1873 and early 1874, Turki was debilitated by illness. In Sharqiya, Salih bin Ali heard a rumor that the sultan had died so he took his forces to Muscat immediately to try to seize the capital. The rumors had been exaggerated, but Turki was unable to mount a vigorous defense. Salih bin Ali negotiated favorable peace terms for the Hinawi with the sultan, and received a personal stipend of $500 per month. The amount of the stipend, nearly twice what Salim and Abdulaziz received, gives a sense of Salih bin Ali's threat and the importance of winning his favor.

In his first year with the renewed Zanzibar subsidy, Turki quickly spent more than $100,000 on allies and rivals yet his rule was not assured. By the summer of 1874, he was borrowing money, and his emergency reserves were depleted. Spending on these "endeavours to pacify the tribes" proved ineffective, and Turki, suffering from both illness and despair, had begun to speak frequently about abdication. He was tired, physically incapacitated, and unable to cope with his enemies any longer.[82] He invited Abdulaziz back from exile to serve as his deputy, and then retired to Gwadar with his own stipend guaranteed from the Zanzibar subsidy. This arrangement lasted only a few months, and Turki returned to claim control of the sultanate. The consul in Muscat, S. B. Miles, supported Turki but had noted before the temporary abdication that Turki's case was "hopeless" because power had "fallen from his grasp." If the British hoped to sustain him, Miles noted, "it must be by some strong measure."[83]

As Salih bin Ali's prestige in the interior grew, the British agents in Muscat and in the Persian Gulf chose a new tack in their policy toward Muscat because of the Harthi chief. Previously they had based their actions on the notion of protecting the maritime peace of the gulf, but had

FIGURE 9.1. Muscat as Saleh bin Ali and his forces approaching from the interior would have seen it. From Emile Allemann, "Mascate," *Le Tour du Monde* 7, no. 8 (1901), 86.

not interfered with land-based fighting. In 1874, however, British agents formulated a new policy in response to Salih bin Ali's attack on Muscat. Officers were not permitted to undertake operations on shore, but they would accede to Turki's requests for assistance and actively assist him "so far as the guns of our vessels of war can reach."[84] British guns could not reach to the interior of Oman, however, and it was there that Salih bin Ali's prestige grew. Salih bin Ali commanded respect as a learned Ibadi and as the successor to the imamate. He increasingly played the role of arbitrator and conciliator in tribal disputes beyond the Harthi. He helped negotiate a truce between rival tribes in Izki (1877) and was asked to settle a murder dispute between the Busaidi and the Bani Rawahi clan (1878) by ruling on blood money.[85] As Salih bin Ali played peacemaker (and enforced the terms of agreements) his reputation and influence grew. These actions, combined with his stipend from Turki, helped him to form alliances and attract followers for his own political (and military) projects. Thus from the mid-1870s until his death in the mid-1890s, Salih bin Ali used his prestige and his wealth to attract a shifting group of allies to his causes. During this time, his own influence waxed and waned relative to the sultan, as both sought to maintain their coalitions. Access to credit was critical to building coalitions as seen in Turki's ability to hold power when the Zanzibar subsidy was renewed. Going forward, Salih bin Ali developed his own line to Zanzibar wealth, carrying out mortgages there and selling property to raise funds.

REBELLION AND DEBT IN THE 1870S

Salih bin Ali and allies from Sharqiya attempted to dislodge Turki by attacking Muscat and Muttrah in 1877 and 1878. These two risings together make clear the political economy of tribal warfare in Oman, and the value of access to credit in Zanzibar. In the 1870s Salih bin Ali was the principal rival to Turki. In Sharqiya, Salih bin Ali held great prestige—a later commentator said that Salih was "stronger in his own sphere than the new Sultan in his."[86] Prestige alone, however, did not result in followers willing to take up arms. Salih bin Ali used strategic alliances and Zanzibar property to threaten Turki's standing. In his attempts to challenge and undermine the sultan, we see the dominance of wealth and the subtleties of tribal politics in confronting Britain, a rising imperial power. Due to the limited funds available in Oman, access to outside wealth was key to the political machinations of the 1870s. Turki bin Said had only been able to overthrow the imamate with aid from the sultan in Zanzibar. For Turki, the Zanzibar subsidy was vital to establishing his rule in the early years, and through guaranteeing this subsidy the British found themselves increasingly intertwined with the sultan's interests in Oman. Yet, as the aftermath of the 1877 and 1878 attacks revealed, neither the sultan nor his British allies could exact retribution from Salih bin Ali and his Harthi clansmen. The Harthi and their chief maintained autonomy through their mastery of the Omani interior and Indian Ocean trade networks.

In June 1877, a force of fifteen hundred men from the Sharqiya tribes of the Harthi, Hijriyin, and the Habus, all under the leadership of Salih bin Ali, descended on Muttrah and Muscat. The attack was not secret. Salih bin Ali had undertaken extensive planning and broadcast his intentions to the sultan and the British agent. Salih bin Ali wrote to the sultan to give him fair warning and told those under his command that they would not strike until Turki had received the letter, out of respect for their previous relationship. Turki's and Salih's relationship had deteriorated in part because Turki was upset by Salih's increasing role as a mediator in disputes. People in the interior sought out Salih rather than the sultan. Salih, who received a yearly allowance of $6,000 had not felt justified in attacking Turki during the previous three years, but renounced that position because "one must take care of himself."[87] He also had to take care of others and bore the expenses of inducements to persuade his allies to join. He had initially tried to convince his confederates that their payment for rising with him would be the plunder of Muscat and Muttrah, but the tribes had insisted on being paid in advance. Salih bin Ali seems to have expended his own resources for this.

The threat of attack in 1877 was the first to occur since the British had stated their policy to support the sultan. Robertson, the British consul at Muscat, warned Salih bin Ali that any action against the two principal cities would be considered "a rebellion against an esteemed ally of the British Government" and that Salih would be responsible for the consequences.[88] Salih bin Ali explained that he had tried to advise Turki, but that the sultan did not heed him. As a result, Salih's followers had taken a dim view of the sultan's subsequent actions. Salih warned the consul that the property of British subjects would be in danger if his men plundered Muttrah. He informed Robertson of the possibility out of his respect for the consul and out of pity for the British subjects. Salih bin Ali recommended they embark their goods until the cessation of hostilities.[89]

As promised, Salih bin Ali and his forces attacked and occupied Muttrah. The British consul and the sultan both realized that this was a serious attack. The attackers overran Muttrah, blocked Muscat from the land, and cut off its water supplies. Robertson noted that it was not simply a mission for "plunder and extortion" but a well-organized coalition of the "fanatical faction" to overthrow Turki's government.[90] On the second day, Turki wrote to the British consul asking for a loan to cover the loss of property and the expense of defending the capital. He emphasized that the disarray of the merchant community meant that he could not borrow from them, so he sought an advance on the Zanzibar subsidy. He put faith in the man-of-war that was arriving and the "lofty protection" of the British.[91] Following the guidelines adopted in 1874, the British did not carry out an operation on land to support Turki, but their navy shelled the town and provided cover for the British subjects to escape Muscat and Muttrah. With the merchants safely out, Robertson warned some of Ibrahim bin Qays and Salih bin Ali's allies that if they persisted on taking Muscat, "the guns of the Man O'War now in port will open fire on you and you are the responsible person."[92] The challengers never entered Muscat, but over the next few days the ship launched shells at the rebel encampment in the valley behind the town.[93] After holding Muttrah for the better part of a week and without capturing Muscat, Salih bin Ali and his allies sued for peace.

Attacks such as this were conflicts over the resources of the state and how they would be distributed. Although overthrowing the government had been the goal of the 1877 siege, failing to achieve this, Salih bin Ali and his Hinawi allies resorted to plunder and extortion. In Muttrah the occupiers had taken "everything within their reach." The leaders of the attack, however, sought to come to financial terms with the sultan. When Salih had negotiated his stipend in 1874, the sultan was compromised by illness and flush with cash from the renewed Zanzibar subsidy. In the aftermath the 1877 blockade, Salih bin Ali demanded a payment of $20,000 for leaving Muttrah, and also insisted on the continuation of the allowances he and Ibrahim bin Qays received. Salih bin Ali failed to recognize, however, that with a British man-of-war on Turki's side, the sultan was in a much stronger negotiating position. Turki refused the request. The British consul was delighted with Turki's newfound pluck and his refusal to agree to "utterly absurd" terms. Moreover, the consul believed that the failed mission would "ruin the reputation of Saleh as an organizer and leader." He judged it as a great setback for the conservative forces in Oman, calling it "undoubtedly the greatest blow" they had sustained since the Imam Azzan bin Qays was killed in 1871.[94] The repercussions of this failed attack, however, were not simply measured in the economy of prestige. The sultan and his British allies both wanted to inflict a pecuniary punishment on the rebels, though for different reasons.

The sultan and the consul cooperated to exact reparations for their own means, and their attempts to level sanctions against the rebels in the Omani interior revealed three strata of economic relationships among the tribes. The sultan wanted to recoup losses—the kinds of expenses for which he borrowed money during the attack—and the British agent in the gulf wanted the defeated rebels to compensate the British subjects (read: Indians) most affected by the siege. Collecting reparations created a contradiction for the British agent who worked under three guiding lemmas in Oman: enforcing the maritime peace, protecting the interests of British subjects, and not interfering with the tribes of Oman. The residents of Muttrah estimated their losses at between eight and fifteen thousand dollars. The British quickly seized on the higher figure, and sought to determine who would pay the reparations and who would (or could) collect them. In the past, the sultan alone bore the brunt of these indemnities. The British officials in the gulf worried that the sultan could not afford the loss (it would "cripple his resources" and invite further attacks) nor could he enforce punishment (without at least a warship present). Thus they had different goals but a shared interest. Turki wanted to recover losses and shore up his government while the British agent wanted to compensate British Indian subjects and make sure Turki did not lose control of the state.

The difficulty in applying economic levers to the interior tribes—al-Habus, al-Hijri, and al-Harthi—was that each of the three had distinct sources of wealth through their relationship to trade and commercial networks. The Habus would be impossible to collect from because they were "a wild tribe" that had no direct relationship with any port. The Hijriyin traded with the Jenebeh at Sur, where they kept "extensive depôts," and thus it would be easy to confiscate the goods and property held by their Jenebeh tribal partners. The Harthi were confounding because of their extensive connections across the Indian Ocean: They did not have trade depots or depend on other groups at Sur. Instead they "carry on operations themselves direct with Zanzibar where they are possessed of considerable wealth and where Saleh bin Ali himself is said to hold some property."[95] The pattern is one that characterizes three types of relationship between Omani tribes and external trade: groups with no direct trade with any port; groups that trade with ports through intermediaries; and groups that trade on their own and have substantial transnational connections. Thus, the sultan was only able to put economic pressure on one group of Arabs: those engaged in trade but dependent on others for access to ports and international commerce. The Hijriyin understood their vulnerable position and were worried about getting their date harvest to the market. They sent a delegation to Turki three months after the attack. Robertson urged Turki not to promise them anything unless they would pay for half of the indemnity from the June attack.[96] The Harthi, however, had a greater degree of autonomy from the state and were less vulnerable to the pressures that the sultan (or his British allies) could bring to bear.

The defeat in 1877 tarnished Salih bin Ali's reputation, had a disastrous effect on his finances, and led him to activate his own transnational network. Salih bin Ali generated a great deal of debt from the attack in 1877. He had tried to recruit allies on the promise of plunder, but they asked to be paid in advance. The return on this speculative investment, however, was poor. They did not capture the capital and they failed to secure a ransom. In addition, Salih bin Ali lost the substantial stipend that the sultan had paid him. In 1878, Salih bin Ali pursued three strategies to bring his finances in order: he sought a subsidy from the sultan; he threatened another rebellion; and he sold property in the Zanzibar market. The first two of these were interrelated. As early as January 1878 Salih bin Ali sent an envoy from the Bani Bu Hassan to Turki seeking a stipend. He was willing to negotiate and asked for $3,000 per year, half the annual subsidy he had received between January 1874 and June 1877. Turki refused and asked that the question never be raised again.[97] Perhaps to give greater force to his request, Salih bin Ali contemplated another uprising. A credible threat boosted the chances of a stipend. Turki was worried that Salih bin Ali would rally the Ibadi conservatives to back Turki's brother, Abdulaziz bin Said, and then replace him with a descendant of the assassinated imam Azzan bin Qays.[98] Turki underestimated the disarray of the former Ibadi alliances. The British officials in the Persian

Gulf were more sanguine, believing that not only had Salih lost influence and prestige, but that his personal resources were "diminished."[99]

Salih bin Ali's ability to raise an armed force to support his causes depended on his finances and his persuasiveness. Several months after his failure in Muscat, Salih bin Ali's prestige seemed to have dipped, undercutting his ability to attract followers. Previously others had valued him for his ability to settle disputes and enforce the terms of the settlement terms, but he had been unable to do so for a murder arbitration. In the latest iteration of a feud that went back to Turki's acquiescence in the murder of al-Khalili and his son, the Bani Rawahi clan were tired of waiting for the Busaidi blood money that Salih bin Ali had arranged. In response, the Bani Rawahi killed a Busaidi man and his attendant.[100] The Hijriyin, who were earlier allies from Sharqiya, were the most susceptible to the sultan's plans for punishment. They made it clear in early 1878 that Salih bin Ali could not count on their assistance.[101] Even among the Harthi, two sheikhs of the tribe reported to Turki in February 1878 that a certain "coolness" existed toward Salih bin Ali.[102] Facing indebtedness and loss of prestige at home, Salih bin Ali turned to Zanzibar.

In the months following the 1877 ill-fated attack on Muscat, given his loss of income and his mounting debt, Salih bin Ali sold property he held in Zanzibar to raise cash. As the same time, a close ally and kinsmen by marriage took out loans in Zanzibar against two properties in Oman. Indeed these actions suggest that Salih bin Ali tapped relatives to use the credit markets in Zanzibar to assist the rebellion or pay for it afterwards. A close look at these two transaction helps us see the dynamic of credit and wealth across Indian Ocean networks.

On the ninth day of Ramadan (September 1877), Salih bin Ali's kinsman Salim bin Isa bin Ali al-Suqri borrowed money in Zanzibar against a property in Oman. He borrowed $3,300 from Likmidas Ladha, a wealthy merchant and portfolio capitalist in Zanzibar. This was the first of two transactions that were unusual both for the extreme distance between the properties and the creditor, and for their connection to the religious and tribal elite in Oman. To secure the loan he pledged a property in al-Dariz, Sharqiya. While many other people in Zanzibar pledged property during this time, the property was generally in East Africa. Furthermore, Salim bin Isa al-Suqri was intimately linked to the Harthi elite and to scholarly networks in Oman. The Suqri were one of the constituent subclans that made up the Harthi, and Salim bin Isa was the nephew of the renowned Said bin Ali al-Suqri, known as *al-'Ālim al-Kabīr* (the great theologian). Said bin Ali al-Suqri was an Ibadi *'alim* and both the teacher and father-in-law of Salih bin Ali. Thus Salim bin Isa, the man carrying out the redeemable sale in Zanzibar during this critical period, was the first cousin of Salih bin Ali's wife.

The house that Salim bin Isa pledged was in al-Dariz, near both al-Qabil, where Salih bin Ali resided, and 'Izz, where Said bin Ali al-Suqri lived. Like these other two settlements, Harthi tribesmen had built al-Dariz, perhaps by extending or renewing the *falaj* in the previous century, sometime between when Salih bin Ali's forbearers dug the *falaj* in al-Qabil (1758) and when Said bin Ali opened the watercourse in 'Izz in 1856.[103] Access to water and *falaj* shares were vital in this part of Sharqiya, and Salim bin Isa also pledged the water rights and productive land attached to the house.[104] Less than two months later, Salim bin Isa borrowed more money and offered as security a different property, a stone house and land at al-Dariz. This loan was only MT$390, but the term was another year. This contract, written by the Zanzibar *qadi* Abdullah bin Ali bin Muhammad al-Mundhri, more clearly (but imperfectly) spells out details of the two properties. For instance, while the contract explains that Sheikh Salim bin Khalfan owned the house to the east of the pledged stone house, the contract states that the person who owned the property south of the pledged land was "the Sheikh." One would need the social context to understand which sheikh. The contract specifies that the pledge does not include usufruct rights.[105] Both debts, acknowledged in Zanzibar but secured with property in Oman, appear at a crucial moment in the Sharqiya region and at a vital juncture for Salih bin Ali. The transactions were completed in September and November 1877, after the defeat in Muscat and before the rising of 1878. While there is no irrefutable evidence to tie these to Salih bin Ali, three factors suggest a connection: the unusual nature (and timing) of these documents, his kinship with those involved, and his own financial straits. In the same vein, the following year Salih bin Ali used the credit markets of Zanzibar to dispose of his own property.

Salih bin Ali's actions in 1878 show that deeply indebted actors could take some steps to redeem their situations, but when facing multiple challenges, insolvency was difficult to overcome. Salih bin Ali sought to rise again in 1878 and challenge Turki. This aborted revolt is not covered in standard accounts even though it reveals tribal tensions and the precariousness of debt for those in interior Oman.[106] Turki's informants warned him in early June to be prepared for an attack. They knew that Salih bin Ali was raising funds to pay tribal levies. He did this by taking advantage of the Zanzibar credit nexus and Harthi network in East Africa to dispose of property that he held in Sharqiya. One of Turki's allies in Sharqiya explained what had happened: "Saleh bin Ali wrote to his tribesmen (at Zanzibar) this year giving them

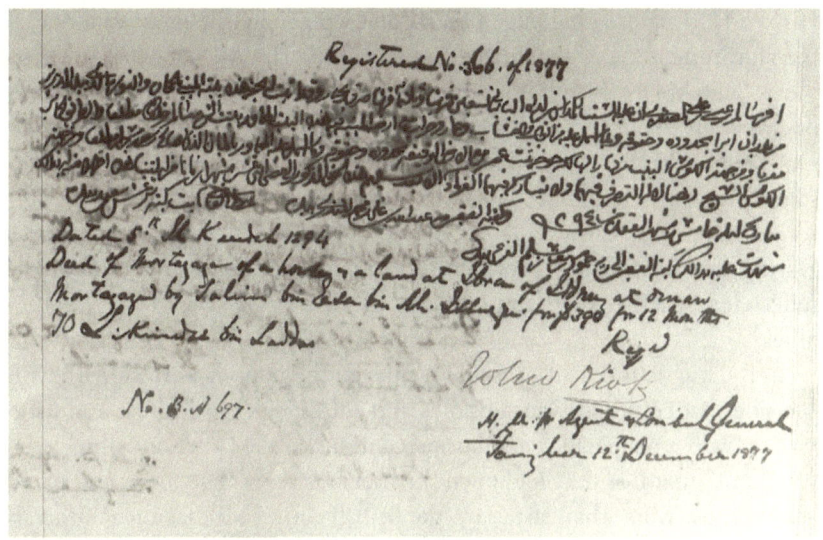

FIGURE 9.2. In 1877, Salim bin Isa al-Suqri in Zanzibar agreed to temporarily sell his rights to a property in Sharqiya, Oman. Registered Deed no. 366 of 1877, AM 3/1, Zanzibar National Archives.

power to dispose of his landed property in 'Izz; and they have sold it accordingly for 17,000 dollars."[107] These rumors flew during the first week of June, around the time sailing ships from Zanzibar would be arriving in Arabian ports. Turki initially doubted the report and the amount because it did not accord with his own information from Zanzibar, but another of his confidants confirmed a week later that Salih had sold the property and realized $16,000.[108] This was more than two and a half times the annual subsidy he had previously received from the sultan.

Although an uprising failed to materialize in 1878, the threat of another challenge to Muscat and the intrigue surrounding it shows the connection between finances, local rivalries, and the commercial anxiety political instability caused. Salih bin Ali had financing in hand but discord among potential allies limited his ability to act. Rumors suggested that Abdulaziz bin Said al-Busaidi, the younger brother and frequent rival of Turki, might join in the attack. Later, discord among the Harthi with their rivals in Sharqiya made an uprising unlikely. One of Turki's al-Harthi allies reported from al-Dariz that Salih himself had said he would rise and "place his dependence on God" but his followers' "courage and boasting have much decreased of late."[109] The Masakira, a Ghafiri group in Ibra that sometimes rivaled the

"Everything Is Pledged to Its Time"   245

Hinawi Harthi, also challenged them, and when a scuffle broke out, one of the Harthi men was killed, further undermining Hinawi resolve.[110] Furthermore, Salih bin Ali's profit from the property he sold was not enough to cover his previous debts and underwrite a new uprising.[111] An informant in al-Dariz who was knowledgeable about the transaction explained that Salih sold his property to a man known to Turki whose son had since taken possession of it.[112] Certainly Salih bin Ali's kin network with the Suqri and other Harthi men in Zanzibar provided him advantages, but the letter does not make clear whether those in possession of the property were Suqri or other allies.

In the fragile moment of 1878, loyalties in the interior were aligned with the side that could provide subsidies and subsistence. In Muscat and Muttrah, however, people took anxious precautions, as they were unwilling to be caught off guard, as they had been the previous year. "The terror and panic are ten times worse than last year," the British consul Miles wrote to officials in the Persian Gulf. Memories of the murders and cruelties committed during the last invasion and anticipation of similar occurrences brought trade to a standstill for a month. Residents abandoned the suburbs of Muscat and Muttrah, and some women and children lived aboard ships. The population was demoralized and lacked confidence in Turki's rule.[113] Outside the capital, Salih bin Ali was not the only one experiencing the gnaw of debt. In the face of the expenses, he seems to have retreated. Meanwhile, Abdulaziz had raised a force on his own to go to Samad and make his way to Muscat.

Even though Salih bin Ali did not engage in Abdulaziz's ill-fated operations in 1878, the threat of Salih's participation led Miles, the British consul in Muscat, to begin to view Salih as a mysterious, fearsome enemy who was the mastermind of all uprisings.[114] Miles realized that Abdulaziz could not be successful without a more influential ally, so he puzzled Salih's nonparticipation, spinning psychological theories. Miles's first theory was that Salih was secretly working against Abdulaziz to prove his own importance. Miles speculated that the Harthi sheikh wanted "to show the country that no rising can succeed unless it has his personal support and superintendence, that he alone in short is capable of organizing a successful rebellion and that his influence must be paramount." He also entertained the idea that Salih bin Ali was playing an elaborate chess game, and that Abdulaziz was just a pawn to test the sultan's position and British support. If Abdulaziz's action elicited no reaction or only a minimal one, Salih bin Ali would then throw his full force behind it.[115] In trying to read Salih bin Ali's position, Miles overlooked the fiscal conditions—the credit and indebtedness—that shaped events in July 1878.

Subsidies were the leading edge of allegiances, and the ability to provide for clients ensured the smooth working of tribal politics in Oman. The tribal politics of the summer months of 1878 came down to which side was able to provide subsidies for the various factions. One of the sites of conflict was in the Sumayl gap, the passage between the mountains that connected the interior to the markets of Muttrah and the political capital at Muscat. Turki had worked to maintain good relations with the dominant tribes of Sumayl because they guarded the pass. In the hot summer of 1878, Turki's forces in the valley jockeyed for control with the Hinawi rebels in Upper Sumayl and other tribes in this area. Turki's son Faysal took charge of securing the alliances that would block access to the Sumayl passes to their enemies. From the field, he wrote to his father, "The best thing for this is money, rice and ammunition."[116] Indeed, the governor of Sumayl, Nasir bin Muhammad al-Busaidi, a key ally in inhibiting an uprising, wrote to one of Turki's wazirs, "As you know my brother I have no funds in hand and for this affair money is necessary." He requested that Turki send money, rice, and powder as soon as possible. Time was of the essence, and money could move faster than goods. "If you have not camels," to carry the loads, he explained, "at least send me the money that I may purchase some here at Semail." The governor suffered a poor budget in part because he had not yet collected taxes on the date harvest.[117] Indeed, summer was the time to harvest dates but the anxiety of rebellion and the economic standstill at Muttrah exacerbated what turned out to be a poor date harvest. This in turn created "steady emigration" to Zanzibar, with an estimated one thousand people leaving on account of the lackluster crop.[118] Those who remained continued to scratch for resources, with conflict at hand. The governor of Sumayl closed his letter to the minister with a reminder that he had asked the sultan "to send me a gun as now is the time to use it."[119] No set battle occurred, but three people were killed in skirmishes and Faysal bin Turki destroyed two houses to punish the rebels and their allies.[120]

While Salih bin Ali's indebtedness influenced his political machinations, Turki took advantage of his absence from the field to press his slight advantage. First, he bought off some of those who had rebelled against him. Rather than direct cash payments that would have put immediate fiscal pressure on him, Turki authorized tax exemptions for important allies.[121] He then contemplated attacking Ibrahim bin Qays at al-Hazm, the fort in al-Rustaq, to try to extinguish the threat from the Qays bin Azzan line, the children of the last Imam. He framed this military and political action in economic terms. Turki would intercept trade with al-Rustaq and block their produce from reaching the market. Even if he could not capture al-Hazm, arguably one of the strongest forts in Oman, he intended to destroy the trees and the *aflaj* surrounding it and inflict as much damage as possible.[122] This brutally destructive practice contravened Ibadi rules of war, and Turki abruptly changed his mind in August for more esoteric reasons: he learned that the dates had already been harvested and that a larger force than he expected awaited. Before returning to Muscat, however, Turki had to pay and dismiss the Arab forces who had joined him.[123] For the sultan, too, stipends and grants underwrote tribal alliances and loyalty.

Thus in the aborted rebellion of 1878, the actions of the sultan and the sheikh highlighted the contingent nature of the tenuous alliances in Oman. Paying subsidies and subsistence for tribal leaders and their followers was an essential requirement of coalition building in the 1870s. The sultan, backed by the British and underwritten by the Zanzibar subsidy, enjoyed a slight upper hand. The sheikh, who commanded the allegiance of many and the respect of all, tried to escape indebtedness and raise rebellion through the credit markets in East Africa. He and his allies were able to tap into readily available cash through absolute sales and mortgages, but in the difficult economic environment of 1878 Salih bin Ali stayed home. In the early days of Ramadan that year, Salih bin Ali explained to a sheikh of the Hijri that he had not sought out hostility toward Turki but had acted at the request of an unnamed person with whom he had since cut allegiances. Perhaps referring to his economic standing he noted, "You are aware of how I am situated." In three days from the date of his writing, al-Suqri's loan and pledged house would be due in Zanzibar. Between the closing lines of Sheikh Salih's letter, it is hard not read the relationship between money, mortgages, and his own ambitions: "There is a limit and end to all things. Everything is pledged to its own time."[124]

A MORTGAGE, A SURPRISE ATTACK, AND RAPPROCHEMENT WITH ZANZIBAR IN THE 1880S

The stalemate of the 1870s was broken in 1883 when Salih bin Ali took advantage of Turki's fumbling alliances and mortgaged his property to lead a sneak attack on Muscat. Turki, in trying to expand his influence into strategic places in the interior, became more intimately involved in local disputes and unwittingly alienated key allies. This created an unexpected opening for Salih bin Ali who mortgaged property to spring into action. His surprise attack on Muscat backfired and became an unexpected boon for Turki in the politics of the interior and in winning the respect of his British allies. The uprising of 1883 and its aftermath also marked a turning point for Turki's relationship with Salih bin Ali and, less directly, with Barghash in Zanzibar. Turki's request for help from Barghash signaled a rapprochement predicated on Turki's lower status. Barghash's subsequently largesse made clear Zanzibar's dominance, and the previously estranged brothers met in Oman in 1888. Both sultans died shortly thereafter, and Salih bin Ali survived them both. But he never led an attack on Muscat after 1883.

In the early 1880s, Salih bin Ali reestablished himself as an important mediator in tribal disputes. He helped achieve peace in 1880 between the Bani Bu Hassan and the Jenebeh on the route to Sur.[125] As for Turki, although a visitor in 1883 described him as a "poor sunken and demoralized creature, afraid each day of being poisoned by his son," the sometimes fragile sultan was vigorously looking beyond Muscat trying to expand his influence in the interior and maintain his rule.[126] Turki's obsession with controlling Wadi Sumayl, the gateway from the interior to Muttrah and Muscat (and an emerging center for growing the dates that were Oman's most commercially successful export), required careful attention to tribal politics. He paid subsidies to the Nidabiyin and the Rahbiyin to hold the passes. In early 1883 he reconsidered his position because of those tribes' ongoing quarrels with the Bani Jabir, who occupied Nidabiyin houses in Sarūr. The Bani Jabir committed the ultimate aggression: cutting down the Nidabiyin date trees. Turki tried unsuccessfully to negotiate a peace and protect his interest in the Wadi Sumayl. In doing so he alienated the Nidabiyin and the Rahbiyin. These former allies defected to Salih bin Ali who was also married to a woman of the Bani Jabir, and suddenly the Harthi chief had a clear path to the capital.[127]

The British suspected Salih bin Ali was a deep strategist and assumed that he had played a very subtle game in creating the disturbance in Wadi Sumayl. Writing a year later, E.C. Ross explained that the quarrel over Sarūr in Wadi Sumayl "has been carefully fomented and increased, almost from the first, by the intrigues of Shaikh Saleh, which subtle mind perceived that if he could separate the two tribes holding the passes . . . he would have gained an important advantage" in challenging Turki. Ross begrudgingly attributed a brilliance to these maneuvers: "Not only did he succeed in this, but he managed to make the quarrel itself the pretext for his rebellious proceedings."[128]

If, as Sheikh Salih had written, everything is pledged it its time, Salih underwrote the 1883 uprising by mortgaging his personal property in July for $9,000. He spread the word that an uprising to support the Nidabiyin would occur after Ramadan.[129] The Sumayl valley was the point of contention, and unsettled allegiances in the region made it ripe for conflict. Salih bin Ali and his forces reached the valley in August, and Turki, preparing to oppose them, sent his son Faysal in September. When Faysal moved into lower Sumayl, Salih and his allies occupied the upper reaches, which were closest to the interior. Salih also used his influence to attract a wide coalition. He joined forces again with Abdulaziz bin Said, the frequently disgruntled pretender to the throne, and formed a key alliance with Juma bin Said al-Miskri of Ibra. The Miskri and the Harthi had a long-simmering feud between upper and lower Ibra, a rivalry that mirrored the larger tribal confederations of the Ghafiri and the Hinawi. While Salih bin Ali had frequently been able to call on the Hinawi tribes of the Sharqiya, Juma bin Said nursed a personal grudge with Turki and used his influence among the Ghafiri to attract some of the tribes to Salih's coalition. (Juma bin Said al-Miskri was also a polarizing figure, and his overtures convinced some tribes that Turki's side must be the correct one.)[130] September became October, and a sharp double-shock earthquake hit Muscat just before afternoon prayers on the thirteenth, rattling doors and windows.[131] Soothsayers and sign seekers would have been justified in predicting that a calamity was near at hand.

A week later, political rumblings came from the interior. Salih bin Ali and his forces passed through the Sumayl valley unmolested after having won key allies through the feints and allegiances of the summer. As they moved toward Muscat, Abdulaziz announced their intentions to capture the city to the British political agent on October 19 so that British subjects could protect themselves and their goods. The sultan scrambled to man his garrisons. Two days later a rebel force of more than eighteen hundred men filtered into the village of Ruwi, a short distance from Muscat, and more followed. Salih bin Ali wrote to the sultan who anticipated an attack the next day. The rebels did not wait. That night, they dressed in black and fanned out across the rocky hills surrounding Muscat. Shortly after midnight they struck at three points of the city's defenses simultaneously, completely surprising the defenders. Their advantage was quickly lost. Turki's recently reinforced garrisons and the city's defensive fortifications counterbalanced the surprise. Turki's soldiers recovered quickly and returned heavy, sustained fire. The attackers fell back.[132]

The failure of the surprise attack presaged the outcome for the invaders, but the denouement lasted several days and underscored the shift in balance of power. Turki wrote to Barghash in Zanzibar asking for money and for him to seize the property there of the rebels. In Muscat, British support for Turki was crucial.[133] The *HMS Philomel* steamed into the harbor the next day and lobbed artillery over the city to strike the rebels' position. The British ship pinned down the attackers and bought time for more of Turki's allies to reach the capital. Salih bin Ali and Abdulaziz were soon outnumbered and withdrew, defeated, all the way back to Sharqiya.[134] Turki had attracted more than three thousand fighters, and Faysal bin Turki led some of the assembled forces to pursue the retreating enemy with the goal of punishing those in Sumayl. Faysal attacked the Nidabiyin and the Rahbiyin, dealing them the ultimate blow of chopping down some of their date groves. The defense of Muscat and revenge in Sumayl enhanced Turki's standing in the country. The wily but unsuccessful tactics of the rebels underscored the British political agent's portrait of Salih bin Ali as a worthy, dangerous opponent.

Salih bin Ali's defeat and Turki's victory in 1883 marked a turning point in the relationship between the two men as well as in the relationship between the sultans of Muscat and Zanzibar. As a result of the 1883 storming of Muscat, Turki agreed to pay stipends to Salih bin Ali and Abdulaziz bin Said. The Harthi leader received only $50 per month, a tenth of what he had received a decade earlier, while the sultan's half-brother was given $200 per month.[135] Clearly, Turki feared Salih bin Ali less than he had in the past. In the years that followed, rumors would fly about Salih bin Ali's intrigues, but the Harthi sheikh did not challenge Turki again. While Salih's indebtedness and personal finances influenced his ability to rebel, another factor was the strong British backing of Turki. Salih bin Ali had seen British intervention in Zanzibar in 1859, in Muscat in 1877 and 1878, and again in 1883. British gunboats and financial backing were difficult for Salih bin Ali and his confederates to overcome. This fact was not lost on Turki. The day after his forces had repelled Salih bin Ali and his allies in 1883, Turki signaled victory by flying British flags from his forts.[136] Following Turki's successful showing, the British also raised their commitment, pledging in 1886 to uphold the sultan's rule and not to tolerate any change of government.[137] In this context, as Turki's internal rivals were diminished, the Muscati sultan's relationship with Barghash, his half-brother and the sultan of Zanzibar, was markedly improved.

RECONCILING SULTANS

The two Busaidi sultans in Oman and Zanzibar established a new relationship in the mid-1880s with a clear hierarchy. Barghash led a modern state and lavished his client Turki with gifts Turki could not reciprocate. This was a new state of affairs. Through the early 1880s, Turki and Barghash had used each other's realm as a place to exile enemies of their own state, especially high officials who had fallen out of favor. Thus Turki deported Seyyid Badr bin Sayf al-Busaidi to Zanzibar in 1877. Badr had served as the governor of the vital port of Suhar but Turki feared that he was becoming too independent and would seize Suhar as his own. Turki imprisoned the governor and then packed him onto the mail steamer for Zanzibar, where members of his family already resided. After more than two years in exile Badr bin Sayf returned, apparently rehabilitated in 1880, and Turki appointed him as governor of Muttrah, the commercial capital.[138] In the other direction, when Barghash sacked two members of the royal family who had served as governors of the important ports of Lamu and Mombasa, he sent them to Muscat in late 1884.[139] These exiles pointed to the cultural continuities and political divisions between Arabia and East Africa. By the time Barghash's dissident governors arrived in Oman in 1884, however, the official relationship between Muscat and Zanzibar had begun to thaw.

In the midst of Turki's tangle with Salih bin Ali in 1883, the sultan had written to Barghash requesting assistance. Turki sought financial support for his resource-poor state, but he also wanted Barghash to cripple his rivals by seizing property they owned in Zanzibar. Turki singled out Juma bin Said al-Miskri of Ibra, who he believed was the ringleader of the disaffected group.[140] This request by Turki acknowledged, implicitly, the way that people in Oman used property in Zanzibar to underwrite political rivalries. Whether or not Barghash seized the property, he eventually sent Turki $15,000, delivered in Barghash's own steamer. Turki was pleased by the support, and sent a shipment of horses to Barghash in December of 1883.[141] Thus began a series of increasingly lavish gift exchanges between the brothers that would continue for the next four years. Remember that Barghash's rival—Majid—had been a close ally of Turki and had assisted him in his escape from India and in his conquest of the imamate in Oman. In addition, Turki had supplanted the conservative Ibadi forces in Oman, a group with which Barghash had long been sympathetic. Barghash had sent some gifts as tokens early in Turki's rule, but he had also vehemently opposed the Zanzibar subsidy, vowing in the early 1870s to send nothing to Muscat. What had changed? By the early 1880s, these men were no longer rivals. Both had solidified their positions and were unquestionably dependent on British support (though Barghash accepted it much more reluctantly). Moreover, the two men were not equals in wealth or power, and Turki had signaled this by subordinating himself and seeking Barghash's help in 1883.

In the exchange of gifts between the sultans of Zanzibar and Muscat, steam-powered ships carried the goods and set the tone, demonstrating clearly that Barghash was the patron and Turki the client. In the 1880s, Barghash's burgeoning fleet of steamships made Muscat a regular port of call. They stopped there on the way to Bombay for trade or on the way to or from Mecca to pick up or discharge pilgrims. When Barghash acquired a new steamship from Hamburg, the *Kilwa*, it stopped in Muscat on its way to East Africa. The same ships brought gifts from Barghash to Turki. Barghash's gifts—gunpowder, cash, and steamships—were tools of modern statecraft, and Turki reciprocated as best he could by sending the traditional trappings of Arab largesse—camels and horses. This unequal exchange pointed to the depressed state of the Muscat economy and the relative wealth of Zanzibar.[142] Thus, when Barghash sent one hundred kegs of gunpowder and $5,000, Turki dispatched thirteen horses and seven camels for his brother. In 1886, Barghash presented Turki with his own steamship, the SS *Sultani*.[143] Turki deployed the ship almost immediately in a display of his own prestige. In July he sent the *Sultani* to Sur, a thriving, outlaw port where the sultan had been unable to collect any duties because of his poor relationships with the chiefs there. In a grand gesture of statecraft, Turki had invited selected leaders from Sur to witness his investiture as a Grand Commander of the State of India, an imperial honor to showcase his power vis-à-vis the British Empire, and had sent his personal steamship to collect them. The *Sultani* delivered the men to Muscat so that they could witness the ceremony. These acts sent the message to his domestic rivals that he enjoyed the support of the Zanzibar sultan and of the British Empire. Yet Turki was limited on the prestige gifts he could bestow. After the gift of the steamship, Turki reciprocated with camels and even more horses (seventeen) for Barghash.[144]

Even as this official rapprochement unfolded, Turki was apprehensive that dissenters in Oman might gain backing in Zanzibar. In this sense, East Africa continued to be an escape valve for Muscat, and access to credit there was still desirable to many Omanis, especially those who hoped to challenge the sultan. In October 1887 a coalition of al-Harthi began to organize against Turki. They collected $2,000 and entrusted it to Salih bin Ali to aid in rebellion. They also planned to send representatives to Zanzibar, presumably to drum up support and add to their working capital. The sultan in Muscat, however, had a much stronger position than he had had in the 1870s. One sign of his greater strength was that he made sure his dissenting subjects could not seek succor from Barghash's ship. He ordered the Harthi present in the port cities of Muscat, Muttrah, and Sur to return to Sharqiya. For good measure, he also imprisoned one of the leaders who, like many of the Harthi elite, owned property in Zanzibar. The dissident was released a week later, after Barghash's ship had sailed from Oman to Zanzibar.[145]

Religious and ideological differences also rippled beneath this emerging relationship, and one of Turki's Ibadi *qadis* fled Muscat under the cover of darkness in 1888. In Zanzibar Barghash fostered a culture of Islamic, and especially Ibadi, learning.[146] In Oman, on the other hand, many Ibadis regarded Turki with suspicion and disdain because of his role in the death of al-Khalili. Salim bin 'Udaym bin Salih al-Rawahi, had been a stalwart in the imamate, "one of the ablest" of its leaders, so he had been a controversial choice for *qadi* of Muttrah when he was appointed in 1880. Salim bin 'Udaym explained that he sought the appointment from Turki because he was poor and needed the employment. The suspicious British agent saw him as a "staunch friend and coadjutator" of Salih bin Ali and guessed that he sought the post in Muttrah to keep a closer eye on the commercial capital for the conservative party.[147] The cause of his sudden, secretive departure eight years later is unknown, but he quickly established himself in Zanzibar as a *qadi* and jurist, writing debt acknowledgments and witnessing ivory deals for freed slaves of powerful men.[148] Whether Salim bin 'Udaym's move was ideological or pecuniary, Zanzibar under Barghash was more attractive to him than Oman under Turki, even when the sultans had reconciled.

The culmination of the newfound closeness of the two sultans was a visit to Muscat by an ailing Barghash in March 1888. Since the death of their father Said bin Sultan in 1856, the rivalry between Muscat and Zanzibar had precluded state visits by the sultans, though Omanis of every other station in life continued to move across the Indian Ocean between these nodes of Said bin Sultan's former domain. A dire situation prompted Barghash's visit. He arrived in Oman in early March in a poor state of health seeking the curative powers of Bowshar hot springs. Despite his illness, Barghash lavished his host with a gift of $50,000 and gave each of Turki's sons $2,000. This generous act was one of his last. He departed Oman on March 17 and died after midnight ten days later, just five hours after his ship landed in Zanzibar. He was buried at daybreak.[149] In Muscat, Turki outlived him by only a few months. He died in early June 1888. Beset by illness much of his adult life, Turki had held onto power for seventeen years through compromises, allowances, and luck.

The year 1888 thus marked a significant turning point for both Zanzibar and Muscat. Despite their deep imbalance in political and financial power, the sultans who ruled each place had followed an oddly parallel career, beginning as ambitious rivals passed over in the wake of their father's death, enduring exile in Bombay, and assuming power in the early 1870s. Both faced internal threats and met them by relying on the financial and military backing of an expanding British Empire. In exchange, both capitulated to British demands to end the slave trade and tolerated British interference in the day-to-day aspects of the sultans' rule. While Turki and Barghash had negotiated terms with the British and attempted to balance their independence, their successors in Muscat and in Zanzibar would be British clients from the beginning. For Turki and for Barghash, their father had extended direct Omani rule over far-flung territories of the western Indian Ocean, but they each ruled only a part of his bifurcated realm. Their reconciliation in the 1880s, and their meeting in the land of their forefathers as both neared death, lent a poetic touch to the final step in the dissolution of the nineteenth-century empire.

SALIH BIN ALI'S SWAN SONG

Salih bin Ali al-Harthi survived his former ally Barghash bin Said and his long-time rival Turki bin Said. Indeed, with new sultans in Muscat and in Zanzibar, Salih bin Ali briefly found room to maneuver again in the 1890s. Even closer and more coordinated cooperation from Zanzibar allowed Salih to mount a significant threat to Muscat. When Turki's son Faysal, the new sultan of Muscat, dabbled in Hinawi politics to support a rival to Salih bin Ali, the canny sheikh struck back. This time, however, Salih bin Ali had the resources to overcome one of his historical weaknesses: lack of direct access to an outside ally.[150] Salih bin Ali's mortgages, property sales, and invocations of kin networks in the 1870s and 1880s all point to self-funded campaigns via the credit markets in East Africa. In the early 1890s, however, direct assistance from the newest sultan of Zanzibar appeared promising.

In Zanzibar a long period of stability gave way to a quick succession of rulers. Despite threats to Majid's rule early in his tenure, Zanzibar had only two sultans between 1856 and 1888. Barghash's successor in 1888, Khalifa bin Said, died in 1890, and the next sultan Ali bin Said died in 1893. The accession of Hamad bin Thuwayni in 1893 rekindled the relationship with Oman, and especially with the Harthi and Sharqiya allies. As the son of Thuwayni, the new Zanzibar sultan had grown up in Oman and as a sultan dreamt of reuniting his grandfather's realm. His wazirs and ministers shared his vision. One of his closest advisors was Hilal bin Amir bin Sultan al-Khanjari al-Harthi from 'Izz in Sharqiya. Hilal's father had assisted the Grand Theologian Said bin Ali al-Suqri in opening the *falaj* to 'Izz in 1856. While Hilal served the sultan in Zanzibar, his brother Muhsin bin Amir remained in 'Izz and became a powerful sheikh and close ally of Salih bin Ali.[151] Thus Hilal bin Amir and the sultan he advised were closely attuned to Omani politics in the interior. They sent a delegation to Oman, not to meet with the sultan, but with Salih bin Ali. In the other direction, many Omani sheikhs sought the new Zanzibar sultan's advice and largesse. The time was ripe in early 1894, and Salih bin Ali sent his son Abdullah along with Muhsin bin Amir, brother to the Zanzibar advisor, to East Africa to plot the overthrow of Faysal. Abdullah bin Salih's trip to East Africa was shorter than his father's sojourn there more than thirty years previously, and the son returned with tools he could use immediately: three large field guns and three hundred barrels of gunpowder.[152] With this strong encouragement, Salih bin Ali maneuvered to gain tribal support in Sharqiya, attract the leadership of the conservative Ibadi *'ulama*, and win over support in Wadi Sumayl to hold open the pass to gain access to Muscat. Three tribes—Bani Siyabiyin, Bani Rahbiyin, and Bani Nidabiyin—all cooperated willingly rather than oppose the powerful chief. The Bani Shahaim, however, needed more convincing, and Salih bin Ali subjugated them in November 1894.[153] While Salih bin Ali's prestige allowed him to play the role of conciliator, his son Abdullah emerged as a leader for the Harthi specifically and the Hinawi confederation in general. After his trip to Zanzibar, Salih bin Ali urged his son Abdullah bin Salih to lead a reconciliation between the dominant tribes of Nizwa and seal a six-month truce. This truce also neutralized some potential opposition to an uprising from Oman's interior.[154] His ability to lead reconciliations, gain strategic advantages, and call on resources overseas were signs of Abdullah's rising star.

FIGURE 9.3. A view from inside Muscat's gates, 1898. From Emile Allemann "Mascate," *Le Tour du Monde* 7, no. 7e (1901), 73.

The Nizwa reconciliation also set the stage for an elaborate ruse to seize Muscat. In February 1895 Abdullah bin Salih, Muhsin bin Amir al-Khanjari (of 'Izz, with the powerful brother in Zanzibar), and a small cadre of sheikhs entered Muscat as Faysal's guests under the pretense of reporting the Nizwa news. As the Bombay press reported, Faysal welcomed them with a cash present of $400 for Abdullah and rice, dates, coffee, "and the famous Muscat 'halwa' for the men."[155] While they accepted this hospitality, they had also arranged for other tribal leaders to enter the gates of Muscat in small groups so as not to arouse suspicion. At the appointed moment Abdullah bin Salih and his confederates launched their attack from within the fortified city, seizing the gates and fanning out through the narrow lanes of the old city. They hunted the sultan and his ministers. Muhammad bin Turki, the sultan's brother, leapt from a second-story window and raced to Fort Mirani to organize the resistance. Sultan Faysal, for his part, fended off his assailants and sought refuge in Fort Jalali on the other arm of the harbor. Thus, with the sultan's forces in the forts and the rebels holding the neighborhoods and streets, a stalemate set in that lasted nearly three weeks. The British, who had played such decisive roles in quelling all of Salih bin Ali's other uprisings, opted for a guarded neutrality, much to Faysal's dismay. Both sides called for reinforcements, and Salih bin Ali, who had masterminded the attack, arrived with additional forces from Sharqiya. They were able to hold Muscat and the nearby Ruwi, but they could not take Muttrah. Faysal, meanwhile, was able to attract men from a wider cross-section of the country, and his forces soon vastly outnumbered the rebels. To win back the city, however, would have required street-by-street and house-by-house fighting. When news reached the city that Faysal's partisans had closed the path from Muscat via Sumayl, some of Salih's supporters began to defect. Faysal, using a time-honored diplomatic maneuver, successfully bought off some of the opposing sheikhs. Negotiations ended the military deadlock on March 9, and Faysal agreed to pay more than $12,000 to the rebels and to pay a stipend to their key allies, the Busaidis of the Azzan bin Qays line.[156]

Although arms and funds from Zanzibar had helped launch the attack, further support was not forthcoming. Zanzibar had become a formal British Protectorate in 1890, another step in the subjugation of the sultanate, and the new administration was slow to catch on to the new sultan's overtures toward Oman after 1893. As these connections came to light, however, they suspected Hilal bin Amir al-Khanjari as the prime mover both in the reunification efforts and in the anti-British sentiment in Zanzibar. They arrested him and exiled him to Oman. The anti-imperial feeling simmered in Zanzibar, however, and the sultan, Hamad bin Thuwayni, encouraged it. When

Hamad was near death in 1896, he called on Khalid bin Barghash, son of the illustrious sultan, and encouraged him to take the throne.[157] When Sultan Hamad died, Khalid bin Barghash seized the palace. After British protestations and some saber rattling, Khalid's two-day reign ended in what jingoistic imperialists have dubbed "The Shortest War in History." While it was short—just twenty minutes—it was not a war but a close-range shelling that destroyed the sultan's palace and the Zanzibar waterfront. One could imagine this was what the British ships would have done to Muscat had Salih bin Ali ever successfully captured the city. In Zanzibar, Khalid bin Barghash escaped to the African mainland; not to the caravan routes that his father's supporters had spilled into in 1859, but to Dar es Salaam and German protection. In Zanzibar, the British installed their favored candidate, Hamud bin Muhammad al-Busaidi, who cooperated with the elaboration of British indirect rule.

In Oman, Salih bin Ali and his forces did not win the battle for Muscat in 1895, but compared to Faysal bin Turki and the British, he lost the least. Faysal bin Turki emerged from the conflict scathed, with the tenuous basis of his rule exposed. A few narrow escapes and the timely arrival of fickle allies from Oman saved his rule, but rebels looted his capital and his previous cooperation with the British yielded no help, only watchful waiting. For their part, the British also lost in the conflict by failing to protect British subjects, influence the sultan, or shape the outcome of the rebellion. To avoid this in the future, the British announced in 1895 that they would not permit attacks on Muscat.[158] While this was short of the protectorate declared in Zanzibar, it signaled intolerance for the volatility of the natural political economy of Oman in which powerful tribal leaders with overseas linkages could regularly raise forces. In 1895, Salih bin Ali and his allies had failed once again to strike quickly and decisively enough to cripple the sultan's rule. They also lacked a coalition outside Sharqiya and among the Ghafiri to affect a large-scale popular revolt. Finally, additional support from Zanzibar never materialized. When the Hinawi forces retired to their date groves, however, they still posed a great threat to the sultan and his rule.[159] For Salih bin Ali, however, it would be his last assault on Muscat. The next year he was wounded in a skirmish and died. His death marked the end of an era, and a generational shift in leadership.

Although his promising son Abdullah died from an illness shortly after the siege in Muscat, Salih's son Isa rose to lead a powerful movement that reshaped Oman. Isa bin Salih and his father's numerous students eschewed taking Muscat, and instead claimed the interior as their own. They established an imamate in 1913 that remained autonomous until 1958, and they retrospectively viewed Salih bin Ali as their own special imam.

The great Omani historian Abdullah bin Humayd al-Salimi dubbed his teacher Salih bin Ali as *al-Imam al-Muhtasib*, which Wilkinson defines as a learned man "with the dependability and integrity to lead and advise the Muslim community until such time as an Imam can be properly elected."[160] From the fall of Qays bin Azzan's imamate in 1871, Salih bin Ali thus stood as a kind of temporizing imam, an unelected leader who could protect the community until a full imam appeared. This designation recognized Salih bin Ali's leadership and justified his military actions. Al-Salimi was not simply a historian of Oman, he himself was Salih bin Ali's devoted student and was one of the principal architects of the revival of the imamate in 1913.[161] Thus al-Salimi's retrospective view of Salih bin Ali as an *imam al-muhtasib* occurred at the very moment that the author was making a case for a new imamate. If, in al-Salimi's view, Salih bin Ali had been buying time for an Ibadi reawakening in the early twentieth century, the moment had come. Salih bin Ali's own belief that everything was pledged to its time suggests he understood historical contingency and the way it fit the arc of his life.

Although Salih bin Ali's last campaign took place amid a British imperial reorganization of the western Indian Ocean, we can see his career as exemplary of a period of uncertain outcomes. His life, like those of Barghash's and Turki's began in an era when the winds shaped patterns of mobility between Arabia and Africa, and ended in an era of steam and expanding global capital. In this light, Salih bin Ali's career paralleled the two sultans. Salih bin Ali had taken part in the scuffles to determine Said bin Sultan's successor in 1859. His exile was not in Bombay, like Barghash and Turki, but self-imposed in Somalia, on the other side of the Indian Ocean littoral. These years were a prelude to his rise to the top of the Harthi tribe and Hinawi confederation and to his short stint as a wazir and pillar of the imamate government. Salih bin Ali's leadership and moral standing drew others to him, and his connections to East Africa funded several uprisings. Salih tapped into the wealth in Zanzibar to capitalize property and try to reform the government of Muscat. At a different time, Salih bin Ali would likely have been much more successful. The creeping encroachment of British interest in Muscat and Zanzibar, however, created insurmountable obstacles. Salih bin Ali was able to invoke the ideals of Ibadi governance, mortgage personal holdings, and raise tribal levies to defeat the sultan, but even this wily, sagacious, and tough Harthi sheikh could not defeat the British Empire.

Epilogue

ON THE THIRD DAY of Eid al-Fitr in December of 2001, I attended a lunch in Al Amirat Seih Dhabi, a suburb of the Omani capital, Muscat. My host Ahmed bin Muhammad bin Khalid al-Barwani had invited me to share a meal with his Barwani clansmen. Ahmed was a halwa seller born in Zanzibar in 1955. He had moved to Oman in 1977 in search of a better life. His story is a twentieth-century complement both to the lost confectioners of Nizwa during the drought in the 1840s, and to the mobility of Thani bin Amir al-Harthi, the humble halwa maker who became the leading agent at Kazeh in the 1850s. Ahmed bin Muhammad's history also serves to frame this book's conclusions. Indeed, the contingent nature of mobility that pertained in the nineteenth century, when individuals in the western Indian Ocean used debt and the infrastructures of kinship to buy time in the face of new challenges, resonates with experiences of Africans and Arabs at the beginning of the twenty-first.

This epilogue narrates Ahmed bin Muhammad's life and context to connect the closing of the nineteenth century to the present day. Ahmed's life highlights a historical irony: Ahmed's father, like many in his generation and the generations before him, fled Oman for the wealth and stability of Zanzibar. Later, Ahmed and thousands of others fled East Africa for the wealth and stability of Oman. This seeming paradox is grounded in the specific contexts of both places and dependent on their historical relationship. In Zanzibar, the Arab sultanate aligned with British indirect rule to create prosperity and privilege for some in the first half of the twentieth century. The violence that surrounded Zanzibar's political independence in the early 1960s, however, fell disproportionately on those of Arab and Indian descent. A bloody revolution in Zanzibar led to the archipelago's hasty union with Tanganyika in 1964, and in the decades that followed many people faced diminishing social and economic possibilities and sought to emigrate. In Oman, on the other hand, the political reunification of the country in 1958 allowed oil production to begin, and a bloodless palace coup in 1970 brought a new sultan to the throne who was committed to using oil revenue to modernize the sultanate and foster Omani nationalism. When emigrants from Africa like Ahmed bin Muhammad arrived, however, they faced the challenges of establishing themselves in a new location and integrating themselves within this new nationalist project. Halwa and kinship helped Ahmed bin Muhammad solve both problems. He became a sweetmeat manufacturer, and, as the chief genealogist of the sprawling Barwani clan, created a family tree that demonstrated the diasporic family's roots in Oman.

Although Ahmed bin Muhammad al-Barwani was not from a wealthy or prominent branch of the family, he established a thriving business in Oman and was happy to trade on the reputation of his kinsmen. The Barwani clan, one branch of the broader Harthi confederation, originated in the Sharqiya region of Oman and gained great importance in East Africa. Men from the clan had been important governors, wealthy merchants, religious leaders, and resistance figures in the nineteenth century. In the twentieth century, Ali bin Muhsin al-Barwani founded the Zanzibar Nationalist Party and became the foreign minister of independent Zanzibar in 1963. As for Ahmed bin Muhammad, his small shop produced delicious, nutty halwa, and when I visited in the days before Eid, the walls were stacked high with fresh containers. Ahmed's confections were well known in Muscat and beyond.[1] Once, someone sent an order to Portsmouth, England, where Jamshid bin Abdullah al-Busaidi, the last sultan of Zanzibar has lived in exile since 1964. Seyyid Jamshid greatly enjoyed this halwa, and when he found out who had made it, he joked that he never expected to eat halwa made by a Barwani.[2] Ahmed tells this story at his own expense, teasing at the discrepancy between the illustriousness of his clan name in East African history and the humbleness of his profession. And if Seyyid Jamshid never expected to eat sweetmeats prepared by a kinsman of his foreign minister, this was but one small part of a life that defied expectation. Jamshid was born in 1929 in the Zanzibar Protectorate during the long reign of his grandfather, Seyyid Khalifa bin Harub (r. 1911–60). Khalifa died in 1960, and his successor, Jamshid's father, died suddenly in 1963. Thus, at age thirty-three, Jamshid became the sultan of Zanzibar several months before independence. Even with those surprising turns of events, he probably did not expect to spend most of his adult life in exile in the United Kingdom. Like the sultans-in-exile and mobile confectioners of an earlier era, mobility and displacements had upended expectations. What were those expectations in the early decades of the twentieth century?

Expectations for those living in the interior of Oman were for modest lives, whereas Zanzibar continued to be a site of aspiration. The father of Ahmed the halwa maker, Muhammad bin Khalid al-Barwani, was born in al-Dariz, in Sharqiya, Oman, during the first decades of the twentieth century. This was a period of drought, great poverty and uncertainty in Oman. The heirs of Salih bin Ali, the Harthi leader of the nineteenth century, abandoned their family home in al-Qabil during this period because of "long continued" drought and moved to the nearby settlement of 'Izz.[3] Zanzibar remained a source of wealth in Oman, but among those who were left out of the flow of money connected to Zanzibar, suspicions and jealousy were rampant. We can see this in the correspondence and legal challenges about control of property that arose at this time. A letter sent in 1902 from al-Rustaq in the interior of Oman to Zanzibar, for instance, reported that there was no news except drought, hunger, war, and injustice "which are prevalent all over and are at their extremes." This correspondence was part of a legal case in which people in Oman challenged their relative in Zanzibar for his sale of a property in Oman to satisfy a debt. The owner sold the property—the plot of land, *falaj* channels that watered it, and the houses—in Zanzibar via a redeemable sale (*bay' khiyār*). The relatives in Oman had served as the caretakers of the property while their kinsman was in Zanzibar. They refused to hand over the farm and disputed the documents that the new owner brought even though they were duly written and witnessed in Zanzibar.[4] The Omani caretaker's letters to the relative in Zanzibar are indignant and include accusations of betrayal. He wanted to believe that the absent owner had only appointed the creditor as an agent to possess that property. He could not fathom that his kinsman had sold the property without giving him the customary right of preemption (*shufa'a*).[5] However, by going to the colonial court in Zanzibar and invoking the heterodox legal system of the western Indian Ocean, the owner undercut claims made by kin and claims grounded in custom. The case also shows that many people in Oman did not benefit from having relatives in Zanzibar, which may have encouraged people to pursue their own opportunities in East Africa.

For those living in the Omani interior, the reemergence of an imamate in the first decades of the twentieth century marked a shift in their political autonomy. This reemergence was, in part, due to the death of the sultan

Faysal bin Turki in 1913. Faysal bin Turki, who had spent part of his childhood destitute in Bombay while his father was in exile, spoke Gujarati and Swahili better than Arabic. He relied heavily on British military and financial support. In 1912, in exchange for a substantial boost to his annual subsidy (which had originated as the Zanzibar subsidy), Faysal granted the British authority to curtail the extensive arms trade in Oman.[6] This trade supplied India's northwest frontier and the Persian Gulf, and while the trade centered on Muscat, tribal sheikhs in the interior also prospered from it.[7] As Landen points out, the 1912 agreement ended gun running to the Persian Gulf and greatly eased British security concerns in the region. For Faysal, however, it resulted in "one of the most dangerous crises ever faced by an Al Bu Sa'id regime." Essentially, the arms deal underscored Faysal's dependence and his willingness to sacrifice national sovereignty for his own well-being. Faysal's actions helped an alliance among Salih bin Ali al-Harthi's former students and his son Isa bin Salih, and in May 1913 they elected an imam. The tribal leaders used Ibadi doctrine to declare Faysal deposed, dissociated (*bara'a*) from the faithful, and without jurisdiction over them. Faysal died in October 1913, and his son Taymur inherited an anemic state with an unfolding civil war.[8] The new imamate allied the sheikhs of the two tribal confederations, the Ghafiri and the Hinawi (under paramount sheikh Isa bin Salih). The period between 1913 and 1920 was perilous. With World War I playing out in the background, Omanis faced severe economic hardship, a deep trade recession, and ongoing skirmishes between the imamate and the sultan's forces. The global influenza epidemic also slammed Oman.

In September 1920 the imamate concluded the Seeb agreement with Sultan Taymur bin Faysal (r. 1913–1932). The agreement, brokered by the British, granted the interior a good degree of autonomy and laid out guarantees for the free passage of people and goods between coast and interior.[9] The agreement makes clear the economic difficulties faced by the people in the region. In earlier correspondence Arabs in the interior had complained about the fall in value of the Maria Theresa dollar and the inflation in prices for food and cloth.[10] The interior tribes had also complained that British interference and blockades had made it impossible for them to oversee their property at the coast or in Zanzibar and had thus created great difficulties in pursuing business and settling claims. Mobility was vital to those in the interior. The Seeb agreement offered something for the interior Omanis led by Isa bin Salih, for the Sultan, and for the British. (Indeed, for the British, political scientist Marc Valeri points out that the Seeb agreement mirrored indirect colonial rule in Africa.[11]) As such, it differed from interior tribes' efforts in the nineteenth century to capture Muscat in order to insure their own autonomy. The Seeb agreement divided the political forces within Oman, isolating the imamate in the interior while the sultan in Muscat remained the nominal hegemon. In the agreement, however, all sides recognized the importance of both movement within Oman and the free passage to enter or leave any towns on the coast.

During this period, in the first half of the twentieth century, Omanis from the interior moved to the more economically promising East Africa, as previous generations had done; but they did so with new technology and encountered new social stratifications. Muhammad bin Khalid left al-Dariz for Zanzibar as a young man during this time and settled in Zanzibar. While some of these movements looked like the nineteenth-century journeys made in dhows, others found themselves on steamers sailing to Zanzibar via Bombay.[12] Those who went to the East African interior traveled over the same territory as their predecessors but they did so not on foot, but on trains. The Germans built their rail line along the central caravan route from the coast to the towns created by Indian Ocean migrants in the nineteenth century. Tabora was a main stop, and the rail terminus was north of Ujiji on the shores of Lake Tanganyika. Twentieth-century migrants from Oman went to places that previous generations of Arabs had settled, but their opportunities on arrival were more limited.

The anthropologist Colette Le Cour Grandmaison pointed out the "hidden stratification" among waves of twentieth century Arab migrants in East Africa that created two groups.[13] Her schema of "rich cousins" and "poor cousins" was based on the geography of settlement on the African mainland, however, and overlooks the stratification within Zanzibar. Le Cour Grandmaison suggested that over the course of the nineteenth century the old Arab families of Zanzibar and the coast became a local elite. Rather than marrying along narrowly patronymic lines or only within their clans, this group intermarried within the new elite. These practices bolstered their accumulation and ongoing control of wealth. The superior situation of those in Zanzibar vis-à-vis those in Oman continued to attract new migrants, but Arabs who came later, especially those who settled in the East African interior, had fewer chances for grand wealth.[14] In Zanzibar, the poor Omanis who arrived in the twentieth century were considered distinct from the Zanzibari Arab elite. This separate group was called *Manga* or *WaManga*. Although some of them could claim kinship ties and become clients of their wealthier relatives, many others could not mobilize capital. They sought short-term engagements as shopkeepers or small landowners to accrue savings and return to Oman.[15] Colonial and popular discourse in Zanzibar stereotyped Manga Arabs as violent and unruly. Indeed, groups of Manga men rioted in 1928 and 1936, and both events resulted in loss of life. Jonathon Glassman attributes the 1928 riots to tensions with Arab Hadrami migrants (both groups were at the margins of Zanzibari society), while political scientist Michael Lofchie suggests that part of the 1928 conflagration was due to a social snub from an Omani Zanzibari family toward an influential Manga Arab.[16] These emerging social stratifications in Zanzibar and across East Africa became increasingly important as nationalist politics picked up steam in the 1950s.

When Ahmed bin Muhammad, the Muscati halwa maker, was born in Zanzibar in 1955, Jamshid's grandfather was the sultan, and high clove prices helped support a booming economy. Unlike the underdeveloped Omani interior his father had left, Ahmed's Zanzibar had three movie theatres that played American westerns and the latest Hindi films. Young people growing up at that time saw themselves as decidedly cosmopolitan.[17] Beneath this cosmopolitan sheen, however, a political and racial storm was brewing, one that would erupt as the Zanzibar protectorate moved on the British-prescribed path to independence.[18] The same year Ahmed bin Muhammad was born, his elite relative Ali Muhsin al-Barwani helped found the Zanzibar Nationalist Party (ZNP). Ali Muhsin's brand of Zanzibar nationalism was nonracial and was based on loyalty to the sultan and the shared values of Islamic civilization.[19] The ZNP's main rival, the Afro-Shirazi Party (ASP), however, made nationalist claims that evoked and elided Zanzibar's Indian Ocean connections.

Both of these strains of nationalist politics in Zanzibar in the 1950s drew on colonial-era ideas of history to hone racial stereotypes. The ZNP invoked European ideals of Arabs as a civilizing force in East Africa to argue for a national ideal centered on being Zanzibari, being Muslim, and being loyal to the sultan. The ASP, however, echoed the language of Victorian abolitionists in their charges against Arabs for the slave trade and the cruelties of slavery. This strain of nationalism also collapsed distinctions between Arabs in Zanzibar, conflating the Arabness of elite families who had been in East Africa for generations with the Arabness of impoverished economic migrants who had come recently from Oman.[20] While the former group included the sultan and many of the leaders of the ZNP, the latter group, the Manga, was much poorer. Lofchie noted that Manga shopkeepers, for example, "in sheer economic terms were much closer to Africans."[21] Manga Arabs gained a thuggish reputation, known for their criminality and their short-term stays in Zanzibar, an echo of the discourse about "Northern Arabs" and their seasonal migration in the nineteenth century. The resulting political discourse ran together nineteenth-century abolitionist language about Arabs as slave traders and twentieth-century stereotypes of violent, impoverished migrants. The result of this rhetoric was the loss of many lives in the 1960s.

In Oman, during the 1950s, however, a different kind of politics was unfolding. With the promise of oil discovery in the interior, the sultan in Muscat, Said bin Taymur (r. 1932–1970), had a much greater incentive than his predecessors to challenge the imamate's hold on the center of the country. He also had much more powerful allies. Petroleum Development (Oman), a subsidiary of the Iraq Petroleum Company (and later, Shell Oil), funded the Muscat and Oman Field Force, a military unit made up of Omanis under British leadership.[22] Oil exploration pushed into the imamate region in the interior, and in 1954 contravened the terms of the Treaty of Seeb by occupying Ibri. In 1955 the Omani Field Force helped the sultan retake the interior with little fighting, nominally unifying the coast and the interior for the first time since the imamate of 1868–71. The imam and the imamate leadership fled the country. In 1956, a century after Said bin Sultan's death, the British ended the Zanzibar subsidy of MT$40,000 that they had been paying to Muscat's ruler since Majid's refusal in the 1860s to honor the terms of the Canning Award. Just as previous sultans had depended on this subsidy to uphold their rule, Said bin Taymur felt the fiscal pinch of its loss. This occurred at the same time the imamate forces reemerged to seize Nizwa and several interior towns in 1957. The sultan thought it was in his best interest to sign an agreement with the British for military support in 1958. This led to the reorganization of the Omani military and the insertion of British officials into the affairs of state. The British Royal Air Force bombed the imamate positions in Jebel Akhdar, and two squadrons of Special Air Service forces seized the key towns of the rebellion in early 1959.[23] The sultan and his British allies defeated the imamate.

As this struggle for control of the interior unfolded, everyday Omanis continued to emigrate for opportunities abroad. The sultan, however, remained committed to strict control of the country and suspicious of outside influences, so his policies discouraged the return of migrants. Throughout the 1950s, however, migration continued to be appealing because the material conditions for most Omanis remained poor. For example, a man who left Sharqiya for East Africa in the 1950s told me that the state of the economy was so bad for his family that they made their own gunpowder because they were unable to purchase it. He immigrated to Zanzibar by dhow, following an uncle who was established there.[24] Others went to the gulf for employment, but the sultan made it difficult for them to return. Those who immigrated to Zanzibar, on the other hand, faced contentious politics on the island in the 1950s.

In Zanzibar, nationalist politics and electoral contests resulted in an escalating series of violent clashes. While Harold McMillan's famous 1961 speech on African decolonization acknowledged the "winds of change" blowing across the continent, Zanzibar experienced them as a monsoon. Zanzibar had become a British protectorate in 1890, and retained the sultan as the titular head of state. In 1911, Seyyid Khalifa bin Harub ascended to the throne and became a very popular sultan. After nearly a half-century of rule, he died in 1960 just as electoral politics cast an uncertain future for the island. Like the quick cycling of sultans after Barghash's death in 1888, the early 1960s saw a rapid succession of three sultans and a tumultuous set of elections to determine which party would control the state in the lead up to independence. Under the new sultan Abdullah bin Khalifa, Zanzibar had two elections in 1961. In January, a hotly contested vote resulted in a parliamentary tie, and in July, a second election led to days of rioting: street-fighting in the city and roaming bands in the countryside. This violence resulted in the death of sixty-eight people, sixty-four of whom were Arabs.[25] In 1963 the final elections for the transition to independence were also contested elections, and while the ASP won a majority of votes, they did not win a majority of districts. The ZNP, led by Ali Muhsin Barwani, formed a government in June 1963 with the Zanzibar and Pemba People's Party over the objections of the ASP. Shortly afterward, Seyyid Abdullah died, and his son Jamshid bin Abdullah, age thirty-three, became sultan. On December 10, Zanzibar became an independent, constitutional monarchy under Sultan Jamshid, the descendant of Seyyid Said bin Sultan who had extended his sovereignty from Muscat to Zanzibar in the 1830s.[26] Jamshid's government was short lived. In January 1964 a group of armed rebels led a revolution that forced Jamshid to flee, installed Abeid Karume, the ASP leader, as president, and began a pogrom against Arabs in Zanzibar. In April 1964, Zanzibar joined with Tanganyika, which had been independent since 1961, to form Tanzania.

The so-called Zanzibar Revolution of 1964 was a cataclysmic event that redefined the relationship between Zanzibar and Oman. In the violent aftermath, many people were killed, with scholarly estimates ranging from three thousand to ten thousand.[27] While violence touched every part of Zanzibar and Pemba, Manga Arabs living in rural areas were disproportionately killed. Sexual violence was rampant, echoing dark threats from the harsh sniping that had taken place in the pages of partisan newspapers during the 1950s.[28] Many people were detained after mass arrests and the new government seized property.[29] The horrors and dispersals of this period remain a watershed for those who survived it.

The revolution in Zanzibar set many people into motion, reinvigorating older patterns of migration, but the politics of nation states limited their movements. While Seyyid Jamshid was able to escape from Zanzibar on the day of the revolt, Kenyan officials denied him entry to Mombasa, and after several days at sea his party was permitted to land at Dar es Salaam. From there he made his way to England and eventually settled in Portsmouth. Many other Arabs, however, were not able to leave immediately or find refuge so readily. The most obvious place for them to seek refuge was in Oman, but the policies of Said bin Taymur strictly limited immigration and only a small number of people were initially admitted.[30]

During the 1960s, many Zanzibari Arabs who were able to escape found themselves stateless. Some could travel under UN passports, while others sought passports as subjects of the imam in exile in Saudi Arabia.[31] Some moved within East Africa, settling in Kenya or even mainland Tanzania. Some sought out relatives who had arrived in Rwanda, Burundi, or the Congo during the early twentieth century. Another group sought refuge in Oman, but many were unable to enter there and instead went to gulf states where new oil wealth offered employment. Many others, like Ahmed bin Muhammad al-Barwani, aged nine at the time of the revolution, and his family remained in Zanzibar where autocratic rule of the Revolutionary Council limited political expression and undercut the archipelago's economy.[32]

Were it not for revolutionary changes in Oman, this diaspora of Zanzibaris might have remained scattered. However, in July 1970, Qabus bin Said, a Sandhurst graduate, overthrew his father in a bloodless palace coup. He pledged to bring development to his people by harnessing the country's oil wealth. He also opened the borders and invited Omanis who had been overseas to return. This was a watershed year for Oman and redefined the modern history of the country. Qabus worked rapidly to scale up development of the country, building roads and schools in a modernization scheme along developmentalist lines. He also initiated a nationalist program that sought to foster an Omani identity rather than tribal or regional ones. After 1970, large numbers of people from East African countries who claimed Omani descent sought entry to Oman. As they settled in the land of their forefathers, they felt pressure to integrate into their new society. East Africans took part in the process of becoming Omanis.

Although emigration from Africa to Oman was initially straightforward, by the early 1980s it was more difficult for those settling in Oman to claim citizenship. The Omani state was relatively open to receiving immigrants in the 1970s with connections to Oman. In addition, as conditions in East Africa, including political repression and declining economic standing, worsened, the booming "miracle" in Oman became increasingly attractive to those who could make claims to Omani nationality. Historian Nathanial Mathews shows that between 1970 and 1983 tens of thousands of people from East Africa moved to Oman and obtained Omani citizenship. Initially, the standard for citizenship for migrants "returning" to Oman was affirmation of tribal membership as vouched by leaders of rooted, resident Omani clans. Ahmed bin Muhammad arrived in Oman from Zanzibar during this time. Genealogies were important in these processes of attesting to kinship, and his father's relatives in Sharqiya could attest to Ahmed's Omani heritage. After 1983, however, the Omani state made it much more difficult for "returnees" to claim citizenship, so East Africans began to use short- and long-term visas to connect with relatives who had immigrated to Oman.[33] Yet even those from Africa with an easy path to citizenship were not all easily incorporated into Omani society. These people—whether they arrived from Zanzibar, Kenya, mainland Tanzania, or the Congo—came to be known generically as Zanzibaris (*Zinjibari*), and Omanis did not always readily accept them.[34]

THE BARWANI GENEALOGIST AND THE RECONFIGURING OF OMAN'S RELATIONSHIP WITH EAST AFRICA

While Ahmed bin Muhammad al-Barwani supported himself as a confectioner in Oman, his all-consuming hobby was the genealogy of the Barwani clan. His work, published as a poster in 2000, contained thousands of names and went back seventeen generations. This genealogical production also had the effect of creating a seamless Barwani clan centered in Arabia with deep historical roots in Oman. Looking at the poster, this unity was apparent, yet these genealogies elided the clan's history of mobility and the fact that the family had achieved much greater prominence in East Africa. For Ahmed bin Muhammad, however, the dense layers of meaning were obvious. Conversation with him about Barwani history is peppered with references to the family tree, which he reads like a topographic map, pointing to fault lines and differences in elevation. He identifies lineages that left Ibadism and became Sunni, a fact that connects to the fallout from the harsh reprisals against the Harthi after 1859. He identifies family members who settled in the Congo in the nineteenth century and only recently moved to Oman. Ahmed bin Muhammad's extensive research created a tree that also elaborates other branches of the family. The tree sets those from Zanzibar, and from Africa more generally, among the members of the clan who had remained rooted in Oman. While other people I interviewed pointed to difficulties in Oman for those who came from East Africa, Ahmed did not. He was upbeat about Oman and about Omanis, and was endlessly excited about the Barwani clan. Thus, while a genealogy, like kinship in general, can be used to support many arguments, this family tree in poster form was an assertion of Omaniness for what had been a widely dispersed Barwani clan. Not unlike the genealogical texts that anthropologist Engseng Ho shows rooted Hadrami scholars from around the Indian Ocean in their Arabian homeland, this genealogy reunited a Barwani family and placed them in the new Oman of Qabus.[35] The poster also advertised their success: the names of the sponsors of the printing revealed prominent, wealthy members of the clan who had achieved success in the new Oman.

The meal I attended at Ahmed's house during Eid was intended as a Barwani family reunion, and he invited an array of Barwanis. As we ate from common plates heaped with rice and meat, Ahmed pointed out clansmen who hailed from Syria, Mozambique, and Kenya. From my own time in East Africa, however, I understood that not all Barwanis could immigrate to Oman. In this clan as in others, many who claimed descent from Omani Arabs remained in East Africa. Some of these cousins waited too long to seek citizenship in Oman while others were content to remain in East Africa. These cousins oversaw family property and, in many cases, received support from their now wealthier relatives overseas. Indeed, while Zanzibar had supported Oman in the nineteenth century, by the late twentieth century, the lines had reversed. Remittances from Oman to Zanzibar became an important source of support for many families. Based on the figures from a single currency exchange in Oman, Omani-Zanzibaris sent the equivalent of 1.9 million Tanzania shillings to Zanzibar in 1985. That number grew geometrically, and in 1992 it was 357.7 million. While these figures indicate an expansion of business for a particular currency exchange, and the data represent only one source, even as a partial and inexact measure it is clear that remittances were flowing from Oman to Zanzibar.[36] Starting in the early 1990s, wealthy Zanzibari-Omanis also began to return to the island to recover family properties seized after 1964 or to build vacation homes. Alongside these remittances and investments, the other element flowing out of Oman (and circulating within the country) was a new set of secular scholarship and memoirs that reinterpreted the history of East Africa.

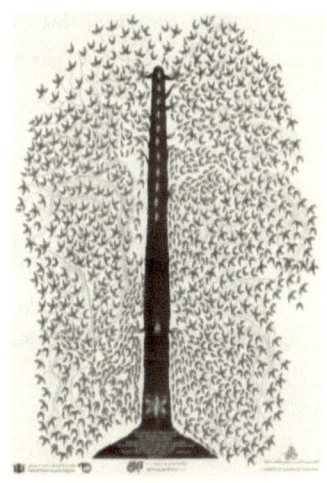

FIGURE 10.1. The Barwani family tree contains more than one-thousand names and seventeen generations. Color poster (26.75" × 38") produced by Ahmed bin Muhammad bin Khalid al-Barwani (2000).

WRITING INDIAN OCEAN HISTORIES FROM OMAN

Ahmed bin Muhammad's published genealogy in Arabic firmly situates the Barwani clan within an Omani national milieu. Other Omanis with East African roots have written in Swahili and English—less frequently Arabic—to publish histories of Oman and East Africa. Indeed, Oman's mini-boom in Swahili-language publications, place the country clearly with the broader Swahiliphone world that was expanded by the nineteenth century patterns of mobility. These publications dispute or reinterpret East African history. After he moved to the gulf in the 1980s, Ali Muhsin Barwani, who began his political life as the longtime editor of the newspaper Mwongozi in Zanzibar in the 1940s and 1950s, wrote pedagogical texts, religious commentaries, and memoirs.[37] His book for Swahili speakers on learning to read Arabic (*Jifunze Kusoma Kiarabu*) addressed a religious goal of helping Swahili speakers read the Quran but also highlighted the linguistic challenges that many East Africans faced as they sought to establish themselves in Oman and the gulf. He believed that anyone who followed the book could read the Quran in two to three weeks and write Swahili in Arabic script. He begins by telling the reader how easy it is and invokes a historical ideal about the wide network of the readers' forbears. He references "our Swahili-speaking ancestors" (*wazee wetu wa Kiswahili*) and situates them on the islands, on the coast, and in the original cities of the interior like Tabora and Kigoma to assert that nearly all of them could read Quran and write Swahili in Arabic script.[38] Ali Muhsin's own English-language memoir makes clear that his sense of the Swahili-speaking

Epilogue ⇝ 271

world was as much influenced by his family history—with numerous ties to the southern Swahili coast and to his uncle, the nineteenth-century ivory trader Rumaliza—as it was by his own experience of being a political prisoner under Julius Nyerere in Tanzania for ten years.

This new Swahili literature coming from Oman addresses, expands, and reinterprets several periods of East African history. They argue for the injustice of colonial rule, the misunderstanding of the Arab presence in East Africa, and the illegitimacy of the Zanzibar revolution. Issa Nasser Issa al-Ismaily's 1999 book *Zanzibar: Kinyang'anyiro na Utumwa* (*Slavery and the Scramble for Zanzibar*), reexamines nineteenth-century expansion and critiques the way that Europeans used anti-slavery disingenuously to justify for the imposition of colonial rule in Africa. Ibrahim Noor Shariff, who has been a professor at both Rutgers and Sultan Qaboos University, has a distinguished record of publications in English and in Swahili about Swahili poetry and identity. Since he moved to Oman, he has become a key intellectual figure in Swahili language publications there—frequently thanked for his editorial assistance and encouragement—and an active participant in online discussion forums.[39] His early scholarship situated Swahili language and people firmly within an African (and Africanist) context. His most recent book *Tanzania na Propaganda za Udini* (*Tanzania and Religious Propaganda*) disputes historical understanding of Bantu dispersion to suggest that Arabs arrived in East Africa before Bantu-language speakers, shows the breadth of social classes among Arabs in East Africa, and pivots to critique the way that Tanzania has discriminated against Arabs and Muslims.

While some of the recent work is more polemical, Harith Ghassany's *Kwaheri Ukoloni, Kwaheri Uhuru! Zanzibar na Mapinduzi ya Afrabia* (*Goodbye Colonialism, Goodbye Freedom!: Zanzibar and the Afrabian Revolution*), published in 2010, is an in-depth reexamination of the revolution in Zanzibar. Ghassany draws on new interviews and extensive research to show the role of Nyerere and mainlanders in the revolution.[40] In doing this, Ghassany draws on the notion of "Afrabia" that was put forward by Ali Mazrui in 1992 to better encapsulate the long history of connection between Africa and Arabia.[41] Ghassany identifies himself as an "Afrabian" and points to his Arabian parentage and a set of African maternal kin. Ali Mazrui, a descendent of the famous Omani-Mombasa family was also an Afrabian in this sense, and the new Swahili historiography from Muscat draws strongly on this tradition.

Publications from Oman—genealogies, histories, and a growing number of memoirs—recast and reinvigorate the history of Oman and East Africa at a particular moment in history. Some of these are triumphalist or nostalgic, while others, like Ghassany's, are quite measured. Their arguments challenge nationalist histories of East Africa and also support a place for Africans within the post-1970 oil-rich Oman by celebrating the country's long maritime and overseas connections. Anthropologist Mandana Limbert, in her ethnography of life in contemporary Oman, argues that Omani nationalism is grounded in specific views of history and an unusual temporal sense of the present moment. The country, with its illustrious maritime past, had been poor before oil, and the recent transformation has produced a kind of wonder. Limbert argues that Omanis perceive that they are in a magical time between Qabus bin Said's deployment of oil wealth to develop the country and a not-so-distant future when the oil runs out and Qabus bin Said dies. As she explains, "Almost every aspect of everyday life was affected by this temporal consciousness and the material conditions of oil wealth."[42] This self-consciousness of time is a modern one, but as this book has suggested, frameworks of time governed Omani Arab and Indian Ocean actors in the past as well. They dealt with uncertainty in their present moment by temporizing and delaying and buying time through mobility and access to credit as they moved between the Omani interior, the Swahili coast, and the African interior. The onset of formal colonialism at the end of the nineteenth century limited their possibilities, and, to some extent, it is this loss that the new Swahili historiography from Oman explores.

THE END OF BUYING TIME

In the eastern region of the Congo Free State in the 1890s, a set of European commanders and their African troops battled against the Congo Arabs for control of trade and production in the region. The Europeans unwittingly challenged a process more than a half-century in the making that had connected central Africa to the western Indian Ocean through networks of credit, mobility, and kinship that transformed environments in Arabia and Africa. The Free State justified its actions on humanitarian and anti-slave trading grounds. They deposed Tippu Tip as the governor, but his son and his close associates fought to defend what they had built in the Congo. In March 1893, Free State forces captured Kasongo, Tippu Tip's former trading headquarters and an important town on one of the Congo River's tributaries. The attackers were surprised by the degree to which the Arabs had transformed this settlement into a cosmopolitan center. All the soldiers acquired new outfits in what was left behind and they slept on carved beds with mosquito nets. The mattresses were covered with silk and satin, and the Europeans found luxuries that they had been denied in their own campaigns, such as candles, sugar, and matches, not to mention silver and glass goblets.

They also saw that the landscape had been radically altered. Miles of forest had been selectively cleared for agriculture; not just rice, but sugar cane, maize, and fruit crops. In key places they left giant trees for shade or land marks. The environmental changes meant that wild game had been driven from the immediate area. In fact, the European invaders struggled to make sense of the place in the Congo River watershed. After sleeping in a large room with a door opening onto an orange grove and beautiful vista, Sydney Hinde, the leader of the force, recalled that "it was hard, on waking, to realise that I was in Central Africa."[43] Indeed, while he was close to the Lualaba River, a source of the Congo, he was not just in central Africa. He was in an outpost of the Indian Ocean world.

As ill-prepared as Hinde and his associates were to make sense of this altered geography at the time, the subsequent history—of colonialism, territorial nation-states, independence movements, and Cold War regional groupings, among other factors—have also erased this nineteenth-century world. This book has attempted to reconstruct the movements and connections of that period to restore a sense of contingency and individual agency that explains what Hinde discovered in Kasongo. One clue should have been the twenty-five tons of ivory that Hinde's men found there.

The global demand for western Indian Ocean products, in the nineteenth century, including ivory, copal, dates, and pearls, helped underwrite the mobility of Africans, Arabs, and Indians during this period. Arab rulers were mobile, and Said bin Sultan's conquest of the Swahili coast from the 1820s and relocation of his capital to Zanzibar after 1832 connected the coasts of the western Indian Ocean under one sovereign and enriched a long-standing circuit of exchange. Those who left Arabia for the Indian Ocean world from the end of the eighteenth and through the nineteenth century did not do so out of obligation to a ruler. The loose political structures of Oman and of the Arab state in Zanzibar gave sultans little direct control over people. Instead, mobility was a response to challenges and constraints including impoverished oasis towns and environmental disasters, from devastating drought to destructive floods. Movement offered temporary respite from pressing concerns, but the uncertainty of life sometimes transformed short-term trips into permanent relocation and, in some cases, extraordinary success.

For the displaced and dispossessed, access to credit was potentially transformative. Credit, construed through Islamic instruments with a long Indian Ocean past, allowed newcomers to take part in the emerging ivory trade. Examining these business transactions also points to the way that everyday people—indigenous Zanzibaris, coastal Swahili people, and freed slaves, among others—could sell property and raise capital. While Indian creditors, like the Zanzibar customs master, generally controlled access to credit, they operated broad portfolios and distributed their risk. The sultans of Oman and Zanzibar depended on access to this credit. Said bin Sultan employed mobile governance to unify a dispersed dominion in the western Indian Ocean, but his sons were increasingly hemmed in after his death in 1856. They were mobile in new ways—Bombay figured prominently as a place of exile and inspiration—and, more than their father, they depended on credit to run sultanates in Muscat and Zanzibar.

Their subjects, however, were much less territorially constrained. While the Arab state tried to establish itself vis-à-vis Swahili elites on the African coast, many people took to the caravan trails. Arabs and Africans walked away from the ocean in search of cheap ivory and new opportunities, but Indian Ocean identities shaped their interactions and settlements. New towns in the interior were trading centers, and they accrued a population of coastal people and African migrants, slowly growing over time. Their increasing populations and prominence gave lie to the myth of return (that all travelers only sojourned temporarily in the interior), and to the assumptions of coastal chauvinism (that Indian Ocean shores were the most desirable place to be). Infrastructures of kinship facilitated movement and settlement in the African interior. Tippu Tip's extraordinary family network makes these infrastructures most clear, but examples of marriages, sibling partnerships, and connections through matrilineal kin, while harder to see for others, offer compelling evidence.

In the western Indian Ocean, manumitted slaves took advantage of credit and mobility, and their own sense of buying time, to make new opportunities for themselves as their business transactions from the 1840s make clear. Islamic manumission has been frequently overlooked, but the practice was entrenched before the new labor economy and antislavery treaties of the midcentury created perverse incentives for insincere manumission. Insincere manumission offended the moral economy of manumission in the western Indian Ocean. Former slaves parlayed both their connections with their patrons' families and their access to land to launch themselves into the economic life of Zanzibar, interior Africa, and the Indian Ocean world. Increased scrutiny of slavery after the 1873 treaty, however, altered Africans' ability to move at sea and created a new round of insincere manumissions. This compromised mobility emerged as an artifact of a British documentary regime that sought to rationalize the place of Indians in East Africa through consular courts and greater consular scrutiny. This moment in history inadvertently created new ways of understanding the Indian Ocean past by requiring the registration of contracts. The contracts and other consular acts reveal that by the 1870s Indian and Arab households were multiracial and mobile.

The clearest examples of the way that time, debt, mobility, kinship, and environment intertwined in the western Indian Ocean are through the biographical lenses applied to the freed African slave Songoro and to the elite Arab tribal leader Salih bin Ali al-Harthi. The first, a former slave, wrangled property holdings in Zanzibar and launched himself into the East African interior. He established a second Zanzibar on Lake Victoria and built the first dhow there. By marrying the sister of a local ruler and establishing an agricultural base, Songoro had the markings of a big man, but he was subordinate to both the Ugandan kingdom and the Nyamwezi warlord Mirambo. He also entangled himself in complex debt relations with his allies, and his attempt to remake the world in his favor led to an untimely demise. Sheikh Salih bin Ali, on the other hand, bided his time well and took maximal advantage of access to credit networks of the western Indian Ocean. His oceanic mobility in youth stood in contrast to the life he built in the economically marginal Sharqiya region of Oman. Salih bin Ali spent a lifetime angling for opportunities to undercut a succession of sultans in Muscat and promote his own interests and those of his Ibadi followers. In the end, however, Salih bin Ali's credit networks and personal charisma were no match for the resources of the British Empire that backed his rival, Turki, and Turki's son Faysal. Salih bin Ali died in Oman three years after Hinde had marveled at the wonders of Kasongo. Salih likely had a much better notion of the large, complex Indian Ocean world than Hinde. Salih bin Ali had taken part in and witnessed the movement of people between the Omani interior and East Africa. He had acknowledged that everything was pledged to its time, and he understood the contingency of his own actions.

Celebrating Eid in Muscat with Ahmed bin Muhammad, the confectioner and genealogist, was a good reminder that the greater forces of history occlude vital periods of the past. Viewed from the present, the western Indian Ocean and its intimate interlinkings no longer fit easily with continental thinking and territorial nation-states. Yet in writing this book, I traveled in Arabia and in East Africa to the oasis towns, the port cities, the caravan depots, and the lakeside outposts mentioned in the Arabic-language contracts that underwrote the broad changes of the nineteenth century. In each of these place, I spoke Swahili, ate halwa, and heard stories about the lives of ancestors and about an Indian Ocean world that is not forgotten.

Notes

ABBREVIATIONS USED IN NOTES

ASCF	Abdul Sheriff Card File
CMI	Church Missionary Intelligencer
FO	Foreign Office
IOR	India Office Records
MAE	Ministère des Affairs Éstrangères
MSA	Maharashtra State Archives
NAI	National Archives of India
PRO	Public Record Office
TBGS	Transactions of the Bombay Geographical Society
TNA	Tanzanian National Archives
ZLR	Zanzibar Law Reports
ZNA	Zanzibar National Archives

INTRODUCTION: TEMPORIZING ACROSS THE INDIAN OCEAN

1. Registered deed 1063 of 1888, AM 12/20, ZNA (originally contracted in 1869).

2. Hermann von Wissmann, *My Second Journey Through Equatorial Africa: From the Congo to the Zambesi, in the Years 1886 and 1887* (London: Chatto & Windus, 1891), 230, 233.

3. François Bontinck, "La Double Traversée de l'Afrique Par Trois 'Arabes' de Zanzibar (1845–1860)," *Études d'Histoire Africaine* 6 (1974), 5–53; Mr. MacQueen, "Notes on African Geography." *Journal of the Royal Geographical Society of London* 15 (1845): 371. https://doi.org/10.2307/1797919.

4. Henry Morton Stanley, *How I Found Livingstone* (London: Sampson Low, Marston & Co., 1895), 380.

5. Fernand Braudel, *The Mediterranean and the Mediterranean World in the Age of Philip II* (Berkeley: University of California Press, 1996), 1:130.

6. See for example: K. N. Chaudhuri, *Trade and Civilisation in the Indian Ocean: An Economic History from the Rise of Islam to 1750* (New York: Cambridge University Press, 1985).

7. The term comes from P. Horden and N. Purcell, "The Mediterranean and 'The New Thalassology,'" *American Historical Review* 111, no. 3 (2006): 723. Markus Vink uses this as a centerpiece for his masterful historiographical essay on the state of Indian Ocean history: "Indian Ocean Studies and the 'New Thalassology,'" *Journal of Global History* 2 (2007): 41–62.

8. K. Wigen, "Introduction [to AHR Forum: Oceans of History]," *American Historical Review* 111, no. 3 (2006): 717–21. As antidote to this, see Vink, "Indian Ocean Studies and the 'New Thalassology,'" 41–62, for historiography, and for historiography-cum-method, and Antoinette Burton et al., "Sea Tracks and Trails: Indian Ocean Worlds as Method," *History Compass* 11, no. 7 (2013): 497–502.

9. Gwyn Campbell, "Introduction: Slavery and Other Forms of Unfree Labour in the Indian Ocean World," in *The Structure of Slavery in Indian Ocean Africa and Asia* (Portland, OR: Frank Cass, 2004), vii–xxxii; Marina Carter, "Slavery and Unfree Labour in the Indian Ocean," *History Compass* 4, no. 5 (2006): 800–13; Richard Eaton, "Introduction," in *Slavery and South Asian History*, ed. Indrani Chatterjee and Richard M. Eaton (Bloomington: Indiana University Press, 2006), 1–16; Jonathon Glassman "The Bondsman's New Clothes: The Contradictory Consciousness of Slave Resistance on the Swahili Coast," *Journal of African History* 32, no. 2 (1991): 277–312; Matthew S. Hopper, *Slaves of One Master: Globalization and Slavery in Arabia in the Age of Empire* (New Haven, CT: Yale University Press, 2015).

10. As a foundational study, Joseph Miller considers West Central Africa, Brazil, and Portugal to demonstrate an integrated system: *Way of Death: Merchant Capitalism and the Angolan Slave Trade, 1730–1830* (Madison: University of Wisconsin Press, 1988). For the specific cases mentioned, see Roquinaldo Ferreira, *Cross-Cultural Exchange in the Atlantic World: Angola and Brazil during the Era of the Slave Trade* (New York: Cambridge University Press, 2012); Kristin Mann, *Slavery and the Birth of an African City: Lagos, 1760–1900* (Bloomington: Indiana University Press, 2007); Mariana P. Candido, *An African Slaving Port and the Atlantic World: Benguela and Its Hinterland* (New York: Cambridge University Press, 2013).

11. Appadurai, "Grassroots Globalization and the Research Imagination," *Public Culture* 12, no. 1 (2000): 7. See also: Martin W. Lewis and Kären Wigen, *The Myth of Continents: A Critique of Metageography* (Berkeley: University of California Press, 1997); and for the study of Africa, Roberts, "Is 'Africa' Obsolete?" *African Arts* 33, no. 1 (2000): 93. This is certainly true of the Indian Ocean, although these transnational approaches assume a global order of nation-states, which did not exist in the Indian Ocean until formal colonialism. See also C. A. Bayly et al., "AHR Conversation: On Transnational History," *American Historical Review* 111, no. 5 (December 2006): 1441–64.

12. Appadurai, "Grassroots Globalization and the Research Imagination," 7.

13. See, for example: Engseng Ho, *The Graves of Tarim: Genealogy and Mobility across the Indian Ocean* (Berkeley: University of California Press, 2006); Thomas R. Metcalf, *Imperial Connections: India in the Indian Ocean Arena, 1860–1920* (Berkeley: University of California Press, 2007); Kerry Ward, *Networks of Empire: Forced Migration in the Dutch East India Company* (New York: Cambridge University Press, 2008); and Pedro Machado, *Ocean of Trade: South Asian Merchants, Africa and the Indian Ocean, c. 1750–1850* (Cambridge: Cambridge University Press, 2014).

14. For the definition of "temporize," I rely on *Oxford English Dictionary Online* (June 2016).

15. I have found William H. Sewell's arguments about structure and agency useful, especially in considering the multiple and overlapping contexts of Indian Ocean actors. I appreciate his acknowledgment of the limited power of agents who can exert "some degree of control" over the social relations in which they are enmeshed and therefore have the ability to "transform those social relations to some degree" (143). This sense of partial or incomplete agency is vital to the idea of buying time, as is the cross-cultural possibility for agents to move between structures and schemas: "Agents are empowered by structures, both by the knowledge of cultural schemas that enables them to mobilize resources and by the access to resources that enables them to enact schemas"; *Logics of History: Social Theory and Social Transformation* (Chicago: University of Chicago Press, 2005), 151.

16. For the hardening of these attitudes: Jonathon Glassman, *War of Words, War of Stones: Racial Thought and Violence in Colonial Zanzibar* (Bloomington: Indiana University Press, 2011).

17. Hofmeyr, "Clare Anderson. Subaltern Lives: Biographies of Colonialism in the Indian Ocean World, 1790–1920," *American Historical Review* 118, no. 3 (2013): 817.

18. Jürgen Osterhammel, *The Transformation of the World: A Global History of the Nineteenth Century* (Princeton, NJ: Princeton University Press, 2015), 48–52.

19. V. Ogle, "Whose Time Is It? The Pluralization of Time and the Global Condition, 1870s–1940s," *The American Historical Review* 118, no. 5 (2013), 1381.

20. Stephen Kern, *The Culture of Time and Space 1880–1918* (Cambridge, MA: Harvard University Press, 1983), 11–15.

21. See, for example: Vanessa Ogle, *The Global Transformation of Time: 1870–1950* (Cambridge, MA: Harvard University Press, 2015); and Roman Loimeier, *Eine Zeitlandschaft in der Globalisierung: Das islamische Sansibar im 19. und 20. Jahrhundert*, 1st ed. (Bielefeld: Transcript-Verlag, 2012). The anthropologist Roman Loimeier's account of landscapes of time (*Zeitlandschaft*) in East Africa notes that specific configurations of time compete with each other and must be negotiated locally. More specifically, one of the measures of hegemony is who is able to authorize the "right" time. Loimeier focuses on the period between the Zanzibar hurricane of 1872, during the reign of Seyyid Barghash, when British power was ascendant, and the revolution in 1964. For contests over time in South Africa, see Keletso Atkins, "'Kafir Time': Preindustrial Temporal Concepts and Labour Discipline in Nineteenth-Century Colonial Natal," *Journal of African History* 29, no. 2 (1988): 229–44.

22. The *falaj* book that tracked these matters in Izki in 1825 recorded shares as small as half of a *sha'īra* (roughly 1/16 of a second), and three people shared this portion of a *sha'īra*! See John C. Wilkinson, *Water and Tribal Settlement in South-East Arabia: A Study of the Aflāj of Oman* (Oxford: Clarendon Press, 1977), 108.

23. Jeremy Prestholdt, *Domesticating the World: African Consumerism and the Genealogies of Globalization* (Berkeley: University of California Press, 2008), 108.

24. Erik Gilbert, *Dhows & the Colonial Economy in Zanzibar, 1860–1970* (Athens: Ohio University Press, 2004).

25. Wilkinson, *Water and Tribal Settlement in South-East Arabia*.

26. David Graeber, *Debt: The First 5,000 Years* (Brooklyn: Melville House, 2011), 122.

27. Robert Campbell, "Tuskers, Trade, and Trypanosomes: The Ecologies of the Victorian Parlor," (Paper presented at the Agrarian Studies Colloquium, Yale University, New Haven, CT, November 12, 2010).

28. Abdul Sheriff, *Slaves, Spices, and Ivory in Zanzibar: Integration of an East African Commercial Empire into the World Economy, 1770–1873* (Athens: Ohio University Press, 1987); Thaddeus Sunseri, *Wielding the Ax: State Forestry and Social Conflict in Tanzania, 1820–2000* (Athens: Ohio University Press, 2009); Hopper, *Slaves of One Master*; Calvin H. Allen, "Sayyids, Shets and Sultans: Politics and Trade in Masqat under the Āl Bū Saʿīd, 1785–1914" (PhD diss., University of Washington, 1980).

29. Fahad Ahmad Bishara, "A Sea of Debt: Histories of Commerce and Obligation in the Indian Ocean, c. 1850–1940" (PhD diss., Duke University, 2012), chapter 2.

30. Jairam Shivji, the customs master before Ladha Damji, had tried to push interest-bearing loans onto an American merchant who needed cash in the late 1840s, offering up to $50,000 at 5 percent with the encouragement to keep it as long as he wished. Ward to Bertram (3 February 1849), Ward's Letter Book, ASCF. The interest rate for Americans and Europeans was standardized to 9 percent in the 1860s. Jablonski to MAE, November 11, 1863, Correspondance Consulaire et Commerciale: Zanzibar II, 324–43 (ASCF).

31. Burton, "Zanzibar; and Two Months in East Africa (1858)," *Blackwood's Edinburgh Magazine* 83 (May 1858): 407. Livingsone to Kirk, 30 October 30, 84/1387, 706, FO.

32. Stanley, *How I Found Livingstone*, 7.

33. Ghislaine Lydon, *On Trans-Saharan Trails: Islamic Law, Trade Networks, and Cross-Cultural Exchange in Nineteenth-Century Western Africa* (Cambridge: Cambridge University Press, 2009), 383.

34. Jonathon Glassman, *Feasts and Riot: Revelry, Rebellion, and Popular Consciousness on the Swahili Coast, 1856–1888* (Portsmouth, NH: Heinemann, 1995).

35. Avner Geif, "Reputation and Coalitions in Medieval Trade: Evidence on the Maghribi Traders" *The Journal of Economic History*, vol. 49, no. 4 (Dec. 1989), 858. For a critique of this see Sebouh Aslanian, *From the Indian Ocean to the Mediterranean: The Global Trade Networks of Armenian Merchants from New Julfa*. (Berkeley: University of California Press, 2011), 185.

36. Burton, *Zanzibar*, 1:263–64; Pelly to Foreign Office, 13 March 1862; 84/1179, 359–61 ASCF, FO.

37. Bishara, "A Sea of Debt."

38. Ho, *The Graves of Tarim*.

39. Anne K. Bang, *Sufis and Scholars of the Sea: Family Networks in East Africa, 1860–1925* (London: Routledge Curzon, 2003); Ho, *The Graves of Tarim*.

40. Pierre Bourdieu, *Outline of a Theory of Practice* (New York: Cambridge University Press, 1977), 34.

41. Richard F. Burton, "The Lake Regions of Central Equatorial Africa, with Notices of the Lunar Mountains and the Sources of the White Nile; Being the Results of an Expedition Undertaken under the Patronage of Her Majesty's Government and the Royal Geographical Society of London, in the Years 1857–1859," *Journal of the Royal Geographical Society of London* 29 (1859): 262.

42. John Comaroff and Jean Comaroff, "On Personhood: An Anthropological Perspective from Africa," *Social Identities* 7, no. 2 (2001): 268.

43. Hollian Wint, "Credible Relations: Indian Finance and East African Society in the Indian Ocean, c. 1860–1940" (PhD diss., New York University, 2016), 20.

44. While important works of environmental history are set in the Indian Ocean—e.g., Richard Grove, *Green Imperialism: Colonial Expansion, Tropical Island Edens, and the Origins of Environmentalism, 1600–1860* (Cambridge: Cambridge University Press, 1995)—a systematic environmental history of the Indian Ocean world is yet to be written. Recent works that touch on the Indian Ocean world include Thaddeus Sunseri, *Wielding the Ax: State Forestry and Social Conflict in Tanzania, 1820–2000* (Athens: Ohio University Press, 2009); Alan Mikhail, *Nature and Empire in Ottoman Egypt: An Environmental History* (Cambridge: Cambridge University Press, 2011); and Greg Bankoff and Joseph Christensen, eds., *Natural Hazards and Peoples in the Indian Ocean World* (New York: Palgrave Macmillan, 2016).

45. Anna Lowenhaupt Tsing, *The Mushroom at the End of the World: On the Possibility of Life in Capitalist Ruins* (Princeton: Princeton University Press, 2015), 5.

46. David Livingstone, *The Last Journals of David Livingstone, in Central Africa, from 1865 to His Death: Continued by a Narrative of His Last Moments and Sufferings, Obtained from His Faithful Servants Chuma and Susi; in Two Volumes*, ed. Horace Waller (London: Murray, 1874), 1:90.

47. Edward Peters, "Quid Nobis Cum Pelago? The New Thalassology and the Economic History of Europe," *Journal of Interdisciplinary History* 34, no. 1 (July 2003): 49–61; Peregrine Horden and Nicholas Purcell, "The Mediterranean And 'the New Thalassology,'" *The American Historical Review* 111, no. 3 (2006): 722–40; Vink, "Indian Ocean Studies and the 'New Thalassology,'" 41–62.

48. Sir Reginald Coupland, *East Africa and Its Invaders, from Earliest Times to the Death of Seyyid Said in 1856* (Oxford: Clarendon Press, 1938) and *The Exploitation of East Africa, 1856–1890: The Slave Trade and the Scramble* (London: Faber and Faber, 1939).

49. Edward Alpers, *Ivory and Slaves in East Central Africa* (Portsmouth, NH: Heinemann, 1975); Abdul Sheriff, *Slaves, Spices, and Ivory in Zanzibar: Integration of an East African Commercial Empire into the World Economy, 1770–1873* (Athens: Ohio University Press, 1987).

50. Norman Robert Bennett, *Arab Versus European: Diplomacy and War in Nineteenth-Century East Central Africa* (New York: Africana Publishing Company, 1986).

51. Glassman, *Feasts and Riots*; Stephen Rockel, *Carriers of Culture: Labor on the Road in Nineteenth-Century East Africa* (Portsmouth, NH: Heinemann, 2006).

52. Robert Geran Landen, *Oman since 1856; Disruptive Modernization in a Traditional Arab Society* (Princeton: Princeton University Press, 1967); M. Reda Bhacker, *Trade and Empire in Muscat and Zanzibar: The Roots of British Domination* (New York: Routledge, 1992).

53. Nile Green, "Rethinking the 'Middle East' after the Oceanic Turn," *Comparative Studies of South Asia, Africa and the Middle East* 34, no. 3 (2014): 556–64. https://doi.org/10.1215/1089201X-2826109.

54. Hopper, *Slaves of One Master*.

55. Metcalf, *Imperial Connections*; Sugata Bose, *A Hundred Horizons: The Indian Ocean in the Age of Global Empire* (Cambridge, MA: Harvard University Press, 2006).

56. Ho, *The Graves of Tarim*; Bang, *Sufis and Scholars of the Sea*.

57. Recently two other excellent scholars have turned their attention to these documents in Zanzibar with wonderful results: Bishara, "A Sea of Debt," and Hollian Wint, "Credible Relations."

CHAPTER 1: DROUGHT AND NEW MOBILITIES
IN THE OMANI INTERIOR

1. S. B. Miles, "On the Border of the Great Desert: A Journey in Oman," *The Geographical Journal* 36, no. 2 (1910): 178.

2. Eventually local goods were replaced with imported cloth from India and the United States. Miles, "On the Border," 176; Wellsted, *Travels in Arabia* (London: Murray, 1840), 1:124.

3. C. S. D. Cole, "An Account of an Overland Journey from Leskhairee to Meskat and the 'Green Mountains' of Oman," in *Transactions of the Bombay Geographical Society*, 8:114; Valerie J. Hoffman, "The Articulation of Ibāḍī Identity in Modern Oman and Zanzibar," *Muslim World* 94 no. 2 (2004): 202.

4. Cole, "An Account of an Overland Journey," 115.

5. M. Rheda Bhacker's account of Saʻid bin Sultan al-Busaidi's move considers Omani and British activity in the gulf and in the Indian Ocean, seeing Saʻid's move as both commercial (access to new markets and new resources) and strategic (establishing suzerainity outside of the post-1820 British sphere in the gulf). *Trade and Empire in Muscat and Zanzibar: Roots of British Domination* (New York: Routledge, 1992).

6. C. S. Nicholls attributed Omani Arab migration in the nineteenth century first to economic opportunities in East Africa and second to the "personal importance" of Seyyid Saʻid bin Sultan, in *The Swahili Coast: Politics, Diplomacy and Trade on the East African Littoral, 1798–1856* (New York: Africana Publishing Corporation, 1971), 378. Randall Pouwells also focused on the person of Saʻid bin Sultan, asserting his secure position in Muscat after 1820 and his great personal wealth as the primary force within the government. When Pouwells addressed immigrants to East Africa, he focused on other Indian Ocean migrants, from Hadramaut (southern Arabia) and Comoros (islands in the western Indian Ocean), in *Horn and Crescent: Cultural Change and Traditional Islam on the East African Coast, 800–1900* (New York: Cambridge University Press, 1987), 99, 103, 111–13.

7. The expert on both the geography of Oman and the Imamate is J. C. Wilkinson, and his two books, *Water and Tribal Settlement in South-East Arabia: A Study of the Aflāj of Oman* (Oxford, UK: Clarendon Press, 1977) and *The Imamate Tradition* (Cambridge: Cambridge University Press, 1987) are the most comprehensive on these subjects. This chapter draws heavily from the magisterial *Water and Tribal Settlement*.

8. To complete the metaphor, the United Arab Emirates sits on the vamp, and Qatar and Bahrain are a tassel on the instep, just below the tongue.

9. Bajada is the zone where outwash fans from mountains come together. Wilkinson, *Water and Tribal Settlement*, 66, 265.

10. Michael Pearson, "Littoral Society: The Concept and the Problem," *Journal of World History* 17, no. 4 (2006): 353–73.

11. Valerie J. Hoffman, *The Essentials of Ibadi Islam* (Syracuse, NY: Syracuse University Press, 2012), 3. As Hoffman has noted, although Ibadis are often lumped within the Kharawij, they see themselves as distinct from this early group of Muslim dissidents.

12. Hoffman, "The Articulation of Ibāḍī Identity," 202, 206. Hoffman has invigorated the study of Ibadism, and her work is part of a growing interest in this once-marginalized sect of Islam. For recent works on this subject see Wilkinson, *Ibadism: Origins and*

Early Development in Oman (Oxford University Press, 2010); and the new series of Studies on Ibadism and Oman edited by Abdulrahman Al Salimi and Heinz Gaube (published by Georg Olms Verlag, 17 vols.)

13. On this point, see Wilkinson, *Water and Tribal Settlement*, 124; and for a full explanation, see Wilkinson, *The Imamate Tradition of Oman*, and Hoffman, *Essentials of Ibadi Islam*, 14.

14. Calvin Allen, "Sayyids, Shets and Sultāns: Politics and Trade in Masqat under the Āl Bū Sa'īd, 1785–1914." (PhD diss., University of Washington, 1978), 28.

15. Robert G. Landen, *Oman since 1856: Disruptive Modernization in a Traditional Arab Society* (Princeton: Princeton University Press, 1967), 111.

16. Ibid., 110.

17. Ibid.

18. Climatic Research Unit of University of East Anglia, "Average Monthly Rainfall for Oman from 1900–2012," The World Bank Group Climate Change Knowledge Portal, http://sdwebx.worldbank.org/climateportal/index.cfm?page=country_historical _climate&ThisCCode=OMN.

19. Wellsted, *Travels in Arabia*, 1:92; Cole, "An Account of an Overland Journey," 115–16; Allen, "Sayyids, Shets and Sultans," 8. For an extensive overview, see Wilkinson, *Water and Tribal Settlement*.

20. "Kanāt," *Encyclopedia of Islam*, 2nd. ed., 4:529a.

21. Wilkinson, *Water and Tribal Settlement*, 91. For the social organization of these spaces, see Paul Bonnenfant, Guilemette Bonnenfant, and Salim ibn Hamad ibn Sulayman al-Harthi. "Architecture and Social History at Mudayrib." *Journal of Oman Studies* 3, no. 2 (1977), 107–35; Paul Bonnenfant and Colette Le Cour Grandmaison. "The Ibra' and Mudayrib Area." *Journal of Oman Studies* 3, no. 2 (1977), 91–4.

22. Wilkinson, *Water and Tribal Settlement*, 97–8.

23. Ibid., 100.

24. Wilkinson cites a story from the Imam Ghassān b. 'Abdullah al-Yahmadi who ruled from 808–823 and had to replace local officials for their failure to properly maintain the *falaj*; Wilkinson, *Water and Tribal Settlement*, 100.

25. Ibid., 264–65.

26. Mandana E. Limbert, *In the Time of Oil* (Stanford, CA: Stanford University Press, 2010), 124–25; Wilkinson, *Water and Tribal Settlement*, 213–15, 258–65.

27. Wilkinson, *Water and Tribal Settlement*, 88, 124. Wilkinson elsewhere offered a low opinion of the general upkeep of the irrigation system in Oman, suggesting that the entire system was built more than 1,200 years ago and that very little has been done to maintain it since then: "It is improbable that this work could have been carried out by the people who now use these irrigation systems, at least not with the levels of skill, knowledge, attitudes, and methods of land organization they currently [mid-to-late 1960s] display" (p. 85).

28. Colette Le Cour Grandmaison, "L'eau du vendredi: Droits d'eau et hiérarchie sociale en Sharqîya (Sultanat d'Oman)." *Études rurales*, no. 93/94 (1984), 35.

29. Ibid., 100.

30. Technically, Said bin Sultan's brother Salim bin Sultan held a coregency with him for two years, from 1804 to 1806.

31. The relationship between these three territories is exemplified by a story from the eighteenth century. When Sayf and Sultan ibna Imam Ahmed rebelled unsuccessfully against their father, they withdrew to Makran. Sayf eventually went to East

Africa, and Sultan eventually returned to Oman where he was a frequent challenge to his brother Said after 1783. Bhacker, *Trade and Empire in Muscat and Zanzibar*, 22–3.

32. In 1847, he married a Persian princess with the hope of securing better relations with the Qajar court. Hamerton to Palmerston, Zanzibar, 26 January 1848, no. 2 of 1848, AA 1/3, ZNA.

33. There is a lively literature on piracy in the gulf that disputes the terms and definitions. See Sultan Muhammad al-Qasimi, *The Myth of Arab Piracy in the Gulf* (London: Croom Helm, 1986); Charles E. Davies, *The Blood-Red Arab Flag: An Investigation into Qasimi Piracy: 1797–1820* (Exeter, UK: University of Exeter Press, 1997); Patricia Risso, "Cross-Cultural Perceptions of Piracy: Maritime Violence in the Western Indian Ocean and Persian Gulf Region During a Long Eighteenth Century," *Journal of World History* 12, no. 2 (2001): 293–94.

34. Bhacker, *Trade and Empire*.

35. Abdul Sheriff, *Dhow Cultures and the Indian Ocean: Cosmopolitanism, Commerce and Islam* (New York: Columbia University Press, 2010).

36. J. C. Wilkinson, "Oman and East Africa: New Light on Early Kilwan History from the Omani Sources," *The International Journal of African Historical Studies* 14, no. 2 (1981).

37. Bhacker, *Trade and Empire*, 81.

38. Mabarak Ali Hinawy, *Al Akida and Fort Jesus, Mombasa*, 2nd. ed. (Nairobi: East African Literature Bureau, 1970), 8.

39. Wilkinson provides a brilliant analysis of what he calls "The Imamate Cycle" in Omani history. In general, "as the ideological basis of the Ibadi Imamate weakens and competition for control of power and wealth grows . . . tribal factionalism revives," leading to collapse of central power and loss of revenue from external trade. For a simple statement of this, see *Water and Tribal Settlement*, 124; and for a full explanation, see *The Imamate Tradition of Oman*. The rule of Said bin Sultan al-Busaidi can certainly be considered part of a "downward" cycle from religious unification under a strong Imam.

40. Calvin Allen focuses on the split of Muscat from Oman and the disjunctures within al-Busaidi rule in contrast to early accounts (Badger, Kelly, Landen, and Lorimer, among others) that saw a fundamental unity in the al-Busaidi state. Calvin H. Allen, Jr., "The State of Masqat in the Gulf and East Africa, 1785–1829," *International Journal of Middle East Studies* 14, no. 2 (1982): 117; Salīl ibn Ruzīk [Ibn Ruzayq], *History of the Imâms and Seyyids of 'Omân*, trans. by George Percy Badger (London: Hakluyt Society, 1871); J. B. Kelly, *Britain and the Persian Gulf, 1795–1880* (Oxford: Oxford University Press, 1968); Landen, *Oman since 1856*; John Gordon Lorimer, *Gazetteer of the Persian Gulf, Oman and Central Arabia*, 8 vols. (Dublin: Irish Academic Press, 1986 [1915]).

41. W. F. W. Owen, *Narrative of Voyages to Explore the Shores of Africa, Arabia and Madagascar: Performed in H. M. Ships Leven and Barracouta under the Direction of Captain W. F. W. Owen, R. N.*, ed. Heaton Bowstead Robinson, (London: R. Bentley, 1833) 1:206–7.

42. Ibid., 1:205.

43. Davies, *The Blood-red Arab Flag*, 237–38.

44. The delegation included a clever qadi from the al-Mauli who matched theological wits with learned Shi'ites at the Persian court. Ibn Ruzīk [Ibn Ruzayq], *History of the Imâms and Seyyids of 'Omân*, 307–12.

45. Davies, *The Blood-red Arab Flag*, 326–29; Ibn Ruzīk [Ibn Ruzayq], *History of the Imāms and Seyyids of 'Omân*, 299.

46. Ibn Ruzīk [Ibn Ruzayq], *History of Imâms and Seyyids*, 315, 320.

47. Ibid., 335.

48. Ibid., 336–37.

49. He used this, for instance, with Nāsir ibn Nabhān al-Kharūsī (1778–1847). Hoffman, "The Articulation of Ibādī Identity," 210. Other Omani leaders had employed this technique. In the fight for control of Oman in the eighteenth century, Muhammad bin Nasir, a challenger for the Imamate, seized a young Imam and his family and kept them hostage as he pursued his campaign. Ibn Ruzīk [Ibn Ruzayq], *History of Imâms and Seyyids*, 114.

50. Cole, "An Account of an Overland Journey," 113.

51. This account draws from J. S. Birks, "The Reaction of Rural Populations to Drought: A Case Study From South East Arabia" 31, no. 4 (1977): 299–305. This account is useful in thinking about the earlier periods of drought in Oman because of the broad continuities in everyday life in Omani society that lasted through the late 1970s. For evidence of these continuities see Christine Eickelman's account of her fieldwork in al-Hamra, Oman, from 1979 to 1980: *Women and Community in Oman* (New York: New York University Press, 1984). Another study carried out in 1982—a time when the Omani domestic labor market offered low wages—pointed out that Omanis undertook menial labor in the gulf to buy land or water shares at home. The long-term continuities of interior communities depending on *falaj* systems have only recently seen significant changes. Robin Brown, Michael M. Horowitz, and Muneera Salem-Murdock, *Social and Institutional Aspects of Oman: A Review of the Literature* (Washington, DC: Agency for International Development, 1982).

52. J. S. Birks, "The Reaction of Rural Populations to Drought, 301–3.

53. Ibid.

54. Ibid., 303.

55. Ibid.

56. Ibid., 299–305.

57. Ibn Ruzīk [Ibn Ruzayq], *History of the Imâms and Seyyids*, 212; Nasser bin Abdulla Al Riyami, *Zanzibar: Personalities and Events (1828–1972)*, trans. Ali bin Rashid Al Abri (Muscat: Beirut Bookshop, 2012), 397.

58. Ibn Ruzīk [Ibn Ruzayq], *History of the Imâms and Seyyids*, 212.

59. Ibid.

60. Wellsted, *Travels in Arabia*, 1:75.

61. Ibid., 49–50.

62. Wilkinson, *Water and Tribal Settlements*, 40–41.

63. Ibid., 40, 259; Wellsted, *Travels in Arabia*, 1:91.

64. E. C. Ross, *Report on the Administration of the Persian Gulf Political Residency and Muscat Political Agency for the year 1875–76* (Calcutta: Foreign Department Printing Press, 1876), 78.

65. PJC Robertson to Lt. Col EC Ross, 20 December 1877, Pol. Dept. 1878, vol. 134, comp. 89, "Muscat Affairs," MSA.

66. Henry Ballantine, *Midnight Marches through Persia* (Boston: Lee and Shepard, 1879), 26. For the global aspects of the gulf's date trade see Matthew Hopper, *Slaves of One Master* (New Haven: Yale University Press, 2015).

67. Allen, "Sayyids, Shets and Sultans," 154.

68. Miles to Ross, 3 September 1878, Pol. Dept. 1878, vol. 134, comp. 89 "Muscat Affairs," MSA.

69. E. C. Ross, Report on the Administration of the Persian Gulf Political Residency and Muscat Political Agency for the year 1877–78 (Calcutta: Foreign Department Press, 1878), 129.

70. Miles, "On the Border of the Great Desert," 160–61.

71. Allen, "Sayyids, Shets and Sultans," 153.

72. Ibid.

73. Nasser bin Abdulla Al Riyami, *Zanzibar*, 397.

74. Claude Markovits, *The Global World of Indian Merchants, 1750–1947: Traders of Sind from Bukhara to Panama* (New York: Cambridge University Press, 2000). Historian Sebouh Aslanian has articulated this idea further to discuss "circulation societies," but this may not be as apt for the open-ended nature of Arab mobility in *From the Indian Ocean to the Mediterranean: The Global Trade Networks of Armenian Merchants from New Julfa* (Berkeley: California University Press, 2011).

CHAPTER 2: THE CUSTOMS MASTER AND
CUSTOMS OF CREDIT IN ZANZIBAR

1. Captain T. Smee, "Observations during a Voyage of Research on the East African Coast, from Cape Guardafui south to the Island of Zanzibar, in the H. C.'s cruiser Ternate" (1811) in R. F. Burton, *Zanzibar: City, Island and Coast* (London: Tinsley Brothers, 1872), 2:469.

2. Ibid., 2:469, 471.

3. Ibid., 473.

4. Hamerton, Report on the Port of Zanzibar, 1844, AA 1/3, ZNA.

5. Maria Theresa dollars, abbreviated as MT$, was the dominant currency of the Indian Ocean region. The currencies in the book are in Maria Theresa dollars unless otherwise indicated.

6. Chhaya Goswami, *The Call of the Sea: Kachchhi Traders in Muscat and Zanzibar, c. 1800–1880* (New Delhi: Orient Blackswan, 2011), 192–93.

7. Alexander Burnes, "On the Maritime Communications of India, as Carried on by the Natives, Particularly from Kutch, at the Mouth of the Indus," *Journal of the Royal Geographical Society of London* 6 (1836): 25.

8. John Studdy Leigh and James S. Kirkman, "The Zanzibar Diary of John Studdy Leigh, Part I," *The International Journal of African Historical Studies* 13, no. 2 (1980): 281–312.

9. Richard P. Waters to Abji bin Siwji [brother of Jairam], Zanzibar, 20 September 1839, in *New England Merchants in Africa: A History Through Documents, 1802 to 1865*, Norman Robert Bennett and George E. Brooks (Brookline, MA: Boston University Press, 1965), 222.

10. C. S. Nicholls, *The Swahili Coast; Politics, Diplomacy and Trade on the East African Littoral, 1798–1856* (New York: Africana Pub. Corp, 1971), 217.

11. Edgar Botsford to Daniel Webster, Received in Washington, November 10, 1842, in Bennett and Brooks, *New England Merchants in Africa*, 222.

12. The definitive work on this is Abdul Sheriff, *Slaves, Spices and Ivory in Zanzibar: Integration of an East African Commercial Empire into the World Economy, 1770–1873* (Athens: Ohio University Press, 1987).

13. These few ultra-rich merchants are easily differentiated from the many Indians in East Africa with whom they may have shared a common religion or region. Most examinations of credit in Zanzibar have taken as foundational the role of Indian merchants (both Hindu Banyans and Ismaili Khoja Muslims). While certainly the largest and most prominent lenders—people like Jairam Sewji, Ladha Damji, and Tharia Topan—were Indian, the range of Indian people in Zanzibar and East Africa was quite wide, and the differences within the groups are equally illustrative of the divisions within society. Where possible, I take pains to disaggregate "Arabs" as a group, and Indians as historical actors should be treated the same way.

14. Hamerton to Malet, 25 October 1849, AA 3/8, ZNA.

15. For point of reference, I include Sheriff's data on the value of export ivory in Maria Theresa dollars. In 1823, one frasila was worth MT$22, which is equivalent to one pound of ivory for MT$0.62. By 1869, the price of ivory was much higher, and one frasila was valued at MT$60, or one pound for MT$1.90. See Sheriff, *Slaves, Spices and Ivory*, 254–55.

16. Hamerton to A. Malet Esq., Chief Secretary to Government Bombay, 25 Oct 1849, Zanzibar, AA 3/8, ZNA. Jairam Sewji bought rupees from Hamerton in exchange for Maria Theresa dollars, at the rate of 215 Rupees per $100, with a 5 percent charge for the exchange. See also Hamerton to A. Malet Esq., Sec to Govt Bombay, 20 April 1846, AA 3/8, ZNA.

17. For an in-depth discussion of the links between the Omani rulers in Zanzibar and the Indian commercial houses, see M. Reda Bhacker, *Trade and Empire in Muscat and Zanzibar: Roots of British Domination* (New York: Routledge, 1992), 176–77.

18. Şevket Pamuk, *A Monetary History of the Ottoman Empire* (Cambridge, UK: Cambridge University Press, 2000), 84.

19. Sheriff, *Slaves, Spices and Ivory*, 65, 87. Ladda Damji, who bought Juma Merikani's ivory in this book's opening vignette, was one of Sewji's associates. Note that the practice of farming the customs to Hindu merchants in Zanzibar closely resembled what Postans found across the Indian Ocean in Sindh. He noted that the Hindu merchant's "command of ready money gives them also a certain power over the rulers, who . . . are too happy to farm its resources to the Soucars (as the Hindu traders are called) for any sum which may be immediately commanded . . . . In these transactions the Hindu always runs the greatest risk of being called upon to disgorge any profits he may amass, and he knows that his bonds and contracts with Mahomedan chiefs are so much waste paper; but he makes his calculations accordingly, and, despite power and despotism, never fails to accumulate wealth at the expense of the profligacy of the rulers." Thomas Postans, *Personal Observations on Sindh: The Manners and Customs of Its Inhabitants, and Its Productive Capabilities with a Sketch of Its History, a Narrative of Recent Events, and an Account of the Connection of the British Government with That Country to the Present Period* (London: Longman, Brown, Green, and Longmans, 1843), 64.

20. John F. Webb to Charles Ward, 27 September 1851, Zanzibar, in Bennett and Brooks, *New England Merchants in Africa*, 488.

21. Ibid., 107.

22. John F. Webb to Michael Shepard, 17 July 1851 (Zanzibar), in Bennett and Brooks, *New England Merchants*, 486–87.

23. Sheriff, *Slaves, Spices and Ivory*, 107.

24. For a comparable set of documents from a later period, see the remarkable collection in Alessandra Vianello and Mohamed M Kassim, eds., *Servants of the Sharia: The Civil Register of the Qadis' Court of Brava, 1893–1900*, 2 vols. (Leiden: Brill, 2006).

25. Registered documents 208, 210, 211, 213, 221, 233, 236, 241–42, 270, 277–81 of 1877, AM 3/1, ZNA. These documents were registered in 1877, but they represent contracts, sales, and business arrangements made in the 1840s.

26. 233 of 1877, 14 Rajab 1261/19 June 1845, AM 3/1, ZNA.

27. 213 of 1877, 15 Jumada al-Thani 1263/30 May 1847, AM 3/1, ZNA

28. A. Werner, "A Swahili History of Pate (Continued)," *Journal of the Royal African Society* 14, no. 55 (1915): 292–95; Nicholls, *The Swahili Coast*, 122–33; Ann Biersteker and Ibrahim Noor Shariff, *Mashairi Ya Vita Vya Kuduhu: War Poetry in Kiswahili Exchanged at the Time of the Battle of Kuduhu* (East Lansing: Michigan State University Press, 1995).

29. Glassman, *Feasts and Riots*, 66.

30. Burton, "The Lake Regions of Central Equatorial Africa," 1:123–34, 302–3; Marek Pawełczak, *The State and the Stateless: the Sultanate of Zanzibar and the East African Mainland: Politics, Economy and Society, 1837–1888* (Warsaw: Instytut Historyczny Uniwersytetu Warszawskiego, 2010); Norman Robert Bennett, *Arab versus European: Diplomacy and War in Nineteenth-Century East Central Africa* (New York: Africana Publishing Company, 1986); Velten, *Safari za Wasuaheli* (Göttingen: Vandenhoeck [und] Ruprecht, 1901), 141n1 points out that the dual title Diwan Mwekambi, and cites Bwana Kheri bin Mwekambi Juma as an example of this usage.

31. Glassman reasons that Bwana Heri's mother was Zigua, from the interior hinterland of Saadani. He bases this on interviews that he conducted. Glassman, *Feasts and Riots*, 65–66, 66n26, 150–51. While this may be true—Muslim men could have multiple wives—the land sale document shows us a patrician Swahili woman who could also have been his mother. This would make Bwana Heri's achievements as a patron and deal maker in the interior all the more impressive. Pawelczak, *The State and the Stateless*, 268–69 also questions Bwana Heri's parentage.

32. This is 278 of 1877, 20 Rajab 1261/24 July 1845, AM 3/1, ZNA; his title is (الصرنج) written in Arabic as *al-saranj*.

33. Derek Nurse and Thomas T. Spear, *The Swahili: Reconstructing the History and Language of an African Society, 800–1500* (Philadelphia: University of Pennsylvania Press, 1985), 82–83.

34. Burton *Zanzibar*, 1:2; John M. Gray, "The Hadimu and Tumbatu of Zanzibar," *Tanzania Notes and Records* 81 and 82 (1977): 135–53

35. Hamerton to "Sir," 13 July 1841, AA 12/1A, ZNA.

36. Nicholls, *Swahili Coast*, 28–29.

37. Aaron Jaffer, "'Lord of the Forecastle': Serangs, Tindals and Lascar Mutiny, c. 1780–1860," in *Mutiny and Maritime Radicalism in the Age of Revolution: A Global Survey* (Cambridge; Cambridge University Press, 2014), 155; G. Balachandran, "South Asian Seafarers and Their Worlds, c. 1870–1930s," in *"Seascapes: Maritime Histories, Littoral Cultures, and Transoceanic Exchanges*, 186–202 (Honolulu: University of Hawai'i Press, 2007); note that the title is in early Swahili dictionaries, see "serénge," a small captain, in J. L. Krapf, *A Dictionary of the Suahili Language* (London: Trüb-

ner and Co., 1882), and "serahangi," in A. C. Madan, *English-Swahili Dictionary* (Oxford: Clarendon Press), 335.

38. Burton, *Zanzibar*, 1:24.

39. Janet J. Ewald, "Crossers of the Sea: Slaves, Freedmen, and Other Migrants in the Northwestern Indian Ocean, c. 1750–1914," *The American Historical Review* 105, no. 1 (2000): 76–77.

40. Nicholls, *The Swahili Coast*, 272.

41. Registered Deed 328 of 1877, 3/1, ZNA. The translations are my own, though I benefited tremendously from the assistance of Adel Allouche, Department of History, Yale University, who helped me decipher the cramped hand as I learned to read these documents.

42. This section draws from the excellent summary in Y. Linant de Bellefonds, "Iḳrār," in *Encyclopaedia of Islam*, 2nd ed., P. Bearman et al., eds (Leiden: Brill, 2007). http://dx.doi.org/10.1163/1573-3912_islam_COM_0357.

43. S. D. Goitein, *A Mediterranean Society: The Jewish Communities of the Arab World as Portrayed in the Documents of the Cairo Geniza* (Berkeley: University of California Press, 1967), 1:250.

44. See the examples in Huda Lutfi, "A Study of Six Fourteenth Century Iqrars from Al-Quds Relating to Muslim Women," *Journal of the Economic and Social History of the Orient* 26, no. 3 (1983).

45. This is because the documents were registered in the consulate. Many more varieties of *iqrār* and other documents likely circulated in the nineteenth century.

46. Goitein, *A Mediterranean Society*, 1:250.

47. Abraham L. Udovitch, *Partnership and Profit in Medieval Islam*, Princeton Studies on the Near East (Princeton: Princeton University Press, 1970).

48. The Koran 2:282, trans. by N. J. Dawood, (London: Penguin Books, 1993).

49. Noor Mohammed, "Principles of Islamic Contract Law," *The Journal of Law and Religion* 6, no. 1 (1988): 117–21.

50. Joseph Schacht, *An Introduction to Islamic Law* (Oxford, UK: Clarendon Press, 1996).

51. See, for instance, S. D. Goitein, "The Documents of the Cairo Geniza as a Source for Islamic Social History," in *Studies in Islamic History and Institutions* (Leiden: Brill, 1966), 284–85. The research that Goitein produced from these documents is masterful (see *A Mediterranean Society*).

52. Udovitch, *Partnership and Profit in Medieval Islam*.

53. The writing and analysis of these formulas to ensure their legality grew into a branch of Islamic knowledge called *'ilm al-shurut*. The prominence of this field lay, to some extent, in the degrees of accuracy it could create, and each school of Islamic law produced volumes of *shurūt* (singular: *shart*) to assist practitioners. One prominent writer, al-Tahāwī, clarified why the accessibility of these documents was important: "Whatever is closer to the comprehension of the commoners (*al-'āmma*) in the works of the shurūt is preferable to us, because the book may be acquired by a commoner who may not understand the (technical) language. Thus we wrote in a manner that is closer to the understanding of the commoners in general, because the elites (al-khāssa) will understand what the commoners understand though the contrary is not the case." Ahmad ibn Muhammad al-Tahāwī, *The Function of Documents in Islamic Law; the Chapters on Sales from Tahawi's Kitab Al-Shurut Al-Kabir*, ed. Jeanette A. Wakin (Albany: State University of New York Press, 1972), 27. These collections of templates were

accessible, but did not limit actions. Formularies could be combined for subtlety and flexibility, so that business people who wished to stay within legal bounds were able to use a number of formulary contracts independently, and each passed legal standards, but the combined effect of all of them would be to do something that was not permitted. J. Schacht, "Ḥiyal," in Bearman et al., *Encyclopaedia of Islam* (Leiden: Brill, 2007). Brill Online. See also Wael B. Hallaq, "Model Shurūṭ Works and the Dialectic of Doctrine and Practice," *Islamic Law and Society* 2, no. 2 (1995): 109–34.

54. This description is based on Lutfi, "A Study of Six Fourteenth Century Iqrars ," 256–57, and, following her references, on Muhammad ibn Shihāb al-Dīn al-Suyūtī, *Jawāhir Al-`uqūd Wa-mu`īn Al-qudāh Wa-al-muwaqqi`īn Wa-al-shuhūd* (Al-Tab`ah, n. d.), 1:17–54.

55. In other places, a fuller name is used for the Hindu trader: Ladha bin Damha bin Tupan. The suffix -ji is an honorific. His *nisba* also periodically changes from al-Baniani to al-Hindi.

56. In 1865 Majid bin Said al-Busaidi explained that the validity of such mortgages relied on five conditions: 1. The people of the house should leave it, and the people to whom it was mortgaged should enter it; 2. The mortgagee should have witnesses of the their taking possession in the presence of the mortgagors; 3. The mortgagee should give it for rent and that the mortgagee should receive the rent; 4. Should the mortgagee alter the house, the mortgagor should not object; and 5. The mortgagee should appoint an agent to receive the house from the mortgagor. R. L. Playfair notes, n. d. [1865], AM 1/1, ZNA.

57. Salim bin Abdullah bin Khamis al-Mazrui mortgage of shamba in Pemba to Budu Liladher, 26 al- Dhu al-Qa'da 1313 [8 May 1896], AC 7/28, ZNA; R. L. Playfair, "Sales of Property When Such Property is Retained in Possession of the Letter," n. d. [c. 1865], AM 1/1, ZNA; Taḥāwī, *The Function of Documents in Islamic Law*; A.-M. Delcambre, "K͟hiyār," in *Encyclopaedia of Islam*, P. Bearman et al., eds. (Leiden: Brill, 2007).

58. Registered documents 102 and 103 of 1877, 12/19, ZNA.

59. J. N. D. Anderson, *Islamic Law in Africa*, 2nd. ed., Cass Library of African Law No. 3 (London: F. Cass, 1970), 49.

60. 4 Zanzibar Law Report 90, as cited in Anderson, *Islamic Law in Africa*, 360.

61. Calvin Allen, "The Indian Merchant Community of Masqat" (*Bulletin of the School of Oriental and African Studies, University of London* 44: 1, 1981), 47.

62. Philip D. Curtin, *Cross-Cultural Trade in World History* (Cambridge: Cambridge University Press, 1984).

CHAPTER 3: SULTANS AT SEA: MOBILITY AND THE OMANI STATES

1. Richard Francis Burton, *Zanzibar: City, Island, and Coast* (London: Tinsley Brothers, 1872), 1:80.

2. R. L. Playfair, "Reminiscences," *Chambers Journal* 2 no. 68 (March 18, 1899): 244.

3. M. Rheda Bhacker provides the broader trade context for this series of events, in *Trade and Empire in Muscat and Zanzibar: Roots of British Domination* (New York: Routledge, 1992), chapter 12.

4. Reginald Coupland, *East Africa and Its Invaders, from the Earliest Times to the Death of Seyyid Said in 1856* (New York: Russell & Russell, 1965); Robert Geran Landen, *Oman since 1856; Disruptive Modernization in a Traditional Arab Society* (Princeton: Princeton University Press, 1967); C. S. Nicholls, *The Swahili Coast; Politics, Diplomacy and Trade on the East African Littoral, 1798–1856* (New York: Africana Publishing Corp., 1971).

5. John C. Wilkinson, *The Imamate Tradition of Oman* (Cambridge: Cambridge University Press, 1987), 169–170.

6. Uzi Rabi, *Emergence of States in a Tribal Society: Oman Under Saʻid Bin Taymur, 1932–1970* (Brighton: Sussex Academic Press, 2011), 24. For comparison to mobile governance in Qing China, see Michael Chang, *A Court on Horseback: Imperial Touring & the Construction of Qing Rule, 1680–1785* (Cambridge, MA: Harvard University Press, 2007).

7. Wilkinson, *Imamate Tradition*, 13; Calvin Allen, "The State of Masqat in the Gulf and East Africa, 1785–1829." *International Journal of Middle East Studies* 14, no. 2 (1982), 117–18.

8. Valerie Hoffman, *The Essentials of Ibadi Islam* (Syracuse, NY: Syracuse University Press, 2012), 25.

9. This line of argumentation is based on Bhacker's *Trade and Empire in Muscat and Zanzibar*, see chapters 5 and 6 for a detailed account.

10. Ibid., 100.

11. E. C. Ross, *Report on the Administration of the Persian Gulf Political Residency and Muscat Political Agency for the Year 1883–84* (Calcutta: Government Printing, India, 1884), 29.

12. Cogan Memorandum on Zanzibar, 5 December 1839, 54/3, 115, FO.

13. The ship was a teak-built frigate with auxiliary steam and thirty-two guns. It was built in Bombay's Mazagon dockyards. Robert Nunez Lyne, *Zanzibar in Contemporary Times: A Short History of the Southern East in the Nineteenth Century* (London: Hurst and Blackett 1905), 45; Burton, *Zanzibar*, 1:267.

14. Calculation based on Bhacker's chart, see *Trade and Empire*, 93.

15. W. S. W. Ruschenberger, *Narrative of a Voyage Round the World: During the Years 1835, 36, and 37, Including a Narrative of an Embassy to the Sultan of Muscat and the King of Siam* (London: R. Bentley, 1838), 69; Ross, *Report on the Administration of the Persian Gulf Political Residency*, 34.

16. Hamerton to My Lord, 31 July 1844, AA 1/3, ZNA.

17. Ross, *Report on the Administration of the Persian Gulf Political Residency*, 34.

18. Said bin Sultan to Hamerton, 1 November 1849, AA 1/3, ZNA.

19. Hamerton to Palmerston, Sec State for Foreign Affairs, 2 November 1849, no. 9, AA 1/3, ZNA.

20. Said bin Sultan to Palmerston, Sec State for Foreign Affairs, 15 Dhu al-Hajj 1265 / 1 November 1849, AA 3/1, ZNA.

21. Captain Atkins Hamerton to A. Malet, 5 November 1849, AA 3/6, ZNA; Hamerton to A. Malet, Chief Sec to Govt Bombay, Muscat, 5 November 1851, AA 3/8, ZNA.

22. Hamerton to A. Malet, Chief Sec to Govt Bombay, Muscat, 5 Nov 1851, AA 3/8, 285–90, ZNA.

23. Chhaya Goswami, *The Call of the Sea: Kachchhi Traders in Muscat and Zanzibar, c. 1800–1880* (New Delhi: Orient Blackswan, 2011).

24. This news of the Queen's takeover of the company in India occasioned great celebrations in Muscat. Thuwayni's guns fired a salute to the queen, and the British Navy returned the salute; the Union Jack flew on the principal flag staffs of the forts of Muscat, "all the influential men residing in the district, of all denominations" boarded a British ship to offer congratulations, and on the shore Hindu merchants provided feasts for all who wished to partake. Commodore Griffith Jenkins, Commanding Persian Gulf Squadron [in Muscat] to GG Wellesley, HM Indian Navy, 10 March 1859, Pol. Dept. vol. 120, comp. 675, MSA.

25. J. B. Kelly, *Britain and the Persian Gulf, 1795–1880* (Oxford: Clarendon Press, 1968), 541.

26. Sa'īd bin 'Alī Mughayri, *Juhaynat al-akhbār fī tārīkh Zanzibār* (Muscat, Oman: Wizārat al-Turāth al-Qawmī, 1979), 308.

27. Capt Felix Jones, IN, Pol Res PG, to Comm. Griffith Jenkins, 25 February 1859, Pol. Dept. 1859, vol. 120, comp. 676, MSA.

28. Grant, "Account of Sheykh Salih bin Ali," 12 May 1884, R15/6/16, IOR.

29. Said al-Hashimy, "Imamate Revival in Oman, 1913–20" PhD diss., University of Leeds, U.K., 1994), 26–27.

30. Bhacker, *Trade and Empire*, 185, 244n35; Mughayri, *Juhaynat al-Akhbar*, 200.

31. Bombay Govt Pol Dept [HL Anderson, Sec] to Wellesley, C-i-C Indian Navy, 15 April 1859, Pol. Dept. 1859, vol. 120, comp. 676, MSA.

32. Rigby to Anderson, Sec Gov Bombay, 24 August 1858, Foreign Dept 29/10 /1858-S.C. 59–60, M(11–5) (from the private collection of Abdul Sheriff), NAI.

33. Rigby to Anderson, Sec Gov Bombay, 24 August 1858, Foreign Dept 29/10 /1858-S.C. 59–60, M(11–5) (from the private collection of Abdul Sheriff), NAI.

34. Emilie Ruete, *An Arabian Princess between Two Worlds: Memoirs, Letters Home, Sequels to the Memoirs, Syrian Customs and Usages*, ed. E. van Donzel (Leiden: Brill, 1993), 342.

35. Her extraordinary memoir is one of the reasons we have such an intimate account of the rebellion. She worked with a literate slave to teach herself to read and write. Ruete, *Arabian Princess*, 186–87.

36. Ruete, *Arabian Princess*, 344.

37. Ibid., 342.

38. Hiskale [Heskiel] to Political Resident, Persian Gulf, 18 May 1859, and Pol Res PG to Anderson, 29 June 1859, Pol. Dept. 121/1859, 325–6, 349–50 (from the private collection of Abdul Sheriff), MSA.

39. Ruete, *Arabian Princess*, 346.

40. Rigby to Bombay, 4 April 1859, FD 17.6.1859-P.C.-5 (from private collection of Abdul Sheriff).

41. Ruete, *Arabian Princess*, 347–49.

42. Ibid., 348.

43. Ibid.

44. Ibid., 352–53.

45. Rigby to Anderson, 12 October 1860, Pol. Dept. 158, 1860, 500–3, MSA.

46. Heskiel Yusuf to Anderson, 16 Rabi al-Thani 1276 / 12 November 1859, Pol. Dept. 1859, vol. 120, comp. 15, MSA.

47. Pelly to Kinloch Forbes, 30 October 1861, Pol Dept 1862, vol. 47, comp 17, MSA.

48. Nile Green, *Bombay Islam, The Religious Economy of the West Indian Ocean, 1840–1915* (Cambridge: Cambridge University Press, 2013), 3.

49. Barghash to Elphinston, 30 March 30 1860, Pol. Dept. 158, 325–32 (from the private collection of Abdul Sheriff), MSA.

50. Pelly to Shaw Stewart, 4 March 1862, no. 141, 12/8, ZNA.

51. Pelly to Shaw Stewart, 4 March 1862, no. 141, 12/8, ZNA.

52. See chapter 8 for more details on Said bin Salim.

53. Pelly to Shaw Stewart, 4 March 1862, no. 141, 12/8, ZNA. This echoes the arguments that anti-slavery advocates made at the end of the nineteenth century: it is possible to end slavery without disturbing the underlying political economy. Fred Cooper, From Slave Cooper, Frederick. *From Slaves to Squatters: Plantation Labor and Agriculture in Zanzibar and Coastal Kenya, 1890–1925* (New Haven: Yale University Press, 1980).

54. Pelly to Kimloch Forbes, 11 November 1862, Pol. Dept. 1862, vol. 47, comp. 206, MSA.

55. Playfair memorandum for Colonel Taylor, n. d. [Sept 1869], AA 3/26, ZNA.

56. Seward to C. Gonne, Sec to Govt Bombay, 18 September 1865, AA 3/26, ZNA.

57. In fact, the ship had been part of an imperial boondoggle in China, later bought by the governor of Bombay to keep it out of the American Civil War, before it was given as a gift to Majid. Horatio Nelson Lay, a private British citizen and a "Chinese-speaking diplomatist," served as the inspector general of the customs under the Chinese government. The Chinese commissioned him to outfit a fleet to help suppress the Taiping rebellion and patrol for pirates and smugglers. While Lay purchased five other practical ships, the "elegantly fitted out" Thule, originally built in 1860 for James Anderson, the managing director of the Peninsular & Oriental Co (a steamship company) was "a slight indulgence." When the fleet (the Lay-Osborn flotilla) reached China in 1863, Lay's unwillingness to hand over the ships to Chinese officers put them in limbo between the British and Chinese governments. The British minister at Peking ordered the ships to India and to London, where they were embargoed, lest they be sold to the American Confederates. Bombay Governor Frere bought the ships in 1865, when the American Civil War was over, and the Government of India bought the Thule and one other ship, which was freighted with imperial hubris and given as a gift to Majid. Majid did not sail back to Zanzibar in the Thule when he departed. The ship was delivered early the next year and presented by none other than David Livingstone to help him curry favor with the sultan. J. Talboys Wheeler, *Summary of Affairs of the Government of India in the Foreign Department from 1864 to 1869* (Calcutta: Office of Superintendent of Government Printing, 1868), 157; John King, "Horatio Nelson Lay, C.B.: A Pioneer of British Influence in the Far East," *Journal of the American Asiatic Society* 14, no. 2 (March 1914): 49–54; Richard N. J. Wright, *The Chinese Steam Navy 1862–1945* (London: Chatham, 2000), 15–19; Frere to Sir Charles Wood, 4 April 1864, in John Martineau, *The Life and Correspondence of the Sir Bartle Frere* (London: John Murray, 1895), 465–66; Caledonian Maritime Research Trust, "Thule," Database of Clyde Built Ships, available at http://www.clydeships.co.uk/.

58. Frere to Sir Charles Wood, 4 April 1864, in John Martineau, *The Life and Correspondence of the Sir Bartle Frere* (London: John Murray, 1895), 465–66.

59. Seward to Gonne, Chief Sec Gov Bombay, 6 February 1866, AA 3/26, ZNA.

60. James R. Brennan and Andrew Burton, "The Emerging Metropolis: A history of Dar es Salaam, circa 1862–2000," in James R. Brennan, Andrew Burton, and Yusuf Lawi, eds., *Dar es Salaam. Histories from an Emerging African Metropolis* (Oxford: African Books Collective, 2007), 16–17.

61. Kelly, *Britain and the Persian Gulf*, 541.

62. British agent at Muscat to Secretary to the Government, Bombay, 8 January 1862, AA 12/8, ZNA.

63. Zāmil Muḥammad al-Rashīd, *Suʿūdī Relations with Eastern Arabia and ʿUmān (1800–1871)* (London: Luzac & Co., 1981), 62, 114.

64. Kelly, *Britain and the Persian Gulf*, 647–48.

65. Ibid., 649.

66. This period, especially the conspiracy surrounding Thuwayni's death, is one that has been disputed in Omani history.

67. Kelly, *Britain and the Persian Gulf*, 651.

68. Wheeler, *Summary of Affairs of the Government of India*, 146–47.

69. Ibid., 148–49.

70. al-Hashimy, "Imamate Revival in Oman," 33.

71. Wilkinson, *Imamate Tradition*, 182.

72. Ali bin Humood bin Muhammad al-Juul to Turki bin Said, 172 of 1869, 12 January, and Said bin Ahmad bin Sayf to Turki bin Said, 173 of 1869, 30 January, Pol. Dept. 1869, no. 89, vol. 4, comp. 446, MSA.

73. [Said bin Muhammad Suliman to Shaykh Muhammad bin Abdullatif, Arab of Bombay] (names not stated in original), n. d. [1869], Pol. Dept. 1869, no. 89, vol. 4, comp. 446, MSA.

74. Disbrowe to Gonne, 8 June 1869, Pol. Dept. 1869, no. 89, vol. 4, comp. 970, MSA.

75. Saloman bin Yacoob (petition on behalf of Turki and family) to H. E. the Gov of Bombay, 19 April 1870, Pol. Dept., vol. 2, no. 92, comp. 8, MSA; Memo from Pol Dept, 5 May 1870, Pol. Dept., vol. 2, no. 92, comp. 8, MSA.

76. Note on back of letter, Turki bin Said to Asst Sec to Govt, 6 June 1870, Pol. Dept. 1870, vol. 2, no. 92, comp. 8, MSA.

77. Memorandum from Venayek Wassoodew, Oriental Translator to Govt, Bombay, 25 August 1870, Pol. Dept. 1870, vol. 2, no. 92, comp. 8, MSA.

78. Turki bin Said to Right Hon the Governor of Bombay, 27 February 1869, Pol. Dept. 1869, vol. 4, no. 89, comp. 44, MSA.

79. Registered deed 1093 of 1888, dated 26 Rajab 1285 / 11 November 1868, AA 12/20, ZNA.

80. Sec to Gov, Pol Dept to Commissioner of Customs, 14 February 1870, Pol. Dept. 1870, vol. 2, no. 92, comp. 348, MSA.

81. Saloman Yacoob, agent in Bombay of Turki bin Said, to His Excellency Sir Seymour Fitzgerald, Gov. and President in Council, n. d. [recd 31 August 1870], Pol. Dept. 1870, vol. 2, no. 92, comp. 1556, MSA.

82. Turki bin Said to Governor of Bombay, 27 February 1869, Pol. Dept. 1869, no. 89, vol. 4, comp. 446, MSA.

83. Turki bin Said to Governor of Bombay, 12 February 1870, Pol. Dept., vol. 2, no. 92, comp. 8, MSA.

84. Saloman Yacoob to H. E. the Gov of Bombay, 19 April 1870, Pol. Dept. 1870, vol. 2, no. 92, comp. 8, MSA.

85. Saloman Yacoob to Oriental Translator to Govt Bombay, 19 July 1870, Pol. Dept. 1870 vol. 2, MSA.

86. Asst Pol Agent at Gwadur to Pol Secretary, Bombay, telegram, 9 March 1870, Pol. Dept., vol. 2, no. 92, comp. 8, MSA.

87. Pelly in Bushire to Foreign Secretary and Pol Secretary, Bombay and Shimla [not respectively], telegram, 10 May 1870, Pol. Dept. 1870, vol. 2, no. 92, comp. 8, MSA.

88. Turki bin Said to Asst Sec to Govt, 25 Rabia al-Awal 1287/ 24 June 1860, Pol. Dept. 1870, vol. 2, no. 92, comp. 8, MSA.

CHAPTER 4: HALWA AND IDENTITY IN THE WESTERN INDIAN OCEAN WORLD

1. Although he is a central character in the expansion of the Indian Ocean world, the name of Thani bin Amir is not clear in the historical record. Burton calls him Snay bin Amir al-Harisi, but I have I have followed Wilkinson's transcription of the name. John C. Wilkinson, *The Arabs and the Scramble for Africa* (Sheffield, UK: Equinox Publishing, 2014), 88. Given other examples of Burton's transcription, such as his references to known members of the Harthi clan as Harisi, this makes the most sense. Bontinck refers to him as Thenei bin Amur. François Bontinck, *L'autobiographie de Hamed ben Mohammed el-Murjebi, Tippo Tip, ca. 1840–1905* (Brussels: Académie royale des Sciences d'Outre Mer, 1974), 185n30. Halwa was a sweet delicacy.

2. Given his profession and the timing of his departure from Oman, Thani might have been one of the halwa makers who abandoned Nizwa during the crushing drought described in chapter 1.

3. M. Guillain, *Documents sur l'histoire, la géographie et le commerce de l'Afrique Orientale*, vol. I (Paris, 1856), 17, 26.

4. Ibid., 40.

5. Thaddeus Sunseri, *Wielding the Ax: State Forestry and Social Conflict in Tanzania, 1820–2000*, (Athens: Ohio University Press, 2009), 1–2.

6. Richard F. Burton, *The Lake Regions of Central Africa* (New York: Dover Publications, 1995), 69.

7. Burton, "The Lake Regions of Central Equatorial Africa," 280, 294.

8. Ibid.

9. Ibid., 181.

10. Burton, *Lake Regions of Central Africa*, 228–29.

11. The primary source for the information on Musa and his brother Sayyan is Burton, *Lake Regions of Central Africa*, 211, 423–24. Burton undoubtedly heard the story from Musa during their time together in Unyanyembe, between 1858 and 1859. John Milner Gray addresses this issue in his account, "Trading Expeditions from the Coast to Lakes Tanganyika and Victoria before 1857," *Tanganyika Notes and Records* 49 (1957): 226–46. His story serves as reference point for other authors on the subject. Were they actually biological brothers? In the earliest recording of the story (1860), Richard Burton identifies them as brothers, based on Burton's interviews with Musa. In Burton's account of his time in Zanzibar (published in 1872), Burton places quotation marks around the word brother. He also moves the date of their entry into Unyamwezi back by five years. Thus, in discussing Musa's activity, Burton wrote, "He and his 'brother' Sayyan, entered the country about 1830." This potentially revises Burton's earlier writing on their relationship and the date of the men's first interior trade venture. Richard Francis Burton, *Zanzibar: City, Island, and Coast* (London: Tinsley Brothers, 1872), vol. I, 339n11.

12. Burton, *Lake Regions of Central Africa*, 227, 229.

13. Burton, "The Lake Regions of Central Equatorial Africa," 181–2.
14. Burton, "The Lake Regions of Central Equatorial Africa," 182, 295.
15. Burton, *Lake Regions of Central Africa*, 263.
16. Burton's text has remained a vital historical source, even with the author's Victorian racism and self-aggrandizement. For more on Burton, see McDow, "Trafficking in Persianness: Richard Burton between Mimicry and Similitude in Indian Ocean and Persianate Worlds," *Comparative Studies of South Asia, Africa and the Middle East*. Vol. 30, no. 3 (2010): 491–511. Like many early ethnologists and scholars of Africa, Burton only gives indirect credit to his informants. For a later but enlightening case, see Ludger Wimmelbücker, *Mtoro bin Mwinyi Bakari: Swahili Lecturer and Author in Germany* (Dar es Salaam: Mkuki na Nyota, 2009).
17. Royal Geographical Society, "Obituary: Sir Richard Francis Burton, K. C. M. G.," Proceedings of the Royal Geographical Society and Monthly Record of Geography, December 12, 1890, 759, 760. Thani was only one of two non-Europeans mentioned in the obituary.
18. Alexander MacKay, "Muscat, Zanzibar, and Central Africa," *Church Missionary Intelligencer and Record* 14, (January 1889): 20.
19. Lewis H. Gann and Peter Duignan, *The Rulers of German Africa, 1884–1914* (Redwood City, CA: Stanford University Press, 1977), 13; Glassman, *Feasts and Riot: Revelry, Rebellion, and Popular Consciousness on the Swahili Coast, 1856–1888* (Portsmouth, NH: Heinemann, 1995), 32; and A. J. Wills, *An Introduction to the History of Central Africa*, 3rd. ed. (Oxford: Oxford University Press, 1973), 76.
20. Henry M. Stanley, *Through the Dark Continent: Or, The Sources of the Nile around the Great Lakes of Equatorial Africa, and Down the Livingstone River to the Atlantic Ocean* (New York: Harper & Brothers, 1878), 1:44.
21. Thomas Spear, "Early Swahili History Reconsidered," *International Journal of African Historical Studies* 33, no. 2 (2000): 257–90; Thomas T. Spear, "Swahili History and Society to 1900: A Classified Bibliography," *History in Africa* 27 (2000): 339–73; Randall Lee Pouwels, "A Reply to Spear on Early Swahili History," *International Journal of African Historical Studies* 34, no. 3 (2001): 639–46; Randall Lee Pouwels, "Bibliography of Primary Sources of the Pre-Nineteenth Century East African Coast," *History in Africa* 29 (2002): 393–411.
22. Monolithic rubrics can obscure more than they reveal, especially when the goal is to understand historical processes by examining how people identified themselves. Norman R. Bennett employs "Arab" for "all Muslim individuals who thought of themselves as Arabs and who participated in the political, economic, and cultural system centering on Zanzibar." Norman R. Bennett, *Arab Versus European: Diplomacy and War in Nineteenth Century East Central Africa* (New York: Africana Publishing Company, 1986), 10. This rubric depends both on knowing whether an individual professed Islam and on having a sense of an individual's self-conception. Further eliding groups, Bennett places Omani Arabs atop a hierarchy, from which flows an "Umani-directed society." He argues that many Africans—including "the Swahili-speaking populations of Zanzibar, Pemba, and the African coastlands, peoples long incorporated into the Muslim world"—shared in the beliefs of this Umani-directed society (Ibid., 5). Glassman's *Feasts and Riot* offers an obvious challenge to this, and Von Oppen provides a thorough critique of the notion of a "Muslim world." Achim von Oppen, "The Making and Unmaking of Boundaries in the Islamic World," *Die Welt des Islams* 41, no. 3

(2001). Swahili-speaking *diwans* (patricians) and townsmen in the nineteenth century took part in the political, economic, and cultural systems linked to Zanzibar, whether they stayed on the coast or traveled to the interior. Still, they struggled to differentiate themselves from the recent Omani arrivals (and recent migrants from upcountry). Beverly Brown, Bennett's student, refers to Muslims generally, with an interest in their trade and influence. The breadth of her account is useful, since she draws a contrast with African peoples living near Lake Tanganyika. See "Muslim Influence on Trade and Politics in the Lake Tanganyika Region," *African Historical Studies* 4, no. 3 (1971): 617–29. Similarly, Marcia Wright and Peter Lary use "Swahili" as an umbrella term and recognize the compromise in this, noting that this heterogeneous group includes people who could also be identified as Arab, Baluchi, Nyamwezi, or Yeke. See "Swahili Settlements in Northern Zambia and Malawi, *African Historical Studies* 4, no. 3 (1971): 547–73.

23. Harry W. Langworthy, "Swahili Influence in the Area between Lake Malawi and the Luangwa River," *African Historical Studies* 4 no. 3 (1971), 579.

24. Glassman, *Feasts and Riot*, chapter 1.

25. Jan-Georg Deutsch, "Notes on the Rise of Slavery & Social Change in Unyamwezi, c. 1860–1900," in *Slavery in the Great Lakes Region of East Africa* (Athens: Ohio University Press, 2007), 78.

26. This is one of the central arguments of Glassman, *Feasts and Riot*.

27. Glassman also makes clear that becoming Mwungwana, Mrima, or Mswahili allowed individuals to evade the control of coastal patricians. Glassman, *Feasts and Riot*, 62.

28. Edward Steere, "On East African Tribes and Languages," *Journal of the Anthropological Institute of Great Britain and Ireland* 1 (1872), cl; Edward Steere, *Collections for a Handbook of the Nyamwezi Language, as Spoken at Unyanyembe* (London: Society for Promoting Christian Knowledge, 1885).

29. Edward Alpers, *Ivory and Slaves: Changing Pattern of International Trade in East Central Africa to the Later Nineteenth Century* (Portsmouth, NH: Heinemann, 1975), 22; Alfred J. Swann, *Fighting the Slave-Hunters in Central Africa: A Record of Twenty-Six Years of Travel and Adventure Round the Great Lakes, and of the Overthrow of Tip-pu-Tib, Rumaliza and Other Great Slave-Traders*, 2nd ed. (London: Frank Cass, 1969), 58.

30. T. Dunbar Moodie and Vivienne Ndatshe, *Going for Gold: Men, Mines, and Migration, Perspectives on Southern Africa* (Berkeley: University of California Press, 1994), 134.

31. Glassman, *Feasts and Riot*, 62.

32. Burton, "The Lake Regions of Central Equatorial Africa," 192.

33. Verney Lovett Cameron, "On His Journey across Africa, from Bagamoyo to Benguela," Proceedings of the Royal Geographical Society of London, 20 no. 4 (1875): 325.

34. Verney Lovett Cameron, *Across Africa* (New York: Harper & Brothers, 1877), 71.

35. Cameron, *Across Africa*, 71–72.

36. New arrived in Zanzibar in April 1862, and his book was published in 1873. Charles New, *Life, Wanderings, and Labours in Eastern Africa. With an Account of the First Successful Ascent of the Equatorial Snow Mountain, Kilima Njaro, and Remarks Upon East African Slavery*, 3rd ed. (London: Frank Cass, 1971), 56.

37. Mervyn W. H. Beech, "Slavery on the East Coast of Africa," *Journal of the Royal African Society* 15, no. 58 (1916): 146n3.

38. Hamed bin Muhammed al-Murjebi, *Maisha ya Hamed bin Muhammed el Murjebi yaani Tippu Tip: kwa maneno yake mwenyewe*, translated by W. H. Whitely (Nairobi: East African Literature Bureau, 1966), 20, 26, 78, 94.

39. Mervyn W. H. Beech, "Slavery on the East Coast of Africa," *Journal of the Royal African Society* 15, no. 58 (1916): 146n3.

40. New, *Life, Wanderings, and Labours*, 56–57.

41. Edward Steere, A *Handbook of the Swahili Language, as Spoken at Zanzibar*, 3rd ed. revised and enlarged by A.C. Madan (London: Society for Promoting Christian Knowledge, 1884), 32, 95, 315.

42. Frederick Johnson, ed., *A Standard Swahili-English Dictionary (Founded on Madan's Swahili-English Dictionary)*, 1st ed. (Nairobi: Oxford University Press, 1999 [1939]), 323.

43. Burton, "The Lake Regions of Central Equatorial Africa," 199, 333.

44. Stephen J. Rockel, *Carriers of Culture: Labor on the Road in Nineteenth-Century East Africa* (Portsmouth, NH: Heinemann, 2006), 6.

45. D. P. Jones to London Missionary Society, 1884, as quoted in Beverly Bolser Brown, "Ujiji: The History of a Lakeside Town. c. 1800–1914" (PhD diss., Boston University, 1973), 100.

46. Burton, *Lake Regions of Central Africa*, 30–31.

47. Ibid.

48. Brown, "Ujiji," 110.

49. Popular biographies of Burton make much of this. Fawn M. Brodie, *The Devil Drives: A Life of Sir Richard Burton* (New York: Norton, 1967); Edward Rice, *Captain Sir Richard Francis Burton: The Secret Agent Who Made the Pilgrimage to Mecca Discovered the Kama Sutra, and Brought the Arabian Nights to the West* (New York: Scribner's, 1990).

50. Burton, "Lake Regions Notices," 12.

51. Richard F. Burton, "Zanzibar; and Two Months in East Africa [Part I]," *Blackwood's Edinburgh Magazine* 83, no. 508 (1858), 211.

52. Ibid., 212.

53. Ibid.

54. Burton, *Lake Regions of Central Africa*, 109.

55. Ibid. Burton used his Latin erudition to connect Roman history to Kidogo's situation. When Burton wrote of Kidogo, "*Natione magis quam ratione barbarus*" (a barbarian more by virtue of his homeland than his intelligence), he referenced the Roman historian Velleius Paterculus's account of Maroboduus, an exceptional German chieftain. Burton referenced a piece of Roman history with striking parallels to the situation that Swahili people faced in relation to the Omani state in the nineteenth century. Facing Roman encroachment, the Germanic tribes migrated to escape and establish themselves elsewhere. Like the Swahili people who moved to the interior, Maoboduus, "resolved to remove his own race far away from the Romans and to migrate to a place where, inasmuch as he had fled before the strength of more powerful arms, he might make his own [arms] all powerful." Velleius Paterculus, *Velleius Paterculus and Res Gestae Divi Augusti* (Cambridge: Harvard University Press, 1924), 272–273. I am grateful to Arden Rogow-Bales for his translation of the Burton fragment above and his reference to Velleius Paterculus's history.

56. Ramji was an assistant to Jairam Shivji, customs master in Zanzibar, and he had traded and fought on the mainland. Burton, *Lake Regions of Central Africa*, 49–50.

57. On the extensive use of debt pawns in the East African Indian Ocean world, see Jan-Georg Deutsch, "Notes on the Rise of Slavery & Social Change in Unyamwezi, c. 1860–1900," in *Slavery in the Great Lakes Region of East Africa*, eds. Henri Mèdard and Shane Doyle (Athens: Ohio University Press, 2007), 76–110; Edward A. Alpers, "Debt, Pawnshop, and Slavery in Nineteenth Century East Africa," in *Bonded Labour and Debt in the Indian Ocean World*, ed. Gwyn Campbell and Alessandro Stanziani (New York: Routledge, 2015).

58. Rigby to H. L. Anderson, Secretary to Government, Bombay, 15 July 1859, in Mrs. Charles E. B. Russell, ed. *General Rigby, Zanzibar and the Slave Trade with Journals, Dispatches, etc.* (London: Allen & Unwin, 1935), 245.

59. Burton, *Lake Regions of Central Africa*, 110.

60. John Hanning Speke, *What Led to the Discovery of the Source of the Nile?* (London: Frank Cass, 1967), 194.

61. For similar negotiations among porters, see Rockel, *Carriers of Culture*.

62. Burton, *Lake Regions of Central Africa*, 258.

63. Ibid., 221.

64. Ibid., 127.

65. Ibid., 133, 183, 201.

66. Ibid., 146.

67. Ibid., 452.

68. Ibid., 432.

69. Ibid., 226; Speke, *What Led to the Discovery*, 195.

70. Speke, *What Led to the Discovery*, 195.

71. Burton compares the Arab merchants in Unyanyembe to the British in India, stating that they "visit but do not colonize." This might come as news to some scholars of South Asia, even though at the time, Burton did not know of the mutiny in India. Burton, *Lake Regions*, 225, 229.

72. Hamed bin Muhammed al-Murjebi, *Maisha ya Hamed bin Muhummed el Murjebi yaani*, W. H. Whitely, trans. (Nairobi: East African Literature Bureau, 1966), 11.

73. Russell, *General Rigby*, 239. Incidentally, Speke's usage of "blackguard" suggests a strong distaste for the people who might be associated with the rebellion. Although it can mean simply a group of people, the sense of the word has more opprobrium. It could include menials, camp-following rabble, vagabonds, loafers, vagrant children, or, interesting in this context, "city Arabs." It could also mean the idle criminal class. See "blackguard," in *The Oxford English Dictionary*, OED Online, http://www.oed.com/view/Entry/19719?rskey=SdPQYq&result=1.

74. Heinrich Brode, *Tippoo Tib, the Story of His Career in Central Africa*, trans. H. Havelock (Chicago: Afro-Am Press, 1969), 10–11, 15.

75. V. L. Cameron, "On His Journey across Africa, from Bagamoyo to Benguela," (Proceedings of the Royal Geographical Society of London, 20, no. 4 (1875): 307.

76. Burton, *Lake Regions*, 225–26.

77. Murjebi, *Maisha*, 13.

78. Ibid., 227.

79. The Arabs who came to the attention of European missionaries and adventurers are the easiest for historians to track, but the movement of Swahili-speaking people

from the coast was at the root of more profound social transformations. See chapter 4 for more on this.

80. David Livingston, *The Last Journals of David Livingstone, in Central Africa, from 1865 to His Death: Continued by a Narrative of His Last Moments and Sufferings, Obtained from His Faithful Servants Chuma and Susi; in two volumes*, 2nd ed. Horace Waller (London: Murray, 1874), 420.

81. The distance from Tabora is not clear. Burton's map indicated that it is seventy miles west northwest. Burton claims it should take five marches over eight days. Burton and Speke used thirteen marches to travel from Tabora to Msene, but only once in this time did they travel for four hours in a day. Burton, *Lake Regions*; W. Wenban-Smith, "Diary of the 1857–1858 Expedition to the Great Lakes," *Tanganyika Notes and Records* 49 (1957), 249. R. W. Beachey inexplicably locates Msene "about 100 miles north of Tabora," in "The East African Ivory Trade in the Nineteenth Century," *Journal of African History* 8, no. 2 (1967), 272n10.

82. Burton, *Lake Regions*, 269.

83. Burton, "Lake Regions Notices," 426; Burton, *Lake Regions*, 271.

84. Burton, "The Lake Regions of Central Equatorial Africa," 188.

85. Burton, *Lake Regions*, 229.

86. Speke, *What Led to the Discovery*, 201.

87. Burton, *Lake Regions*, 269; and Roy Bridges, "Decline and Fall of Arab Power, Review of Norman Robert Bennett, Arab versus European. Diplomacy and War in Nineteenth Century East Central Africa," *Journal of African History* 28, no. 2 (1987), 313–14.

88. Burton, *Lake Regions*, 269–73.

89. Ibid., 229.

90. Ibid., 269.

91. Ibid., 272.

92. Ibid., 271.

93. Ibid., 109., Speke, *What Led to the Discovery*, 201.

94. Thomson, *To the Central African Lakes and Back*, vol. II, 91.

95. Burton *Lake Regions of Central Africa*, 262.

96. Ibid., 362–63.

97. S. B. Miles, "Across the Green Mountains of Oman," *The Geographical Journal* 18, no. 5 (1901), 468, and "Notes on the Tribes of 'Oman by Lieutenant-Colonel S. B. Miles," [1881] Reprinted in *Annals of Oman* (Cambridge: Oleander Press, 1984), 98; John Gordon Lorimer *Gazetteer of the Persian Gulf, 'Oman, and Central Arabia* (Dublin: Irish Academic Press, 1986), 2a: 296–97; Thomas, *Alarms and Excursions in Arabia* (Indianapolis: Bobbs-Merrill Co. Publishers, 1931), 153; J. C. Wilkinson, "Bayasirah and Bayadir," *Arabian Studies* 1 (1974), 76; R. B. Serjeant, "Fisher-Folk and Fish-Traps in al-Bahrain," *Bulletin of the School of Oriental and African Studies, University of London* 31 (1968), 486; Randall Lee Pouwels, *Horn and Crescent: Cultural Change and Traditional Islam on the East African Coast, 800–1900* (New York: Cambridge University Press, 1987), 118–19.

98. Andre Wink, *Al-Hind, The Making of the Indo-Islamic World* (Leiden: Brill, 1991), 69.

99. James McNabb Campbell and R. E. Enthoven, eds., *Gazetteer of the Bombay Presidency*, (Bombay: Government Central Press, 1896), 1:516n5.

100. Wilkinson, "Bayasirah and Bayadir," 80.

101. "Racial Classes in Oman: (3) Beesari," March 21, 2009, http://realityinoman.wordpress.com/2009/03/21/racial-classes-in-oman-3-beesari/.
102. S. B. Miles, "Across the Green Mountains of Oman," 468.
103. For details of south Arabian caste systems, see Bertram Thomas and Arthur Keith, *Arabia Felix: Across the Empty Quarter of Arabia* (London: Readers' Union, 1938), 12, 26.
104. S. B. Miles, "Notes on the Tribes of 'Oman," 98.
105. Lorimer, *Gazetteer of the Persian Gulf, 'Oman, and Central Arabia*, 2a: 297.
106. John Peterson, *Historical Muscat an Illustrated Guide and Gazetteer* (Leiden: Brill, 2007), 39, 42–3, 47, 62, 84, 102–3, 107–8, 110–11.
107. Lorimer, *Gazetteer of the Persian Gulf, 'Oman, and Central Arabia*, 2a: 297.
108. Wilkinson, *Water and Tribal Settlement in South-East Arabia: A Study of the Aflaj of Oman* (Oxford: Clarendon Press, 1977), 231, 251.
109. "Ameua Waarabu kadha wa kadha na Wabisar na watu wa mrima." Murjebi, *Maisha*, 20.
110. S. B. Miles, "Across the Green Mountains of Oman," 468.
111. Brode, *Tippoo Tib*, 11; Bertram Thomas, *Alarms and Excursions in Arabia*, 153
112. Thomas, *Alarms and Excursions*, 151–53.
113. Ibid., 153.
114. Pouwels, *Horn and Crescent*, 118–19.
115. Abdallah Salih Farsy, *Seyyid Said Bin Sultan: Joint Ruler of Oman and Zanzibar (1804–1856)* (New Delhi: Lancers, 1986), 52–53.
116. Book of Consular Acts, Acts 788 and 789 of 1878, AA 12/26, ZNA.
117. Some practices of freeing slaves were insincere and fraudulent. See chapter 7 for details.
118. Registered Deed 32 of 1879, 4 Rabi'a al-Thani 1296 / 12 May 1879, AM 3/2, ZNA.
119. Brode, *Tippoo Tib*, 21. In the original German, Brode wrote that the *bayasirah* were not of "reinem Rasseblut" (pure or unadulterated racial blood).
120. Ibid, xi.
121. Burton, *Lake Regions of Central Africa*, 263.
122. John Craven Wilkinson, *The Arabs and the Scramble for Africa*, 91–92.
123. Brode, *Tippoo Tib*, 21.
124. Sheriff, *Slaves, Spices and Ivory in Zanzibar: Integration of an East African Commercial Empire into the World Economy, 1770–1873* (Athens: Ohio University Press, 1987).
125. Sayf Muhammad Sulayman al-Jabri, Tabora, interview with the author, September 2001.
126. Bennett, *Arab Versus European*, 235–44.
127. The story of his death is, in fact, a tragic one. As the Arabs fled the Belgian forces, Muhammad bin Khamis realized that his teenage son Khamis was not there, so he returned to rescue him. Both father and son were killed by the Belgian forces. Interview with Sayf Muhammad Sulayman al-Jabri, Tabora, September 2001.
128. Murjebi, *Maisha*, 26–27; Sayf Muhammad Sulayman al-Jabri, interview with the author, August 14, 2002, Tabora, Tanzania.
129. See, for example, the 1886 letter introducing the bearer as an envoy of Barghash. Holmwood (for Kirk) to Sulayman b. Zuhayr al-Jabri of Uganda, 1304/1886, AA 5/11-99, ZNA.

130. Sayf Muhammad Sulayman al-Jabri, interview with the author, August 14, 2002, Tabora, Tanzania.

131. Registered deed 733 of 1885, Sulayman bin Zahir al-Jabri (from Tharia Topan), Ibrahim and Abbas walad Muhammad bin Ali al-Kasmiri agents of Sulayman bin Zahir al-Jabri (from Tharia Topan), 866 of 1886, 1304, Ibrahim and Abbas walad Muhammad bin Ali al-Kasmiri, agents of Sulayman bin Zahir al-Jabri (from Tharia Topan), 1039 of 1887, 1305; Sulayman bin Zahir al-Jabri (from Sewa Haji), 29 Dhu al-Hijja 1302 / 8 October 1885, 1080 of 1888, AA 12/20, ZNA.

132. Alexina Harrison, *A. M. Mckay: Pioneer Missionary of the Church Missionary Society to Uganda* (New York: A. C. Armstrong and Son, 1890), 423n1; B. G. Martin, *Muslim Brotherhoods in Nineteenth Century Africa* (Cambridge: Cambridge University Press, 1976), 167, 230n167. Bennett, *Arab Versus European*, 204, 206, 209. These accounts differ on the dates of Mwanga's exile. According to Martin, the correct date is 1888.

133. Murjebi, *Maisha*, 26–27.

134. This could be the sibling of another trusted servant, Farhani bin Othman, who oversaw one of the districts of Tabora. C. Velten, *Swahili Prose Texts: A Selection from the Material Collected by Carl Velten from 1893 to 1896*, ed. Lyndon Harries (Oxford: Oxford University Press, 1965), 238.

135. This account comes from a series of interviews with Sayf Muhammad Sulayman al-Jabri in Tabora, September 2001 and August 2002.

136. "Kafā'a," *The Encyclopedia of Islam*, new ed. (Leiden: Brill), 4:404. For more on *kafā'a* in the Omani and Zanzibari contexts, see Mandana Limbert, "Of Ties and Time: Sociality, Gender and Modernity in an Omani Town" (PhD diss., University of Michigan, 2002), especially chapter 6, "Gender, Race and Genealogy: Being and Becoming Bahlawi," which also includes a story of near marriage (266). I am grateful to Mandana Limbert for her stimulating discussion of these topics. See also Elke Stockreiter's book, *Islamic Law, Gender, and Social Change in Post-Abolition Zanzibar* (New York: Cambridge University Press, 2015).

137. J. C. Wilkinson, "Bayasirah and Bayadir," *Arabian Studies* 1 (1974): 86.

138. This supposition is based on the marriage patterns at the time, that her mother was not mentioned in several versions of the story told over a year apart, and my knowledge of the interviewee's own family line.

139. Sayf Muhammad Sulayman al-Jabri, Tabora, interview with the author, Tanzania, August 14, 2002.

140. See for instance the debt contracted by Salum Sa'ad Khamis Khadim from Sewa Haji, registered deed 1075 of 1888, 29 Moharram 1305, AA 12/20, ZNA; and the series of mortgages taken out by Hamdan Shwain Salmun Khadim al-Harthi, registered deeds 1096–98 of 1888, AA 12/20, ZNA.

141. G50/28-LR, 127, TNA, includes both men. Sulayman bin Sleyum is also mentioned in G50/29-LR 1907, 73–74. The fact that the Germans identified him as an Arab demonstrates how the shades of Arab identity collapsed over time.

142. Most people in Tabora have little invested in the precolonial or early colonial history of the region. Those who had some knowledge also had a link to one of the families who had been prominent. These few descendants preserve an older sense of Arab identity in the interior of East Africa. Many of those in East Africa with strong links to Oman have migrated to Muscat in the years since 1970, when the country's new ruler welcomed overseas Omanis and their descendants. Interviews with Hemed

Ali Sulayman al-Murjebi, 12, 13, 14 September 2001; Sulayman Ali Sulayman al-Murjebi, 12, 13, 14, 17 September 2001; Hashil Mohd Hashil al-Toq 17 September 2001; Nalin Patel, 18 September 2001; Sayf Muhammad Sulayman al-Jabri, 24 September 2001; Kabango Rubange, 11 August 2002; Abdullah Said Fundikira, 12 August 2002, all in Tabora, Tanzania.

CHAPTER 5: TIPPU TIP'S KIN, FROM OMAN
TO THE EASTERN CONGO

1. "Central Africa's Richest Man," *Atlanta Constitution*, September 8, 1886; "Sights at Antwerp's Fair," *New York Times*, August 5, 1894. The *Times* report took great pains to show how much less impressive the Antwerp offerings were compared to Chicago's blockbuster World's Fair the year before.

2. Moore, *Ivory: Scourge of Africa* (New York: Harper & Bros., 1931), 67. American and European writers seized on dramatic (and often contradictory) language to write about Tippu Tip because they were unable to fit him neatly into preexisting categories. Alan Moorehead said so explicitly: "Tippu Tib . . . is not a character who can be understood in Western terms, for he was a gangster of the most brutal kind with all the attributes of a scholarly and distinguished gentleman. He was tall, dark-skinned, black-bearded and very good-looking, an authoritative figure, beautifully dressed, intelligent to talk to, a pirate of considerable charm and delicacy." Moorehead, *The White Nile* (Harper Collins, 2000), 159.

3. Ḥāmid ibn Muḥammad al- Murjebi. *L'autobiographie de Hamed ben Mohammed el-Murjebi Tippo Tip (ca. 1840–1905)* ed. François Bontinck (Bruxelles, 1974); Brode, *Tippoo Tib: The Story of His Career in Central Africa*, trans. H. Havelock (Chicago: Afro-American Press, 1969); Hamed bin Muhammad al-Murjebi, *Maisha ya Hamed bin Muhammed el Murjebi yaani Tippu Tip: kwa maneno yake mwenyewe*, trans. W. H. Whitely (Nairobi: East African Literature Bureau, 1966). He was also mentioned frequently by contemporary missionaries and travelers and credited with helping them in various difficulties. See, for instance, Edward C. Hore, *Tanganyika: Eleven Years in Central Africa* (London: Edward Stanford, 1892), viii–ix.

4. See Jeremy Prestholdt, "East African Consumerism," in *Domesticating the World: African Consumerism and the Genealogies of Globalization* (Berkeley: University of California Press, 2008).

5. Lawrence Stone noted that "family history is inextricably involved in the great issue of the change from traditional to modern society. . . . There is hardly a single one of these transformations in which the family has not played a key role as agent, subject, catalyst, or transmitter of changing values and experience." See "Family History in the 1980s: Past Achievements and Future Trends," *Journal of Interdisciplinary History* 12 (1981): 82.

6. Norman Robert Bennett, *Arab Versus European: Diplomacy and War in Nineteenth-Century East Central Africa* (New York: Africana Publishing Company, 1986), 112–13.

7. Johannes Fabian, *Out of Our Minds: Reason and Madness in the Exploration of Central Africa* (Berkeley: University of California Press, 2000).

8. Walter Thaddeus Brown, "A Pre-Colonial History of Bagamoyo: Aspects of the Growth of an East African Coastal Town" (PhD diss., Boston University, 1971), 181,

seems to take this point from Emil Quaas, "Die Szuri's, Die Kuli's Und Die Sclavan in Zanzibar," *Zeitschrift Für Allgemeine Erdkunde* 9 (neue Folge) (1860): 356; James Christie, *Cholera Epidemics in East Africa from 1821 till 1872* (London: Macmillan & Co., 1876), 337.

9. R. Fox, *Kinship and Marriage: An Anthropological Perspective* (Harmondsworth: Penguin, 1967), 10.

10. Anthropologist Emily Margaretten provided invaluable insight into my formulation of this chapter. Her own work deals with fictive kinship in contemporary South Africa.

11. Pierre Bourdieu, *Outline of a Theory of Practice* (New York: Cambridge University Press, 1977), 33–34.

12. Lewis Henry Morgan to the Honorable Edwin B. Morgan, 8 January 1859, in Carter Woods, L. H. Morgan, and E. B. Morgan. "Lewis Henry Morgan To Edwin B. Morgan." *New York History* 31, No. 2 (1950), 182; Leslie A. White, "Father of American Anthropology," *The Scientific Monthly* 77, no. 6 (1953), 323; Carter A. Woods, "Some Further Notes on Lewis Henry Morgan," *American Anthropologist*, New Series, 47, no. 3 (1945), 463.

13. Thomas R. Trautmann, "Morgan, Lewis Henry," American National Biography Online, accessed 4 January 2008, http://www.anb.org/articles/14/14-00423.html.

14. B. Malinowski, "Kinship," *Man*, 30 (Feb. 1930), 19.

15. See F. Rosenthal, "Nasab." *Encyclopaedia of Islam*, ed. P. Bearman et al. (Leiden: Brill, 2008), http://www.encislam.brill.nl/subscriber/entry?entry=islam_SIM-5807.

16. For an excellent overview of work in the study of kinship, which heavily influenced my understandings, see Michael G. Peletz, "Kinship Studies in Late Twentieth-Century Anthropology," *Annual Review of Anthropology* 24 (1995): 343.

17. Bourdieu, *Outline of a Theory of Practice*, 34.

18. John Comaroff and Jean Comaroff, "On Personhood: An Anthropological Perspective from Africa," *Social Identities* 7, no. 2 (2001): 268.

19. It should be noted that *bin*, meaning "son of," is used more commonly in East Africa than the proper Arabic *ibn*, though their meanings are the same.

20. This is based on a copy of a Murjebi family tree handwritten in Arabic script. Sulayman bin Ali bin Sulayman al-Marjebi supplied this in September 2001. A copy is in the author's possession. Henceforth referenced as Murjebi Family Tree.

21. Jacqueline Sublet, "Nisba," *Encyclopaedia of Islam*, ed. P. Bearman et al. (Leiden: Brill, 2008), http://www.encislam.brill.nl/subscriber/entry?entry=islam_COM-0866.

22. Ibid.

23. Murjebi Family Tree.

24. Registered deed 261 of 1869, AM 1/1, ZNA. As a witness to his uterine brother's loan the same year, he identified himself with nisba but four names: Hamed bin Muhammad bin Juma bin Rajab. Registered deed 258 of 1869, AM 1/1, ZNA.

25. Raphael Patai, "The Structure of Endogamous Unilineal Descent Groups," *Southwestern Journal of Anthropology* 21, no. 4 (1965): 335. The material preceding the quotation explains the extent to which the author believed this: "Descent is important in the Middle East for establishing the ascribed status of an individual, for providing him with the basis of his claim to position, occupation, property, a girl's hand, economic help, armed support, social, legal, or religious functions, a seat in council, membership in larger social units, etc. In all this, and in many more respects or

purposes, a man's patrilineal descent counts for everything; his matriline counts for nothing."

26. The debate between Patai, on the one hand, and Murphy and Kasdan, on the other, in the *Southwestern Journal of Anthropology* provides insight into the way the debate over Arab kinship and descent began to shift in the second half of the twentieth century. See Robert F. Murphy and Leonard Kasdan, "Agnation and Endogamy: Some Further Considerations," *Southwestern Journal of Anthropology* 23, no. 1 (1967): 1–14, and "The Structure of Parallel Cousin Marriage," *American Anthropologist* 61, no. 1 (1959): 17–29; Patai, "The Structure of Endogamous Unilineal Descent Groups."

27. Interview with Sulayman Ali Sulayman al-Murjebi and Hemed Ali Sulayman al-Murjebi, 12, 13, and 14 September 2001, Tabora, Tanzania.

28. Murjebi Family Tree. The handwritten family tree states in Arabic, "The young man Rajab bin Muhammad bin Said al-Murjebi came from Oman in the region of Adam."

29. For more on Mbwamaji, see Rockel, *Carriers of Culture: Labor on the Road in Nineteenth-Century East Africa* (Portsmouth, NH: Heinemann, 2006), 47–48, 135.

30. Brode, *Tippoo Tib*, 7.

31. Murjebi, *Maisha*, 28–29.

32. Ibid., 20–21, 28–29.

33. Ibid., 28–29. Livingstone dealt frequently with Muhammad bin Saleh al-Nabhani, whom he referred to by his African name, Mpamari. Livingstone met him on November 21, 1867. Livingstone, *Last Journals*, 201. At one point, Livingstone had traveled with him so frequently, the he was afraid that local people had confused them. See Livingstone, *Last Journals*, 234.

34. Murjebi Family Tree. The connection with Bint Juma al-Nabhani remained cogent for several generations. In the second half of the nineteenth century, Salum bin Saleh al-Nabhani lived in Mfuto, Unyamwezi, and when Tippu Tip went there in the early 1870s he identified Salum bin Saleh as *ndugu yetu*, "our kinsman." See Murjebi, *Maisha*, 40–41.

35. Mirambo, the notorious chief who opposed the Arabs of Tabora, was the descendent of Moura, and it was he who related this story to Muhammad bin Juma, Tippu Tip's father. Ibid., 98–101.

36. Murjebi Family Tree.

37. Murjebi, *Maisha*, 12–13.

38. Moore, *Ivory: Scourge of Africa*, 11.

39. Ibid.

40. In writing about his father, Hamed bin Muhammad uses heavily Arabic-inflected Swahili to note that the people with him were *aulad ammu*, or the sons (*awlad*) of his paternal uncles (*ammu*). Murjebi, *Maisha*, 14–15.

41. Ibid.

42. William Beardall, "Exploration of the Rufiji River under the Orders of the Sultan of Zanzibar," *Proceedings of the Royal Geographical Society and Monthly Record of Geography* 3, no. 11 (1881): 653; Murjebi, *Maisha*, 9.

43. Herbert Ward, *Five Years with the Congo Cannibals*, (London: Chatto & Windus, 1891), 188.

44. Murjebi, *L'autobiographie*, 179n2; Murjebi, *Maisha*, 66–69, 72–73. Bontinck does not explain how he concluded that this Masoud al-Wardi was the father of Muhammad bin Masoud. A business document from the Zanzibar archives suggests,

instead, that Muhammad bin Masoud's full name was Muhammad bin Masoud bin Muhammad al-Wardi. (See Registered Deed 1010 of 1887, 15 Dhu al-Qa'da 1304/ 4 August 1887, AA 12/20, ZNA.) From Burton's account, it is difficult to understand how a trained Arabist could have mistaken the name; however, Masoud's age seems appropriate. Burton met Masoud bin Musallam al-Wardi in Karira on Boxing Day 1857. He described Masoud as an "old man" who was a member of the Bani Bu Ali. Burton developed a close relationship with Masoud, who undertook a dangerous errand to retrieve some of Burton's lost notebooks. Masoud had personal knowledge of a British expedition in the Omani interior in 1821. Burton, *Lake Regions of Central Africa*, 224, 267. In that year a British force under the command of Lionel Smith revenged a grave defeat. The previous year, Said bin Sultan had sought British assistance in putting down the Bani Bu Ali who he suspected of Wahhabi tendencies. The Bani Bu Ali laid waste to the attacking force of Arabs and eight hundred British Indian soldiers under British Captain Thompson. The next year, Lionel Smith's much stronger force of three thousand men landed at Sur and marched fifty miles into the interior. They defeated the Bani Bu Ali, captured the sheikh and several of the principal men, and sent them to Bombay for two years. When the men returned from India, the British gave them presents and funds to rebuild their town. When Wellsted arrived in 1835, he was received quite generously as an Englishman. The Bani Bu Ali promised him that should he return, they would build him a house like those in India. Wellsted, *Travels in Arabia* (London: Murray), 1:54–59, 84.

45. Registered deeds 893 and 894 of 1887, 16 Rabi'a al-Thani 1304/ 11 January 1887, AA 12/20, ZNA.

46. Murjebi, *Maisha*, 138–41. These included his new business partner Muhammad bin Khalfan al-Barwani, also known as Rumaliza. See Deeds 451 and 452 of 1883, AM 8/1, ZNA.

47. Registered deeds 930 of 1887, 29 Jumada al-Awal 1304 / 22 February 1887, AA 12/20, ZNA.

48. Murjebi, *Maisha*, 46–49.

49. Ward, *Five Years with the Congo Cannibals*, 174.

50. Murjebi, *Maisha*, 108–111.

51. Ibid., 96–99.

52. Jérôme Becker, *La vie en Afrique, ou, Trois ans dans l'Afrique centrale* (Paris: J. Lebègue, 1887), 2:44.

53. Murjebi, *Maisha*, 120–121.

54. Ibid., 132–133.

55. Ibid., 140–141.

56. Patai, "The Structure of Endogamous Unilineal Descent Groups," 335.

57. Whitely's English translation simply calls them uncles. The relationships become clearer in the original text because the Swahili word "mjomba" signifies maternal uncles. Murjebi, *Maisha*, 9.

58. Patai, "The Structure of Endogamous Unilineal Descent Groups," 338.

59. Murjebi, *Maisha*, 66–69, 72–73.

60. Ibid., 66–69.

61. Ward, *Five Years with the Congo Cannibals*, 183.

62. Richard Francis Burton, *Zanzibar: City, Island, and Coast* (London: Tinsley Brothers, 1872), 394. The marriage of an Arab man to his father's brother's daughter "is the most emphatic expression of patrilineal endogamy" and has been held up as the

ideal type of Arab marriage. Patai, "The Structure of Endogamous Unilineal Descent Groups," 329.

63. Tippu Tip's biographer, Heinrich Brode, notes only that a husband divorcing a wife was "a common occurrence among Arabs." Brode, *Tippoo Tib*, 8.

64. See Jonathon Glassman, "Social Rebellion and Swahili Culture: The Response to German Conquest of the Northern Mrima, 1888–1890" (PhD diss., University of Wisconsin–Madison, 1988), chapter 4.

65. Registered deeds 258, 259, and 260 of 1869, AM 1/1, ZNA.

66. Ward calls his uncles Bushir and Abdulla bin Habib his cousins, but notes their key role in protecting him and attacking those who attacked him. Ward, *Five Years with the Congo Cannibals*, 180.

67. Murjebi, *Maisha*, 22–25.

68. Ibid., 24–25.

69. Ibid., 54–55, 74–75. The others killed in the attack suggest the relative size of the caravan and its makeup. Bushir bin Habib (an Arab), ten Waungwana (coastal or interior Muslims), and fifty Wanyamwezi also died in the attack. Some others escaped and reported the losses to Hamed bin Muhammad.

70. Verney Lovett Cameron, *Across Africa* (New York: Harper & Brothers, 1877), 174–75. Bontinck suggests that this is indeed Tippu Tip's uncle, but there is no conclusive evidence. Bontinck, *L'autobiographie*, 179n3. The fact that Cameron identified others as "Arab" and "half-caste" and called Abdullah bin Habib an Mrima demonstrates the great phenotypic variety of Arab and coastal traders. Abdullah's inability to explain routes and quantify the number of marches for Cameron may suggest that he had not traveled as much as Tippu Tip.

71. Cameron, *Across Africa*, 218.

72. Murjebi, *Maisha*, 96–99, 106–107. This is almost certainly the man listed as Hamud bin Said bin Salim al-Wardi in a deed of debt from 1886, see Registered Deed 860 of 1886, 18 Dhu al-Hijja 1303 / 16 September 1886, AA 12/20, ZNA, in which Hamud bin Said bin Salim al-Wardi pledges a debt to Gopal Tukursi on. In his account, Bontinck suggests that this man, Hamed bin Said al-Wardi, may be the same Humadi bin Said who was convicted of slave trading between Mozambique and Madagascar in 1876. The convicted slaver was identified by the *nisba* al-Wardi. Besides a similar name, no other evidence seems to support this interpretation. James Frederick Elton, *Travels and Researches among the Lakes and Mountains of Eastern and Central Africa*, ed. Henry Bernard Cotterill (London: Murray, 1879), 170.

73. Burton, *Lake Regions of Central Africa*, 309; Waqf dated 7 Safar 1300 / 17 December 1882, HD 5/2, ZNA. An account of sending income from the property to Oman is found in HD 5/61, ZNA. See also Bissell, "Stone Town Database," House #561, for additional details on the property. The religious endowment attached to this house was later contested in the case Suleman bin Ahmed vs. Salem bin Abdulla al-Wardi (1910), in 1 Zanzibar Law Reports 328, which noted that the waqf had been established to defend the Wardi tribe "from any ruler who attempts to exact taxes from them." As noted in Chris Jones, "Plus ça change, plus ça reste le meme? The New Zanzibar Land Law Project," *Journal of African Law* 40, no. 1 (1996): 32n75.

74. I am grateful to Emily Margaretten for making me aware of the anthropological literature on siblingship, including her own excellent study of street youth in South Africa: *Street Life Under a Roof: Youth Homelessness in South Africa* (Urbana, IL: University of Illinois Press, 2015).

75. Other sibling partnerships included some of the first Indian Ocean merchants to reach Unyanyembe (see discussion on the Khoja brothers Musa Mzuri and Sayyan in chapter 4); governors of the Arab settlement there (Abdallah and Shaykh bin Nasib bin Shaykh al-Mutafi) and numerous traders who traveled far past Unyanyembe into the Congo Basin. Furthermore, sibling partnerships between the coast and the interior were also common. Consider for instance Said bin Salim al-Lamki, Burton's caravan leader who became the Arab governor at Unyanyembe and his brother Ali bin Salim based in Bagamoyo.

76. The prison in Zanzibar in the late nineteenth century was also known as *kumbakumba*. Katrin Bromber, ed., *The Jurisdiction of the Sultan of Zanzibar and the Subjects of Foreign Nations* (Würzburg: Ergon-Verl., 2001), 53.

77. Murjebi, *Maisha*, 16–19.

78. Brode, *Tippoo Tib*, 13; Murjebi, *L'autobiographie*, 187n140.

79. Brode, *Tippoo Tib*, 13.

80. Murjebi, *Maisha*, 16–19.

81. Ibid., 36–37, 52–53, 108–109.

82. Marcia Wright and Peter Lary, "Swahili Settlements in Northern Zambia and Malawi," *African Historical Studies* 4, no. 3 (1971): 555–56.

83. Murjebi, *Maisha*, 106–107.

84. Ibid., 98–99.

85. Registered deed 1010 of 1887, 15 Dhu al-Qaʻda 1304 / 2 August 1887, AA 12/20, ZNA.

86. Hamed bin Muhammad to Muhammad bin Masoud [al-Wardi], c. August 1888 (received in Zanzibar 21 December 1888) reprinted in Murjebi, *L'autobiographie*, 165–66. Bontinck notes that the letters were mislabeled in *Archives Africaines*, Bruxelles, A.E., 75 (211). The letter quoted here was recorded as being to both Muhammad bin Masoud and Sayf bin Hamed, but of the two letters, the first letter was only to Muhammad bin Masoud and the second letter was only to Sayf bin Hamed. The content of the letters supports this difference.

87. James S. Jameson, *The Story of the Rear Column of the Emin Pasha Relief Expedition* (New York: Negro Universities Press, 1969), 213; H. R. Fox Bourne, *On the Other Side of the Emin Pasha Relief Expedition* (London: Chatto & Windus, 1891), 25; J. R. Werner, *A Visit to Stanley's Rearguard at Major Barttelot's Camp on the Aruhwimi, with an Account of the River-Life on the Congo* (London: W. Blackwood and Sons, 1889), 252. Bourne later (mistakenly?) identifies Bwana Nzige as Tippu Tip's "brother-in-law and partner." H. R. Fox. Bourne, *Civilisation in Congoland: A Story of International Wrong-Doing* (London: P. S. King & Son, 1903), 86.

88. Jameson, *The Story of the Rear Column of the Emin Pasha Relief Expedition*, 127.

89. Werner, *A Visit to Stanley's Rearguard at Major Barttelot's Camp on the Aruhwimi*, 251. Bennett, *Arab versus European*, 115.

90. Murjebi, *Maisha*, 80–81.

91. Ibid., 80–83. From the early 1860s, British India led the world in rice exports and Bengal was its most productive region. Produce was sent into the Indian Ocean trade through the port at Calcutta. See H. J. S. Cotton "The Rice Trade in Bengal," *Calcutta Review* 58 (1874): 171–88, and "The Rice Trade of the World," *Calcutta Review* 58 (1874): 267–302. In Arabia of the 1830s, ships came directly to Jeddah from Calcutta laden with Bengali rice, sugar, and muslin. Wellsted, "Observations on the

Coast between Ras Mohammed and Jedda," *Journal of the Royal Geographical Society of London* 6 (1836): 90. Bontinck notes that two contemporary observers in East Africa (Speke and Maloney) invoked the same comparisons. Murjebi, *L'autobiographie*, 245–46n303. This suggests that "producing rice like Bengal" was something of a trope in the cosmopolitan Indian Ocean world.

92. Bennett, *Arab versus European*, 115.

93. Murjebi, *Maisha*, 90–93.

94. *Hamwambia Muhammad bin Said; Mimi ntasafiri, nawe nyuma yangu pakia watu na pembe, uende Tanganyika. Hawachia safari yeye Muhammed bin Said wa Said bin Sultan el Gheithi.* Ibid., 94–95. "I told Muhammad Said, I will travel, and you'll be behind me loading the people and ivory, then go to Tanganyika. I left him, Muhammad bin Said, and Said bin Sultan el-Gheithi behind." Whitely flattens this in his translation and thus renders Muhammad bin Said and Said bin Sultan equal, when the Swahili text places direct emphasis on Bwana Nzige.

95. Bennett, *Arab versus European*, 115; Werner, *A Visit to Stanley's Rearguard at Major Barttelot's Camp on the Aruhwimi*, 234.

96. Sidney Langford Hinde, *The Fall of the Congo Arabs* (London: Methuen & Co., 1897), 174, 180.

97. Ibid., 183–88.

98. Murjebi, *Maisha*, 39. Tippu Tip transliterates the name as Salum bin Abdullah, thought by generation, wealth, and Oman-Zanzibar connections, this is likely to be Salim bin Abdullah (b.c. 1835).

99. Brode, *Tippoo Tib*, 24.

100. Murjebi, *Maisha*, 32–33.

101. Registered Deeds 328 and 329 of 1877, 3/1, ZNA.

102. Unpublished notebook of Barwani family history and genealogy. Contains , "Shajarat L'qabīlati Al-Barawana [Al-Barwani Family Tree]." A copy is in the author's possession. Henceworth, Barwani Notebook.

103. Ali ibn Muḥsin al-Barwānī, *Conflicts and Harmony in Zanzibar: Memoirs* (Dubai: n.p., 1997). When I interviewed Ali Muhsin at his daughter's home, I did not ask him about this directly, but I did explain my research interests, and he did not make this connection. Interview, Ali Muhsin al-Barwani, 2 December 2001, Muscat, Oman.

104. Tippu Tip explained that he was in Tabora with his father just after those who fled Zanzibar in 1859 arrived. Perhaps a marriage was arranged then, when Tippu Tip's father was strong and perhaps able to offer succor to those Arab refugees. Murjebi, *Maisha*, 14–15.

105. For this pattern in the twentieth century, see Colette Le Cour Grandmaison, "Rich Cousins, Poor Cousins: Hidden Stratification among the Omani Arabs in Eastern Africa," *Africa: Journal of the International African Institute* 59, no. 2 (1989): 176–84.

106. Barwani Notebook and "Shajarat L'qabīlati Al-Barawana [Al-Barwani Family Tree]." This unpublished notebook of Barwani family history details the births and deaths of several generations beginning in earnest with Abdullah bin Salim and his brother Isa. The focus of the work is on the descendants of these two brothers who made up the core of the Awlad Baghan, or the sons of Baghan, a neighborhood in Zanzibar. The other al-Barwani family tree listed here is based on several generations of collected information and has most recently (2000) been published by Ahmed bin Muhammad bin Khalid al-Barwani as a huge poster that contains, in some case eigh-

teen generations. This work, however, includes only men. An image of the more recent (2000) Barwani family tree is reproduced in the epilogue of this book.

107. The name Nangomwa, the father of Abdullah's wife, suggests a Makonde origin. Makonde speaking people lived on the southern end of the Swahili coast near the Ruvuma River. For a Makonde chief named Nangomwa, see J. Gus Liebenow, *Colonial Rule and Political Development in Tanzania: The Case of the Makonde* (Evanston: Northwestern University Press, 1971), 92.

108. Emily Ruete, *An Arabian Princess between Two Worlds: Memoirs, Letters Home, Sequels to the Memoirs*, ed. by E. van Donzel (Leiden: Brill, 199), 154–155.

109. A Swahili text from the nineteenth century notes, *Suria . . . akapewa chumba chake kama mke.* (A concubine . . . was given her own room like a wife [would be]). See Harries, *Swahili Prose Texts: A Selection from the Material Collected by Carl Velten from 1893 to 1896* (London: Oxford University Press, 1965), 66. The English agents at Zanzibar were never particularly exercised about the status of concubines, and when the British freed the slaves in the 1890s after declaring a protectorate in Zanzibar, concubines were the last to be freed (more than a decade later). What did, however, annoy the British consul Hamerton were two white English concubines who lived with the captain and sailing master of one of Said bin Sultan's ships. Hamerton to [Bombay], 2 January 1844, AA 1/3, ZNA; Hamerton to Secretary of State for Foreign Affairs, 24 March 1845 AA 1/3, ZNA. In the latter missive, Hamerton reports that he forbid the two men from bringing the women to his house, he estimated that "as to respecting his [the Sultan's] people I do not recollect ever having even been what could be termed unkind to any of them except my having forbid . . . [them] to come themselves or bring to my house at any time or on any pretense whatever either of these women—and positively this is the only thing of an unpleasant nature that I recollect ever having taken place between me and any of the Imam's people."

110. Barwani Notebook.

111. Murjebi, *Maisha*, 114–117. Although Rumaliza's reputation in European eyes was sullied by his role in defending the Arab position in the Congo in the 1890s, the missionary Hore praised him "for hospitality, for aid in imminent peril, and frequent assistance and information." Hore, *Tanganyika*, vii–ix.

112. Barwani, "Barwani Family."

113. Murjebi, *Maisha*, 106–107.

114. Ibid. Of course Tippu Tip's account is critical of Rumaliza because of their ongoing dispute over the dissolution of their partnership.

115. Barwani, "Barwani Family." Ali bin Isa owned a very large house in Shangani, Zanzibar, and it has been suggested that he was tied to the slave trade. AA HD3/31, ZNA; CS Smith to Kirk from Kilwa Kivinje, 14 July 1884, AA 10/1, ZNA.

116. Murjebi, *Maisha*, 42–43, 106–107; Beverly Bolser Brown, "Ujiji: The History of a Lakeside Town c. 1800–1914" (PhD diss., Boston University, 1973), 119.

117. Murjebi, *Maisha*, 116–117.

118. Harrison, *A. M. McKay: Pioneer Missionary of the Church Missionary Society to Uganda* (New York: A.C. Armstrong and Son, 1904), 359. A person from Buganda was a Muganda, plural Baganda.

119. Murjebi, *Maisha*, 12–13.

120. Ibid.

121. Ibid, 14–15. He referred to the man who had been killed as "mjombawe," a maternal uncle of Karunde.

122. Ibid., 14–15.
123. Ibid.
124. Ibid.
125. Interviews with Abdullah Said Fundikira, 12 August 2002, and Hemed Ali Sulayman al-Murjebi, 12–14 September 2001, Tabora, Tanzania.
126. Cameron, *Across Africa*, 174.
127. F. Bontinck, "La Double Traversée De L'afrique Par Trios 'Arabers' De Zanzibar (1845–1860)," *Études d'Histoire Africaine* 6 (1974): 3–50.
128. Cameron, *Across Africa*, 424.
129. Swann, *Fighting Slave Hunters Hunters in Central Africa: A Record of Twenty-Six Years of Travel & Adventure Round the Great Lakes and of the Overthrow of Tip-pu-Tib, Rumaliza and Other Great Slave-Traders* (London: Frank Cass, 1969), 271.
130. Burton, *Lake Regions of Central Africa*, 184.
131. Marriage contract between Halfani bin Mangulmani and Kalapaka bin Lungumi, 21 Safar 1305 / 7 November 1887 in C. G. Büttner, *Suaheli-Schriftstücke in Arabischer Shrift*, Lehrbucher des Seminars für Oreintalische Sprachen in Berlin, vol. X, (Stuttgart and Berlin: W. Spemann 1892), 87. See also Büttner, *Anthologie aus der Suaheli-litteratur: Gedichte und Geschichten der Suaheli*. (Berlin: Felber, 1894).
132. William Tozer, Missionary Bishop, to Kirk, 3 July 1871, AA 2/8, ZNA.
133. Ibid.
134. Sarah Mirza and Margaret Strobel, eds., *Muslim Women in Mombasa, 1890–1975*, Bloomington: Indiana University Press, 43.
135. Burton, *Zanzibar*, 1:394.

CHAPTER 6: FREED SLAVES: MANUMISSION AND MOBILITY BEFORE 1873

1. Thomas Boteler, *Narrative of a Voyage of Discovery to Africa and Arabia Performed in His Majesty's Ships "Leven" and "Barracouta" from 1821 to 1826, under the Command of Capt. F. W. Owen, R. N.* (London: R. Bentley, 1835), 2:224.
2. The three most important books on the plantation economy are: Frederick Cooper, *Plantation Slavery on the East Coast of Africa* (New Haven: Yale University Press, 1977); Abdul Sheriff, *Slaves, Spices and Ivory in Zanzibar: Integration of An East African Commercial Empire Into the World Economy, 1770–1873* (Athens: Ohio University Press, 1987); and Jonathon Glassman, *Feasts and Riot: Revelry, Rebellion, and Popular Consciousness on the Swahili Coast, 1856–1888* (Portsmouth, NH: Heinemann, 1995). On freed slaves in the twentieth century, see Laura Fair, *Pastimes and Politics: Culture, Community, and Identity in Post-Abolition Urban Zanzibar, 1890–1945* (Athens: Ohio University Press, 2001), especially chapter 3.
3. Register of Freed Slaves, 1860–74, 1871–88, AA 12/3, ZNA; Released slave register, AB 71/9, ZNA; E. A. Alpers, "The Story of Swema: Female Vulnerability in Nineteenth-Century East Africa," in *Women and Slavery in Africa*, eds. Claire Robertson and Martin A. Klein (Madison: University of Wisconsin Press, 1983), 186; A. C. Madan, *Kiungani: Or, Story and History From Central Africa* (London: G. Bell & Sons, 1887).
4. Jonathon Glassman, "The Bondsman's New Clothes: The Contradictory Consciousness of Slave Resistance on the Swahili Coast," *Journal of African History* 32,

no. 2 (1991), 277, 296–97, 309; Gwyn Campbell, "Introduction: Slavery and Other Forms of Unfree Labour in the Indian Ocean World," in *The Structure of Slavery in Indian Ocean Africa and Asia*, ed. Gwyn Campbell (Portland, OR: Frank Cass, 2004), xxii.

5. Glassman, "The Bondsman's New Clothes."

6. Hamerton, "Details of Population and Extent of Slave Trade," 2 January 1844, AA 1/3, ZNA; C. S. Nicholls, *The Swahili Coast; Politics, Diplomacy and Trade on the East African Littoral, 1798–1856* (New York: Africana Pub. Corp, 1971), 207–8.

7. For more on the centrality of Europeans to the slave trade, see Sir Reginald Coupland *The Exploitation of East Africa, 1856-1890: The Slave Trade and the Scramble*, (London: Faber and Faber, 1968), 4; see also Roland Oliver, *The Missionary Factor in East Africa*, 2nd ed. (London: Longman, 1970), and *Sir Harry Johnstone and the Scramble for Africa* (New York: St. Martin's Press, 1958); Robert Nunez Lyne, *An Apostle of Empire: Being the Life of Sir Lloyd William Mathews, K.C.M.G.* (London: George Allen and Unwin, 1936). On the British and German attempts to mitigate the end of slavery, see Frederick Cooper, *From Slaves to Squatters: Plantation Labor and Agriculture in Zanzibar and Coastal Kenya, 1890–1925* (New Haven: Yale University Press, 1980); and Jan-Georg Deutsch, *Emancipation without Abolition in German East Africa, c. 1884–1914* (Athens: Ohio University Press, 2006). For more on the agency of slaves, see Glassman, "The Bondsman's New Clothes"; and Fred Morton, *The Children of Ham: Freed Slaves and Fugitive Slaves on the Kenya Coast, 1873–1907* (Boulder, CO: Westview Press, 1990).

8. Ghislaine Lydon, "Slavery, Exchange and Islamic Law: A Glimpse from the Archives of Mali and Mauritania," *African Economic History*, no. 33 (2005), 121, 142nn17–18. Lydon cites, in particular, U. Mitter, "Unconditional Manumission of Slaves in Early Islamic Law: A Hadîth Analysis," in *The Formation of Islamic Law*, ed. W. B. Hallaq (Burlington, VT: Ashgate, 2004).

9. *The Koran*, trans. by N. J. Dawood, (London: Penguin Books, 1993), 24:33. On the status of freed slaves, see Patricia Crone, *Roman, Provincial and Islamic Law: The Origins of the Islamic Patronate* (Cambridge: Cambridge University Press, 2002), especially chapter 3. For a critique of Crone's overall thesis and further insight into *walā' al-'itiq*, see Wael B. Hallaq, "The Use and Abuse of Evidence: The Question of Provincial and Roman Influences on Early Islamic Law," *Journal of the American Oriental Society*, 110, no. 1 (January–March 1990), 79–91.

10. On a single ideology, see Glassman, "The Bondsman's New Clothes," 279, which challenges the functionalist assumptions upon which the Meirs and Kopytoff thesis is built. An overview of other Islamic contexts is here: William Gervase Clarence-Smith, *Islam and the Abolition of Slavery* (New York: Oxford University Press, 2006).

11. See Nūr al-Dīn 'Abdullah bin Ḥumayd as-Sālimī, *Jawābāt al-Imām As-Sālimī*, ed. 'Abd al-Sitar Abu Ghadda (Badīya: Maktabat al-Imām Sālimī, 2010), vol. 4: 35, 76–77, 437–8, among others.

12. Registered Deed 303 of 1877, 6 Shawal 1294 / 14 October 1877, AM 3/1, ZNA.

13. Nūr al-Dīn 'Abdullah bin Ḥumayd al-Sālimī, *Jawābāt al-Imām As-Sālimī*, 4:35, 93.

14. 'Umar al-Naqar, "Arabic Materials in the Government Archives of Zanzibar," *History in Africa* 5 (1978), 379; John Hanning Speke, *Journal of the Discovery of the Source of the Nile* (Edinburgh: W. Blackwood and Sons, 1863), xxvi; W. Cope Devereux, *A Cruise in the "Gorgon": Or Eighteen Months on H. M. S. "Gorgon," Engaged*

in the Suppression of the Slave Trade on the East Coast of Africa (London: Bell and Daldy, 1869), 107.

15. Deed executed by Mubarak bin Khalfan bin Mohammed el-O'Saji, certified by Barghash bin Said, and duly witnessed on the night of 19 Rabia el Awal 1292 / 25 April 1875, Inclosure in Kirk to Darby, 62 of 1875, 27 April 1875, c. 1588, Slave Trade No. 4 (1876), Correspondence with British Representatives and Agents Abroad, and Reports from Naval Officers, relating to the Slave Trade, *Accounts and Papers of the House of Commons*, vol. 70 (1876), London.

16. Al-Naqar, "Arabic Materials," 379.

17. Humphrey J. Fisher, *Slavery in the History of Muslim Black Africa* (New York: New York University Press, 2001), 72; Reg. Deed 303/1877, 6 Shawal 1877 / 14 October 1877, AM 3/1, ZNA; Mtoro bin Mwinyi Bakari, *The Customs of the Swahili People*, trans. and ed. J. W. T Allen (Berkeley: University of California Press, 1981), 176.

18. Nūr ad-Dīn 'Abdullah bin Ḥumayd as-Sālimī, *Jawābāt al-Imām As-Sālimī*, 4:133.

19. David Livingstone, *The Last Journals of David Livingstone in Central Africa*, ed. Horace Waller (New York: Harper & Brothers, 1875), 173, 422. Note that Livingstone calls him Hamees Wodin Tagh.

20. Livingstone, *Last Journals*, 1:231–32. These hunters were valued for their skill in bringing down elephants. Magical knowledge and command of special medicines added to their power. Paul Reichard, "Das afrikanische Elfenbein und sein Handel," *Deutsche Geographische Blätter* 12 (1889), 139.

21. Mtoro, *Customs of the Swahili People*, 175; Nūr al-Dīn 'Abdullah bin Ḥumayd al-Sālimī, *Jawābāt al-Imām As-Sālimī*, 4:76.

22. "Statement of Mariam," March 6, 1846, included in Hamerton to Willoughby, 23 April 1846, FD-13/6/1846-F.C.-138, National Archives of India (NAI).

23. Devereux, *A Cruise in the "Gorgon,"* 107; Glassman, "The Bondsman's New Clothes," 304, 311.

24. Hamerton to Palmerston, 20 August 1850, AA 1/3, ZNA.

25. John C. Wilkinson, *The Imamate Tradition of Oman*, (Cambridge: Cambridge University Press, 1987); Hamerton to Palmerston, 20 August 1850, AA 1/3, ZNA.

26. For general reference on this trade, see G.S.P. Freeman-Grenville, *The French at Kilwa Island: An Episode in Eighteenth-century East African History* (Oxford : Clarendon Press, 1965); Thomas Vernet, "La première traite française à Zanzibar: le journal de bord du vaisseau l'Espérance, 1774–1775," in C. Radimilahy and N. Rajaonarimanana (eds.), *Civilisationbs des mondes insulaires* (2015): 477–521.

27. Hamerton to Palmerston, 24 September 1851, AA 1/3, ZNA.

28. Ibid. This "free" labor system was known as *rachat préalable* or "slave ransoming," and the primary literature is in French: François Renault, *Libération d'esclaves et nouvelle servitude* (Abidjan: Les Nouvelles Éditions Africaines, 1976) and Sudel Fuma, "Le servilisme à la place du concept d'engagisme pour définer le statut des travailleurs immigrés ou affranchis après l'abolition de l'esclavage en 1848," (2001) available at https://histoire974.wordpress.com/2016/01/19/le-servilisme-a-la-place-du-concept-dengagisme-pour-definir-le-statut-des-travailleurs-immigres-ou-affranchis-apres-labolition-de-lesclavage-en-1848-sudel-fuma/. I am grateful to one of Ohio University Press's anonymous reviewers for these references.

29. Nicholls, *Swahili Coast*, 197–99; Hamerton to Palmerston, 24 September 1851, AA 1/3, ZNA.

30. Hamerton to Wyville, 13 March 1851 AA 1/3, ZNA.

31. Hamerton to Aberdeen, 23 April 1846, AA 1/3, ZNA; Hamerton to Wyville, March 1851, AA 1/3. ZNA; Hamerton to Palmerston, 24 September 1851, AA 1/3, ZNA.

32. Lauren Benton, "Legal Spaces of Empire: Piracy and the Origins of Ocean Regionalism," in *Comparative Studies in Society and History* 47, no. 4 (2005), 706–13.

33. Arab opinion reported in Hamerton to Palmerston, 24 September 1851, AA 1/3, ZNA; Said bin Sultan to Clarendon [Hamerton's translation], n. d., enclosed in Hamerton to Earl of Clarendon, 13 April 1854, AA 1/3, ZNA.

34. See the examples in Khamis Salim and Abdurahman Juma, *Zanzibar Slave Memory* [Zanzibar]: [publisher not identified], 2005.

35. Mtoro, *Customs of Swahili People*, 177; Devereux, *A Cruise in the "Gorgon,"* 107–8; Reg. Deed 303/1877, 6 Shawal 1877 / 14 October 1877, AM 3/1, ZNA. Prestholdt has compared carrying writings to the amulets worn by Swahili people to protect them from harm. See Jeremy Prestholdt, *Domesticating the World: African Consumerism and the Genealogies of Globalization* (Berkeley: University of California Press, 2008), 135. For more on the comingling of Islamic and African traditions in the nineteenth-century amulets of the Swahili coast, see Mtoro, *Customs of Swahili People*, 60–62.

36. August H. Nimtz provides a good example of this from mainland Tanganyika, in which a slave freed in the nineteenth century by a prominent family was able to claim support in the 1930s, see *Islam and Politics in East Africa: the Sufi Order in Tanzania* (Minneapolis: University of Minnesota Press, 1980), 99–100. Matthew Hopper has analyzed similar claims among freed slaves in the Persian Gulf, see *Slaves of One Master: Globalization and Slavery in Arabia in the Age of Empire* (New Haven: Yale University Press, 2015).

37. Elke Stockreiter, "Tying and Untying the Knot: Kadhi's Courts and the Negotiation of Social Status in Zanzibar Town, 1900–1963" (PhD diss., School of Oriental and African Studies, 2008), 271–72; Reg. Deed 242/1877, AM 3/1, ZNA.

38. Registered deed 342 of 1877, AM 3/1, ZNA; Livingston to Kirk, 18 November 1871, ARC 4/23, ZNA.

39. Mtoro, *Customs of Swahili People*, 15; Prestholdt, *Domesticating the World*, chapter 5.

40. Reg. Deed 221/1877, 29 Dhu al-Qa'da 1263 / 7 November 1847, AM 3/1, ZNA; Sa'īd b. Alī al-Mughayrī, *Juhaynat al-Akhbār fīTa'rīkh Zinjibār*, 4th ed. (Muscat, Oman: Ministry of National Heritage and Culture, 2001), 77; Reg. Deed 237/1877, 3 Safar 1263 / 21 January 1847; Reg. Deed 241/ 1877, 22 Rajab 1262 / 15 July 1846; AM 3/1, ZNA.

41. Calvin Allen, "Seyyids, Shets, and Sultans" (PhD diss., University of Washington, 1978), 72.

42. [Waqf's information sheet], n.d., Ledger Folio 10, HD 4/34, ZNA. Although his name is properly al-Aghbari or al-Aghbri, based on the Arabic, the mosque and his pious endowments have been recorded as "Lagbri" in the English language records. Interview with caretaker of al-Aghbari mosque, Forodhani, Zanzibar, January 7, 2010; Paola Costa with Eros Baldissera, *Historic Mosques and Shrines of Oman* (Oxford: Archeopress, 2001), 222, quoting Holy Quran, Surah xxiv, 37.

43. The people who attested to be freed slaves of al-Aghbari (and the year they concluded contracts) include Maktub (1857); Rajab (1857); Fundi Warya bin Makabangi (1857); the brothers Juma bin Swedan (1869) and Amur bin Swedan (1870–71); Salim bin Barut (1870): Fatma bin Khairi (1871): and Salim bin Maktub (1871). In some cases, it is not clear whether the person listed was freed or whether his or her parent

was freed. That is, in the generic case: A the son of B freed slave of C the son of D, there is some ambiguity between [(A the son of B) freed slave of C the son of D] and [A the son of (B freed slave of C the son of D)]. The patterns of land ownership—e. g., the former slaves owning plots adjacent to each other—suggest that Said bin Muhammad or his heirs subdivided larger properties to grant smaller plots to slaves upon manumission.

44. Reg. Deed 215/1877, 15 Sha'ban 1273 / 10 April 1857, AM 3/1, ZNA; Glassman, "The Bondsman's New Clothes," 292. Some al-Barwani identified themselves as belonging to this neighborhood, calling themselves "Awlad Baghan," or the sons of Baghani. For additional information on the al-Barwani clan and their connections to Oman, see Thomas F. McDow, "Arabs and Africans: Commerce and Kinship from Oman to the East African Interior, c. 1820–1900" (PhD diss., Yale University, 2008); Joseph Barlow Felt Osgood, *Notes of Travel: Or, Recollections of Majunga, Zanzibar, Muscat, Aden, Mocha, and Other Eastern Ports* (Salem, MA: George Creamer, 1854), 28; Richard Francis Burton, *Zanzibar: City, Island, and Coast* (London: Tinsley Brothers, 1872), 1:86; Abdalla Saleh Farsi, *Seyyid Said Bin Sultan: The Joint Ruler of Oman and Zanzibar (1804–1856)* (New Delhi: Lancers Books, 1986), 49.

45. Reg. Deed 215/1877, 15 Sha'ban 1273 / 10 April 1857, AM 3/1, ZNA; Felicitas Becker, "Cosmopolitanism Beyond the Towns: Rural-Urban Relations in the History of the Southern Swahili Coast in the Twentieth Century," in *Struggling with History: Islam and Cosmopolitanism in the Western Indian Ocean*, eds., Edward Simpson and Kai Kresse (New York: Columbia University Press, 2008), 263.

46. James Christie, *Cholera Epidemics in East Africa* (London: MacMillan and Co., 1876), 303; Reg. Deed 149/1877, 6 Sha'ban 1294 / 16 August 1877, AA 12/19, ZNA.

47. Reg. Deed 276/1877, 4 Dhu al-Qa'dah 1286 / 2 May 1870, AM 3/1, ZNA; Anne K. Bang, *Sufis and Scholars of the Sea: Family Networks in East Africa, 1860–1925* (London: Routledge, 2003), 25–27; Anne Bang, "Cosmopolitanism Colonised?" in *Struggling with History: Islam and Cosmopolitanism in the Western Indian Ocean*, eds., Edward Simpson and Kai Kresse (New York: Columbia University Press, 2008), 170–71; Sugata Bose, *A Hundred Horizons: The Indian Ocean in the Age of Global Empire* (Cambridge, MA: Harvard University Press, 2006), esp. chapter 1.

48. Fair, *Pastimes and Politics*, chapter 3.

49. Farsi, *Seyyid Said Bin Sultan*, 51; Johann Ludwig Krapf, *A Dictionary of the Suahili Language* (London: Trübner and Co., 1882), 163, 328; Garth Andrew Myers, "Early History of the 'Other Side' of Zanzibar Town," in *The History and Conservation of Zanzibar*, ed. Abdul Sheriff (London: James Currey, 1995), 44n33, n36. Krapf differentiates *kiunga* (fruit trees) and *shamba* (land cultivated with grains). The words meaning "plantation close to town" changed over time, and came to mean "suburbs" or "outskirts." A. C. Madan, *English-Swahili Dictionary*, 2nd ed. (Oxford: Clarendon Press, 1902), 268, 399. Freed slaves who received property included: Salim bin Maktūb, Reg. deed 226/1877, 20 Jumada al-Awal 1288 / 9 July 1871, AM 3/1, ZNA; Fatima bint Khairi, Reg. deed 231/1877, 14 Jumada al-Akhir / 31 August 1871; Amur bin Swedan, Reg. deed 284/1877, 20 Jumada al-Awal / 9 July 1871.

50. Emily Key, "A Drive through the Island," *Central Africa: A Monthly Record of the Work of the Universities Mission* 154 (1895), 160.

51. Myers, "Early History of the 'Other Side,'" 36–38. Myers suggests that slave owners used the properties "for labor control and the reproduction of slave labor in the town." Fair, *Pastimes and Politics*, 110–18.

52. Farsi, 36–37. Said bin Sultan was wary of Sulayman's power: "His Highness fears him much but he is not at present in a situation to openly displease him in the event of its pleasing God to call the Imam," i.e., if Said were to die; Hamerton to Aberdeen, 25 October 1845, AA 1/3, ZNA; Queen Smeka of the Sackalavas to Said bin Sultan, September/October 1841, AA 12/1A, ZNA; Reg. Deed 8/1865, AM 1/1, ZNA; Reg. Deed 177/1877, AA 12/19, ZNA.

53. Hamerton to Mauritius, 4 October 1841, and Said bin Sultan to Mauritius, 9 October 1841, FO 54/5.

54. V. L. Cameron, *Across Africa* (New York: Harper & Brothers, 1877), 61, 67–73; Alexandre Le Roy, *A travers le Zanguebar: voyage dans l'Oudoé, l'Ouzigoua, l'Oukwéré et l'Ousagara* (Lyon: Bureaux des Missions catholiques, 1884), 84–85; Isaria Kimambo and A. J. Temu, eds., *A History of Tanzania* (Nairobi: East African Pub. House, 1986), 63; Norman R. Bennett, *Arab Versus European: Diplomacy and War in Nineteenth Century East Central Africa* (New York: Africana Publishing Company, 1986), 65.

CHAPTER 7: ACTS FOR CONSULS AND CONSULAR ACTS: DOCUMENTS, MANUMISSION, AND OCEAN TRAVEL AFTER 1873

1. Kirk to Bombay Government, 22 April 1873, 84/1357, FO.

2. Gavin's account of how this treaty came about and why Frere, the former governor of Bombay, led the negotiations, is admirable for its attention to politics in Muscat and Zanzibar. R. J. Gavin, "The Bartle Frere Mission to Zanzibar, 1873," *The Historical Journal* 5, no. 2 (1962): 122–48.

3. In April 1873 Seyyid Turki, ruler of Muscat, had agreed to a similar treaty but more sanguinely.

4. Sheriff, *Slaves, Spices, and Ivory in Zanzibar: Integration of an East African Commercial Empire into the World Economy, 1770–1873* (Athens: Ohio University Press, 1987), 237.

5. Historian Bhavani Raman has argued that in nineteenth-century India, a government of clerks and bureaucracy formed "a document raj." In this bureaucracy, the micropractices of writing were not just the technological basis for the modern state, but an essential ingredient of the protocol of law that underwrote that state. My formulation derives from this set of ideas. Bhavani Raman, *Document Raj: Writing and Scribes in Early Colonial South India* (Chicago: University of Chicago Press, 2012).

6. Doulton, "The Royal Navy's Anti-Slavery Campaign in the Western Indian Ocean," 26–27, 42.

7. Lt Col S.B. Miles (Muscat) to Kirk (Zanzibar), 20 June 1881, AA 2/30, ZNA, includes "Statement of Mabrook, a Slave."

8. For many examples, see the released slave lists, AB 71/9, ZNA.

9. Prideaux to HM's Prin. Sec of State for Foreign Affairs, 10 September 1874, AA 2/14, ZNA. This group of Africans became known as "Zanzibaris" in Natal and were an anomalous African group under Apartheid. In the 1960s they were classified not as Black but as "Other Asiatics." Preben Kaarsholm, "Zanzibaris or Amakhuwa? Sufi Networks in South Africa, Mozambique and the Indian Ocean," *Journal of African History* 55, no. 2: 193–94.

10. Jeremy Prestholdt, *Domesticating the World: African Consumerism and the Genealogies of Globalization* (Berkeley: University of California Press, 2008).

11. A. S. G. Jayakar, "Medical Topography of Muscat," in *Report of the Administration of the Persian Gulf Political Residency and Muscat Political Agency for the Year 1876–77* (Calcutta: Government of India, Foreign Department, 1877), 101–2. A few years earlier, a British physician had claimed, "the bulk of the population of Muscat consists of Beloochees and Africans," but his own statistics suggested an inversion of Jayakar's numbers, with Baluchis at just over a quarter of the population, and Africans at almost an eighth. His total population was 17,045, less than half of Jayakar's estimate. C. T. Peters, "Medico-Topographical Report of Muscat," *Transactions of the Medical and Physical Society of Bombay* 12 (1876): 164–65.

12. Pengelly, Muscat, to A. Kinlock Forbes, 100 of 1861, 10 December 1861, AA 12/8, ZNA.

13. C. T. Peters, "Medico-Topographical Report of Muscat," 163; Salma Samar Damluji, *The Architecture of Oman* (Reading: Garnet Publishing, 1998), 325.

14. [Released slave list], nos. 255–66, 1874/5, AB 71/9, ZNA.

15. Abdul Sheriff, *Slaves, Spices & Slavery in Zanzibar*, 234–35.

16. Elizabeth McMahon, "Trafficking and Reenslavement: The Social Vulnerability of Women and Children in Nineteenth-Century East Africa," in *Trafficking in Slavery's Wake: Law and the Experience of Women and Children*, eds. Benjamin N. Lawrance and Richard L. Roberts (Athens: Ohio University Press, 2012), 29–31.

17. Edward Steere also lists this term as a synonym for northern Arabs, the seasonal traders who came to Zanzibar, see *A Handbook of the Swahili Language as Spoken at Zanzibar* (London: Bell & Daldy, 1870), 394; Charles New, *Life, Wanderings, and Labours in Eastern Africa: With an Account of the First Successful Ascent of the Equatorial Snow Mountain, Kilima Njaro and Remarks upon East African Slavery*, 3rd ed. (London: F. Cass, 1971), 35.

18. Lt Col S.B. Miles (Muscat) to Kirk (Zanzibar), 20 June 1881, AA 2/30, ZNA; includes "Statement of Mabrook, a Slave."

19. My thinking about passports has been shaped by Mark Salter, *Rights of Passage: The Passport in International Relations* (Boulder, CO: Lynne Rienner, 2003); and John Torpey, *The Invention of the Passport: Surveillance, Citizenship and the State* (Cambridge: Cambridge University Press, 2000). Note also that the connections to contemporary trafficking also rely on working within the rules in place: Kevin Bales and Jody Sarich, "Afterword: The Paradox of Women, Children, and Slavery," in *Trafficking in Slavery's Wake: Law and the Experience of Women and Children*, eds. Benjamin N. Lawrance and Richard L. Roberts (Athens: Ohio University Press, 2012), 246–48.

20. Lindsay Doulton has written an excellent dissertation on this, see *The Royal Navy's Anti-Slavery Campaign in the Western Indian Ocean, c. 1860–1890: Race Identity, and Empire* (PhD diss., University of Hull, 2010). For accounts of the earlier period (that Doulton analyzes as well), see G. L. Sullivan, *Dhow Chasing in Zanzibar Waters and on the Eastern Coast of Africa: Narrative of Five Years' Experiences in the Suppression of the Slave Trade* (London: Sampson Low, Marston, Low & Searle, 1873); and P. H. Colomb, *Slave-catching in the Indian Ocean: A Record of Naval Experience* (London: Longmans, 1873).

21. Majid bin Said bin Sultan to Rigby, 26 July 1861, AA2/4, ZNA.

22. Calvin H. Allen, "The Indian Merchant Community of Masqat," *Bulletin of the School of Oriental and African Studies, University of London* 44, no. 1 (1981): 40–46.

23. William Wilson Hunter, et al., eds., *Imperial Gazetteer of India* (Oxford: Clarendon Press, 1909), 4:82.

24. Reda Bhacker, *Trade and Empire in Muscat and Zanzibar: Roots of British Domination* (London: Routledge, 1992), 72–74, 166–67. Bhacker's account illustrates the process of making Indians into British subjects, as this phenomenon supports his argument about the declining role of Omani commerce in the western Indian Ocean. In the years preceding his 1869 proclamation, the Rao of Kutch had written to British officials on behalf of his subjects, forwarding petitions or complaining about the treatment of Kutchis. See, for instance, ZNA AA 2/2, translated from a letter from H. H. the Rao of Kutch to the Acting Political Agent in Kutch, January 14, 1859.

25. Frere to Lord Granville, no. 4, 10 January 1873, AA 1/10, ZNA.

26. Rigby to Secretary to Bombay Government, 14 September 1860, AA 12/2, ZNA. See also Hollian Wint, "Credible Relations: Indian Finance and East African Society in the Indian Ocean, c. 1860–1940" (PhD diss., New York University, 2016) for a much more in-depth view.

27. Consular Court Cases, 5 April 1865, AA 3/11, ZNA. In this case, a Khoja man was found guilty of receiving slaves in a "mortgage" contract.

28. 233 of 1877, 14 Rajab 1261 / 19 June 1845, AM 3/1, ZNA.

29. Prideaux to Sec to the Govt of India, Calcutta, 12 September 1874, AA 2/14, ZNA.

30. Ibid.

31. Ibid.

32. Finding guides identify this file as covering the years 1859 to 1861, and it is said to include: "Outward letters including shipping returns, tables of money, weights and measures, rates of exchange." Most of the volume is comprised of Rigby's outward letters, but included in the back is a small collection of notes on civil cases, heard in the consular court between 1863 and 1867. This particular case was heard on April 30, 1867 (AA 2/4, ZNA).

33. Case of 13 May 1867, AA 2/4, ZNA.

34. Prideaux to Sec to the Govt of India, Calcutta, 12 September 1874, AA 2/14, ZNA.

35. Administrator of Soomar [Sumar] Widani vs. Abdulla bin Raschid [al-Ghaythi], Case 79 of 1878, HC 7/98, ZNA.

36. This is based on the approved Ibadi practice of *taqiyya*, which permitted adherents to dissimulate their convictions in the case of religious persecution or in situations where harm was possible. Ibadi scholarship suggested that *taqiyya* was a necessary part of religion. Jumayyil bin Khamis wrote in his *Kāmūs al-sharī'a* (published in Zanzibar in the 1880s) that "*taqiyya* is a cloak for the believer: he has no religion who has no *taqiyya*." For a summary of the principles of *taqiyya*, see R. Strothmann and Moktar Djebli, "Taḳiyya," in *Encyclopaedia of Islam*, 2nd ed., eds. P. Bearman, et al., http://dx.doi.org/10.1163/1573-3912_islam_SIM_7341.

37. Prideaux "Administrative Report of the Political Agent and Consul General at Zanzibar for the year 1873 and 1874," AA 2/15, ZNA. In each of these years, three or four suits were brought with no money claimed. The fact that this number stays steady,

while the total number tremendously increased, suggests the consistency of the measure. The years 1872 to 1874 are those for which records are most readily available.

38. Ibid. This table does not include the total fees paid to the court, which roughly tripled over these three years.

39. Ibid.

40. Ibid.

41. Salter, *Rights of Passage*, 2.

42. Here I paraphrase from and draw on the persuasive arguments of John Torpey, *The Invention of the Passport*.

43. Consular Acts 26 and 27 of 1877, 9 January 1877, AA 12/26, ZNA.

44. Hamerton (Zanzibar) to C. Wyville, C-in-C, HM ships and vessels of war, Cape Good Hope station; 13 March 1851, 1/3, ZNA.

45. See, for example, Consular Acts 174–177 for contracts between Indian men and four presumably African women. AA 12/26, ZNA.

46. Consular Acts 269–271, 21 February 1879, AA 12/26, ZNA.

47. Janet J. Ewald, "Crossers of the Sea: Slaves, Freedmen, and other Migrants in the Northwestern Indian Ocean, c. 1750–1914," *The American Historical Review* 105, no. 1 (February 2000), 76–77. See, for example, Consular Act 361 of 1879, 14 March 1879, AA 12/26, ZNA.

48. Hatim M. Amiji,"The Bohras of East Africa," *Journal of Religion in Africa*, 7, fasc. 1 (1975), 37.

49. Kazi Shahabudin to Kaye, 14 February 1870, CP 44/2314, FO. His information was based on that of a Batia trader who had lived in East Africa for seven years. Burton—ever saucy—claimed that, in the late 1850s, "no honest Hindi Moslem would take his women-folk to Zanzibar," because of the "huge attractions and enormous temptations" that African men offered. Burton, *A Plain and Literal Translation of the Arabian Nights' Entertainments: Now Entitled The Book of the Thousand Nights and a Night* (Burton Club, 1885), 1:6.

50. In late twentieth-century Gujarati, this word carried negative connotations, see Agehananda Bharati, *Asians in East Africa: Jayhind and Uhuru* (Chicago: Nelson-Hall Co., 1972). In late 2015 and early 2016, the world *chotara* was used pejoratively in Zanzibar after the disputed election of October 2015. In the political discourse, *chotara* was used to attack the opposition party, referencing their mixed-race supporters, people with Arab or Indian descent.

51. Walter Brown, "The Politics of Business: Relations between Zanzibar and Bagamoyo in the Late Nineteenth Century," *African Historical Studies* 4, no. 3 (1971), 631–43.

52. Kazi Shahabudin to Kaye, 14 February 1870. His information was based on Batia traders who had lived in east Africa for seven years.

53. Case 11 of 1880, HC 1/37, ZNA.

54. For a much more extensive treatment of this topic see Wint, "Credible Relations."

55. Pelly to Shaw Stewart, 10 July 1862, AA 12/8 Comp 16, ZNA.

56. Estate of Late Jesa Damani, 102 of 1878, AA 7/5, ZNA.

57. Estate of Sumar Widani, AA 7/5, ZNA.

58. See, for example, Fazel Isa's deals with Ambari, Mgindo, and Msafiki. Nyassa, 22 January 1879 nos. 56 and 57 for one year; 9 September 1878, no. 1109, Virji Somji and Khamis, Zanzibar, for seven months.

59. Consular Acts 549 of 1877, 27 August, 1877, AA 12/26, ZNA.
60. Consular Acts 545 of 1877, 25 August, 1877, AA 12/26, ZNA.
61. Consular Acts 1188 and 1189 of 1878, 14 October 1878, AA 12/26, ZNA. It is interesting that the consular writer affirmed the previous relationship of master and slave between Visram and the unnamed person, even though the visit was meant to affirm the signature on the certificate of freedom.
62. J. G. Lorimer, *Gazetteer of the Persian Gulf, 'Oman, and Central Arabia* (Calcutta: Superintendent of Government Printing, 1908), 2A, 741–42. This does not mean men as the generic for all people. They were enumerated in terms of fighting strength.
63. Registered deed 221 of 1877, Dated 29 Dhu al-Qa'da/ 7 November 1847, AM 3/1, ZNA. In this document, Twakkali *Sarih* Haramil bin Said al-Ghaythi sells a *shamba* at Bonde Mzinga, Zanzibar to Jairam Sewji.
64. 29 of 1866, AM 1/1, ZNA; 17 of 1866, AM 7/1, ZNA; *shamba* in Mwera 167 of 1868, AM 1/1, ZNA.
65. Emilie Ruete, *Memoirs of an Arabian Princess from Zanzibar* (Zanzibar: The Gallery Publications, 1998), 150. This passage is missing from the first English publication, and the scholarly edition conveys that plantation overseers "who mostly immigrate from Omân while quite poor, can return home with considerable wealth after some years." Ruete, *An Arabian Princess between Two Worlds: Memoirs, Letters Home, Sequels to the Memoirs: Syrian Customs and Usages*, ed. by E. van Donzel (Leiden: Brill, 1993), 357.
66. SB Miles to EC Ross, 14 January 1878, MSA Pol Dept 1878, Vol 134, Comp 89 "Muscat Affairs."
67. Abdulaziz bin Said to Miles, 8 July 1878, MSA Pol Dept 1878, Vol 134, Comp 89 "Muscat Affairs."
68. SB Miles to EC Ross, 3 September 1878, MSA Pol Dept 1878, Vol 134, Comp 89 "Muscat Affairs."
69. 574 of 1878, 30 Rajab 1295 / 30 July 1878, AM 3/1, ZNA.
70. Consular Acts 604 and 605 of 1879, 24 April 1879; and 622 and 623 of 1879, 20 April 1879.
71. Robert Codrington, "The Central Angoniland District of the British Central Africa Protectorate," *The Geographical Journal* 11, no. 5 (May 1898), 516; Henry Rowley, *The Story of the Universities' Mission to Central Africa: From Its Commencement, Under Bishop Mackenzie, to Its Withdrawal from Zambesi* (London: Saunders, Otley and Co., 1867), 26, 246; David Livingstone and Charles Livingstone, *Narrative of an Expedition to the Zambesi and Its Tributaries: And of the Discovery of the Lakes Shirwa and Nyassa, 1858–1864* (New York: Harper and Bros: 1866), 126–28; Edward Steere, "On East African Tribes and Languages," *The Journal of the Anthropological Institute of Great Britain and Ireland* 1 (1872), cxliii.
72. Steere, *Handbook of the Swahili Language*, v; Steere's normative view of language was in keeping with nineteenth-century missionary linguists.
73. Rigby to Anderson, 15 October 1858, Abdul Sheriff Card Archive: Pol. Dept., 120/1859, MSA, 131–33, 135.
74. Eugène de Froberville "Notes sur les Va-Ngindo," *Bulletin de la Société de Géographie*, 4.me Série, 3 (1852), 425–43.
75. Prideaux to HM's Princ Sec of State for FA, London, Outward Letters, 19 September 1874, AA 2/14, ZNA.

76. Sullivan, *Dhow Chasing*, 177–179; Hopper, *Slaves of One Master: Globalization and Slavery in Arabia in the Age of Empire* (Yale University Press, 2015), 167.

77. Marek Pawełczak, *The State and the Stateless: the Sultanate of Zanzibar and the East African Mainland: Politics, Economy and Society, 1837–1888* (Warsaw: Instytut Historyczny Uniwersytetu Warszawskiego, 2010), 191, quoting Steere. For a detailed discussion of the Ngindo and Nguni-speakers, see Pawełczak, *The State and the Stateless*, 164–67, et seq.

78. These scarifications and other bodily ornamentation typically appeared on Africans who had been born free and enslaved later. This concept and practice has been given more attention in the Atlantic world—where they have been used to reconstruct slave communities of origins—than the Indian Ocean. Michael Gomez, *Exchanging Our Country Marks: The Transformation of African Identities in the Colonial and Antebellum South* (Chapel Hill: University of North Carolina Press, 1998).

79. Consular Acts 604 and 605 of 1879, 24 April 1879; and 622 and 623 of 1879, 20 April 1879, AA 12/26, ZNA.

CHAPTER 8: A DHOW ON LAKE VICTORIA

1. As such this detailed analysis builds on and elaborates earlier biographical works from this period, including A.D. Roberts, "The History of Abdullah Ibn Suliman," *African Social Research*, no. 4 (1967): 241–70; Lyndon Harries, ed. and trans., *Swahili Prose Texts: A Selection from the Material Collected by Carl Velten from 1893 to 1896* (London: Oxford University Press, 1965), 235–259; and Donald Herbert Simpson, *Dark Companions: The African Contribution to the European Exploration of East Africa* (New York: Barnes & Noble Books, 1976). Simpson's work is an early contribution to excavating the stories of nonelites. Its focus on European exploration misses other activities by Africans.

2. Said bin Salim al-Lamki to Barghash, 7 Moharram 1295 / 4 January 1878, enclosed in Kirk (Zanzibar) to Earl of Derby, 10 February 1878, Slave trade. No. 1 (1879). Correspondence with British Representatives and Agents Abroad, and Reports from Naval Officers relating to Slave Trade, C.2422 (Parliamentary Papers 1879, LXVI).

3. The clan nisba is al-Ma'uli (المعولي). For Msabbah, see Registered Deeds 1279 and 1280 of 1887, ARC 3/19, ZNA. For Songoro, see Registered Deeds 8 and 199 of 1868, AM 1/1, ZNA.

4. Smith to CMS, 27 November 1877, CMI 1878, 418.

5. Charles E. Davies, *The Blood-Red Arab Flag: An Investigation Into Qasimi Piracy, 1797–1820* (Exeter University Press, 1997), 237–38.

6. Salīl ibn Razīk [Ibn Ruzayq], *History of the Imâms and Seyyids of 'Omân*, trans. George Percy Badger (London: Printed for the Hakluyt Society, 1871), 307–12.

7. Davies, *The Blood-Red Arab Flag*, 326–29; Razīk, *History of the Imâms and Seyyids*, 299.

8. Razīk, *History of the Imâms and Seyyids*, 315, 320.

9. Ibid., 335.

10. Ibid., 336–37.

11. William Harold Ingrams, "Burton Memorial Lecture: From Cana (Husn Ghorab) to Sabbatha (Shabwa): The South Arabian Incense Road," *Journal of the Royal Asiatic Society of Great Britain and Ireland* no. 2 (1945): 169, and *Arabia and the Isles*,

etc. (London: J. Murray, 1942), 30–31. An inscription on the Lamu fort names Muhammad bin Nasir al-Mauli as the first governor there, between 1812/13 and 1828/29. G.S.P Freeman-Grenville and B.G. Martin, "A Preliminary Handlist of the Arabic Inscriptions of the Eastern African Coast." *Journal of the Royal Asiatic Society of Great Britain and Ireland*, no. 2 (1973), 110.

12. Registered deed 281 of 1877 (originally dated 1264 / 1849), AM 3/1, ZNA.

13. As chapter 6 shows, many Arabs in Zanzibar freed slaves either during their lifetimes or at their deaths.

14. Waqf Commissioners for Zanzibar vs. Wallo Ramchor, Civil Case 1333 of 1907, 1, 230, ZLR. This case was important for land tenure and the place of Islamic law in colonial Zanzibar.

15. Waqf Commissioners for Zanzibar vs. Wallo Ramchor, Civil Case 1333 of 1907, 1, 230–31, ZLR.

16. HC 7/265, ZNA; Edward Steere, *A Handbook of the Swahili Language as Spoken at Zanzibar* (London: Bell & Daldy, 1870), 13, 346.

17. James Augustus Grant, *A Walk across Africa, or Domestic Scenes from my Nile Journal* (London: William Blackwood and Sons, 1864), 70–71. Toyin Falola and Paul E. Lovejoy, "Pawnship in Historical Perspective," in Falola and Lovejoy, eds., *Pawnship, Slavery, and Colonialism in Africa* (Trenton, New Jersey: Africa World Press, Inc., 2003), 2.

18. Ibid., 160.

19. Smith Diary Entry, 18 November 1877, CMI 1878; J. M. Gray, "Arabs on Lake Victoria. Some Revisions." *Uganda Journal* (1958): 76.

20. Registered deed 1279 of 1887, 5 January 1887, ARC 3/19, ZNA.

21. Grant, *A Walk across Africa*, 71.

22. Consular Court Cases, 27 July 1861, AA 3/11, ZNA; Pelly to Shaw Stewart, no. 226 re Van Der Decken, Comp 17, 28 June 1862, AA 12/8, ZNA.

23. Registered deed 1280 of 1887 included in HC 7/265, ZNA.

24. Registered deed 8 of 1866, AM 1/1, ZNA; "Lagbri and Vuga Wakf," HD5/9, ZNA.

25. Registered deed 1279 of 1887, ARC 3/19, ZNA.

26. Price based on Abdul Sheriff's table in *Slaves, Spices, and Ivory in Zanzibar: Integration of an East African Commercial Empire into the World Economy, 1770–1873* (Athens: Ohio University Press, 1987), Appendix B.

27. Ibid.

28. Mrs. Charles E. B. Russell, ed., *General Rigby, Zanzibar and the Slave Trade with Journals, Dispatches, etc.* (London: Allen & Unwin, 1935), 239. Incidentally, Speke's usage of "blackguard" suggests strong distaste for the people who may have been associated with the rebellion. Although this word can simply mean a group of people, its general sense has much more opprobrium: menials, camp-following rabble, vagabonds, loafers, vagrant children, idle criminals, or, interesting in this context, "city Arabs." See "blackguard," in *The Oxford English Dictionary*, 2nd ed. (Oxford: Oxford University Press, 1989), http://dictionary.oed.com/cgi/entry/50022974.

29. This section draws from Richard J. Reid, "Mutesa and Mirambo: Thoughts on East African Warfare and Diplomacy in the Nineteenth Century," *International Journal of African Historical Studies*, 31, no. 1 (1998): 73–89; see also Norman R. Bennett, *Mirambo of Tanzania, 1840?–1884* (New York: Oxford University Press, 1971).

30. Norman R. Bennett, *Mirambo of Tanzania, 1840?–1885* (New York: Oxford University Press, 1971), 167.
31. Reid, "Mutesa and Mirambo," 91.
32. Sheriff, *Slaves, Spices and Ivory*, 180–1.
33. Reid, "Mutesa and Mirambo," 76.
34. Speke's claim was controversial at the time, but his essential findings have borne out; Smith to CMS, 27 August 1877, CMI 1878, 158.
35. Lieutenant Shergold Smith, Diary, 22 October 1877, CMI 1878, 530.
36. Henry M. Stanley, *Through the Dark Continent* (New York: Harper, 1878), 1:149; Smith to CMS, 11 December 1877, CMI 1878, 703.
37. Smith to CMS, 27 November 1877, CMI 1878, 419; Stanley, *Through the Dark Continent*, 1:143.
38. Stanley, *Through the Dark Continent*, 1:144, 146.
39. Smith to CMS, 10 December 1877, CMI 1878, 702–3.
40. Smith to CMS, 10 December 10, 1877, CMI 1878, 703.
41. Gerald W. Hartwig, "A Cultural History of the Kerebe of Tanzania to 1895" (PhD diss., Indiana University, 1971), 164, 209–10.
42. Ibid., 192.
43. Henry M. Stanley, *Through the Dark Continent* (New York: Harper, 1878), 1:254; Eunice Chacker, "Early Arab Contacts with Ukerewe," *Tanzania Notes and Records* 68 (1968):78; for a unique view of kinship and social relations in Ukerewe, see the novel written in the local vernacular and translated to Swahili and English. Aniceti Kitereza and Gabriel Ruhumbika, *Mr. Myombekere and his wife Bugonoka, their Son Ntulanalwo and Daughter Bulihwali: The Story of an Ancient African Community* (Dar es Salaam, Tanzania: Mkuki na Nyota Publishers, 2002).
44. Wilson to CMS, 26 July 1877, CMI 1878.
45. Hartwig, "A Cultural History of the Kerebe," 205.
46. Gerald W. Hartwig, "Victoria Nyanza as Trade Route," *Journal of African History* 11, no. 4 (1970): 542.
47. Verney Lovett Cameron, *Across Africa* (New York: Harper, 1977), 1:150–1.
48. Said bin Salim al-Lemki to Bargash, 29 al-Qaeda 1288, in "Dr. Livingstone: News of His Safety," *Proceedings of the Royal Geographical Society of London* 16, no. 5 (1871–72): 386. Note that his tribal name (*nisba*) is mistakenly listed as "el Kemki" and "el Kempi."
49. Recall that Burton chided him for his obsession with genealogy and kinship. See chapter 4 for details.
50. Jonathan Ludwig Krapf, *A Dictionary of the Suahili Language* (London: Trübner and Co., 1882), 424.
51. Said bin Majid bin Said to Bargash and Shaykh bin Nasib to Barghash, both 28 al-Qaeda 1288, in "Dr. Livingstone: News of His Safety," *Proceedings of the Royal Geographical Society of London* 16, no. 5 (1871–72): 386.
52. Cameron, *Across Africa*, I:151–52.
53. Sir Reginald Coupland, *The Exploitation of East Africa, 1856–1890: The Slave Trade and the Scramble* (London: Faber and Faber, 1939), 259.
54. Elton to Principal Sec of State for Foreign Affairs, Foreign Office, London and CA Aitchison, Sec Govt of India, 24 December 1874, AA 2/14, ZNA; Cameron, *Across Africa*, I:151–52.
55. Sherrif, *Slaves, Spices and Ivory*, 194.

56. Stanley, *How I Found Livingstone* (London: Sampson Low, Marston & Co., 1895), 266, 271; AM 3/1, 241–42, ZNA.

57. Sherrif, *Slaves, Spices and Ivory*, 194; Reid, "Mutesa and Mirambo," 77–78.

58. Stanley *Through the Dark Continent*, 1:254.

59. Francis Pocock to his parents, 15 May 1875, in Henry M. Stanley, *Stanley's Despatches to the New York Herald, 1871–1872, 1874–1877*, ed. Norman R. Bennett (Boston: Boston University Press, 1970), 469.

60. Ibid., 1:114.

61. Tim Jeal, *Stanley: The Impossible Life of Africa's Greatest Explorer* (New Haven: Yale University Press, 2007), 160.

62. Stanley, 4 December 1875, *The Daily Telegraph*, November 15, 1875 in Henry M. Stanley, *Stanley's Despatches to the New York Herald, 1871–1872, 1874–1877*, ed. Norman R. Bennett (Boston: Boston University Press, 1970), 208.

63. Smith to CMS, 27 August 1877, CMI 1878, 159.

64. Stanley, *Through the Dark Continent*, 2:67.

65. Smith to Kirk 14 October 1877, in Kirk to Earl of Derby, 7 January 1878, no. 234, House of Commons, *Parliamentary Papers* 66 (1879): 169. He does offer a contradictory point six weeks later when, after meeting hostile fisherman near Mwanza, Smith explained that their enmity was caused by an ongoing dispute with Kaduma of Kagei. Smith averred that these men might have been escaped slaves from Songoro and others.

66. Tim Jeal calls him al-Barwani, see Stanley, *How I Found Livingstone*, 172.

67. Stanley, *How I Found Livingstone*, 198, 278–79.

68. Letter from Stanley, 14 April 1875, in Mtesa's Capital, Uganda, in Stanley, *Stanley's Despatches*, ed. Norman R. Bennett (Boston: Boston University Press, 1970), 225.

69. Ibid.

70. Within days of the publication of Stanley's letter in the *Telegraph* on November 15, 1875, the CMS received applications for a trip to Uganda and offers of financial support for the mission. Eight days after publication of the letter, they adopted a resolution to pursue the mission with £5,000 from an anonymous donor. Eugene Stocke, *The History of the Church Missionary Society, Its Environment, Its Men and Its Work* (London: The Church Missionary Society, 1899), 3:95–96.

71. C. T. Wilson and Robert William Felkin, *Uganda and the Egyptian Soudan* (S. Low, Marston, Searle, & Rivington, 1882) 1:85.

72. Lieutenant Shergold Smith, Diary, 22 October 1877, CMI 1878, 530.

73. Wilson and Felkin, *Uganda and the Egyptian Soudan*, I:89–90.; Chacker, "Early Arab Contacts with Ukerewe," 83.

74. CMI 1877, 755.

75. CMI 1877, 753.

76. CMI 1877, 755.

77. CMI 1877, 754.

78. "Further News from Lake Victoria," CMI 1878, 379; Chacker, "Early Arab Contacts with Ukerewe," 84.

79. "Further News from Lake Victoria," CMI 1878, 380–1.

80. Smith, Diary 15 November 1877, CMI 1878, 422.

81. Ibid., 19 November 1877, 424.

82. C. T. Wilson to CMS, 22 February 1877, CMI 1878, 151.

83. Shergold Smith to CMS, 27 August 1877, CMI 1878, 159 6 November 1877, CMI 1878, 420, and 27 November 1877, CMI 1878, 418.

84. C. T. Wilson to CMS, 22 February 1877, CMI 1878, 151; Shergold Smith to CMS, 28 August 1877, CMI 1878, 156–7; Smith to CMS, 27 November 1877, CMI 1878, 418. Although Smith considered this "true savage warfare," he speculated about the nature of "civilized warfare" in light of the Christian Russians' butchery of the Turkomens while capturing the Khiva Khanate, and the Muslim Turks who slaughtered Bulgarians in response to the April Uprising. He called these acts "civilized butchery and refined murder!"; see CMI 1878, 421.

85. Smith, 23 and 25 November 1877, CMI 1878, 426; Chacker, "Early Arab Contacts with Ukerewe," 84.

86. Chacker, "Early Arab Contacts with Ukerewe," 84.

87. Wilson and Felkin, *Uganda and the Egyptian Soudan*, 1:121; Lukonge later justified his attack by noting that Songoro had removed his sister (Songoro's wife) from the island. Lukonge also said that the missionaries refused to abandon Sangoro.

88. Said bin Salim al-Lamki to Barghash, 7 Moharram 1295 / 4 January 1878, enclosed in Kirk (Zanzibar) to Earl of Derby, 10 February 1878, Slave trade. No. 1 (1879). Correspondence with British Representatives and Agents Abroad, and Reports from Naval Officers relating to Slave Trade, C.2422 (Parliamentary Papers 1879, LXVI).

89. Gerald W. Hartwig, "Bukerebe, the Church Missionary Society, and East African Politics, 1877–1878," *African Historical Studies* 1, no. 2 (1968): 211.

90. Barghash vs Jairam Sewji, Case 141 of 1887, HC 7/265, ZNA.

91. Fahad Ahmad Bishara, "A Sea of Debt: Histories of Commerce and Obligation in the Indian Ocean, C. 1850–1940" (PhD diss., Duke University, 2012).

92. Waqf Commissioners for Zanzibar vs. Wallo Ramchor, Civil Case 1333 of 1907, ZLR 1, 230.

CHAPTER 9: "EVERYTHING IS PLEDGED TO ITS TIME": SALIH BIN ALI, DEBT, AND REBELLION IN THE OMANI INTERIOR

1. Grant to Ross, 12 May 1884, R15/6/16, 24–25, IOR; Graeme M. Bannerman, "Unity and Disunity in Oman, 1895–1920" (PhD diss., University of Wisconsin–Madison, 1976), 33.

2. Grant to Ross, 12 May 1884, 34–35, R15/6/16, IOR; Said bin M. bin S. Al-Hashimy, "Shaikh Salih Bin Ali Al-Harthy and His Social and Political Role (1250\1834–1314\1896)," *Journal of the Gulf and Arabian Peninsula Studies* 33, no. 125 (2007); Nūr al-Dīn 'Abdullāh bin Ḥumayd Al-Sālimī, Tuḥfat al-a'yn bi-sīrat ahl 'Umān, 1:104, 247–9.

3. His full name was Sālih bin 'Alī bin Nāsir bin 'Isa bin Sālih bin 'Isa bin Rāshid bin Sa'īd bin Rajab bin Rāshid bin Sālim bin Muhammad al-Sumrī al-Ḥārthī. Said bin M. bin S. Al-Hashimy, "Shaikh Salih Bin Ali Al-Harthy" (2007).

4. Paul Bonnenfant, Guillemette Bonnenfant, and Salim ibn Hamad ibn Sulayman al-Harthi, "Architecture and Social History at Mudayrib," *The Journal of Oman Studies* 3, no. 2 (1977): 108–9; Paulo M. Costa and Eros Baldissera, *Historic Mosques and Shrines of Oman* (Oxford: Archaeopress, 2001), 253–54. The mosque is now known as Masjid al-Qadim (the old mosque). In addition to this historical information, the

mihrab (the semicircular niche in a wall of a mosque that shows the direction of Mecca) also contains Islamic exhortations, freely adapted lines from an ancient poet, and a magical square for protection. Costa argues that this *mihrab* also displays a continuity of technique with mosques in the Sema'il valley, including the Aghbari mosque, which has its own connection to East African wealth as detailed in chapter 6.

5. J. R. Wellsted, *Travels in Arabia*, vol. I (London, John Murray, 1838), 98.

6. W. Christopher, "Extract from a journal kept during a partial enquiry into the present resources and state of North Eastern Africa, with Memoranda," *Transactions of the Bombay Geographical Society* 6 (1844): 38384; Hamerton to Willoughby, 20 March 1844 and 14 April 1845, AA 3/6, ZNA; E. C. Ross, *Report on the Administration of the Persian Gulf Political Residency and Muscat Political Agency for the Year 1883–84* (Calcutta: Government Printing Office, 1884), 32; J. C. Wilkinson, "al-Hārithī," in *Encyclopaedia of Islam*, 2nd ed., Brill Online, 2013. Scholars disagree on some basic facts about this fascinating man. Al-Hashimy suggests that it was Salih bin Ali's grandfather who was killed, and he puts the year at 1834 ("Shaikh Salih Bin Ali Al-Harthy," 188); Marel Pawełczak identifies Ali bin Nasir as al-Busaidi and suggests that he served intermittently until 1880; see *The State and the Stateless. The Sultanate of Zanzibar and the East African Mainland: Politics, Economy and Society, 1837–1888* (Warsaw: SOWA, 2010), 236; a different Ali bin Nasir served as governor of Mombasa in the late 1860s. See Kirk to Foreign Office, 22 May 1869, 84/1307, FO; Burton claims that Ali bin Nasir, while serving as the governor of Mombasa, inveigled Africans near the city to borrow grain during a famine, making them pledge their children as collateral. When they were unable to repay their loans, he sold the children as slaves. As Burton tells it, Ali bin Nasir was captured during the battle at Siyu. He was recognized by his captors, who tormented his sons and mutilated him before killing him. Richard F. Burton, *Zanzibar: City, Island, and Coast* (London: Tinsley Brothers, 1872), 2:100.

7. Valerie J. Hofmann, "The Articulation of Ibadi Identity in Modern Oman and Zanzibar," *The Muslim World* 94, no. 2 (April 2004): 201–16.

8. Grant to Ross, 12 May 1884, R15/6/16, 24–25, IOR.

9. Pol. Resident to Anderson, 29 June 1869, Pol. Dept. 1859, vol. 121, 325–26, 349–50 (from the private collection of Abdul Sheriff), MSA.

10. Emily Ruete, *Arabian Princess between Two Worlds: Memoirs, Letters Home, Sequels to the Memoirs: Syrian Customs and Usages*, ed. E. J. van Donzel (Leiden: Brill, 1993), 342.

11. Ruete, *Arabian Princess*, 352–53.

12. Pelly to Shaw Stewart Esq, 2 July 1862, Pol. Dept. 1862, vol. 47, no. 299, comp. 17, MSA; Rigby to Bombay, 5 October 1861, FD-23.12.1859–S.C.-II/12 (L&P&S/9/38) (from the private collection of Abdul Sheriff), NAI.

13. Mrs. Charles E. B. Russell, ed., *General Rigby, Zanzibar and the Slave Trade with Journals, Dispatches, etc.* (London: George Allen & Unwin, Limited, 1935), 239.

14. Edward A. Alpers, *East Africa and the Indian Ocean* (Princeton, NJ: Markus Wiener Publishers, 2009), 65, 67. For intricate details of the trade for a lightly later period, see Alessandra Vianello and Mohamed M Kassim, *Servants of the Sharia: The Civil Register of the Qadis' Court of Brava, 1893–1900* (Leiden; Boston: Brill, 2006).

15. Christopher, *Transactions of the Bombay Geographical Society*, VI, 385–87 (from the private collection of Abdul Sheriff).

16. Fabens to Smith, 25 October 1844, Fabens, box 3, Peabody Essex Museum.

17. Pol. Dept. 186, vol. 138, 106–14, MSA; FD-IO/1868–PolA-388-9 (from the private collection of Abdul Sheriff), NAI.

18. Valerie Hoffman, "In His (Arab) Majesty's Service: The Career of a Somali Scholar and Diplomat in Nineteenth-Century Zanzibar," in *The Global Worlds of the Swahili: Interfaces of Islam, Identity and Space in 19th and 20th-Century East Africa*, eds. Roman Loimeier and Rüdiger Seesemann (Berlin: LIT Verlag, 2006), 256. According to B. G. Martin, his teachers were two local men, Sayyid Abu Bakr al-Mihdar (linked, Martin speculates, to the Mihdar sayyids of Tarim in the Hadhramaut) and Hajj 'Alī b. 'Abd al-Rahman, and one North African, Sayyid Ahmad al-Maghribī. B. G. Martin, "Notes on Some Members of the Learned Classes of Zanzibar and East Africa in the Nineteenth Century," *African Historical Studies* 4, no. 3 (1971): 537–38.

19. Hamad bin Sulayman al-Busaidi said this, and Shaykh Abdulaziz recorded it in his autobiography. Valerie Hoffman, "In His (Arab) Majesty's Service," 256.

20. Anne Bang, *Islamic Sufi Networks in the Western Indian Ocean (c. 1880–1940): Ripples of Reform* (Leiden: Brill, 2014), 34–35; B. G. Martin, "Notes on Some Members of the Learned Classes," 538; Roman Loimeier and Rüdiger Seesemann, eds., "Amina Ameir Issa, The Legacy of Qādirī Scholars in Zanzibar," in *The Global Worlds of the Swahili: Interfaces of Islam, Identity and Space in 19th and 20th-Century East Africa* (Berlin: LIT Verlag, 2006), 343–61.

21. Muḥammad bin 'Abdallāh ibn Ḥumayyid al-Sālimī, *Nahḍat al A'yān bī-Ḥuriyyat 'Umān* (Beirut: Dar al-Jil, 1998), 68.

22. Anne Bang, *Islamic Sufi Networks*, 50.

23. B. G. Martin, "Muslim Politics and Resistance to Colonial Rule: Shaykh Uways B. Muhammad Al-Barawi and the Qadiriya Brotherhood in East Africa," *Journal of African History* 10, no. 3 (1969): 473–474.

24. Paul Bonnenfant, Guillemette Bonnenfant, and Salim ibn Hamad ibn Sulayman al-Harthi, "Architecture and Social History at Mudayrib," *Journal of Oman Studies* 3, no. 2 (1977): 107–35.

25. Ibid., 117–18; al-Hashimy, "Shaikh Salih bin Ali Al-Harthy," 191, 192, 195. The date of the marriage is based on the fact that one of their four children, Isa bin Salih, was born in January 1874. al-Sālimī, *Nahḍat al A'yān bī-Ḥuriyyat 'Umān*, 66.

26. al-Hashimy, "Shaikh Salih bin Ali Al-Harthy," 192. They had four children together but we only know the birthdates of the sons. The elder son, Abdullah, was born in 1875.

27. al-Hashimy, "Shaikh Salih bin Ali Al-Harthy," 196.

28. al-Hashimy, "Imamate Revival in Oman," 30; Valerie Hoffman, *The Essentials of Ibadi Islam* (Syracuse, NY: Syracuse University Press, 2012), 25.

29. J. B. Kelly, *Britain and the Persian Gulf, 1795–1880* (Oxford: Clarendon Press, 1968), 651.

30. Said al-Hashimy, "Imamate Revival in Oman, 1913–20," 30; Kelly, *Britain and the Persian Gulf*, 657.

31. Wellsted, *Travels in Arabia*, I: 51.

32. Pelly, Pol Res PG to Gonne, 26 October 1867, Pol. Dept. 1868, vol. 2, no. 84, MSA.

33. Ibid.

34. al-Hashimy, "Imamate Revival in Oman," 30.

35. Robert Geran Landen, *Oman since 1856: Disruptive Modernization in a Traditional Arab Society* (Princeton: Princeton University Press, 1967), 294–95.

36. Hamid ibn Muhammad Ruzayq, *History of the Imâms and Seyyids of 'Omân*, trans. G. P. Badger (London: The Hakluyt Society, 1871), 7–8.

37. Wilkinson, *Imamate Tradition*, 3–6.

38. Amal Nadim Ghazal, "Islam and Arabism in Zanzibar: The Omani Elite, the Arab World and the Making of an Identity, 1880s–1930s" (PhD diss., Department of History and Classics, University of Alberta, Edmonton, 2005), 67.

39. Acting Pol Agent, Muscat to Gonne [Bombay], 14 November 1868, Pol. Dept. 1869, vol. 156, 89–92 (from the private collection of Abdul Sheriff), MSA.

40. Acting Pol Agent, Muscat to Gonne [Bombay], 14 November 1868, Pol. Dept. 1869, vol. 156, 89–92 (from the private collection of Abdul Sheriff), MSA.

41. FD 2/1869, Pol A-50/I, NAI.

42. Said bin Ahmed bin Sayf to Turk bin Said, 5 Feb 1869, 170 of 1869, comp. 446, MSA.

43. Landen, *Oman since 1856*, 300–1.

44. [Said bin Muhammad Suliman to Shaykh Muhammad bin Abdullatif, Arab of Bombay] [names not stated in original], n. d. 1869, Pol. Dept., vol. 89, no. 4, comp. 446, MSA; Registered deed 516 of 1875, 12/19, ZNA.

45. Sir Bartle Frere gives a succinct overview of this history in his memorandum to the Indian government on 2 May 1873, Muscat Affairs 1869–1892, Muscat Precis, L/PS/20/C229, 46v, IOR.

46. Atkinson, Ag Pol Agent, Muscat to HBM Pol Agent Zanzibar, 520 of 1868, 18 November, Pol. Dept. 1868, vol. 1, no. 84, comp. 1346, MSA.

47. Abdulaziz bin Said to Barghash bin Said, n.d. [late January 1870], FO 84/1344.

48. Muhammad bin Azan to Turki bin Said, 6 January 1869; Said bin Ahmad bin Sayf to HH Turki bin Said, 173 of 1869, 30 Jan 1869; and Said bin Ahmed bin Sayf to Turki bin Said, 170 of 1869, 5 Feb 1869, Pol. Dept. 1869, vol. 4, no. 89, comp. 44, MSA.

49. Wilkinson, *Imamate Tradition*, 237.

50. Muhammad bin Sirhan et al to Turki bin Said, 1 January 1869, 168 of 1869, Pol. Dept. 1869, vol. 4, no. 89, comp. 44, MSA.

51. Turki bin Said to Right Hon the Governor of Bombay, 27 February 1869, Pol. Dept. 1869, vol. 4, no. 89, comp. 44, MSA.

52. Registered deed 1093 of 1888, 26 Rajab 1285/11 November 1868, AA 12/20, ZNA.

53. Turki bin Said to Right Hon the Governor of Bombay, 27 February 1869, Pol. Dept. 1869, vol. 4, no. 89, comp. 44, MSA.

54. Majid bin Said al Busaidi, Zanzibar, to Turki bin Said al Busaidi, 25 December 1868, 174 of 1869, MSA.

55. Said bin Ahmad bin Sayf to HH Turki bin Said, 30 January 1869, 173 of 1869, and Said bin Ahmed bin Sayf to Turki bin Said, 5 February 1869, 170 of 1869, Pol. Dept. 1869, no. 89, vol. 4, comp. 446, MSA.

56. Kirk to Gonne, 29 April 1869, Pol. Dept. 154 of 1869, 20–26, MSA.

57. Acting Pol Agent Muscat to Gonne, 14 November 1868, Pol. Dept. 156 of 1869, 89–92, MSA.

58. Kelly, *Britain and the Persian Gulf*, 705; Majid sent Rs. 20,000 via a bill of exchange through the firm of Jairam Shivji in August 1870. With his financial incentives, Majid also encouraged Turki to ally with Abdullah bin Faysal, the Wahhabi leader, to capture Suhar.

59. Govt of India [to ?]: Extract on Turki's acceptability, 17 February 1869, MSA.

60. Kelly, *Britain and the Persian Gulf*, 705–6.
61. Ibid., 706–7.
62. Hilal bin Hamed to Barghash bin Said, 28 Ramadan 1287 / 22 December 1870, 169–70, FO 84/1344.
63. Salih bin Ali to Barghash bin Said, 11 Ramadan 1287 / 5 December 1870, 167–68, FO 84/1344.
64. Said bin Khalfan al-Khalili to Barghash bin Said, 11 Ramadan 1287 / 5 December 1870, 168–69, FO 84/1344.
65. Abdulaziz bin Said to Barghash bin Said, n.d. [December 1870], 171–72, FO 84/1344.
66. Whether Sayf bin Sulayman was al-Riyami or al-Busaidi is unclear. Kelly and Salimi each offer a different name. See Said al-Hashimy, "Imamate Revival in Oman, 1913–20."
67. The bureaucratic debate over sinking this ship stayed afloat for some years, with the aggressive action becoming a divisive point over British and British Indian policy toward Muscat and in the Gulf of Oman. See Muscat Affairs 1869–1892, Muscat Precis, L/PS/20/C229, 45–58, IOR.
68. Kelly, *Britain and the Persian Gulf*, 708; Muscat Affairs 1869–1892, Muscat Precis, L/PS/20/C229, 32 and 45, IOR.
69. Ibid., 35, 44.
70. Ibid., 36R.
71. British Library, India Office Records and Private Papers, Muscat Affairs 1869–1892, L/PS/20/C229, 49v–50r, IOR.
72. Sir Bartle Frere, Memorandum to the Indian government, 2 May 1873, Muscat Affairs 1869–1892, Muscat Precis, L/PS/20/C229, 51r, IOR. For more on the Khoja split in Oman, see Allen, "Seyyids, Shets, and Sultans," 123–24, and for broader context, Teena Purohit, *The Aga Khan Case: Religion and Identity in Colonial India* (Cambridge: Harvard University Press, 2012).
73. Sir Bartle Frere gives a succinct overview of this history in his memorandum to the Indian government on 2 May 1873, Muscat Affairs 1869–1892, Muscat Precis, L/PS/20/C229, 46v, IOR.
74. Ibid., 35, 43.
75. Ibid., 47r.
76. Ibid., 46r.
77. Ibid., 47r
78. Ibid., 47r–v.
79. Ibid., 49r.
80. Ibid., 51r.
81. Muscat Affairs 1869–1892, Muscat Precis, L/PS/20/C229, 50v, IOR.
82. Ibid., 65v, 67r.
83. Ibid., 67r.
84. From 13 August 1874, Muscat Affairs 1869–1892, Muscat Precis, L/PS/20/C229, 68[?], IOR.
85. PJC Robertson Esq, Off Pol Agent and Consul Muscat, to Lt Col EC Ross, HBMs Resident PG, 6 December 1877, and Shaykh Hamed bin Said al-Harthi to Sayyid Turki [Robertson's translated purport], 4 December 1877.
86. George Rentz, *Oman and the South-eastern Shore of Arabia* (Reading, UK: Ithaca Press, 1997), 35.

87. Saleh bin Ali al-Harthi to Sayyid Turki, 7 June 1877, Pol. Dept. vol. 129, comp. 1243, MSA.

88. Robertson, HBM's Pol Agent and Consul, Muscat, to Saleh bin Ali al-Harthi, 7 June 1877, Pol. Dept. vol. 129, comp. 1243, MSA.

89. Saleh bin Ali al-Harthi to HBM's Pol Agent and Consul, Muscat [Robertson's translation], 7 June 1877, Pol. Dept. vol. 129, comp. 1243, MSA.

90. P. Robertson Esq, Officiating HBM's Pol Agent and Consul Muscat, to Lt Col Prideaux, Officiating HBM's Political Agent in the Persian Gulf, Bushire, 21 June 1877, Pol. Dept. vol. 129, comp. 1243, MSA.

91. Sayyid Turki to HBM's Political Agent and Consul, Muscat [translated purport by Robertson], 15 June 1877, Pol. Dept. vol. 129, comp. 1243, MSA.

92. Robertson to Ibrahim bin Qais and the Hinawi Sheikhs, 16 June 1877, Pol. Dept. vol. 129, comp. 1243, MSA.

93. P. Robertson Esq, Officiating HBM's Pol Agent and Consul Muscat, to Lt Col Prideaux, Officiating HBM's Political Agent in the Persian Gulf, Bushier, 21 June 1877, Pol. Dept. vol. 129, comp. 1243, MSA.

94. Ibid.

95. Lt Col SB Miles to Lt Col EC Ross, 4 January 1878, Pol. Dept. 1878, vol. 124, comp 89, MSA.

96. Memorandum by Lt Col EC Ross, HBMs Pol Agent in the Persian Gulf, 8 December 1877, Pol. Dept. 1878, vol. 124, comp. 89, MSA.

97. Lt Col SB Miles to Lt Col EC Ross, 14 January 1878, Pol. Dept. 1878, vol. 124, comp. 89, MSA.

98. Turki to Miles, 5 February 1878, Pol. Dept. 1878, vol. 124, comp. 89, MSA.

99. Miles to Ross, 8 February 1878, Pol. Dept. 1878, vol. 124, comp. 89, MSA.

100. Miles to Ross, 2 May 1878.

101. Said bin Khalfan bin Mubarak al-Hijri [Hejri] to Sayyid Turki, 8 January 1878, Pol Dept. 1878, vol. 124, comp. 89, MSA.

102. Shaykh Hussayn bin Muhammad al-Harthi and Shaylkh Hamad bin Said al-Harthi to Turki bin Said, 16 February 1878, Pol. Dept. 1878, vol. 124, comp. 89, MSA.

103. Bonnenfant et al., "Architecture and Social History at Mudayrib," 118.

104. Deed no. 324 of 1877, dated 9 Ramadan 1294/16 September 1877, AM 3/1, ZNA. Lakimidas Ladha was the son of Ladha Damji. Charles New, *Life, Wanderings, and Labours in Eastern Africa. With An Account of the First Successful Ascent of the Equatorial Snow Mountain, Kilima Njaro, and Remarks Upon East African Slavery*, 3rd ed. (London: Cass, 1971). The contract, written by Hamad bin Said bin Hamad al-Mawli, a scribe (and minor qadi) active in 1870s, does not provide clear details of the location of the property, it does mention the borrower's famous uncle.

105. Registered Deed no. 366 of 1877, dated 5 Dhu al-Qa'da 1294/10 November 1877, AM 3/1, ZNA.

106. This account is absent from Landen, *Oman since 1856*, and George Rentz, *Oman and the South-eastern Shore of Arabia*.

107. Hamad bin Said al-Harthi to Said bin Turki, 7 June 1878, Pol. Dept. 1878, vol. 134, comp. 89, MSA.

108. Miles to Ross, 12 June 1878; Shaykh Ali bin Nasir to Turki bin Said, 15 June 1878, Pol. Dept. 1878, vol. 134, comp 89, MSA.

109. Hamad bin Said al-Harthi to Turki bin Said, 21 June 1878, Pol. Dept. 1878, vol. 134, comp. 89, MSA.

110. Ali bin Nasir Hameyd and Said bin Majid bin Muhammad al-Maskeri, 24 June 1878, Pol. Dept. 1878, vol. 134, comp. 89, MSA.

111. Sheikh Ali bin Nasir to Turki bin Said, 15 June 1878; Miles to Ross, 19 June 1878, Pol. Dept. 1878, vol. 134, comp. 89, MSA.

112. Hamad bin Said al-Harthi to Turki bin Said, 21 June 1878.

113. Miles to Ross, 18 July 1878, Pol. Dept. 1878, vol. 134, comp. 89, MSA.

114. Miles to Ross, 10 July 1878.

115. Miles to Ross, 18 July 1878.

116. Faysal to Turki, 21 July 1878.

117. Nasir bin Muhammad bin Said al-Busaidi, Gov of Semail to Sayyid Said bin Muhammad [al-Busaidi, the Minister/wazir], 25 July 1878, Pol. Dept. 1878, vol. 134, comp. 89, MSA.

118. E. C. Ross, *Report on the Administration of the Persian Gulf Political Residency and Muscat Political Agency for the Year 1878–79*, 129.

119. Nasir bin Muhammad bin Said al-Busaidi, Gov of Semail, to Sayyid Said bin Muhammad [al-Busaidi, the Minister/wazir], 25 July 1878, Pol. Dept. 1878, vol. 134, comp. 89, MSA.

120. Faysal to Turki, 24 July 1878 and 7 August 1878, Pol. Dept. 1878, vol. 134, comp. 89, MSA.

121. Shaykh Ali bin Jaber to Turki bin Said, 7 August 1878, MSA, Pol. Dept. 1878, vol. 134, comp. 89, MSA.

122. Miles to Ross, 15 August 1878, Pol. Dept. 1878, vol. 134, comp. 89, MSA.

123. Wilkinson, *Water and Tribal Settlement in South-East Arabia: A Study of the Aflāj of Oman* (Oxford: Clarendon Press, 1977), 264–65; Miles to Ross, 21 August 1878, Pol. Dept. 1878, vol. 134, comp. 89, MSA.

124. Saleh bin Ali al-Harthi to Msellem bin Abeyd al-Hejri, 4 September 1878, Pol. Dept. 1878, vol. 134, comp. 89, MSA.

125. Grant to Ross, 25 October 1880, no. 348 of 1880, R15/6/13, IOR.

126. H. A. Birks, *The Life and Correspondence of Thomas Valpy French, First Bishop of Lahore* (London: John Murray, 1895), 2:44.

127. E. C. Ross, *Report on the Administration of the Persian Gulf Political Residency and Muscat Political Agency for the Year 1883–84*, 17; Landen, *Oman since 1856*, 337–38.

128. Ross, *Report on the Administration*, 1883–84, 17.

129. Ibid.; Landen, *Oman since 1856*, 336.

130. Ross, *Report on the Administration*, 1883–84, 17–18.

131. Diary entry, 13 October 1883, R/15/6/14, IOR.

132. Ross, *Report on the Administration*, 1883–84, 18.

133. Diary entry 23 November 1883, Kirk to Sec to Gov India, Foreign Dept, Calcutta, 23 November 1883, Zanzibar, no 69/1883, R15/6/14, IOR.

134. Ibid.

135. Landen, *Oman since 1856*, 361.

136. Diary entry 10 October 1883, R/15/6/14, IOR; Political Diary of Muscat Agency, 1881–1889.

137. Landen, *Oman since 1856*, 340.

138. Miles to Ross, 7 March 1878, and PJC Robertson to Ross, 12 December 1877, Pol. Dept. 1878, vol. 134, comp. 89, MSA; Grant, Admin Report of the Pol Agency Muscat for the year 1879–80; R15/6/13, IOR.

139. Diary entry 12 November 1884, Political Diary of Muscat Agency, 1881–1889, R15/6/14, IOR.

140. Diary entry 23 November 1883, Kirk to Sec to Gov India, Foreign Dept, Calcutta, 23 November 1883, Zanzibar, no 69/1883, R15/6/14, IOR.

141. Miles to Resident, Bushire (916/84), 9 January 1884, R15/6/14, IOR; Political diary entries December 22 and 25, 1883; Gift also listed as Rs. 32,000 in Muscat Affairs 1869–1892, 130r, L/PS/20/C229, IOR.

142. Several waqf funds were set up in Zanzibar at this time for the benefit of poor people living in Oman. Often these were established by wealthy men to help the poor of their tribe in Oman. HD 5/27 and HD 5/61, ZNA.

143. This was not a new ship. It had been repaired in Bombay in 1874 and Barghash had used it in 1882 to send troops to the coast north of Mombasa. Prideaux to Sec to Govt Bombay, 15 September 1874, AA 3/14, ZNA; T. H. R. Cashmore, "Sheikh Mubarak bin Rashid," in *Leadership in Eastern Africa: Six Political Biographies*, ed. N. R. Bennett (Brookline, MA: Boston University Press, 1968), 118.

144. Political diary entries for 11 July 1886 and 4 December 1886, R15/6/14, IOR.

145. Political diary 31 October 1887 and 11 November 1887, R15/6/14, IOR. The seller in this case is Said bin Salim bin Rashid al-Barwani, 340 of 1881, AM 3/2, ZNA.

146. Anne K. Bang, *Sufis and Scholars of the Sea: Family Networks in East Africa, 1860–1925* (London: Routledge, 2003); Ghazal, "Islam and Arabism in Zanzibar: The Omani Elite, the Arab World and the Making of an Identity, 1880s–1930s" (PhD diss., Department of History and Classics, University of Alberta, Edmonton, 2005).

147. Political diary 12 January 1888, R15/6/14, IOR; Landen, *Oman since 1856*, 305; Miles to Ross, 22 November 1880 (393/1880), R15/6/13, IOR; Ghazal claims that he left Oman in 1878 but does not cite a source (see "Islam and Arabism in Zanzibar," p. 55). The British archives do not support this view.

148. Registered deeds 1131 and 1116 of 1888, AA 12/20, ZNA.

149. Remember that his father died at sea and Barghash was one of the conspirators who hoped to bring the body ashore for burial. Muscat Affairs 1869–1892, Muscat Precis, 139v, L/PS/20/C229, IOR; Euan-Smith to Marquis of Salisbury, Zanzibar, 31 May 1888, no. 24, in Great Britain, Parliament, 1888, *Further Correspondence Respecting Germany and Zanzibar* (C. 5603).

150. Landen, *Oman since 1856*, 336.

151. Bonnenfant et al., "Architecture and Social History," 117–118; Bannerman, "Unity and Disunity," 38.

152. Bannerman, "Unity and Disunity," 38; Ghazal, "Islam and Arabism in Zanzibar," 73; Sa'īd bin 'Alī al- Mughayrī, *Juhaynat al-akhbār fī tārīkh Zanzibār* (Muscat, Oman: Wizārat al-Turāth al-Qawmī, 1979).

153. Bannerman's analysis of this uprising and the clear implications it had for the separatist movements of the twentieth century is excellent. I have drawn from his analysis and narrative in the section that follows. Bannerman, "Unity and Disunity," 43.

154. Bannerman, "Unity and Disunity," 44.

155. Samuel M. Zwemer, *Arabia: The Cradle of Islam: Studies in the Geography, People and Politics of the Peninsula, with An Account of Islam and Mission–work*, 2nd ed. (New York: F. H. Revell Company, 1900), 203.

156. Bannerman, "Unity and Disunity," 50–52, 59.

157. Ghazal, "Islam and Arabism in Zanzibar," 73; al-Mughayrī, *Juhaynat*, 377–78.

158. Rentz, *Oman and the South-Eastern Shore of Arabia*, 38.
159. Bannerman, "Unity and Disunity," 59–65.
160. Wilkinson, *Imamate Tradition*, 162, 238. Al-Salimi used this designation in his introduction to a collection of Ali bin Salih's writings that were arranged in 1916–17, after the death of both men, called *Ayn al-maṣāliḥ* (Damascus n.d.). Later historians used *Imam al-Muhtasib* as a title for Salih ibn Ali. Muḥammad bin ʿAbdallāh ibn Ḥumayyid al-Sālimī, *Nahḍat al Aʿyān bī-Ḥuriyyat ʿUmān* (Beirut: Dar al-Jil, 1998), 62–63.
161. J. C. Wilkinson, "al-Sālimī," *Encyclopaedia of Islam, Second Edition*, edited by P. Bearman, Th. Bianquis, C. E. Bosworth, E. van Donzel, W. P. Heinrichs, http://dx.doi.org/10.1163/1573-3912_islam_SIM_6551.

EPILOGUE

1. Priyanka Sacheti, "Sweet temptations," Gulf News, 3 May 2007, http://gulfnews.com/leisure/food/sweet-temptations-1.25094.
2. Interview with Ahmed bin Muhammad al-Harthi, December 2001.
3. J. G. Lorimer, *Gazetteer of the Persian Gulf, 'Omān, and Central Arabia*, 2 vols., (Calcutta: Superintendent of Government Printing: 1908), 2a: 743.
4. Saleh bin Sulayman bin Saleh al-Jadidi al-Shibeni [in Oman] to Abdullah bin Sallam [bin Masoud al-Shaqsi, presumably], 23 Rabia al Awal 1320 / 30 June 1902, case no. 58 of 1909, HC 5/14, ZNA.
5. Case no. 58 of 1909, HC 5/14, ZNA.
6. Robert Geran Landen, *Oman since 1856: Disruptive Modernization in a Traditional Arab Society* (Princeton: Princeton University Press, 1967), 390–91; George Rentz, *Oman and the South-Eastern Shore of Arabia* (Reading, UK: Ithaca Press, 1997), 48.
7. Paul W. Harrison arrived in Muscat in 1909 and traveled to the interior early in his stay. He noticed the impact of the trade in both places. See *Doctor in Arabia* (New York: John Day, 1940), 20–21 and 32.
8. Landen, *Oman since 1856*, 394–95; Landen bases much of his account on Gertrude Bell's 1916 report, which comprises a chapter in her book *The Arab War: Confidential Information for General Headquarters from Gertrude Bell* (London: Golden Cockerel Press, 1940), see chapter 3, "The Rebellion against the Sultan of Muscat."
9. Landen, *Oman since 1856*, 397–400.
10. Letter from June 1915, Bell, *The Arab* War, 25.
11. Marc Valeri, *Oman: Politics and Society in the Qaboos State* (New York: Columbia University Press, 2009), 33.
12. Villiers dhow journey from the gulf to East Africa in 1939 was not simply nostalgic. Dhows continued to be vital to transregional trade through the 1950s. Some passengers also took steamships. Alan Villiers, *Sons of Sinbad: An Account of Sailing with the Arabs in Their Dhows, in the Red Sea, around the Coasts of Arabia, and to Zanzibar and Tanganyika; Pearling in the Persian Gulf; and the Life of the Shipmasters, the Mariners of Kuwait* (London: Hodder & Stoughton, 1940); Erik Gilbert, *Dhows and the Colonial Economy of Zanzibar, 1860–1970* (Athens: Ohio University Press), 2004; Saʿūd ibn Aḥmad Āl Bū Saʿīdī, Patricia Groves, and Jane Jaffer, *Memoirs of an Omani Gentleman from Zanzibar* (Muscat: Hatim Al Taie, 2012).

13. Colette Le Cour Grandmaison, "Rich Cousins, Poor Cousins: Hidden Stratification among the Omani Arabs in Eastern Africa," *Africa* 59, 2 (1989), 181.

14. Colette Le Cour Grandmaison, "Rich Cousins, Poor Cousins: Hidden Stratification among the Omani Arabs in Eastern Africa," *Africa* 59, no. 2 (1989), 181–82.

15. Michael Lofchie, *Zanzibar: Background to Revolution* (Princeton: Princeton University Press, 1965), 78–79.

16. Glassman, *War of Words, War of Stones: Racial Thought and Violence in Colonial Zanzibar* (Bloomington: Indiana University Press, 2011), 194–99; Lofchie, *Background to Revolution*, 205n21.

17. Ahmad Gurnah, "Elvis in Zanzibar," in *The Limits of Globalization*, ed. Alan Scott (New York: Routledge, 1997).

18. Glassman, *War of Words*, 6–7.

19. Glassman, "Sorting out the Tribes," 405.

20. Glassman, "Sorting out the Tribes."

21. Lofchie, *Background to Revolution*, 189.

22. Calvin H. Allen and W. Lynn Rigsbee, *Oman under Qaboos: From Coup to Constitution, 1970–1996* (Portland, OR: Frank Cass, 2000), 13.

23. Ibid., 19–22.

24. Interview with Seif Mohamed Salum al-Toqi, 2001.

25. Lofchie *Background to Revolution*, 199–204.

26. Prince Philip represented the British monarchy at the handover ceremony, sharing witty asides with Jamshid before flying to Kenya for its independence ceremony. Brian Tetley, *The Story of Mohamed Amin* (Niles, IL: Master Publishing, 2013), 25.

27. Glassman points out that the estimates vary widely depending on the source and are "often shaped by the author's attitude toward the revolution. " Apologists tend to minimize the numbers, opponents inflate them. Glassman, *War of Words*, 374n1.

28. Glassman, *War of Words*, 212, 278.

29. Lofchie, *Background to Revolution*, 257.

30. Nathanial Mathews, "The Zinjibari Diaspora, 1698–2014: Citizenship, Migration and Revolution in Zanzibar, Oman and the Post-War Indian Ocean" (PhD diss., Northwestern University, 2016), 145–46.

31. Mathews, "Zinjibari Diaspora," 125–26, 137.

32. G. Thomas Burgess, Ali Sultan Issa, and Seif Sharif Hamad, *Race, Revolution, and the Struggle for Human Rights in Zanzibar: The Memoirs of Ali Sultan Issa and Seif Sharif Hamad* (Athens: Ohio University Press, 2009), 23–25.

33. Mathews, "Zinjibari Diaspora," esp. Introduction and chapter 4.

34. Nafla S. Kharusi, "The ethnic label Zinjibari: Politics and language choice implications among Swahili speakers in Oman," *Ethnicities* 12, no. 3 (June 2012), 340–43.

35. Engseng Ho, *The Graves of Tarim: Genealogy and Mobility across the Indian Ocean*. (Berkeley: University of California Press, 2006), especially part II, "Genealogical Travel," 97–194.

36. Mohammed Bakari, *The Democratisation Process in Zanzibar: A Retarded Transition* (Hamburg: GIGA, 2001), 195.

37. P. J. L. Frankl, "Obituary: Ali Muhsin Al-Barwani," *British Journal of Middle Eastern Studies* 33, no. 2 (1 November 2006).

38. Ali Muhsin Barwani, *Jifunze Kusoma Kiarabu Kwa Wiki Tatu* [Learn to Read Arabic in Three Weeks] (Dubai: n.p., 1999), http://quranitukufu.net/Jifunze/index.htm. Note that to achieve similar religious goals, Ali Muhsin translated the Quran

into Swahili. For the value of this project see P. J. L. Frankl, "Review of *Tarjama ya al-Muntakhab Katika Tafsiri ya Qur'ani Tukufu*, by Ali Muhsin al-Barwani." *British Journal of Middle Eastern Studies* 25, no. 1 (1998): 191–93.

39. Ibrahim Noor Shariff has written numerous journal articles about Swahili poetry in English; co-authored two books in English, and published a volume in Swahili on Swahili poetry. Alamin M. Mazrui and Ibrahim Noor Shariff, *The Swahili: Idiom and Identity of an African People* (Trenton: Africa World Press, 1994); Ann Joyce Biersteker and Ibrahim Noor Shariff, *Mashairi Ya Vita Vya Kuduhu: War Poetry in Kiswahili Exchanged at the Time of the Battle of Kuduhu* (East Lansing: Michigan State University Press, 1995); Ibrahim Noor Sharif, *Tungo Zetu: Msingi wa Mashairi na Tungo Nyingenezo* (Trenton: The Red Sea Press, 1988).

40. Ghassany's work has been widely circulated in Zanzibar and read by leaders of the two main political parties, though members of the Civic United Front have been more sympathetic to its view. Marie-Aude Foúeré, "Recasting Julius Nyerere in Zanzibar: The Revolution, the Union and the Enemy of the Nation." *Journal of Eastern African Studies* 8, no. 3 (2014): 484–85.

41. Ali Mazrui, "Afrabia: Africa and the Arabs in the New World Order" *Ufahamu: A Journal of African Studies* 20 no. 3 (1992): 51–62.

42. Mandana E. Limbert, *In the Time of Oil: Piety, Memory and Social Life in an Omani Town* (Stanford: Stanford University Press, 2010), 13.

43. Sidney Hinde, *The Fall of the Congo Arabs* (London: Methuen & Co., 1897), 183–88.

Bibliography

Āl Bū Saʿīdī, Saʿūd ibn Aḥmad, Patricia Groves, and Jane Jaffer. *Memoirs of an Omani Gentleman from Zanzibar*. Muscat: Hatim Al Taie, 2012.
al-Qasimi, Sultan Muhammad. *The Myth of Arab Piracy in the Gulf*. London: Croom Helm, 1986.
Allemann, Emile. "Mascate." *Le Tour du Monde* 7, no. 7e (1901).
Allen, Calvin H. "Sayyids, Shets and Sultāns: Politics and Trade in Masqat under the Āl Bū Saʿīd, 1785–1914." PhD diss., University of Washington, 1978.
———. "The State of Masqat in the Gulf and East Africa, 1785–1829." *International Journal of Middle East Studies* 14, no. 2 (1982): 117–27.
———. "The Indian Merchant Community of Masqat," *Bulletin of the School of Oriental and African Studies, University of London* 44, no. 1 (1981): 39–53.
Allen, Calvin H., and W. Lynn Rigsbee. *Oman under Qaboos: From Coup to Constitution, 1970–1996*. Portland, OR: Frank Cass, 2000.
Alpers, Edward A. "Debt, Pawnship, and Slavery in Nineteenth Century East Africa." In *Bonded Labour and Debt in the Indian Ocean World*, edited by Gwyn Campbell and Alessandro Stanziani, 31–44. New York: Routledge, 2015.
———. *East Africa and the Indian Ocean*. Princeton, NJ: Markus Wiener Publishers, 2009.
———. *Ivory and Slaves: Changing Pattern of International Trade in East Central Africa to the Later Nineteenth Century*. Portsmouth, NH: Heinemann, 1975.
———. "The Story of Swema: Female Vulnerability in Nineteenth-Century East Africa." In *Women and Slavery in Africa*, edited by Claire C. Robertson and Martin A. Klein, 185–219. Madison: University of Wisconsin Press, 1983.
Amiji, Hatim M. "Some Notes on Religious Dissent in Nineteenth-Century East Africa." *African Historical Studies* 4, no. 3 (1971): 603–16.
———. "The Bohras of East Africa," *Journal of Religion in Africa*, 7, fasc. 1 (1975): 27–61.
Anderson, J. N. D. *Islamic Law in Africa*. London: Frank Cass, 1970.
Appadurai, Arjun. "Grassroots Globalization and the Research Imagination." *Public Culture* 12, no. 1 (Winter 2000): 1–19.
Aslanian, Sebouh. *From the Indian Ocean to the Mediterranean: The Global Trade Networks of Armenian Merchants from New Julfa*. Berkeley: University of California Press, 2011.
Atkins, Keletso E. "'Kafir Time': Preindustrial Temporal Concepts and Labour Discipline in Nineteenth-Century Colonial Natal." *Journal of African History* 29, no. 2 (1988): 229–44.

Austin, Gareth, and Kaoru Sugihara. *Local Suppliers of Credit in the Third World, 1750–1960*. New York: St. Martin's Press, 1993.

Bakari, Mohammed Ali. *The Democratisation Process in Zanzibar: A Retarded Transition*. Hamburg: GIGA, 2001.

Balachandran, G. "South Asian Seafarers and Their Worlds: c. 1870–1930s." In *Seascapes: Maritime Histories, Littoral Cultures, and Transoceanic Exchanges*, edited by Jerry H. Bentley, Renate Bridenthal, and Kären Wigen, 186–202. Honolulu: University of Hawai'i Press, 2007.

Bales, Kevin, and Jody Sarich. "Afterword: The Paradox of Women, Children, and Slavery." In *Trafficking in Slavery's Wake: Law and the Experience of Women and Children*, edited by Benjamin N. Lawrance and Richard L. Roberts, 241–53. Athens: Ohio University Press, 2012.

Ballantine, Henry. *Midnight Marches through Persia*. Boston: Lee and Shepard, 1879.

Bang, Anne. "Cosmopolitanism Colonised?" In *Struggling with History: Islam and Cosmopolitanism in the Western Indian Ocean*, edited by Edward Simpson and Kai Kresse, 167–88 New York: Columbia University Press, 2008.

———. *Islamic Sufi Networks in the Western Indian Ocean (c. 1880–1940): Ripples of Reform* Leiden, Boston: Brill, 2014.

———. *Sufis and Scholars of the Sea: Family Networks in East Africa, 1860–1925*. London: Routledge, 2003.

———. "Sufis and Scholars of the Sea: The Sufi Family Networks of Ahmad Ibn Sumayt and the Tariqa Alawiyya in East Africa c. 1850–1925." PhD diss., University of Bergen, 2000.

Bankoff, Greg, and Joseph Christensen, eds. *Natural Hazards and Peoples in the Indian Ocean World*. New York: Palgrave Macmillan, 2016.

Bannerman, M. Graeme. "Unity and Disunity in Oman, 1895–1920." PhD diss., University of Wisconsin–Madison, 1976.

Barwani, Ali ibn Muḥsin al-. *Conflicts and Harmony in Zanzibar: Memoirs*. Dubai, n.p. 1997.

———. *Jifunze Kusoma Kiarabu Kwa Wiki Tatu* [Learn to Read Arabic in Three Weeks]. Dubai: n.p., 1999.

Bayly, C. A., Sven Beckert, Matthew Connelly, Isabel Hofmeyr, Wendy Kozol, and Patricia Seed. "AHR Conversation: On Transnational History." *American Historical Review* 111, no. 5 (December 2006): 1441–64.

Beachey, R. W. "The East African Ivory Trade in the Nineteenth Century." *Journal of African History* 8, no. 2 (1967).

Beardall, William. "Exploration of the Rufiji River under the Orders of the Sultan of Zanzibar." *Proceedings of the Royal Geographical Society and Monthly Record of Geography* 3, no. 11 (1881): 641–56.

Bearman, P., Th. Bianquis, C. E. Bosworth, E. van Donzel and W. P. Heinrichs, eds. *Encyclopaedia of Islam*. Leiden: Brill, 2007.

Becker, Felicitas. "Cosmopolitanism beyond the Towns: Rural-Urban Relations in the History of the Southern Swahili Coast in the Twentieth Century." In *Struggling with History: Islam and Cosmopolitanism in the Western Indian Ocean*, edited by Edward Simpson and Kai Kresse. New York: Columbia University Press, 2008.

Becker, Jérôme. *La vie en Afrique, ou, Trois ans dans l'Afrique centrale*. 2 vols. Paris: J. Lebègue, 1887.

Beech, Mervyn W. H. "Slavery on the East Coast of Africa." *Journal of the Royal African Society* 15, no. 58 (1916): 145–49.
Bell, Gertrude. *The Arab War: Confidential Information for General Headquarters from Gertrude Bell*. London: Golden Cockerel Press, 1940.
Bennett, Norman R. "The Arab Power of Tanganyika in the Nineteenth Century." PhD diss., Boston University, 1961.
———, ed. *Leadership in Eastern Africa; Six Political Biographies*. Brookline, MA: Boston University Press, 1968.
———. *Mirambo of Tanzania, 1840?–1884*. New York: Oxford University Press, 1971.
———. *Arab versus European: Diplomacy and War in Nineteenth-Century East Central Africa*. New York: Africana Publishing Company, 1986.
Bennett, Norman Robert, and George E. Brooks. *New England Merchants in Africa: A History through Documents, 1802 to 1865*. Brookline, MA: Boston University Press, 1965.
Benton, Lauren. "Legal Spaces of Empire: Piracy and the Origins of Ocean Regionalism." *Comparative Studies in Society and History* 47, no. 4 (2005): 700–24.
Bhacker, M. Reda. *Trade and Empire in Muscat and Zanzibar: Roots of British Domination*. New York: Routledge, 1992.
Bharati, Agehananda. *The Asians in East Africa; Jayhind and Uhuru*. Chicago: Nelson-Hall Co., 1972.
Biersteker, Ann Joyce, and Ibrahim Noor Shariff. *Mashairi Ya Vita Vya Kuduhu: War Poetry in Kiswahili Exchanged at the Time of the Battle of Kuduhu*. East Lansing: Michigan State University Press, 1995.
Binning, Robert Blair Munro. *A Journal of Two Years' Travel in Persia, Ceylon, etc.* London: Wm. H. Allen and Co., 1857.
Birks, H. A. *The Life and Correspondence of Thomas Valpy French, First Bishop of Lahore*. Vol. 2. London: J. Murray, 1895.
Birks, J. S. "The Reaction of Rural Populations to Drought: A Case Study from South East Arabia." *Erdkunde* 31, no. 4 (1977): 299–305.
Bishara, Fahad Ahmad. "A Sea of Debt: Histories of Commerce and Obligation in the Indian Ocean, c. 1850–1940." PhD diss., Duke University, 2012.
———. "Paper Routes: Inscribing Islamic Law across the Nineteenth-Century Western Indian Ocean." *Law and History Review* 32, no. 4 (2014): 797–820.
Bissell, William C. Municipal Assessment Files Database [Zanzibar]. Unpublished. 1995.
Boehm, Edgar Collins. *The Persian Gulf and South Sea Isles*. London: Horace Cox, 1904.
Bonnenfant, Paul, Guilemette Bonnenfant, and Salim ibn Hamad ibn Sulayman al-Harthi. "Architecture and Social History at Mudayrib." *Journal of Oman Studies* 3, no. 2 (1977): 107–35.
Bonnenfant, Paul, and Colette Le Cour Grandmaison. "The Ibra' and Mudayrib Area." *Journal of Oman Studies* 3, no. 2 (1977): 91–94.
Bontinck, François. *L'autobiographie de Hamed ben Mohammed el-Murjebi, Tippo Tip, ca. 1840–1905*. Brussels: Académie royale des Sciences d'Outre Mer, 1974.
———. "La Double Traversée de l'Afrique Par Trois 'Arabes' de Zanzibar (1845–1860)." *Études d'Histoire Africaine* 6 (1974): 5–53.
Bose, Sugata. *A Hundred Horizons: The Indian Ocean in the Age of Global Empire*. Cambridge, MA: Harvard University Press, 2006.

Boteler, Thomas. *Narrative of a Voyage of Discovery to Africa and Arabia Performed in His Majesty's Ships "Leven" and "Barracouta" from 1821 to 1826, under the Command of Capt. F. W. Owen, R. N.* 2 vols. (London: R. Bentley, 1835).

Bourdieu, Pierre. *Outline of a Theory of Practice.* New York: Cambridge University Press, 1977.

Bourne, H. R. Fox. *Civilisation in Congoland: A Story of International Wrong-Doing.* London: P. S. King & Son, 1903.

———. *The Other Side of the Emin Pasha Relief Expedition.* London: Chatto & Windus, 1891.

Braudel, Fernand. *The Mediterranean and the Mediterranean World in the Age of Philip II.* Berkeley: University of California Press, 1995.

Brennan, James R. and Andrew Burton. "The Emerging Metropolis: A history of Dar es Salaam, circa 1862–2000." In *Dar es Salaam: Histories from an Emerging African Metropolis*, edited by James R. Brennan, Andrew Burton, and Yusuf Lawi. 13–75. Oxford: African Books Collective, 2007.

Bridges, Roy. "Decline and Fall of Arab Power, review of Norman Robert Bennett, Arab versus European. Diplomacy and War in Nineteenth Century East Central Africa." *Journal of African History* 28, no. 2 (1987): 313–14.

Brode, Heinrich. *Tippoo Tib, the Story of His Career in Central Africa.* Translated by H. Havelock. Chicago: Afro-American Press, 1969.

Bromber, Katrin. *The Jurisdiction of the Sultan of Zanzibar and the Subjects of Foreign Nations.* Würzburg: Ergon-Verlag, 2001.

Brown, Beverly. "Muslim Influence on Trade and Politics in the Lake Tanganyika Region." *African Historical Studies* 4, no. 3 (1971): 617–29.

Brown, Beverly Bolser. "Ujiji: The History of a Lakeside Town, c. 1800–1914." PhD diss., Boston University, 1973.

Brown, Robin, Michael M. Horowitz, and Muneera Salem-Murdock. *Social and Institutional Aspects of Oman: A Review of the Literature.* Washington, DC: Agency for International Development, 1982.

Brown, Walter T. "The Politics of Business: Relations between Zanzibar and Bagamoyo in the Late Nineteenth Century." *African Historical Studies* 4, no. 3 (1971): 631–43.

———. "A Pre-Colonial History of Bagamoyo: Aspects of the Growth of an East African Coastal Town." PhD diss., Boston University, 1971.

Burgess, G. Thomas, Ali Sultan Issa, and Seif Sharif Hamad. *Race, Revolution, and the Struggle for Human Rights in Zanzibar: The Memoirs of Ali Sultan Issa and Seif Sharif Hamad.* Athens: Ohio University Press, 2009.

Burnes, Alexander. "On the Maritime Communications of India, as Carried on by the Natives, particularly from Kutch, at the Mouth of the Indus." *Journal of the Royal Geographical Society of London* 6 (1836): 23–29.

Burton, Antoinette, Madhavi Kale, Isabel Hofmeyr, Clare Anderson, Christopher J. Lee, and Nile Green. "Sea Tracks and Trails: Indian Ocean Worlds as Method." *History Compass* 11, no. 7 (2013): 497–502. https://doi.org/10.1111/hic3.12060.

Burton, Richard F. "The Lake Regions of Central Equatorial Africa, with Notices of the Lunar Mountains and the Sources of the White Nile; Being the Results of an Expedition Undertaken under the Patronage of Her Majesty's Government and the Royal Geographical Society of London, in the Years 1857–1859." *Journal of*

the *Royal Geographical Society of London* 29 (1859): 1–454. https://doi.org/10.2307/1798278.
———. *A Plain and Literal Translation of the Arabian Nights' Entertainments Now Entitled, The Book of the Thousand Nights and a Night*. London: Burton Club, 1885.
———. *The Lake Regions of Central Africa*. New York: Dover Publications, 1995.
———. "Zanzibar; and Two Months in East Africa (1858)." *Blackwood's Edinburgh Magazine* 83 (May 1858), 200–24.
———. *Zanzibar: City, Island, and Coast*. 2 vols. London: Tinsley Brothers, 1872.
Büttner, Carl Gotthilf. *Anthologie aus der Suaheli-litteratur: Gedichte und Geschichten der Suaheli*. Berlin: Felber, 1894.
———. *Suaheli-Schriftstücke in Arabischer Shrift*, Lehrbucher des Seminars für Oreintalische Sprachen in Berlin, vol. X, Stuttgart and Berlin: W. Spemann 1892.
Buyers, Christopher. "Oman." In *The Royal Ark: Royal and Ruling Houses of Africa, Asia, Oceania and the Americas*. n.d. http://www.royalark.net/Oman/oman.htm.
Caledonian Maritime Research Trust. "Clyde Built Ships." http://www.clydeships.co.uk/.
Cameron, Lieut. V. L. "Lieut. Cameron's Letters Detailing the Journey of the Livingstone East Coast Expedition from Lake Tanganyika to the West Coast of Africa." *Proceedings of the Royal Geographical Society of London* 20, no. 2 (1875): 117–34. https://doi.org/10.2307/1799874.
Cameron, V. L. "On his Journey across Africa, from Bagamoyo to Benguela." *Proceedings of the Royal Geographical Society of London* 20, no. 4 (1875): 304–28.
Cameron, Verney Lovett. *Across Africa*. New York: Harper & Brothers, 1877.
Campbell, Gwyn. *Abolition and Its Aftermath in Indian Ocean Africa and Asia*. New York: Routledge, 2005.
———, ed. *Bonded Labour and Debt in the Indian Ocean World*. Abingdon, UK: Routledge, 2015.
———, ed. *The Structure of Slavery in Indian Ocean Africa and Asia*. London: Frank Cass, 2004.
Campbell, James McNabb, and R. E. Enthoven. *Gazetteer of the Bombay Presidency*. Vol. 1. Bombay: Government Central Press, 1877.
Campbell, Robert. "Tuskers, Trade, and Trypanosomes: The Ecologies of the Victorian Parlor." Paper presented at the Agrarian Studies Colloquium, Yale University, New Haven, CT, November 12, 2010.
Candido, Mariana P. *An African Slaving Port and the Atlantic World: Benguela and Its Hinterland*. New York: Cambridge University Press, 2013.
Carter, J. R. L. *Tribes in Oman*. London: Peninsular Pub., 1982.
Carter, Marina. "Slavery and Unfree Labour in the Indian Ocean." *History Compass* 4, no. 5 (2006): 800–13.
Chacker, Eunice A. "Early Arab and European Contacts with Ukerewe." *Tanzania Notes and Records*, no. 68 (1968): 75–86.
Chang, Michael G. *A Court on Horseback: Imperial Touring & the Construction of Qing Rule, 1680–1785*. Cambridge, MA: Harvard University Press, 2007.
Chaudhuri, K. N. *Trade and Civilisation in the Indian Ocean: An Economic History from the Rise of Islam to 1750*. New York: Cambridge University Press, 1985.

Christie, James. *Cholera Epidemics in East Africa, from 1821 till 1872.* London: Macmillan & Co., 1876.
Christopher, W. "Extract from a journal kept during a partial enquiry into the present resources and state of North Eastern Africa, with Memoranda." *Transactions of the Bombay Geographical Society* 6 (1844): 375–402.
Church Missionary Society. *The Church Missionary Intelligencer and Record,* 1876.
Clarence-Smith, William Gervase. *Islam and the Abolition of Slavery.* New York: Oxford University Press, 2006.
Codrington, Robert. "The Central Angoniland District of the British Central Africa Protectorate." *Geographical Journal* 11, no. 5 (1898): 509–22.
Cole, C. S. D. "An Account of an Overland Journey from Leshkairee to Muscat and the 'Green Mountains' of Oman." *Transactions of the Bombay Geographical Society* 8 (1849): 106–18.
Colomb, Philip Howard. *Slave-Catching in the Indian Ocean, a Record of Naval Experiences.* London: Longmans, Green and Co, 1873.
Comaroff, John, and Jean Comaroff. "On Personhood: An Anthropological Perspective from Africa." *Social Identities* 7, no. 2 (2001): 267–83.
Cooper, Frederick. *From Slaves to Squatters: Plantation Labor and Agriculture in Zanzibar and Coastal Kenya, 1890–1925.* New Haven: Yale University Press, 1980.
———. *Plantation Slavery on the East Coast of Africa.* New Haven: Yale University Press, 1977.
Costa, Paolo, and Eros Baldissera. *Historic Mosques and Shrines of Oman.* Oxford: Archaeopress, 2001.
Cotton, H. J. S. "The Rice Trade in Bengal." *Calcutta Review* 58 (1874): 171–88.
———. "The Rice Trade of the World." *Calcutta Review* 58 (1874): 267–302.
Coupland, Reginald. *East Africa and Its Invaders: From the Earliest Times to the Death of Seyyid Said in 1856.* Oxford: Clarendon Press, 1938.
———. *The Exploitation of East Africa, 1856–1890: The Slave Trade and the Scramble.* London: Faber and Faber, 1939.
Cox, Percy. "Some Excursions in Oman." The Geographical Journal, Vol. 66, No. 3 (Sep., 1925): 193–221.
Crone, Patricia. *Roman, Provincial, and Islamic Law: The Origins of the Islamic Patronate.* Cambridge: Cambridge University Press, 1987.
Curtin, Philip D. *Cross-Cultural Trade in World History.* New York: Cambridge University Press, 1984.
Damluji, Salma Samar. *The Architecture of Oman.* Reading: Garnet Publishing, 1998.
Davies, Charles. *The Blood-Red Arab Flag: An Investigation into Qasimi Piracy, 1797–1820.* Exeter: University of Exeter Press, 1997.
Dawood, N. J, trans. *The Koran.* New York: Penguin Books, 1993.
Delcommune, Alexandre. *Vingt années de vie africaine: récits de voyages d'aventures et d'exploration au Congo Belge, 1874–1893.* 2 vols. Brussels: Ferdinand Larcier, 1922.
Deutsch, Jan-Georg. *Emancipation without Abolition in German East Africa, c. 1884–1914.* Athens: Ohio University Press, 2006.
———. "Notes on the Rise of Slavery and Social Change in Unyamwezi, c. 1860–1900." In *Slavery in the Great Lakes Region of East Africa,* edited by Henri Mèdard and Shane Doyle, 76–110. Athens: Ohio University Press, 2007.
Devereux, William Cope. *A Cruise in the "Gorgon," or Eighteen Months on H. M. S. "Gorgon," Engaged in the Suppression of the Slave Trade on the East Coast of Af-*

rica: Including a Trip up the Zambesi with Livingstone. London: Bell and Daldy, 1869.
Doulton, Lindsay. "The Royal Navy's Anti-Slavery Campaign in the Western Indian Ocean, c. 1860–1890: Race, Empire and Identity." PhD diss., University of Hull, 2010.
Eaton, Richard. "Introduction." In *Slavery and South Asian History*, edited by Indrani Chatterjee and Richard M. Eaton, 1–16. Bloomington: Indiana University Press, 2006.
Eickelman, Christine. *Women and Community in Oman*. New York: New York University Press, 1984.
Elton, James Frederick. *Travels and Researches among the Lakes and Mountains of Eastern and Central Africa*. Edited by Henry Bernard Cotterill. London: Murray, 1879.
Ewald, Janet J. "Crossers of the Sea: Slaves, Freedmen, and Other Migrants in the Northwestern Indian Ocean, c. 1750–1914." *American Historical Review* 105, no. 1 (2000): 69–91.
Fabian, Johannes. *Out of Our Minds: Reason and Madness in the Exploration of Central Africa*. Berkeley: University of California Press, 2000.
Fair, Laura. *Pastimes and Politics: Culture, Community, and Identity in Post-Abolition Urban Zanzibar, 1890–1945*. Athens: Ohio University Press, 2001.
Falola, Toyin, and Paul E. Lovejoy, "Pawnship in Historical Perspective." In *Pawnship, Slavery, and Colonialism in Africa*, Toyin Falola and Paul Lovejoy, eds., 1–27. (Trenton, New Jersey: Africa World Press, Inc., 2003), 2.
Farsy, Abdallah Salih. *Seyyid Said Bin Sultan: Joint Ruler of Oman and Zanzibar (1804–1856)*. New Delhi: Lancers Books, 1986.
Ferreira, Roquinaldo Amaral. *Cross-Cultural Exchange in the Atlantic World: Angola and Brazil during the Era of the Slave Trade*. New York: Cambridge University Press, 2012.
Fisher, Humphrey J. *Slavery in the History of Muslim Black Africa*. New York: New York University Press, 2001.
Fleisher, Jeffrey, Paul Lane, Adria LaViolette, Mark Horton, Edward Pollard, Eréndira Quintana Morales, Thomas Vernet, Annalisa Christie, and Stephanie Wynne-Jones. "When Did the Swahili Become Maritime? *American Anthropologist* 117, no. 1 (March 2015): 100–15. https://doi.org/10.1111/aman.12171.
Marie-Aude Foüeré, "Recasting Julius Nyerere in Zanzibar: The Revolution, the Union and the Enemy of the Nation." *Journal of Eastern African Studies* 8, no. 3 (2014): 478–496.
Fox, R. *Kinship and Marriage: An Anthropological Perspective*. Harmondsworth: Penguin, 1967.
Frankl, P. J. L. "Obituary: Ali Muhsin Al-Barwani." *British Journal of Middle Eastern Studies* 33, no. 2 (November 1, 2006): 263–65. https://doi.org/10.1080/13530190600953641.
———. "Review of *Tarjama ya al-Muntakhab Katika Tafsiri ya Qur'ani Tukufu*, by Ali Muhsin al-Barwani." *British Journal of Middle Eastern Studies* 25, no. 1 (1998): 191–93.
Freeman-Grenville, G. S. P., and B. G. Martin. "A Preliminary Handlist of the Arabic Inscriptions of the Eastern African Coast." *Journal of the Royal Asiatic Society of Great Britain and Ireland*, no. 2 (1973): 98–122.

Freeman-Grenville, G.S.P. *The French at Kilwa Island: An Episode in Eighteenth-century East African History.* Oxford: Clarendon Press, 1965.

de Froberville, Eugène. "Notes sur les Va-Ngindo." *Bulletin de la Société de Géographie* 4, no. 3 (1852): 425–43.

Gann, Lewis H., and Peter Duignan. *The Rulers of German Africa, 1884–1914.* Redwood City, CA: Stanford University Press, 1977.

Gavin, R. J. "The Bartle Frere Mission to Zanzibar, 1873." *Historical Journal* 5, no. 2 (1962): 122–48.

Ghassany, Harith. *Kwaheri ukoloni, kwaheri uhuru! Zanzibar na mapinduzi ya Afrabia* (Goodbye Colonialism, Goodbye Freedom! Zanzibar and the Afrabian Revolution). N.p., 2010. https://kwaheri.files.wordpress.com/2010/05/kwaheri-ukoloni-kwaheri-uhuru.pdf.

Ghazal, Amal Nadim. "Islam and Arabism in Zanzibar: The Omani Elite, the Arab World and the Making of an Identity, 1880s–1930s." PhD diss., University of Alberta, Edmonton, 2005.

Gilbert, Erik. *Dhows and the Colonial Economy in Zanzibar, 1860–1970.* Athens: Ohio University Press, 2004.

Glassman, Jonathon. "The Bondsman's New Clothes: The Contradictory Consciousness of Slave Resistance on the Swahili Coast." *Journal of African History* 32 (1991): 277–312.

———. *Feasts and Riot: Revelry, Rebellion, and Popular Consciousness on the Swahili Coast, 1856–1888.* Portsmouth, NH: Heinemann, 1995.

———. "Social Rebellion and Swahili Culture: The Response to German Conquest of the Northern Mrima, 1888–1890." PhD diss., University of Wisconsin–Madison, 1988.

———. "Sorting out the Tribes: The Creation Of Racial Identities In Colonial Zanzibar's Newspaper Wars" *Journal of African History*, 41 (2000), 395–428.

———. *War of Words, War of Stones: Racial Thought and Violence in Colonial Zanzibar.* Bloomington: Indiana University Press, 2011.

Goitein, S. D. *A Mediterranean Society the Jewish Communities of the Arab World as Portrayed in the Documents of the Cairo Geniza.* 6 vols. Berkeley: University of California Press, 1967–1993.

———. *Studies in Islamic History and Institutions.* Leiden: Brill, 1966.

Gomez, Michael. *Exchanging Our Country Marks: The Transformation of African Identities in the Colonial and Antebellum South.* Chapel Hill: University of North Carolina Press, 1998.

Goswami, Chhaya. *The Call of the Sea: Kachchhi Traders in Muscat and Zanzibar, C. 1800–1880.* New Delhi: Orient Blackswan, 2011.

Grant, James Augustus. *A Walk across Africa: Or, Domestic Scenes from My Nile Journal.* London: William Blackwood and Sons, 1864.

Gray, John Milner. "Arabs on Lake Victoria. Some Revisions." *Uganda Journal* (1958), 76–81.

———. "The Hadimu and Tumbatu of Zanzibar." In *Tanzania Notes and Records.* (1977): 81–82.

———. "Trading Expeditions from the Coast to Lakes Tanganyika and Victoria before 1857." *Tanganyika Notes and Records* 49 (1957): 226–46.

Graeber, David. *Debt: The First 5,000 Years.* Brooklyn: Melville House, 2011.

Greif, Avner. "Reputation and Coalitions in Medieval Trade: Evidence on the Maghribi Traders." *The Journal of Economic History*, vol. 49, no. 4 (Dec., 1989): 857–82.
Green, Nile. *Bombay Islam: The Religious Economy of the West Indian Ocean, 1840–1915*. Cambridge: Cambridge University Press, 2013.
———. "Rethinking the 'Middle East' after the Oceanic Turn," *Comparative Studies of South Asia, Africa and the Middle East* 34, no. 3 (2014): 556–64. https://doi.org/10.1215/1089201X-2826109.
Grove, Richard. *Green Imperialism: Colonial Expansion, Tropical Island Edens, and the Origins of Environmentalism, 1600–1860*. New York: Cambridge University Press, 1995.
Gurnah, Ahmad. "Elvis in Zanzibar." In *The Limits of Globalization*, Alan Scott, ed., New York: Routledge, 1997.
Guillain, C. *Documents sur l'histoire, la géographie et le commerce de l'Afrique orientale*. Vol 1. Paris, 1856.
Hallaq, Wael B. "Model Shurūṭ Works and the Dialectic of Doctrine and Practice." *Islamic Law and Society* 2, no. 2 (1995): 109–34.
———. "The Use and Abuse of Evidence: The Question of Provincial and Roman Influences on Early Islamic Law." *Journal of the American Oriental Society* 110, no. 1 (1990): 79–91.
Harms, Robert W., Bernard K. Freamon, and David W. Blight. *Indian Ocean Slavery in the Age of Abolition*. New Haven: Yale University Press, 2013.
Harries, Lyndon, ed and trans. *Swahili Prose Texts: A Selection from the Material Collected by Carl Velten from 1893 to 1896*. London: Oxford University Press, 1965.
Harrison, Alexina. *A. M. MacKay: Pioneer Missionary of the Church Missionary Society in Uganda*. New York: A. C. Armstrong and Son, 1904.
Harrison, Paul W. *Doctor in Arabia*. New York: John Day, 1940.
Hartwig, Gerald W. "A Cultural History of the Kerebe of Tanzania to 1895." PhD diss., Bloomington: Indiana University, 1971.
———. "Bukerebe, The Church Missionary Society, and East African Politics, 1877–1878." *African Historical Studies* 1, no. 2 (1968): 211–32. doi:10.2307/216396.
———. "Victoria Nyanza as Trade Route." *Journal of African History* 11 (1970): 535–52.
Hāshimy, Saʿīd bin Muḥammad bin Saʿīd al-. "Shaikh Salih Bin Ali Al-Harthy and His Social and Political Role (1250\1834–1314\1896)." *Journal of the Gulf and Arabian Peninsula Studies* 33, no. 125 (2007): 177–229.
———. "Imam Sālim b. Rāshid and the Imamate Revival in Oman, 1331/1913–1338/1920." PhD diss., Leeds: University of Leeds, 1994.
Hinawy, Mbarak Ali. *Al-Akida and Fort Jesus, Mombasa*. 2nd ed. Nairobi: East African Literature Bureau, 1970.
Hinde, Sidney Langford. *The Fall of the Congo Arabs*. London: Methuen & Co., 1897.
Ho, Engseng. *The Graves of Tarim: Genealogy and Mobility across the Indian Ocean*. Berkeley: University of California Press, 2006.
Hoffman, Valerie J. "The Articulation of Ibāḍī Identity in Modern Oman and Zanzibar." *The Muslim World* 94, no. 2 (2004): 201–16.
———. *The Essentials of Ibadi Islam*. Syracuse, NY: Syracuse University Press, 2012.
———. "In His (Arab) Majesty's Service: The Career of a Somali Scholar and Diplomat in Nineteenth Century Zanzibar." In *The Global Worlds of the Swahili: Interfaces*

of Islam, Identity and Space in 19th- and 20th-Century East Africa. Berlin: LIT Verlag, 2006.

Hofmeyr, Isabel. "Clare Anderson. Subaltern Lives: Biographies of Colonialism in the Indian Ocean World, 1790–1920." American Historical Review 118, no. 3 (2013): 817–18. https://doi.org/10.1093/ahr/118.3.817.

Hopper, Matthew S. "The African Presence in Arabia: Slavery, the World Economy, and the African Diaspora in Eastern Arabia, 1840–1940." PhD diss., University of California, Los Angeles, 2006.

———. "Cyclones, Drought, and Slavery: Environment and Enslavement in the Western Indian Ocean, 1870s to 1920s." In Natural Hazards and Peoples in the Indian Ocean World, 255–82. New York: Palgrave Macmillan, 2016.

———. Slaves of One Master: Globalization and Slavery in Arabia in the Age of Empire. New Haven: Yale University Press, 2015.

Horden, P., and N. Purcell. "The Mediterranean and 'the New Thalassology.'" American Historical Review 111, no. 3 (2006): 722–40. https://doi.org/10.1086/ahr.111.3.722.

Hore, Edward C. "An Arab Friend in Central Africa." The Chronicle of the London Missionary Society, (August 1891), 235–238.

———. Tanganyika: Eleven Years in Central Africa. London: Edward Stanford, 1892.

Hunter, William Wilson, ed. Imperial Gazetteer of India. Vol. 4. Oxford: Clarendon Press, 1909.

Iliffe, John. A Modern History of Tanganyika. Cambridge: Cambridge University Press, 1979.

Ingrams, William Harold. "Burton Memorial Lecture: From Cana (Husn Ghorab) to Sabbatha (Shabwa): The South Arabian Incense Road." Journal of the Royal Asiatic Society of Great Britain and Ireland, no. 2 (1945): 169–85.

———. Arabia and the Isles. London, 1942.

Ismaily, Issa Nasser Issa al-. Zanzibar: kinyang'anyiro na utumwa (Slavery and the Scramble for Zanzibar). Ruwi, Sultanate of Oman: I. N. I. Al-Ismaily, 1999.

Jaffer, Aaron. "'Lords of the Forecastle': Sernags, Tindals, and Lascar Mutiny, c. 1780–1860." In Mutiny and Maritime Radicalism in the Age of Revolution: A Global Survey, edited by Clare Anderson, Niklas Frykman, Lex Heerma van Voss, and Marcus Rediker. Cambridge UK: Cambridge University Press, 2013.

Jameson, James S. The Story of the Rear Column of the Emin Pasha Relief Expedition. New York: Negro Universities Press, 1969.

Jayakar, A. S. G. "Medical Topography of Muscat." In Report of the Administration of the Persian Gulf Political Residency and Muscat Political Agency for the Year 1876–77. Calcutta: Government of India, Foreign Department, 1877.

———. "'Ománee Proverbs." Journal of the Bombay Branch of the Royal Asiatic Society 21 (1904): 435–98.

Jeal, Tim. Stanley: The Impossible Life of Africa's Greatest Explorer. New Haven: Yale University Press, 2007.

Johnson, Frederick, ed. A Standard Swahili-English Dictionary (Founded on Madan's Swahili-English Dictionary). Nairobi: Oxford University Press, 1999 [1939].

Jones, Chris. "Plus Ça Change, Plus Ça Reste Le Même? The New Zanzibar Land Law Project." Journal of African Law 40, no. 1 (1996): 19–42.

Preben Kaarsholm, "Zanzibaris or Amakhuwa? Sufi Networks in South Africa, Mozambique and the Indian Ocean," Journal of African History 55, no. 2: 191–210.

Kelly, J. B. Britain and the Persian Gulf. 1795–1880. Oxford: Clarendon Press, 1968.

Kern, Stephen. *The Culture of Time and Space 1880–1918*. Cambridge, MA: Harvard University Press, 1983.
Key, Emily. "A Drive through the Island." *Central Africa: A Monthly Record of the Work of the Universities Mission* 154 (1895): 158–160.
Kharusi Nafla S. "The ethnic label Zinjibari: Politics and language choice implications among Swahili speakers in Oman." *Ethnicities* 12, no. 3 (June 2012): 335–353.
Kimambo, Isaria N., and A. J. Temu, eds. *A History of Tanzania*. Nairobi: East African Pub. House, 1986.
King, John. "Horatio Nelson Lay, C. B.: A Pioneer of British Influence in the Far East." *Journal of the American Asiatic Association* 14, no. 2 (1914): 49–54.
Kitereza, Aniceti, and Gabriel Ruhumbika. *Mr. Myombekere and his wife Bugonoka, their Son Ntulanalwo and Daughter Bulihwali: The Story of an Ancient African Community*. Dar es Salaam, Tanzania: Mkuki na Nyota Publishers, 2002.
Krapf, Jonathan Ludwig. *A Dictionary of the Suahili Language*. London: Trübner and Co., 1882.
Landen, Robert Geran. *Oman since 1856: Disruptive Modernization in a Traditional Arab Society*. Princeton: Princeton University Press, 1967.
Langworthy, Harry W. "Swahili Influence in the Area between Lake Malawi and the Luangwa River." *African Historical Studies* 4, no. 3 (1971): 575–602.
Lawrance, Benjamin N., and Richard L. Roberts, eds. *Trafficking in Slavery's Wake: Law and the Experience of Women and Children*. Athens: Ohio University Press, 2012.
Le Cour Grandmaison, Colette. *Hiğrāt al-Ḥurṭ ilā awāsiṭ al-qārra al-Ifrīqiyya*. Masqaṭ: Wizārat al-Turāṯ al-Qawmī wa-al-Ṯaqāfa, 1984.
———. "L'eau du vendredi: Droits d'eau et hiérarchie sociale en Sharqîya (Sultanat d'Oman)." *Études rurales*, no. 93/94 (1984): 7–42.
———. "Rich Cousins, Poor Cousins: Hidden Stratification among the Omani Arabs in Eastern Africa." *Africa* 59, no. 2 (1989): 176–84.
———. "Spatial Organization, Tribal Groupings and Kinship in Ibra'." *Journal of Oman Studies* 3, no. 2 (1977): 95–106.
Le Roy, A. *À Travers Le Zanguebar: voyage dans l'Oudoé, l'Ouzigoua, l'Oukwéré et l'Ousagara*. Lyon: Bureaux des Missions catholiques, 1884.
Leigh, John Studdy, and James S Kirkman. "The Zanzibar Diary of John Studdy Leigh, Part I." *International Journal of African Historical Studies* 13, no. 2 (1980): 281–312.
———. "The Zanzibar Diary of John Studdy Leigh, Part II." *International Journal of African Historical Studies* 13, no. 3 (1980): 492–507.
Lewis, Martin W., and Kären E. Wigen. *The Myth of Continents: A Critique of Metageography*. Berkeley: University of California Press, 1997.
Liebenow, J. Gus. *Colonial Rule and Political Development in Tanzania: The Case of the Makonde*. Evanston, IL: Northwestern University Press, 1971.
Limbert, Mandana E. *In the Time of Oil: Piety, Memory, and Social Life in an Omani Town*. Stanford, Calif.: Stanford University Press, 2010.
———. "Of Ties and Time Sociality, Gender and Modernity in an Omani Town." PhD diss., University of Michigan, 2002.
Livingstone, David. *The Last Journals of David Livingstone, in Central Africa, from 1865 to His Death: Continued by a Narrative of His Last Moments and Sufferings*,

Obtained from His Faithful Servants Chuma and Susi; in Two Volumes. Edited by Horace Waller. New York: Harper & Brothers, 1875.

Livingstone, David, and Charles Livingstone. *Narrative of an Expedition to the Zambesi and Its Tributaries: And of the Discovery of the Lakes Shirwa and Nyassa, 1858–1864.* New York: Harper & Bros., 1866.

Lofchie, Michael. *Zanzibar: Background to Revolution.* Princeton: Princeton University Press, 1965.

Loimeier, Roman. *Eine Zeitlandschaft in der Globalisierung: Das islamische Sansibar im 19 und 20. Jahrhundert.* 1st ed. Bielefeld: Transcript, 2012.

Loimeier, Roman, and Rüdiger Seesemann, eds. *The Global Worlds of the Swahili: Interfaces of Islam, Identity and Space in 19th- and 20th-Century East Africa.* Berlin: Lit, 2006.

Lorimer, John Gordon. *Gazetteer of the Persian Gulf, 'Omān, and Central Arabia.* 2 vols. Calcutta: Superintendent of Government Printing, 1908.

Lutfi, Huda. "A Study of Six Fourteenth Century Iqrars from Al-Quds Relating to Muslim Women." *Journal of the Economic and Social History of the Orient* 26, no. 3 (1983): 246–94.

Lydon, Ghislaine. *On Trans-Saharan Trails: Islamic Law, Trade Networks, and Cross-Cultural Exchange in Nineteenth-Century Western Africa.* 1st edition. New York: Cambridge University Press, 2009.

———. "Slavery, Exchange and Islamic Law: A Glimpse from the Archives of Mali and Mauritania." *African Economic History*, no. 33 (2005): 117–48.

Lyne, Robert Nunez. *An Apostle of Empire. Being the Life of Sir Lloyd William Mathews, K.C.M.G.* London: G. Allen & Unwin, 1936.

———. *Zanzibar in Contemporary Times: A Short History of the Southern East in the Nineteenth Century.* London: Hurst and Blackett, 1905.

Machado, Pedro. *Ocean of Trade: South Asian Merchants, Africa and the Indian Ocean, c. 1750–1850.* Cambridge: Cambridge University Press, 2014.

MacKay, Alexander. "Muscat, Zanzibar, and Central Africa." *Church Missionary Intelligencer and Record* 14, (January 1889): 19–24.

MacQueen, Mr. "Notes on African Geography." *Journal of the Royal Geographical Society of London* 15 (1845): 371. https://doi.org/10.2307/1797919.

Madan, A. C. *English-Swahili Dictionary.* Oxford: Clarendon Press, 1903.

———. *Kiungani; Or, Story and History from Central Africa.* London: G. Bell & Sons, 1887.

Malinowski, B. "Kinship." *Man,* 30 (Feb., 1930): 19–29.

Mann, Kristin. *Slavery and the Birth of an African City: Lagos, 1760–1900.* Bloomington: Indiana University Press, 2007.

Margaretten, Emily. *Street Life under a Roof: Youth Homelessness in South Africa.* Urbana, IL: University of Illinois Press, 2015.

Markovits, Claude. *The Global World of Indian Merchants, 1750–1947.* New York: Cambridge University Press, 2000.

Martin, B. G. "Muslim Politics and Resistance to Colonial Rule: Shaykh Uways B. Muhammad Al-Barawi and the Qadiriya Brotherhood in East Africa." *Journal of African History* 10, no. 3 (1969): 471–86.

———. *Muslim Brotherhoods in Nineteenth-Century Africa.* New York: Cambridge University Press, 1976.

———. "Notes on Some Members of the Learned Classes of Zanzibar and East Africa in the Nineteenth Century." *African Historical Studies* 4, no. 3 (1971), 537–38.
Martineau, John. *The Life and Correspondence of Sir Bartle Frere*. London: John Murray, 1895.
Mathews, Nathaniel "The Zinjibari Diaspora, 1698–2014: Citizenship, Migration and Revolution in Zanzibar, Oman and the Post-War Indian Ocean" (PhD diss., Northwestern University, Evanston, Illinois, 2016).
Mazrui, Alamin M. and Ibrahim Noor Shariff. *The Swahili: Idiom and Identity of an African People*. Trenton: Africa World Press, 1994.
Mazrui, Ali. "Afrabia: Africa and the Arabs in the New World Order" *Ufahamu: A Journal of African Studies* 20, no. 3 (1992): 51–62.
McDow, Thomas F. "Deeds of Freed Slaves: Manumission and Economic and Social Mobility in Pre-Abolition Zanzibar." In *Indian Ocean Slavery in the Age of Abolition*, 162–179 New Haven: Yale University Press, 2013.
———. "Trafficking in Persianness: Richard Burton between Mimicry and Similitude in Indian Ocean and Persianate Worlds." *Comparative Studies of South Asia, Africa and the Middle East*. Vol. 30, no. 3 (2010), 491–511.
———. "Arabs and Africans: Commerce and Kinship from Oman to the East African Interior, c. 1820–1900." PhD diss., Yale University, 2008.
McMahon, Elizabeth. "Trafficking and Reenslavement: The Social Vulnerability of Women and Children in Nineteenth-Century East Africa." In *Trafficking in Slavery's Wake: Law and the Experience of Women and Children*, edited by Benjamin N. Lawrance and Richard L. Roberts, 29–44. Athens: Ohio University Press, 2012.
Metcalf, Thomas R. *Imperial Connections: India in the Indian Ocean Arena, 1860–1920*. Berkeley: University of California Press, 2007.
Mikhail, Alan. *Nature and Empire in Ottoman Egypt: An Environmental History*. New York: Cambridge University Press, 2011.
Miller, Joseph. *Way of Death: Merchant Capitalism and the Angolan Slave Trade, 1730–1830*. Madison: The University of Wisconsin Press, 1988.
Miles, S. B. "Across the Green Mountains of Oman." *Geographical Journal* 18, no. 5 (1901): 465–98.
———. "Notes on the Tribes of 'Oman by Lieutenant-Colonel S. B. Miles." In *Annals of Oman*, 97–112. Cambridge: Oleander Press, 1984.
———. "On the Border of the Great Desert: A Journey in Oman." *Geographical Journal* 36, no. 2 (1910): 159–78. https://doi.org/10.2307/1777694.
———. "On the Border of the Great Desert: A Journey in Oman (Continued)." *The Geographical Journal* 36, no. 4 (1910): 405–25. https://doi.org/10.2307/1777049.
———. *The Countries and Tribes of the Persian Gulf*. Reading: Garnet Publishing, 1994.
———. *Report on the Administration of the Persian Gulf Political Residency and Muscat Political Agency for 1885–86*. Calcutta: Superintendent of Government Printing, 1886.
Mirza, Sarah and Margaret Strobel, eds., *Muslim Women in Mombasa, 1890–1975*. Bloomington: Indiana University Press, 1989.
Mitter, U. "Unconditional Manumission of Slaves in Early Islamic Law: A Hadîth Analysis." In *The Formation of Islamic Law*, edited by W. B. Hallaq, 115–52. Burlington, VT: Ashgate, 2004.

Mohammed, Noor. "Principles of Islamic Contract Law." *Journal of Law and Religion* 6, no. 1 (1988): 115–30.
Moodie, T. Dunbar, and Vivienne Ndatshe. *Going for Gold: Men, Mines, and Migration*. Berkeley: University of California Press, 1994.
Moore, Ernst D. *Ivory, Scourge of Africa*. New York: Harper & Bros., 1931.
Moorehead, *The White Nile*. New York: Harper Collins, 2000.
Moritz, B. *Sammlung arabischer Schriftstücke aus Zanzibar und Oman*. Lehrbucher des seminars fur Orientalische Sprachen zu Berlin 9. Stuttgart; Berlin: Spemann, 1892.
Morton, Fred. *The Children of Ham: Freed Slaves and Fugitive Slaves on the Kenya Coast, 1873–1907*. Boulder, CO: Westview Press, 1990.
Mtoro bin Mwinyi Bakari. *The Customs of the Swahili People: The Desturi za Waswahili of Mtoro bin Mwinyi Bakari and other Swahili Persons*. Translated by J. W. T. Allen. Berkeley: University of California Press, 1981.
Mughayrī, Sa'īd bin 'Alī. *Juhaynat al-akhbār fī tārīkh Zanzibār*. Muscat, Oman: Wizārat al-Turāth al-Qawmī, 1979.
Murjebi, Hamed bin Muhammed al-. *Maisha ya Hamed bin Muhammed el Murjebi yaani Tippu Tip: kwa maneno yake mwenyewe*. Translated by W. H. Whitely. Nairobi: East African Literature Bureau, 1966.
———. *L'autobiographie de Hamed ben Mohammed el-Murjebi Tippo Tip (ca. 1840–1905)*. Edited by François Bontinck. Bruxelles, 1974.
Murphy, Robert F., and Leonard Kasdan. "The Structure of Parallel Cousin Marriage." *American Anthropologist* 61, no. 1 (1959): 17–29.
———. "Agnation and Endogamy: Some Further Considerations." *Southwestern Journal of Anthropology* 23, no. 1 (1967): 1–14.
Myers, Garth Andrew. "Early History of the 'Other Side' of Zanzibar Town." In *The History and Conservation of Zanzibar*, edited by Abdul Sheriff, 30–45. London: James Currey, 1995.
Naqar, 'Umar al-. "Arabic Materials in the Government Archives of Zanzibar." *History in Africa* 5 (1978): 377–82.
New, Charles. *Life, Wanderings, and Labours in Eastern Africa: With an Account of the First Successful Ascent of the Equatorial Snow Mountain, Kilima Njaro and Remarks upon East African Slavery*. 3rd ed. London: Frank Cass, 1971.
Nicholls, C. S. *The Swahili Coast; Politics, Diplomacy and Trade on the East African Littoral, 1798–1856*. New York: Africana Pub. Corp., 1971.
Nimtz, August H. *Islam and Politics in East Africa the Sufi Order in Tanzania*. Minneapolis: University of Minnesota Press, 1980.
Nurse, Derek, and Thomas T. Spear. *The Swahili: Reconstructing the History and Language of an African Society, 800–1500*. Philadelphia: University of Pennsylvania Press, 1985.
Ogle, Vanessa. *The Global Transformation of Time: 1870–1950*. Cambridge, MA: Harvard University Press, 2015.
———. "Whose Time Is It? The Pluralization of Time and the Global Condition, 1870s–1940s." *The American Historical Review* 118, no. 5 (2013), 1376–1402.
Oliver, Roland Anthony. *Sir Harry Johnston and the Scramble for Africa*. New York: St. Martin's Press, 1958.
———. *The Missionary Factor in East Africa*. 2nd ed. London: Longman, 1970.

O'Neill, Thomas. *Sketches of African Scenery, from Zanzibar to the Victoria Nyanza: Being a Series of Coloured Lithographic Pictures, from Original Sketches by the Late Mr. Thomas O'Neill, of the Victoria Nyanza Mission of the Church Missionary Society.* London: Church Missionary House, 1878.

Osgood, Joseph Barlow Felt. *Notes of Travel: Or, Recollections of Majunga, Zanzibar, Muscat, Aden, Mocha, and Other Eastern Ports.* Salem, MA: George Creamer, 1854.

Osterhammel, Jurgen. *The Transformation of the World: A Global History of the Nineteenth Century.* Princeton: Princeton University Press, 2015.

Owen, W. F. W. *Narrative of Voyages to Explore the Shores of Africa, Arabia and Madagascar: Performed in H. M. Ships Leven and Barracouta under the Direction of Captain W. F. W. Owen, R. N.* London: Richard Bentley, 1833.

Pamuk, Şevket. *A Monetary History of the Ottoman Empire.* Cambridge: Cambridge University Press, 2000.

Patai, Raphael. "The Structure of Endogamous Unilineal Descent Groups." *Southwestern Journal of Anthropology* 21, no. 4 (1965): 325–50.

Paterculus, Velleius. *Velleius Paterculus and Res Gestae Divi Augusti.* Cambridge: Harvard University Press, 1924.

Pawełczak, Marek, and Instytut Historyczny Uniwersytetu Warszawskiego. *The State and the Stateless: The Sultanate of Zanzibar and the East African Mainland; Politics, Economy and Society, 1837–1888.* Warsaw: SOWA, 2010.

Pearson, M. N. "Littoral Society: The Concept and the Problems." *Journal of World History* 17, no. 4 (2006): 353–73. https://doi.org/10.1353/jwh.2006.0059.

———. *The Indian Ocean.* London: Routledge, 2003.

———. *Port Cities and Intruders: The Swahili Coast, Indian, and Portugal in the Early Modern Era.* Baltimore: Johns Hopkins University Press, 1998.

Peletz, Michael G. "Kinship Studies in Late Twentieth-Century Anthropology." *Annual Review of Anthropology* 24 (1995): 343.

Peters, C. T. "Medico-Topographical Report of Muscat." *Transactions of the Medical and Physical Society of Bombay* 12 (1876): 152–74.

Peters, Edward. "Quid Nobis Cum Pelago? The New Thalassology and the Economic History of Europe." *Journal of Interdisciplinary History* 34, no. 1 (2003): 49–61.

Peterson, John. *Historical Muscat an Illustrated Guide and Gazetteer.* Leiden: Brill, 2007.

Playfair, R. L. "Reminiscences." *Chambers Journal* 2, no. 68 (1899): 289–292.

Porter, J. D. *Oman and the Persian Gulf, 1835–1949 ['Umān Wa-Al-Khalīj Al-Fārisī, 1835–1949].* Salisbury, NC: Documentary Publications, 1982.

Postans, Thomas. *Personal Observations on Sindh: The Manners and Customs of Its Inhabitants, and Its Productive Capabilities with a Sketch of Its History, a Narrative of Recent Events, and an Account of the Connection of the British Government with That Country to the Present Period.* London: Longman, Brown, Green, and Longmans, 1843.

Pouwels, Randall Lee. "A Reply to Spear on Early Swahili History." *International Journal of African Historical Studies* 34, no. 3 (2001): 639–46.

———. "Bibliography of Primary Sources of the Pre-Nineteenth Century East African Coast." *History in Africa* 29 (2002): 393–411.

———. *Horn and Crescent: Cultural Change and Traditional Islam on the East African Coast, 800–1900.* New York: Cambridge University Press, 1987.

Prestholdt, Jeremy. *Domesticating the World: African Consumerism and the Genealogies of Globalization*. Berkeley: University of California Press, 2008.
Purohit, Teena. *The Aga Khan Case: Religion and Identity in Colonial India*. Cambridge: Harvard University Press, 2012.
Quass, Emil. "Die Szuri's, Die Kuli's Und Die Sclaven in Zanzibar." *Zeitschrift Für Allgemeine Erdkunde* IX (neue Folge) (1860): 421–60.
Rabi, Uzi. *Emergence of States in a Tribal Society: Oman Under Sa'īd Bin Taymur, 1932–1970*. Brighton: Sussex Academic Press, 2006.
Raman, Bhavani. *Document Raj: Writing and Scribes in Early Colonial South India*. Chicago: University of Chicago Press, 2012.
Rashīd, Zāmil Muḥammad. *Su'ūdī Relations with Eastern Arabia and 'Umān (1800–1871)*. London: Luzac & Co., 1981.
Reichard, Paul. "Das afrikanische Elfenbein und sein Handel." *Deutsche Geographische Blätter* 12 (1889): 132–168.
Reid, Richard J. "Mutesa and Mirambo: Thoughts on East African Warfare and Diplomacy in the Nineteenth Century." *International Journal of African Historical Studies* 31, no. 1 (1998): 73–89.
Rentz, George. *Oman and the South-Eastern Shore of Arabia*. Reading, UK: Ithaca Press, 1997.
Rigby, Christopher Palmer, and Charles E. B Russell. *General Rigby, Zanzibar, and the Slave Trade, with Journals, Dispatches, etc*. London: Allen & Unwin, 1935.
Risso, Patricia. "Cross-Cultural Perceptions of Piracy: Maritime Violence in the Western Indian Ocean and Persian Gulf Region During a Long Eighteenth Century." *Journal of World History* 12, no. 2 (2001): 293–319.
———. *Merchants and Faith: Muslim Commerce and Culture in the Indian Ocean*. Boulder, CO: Westview Press, 1995.
Riyami, Naṣser bin Abdulla Al. *Zanzibar Personalities and Events (1828–1972)*. Translated by Ali bin Rashid Al Abri. Muscat: Beirut Bookshop, 2012.
Roberts, A. D. "The History of Abdullah Ibn Suliman." *African Social Research*, no. 4 (1967): 241–70.
Roberts, Allen F. "Is 'Africa' Obsolete?" *African Arts* 33, no. 1 (2000): 1–94. https://doi.org/10.2307/3337744.
Robertson, Claire C., and Martin A. Klein, eds. *Women and Slavery in Africa*. Madison: University of Wisconsin Press, 1983.
Rockel, Stephen J. *Carriers of Culture: Labor on the Road in Nineteenth-Century East Africa*. Portsmouth, NH: Heinemann, 2006.
Ross, E. C. *Report on the Administration of the Persian Gulf Political Residency and Muscat Political Agency for the year 1875–76*. Calcutta: Foreign Department Printing Press, 1876.
———. *Report on the Administration of the Persian Gulf Political Residency and Muscat Political Agency for the year 1877–78*. Calcutta: Foreign Department Press, 1878.
———. *Report on the Administration of the Persian Gulf Political Residency and Muscat Political Agency for the Year 1878–79*. Calcutta: Superintendent of Government Printing, 1880.
———. *Report on the Administration of the Persian Gulf Political Residency and Muscat Political Agency for the Year 1880–81*. Calcutta: Foreign Department Press, 1881.

———. *Report on the Administration of the Persian Gulf Political Residency and Muscat Political Agency for the Year 1881–82.* Calcutta: Superintendent of Government Printing, 1882.
———. *Report on the Administration of the Persian Gulf Political Residency and Muscat Political Agency for the Year 1882–83.* Calcutta: Superintendent of Government Printing, 1883.
———. *Report on the Administration of the Persian Gulf Political Residency and Muscat Political Agency for the Year 1883–84.* Calcutta: Government Printing, 1884.
———. *Report on the Administration of the Persian Gulf Political Residency and Muscat Political Agency for the Year 1884–85.* Calcutta: Superintendent of Government Printing, 1885.
Rowley, Henry. *The Story of the Universities' Mission to Central Africa from Its Commencement under Bishop Mackenzie to Its Withdrawal from the Zambesi, by the Rev. Henry Rowley.* London: Saunders, Otley and Co, 1867.
Royal Geographical Society. "Dr. Livingstone: News of His Safety." *Proceedings of the Royal Geographical Society of London* 16, no. 5 (1871): 379–387.
Ruete, Emilie. *Memoirs of an Arabian Princess.* Edited by Lionel Strachey. New York: Doubleday, 1907.
———. *An Arabian Princess between Two Worlds: Memoirs, Letters Home, Sequels to the Memoirs: Syrian Customs and Usages.* Edited by E. van Donzel. Leiden: Brill, 1993.
Ruschenberger, W. S. W. *Narrative of a Voyage Round the World: During the Years 1835, 36, and 37: Including a Narrative of an Embassy to the Sultan of Muscat and the King of Siam.* London: R. Bentley, 1838.
Russell, Mrs. Charles E. B., ed. *General Rigby, Zanzibar and the Slave Trade with Journals, Dispatches, etc.* London: Allen & Unwin, 1935.
Saavedra Casco, José Arturo. *Utenzi, War Poems, and the German Conquest of East Africa: Swahili Poetry as a Historical Source.* Trenton, NJ: Africa World Press, 2007.
Salīl ibn Ruzīk [Ibn Ruzayq]. *History of the Imâms and Seyyids of 'Omân.* Translated by George Percy Badger. London: Hakluyt Society, 1871.
Salim, Khamis, Abdurahman Juma, Zanzibar, and Makumbusho Idara ya Nyaraka na Mambo ya Kale. *Zanzibar Slave Memory.* [Zanzibar]: [publisher not identified], 2005.
Salimi, Abdulrahman Al and Hans Gaube, eds. Studies on Ibadism and Oman, 17 vols. Hildesheim: Georg Olms Verlag.
Sālimī, Nūr al-Dīn 'Abdullah bin Ḥumayd al-. *Jawābāt al-Imām al-Sālimī.* ed. by 'Abd al-Sitar Abu Ghadda. 6 vols. Badīya: Maktabat al-Imām al-Sālimī, 1999.
Sālimī, Muḥammad bin 'Abdallāh ibn Ḥumayd al-. *Nahḍat al A'yān bī-Ḥuriyyat 'Umān.* Beirut: Dar al-Jil, 1998.
Salter, Mark B. *Rights of Passage: The Passport in International Relations.* Boulder, CO: Lynne Rienner Publishers, 2003.
Schacht, Joseph. *An Introduction to Islamic Law.* Oxford [Oxfordshire]: Clarendon Press, 1996.
Serjeant, R. B. "Fisher-Folk and Fish-Traps in Al-Baḥrain." *Bulletin of the School of Oriental and African Studies, University of London* 31, no. 3 (1968): 486–514.
Sewell, William H. *Logics of History: Social Theory and Social Transformation.* Chicago: University of Chicago Press, 2005.

Shaham, Ron. "Masters, Their Freed Slaves, and the Waqf in Egypt (Eighteenth-Twentieth Centuries)." *Journal of the Economic and Social History of the Orient* 43, no. 2 (2000): 162–88.
Shariff, Ibrahim Noor. *Tanzania na Propaganda za Udini (Tanzania and Religious Propaganda)*. N.p., 2014.
———. *Tungo Zetu: Msingi wa Mashairi na Tungo Nyingenezo*. Trenton: The Red Sea Press, 1988.
Sheriff, Abdul. *Dhow Cultures of the Indian Ocean: Cosmopolitanism, Commerce and Islam*. New York: Columbia University Press, 2010.
———. *Slaves, Spices, and Ivory in Zanzibar: Integration of an East African Commercial Empire into the World Economy, 1770–1873*. Athens: Ohio University Press, 1987.
———, ed. *The History and Conservation of Zanzibar Stone Town*. London; Athens: Dept. of Archives, Museums & Antiquities in association with J. Currey; Ohio University Press, 1995.
Sheriff, Abdul, and Engseng Ho, eds. *The Indian Ocean: Oceanic Connections and the Creation of New Societies*, 2014.
Simpson, Donald Herbert. *Dark Companions: The African Contribution to the European Exploration of East Africa*. New York: Barnes & Noble Books, 1976.
Simpson, Edward, and Kai Kresse. *Struggling with History: Islam and Cosmopolitanism in Western Indian Ocean*. London: Hurst & Company, 2007.
Smee, Captain T. "Observations during a Voyage of Research on the East African Coast, from Cape Guardafui south to the Island of Zanzibar, in the H. C.'s cruiser Ternate." In *Zanzibar: City, Island and Coast*, R. F. Burton, vol. 2, 458–493. 2 vols. London: Tinsley Brothers, 1872.
Spear, Thomas. "Early Swahili History Reconsidered." *International Journal of African Historical Studies* 33, no. 2 (2000): 257–90.
———. "Swahili History and Society to 1900: A Classified Bibliography." *History in Africa* 27 (2000): 339–73.
Speke, John Hanning. *Journal of the Discovery of the Source of the Nile*. Edinburgh; London: W. Blackwood and Sons, 1863.
Stanley, Henry M. *How I Found Livingstone*. London: Sampson Low, Marston & Co., 1895.
———. *Through the Dark Continent: Or, The Sources of the Nile around the Great Lakes of Equatorial Africa, and down the Livingstone River to the Atlantic Ocean*. 2 vols. New York: Harper & Brothers, 1878.
———. *Stanley's Despatches to the New York Herald, 1871–1872, 1874–1877*. Edited by Norman R. Bennett. Boston: Boston University Press, 1970.
Steere, Edward. *A Handbook of the Swahili Language as Spoken at Zanzibar*. London: Bell & Daldy, 1870.
———. *Collections for a Handbook of the Nyamwezi Language, as Spoken at Unyanyembe*. London: Society for Promoting Christian Knowledge, 1885.
———. *Collections for a Handbook of the Yao Language*. London: Society for Promoting Christian Knowledge, 1871.
———. "Mohammedanism in Zanzibar." *Mission Life: Or Home and Foreign Church Work* 1 (February 1870): 140–47.
———. "On East African Tribes and Languages." *The Journal of the Anthropological Institute of Great Britain and Ireland* 1 (1872): cxliii–cliv. https://doi.org/10.2307/2841297.
———. *Swahili Tales, as Told by Natives of Zanzibar*. London: Bell & Daldy, 1870.

Stock, Eugene. *The History of the Church Missionary Society: Its Environment, Its Men and Its Work*. 4 vols. London: Church Missionary Society, 1899.
Stockreiter, Elke. *Islamic Law, Gender, and Social Change in Post-Abolition Zanzibar*, New York: Cambridge University Press, 2015.
Stockreiter, Elke Elisabeth. "Tying and Untying the Knot: Kadhi's Courts and the Negotiation of Social Status in Zanzibar Town, 1900–1963." PhD Diss, School of Oriental and African Studies, University of London, 2008.
Stone, Lawrence. "Family History in the 1980s: Past Achievements and Future Trends." *Journal of Interdisciplinary History* (1981): 51–87.
Sullivan, G. L. *Dhow Chasing in Zanzibar Waters and on the Eastern Coast of Africa: Narrative of Five Years' Experiences in the Suppression of the Slave Trade*. London: Sampson Low, Marston, Low & Searle, 1873.
Sunseri, Thaddeus. *Wielding the Ax: State Forestry and Social Conflict in Tanzania, 1820–2000*. Athens: Ohio University Press, 2009.
Suyūṭī, Muhammad ibn Shihāb al-Dīn al-. *Jawāhir Al-ʿuqūd Wa-muʿīn Al-qudāh Wa-al-muwaqqiʿīn Wa-al-shuhūd*. Al-Tabʿah 2, n.d., vol. 1, 17–54.
Swann, Alfred J. *Fighting the Slave-Hunters in Central Africa: A Record of Twenty-Six Years of Travel and Adventure Round the Great Lakes and of the Overthrow of Tippu-Tib, Rumaliza and Other Great Slave-Traders*. London: Frank Cass, 1969.
Tahawi, Ahmad Ibn Muhammad al-. *The Function of Documents in Islamic Law: The Chapters on Sales from Tahawi's Kitab Al-Shurut Al-Kabir*. Edited by Jeanette A. Wakin. Albany: State University of New York Press, 1972.
Tetley, Brian. *The Story of Mohamed Amin*. Niles, IL: Master Publishing, 2013.
Thomas, Bertram. *Alarms and Excursions in Arabia*. Indianapolis: Bobbs-Merrill Co. Publishers, 1931.
Thomas, Bertram, and Arthur Keith. *Arabia Felix: Across the Empty Quarter of Arabia*. London: Readers' Union, 1938.
Torpey, John. *The Invention of the Passport: Surveillance, Citizenship, and the State*. New York: Cambridge University Press, 2000.
Trautmann, Thomas R. "Morgan, Lewis Henry." American National Biography Online. http://www.anb.org/articles/14/14-00423.html.
Tsing, Anna Lowenhaupt. *The Mushroom at the End of the World: On the Possibility of Life in Capitalist Ruins*. Princeton: Princeton University Press, 2015.
Udovitch, Abraham L. *Partnership and Profit in Medieval Islam*. Princeton: Princeton University Press, 1970.
Valeri, Marc. *Oman: Politics and Society in the Qaboos State*. New York: Columbia University Press, 2009.
Vansina, Jan. *Kingdoms of the Savanna*. Madison: University of Wisconsin Press, 1966.
Vaughan, J. H. *The Dual Jurisdiction in Zanzibar*. Zanzibar: Government Printer, 1935.
Velten, Carl. *Safari za Wasuaheli*. Göttingen: Vandenhoeck [und] Ruprecht, 1901.
Vianello, Alessandra, and Mohamed M Kassim. *Servants of the Sharia: The Civil Register of the Qadis' Court of Brava, 1893–1900*. 2 vols. Leiden: Brill, 2006.
Vernet, Thomas. "La première traite française à Zanzibar: le journal de bord du vaisseau l'Espérance, 1774–1775." In *Civilisationbs des mondes insulaires*, C. Radimilahy and N. Rajaonarimanana, eds. 477–521, 2015.
Villiers, Alan. *Sons of Sinbad: An Account of Sailing with the Arabs in Their Dhows, in the Red Sea, around the Coasts of Arabia, and to Zanzibar and Tanganyika;*

Pearling in the Persian Gulf; and the Life of the Shipmasters, the Mariners of Kuwait. London: Hodder & Stoughton, 1940.

Vink, Markus P. M. "Indian Ocean Studies and the 'New Thalassology.'" *Journal of Global History* 2, no. 1 (2007): 41–62.

von Oppen, Achim "The Making and Unmaking of Boundaries in the Islamic World." *Die Welt des Islams* 41, no. 3 (2001): 277–86.

Ward, Herbert. *Five Years with the Congo Cannibals.* London: Chatto & Windus, 1891.

———. *My Life with Stanley's Rear Guard.* New York: C. L. Webster, 1891.

Ward, Kerry. *Networks of Empire: Forced Migration in the Dutch East India Company.* New York: Cambridge University Press, 2009.

Wellsted, J. R. *Travels in Arabia.* 2 vols. London: Murray, 1838.

———. "Observations on the Coast of Arabia between Ras Mohammed and Jiddah." *Journal of the Royal Geographical Society of London* 6 (1836): 51–96.

———. *Travels to the City of the Caliphs, along the Shores of the Persian Gulf and the Mediterranean. Including a Voyage to the Coast of Arabia, and a Tour on the Island of Socotra.* 2 vols. London: H. Colburn, 1840.

Wenban-Smith, W. "Diary of the 1857–58 Expedition to the Great Lakes." *Tanganyika Notes and Records* 49 (1957): 247–56.

Werner, A. "A Swahili History of Pate (Continued)." *Journal of the Royal African Society* 14, no. 55 (1915): 278–97.

Werner, J. R. *A Visit to Stanley's Rearguard at Major Barttelot's Camp on the Aruhwimi: With an Account of the River-Life on the Congo.* Edinburgh: W. Blackwood and Sons, 1889.

Wheeler, James Talboys. *Summary of Affairs of the Government of India in the Foreign Department from 1864 to 1869.* Calcutta: Office of the Superintendent of Government Printing, 1868.

White, Leslie A. "Father of American Anthropology." *The Scientific Monthly* 77, no. 6 (1953): 323.

Wigen, K. "Introduction." *The American Historical Review* 111, no. 3 (2006): 717–21. https://doi.org/10.1086/ahr.111.3.717.

Wilkinson, J. C. "Bayasirah and Bayadir." *Arabian Studies* 1 (1974): 75–85.

———. "Oman and East Africa: New Light on Early Kilwan History from the Omani Sources." *International Journal of African Historical Studies* 14, no. 2 (1981): 272–305. https://doi.org/10.2307/218046.

Wilkinson, John C. *The Imamate Tradition of Oman.* Cambridge: Cambridge University Press, 1987.

———. *Ibâdism: Origins and Early Development in Oman.* Oxford: Oxford University Press, 2010.

———. *The Arabs and the Scramble for Africa.* Sheffield, UK: Equinox Publishing, 2014.

———. *Water and Tribal Settlement in South-East Arabia: A Study of the Aflāj of Oman.* Oxford: Clarendon Press, 1977.

Wills, A. J. *An Introduction to the History of Central Africa.* London: Oxford University Press, 1973.

Wilson, C. T, and Robert William Felkin. *Uganda and the Egyptian Soudan.* 2 vols. London: S. Low, Marston, Searle, & Rivington, 1882.

Wimmelbücker, Ludger. *Mtoro Bin Mwinyi Bakari (c. 1869–1927): Swahili Lecturer and Author in Germany.* Dar es Salaam: Mkuki na Nyota Publishers, 2009.

Wink, André. *Al-Hind, the Making of the Indo-Islamic World*. Leiden: E. J. Brill, 1991.
Wint, Hollian. "Credible Relations: Indian Finance and East African Society in the Indian Ocean, C. 1860–1940." PhD diss., New York University, 2016.
Wissmann, Hermann von. *My Second Journey Through Equatorial Africa: From the Congo to the Zambesi, in the Years 1886 and 1887*. London: Chatto & Windus, 1891.
Woods, Carter A. "Some Further Notes on Lewis Henry Morgan," *American Anthropologist*, New Series, 47, no. 3 (1945): 462–64.
Woods, Carter, L. H. Morgan, and E. B. Morgan. "Lewis Henry Morgan To Edwin B. Morgan." *New York History* 31, No. 2 (1950): 177–88.
Wright, Marcia, and Peter Lary. "Swahili Settlements in Northern Zambia and Malawi." *African Historical Studies* 4, no. 3 (1971): 547–73.
Wright, Richard N. J. *The Chinese Steam Navy 1862–1945*. London: Chatham, 2000.
Zanzibar, and Zanzibar Protectorate. *Zanzibar Law Reports*. London; Zanzibar; Zanzibar Government Printer; Waterlow, n.d.
Zwemer, Samuel Marinus. *Arabia: The Cradle of Islam; Studies in the Geography, People and Politics of the Peninsula, with an Account of Islam and Mission-Work*. 2nd ed. New York: F. H. Revell Co., 1900.

Index

Individuals are listed by first name, except for scholars, Europeans, and Americans, who are listed by last name.

Abdulaziz bin Said al-Busaidi ('Abd al-'Azīz bin Sa'īd al-Busa'īdī): alliance with Bargash, 73, 76; alliance with Salih bin Ali, 245–246, 250–251; intrigue in Oman, 232–235, 237, 242
Abdullah bin Rashid al-Ghaythi ('Abd Allah bin Rāshid), 173–174
Abdullah bin Salim al-Barwani al-Harthi ('Abd Allah bin Sālim al-Barwānī al-Ḥārthī), 72–73, 138–139, 219–220, 224, 309n106
Abu Dhabi, 27, 66, 78, 83
Afro-Indian families, 166, 178–180, 182
Ali bin Muhsin al-Barwani ('Alī bin Muḥsin al-Barwānī), 261, 265, 267, 271
Ali bin Nasir al-Harthi ('Alī bin Naṣir al-Ḥarthī), 216–217, 326n6
Allen, Calvin, 159, 284n40
Amran bin Masoud al-Barwani ('Amrān bin Mas'ūd) al-Barwānī), 104, 203–204
antislavery treaties, 145, 153–154, 164; Treaty of 1822, 37, 154, 165; Treaty of 1845, 37, 149, 154–155; Treaty of 1873, 21–22, 165–6, 168–170, 174–175, 180, 188, 205, 235
Arab identity, 21, 192; in African interior, 87, 91–92, 94, 113, 275; disaggregation of, 107–109, 111, 115–116, 264; vis-a-vis Swahili identity, 92, 95, 97, 99, 272, 275; twentieth century, 264–264, 268
Arabs, Northern, 155, 169, 230, 265, 317n17
Asiatic Articles, 54, 179
Awlad Salim (Awlād Sālim, Arab clan), 183–184
Azzan bin Qays al-Busaidi ('Azzan bin Qays al-Busa'īdī), 79–80, 225; as imam, 81, 83, 226, 228, 230, 235, 241

Baghani, 159–160, 315n44
Bang, Anne, 75
Bani Jabir (al-Jabrī, clan), 229, 249
Barawa, 45, 218, 220–222

bara'a (Ibadi dissociation), 221, 263
Barghash bin Said al-Busaidi (Barghash bin Sa'īd al-Busa'īdī), 167, 259; and mainland settlements, 196, 202–4, 213; and Omani politics, 229, 231–232, 234, 236, 249–250; rebellion and exile, 70–75, 219–220; reconciliation with Turki, 251–255; and 1873 treaty, 165–6, 187, 205; and death of Said bin Sultan, 62–63, 67, 69, 85, 138; as sultan, 143, 221; will of, 150–151, 313n15
Barwani, al- (al-Barwānī, Arab clan), 136–140, 142, 159, 203, 221–222, 224, 260–262, 265, 268–271, 309n102, 309n106, 315n44.
    See also first names for individuals
baysari (pl. bayāsirah), 16, 87, 107–112, 114–115, 301n119
bay' al-iqāla, 59. See also bay' khiyār
bay' khiyār (optional or redeemable sale), 13, 59, 262
Benadir Coast, 45, 132, 218, 220–222
Bennett, Norman R., 119, 296n22
Benton, Lauren, 155
Bishara, Fahad, 214
Bombay, 27, 218; administrative post, 53, 71, 83, 87, 152, 226–227, 293n57; financial hub, 2, 47, 66, 196, 235; model city, 75–77; site of exile, 15, 63, 69, 74–75, 81–84, 85, 220, 228–230, 254, 263, 275, 306n44
Brennan, James, 77
Bugandan kingdom, 88, 126, 195, 197, 199, 200, 202, 204, 211; Christian missionaries and, 206, 209–210, 213; Islam and, 113, 140
Buraimi Oasis, 27, 78–79, 81, 218, 231
Burton, Andrew, 77
Burton, Richard: caravan dynamics, 17, 99–108; ethnographer, 53, 97, 129, 201, 295n11, 295n16, 298n55, 306n44, 319n49, 326n6; Thani bin Amir and, 86, 89, 92, 110–112, 295n1

359

buying time (temporizing strategies), 5, 8–11, 50, 59, 273, 279n15; freed slaves, 146, 191, 211, 275; mobility, 62; in East Africa, 65, 87, 139, 187; in Oman, 33, 42, 79, 81, 225, 236, 250, 259–260
Bwana Heri bin Juma al-Mafazii, 52, 53, 288
Bwana Nzige (Muḥammad bin Saʿīd al-Murjebī), 126, 132–135, 308n87, 309n94

Cameron, Verney Lovett, 104–105, 130–131, 203, 307n70
Canning Award, 63, 75, 77–78, 80, 82, 224, 227, 235, 266
Chang, Michael, 291n6
chotara, 179–180, 319n50
Christian Missionary Society (CMS), 207–213, 324n70
Churchill, Henry Adrian, 172, 186
coastal chauvinism, 15, 87, 90–91, 275
concubines, 68, 88–89, 99, 114, 128, 137–139, 179–182, 206, 310n109. See also *suria*
Congo, eastern, 4, 21, 26, 94, 96, 113, 127–128, 151, 197
Congo Free State, 112, 117, 127, 135–136, 273
consular acts, 171, 173, 175, 178–179, 181–182, 187, 189, 276, 320n61
contracts: as sources, 7, 19, 44–45, 60, 191–192; formal elements of, 1–2, 10, 12–14, 55–57, 175, 244, 290n53; ivory, 1–2, 4, 55, 56, 157, 162, 191–192; marriage, 142–143, 181; slavery and labor, 148, 155–157, 171, 177–179, 181–182
copal, 4, 12, 61, 87, 274
courts, consular, 11, 14, 20, 21, 166, 170–175, 181, 188–189, 214, 275, 318n32
courts, qadi, 12, 14, 59, 173–175, 188, 195, 214. See also qadi courts
customs (revenues, farming, collecting), 83, 222, 287n19; Zanzibar, 35, 47–50, 69, 178, 214, 226, 232, 236, 280n30

Daramumba, 128–129
Dar es Salaam, 63, 77, 85, 258, 268
Dariz, al-, 243–246, 262, 264
date production, 10, 12, 31–32, 38–42, 60, 65, 169, 184, 242, 247–249, 274
debt, 5, 7, 12–14, 56–58, 69, 171–175, 209–210, 214, 215–216, 243–244
documentary regime, 21, 166, 168–170, 175–176, 178–179, 182, 184, 186, 188–189, 275, 316n5
drought, 185, 262
Dubai, 27, 80, 81, 83

Ebji Shivji, 51, 178, 182
emigration from Oman, 20, 24, 34, 37, 40–42, 80, 113, 139, 193, 247, 266–267
Ewald, Janet, 54, 179

Fabian, Johannes, 119
Fair, Laura, 161–162
falaj (irrigation channel; plural *aflāj*), 31–33, 38–40, 42, 216–217, 223, 244, 248, 255, 262
Farhan (Chief of Rehenneko), 163–164
Faysal bin Turki al-Busaidi, 216, 247, 250–251, 255–258, 263
freed slaves, 12, 15–16, 21–22, 111, 115, 145–146, 156–164, 185–188, 192–194, 213–214, 228
Frere, Bartle, 165, 171, 235, 236, 293n57, 316n2, 328n45
Fundikira, 124, 140–141

Ghafiri (Ghāfrī, Omani tribal faction), 224, 231, 245, 250, 258, 263
Ghaythi, al- (Arabic clan), 157–158, 173, 183–185. See also *first names for individuals*
Ghuyuth. See al-Ghaythi
Glassman, Jonathon, 53, 92, 94, 129, 152, 265, 279n16, 288n31, 297n27, 312n10, 334n27
Grant, James A., 103, 191, 194–196
Gujarati, 55, 108–109, 179, 263, 319n50
Gwadar, 27, 65, 83, 218, 237

Halima (freed slave), 183–187
halwa (sweetmeat), 7, 24–26, 33, 43, 86, 88, 89, 107, 112, 169, 257, 260–62, 276
Hamed bin Muḥammad al-Murjebi. See Tippu Tip
Hamerton, Atkins, 53, 67–69, 147, 154–156, 310n109
Harthi, al- (al-Ḥārthī, Arabic clan), 62, 65, 69–74, 84, 86, 104, 111, 132, 136–138, 183–184, 215–217, 219–220, 221–222, 224–227, 239, 241–245, 250–251, 255, 261–262. See also *first names for individuals*
Harthi leaders murdered, 84, 220
Hilal bin ʿAmir bin Sultan al-Khanjari al-Harthi, 255, 257
Hilal bin Said al-Busaidi (Hilāl bin Saʿīd al-Busaʿīdī), 63, 66–69, 74, 84, 127
Hinawi (Hināwī, Omani tribal faction), 215, 224, 226, 228, 234, 237, 240, 246–247, 250, 255–256, 258–259, 263
Hinde, Sydney, 136, 274, 276
Hopper, Matthew, 285n66, 314n36

360 ⇝ Index

Ibadism (Ibaḍiyya), 28, 29–31; doctrine, 32, 150–151, 173–174, 221–222, 248, 259, 263, 318n36; East Africa, 75, 269; history, 64, 226; and Omani politics, 36, 78, 80, 81, 84, 154, 215–217, 225, 229, 233, 238, 253–254, 284n39
Ibra (Ibrā'), 42, 137, 139, 183, 223, 245, 250
Ile de Bourbon, 154, 156
Ile de France, 154. *See also* Mauritius
imamate: Ibadi ideal, 25, 28–30, 64, 226; 1868–71, 81–84, 216, 222–223, 227–235, 239, 254; 1913–58, 259, 262–264, 266, 284n39
Indians as British subjects, 170, 318n24; courts and, 21, 166, 171, 173–174, 175; in East Africa, 75, 236; in Oman, 8, 79, 225, 240–241, 250, 258; slavery and, 51, 172, 180, 188–189
interest (usury, *riba*), 1, 13, 49, 55–56, 59–60, 196, 280n30
iqrār (acknowledgement), 13, 56–59, 289n45
ivory: caravan trade, 12, 86–88, 113, 117–118, 139, 157, 179, 197–198, 201–204; as commodity, 7–8, 12, 48, 211–212, 274–275; environmental history, 18, 197; transactions, 1–2, 4–5, 10–11, 56, 58, 130, 164, 194–196
'Izz, 223, 244–245, 255, 257, 262

Jairam Shivji, 46–55, 60, 69, 157–158, 160, 171; firm of, 49–50, 83, 195–196, 214, 229–230, 280n30, 328n58
Jamshid bin Abdullah al-Busaidi (Jamshīd bin 'Abd Allah al-Busa'īdī), 261, 267–268, 334n26
Juma bin Salim al-Bakri (Jum'a bin Sālim al-Bakrī, Juma Merikani), 1–5, 10–13, 15–17, 20, 23, 26, 58, 113, 197
Juma Merikani. *See* Juma bin Salim al-Bakri

Kaduma, 199–201, 205, 207, 209, 324n65
kafā'a (sufficiency in marriage), 114, 129, 136
Kagei, 191, 197–202, 204–209, 212–213, 218
Karunde, 124, 140–141
Kasongo, 127, 134–136, 197, 273–274, 276
Kazeh. *See* Tabora
Kelly, John Barrett, 230, 329n66
Khalifa bin Harub al-Busaidi (Khalīfa bin Ḥārub), 261, 267
Khamis bin Abdullah, 206
Khamis wad Mtaa, 151
Khoja (Indian Muslims): in East Africa, 15, 112, 119, 124, 152, 171, 180–181, 287n13, 308n75; in Oman, 80, 235, 329n72
Khole bin Said, 73
Kilwa, 14, 35, 99, 126, 152–154, 168, 180, 184, 186, 221
kinship: 16–17, 120–121; Arab notions of, 118–119; fictive, 129, 138, 124; genealogy and, 261, 269, 270; in practice, 21, 124, 131–132, 190–191, 201, 213, 223, 234, 264, 275
Kirk, John, 165–166, 174, 187, 236
Kumbakumba, 132, 308. *See also* Muhammad bin Masoud al-Wardi
Kutch, 4, 15, 36, 47–49, 69, 80, 153, 171, 173, 178–179, 318n24

Ladha Damji, 1, 4, 12–15, 23, 58, 74, 287n13
Lagbari (al-Aghbari), 314n42. *See also* Said bin Muhammad al-Aghbari
Lakimidas Ladha, 330n104
Lamu, 52, 68, 126, 181, 193, 218; prisoners in, 74, 84, 220
Limbert, Mandana, 273, 302n136
Livingstone, David, 13, 18, 105, 123, 151, 205, 207, 293n57, 305n33
London Missionary Society (LMS), 93, 142
Lukonge (Rukonge), 199–201, 208–213, 325n87

Mabrook (freed slave), 168–169, 175, 177
MacKay, Alexander, 90
Madagascar, 34, 36, 99, 153, 160, 163, 203
Majid bin Said al-Busaidi (Mājid bin Sa'īd al-Busa'īdī), 69, 75, 138, 170, 186, 219, 221–222, 225, 228–229, 290n56
Makran Coast, 27, 34, 65, 77, 85, 237, 283n31
Manah (Manaḥ), 38, 39
Mandvi, 48, 171
manumission, 51, 145–147, 162, 166, 175–176, 184, 187–188, 275; insincere, 21, 22, 154–156, 164, 168–170, 177–178; Islamic, 21–22, 146–147, 148–153, 156, 158, 164, 189
marriage: as a strategy, 34, 94; in East African interior, 140–144; Indians and, 179–182; kin linkages and, 16–17, 121, 125, 129–130, 136–139, 201, 223–224; in Oman, 223–224; prohibitions against, 107, 112, 114
Martin, Bradford G., 221, 302n132
Mascarenes, 15, 186
Mauli, al- (al-Ma'ulī, Arab tribe), 36, 191–194, 214. *See also* Talib bin Abdullah al-Mauli
Mauritius, 153–155
Mazrui (Mazari'a, Arab clan), 35, 45, 52, 65, 272
Mazungera (Zaramo chief), 87–88
merikani (American cotton sheeting), 1, 2, 13, 50, 105, 108, 195, 201, 208, 211, 263
Miles, Samuel B., 24, 109, 237, 246
Mirambo, 113, 127, 191, 197–198, 202–204, 206, 212–214, 276, 305n35

Index 361

mobility, 14–16, 121, 221, 260; to East African interior, 87, 96, 111–113; limits on, 81, 83–84, 166, 169, 182, 188–189; from Oman, 33, 38, 43, 159, 192, 259, 263; as strategy, 53–54, 62–63, 67–69, 76, 80, 93, 163, 216, 273–276
Mombasa, 35, 45–46, 52, 65, 126, 217, 218, 268, 272
Moza bint Jabr al-Jabria, 223
Moza bint Khalfan al-Barwani (Muza bint Khalfān al-Barwānīa), 122, 139
Msabbah and Songoro, 190–214
Msene, 104–106, 126, 300n81
Muhammad bin Gharib (Muḥammad bin Ghārib), 157
Muhammad bin Juma al-Murjebi (Muḥammad bin Jum'a), 123–125, 127, 129–130, 140–141
Muhammad bin Khalfan al-Barwani. See Rumaliza
Muhammad bin Masoud al-Wardi (Muḥammad bin Masʿūd al-Wardī, Kumbakumba), 125, 126, 129–130, 132–133, 305n44
Muhammad bin Said al-Murjebi, 126, 132–135, 308n87, 309n94
Mumbai. See Bombay
Murjebi, al- (Arab clan), 117, 122–124, 126–127, 129, 132–134, 140, 197, 304n20. See also first names for individuals
Musa Mzuri, 88, 124, 295n11, 308n75
Muscat, 15, 253; capital moved to, 30, 36, 64; description and geography, 27–29, 40, 218, 236, 250, 263; inhabitants, 37, 39, 41, 47, 80–81, 109, 168–170, 225, 245–246, 292n24; sieges of, 84, 184, 216, 232–233, 237–240, 250–251, 255–258; split from Zanzibar, 62–63, 69–71, 224, 254
Mutesa, 197–198, 206–207, 209, 211, 213
Muttrah, 218; as commercial capital, 36, 39–40, 254; description and geography, 28–29, 109; sieges of, 80–81, 232–233, 239–241, 246–247, 257
Mwinyi Kheri (of Ujiji), 141
Mwinyi Kidogo, 99, 100, 102–104, 107–108, 196
Mwinyi Mkuu (traditional ruler of Zanzibar), 53, 163
mwungwana (pl. *waungwana*), 93–97

nahda, 75, 221
Napoleonic Wars, 50, 66, 154
Ng'ambo, 160–162, 193
Ngindo (pl. Wangido, ethnic group), 186–187

Nizwa: description and geography, 1–2, 15, 109, 218; drought in, 24–26, 33, 38–39, 58, 86; imamate and, 30, 36, 64; Omani politics and, 231, 256–257, 266
Nyamwezi (pl. Wanyamwezi, ethnic group), 21, 86, 92–97, 112–113, 123–124, 140–141, 197–198, 297n22, 307n69
Nyamwezi (place), 88, 100, 103, 125, 195–197, 295n11. See also Unyamwezi
Nyangwe, 126–127, 135, 197
Nyaso, 141

O'Neill, Thomas, 207, 209, 211, 212–213

patron-client relations, 5, 71, 115, 166, 252; debt and, 13–14, 22, 46, 126, 175, 194; manumission and, 146–150, 162–164, 177, 188–189; slavery and, 152, 205
Pelly, Lewis, 75–76, 79–81, 172, 180, 195, 225–226, 233
piracy, 35, 66, 155, 284n33, 293n57
Playfair, Robert L., 76, 172
Prestholdt, Jeremy, 10, 168, 314n35
Prideaux, William F., 172, 174–175

Qabil, al- (al-Qābil), 216–217, 123, 244, 262
qadi courts, 12, 14, 59, 173–175, 188, 195, 214
qadis as scribes, 156, 244, 254, 330n104
Qays bin Azzan bin Qays al-Busaidi (Qays bin ʿAzzan bin Qays al-Busaʿīdī), 66, 78, 247, 259

rahnan maqbuḍan (sale with pledged property), 13, 59
Raman, Bhavani, 316n5
Ras al-Khayma, 36, 66, 78, 192
Rashid bin Amur al-Ghaythi (Rāshid bin ʿAmur), 183–186
Rebellion of 1859, 21, 63, 69, 71, 74–75, 196, 217, 219–222, 292n35
Reid, Richard, 197–198
Rigby, Christopher P., 70, 73, 170, 172, 178, 180, 220, 225
Ross, Edward Charles, 249
ruga-ruga, 198, 203
Rumaliza (Muhammad bin Khalfān al-Barwani), 139–142, 272, 306n46, 310n111, 310n114

Said bin Ahmad al-Busaidi (Saʿīd bin Aḥmad), 47
Said bin Ali al-Suqri (Saʿīd bin ʿAlī al-Ṣuqrī, al-ʿAlīm al-Kabīr), 223, 243–244, 255
Said bin Habib al-Afifi, 141

Said bin Khalfan al-Khalili (Saʿīd bin Khalfān al-Khalīlī), 78, 84, 217, 225–226, 232
Said bin Muhammad al-Aghbari (Saʿīd bin Muḥammad), 145, 149–150, 158–159, 314n42
Said bin Salim al-Lamki (Saʿīd bin Sālim), 17, 99–100, 102–103, 107–108, 202–203, 213, 308n75
Said bin Sultan al-Busaidi (Saʿīd bin Sulṭan), children of, 68, 69, 127; death of, 61–63, 85; domestic politics, 34–37, 49–50, 52, 87–88, 155–156, 159, 192, 283n30, 306n44, 316n52; Ibadism and, 64, 154, 226; marriages, 138; mobile governance, 65–67, 274–275; moving capital to Zanzibar, 8, 21, 26, 45, 47, 163; will of, 150, 156
Said bin Umar bin Muhammad al-Kharusi (Saʿīd bin ʿUmar bin Muḥammad al-Kharūsī), 55–56, 58
Salih bin Ali al-Harthi (Ṣaliḥ bin ʿAlī al-Ḥarthī), 22, 72, 184, 215–229, 231–234, 237–263, 276
Salim bin Abdullah al-Barwani (Sālim bin ʿAbd Allah al-Barwānī), 65, 137, 139
Salim bin Isa bin Ali al-Suqri (Sālim bin ʿIsa bin ʿAlī al-Ṣuqrī), 243–245
Salim bin Thuwayni al-Busaidi (Sālim bin Thuwaynī al-BusaʿIdī), 80–81, 224–227, 229, 234, 237
Salme bin Said al-Busaidi (Salma bin Saʿīd al-Busaʿīdīa), 71–73, 143, 183
sarih (ṣarīḥ), 145–146, 157–158, 194. *See also* Freed slaves
Sayf bin Hamed al-Murjebi (Sayf bin Hamed), 127, 133
Seeb Agreement (1920), 263–264, 266
serang, 53–54
Seward, Edward, 173, 183
Sharqiya: description and geography, 29, 41; links to East Africa, 136–137, 158, 183–184, 243–245, 255–256, 261, 266, 269; Omani politics and, 37, 215–217, 225, 228, 239, 250–253
shenzi (*ushenzi, mshenzi, washenzi*), 93–94, 203
Sheriff, Abdul, 166, 203, 287n12
Shorkah bin Omah, 163
Smith, Shergold, 207–208, 210–213
Sokomuhogo, 160
Somalia, 45, 126, 132, 217, 218, 220–223
Songoro and Msabbah, 190–214
Speke, John Hanning, 17, 97, 99–100, 102–104, 106, 150, 195–196, 198, 220
Stanley, Henry Morton, 13, 91, 191, 204–207
Stanley Falls, 134, 135

Steere, Edward, 93, 185
Suhar, 27, 69, 79–80, 83, 225, 230, 328n58
Sulayman bin Habib (Sulaymān bin Ḥabīb), 111
Sulayman bin Sleyum (Sulayman Chai), 113, 115
Sulayman bin Zahir al-Jabri (Sulaymān bin Ẓāhir), 113–115
Sumar Widani, 173, 181
Sur, 27, 29, 45, 79, 80, 153, 155, 230–231, 242, 253, 305n44
suria (pl. *masuria*; concubine), 68, 88–89, 99, 114, 128, 137–138, 179–182, 206, 310n109
Swahili, identity, 21, 52–53, 87, 92–93, 95–96, 97–104, 105–107, 115–116, 185–187, 203, 271–273, 297n22
Swahiliphone world, 8, 271

Tabora (originally known as Kazeh), 199, 218, 264; founding, 86–90; inhabitants, 111–115, 140, 141, 203; as Indian Ocean settlement, 94, 104–108, 124–127, 197, 220, 27
Talib bin Abdullah al-Mauli (Ṭālib bin ʿAbd Allah al-Maʿūlī), 191–194
taqiyya (Ibadi dissimilation), 174, 318n36
Thani bin Amir al-Harthi (Snay bin Amir), 86–90, 92, 100, 107–108, 111–112, 115–116, 260, 295n1
Tharia Topan, 126, 130, 184, 287n13
Tippu Tip (Ḥamed bin Muḥammad bin Jumʿa al-Murjebī), 21, 118; career, 197, 273; as ethnographer, 95, 110–112, 309n104; kinship, 117–144
treaties, antislavery. *See* antislavery treaties
Tumbatu, 46, 51, 53–54, 126
Turki bin Said al Busaidi (Turkī bin Saʿīd al-BusaʿIdī), 66, 69, 72, 219, 225; in exile, 63, 80–81, 82–85, 228–233; as sultan, 22, 184, 216, 234–251, 252–255, 259, 316n3

Ujiji, 99, 107, 126, 139, 141–142, 197, 202, 264
Ukewere, 22, 126, 197–202, 208–209, 211–213
Unyamwezi, 88, 100, 103, 125, 195–197, 295n11
Unyanyembe (area of Unyamwezi), 88–89, 92, 103–107, 125, 127, 141, 196–198, 201–206, 208, 213, 299n71

Venayek Wassoodew, 82, 84

Wadi Maʿawil, 36, 37, 192–193
Wahhabi, 7, 35–37, 66, 78–81, 83, 192, 224, 306n44
walāʾ al-ʿatiq, 148, 150, 156, 157, 312n9
waqf (pl. *awqaf*), 33, 131, 193, 195, 214, 307n73, 314n42

Wardi, al- (Arab clan), 124, 125, 128–132, 305n44, 307n73. *See also first names for individuals*
waungwana, 93–97. See also *mwungwana*
Wellsted, James R., 31–32, 306n44
Wilkinson, John C., 29, 33, 109–110, 229, 295n1

Yao (pl. Wayao, ethnic group), 93, 103, 184–187

Zanzibar: Omani capital, 8, 21, 26, 49–50, 53, 60, 65–67, 70–72, 86–87, 103, 222, 255, 274; revolution, 22, 31, 261, 267–268, 272; subsidy, 83, 224–226, 228–230, 234–237, 239–242, 248, 252, 263, 266; urban development of, 46, 75, 77, 131, 146–147, 158–162, 166, 193, 194, 205, 214
Zuwayna bin Muhammad al-Kiyumi, 113–115

www.ingramcontent.com/pod-product-compliance
Lightning Source LLC
Chambersburg PA
CBHW020054020526
44112CB00031B/149